AMERICAN NATIONAL SECURITY

A reader in theory and policy

AMERICAN

Edited by **Morton Berkowitz**
BROOKLYN COLLEGE, THE CITY UNIVERSITY OF NEW YORK

and **P. G. Bock**
INTERNATIONAL ENCYCLOPEDIA
OF THE SOCIAL SCIENCES

with a Preface by Heinz Eulau

NATIONAL SECURITY

A Reader in

Theory and Policy

THE FREE PRESS, NEW YORK

Collier-Macmillan Limited, London

To our parents

Preface

"National security" has become one of those arenas of public action in which the needs of policy formulation and determination, on the one hand, and the need of scientific inquiry, on the other hand, confront each other in the expectation that a merger is both desirable and possible. Although the discipline of political science has been traditionally concerned with problems of public policy, scholars primarily committed to prescription have often stood apart from scholars primarily interested in description and explanation.

Of course, the relationship between prescription, or statements of value, and description, or statements of fact, is an epistemological issue as unsolved as ever. But the mere fact that the philosophical problem remains a riddle need not prevent us from proceeding as if it had been solved. It certainly has not kept economists from concerning themselves with issues of public policy, and from shedding on these issues as much theoretical light as the science of economics permits at any given stage of its development. Indeed, one might argue that, among other reasons, it has been the involvement of economic theorists in contemporary economic issues that has contributed to the great theoretical sophistication of economics as well as to its great influence in public-policy making. By way of contrast, political science is underdeveloped, and political scientists play only minor or marginal roles in the processes of policy formation at all levels and in all branches of government.

It is probably symptomatic of the intellectual unrest in political science that younger scholars are increasingly attracted by the "policy science" approach that stresses the interdependence of theory and practice. Indeed, many of those coming into political science are initially attracted by their desire to find solutions to those real-life social and political problems demanding therapeutic treatment. Zeal for change and reform of political conditions is not an unjustifiable motivation for wanting to become a scholar, provided those who are so motivated recognize (as they sometimes do not) that *ira* must be accompanied by *studium*, that the would-be policy scientist must also subject himself to the requirements of scientific rigor and discipline. Policy advice may be premature or even false if it is not grounded in valid theoretical effort and reliable empirical research. All too often those with high policy affect but low scientific competence are lost both to the national manpower pool primarily involved in policy formation and to the pool primarily engaged in academic research.

That national security policy is a critical area of public concern may be taken for granted. The flood of literary outpourings by journalists, independent commentators, government officials, churchmen, and scholars attests to the importance of the subject. Not all of this work deserves either public or scholarly attention. But some of it is sufficiently sophisticated and systematic to call for careful inspection. Bringing a selection of the best of these materials together in a single volume is a welcome contribution to the future of both policy formation and scientific research in the arena of national security.

Admittedly, books of readings rank generally low among publications that define scholarly reputations. This is as it should be. But there are exceptions, and these exceptions are rare enough to earn the anthologist the respect and gratitude of his peers. Among the exceptions is the "Reader," which, like the present work, constitutes an intellectual challenge at the frontiers of knowledge. Morton Berkowitz and Peter Bock deserve our esteem for having brought together their readings on national security from the dual perspective of policy and research, and for having imaginatively concatenated them through a set of useful introductory notes. One might quarrel with particular selections, one might disagree with some of their introductory commentary, or one might be somewhat less sanguine about the prospects of "national security" as a subfield of international relations. But one cannot but admire their enthusiastic belief that national security offers more than simply a convenient handle for coming to grips with the otherwise porous study of international politics. This collection not only solidifies old ground, but also opens up new vistas, and it will serve as a guidepost toward the interdisciplinary and systematic study of international relations.

Heinz Eulau

Institute for Advanced Studies
Vienna, Austria
October, 1964

Introduction

THE UNINTERRUPTED CRISIS IN WORLD POLITICS since the end of World War II has led to a minor revolution in the study and teaching of politics, particularly international relations and foreign policy, in the United States. The increased tempo of international change at first led to an emphasis on the "policy approach"—the attempt to use information provided by the social sciences in the formulation of immediate responses to the rapid succession of international crises confronting the United States. This essentially pragmatic approach, firmly rooted in traditional American values, proved suggestive but could not adequately explain a world in which fundamental change had become a commonplace. It did, however, lead to a new awareness that a hard and painstaking search for theoretical first principles must be undertaken.

Typical of this search has been the increased attention paid by scholars to a vaguely defined area called "national security"—usually located somewhere in the academic discipline of international relations. This development logically followed the emergence of international relations from within the broader field of political science. In both cases the same factors encouraged specialization—the growing complexity of international affairs and the increasingly self-conscious involvement of the United States as the leader of a world system. An army of specialists in the government, in independent research institutions, and at universities, began working in such basic areas as the choice of military strategies and appropriate weapons systems; the allocation of economic resources to competing defense and nondefense needs; the role of scientists in national policy-making; the political setting for strategic decision-making; the problem of alliances and coalitions; the technical, economic, and political challenges of disarmament; the institutions and techniques for international cooperation and the creation of a world community.

The search for objective criteria inevitably led the experts to analyze the theoretical foundations of national security policy. The resulting clarification of goals, definition of research areas, and sharpening of methodological tools all helped to create the images of an emerging concept and a developing field of study.

However, even with the rapid rate of growth, there has been little or no integration of the major research probes and theoretical formulations undertaken in the last decade. Although lack of coordination is characteristic of the entire discipline of international relations, it is particularly pronounced in the field of national security because of the newness of the subject and the wide dispersion of its investigators, who belong to different academic disciplines, research institutions, and government departments. Nevertheless, a careful look at the relevant literature shows some general areas of agreement about the substance and scope of the problems and some discernible directions which research has been taking. The major purpose of this book is to focus on these areas of agreement and research directions. This enables us to offer a tentative definition of the concept of national security and to outline its scope and limits as a field of study.

National security can be most fruitfully defined as *the ability of a nation to protect its internal values from external threats*. Most of the significant work views the concept in this way, either implicitly or explicitly. There is an almost unanimous agreement that a nation possesses security when it can protect some core values, even though there may be much disagreement on precisely what these values are. There is also a consensus that although a nation may be threatened from both the inside and the outside, national security focuses primarily on external dangers; subversion, in this context, is merely the extension of a threat from abroad. Needless to say, the perception of external threats can lead both to offensive and defensive behavior of states. Thus, nearly every action taken by a state has been connected by its leaders to the maintenance of internal values. Such obviously expansionist policies as "Manifest Destiny" or "Lebensraum" were justified in terms of the protection and promotion of existing American and German economic institutions and values.

As an academic discipline, national security may be described as the study of how nations can and do make those decisions and policies designed to maximize the protection of their internal values from external threats. Seen in this way, national security becomes a subfield of international relations, especially when we divide the latter into two basic areas—one concerned with the analysis of the international system, the other concerned with the process by which the system's actors reach decisions about their behavior. One is concerned with the way states interact, the other focuses mainly on how they act. The subfield of national security pre-empts most of the material falling into the second category.

Two questions immediately come to mind: Is national security, then, simply a restatement of the more traditional concept of the national interest? Is the field of national security simply the study of foreign policy, in modern dress?

National security, as defined above, is closely related to, and in fact has evolved from, the idea of national interest. However, the phrase "national interest" has usually meant nothing more than the sum of all the policies and activities of a state which might bring it some advantage. Most studies of the national interest have merely attempted to identify specific positions and actions advantageous to a particular state in various parts of the world. They usually spoke of "the interest of the United States (or some other country) in Latin America (or in the Middle East, Africa, or Outer Space)," and went on to criticize existing policies and prescribe desirable alternatives. Very little attention was paid to the general premises and values underlying these specific interests and joining them in a coherent, integrated pattern. This neglect characterized equally the the work of academicians and the pronouncements of policy-makers. However, national security, as defined above, focuses precisely on that underlying principle which systematically joins the various activities of states. Whatever previous attempts were made to provide systematic analyses generally equated *the* national interest with the quest for power—military, economic, or political. This approach had two serious drawbacks, which the concept of national security may overcome.

First, the concept of power was seldom defined with any degree of precision, making it almost useless as an analytic tool. Too often it tended to be treated as an end in itself. Thus, for example, Strausz-Hupé and Possony state that "Foreign policy aims at the acquisition of optimum, and sometimes maximum power" and then define, as a special type, states that are "driven by a particularly pronounced dynamism, i.e., an urge toward power accumulation." (*International Relations*, 1950, pp. 2, 9). This mystical conception of an "urge toward power" must be conjured up whenever national power is treated as a value rather than a means for the protection of values, that is, a means for the attainment of national security.

Second, once defined, no matter how vaguely, power proved too narrow a concept. Since an increase in one nation's power means a decrease in another's, the power orientation naturally implies the clash of distinct sets of interests, with no real chance of resolution except through the victory of one over the other (a zero-sum game). The security orientation presented here, while encompassing the concerns of power, adds a further dimension: the consideration of common international interests which could result in the simultaneous increase of the security of a number of, or even all, nations (a non-zero-sum game).

In addition to serving as a guide for national policy, the concept of the national interest has too often been used by its advocates as a means for defining and choosing those values which are national, and therefore "desirable," as opposed to those which are subnational, and therefore "selfish" and "undesirable." This entanglement in an inevitably subjective and value-laden process of choice is probably the major reason for the elusiveness and ambiguity of the concept and for its uselessness as an analytic tool. The concept of national security, on the other hand, while tied to specific national values which must be protected, does not attempt to define or choose among the desirable and undesirable ones. Rather, it accepts the prevailing values as determined by political processes within the national system and concerns itself exclusively with the means of protecting them. National security is, therefore, a far less value-laden concept than national interest, and the outlook for its operational definition is considerably brighter, as some of our selections indicate.

The study of foreign policy has traditionally concentrated upon the institutions and processes by which individual countries take actions to further their specific national interests in different geographic areas. This emphasis on the distinctness of each nation's specific interests is a reason why meaningful comparative analysis of national foreign policies has been so slow to develop. National security includes much of the subject matter of foreign policy but focuses precisely on common elements and uniformities in the policies of all nations, thus encouraging the development of systematic comparison.

The national security approach has another advantage: it avoids the misleading dichotomy between internal and external policy which typifies the traditional study of foreign policy. National security joins the two by envisaging both domestic and international policy as designed to protect the same set of values, and ultimately to preserve the national system as a whole. In this sense, the field of national security, while focusing on the external aspect of systems maintenance, allows us to see this aspect as an integral part of a larger problem, and may also contribute to the development of the "systems analysis" approach to politics.

This treatment of national security as a concept and as a field of study is reflected in the organization of our Reader. Part I should give the reader some sense of the important distinction between the *concepts* of national interest and national security by showing the evolution of the former and the emergence of the latter. Parts II and III, taken together, outline the scope of the *field*. Part II reflects the view of national security as a zero-sum game focusing upon the means of maximizing national power within conflict situations. Part III suggests that national security may also be viewed as a non-zero-sum game, emphasizing the growth of international cooperation and the minimization of national power as the road to security. The substantive concerns represented in Part III have not ordinarily been included in readers on national security. Their inclusion reflects our earlier suggestion about the difference between the concepts of national security and national interest. Part IV offers tools by which the area of study previously defined may be investigated. The contributions of these selections are primarily methodological, suggesting ways of reaching a greater clarity and precision in defining both the concept and the field of national security.

The most difficult problem for the anthologist is the selection of a limited number of writings that will be representative of a broad range of scholarship. Our selections, needless to say, are not exhaustive. Since they could not be, we believe it essential to spell out the criteria that guided us in making our choices and the features that distinguish this Reader from other collections containing similar materials.

First, we decided to sacrifice some comprehensiveness and selected only entire articles or self-contained sections of articles or books. This had the advantage of presenting the authors' full views on the topics included, but naturally meant that some pertinent topics had to be omitted, even though appropriate readings were available.

Second, in order to avoid a mere "laundry list" of articles, which would leave the field as uncharted as before, each of the readings was chosen for the contribution it makes to our conceptual scheme. Each is meant to give the student some sense of a cohesive body of work and to indicate the contours of the terrain that still remains to be charted. The introductory notes at the beginning of each Part indicate the specific place of each selection in our over-all scheme.

Third, we tried to include those articles that help to merge the separate strands of the development of the field at a level of sophistication that will be of some lasting use in teaching and research. We have therefore *excluded* most of the material which deals with current, short-range policies designed to meet specific challenges in different parts of the world. No selections are devoted, for example, to the analysis of individual crises, such as Vietnam, Cuba, or Berlin.

Fourth, even though most of the articles are written by American authors, we attempted to choose only those readings which could have a comparative application to the security policies of other actors in the international system.

Fifth, in order to reflect the interdisciplinary character of the new field of national security, we were careful to select writings representative of the work of political scientists, economists, sociologists, social psychologists, historians, mathematicians, and physicists.

Finally, we have appended a bibliography which is intended to do more than simply suggest further readings. It follows the organization of the Reader and will serve as a guide to those relevant topics which lack of space forced us to omit. Together with the reprinted selections, it should give the student a fuller sense of the scope, variety, and lines of development of the literature in this field.

We feel that this Reader is well suited for a variety of purposes. It may be used as a text for courses in national security, international politics, and foreign policy. Courses in national security are being offered at an ever growing number of universities and colleges, both within specific departments and in interdisciplinary programs. The Reader should also be useful to all people and agencies involved with the formulation, consideration, and execution of national security policy.

It is our hope that this Reader will fill an important function by bringing together some of the most significant contributions to theory and policy in the rapidly growing field of national security, so that those working within the field may be left with a sense of what has already been accomplished and what has yet to be done.

It is impossible, of course, to thank all the people responsible for this book. We should like, however, to single out our teacher and friend Professor William T. R. Fox first stimulating our interest in the problems of American security, and our colleague and friend, Professor A. F. K. Organski, for his helpful criticism and advice. We also gratefully acknowledge our debt to all the authors and publishers whose works are represented in this Reader. Individual acknowledgments appear at the beginning of each selection, but we should like to make special mention of our gratitude to Dr. Anatol Rapoport, who kindly allowed us to use a previously unpublished paper. Our personal thanks go to Martin Kessler of The Free Press for his patience and encouragement and to Frances Woodley and Linda K. Bock for their help in preparing the manuscript.

M. B.
P. G. B.

Contributors

CHADWICK F. ALGER
Associate Professor of Political Science, Northwestern University
Author of articles on international relations and organizations

GABRIEL A. ALMOND
Professor of Political Science, Stanford University
Author of The American People and Foreign Policy (*1950*) *and* The Appeals of Communism (*1954*); *coauthor (with James S. Coleman) of* The Politics of the Developing Areas (*1960*)

HAROLD J. BARNETT
Professor of Economics, Washington University (St. Louis)
Author of Scarcity and Growth: Economics of Natural Resource Availability (*1963*)

CHARLES A. BEARD
Distinguished American historian and political scientist
Author of Economic Interpretation of the Constitution *and* The Rise of American Civilization

P. M. S. BLACKETT
Nobel Prize laureate in physics
Author of Fear, War and the Bomb *and* Studies in War

KENNETH E. BOULDING
Professor of Economics, University of Michigan
Author of Conflict and Defense (*1962*) *and coauthor (with Emile Benoit) of* Economic Consequences of Disarmament

BERNARD BRODIE
Senior Staff Member, The RAND Corporation
Author of Strategy in the Missile Age (*1959*)

GRENVILLE CLARK
International lawyer, New York City
Coauthor (with Louis Sohn) of World Peace Through World Law

INIS L. CLAUDE, JR.
Professor of Political Science, University of Michigan
Author of many articles and of Swords into Plowshares: Problems and Progress of International Organization (*1956*) *and* Power and International Relations (*1962*)

KARL DEUTSCH
Professor of Political Science, Yale University
Author of Nerves of Government (*1963*) *and* Political Community at the International Level (*1954*); *coauthor of* Political Community and the North Atlantic Area (*1958*)

CHARLOTTE AND GEORGE DYER
Directors of the Dyer Institute of Inter-disciplinary Studies and instructors in political science, University of Pennsylvania

ALAIN C. ENTHOVEN
Deputy Assistant Secretary of Defense (Systems Analysis), Department of Defense
Coauthor (with Henry S. Rowen) of Defense Planning and Organization *and contributor to* The Economics of Defense in the Nuclear Age (*1960*)

xv

LOUIS HENKIN
: *Hamilton Fish Professor of International Law and Diplomacy, Columbia University*
: Author of Arms Control and Inspection in American Law (*1958*) *and editor of* Arms Control: Issues for the Public

CHARLES J. HITCH
: *Assistant Secretary of Defense, Department of Defense*
: Coeditor (*with Roland Neely McKean*) *of* The Economics of Defense in the Nuclear Age (*1960*)

MARVIN HOFFENBERG
: *Head, Cost Department, Aerospace Corporation*

SAMUEL P. HUNTINGTON
: *Professor of Government, Harvard University*
: Author of The Soldier and the State (*1957*) *and* The Common Defense (*1962*)

FRED C. IKLÉ
: *Staff Member, The RAND Corporation, and Visiting Lecturer, Center for International Affairs, Harvard University*
: Author of The Social Impact of Bomb Destruction (*1958*)

PHILIP C. JESSUP
: *International Court of Justice, The Hague*
: Author of Transnational Law (*1956*) *and* The Use of International Law (*1959*), *and editor of* Atoms for Power (*1958*)

STEPHEN B. JONES
: *Professor of Geography, Yale University*
: Author of Geography and World Affairs (*1950*)

MORTON A. KAPLAN
: *Associate Professor of Political Science, University of Chicago, and research member of The Hudson Institute*
: Author of System and Process in International Politics (*1957*)

JAMES E. KING, JR.
: *Treasurer of The RAND Corporation*

KLAUS KNORR
: *Director, Center of International Studies, Princeton University*
: Author of War Potential of Nations (*1956*) *and* NATO and American Security (*1959*)

HOWARD E. KOCH, JR.
: *Assistant to Robert C. North, Stanford University*

HAROLD D. LASSWELL
: *Edward J. Phelps Professor of Law and Political Science, Yale University*
: Author of Psychopathology and Politics, World Politics and Personal Insecurity, Power and Society, Power and Personality, Politics: Who Gets What How, *and* The Future of Political Science

WASSILY W. LEONTIEF
: *Henry Lee Professor of Economics, Harvard University*
: Author of The Structure of the American Economy (*1951*)

ROLAND NEELY MCKEAN
: *Research economist, The RAND Corporation*
: Coeditor (*with Charles J. Hitch*) *of* The Economics of Defense in the Nuclear Age (*1960*)

HANS J. MORGENTHAU
: *Professor of Political Science, University of Chicago*
: Author of In Defense of the National Interest (*1951*) *and* Politics Among Nations (*1948*)

GUNNAR MYRDAL
: *University of Stockholm*
: Author of An American Dilemma (*1940*), The International Economy: Problems and Prospects (*1956*), Beyond the Welfare State (*1960*), *and* Challenge to Affluence (*1963*)

ROBERT C. NORTH
: *Professor of Political Science, Stanford University, and Director, Project on International Conflict and Integration*
: Author of Moscow and Chinese Communism (*1953*)

CHARLES E. OSGOOD

Professor of Psychology, The University of Illinois
Author of Alternative to War or Surrender (*1962*)

ROBERT E. OSGOOD

Professor of Political Science, University of Chicago
Author of Ideals and Self-Interest in America's Foreign
Relations (*1953*) *and* Limited War (*1957*)

DON K. PRICE

Professor of Government and Dean, Graduate School of Public
Administration, Harvard University
Author of Government and Science (*1954*) *and editor of*
Secretary of State (*1960*)

ANATOL RAPOPORT

Professor of Mathematical Biology, Mental Health Research
Institute, University of Michigan
Author of Fights, Games and Debates (*1960*) *and* Strategy
and Conscience (*1964*)

WILLIAM H. RIKER

Chairman, Department of Political Science, University of
Rochester
Author of Democracy in the United States (*1953*), Soldiers
of the States (*1957*), *and* The Theory of Political Coalitions
(*1962*)

HENRY S. ROWEN

Economist and Deputy Assistant Secretary of Defense (Planning
and N.S.C.), Department of Defense

THOMAS C. SCHELLING

Professor of Economics, Harvard University
Author of Strategy of Conflict (*1960*) *and* International
Economics (*1958*); *coauthor (with Morton H. Halperin) of*
Strategy and Arms Control (*1961*)

WARNER R. SCHILLING

Associate Professor, Columbia University
Coauthor of Strategy, Politics, and Defense Budgets (*1962*)

HOWARD J. TAUBENFELD

Professor of International Law, Southern Methodist University

ARNOLD WOLFERS

Director, Washington Center of Foreign Policy Research,
Johns Hopkins University
Author of The Anglo-American Tradition in Foreign
Affairs (*1956*) *and editor of* Alliance Policy in the Cold War
(*1959*)

RONALD J. YALEM

Associate Professor of International Relations, School of
International Relations, University of Southern California

DINA A. ZINNES

Assistant to Robert C. North, Stanford University

Contents

AMERICAN NATIONAL SECURITY

A reader in theory and policy

Part One

National security: a concept emerges

Introductory note

The question implicit in much of the traditional writing on foreign policy has been:
What are the enduring interests and values toward which nations seek to orient their
external policies? Most early authors did not try to define or analyze the concept of
the national interest, or even to list systematically the different national interests. At
best, such "national interests" were described as being larger in scope and more enduring
in time than the interests of subnational groups. In addition, many writers concentrated on
giving value-laden prescriptions for what a particular country's interest should be in
different parts of the world. The few attempts to explore the concept analytically, and to
identify the interrelationships of its components, usually took the form of assigning
overwhelming importance to a single factor, which overshadowed all the others, thus
creating the illusion of systematic order.

Beard, for example, assigns supreme value to the self-interest of the dominant
economic classes in society. Through superior material and intellectual resources, such
dominant groups usually succeeded in identifying their own self-interest with the national
interest to such an extent that it is accepted by most other groups in society. The writers
surveyed by Jones all share the assumption that the geographic position of a nation is the
most fundamental factor in determining its national interest. According to Morgenthau,
the only clear meaning which can be assigned to the national interest is that nations always
act or always should act to maximize their power over other nations. On the surface,
Morgenthau's position may appear simply as another example of a monistic interpretation
of the national interest. Upon closer inspection, it turns out to be a much more ambitious
attempt, seeking to integrate the various components of the national interest into the
single concept of power. The net result, however, is confusion rather than comprehensiveness,
because the term power is never adequately defined or described and is not used
consistently.

The dissatisfaction with such treatments of the national interest is clearly reflected
in the article by Wolfers. This contribution dissects the ambiguity underlying most of
past and recent writings about the national interest, or the national security interest.

I

Wolfers discusses the relationship between national security and social values and then goes on to suggest that the concept of national security, to be a meaningful guide for action, must be used with far greater precision and specificity.

Morton Kaplan's contribution is one of the most ambitious recent attempts to use the methods of modern systems analysis in an effort to shed light on this particular problem. The article reflects the recent trend to study all aspects of the behaviour of societies as part of a total pattern which constitutes a system. National interest is therefore regarded as simply one aspect—albeit an important one—of the over-all problem of system maintenance. The article shows the close links between the security of the national system and the security of subnational groups, and comes close to our notion of the concept of national security.

Charles A. Beard

The idea of national interest

"FOREIGN POLICIES are not built upon abstractions. They are the result of practical conceptions of national interest arising from some immediate exigency or standing out vividly in historical perspective."[1] In this brief sentence, Charles E. Hughes, speaking as Secretary of State, presented the central conception of modern diplomacy, and it may be added that in practice he applied it with striking precision.

Although especially pointed in statement, the formula of Secretary Hughes was not new to American thought. It reaffirmed an old doctrine accepted, as we shall see, by leaders among the founders of the American Republic, and it gave conservative and official sanction to a creed which had been refurbished during the closing years of the nineteenth century by Alfred T. Mahan, the philosopher of the sea power in history. Indeed, if there is any system at all beneath the voluminous writings of Mahan, it is that national interest is the prime consideration in foreign policy. In one place, he flatly declared: "Self-interest is not only a legitimate, but a fundamental cause for national policy; one which needs no cloak of hypocrisy. As a principle it does not require justification in general statement, although the propriety of its application to a particular instance may call for demonstrations. . . . Not every saying of Washington is as true now as it was when uttered, and some have been misapplied; but

it is just as true now as ever that it is vain to expect governments to act continuously *on any other ground than national interest*. They have no right to do so, being agents and not principals."[2]

On another occasion, Mahan confirmed this doctrine of national interest in a manner somewhat more sweeping, though similar: "It is as true now as when Washington penned the words, and always will be true, that it is vain to expect nations to act consistently from any other motive than that of interest. That, under the name of Realism, is the frankly avowed policy of German statecraft. It follows from this directly that the study of interests—international interests—is the one basis of sound, provident policy for statesmen. . . . Governments are corporations, and corporations have no souls . . . must put first the interests of their own wards . . . their own people."[3]

As Mahan implies, the conception of national interest as the principal rule of diplomacy is not confined to the United States. It is to be found in the *Realpolitik* elaborated by German writers on international relations, in the documents that pour from the chancelleries of other European countries, and in the ceremonial usages of the Orient. From the Italian dispatches of the sixteenth century to the state papers of the latest crisis it appears with striking insistence. On July 31, 1914, when with a grim foreboding of future events the German

Reprinted with permission from Charles A. Beard, *The Idea of National Interest, An Analytical Study in American Foreign Policy*, with the collaboration of G. H. E. Smith, New York, The Macmillan Company, 1934. © 1934 by C. A. Beard; renewed 1962 by W. Beard, Mrs. M. B. Vagts, and G. H. E. Smith.

ambassador in Paris asked the French minister for foreign affairs, "What the attitude of France would be in case of war between Germany and Russia," the minister prepared in reply the laconic formula: "France will have regard to her interests."[4] The following day, when the neutrality of Luxemburg was threatened by Germany, the French minister informed his representative in the duchy that such an act "would compel France from that time to be guided in this matter by care for her defense and her interests."[5]

Even Soviet Russia, though committed broadly to the principle of communist internationalism, does not contemplate, in any case at present, the loss of her identity in a world society composed of individuals ruled from one center of power, but operates on considerations arising from state, if not national, interest. Her position is thus officially declared by Karl Radek, editor of *Izvestia*, the organ of the Communist party in Soviet Russia: "The Soviet Union is strong enough to defend her territorial integrity and her interests. Concentrating her efforts on building up peaceful industries for meeting the needs of her own population, keeping aloof from armed interference with the affairs of foreign nations, the Soviet Union will seek a peaceful settlement of all conflicts which may arise between her and her neighbors. She will base her policy exclusively on her own interests, which correspond with the interests of peace both in the East and in Europe. But she will know how to defend her vital rights. Those who think that she will sacrifice them because she is afraid of a conflict are just as wrong as those who believe that she will become a tool of foreign interests."[6]

Although none of the thinkers and statesmen who thus present the doctrine of national interest speak in the language of exact science, they apparently conceive interest as a reality open to human understanding and as a kind of iron necessity which binds governments and governed alike. It binds them so closely that there is no escape, except possibly for an insignificant minority; it cuts across the social divisions reflected in political parties and compels "a united front"—an integrated, totalitarian State. Such, at least, was the contention of President Taft and President Coolidge (*The Idea of National Interest*, pp. 119, 132), and it was positively formulated in the address by Secretary Hughes from which the opening lines of this chapter are taken.

After saying that foreign policies are the result

of practical conceptions of national interest, Mr. Hughes continued: "When long maintained, they express the hopes and fears, the aims of security or aggrandizement, which have become dominant in the national consciousness, and thus transcend party divisions and make negligible such opposition as may come from particular groups. They inevitably control the machinery of international accord which works only within the narrow field not closed by divergent ambitions or as interest yields to apprehension or obtains compensation through give and take. Statesmen who carry the burdens of empire do not for a moment lose sight of imperial purposes and requirements." While this is not a deterministic sequence, in the scientific sense of the terms, it has some characteristics of the inexorable: the practical conceptions of it; when long maintained, policy becomes an inescapable rule for the nation—a rule written in the nature of things, partaking, it would seem, of the stern mandate imposed by the law of gravitation.[7]

National interest: a modern conception

ALTHOUGH employed as if it were a fixed principle, somewhat like the law of gravitation, the idea of national interest is, relatively speaking, a newcomer among the formulas of diplomacy and international morality. In the nature of things it could not have served the statesmen of antiquity. In that long period of history the relations of states and peoples were not conducted according to any system of international law and diplomacy. Egyptians, Persians, Jews, Greeks, and Romans did not freely grant to other peoples that equality which, though crude and imperfect in practice, is accepted in theory among the great states of modern times, nor did they conceive of their world as a family of nations or balance of power. Substantial interests were pursued, no doubt, by one powerful state or empire after another. Both negotiation and arms were employed to realize these interests. The argument of gain was abundantly used to induce soldiers and the populace to make war on neighboring societies. But, since there were no systematic relations, there was no common formula, accepted by all, on which relations were expected to turn. So far as the Romans needed verbal justification for the deed, they found it in *utilitas rei publicæ* or in *rei publicæ ratio et utilitas*.[8]

Nor in the early middle ages were circumstances favourable to the development of the conception of national interest. The teachings of Christianity, from which policies of state, so far as they were articulate, and rules for private conduct were frequently drawn, lent no countenance to the idea. Christians did, to be sure, render unto Caesar the things that were Caesar's; they admitted that there was no power save from God; and they sanctioned prayers for the magistrates and for the good of the Roman state. "But," as Westermarck truly says, "the emperor should be obeyed only as long as his commands do not conflict with the law of God —a Christian ought rather to suffer like Daniel in the lion's den than sin against his religion; and nothing is more foreign to him than affairs of state. Indeed in the whole Roman Empire there were no men who so entirely lacked in patriotism as the early Christians. They had no affection for Judea, they soon forgot Galilee, they cared nothing for the glory of Greece and Rome. When a judge asked them which was their country, they said in answer, 'I am a Christian.' And long after Christianity had become the religion of the Empire, St. Augustine declared that it matters not, in respect of this short and transitory life, under whose dominion a mortal man lives, if only he be not compelled to acts of impiety or injustice. Later on, when the Church grew into a political power independent of the State, she became a positive enemy of national interests. In the seventeenth century a Jesuit general called patriotism 'a plague and the most certain death of Christian love!' "9

For centuries after the Roman Empire was shattered, there were no national states. Wandering tribes led by war lords conquered, divided, and fought over fragments of the former Roman dominion. The milling around of nomadic peoples and tribes gradually slowed down and small states soon arose, but they were not national states. They were feudal principalities ruled over by war lords supported by their military retainers. These fragments were divided, combined, and handed about with little or no respect for race, language, geography, or trade. Slowly the feudal holdings coalesced into larger duchies, principalities, and kingdoms; the war lords became dukes, princes, and kings; their power and right to rule gradually came to rest upon a broad acceptance of the perpetuation of noble blood and lineage.

The tie which bound the active part of the population, namely, the various grades of feudal lords, was a personal tie of allegiance, not a bond with the earth or people. "To a man of the middle ages 'his country' meant little more than the neighborhood in which he lived. The first duty of a vassal was to be loyal to his lord; but no national spirit bound together the various barons of one country. A man might be the vassal of the King of France and of the King of England at the same time; and often, from caprice, passion, or sordid interest, the barons sold their services to the enemies of the kingdom.... Far from being, as M. Gautier asserts, the object of an express command in the code of chivalry, true patriotism had no place there at all. It was not known as an ideal, still less did it exist as a reality, among either knights or commoners. As a duke of Orleans could bind himself by a fraternity of arms and alliance to a duke of Lancaster, so English merchants were in the habit of supplying nations at war with England with provisions bought at English fairs, and weapons wrought by English hands."10

Strictly speaking, neither secular *Politik* nor reason of state is to be found in the philosophy of the early middle ages.11 The barbarian invaders brought with them the tribal gods of war, but no large conceptions of government. They were led by commanders whose motive was plain conquest and booty, with no ethical trimmings or fine-spun notions of policy. *Am Anfang war die Tat*; in the beginning was the deed. And the deed alone was sufficient, because in the raw struggle for life, the war lords did provide for their followers an acceptable measure of subsistence and protection by their own skill in achieving a crude social organization and in manipulating it through the incessant conflicts of the middle ages. Not until after some assurance of bare survival was attained did it become necessary to go beyond the deed and establish some reason for it. The dominant interest of the lords who conquered and built extensive states, as of the vassals who followed them, was the seizure of new lands, the collection of booty, and the levying of taxes. Not until war lords were converted to Christianity and surrounded themselves with clerics who could read and write were they bothered about explanations or justifications of their own actions, or of the system in which they found themselves.

The purpose was unvarnished and was not challenged until the ethics of Christianity came into vogue, and later the revived ethics of the pagan writers of Greece and Rome. Christianity itself was often employed in the early middle ages as a covering justification for wars against infidels and heretics, although such wars almost invariably promised and yielded rich earthly returns. After Clovis, convinced that the God of the Christians had aided him in winning the battle of Strassburg against the Alemanni, was baptized with his whole army, he served the "true faith" by conquering the King of the Burgundians who clung to "the Arian heresy." Then, finding that the "fair lands of Aquitaine" were also in the hands of "unbelieving Arians," Clovis combined religious motives with conquest and exploitation. The subjugation of England by William of Normandy had papal approval; from time to time the pope lent aid to one Christian king against another for reasons of ecclesiastical politics; and after the pope and high dignitaries of the Church acquired large domains themselves they frequently sanctioned wars among Christians for practical reasons.

But neither the Church nor Christian writers, as such, could consistently lend any support to one Christian king against another or furnish any philosophy of politics to sustain the pretensions of particular monarchs or the secular claims which, in time, came to be covered by the phrase dynastic interests. The pope might give aid and comfort to one king against another less loyal or compliant, but not on any theory of royal or national advantage. He might, on a rare occasion, prefer the growth of the Holy Roman Empire to the development of independent and recalcitrant kingdoms, but in his eyes one faithful monarch stood on the same footing as all others.

Indeed the weight of the Church was, on the whole, against the spread of centrifugal influences under the cover of dynastic and national enterprise. Of necessity this was true. In organization, faith, and conception, the Church was universal, at least for Europeans. Its clergy formed one intellectual and religious brotherhood, spoke and wrote in one tongue—Latin, and thought in terms of an all-embracing union of the faithful. Though clerks often served kings, sometimes too well for the good of the Church, they could not throw off their greater loyalty to the papacy and write a philosophy of nationalism in any form. "To place worldly interests above the claims of the Church was impious. When Machiavelli declared that he preferred his country to the safety of his soul, people considered him guilty of blasphemy; and when the Venetians defied the papal thunders by averring that they were Venetians in the first place and only Christians in the second, the world heard them with amazement."[12]

The conception of dynastic interest

EVIDENTLY, then, the Christian faith, if open to various interpretations, could furnish no formula adequate to the requirements of any particular political interests under the hegemony of the Church during the middle ages. In the circumstances, individual overlords and monarchs found in secular life other sanctions to serve them in their struggle for power, riches and domain. At length, "the will of the prince" and later "dynastic interest" appeared as convenient formulas for secular rulers, as feudal principalities were merged into rising states. Thus the idea of fealty to the overlord expanded into loyalty to the king or reigning house; and the support thus established was further strengthened by the employment of mercenaries to be sustained by growing tax levies.

At first, these sanctions were assumed and frankly employed as such, without a covering of popular ideology. Under the law of God and nature, the will of the prince was supreme—in the legal theory of the middle ages. If the prince waged war, made alliances, annexed territories, and adopted diplomatic policies, that was sufficient for his subjects, at least, as long as it was sufficient. For centuries, accordingly, the relations of European countries turned wholly or chiefly on princely or dynastic considerations and such interests meant in substance increases in territory, vast accumulations of personal property, fortunate family alliances, and bitter personal and family rivalries; and, in the later period, the enlargement of royal revenues through the enrichment of merchants and agriculturists. Ambassadors appeared as royal agents, and royal agents they remained as long as kings retained absolute dominion.

It would be a mistake, accordingly, to follow the theorists and treat the formula, "dynastic interest," as if it were an ideal and logical system of thought, consistent in all its parts and regularly employed by statesmen as a controlling principle to the exclusion of practical considerations. In fact, it covered substantial realities and was seldom, if ever, invoked in the collective actions of monarchs before the appearance of the republican specter. At bottom and stripped of all trappings, dynastic interest originally meant the interest of each monarch in holding fast to the territories and privileges which he already possessed, in keeping a firm grip upon the activities of his subjects, in extending his domains at the expense of his neighbors, and in the aggrandizement and perpetuation of his house. All this brought riches in lands, palaces, chattels, and money, quite as material as those collected by, let us say, modern merchants engaged in a foreign trade, for the protection of which national interest is invoked. Dynastic interest as a general principle came to the front only when revolutionary republics and restless populations drove frightened monarchs to make common cause to stave off impending eclipse.

All formulas associated with dynastic diplomacy thus had their basis in the realities of dynastic interest. The elaborate language of royal and imperial intercourse deceived no one within the circle; the ambassador in glittering court costume could work as hard at gaining a crumb of territory for his avaricious lord as a black-coated minister of modern times does in winning an oil concession abroad for those whom his government serves at home. The transition from the diplomacy of dynastic interest to that of national interest did not mark, therefore, as great a break as the change in pomp and circumstance would seem to indicate.

To trace the rise and decline of "dynastic interest" as a diplomatic formula would require a rewriting of European history for centuries and obviously lies outside the scope of this inquiry. Yet it is relevant to speak of the doom of that conception and to give a practical illustration of the manner in which it was finally blotted out, for practical purposes, by the triumph of cold, impersonal, national interest.

That the diplomacy of dynastic interest was sinking into oblivion near the close of the nineteenth century was made clear, even to its defenders, by the secret negotiations which went on in Europe over the coming war between the United States and Spain. When in the autumn of 1897, General Woodford, the American Minister at Madrid, presented to the Spanish government a protest against its conduct in Cuba and demanded a cessation of hostilities, the German Emperor, William II, was moved by a surge (*Aufwallung*) of feeling for monarchical solidarity to raise with the German Foreign Office the issue of intervention in behalf of Spain by the European states, possibly by the

Continental states only, whose monarchical form of government, he thought, would be threatened by the independence of Cuba. There were even rumors in the press that the Kaiser might address a note to the Government of the United States in the same tone as his famous dispatch during the Transvaal affair a short time before. At all events he was profoundly stirred by the peril to the dynastic interest inherent in the Spanish-American controversy.[13]

But as soon as the Kaiser took up the question with his foreign office, his ardor for action in support of dynastic interest was immediately chilled by the cold waters of commercial interest. Although there was no lack of sympathy for the dynastic principle in Berlin, the futility of acting upon it directly was speedily demonstrated. With due display of tact, Herr von Bulow telegraphed, for the Kaiser's information, that he hoped, in seeking to meet the intentions of the All Highest, to prevent England and France—in case of common action in favor of Spain—from holding off themselves and gaining economic advantages at Germany's expense. If England and France stood aside, he said, the result of common action would not only be doubtful but could bring positive harm to Germany in the form of adverse political and economic consequences.

Then Herr von Bulow came down to the nub of the matter. He recalled for the Kaiser's benefit that the English exports to America amounted to $170,000,000, German to $94,000,000, and French to $66,000,000; while American exports to England totalled $406,000,000, to Germany $97,000,000, and to France $47,000,000. He also directed the attention of His Majesty to the fact that the new American tariff law authorized the President of the United States to grant special favors to foreign countries through reciprocal agreements. Such was Germany's economic position considered in dollars and marks equivalents. On the other hand, Russian, Austro-Hungarian, and Italian trade and shipping interests were far below those of England, Germany, and France. Five words of sympathy for the Kaiser's dynastic interest; a whole note on the politics and economics of commercial interest. Perhaps the proportion of words represented the weight of dynastic interest in the scales of diplomacy in the new capitalistic age. Herr von Bulow was adroit in dealing with William II, but clear and firm.

In transmitting this paper to His Imperial Majesty, Prince zu Eulenburg, of the Kaiser's retinue, agreed sympathetically with the monarchical principle, expressed doubts about the cooperation of England and France, and hinted that a secret suggestion from Germany to Austria would perhaps be the right way to proceed. He added that Austria was the state from which a proposal in favor of Spain would naturally come. The Austrian Minister, Count Goluchowski, had continually made efforts to interest Germany in the matter, and it would be well if he, reasonably sure of Germany's approval, would take over the business of initiation in favor of the Queen-Regent at Madrid. For this plan Prince zu Eulenburg had the endorsement of William II. It depended, he said, upon the realities of the situation. One must choose the most effective method for reaching the goal. Should there be difficulty in enlisting the support of the French Republic for the dynastic principle, it might be possible to unite the powers on another platform, namely, that their colonial possessions ought to be protected against overseas covetousness (*Begehrlichkeiten*). Evidently dynasties were not strong enough to assert themselves openly in their own defense; commercial interests were more powerful; yet by indirection the latter might be used for dynastic ends. Things had changed fundamentally since the allied monarchs moved upon the French Republic after the outbreak of the first Revolution.

In response to Prince zu Eulenburg's expression of views, Herr von Bulow etched the realities of the situation in sharper lines. In order to help the Spanish monarchy without bringing economic and political injuries to Germany, it was desirable, on the one hand, to act if possible with England and France; in any case, with France, against America; and, on the other hand, to avoid the assumption of leadership themselves. How was France to be enlisted? The French were financially and economically more deeply involved in Spain than were the Germans, while an injury to American relations would affect Germany more seriously than it would France. Russia and Austria-Hungary had only slight economic interests in the United States, as compared with Germany, France, and England, and would risk next to nothing in seeking to block American action in Cuba. Given this situation, von Bulow thought that it would be most satisfactory to Germany if France and Russia, or France alone, or England alone, would take the initiative. Perhaps the goal would be reached quickest if Germany, with complete secrecy, should approach the Vienna cabinet— the natural attorney for the Spanish Queen-Regent—with the proposal that Austria make sure of French, Russian, and English support for common procedure in favor of Spain against the United States—"in accordance with the measure of the All Highest's command." To this solution of the problem, the Kaiser gave his approval in a marginal note on the document. Thus it was generally agreed in German governing circles that independent action by Germany in behalf of the dynastic principle would arouse jealousy in England and France and run against German interests. The dynastic principle was precious, of course, but economic considerations were regarded as "decisive in controversies between Europe and America," and all diplomatic shuffling had to be done within the frame set by economic interests.

It would be irrelevant to trace the tortuous windings of European diplomats in their efforts to protect dynastic interest while safeguarding economic interest. Sufficient for the purposes of the study is the summary: None of the governments or monarchs who spent days and weeks in fruitless negotiations behind the scenes could or at least dared to risk practical interests in an effort to uphold the dynastic principle or the fortunes of any dynasty. The dusk of dynastic interest had come; and darkness fell upon it at the end of the World War.

Incidentally, during the negotiations, the principle of universality, represented by the Church, was likewise defied, for all efforts of the pope to save the Spanish house from war were equally futile. On the one side, he entered into the secret negotiations of royal governments and, on the other, he sought to bring direct pressure upon President McKinley through Archbishop Ireland. This, too, came to nothing. The Church Universal was as powerless as William II or Queen Victoria to prevent the war or save the Spanish dynasty from the humiliation of defeat. Like its ancient associate and frequent foe, monarchy, the Church had become impotent in the presence of conflicting national interests.

The abandonment of the dynastic conception was not due, therefore, to a sudden substitution of ideas. In the long process leading up to its eclipse there had been a decided shift in substantial interests. As we have seen, dynastic interest originally meant the interest of the particular monarch in holding fast to the territories he already possessed, in extending his domains, and in the aggrandizement of his house. Dynastic interest was not an abstraction springing from the realm of pure reason and employed as such to move governments, armies, and navies. It embraced, in fact, lands, palaces, goods, chattels, and revenues differing in degree rather than in kind from those enjoyed by the subjects of monarchs, though clothed in the majesty of public law. And long before the age of the dynasts had drawn to a close, they were subjected to the restrictions and pressure of other interests which were growing up among their peoples—interests quite apart from, if not in conflict with, the mere maintenance of ruling families and their personal advantages. Hence the transition from dynamic to national interest was not as sharp as the outward history of monarchies would seem to imply to superficial observers. Although the change had far-reaching repercussions in externalities, it was primarily an internal transformation, involving principally the question: For whose benefit is diplomacy carried on and whose will is to determine the policy and exercise the greatest control?

Reason of state as the pivot of diplomacy

CLOSELY associated, though by no means identical, with the formula of dynastic interest is that of *ragione di stato, raison d'état, Staatsräson,* reason of state. In searching for the origin of this concept we are carried back to Machiavelli. While it is true that he did not compress his system of politics into this or any other slogan, he undoubtedly laid the foundation upon which all later systems of state-reason were built. Although the term was widely used in many senses, good and bad, justifying both low intrigue and high measures of public welfare, the system of politics to which the name of Machiavellianism was popularly given carried definite connotations in the minds of realistic statesmen. It meant maintaining in power the practicing government, whether republican or royal, crushing dangerous opposition at home, extending dominion and influence abroad, and enriching the ruling class of the state. In the attainment of these great ends all means were justified—intrigue, bribery, secret alliances, wars, annexations, and indemnities. Obviously such a system of politics can work effectively only under a regime of secrecy—*arcana imperii*; it is incompatible with parliamentary institutions, published treaties, and a free press. Moreover, however cynically

pursued by many modern statesmen, it runs counter to many sentiments which interfere with, if they do not block, its effective functioning.

In its diluted forms, reason of state provided no practical guide to statesmen, no fulcrum for diplomacy, no working basis for international relations. It was largely an opportune device, a defense mechanism, too uncertain in its application to give continuity or unity to diplomatic practice. In the hands of Giovanni Botero, *ragione di stato* is a combination of Machiavellian shrewdness and respect for religious institutions. Ammirato was equally, or even more vague, for he defined reason of state as nothing more than the *contravenzione di ragione ordinaria per rispetto di publico benefitio o vero per rispetto di maggiore e più universal ragione.*[14] Obviously such abstractions furnish no guide for statesmen in dealing with concrete situations.

Nor have any of the efforts in modern Europe to give working substance to state-reason been more successful. When Meinecke says that state-reason consists of the maxims of state affairs, the law of state motion, telling statesmen what they must do to maintain the state in health and strength, he does not illuminate the path of diplomats confronted by imperial and trade rivalries, foreign investments, intergovernmental debts, defaulted bonds, or disorders in backward countries. Hence the use of reason of state, either in the Machiavellian sense or as modified by later interpretations, has slowly dropped out of the documents of practical politics. It now abides mainly with closet philosophers. When foreign offices, confronted by inconvenient questions from parliamentary bodies, decline to give out information they do not appeal to any reason of state, but to the new slogan, "public interest."[15]

Naturally, the decline in the use of such *termini technici* came first in countries like England and Holland where monarchies were early challenged by popular bodies. In absolute monarchies, possessing supreme and exclusive governing power, the term "state reason" could be easily used to fortify the position of rulers and their bureaucracies. There the idea, equivalent to *suprema lex*, order, royal command, was unanswerable and final. But in England the case was different. Attempts of the Stuarts to fasten authoritarian concepts upon the estates of the realm failed utterly. The English Parliament, accustomed to argumentation and to answering royal ministers and even kings in sharp language, would have none of the absolute irresponsibility that hid itself behind *raison d'état*. For, at bottom, state reason meant that the monarch and a small group of persons around him claimed omniscience with respect to the state's true interest. With the establishment of parliamentary supremacy, the idea of state reason and state interest became largely obsolete in England, surviving longest in the language of the courts of law in dealing with high treason and other state cases. As use of the term declined, such notions as the interest of England, the public interest, and national interest took its place.

The formula of national honor

AMONG the reasons of state, peculiarly appropriate to feudal orders and monarchies, there early appeared a formula known as the "honor of the prince," which was easily transformed, with the growth of democracy, into the idea of "national honor." As its Latin origin implies, the term "honor" was associated with the requirements of rank; an *honestus vir* was a man of high status, possessing property in keeping with his condition; and certain signs and ceremonies of respect, such as salutations and genuflections, were associated with his position in society. In feudal times the characteristics of honor were found in the *code duello*. Ordinarily they did not pertain to pecuniary matters but to insults, aspersions of character, defamation, signs of contempt, and the virtue of women. To give a king's ambassador a lower place at a public spectacle or at a conference table than His Majesty felt proper in view of his conceptions of grandeur and position was an affront to his honor, to his dignity and his status.[16] From feudal and monarchical orders the formula passed over to republics and democracies and was widely employed in political and diplomatic usage and literature.

Like other slogans of politics, the term was never minutely analyzed or defined, but it was treated as covering something transcending in nature all material and economic interests. Indeed from the standpoint of national honor, the latter were deemed ignoble, and appeals to them unworthy of patriotism. This did not mean that statesmen who employed the term national honor were more opposed than princes to wars for material interests; on the contrary, in their opinion, national honor often coincided with winning substantial advantages by arms; yet, as a rule, exponents of the code were inclined to regard with contempt arguments against war based on the pecuniary consideration that war does not "pay."

In many instances, however, "honor" provided a convenient manoeuvring ground for the attainment of economic or political advantage. A cause in which economic matters were involved was not to be rejected, if questions of national honor could also be drawn into the scene, but honor was the supreme concern. The case was clearly put in an address before the Naval War College in 1897 by Theodore Roosevelt, whose public papers and private writings are strewn with the terms "righteousness" and "national honor." In calling for battleships as against arbitration treaties, he said: "A really great people, proud and high spirited, would face all the disasters of war rather than purchase that base prosperity which is bought at the price of national honor.... We ask for a great navy partly because we think that the possession of such a navy is the surest guaranty of peace, and partly because we feel that no national life is worth having if the nation is not willing, when the need shall arise, to stake everything on the supreme arbitrament of war and to pour out its blood, its treasure, and tears like water rather than submit to the loss of honor or renown."[17]

So widely spread was the conception of national honor as the supreme consideration of diplomacy and international relations, in republican America no less than in imperial Germany, that the Hague Conference of 1899 placed it first on the reservations of states. In recommending that parties unable to settle controversies by negotiation should submit them to inquiry by an impartial commission, the Conference included only matters "involving neither honor nor vital interest." For many years thereafter it was customary for governments in drawing arbitration treaties to make similar reservations. That signed by Great Britain and the United States, in 1908, for example, in stipulating that certain differences should be referred to the Hague Tribunal, contained the significant addendum: "Provided, nevertheless, that they do not affect the vital interests, the independence, or the honor of the two contracting states." As the follower of the *code duello* could not submit a matter touching his pride to a court of law in an action for pecuniary damages, so no nation could suffer the arbitration of any point involving honor. As Lord John Russell said, in speaking of the Alabama claims: "That is a question of honor which we will never arbitrate, for England's honor can never be made the subject for arbitration."[18]

Yet on close scrutiny the meaning of national honor in concrete terms proved to be exceedingly elusive. Mr. Perla's symposium of opinions on the subject, published in 1918, revealed an array of diverse and conflicting ideas respecting the content of the phrase, the association of pecuniary interests with it, the occasions on which it should be invoked, and the means of satisfaction. In his careful analysis the irrationality and emotional perils of the concept stood clearly revealed.

As trade, commerce, and other economic relations became increasingly the major subject matters with which international questions were associated, and as the exercise of national sovereignty changed from the personal control of a monarch to that of a popular representative body, the formula of national honor became more and more inadequate. So long as pride, dignity, position, the aggrandizement of royal families and their retinues, and similar matters of personal and emotional content constituted significant subjects of international discourse, the mere assertion of national honor was sufficient. By their very nature such matters were not debatable. Each personal sovereign and later each sovereign nation was the sole judge of its own conduct. There was no basis, no objective standard, for calling these matters into question and settling them.

When, however, economic issues gained a preponderence in international relations, much of the ground upon which the original conception of national honor rested was destroyed. Economic questions, treating of material things, of industry, trade, tariffs, exchange, and the like, are open to statistical enumeration, to reason and logic, to debate and persuasion. Acceptable standards can be applied, and differences of opinion do not involve any indictment of opponents on principles of honor. The very nature of such questions usually precludes their absolute determination at the will of, or by the action of, a single person or a small group. At all events, the use of reason is not excluded.

As soon as the prime subject matters of international intercourse took economic forms, the views and standards of many different peoples and groups became applicable, without insult to any; and "honor" in this connection became debatable, was stripped of absolutism. Moreover, since it was generally impossible to raise an issue of honor that did not also involve pecuniary risks, losses, or gains, it was increasingly difficult to keep pecuniary calculations from entering into the weighing of honor, openly or secretly. It was almost impossible to isolate pure "honor" and avoid imputations of interest. Thus honor as a single, insulated pivot of diplomacy was deprived of its finality.

As time passed, statesmen were led to lay diminishing emphasis on a formula that defied rational analysis, that had its sanction mainly in emotion and ceremony.[19] Perhaps they discerned a certain inconsistency, if not irony, in treaties by which "honorable" governments, which *ipso facto* could not insult one another, reserved from pacific settlement questions of insult against one another. At all events, the phrase, "national honor," already declining in efficacy prior to the World War, was abandoned in some respects and materially altered in others in the post-war years. The emotional and sentimental complex of national honor has not wholly disappeared; nor are appeals to it wanting in lighter political literature;[20] but as a working formula for international action it has become of distinctly secondary importance.[21]

The later arbitration treaties omit it. The climax is reached in the Kellogg Pact which condemns recourse to war for the solution of international difficulties, binds the signatories to renounce it as an instrument of national policy in their relations with one another, and obligates them to seek the pacific settlement of "all disputes or conflicts of whatever nature or of whatsoever origin they may be." The *code duello* is renounced and even matters of national honor are to be adjusted by peaceful processes, without recourse to arms. The transition from the sentiments of feudalism to the philosophy of calculation has been completed—in the pretensions of contemporary diplomacy.

The rise of the idea of national interest

RESPONSIVE to the ever-changing physical conditions of the world, the character and occupations of its people, and the political and economic structure of society, the old formulas of international relations—will of the prince, dynastic interests, reason of state, and national honor—came into being, served their respective purposes in a rough way, and passed into history. Most of these formulas are today either entirely abandoned as pivots or fulcra of diplomacy, or their form is so radically altered to render their operation and influence indirect and of minor importance. No diplomat is any longer seriously disturbed by the will of the prince.[22] Dynastic interests have long since passed into the discard with the eclipse of monarchical rule. State-reason and the feudalistic conceptions of national honor have broken down completely under the impact of economic relations and popular control of government. All these formulas now appear too abstract, too unreal, and too remote from modern conditions to be effective. In the light of modern demands for a foreign policy truly expressive of realities, stable, consistent, and capable of being handled by logical and analytical methods, these old formulas, with their personal associations, their emotional content, their uncertainties and needless hazards, are recognized as deficient.

With the emergence of the national state system, the increase in influence of popular political control, and the great expansion of economic relations, the lines of a new formula— "national interest"—were being laid down. The process by which the new formula came into general use was largely evolutionary, many of the elements of the old formulas, after much reinterpretation and adaptation, being incorporated in it. National interest, as a pivot of diplomacy, is now almost universally employed in international relations. Indeed, it may be said that national interest—its maintenance, advancement, and defense by the various means and instrumentalities of political power— is the prime consideration of diplomacy. The term evidently appeals to men of affairs as susceptible of rational comprehension, concrete definition, and specific usage. Unlike the abstractions and vagaries of the old formulas, national interest seems to bear a clear and positive relation to the tangibles which are the major concern of the modern world, especially to economic operations that can be cast or reflected in particular and general balance sheets.

Although no microscopic history of the idea of national interest has yet been written, some tentative conclusions respecting its origin and development are permissible. The term "interest" is old, being a derivation from the Latin. The word means: it concerns; it makes a difference to, or is important with reference to, some person or thing: *interest omnium recte facere*. In the middle ages, when religious affairs were the chief preoccupation of the intellectual class, it was often employed in spiritual relations—"the heavenly interests of mankind"—and did not necessarily carry material implications. With the spread of secularism and commerce it took on tangible substance—"worldly interests," as contrasted with things of the spirit. With the rise of political economy the term assumed material connotations, thrusting other usages into the background. In some circles it was employed in an invidious sense, in attacks on "vested interests," but the word of aspersion was often accepted by the aspersed; and statesmen were not ashamed to speak of "dollar" diplomacy. While the word retains, and may rightly retain, much of its ancient flavor, whenever it appears in diplomatic and political negotiations it can generally be broken down into substantial elements.

At all events, the use of national interest in diplomacy is particularly associated in time with the rise and growth of the national commercial state, and with the evolution of republican control over national affairs. The nations of Western Europe had scarcely emerged from the chaos of feudalism under the leadership of strong monarchs, when the era of discovery and world commerce opened. If nations were built up by dynastic interests, they soon broke the mold and outran the purposes of their makers. "Princes rule peoples," said the Duke de Rohan in 1638, "and interests dominate the princes." In the beginning the "interests" that ruled princes were interests as conceived by the princes and agreeable to them. As long as the prince merely commanded small groups of fighting men, he could freely consult his own pleasure and will; but as commerce increased, towns flourished, and society became compactly knit in an economic mesh, the prince himself became a victim of interests. National interest was largely developed through the compromise between interests dynastically conceived and interests as interpreted and enforced by the rising class power, and later by popular power.

This change in affairs was apparently observed first, and not strangely, in the commercial cities of Italy, and the philosophy of it was outlined in the documents known as the "Italian Relations"—reports of Italian ambassadors from the other countries of Europe. Commercial in interest and compelled to employ every possible stratagem to preserve themselves against destruction by powerful foes, the Italian cities sent out diplomatic agents who were, of necessity, realistic in their approach. These ministers reported not only on the intrigues of courts, but also on industry, commerce, legislation, and the customs and prejudices of peoples. By the middle of the sixteenth century they reached the conclusion that the great movements of politics sprang from deeply rooted forces of life, that the impersonal *interessi di stato* controlled the relations of states with one another, that each state was driven by the egoism of its own needs and interests, and that all other motives of policy were secondary.[23]

From Italy, it seems, the doctrine of interest spread to France where it was reformulated for French usage by powerful writers during the first half of the seventeenth century. While direct connections are not yet established, it is not without significance that one of the thinkers of the new direction, Duke de Rohan, spent some time in Italy before he wrote his treatise, "De l'Interest des Princes et Estats de la Chrestienté" (1638). In due course the idea of national interest became associated with the concept of dynastic interest in various parts of Europe, giving wider content to that ancient historic formula.

Across the Channel in England, where dynastic interest was early subdued to parliamentary control and reason of state was early recognized as a mere covering formula for monarchical and bureaucratic pretensions the idea of "England's interest," "public interest," and "national interest" found a hospitable home by the end of the seventeenth century. Parliamentarians, publicists, and representatives of ruling classes used the new concept freely as equivalent to the sum of particular interests or a balance of interests in society. In this way they justified policies of government, on the comfortable assumption that a harmony of interests existed, that interest, though often mistaken, could "never lie"—to use the phrase of an old writer—and that national interest could be disclosed by adding together the dominant interests. As the circle of governing classes widened, the circle of interested parties widened, and the interest of society, meaning the vocal and efficient sections of it, supplanted the interest of the dynasty.

In the English colonies beyond the Atlantic, where feudal and monarchical sentiments became attenuated as the population grew, state reason was early regarded with suspicion, and popular interests bulked large in the thought of public men.[24] In their resistance to the British government, Americans acquired a habit of using terms like "the people," "the nation," or "the common-

wealth" when speaking of *res publicæ* in a laudatory sense and of referring to government or state when employing derogatory language.[25] To Americans the state appeared as "a cold monster." As the British official class in the colonies and the British Admiralty increased their pressures on American economic life, under pretense of a general British interest,[26] the provincials developed a sense of community, local, or collective interest as against the weight above. Dynastic interest and state reason had no roots in the American heritage, and British usage had prepared the way for a transition to commonwealth or national interest.

Even from this cursory survey it seems evident that the transition from feudal formulas to the conception of national interest was not marked by a sharp break in ideas, akin to the opposition between the Ptolemaic and Copernican systems. It was a gradual transition from formula to formula. The conception of *unity* associated with dynastic interest remained. An element of compelling *absolutism* was retained: national interest was no less sovereign and inexorable than the will of the prince. Although national interest was opposed to dynastic interest, its official interpreters might exclude the nation from knowledge of specific operations in foreign affairs on grounds of "the public interest." The main citadel of the *arcana imperii* stood unscathed.

If the transition marked no sharp break, however, it was swift. As European commerce expanded to all parts of the world, wars between reigning families over territories in Europe became entangled with wars over colonies, backward places, and trade, thus spreading to the ends of the earth. Meanwhile commerce flourished, capital accumulated, and the trading classes rose in numbers and wealth until they overshadowed the aristocracies of the soil. Monarchs were gradually subdued by parliaments in which the middle class gained ascendancy. Monarchies became republican nations in fact, if not also in name. Science undermined the intellectual authority of the clergy who were concerned, theoretically at least, with otherworldly interests. Competition between capitalist countries for raw materials and markets became sharper and sharper. Political economy was transformed into economics, the science of private gain. Darwinism introduced a principle which was interpreted as implying an eternal struggle for existence on a material plane, as lending biological sanction to the primary significance of material interests. The church was divorced from the state and the desiderata of politics became fundamentally secular. At last the way was prepared for the unquestioned supremacy of national interest in international relations and of the idea as the guide to national action.

Yet no one has explored the nature and implications of the new formula. If citizens are to support the government which prosecutes it, soldiers are to die for it, and foreign policies are to conform to it, what could be more appropriate than to ask: What is national interest? An inquiry into the substance of the formula becomes a pressing task of political science. A beginning may be made with a study of the idea in the United States.

The problem

THE problem presented by the proposed inquiry is not one in exact science—an examination of a deterministic sequence, a physical process under law which can be expressed by a differential equation. Nor is it a problem of philology to be solved by an excursion in etymology, resulting in a dictionary definition. The question—what is national interest?—can be answered, if at all, only by exploring the use of the formula by responsible statesmen and publicists and by discovering the things and patterns of conduct—public and private—embraced within the scope of the formula. The problem, then, can be expressed in terms of formula, things, and patterns of conduct. Where the formula appears in the usages of statecraft it is appropriate to explore the substance covered by it. Where the things and patterns of conduct covered by it appear, with or without the formula, it is appropriate to relate them to the conception of national interest; for obviously statesmen do not always pronounce the formula every time they operate under the conception. Only in this way can unity of these, continuity of practice, diversity of interpretation, and possible upshot be kept steadily in view until general conclusions are reached.

Of necessity the initial procedure must be historical, for the term, national interest, has been extensively employed by American statesmen since the establishment of the Constitution. The formula is an idea which has been developed in a long course of years. Conceivably, to be sure, a shallow time-depth could be taken—the use of the term during the past six months, the past ten years, or the past fifty years; but any such segmentation of history would be arbitrary. It would leave out of account relevant practices, usages, thought, and traditions which cannot be excluded if the fullness of the theme is to be covered. Yet there must be a beginning; and the break made in American institutional history by the establishment of the Constitution affords a starting point which is more than merely convenient. The adoption of the Constitution marked a new concentration of efficient forces in American politics, the creation of new machinery for giving expression to those forces in foreign affairs, and the cooperation of leading statesmen in laying down fundamental lines of foreign policy for the future. Moreover, it is within the framework of the Constitution that foreign policies coming under the head of national interest are still formulated and carried into execution.

Other considerations call for historical procedure. The formula, national interest, embraces two terms—national and interest. Now, it is a matter of common knowledge that the American nation was not created at one stroke in 1776 or in 1787. It is the product of a long historical development. Although the term nation was freely used by the Fathers, by Jefferson as well as Hamilton, it later came under a cloud, as the existence of the nation was challenged by those advocates of states' rights who placed loyalty to their respective commonwealths above loyalty to "the general government," as it was often called. Not until the great decision of 1865 was the issue settled and the existence and supremacy of the nation assured against all doubts and opposition, political or military. Thus, although the nation of the Fathers perdured and survived the trial by battle, the use of the term "national" in connection with "interest" rose and fell with the fortunes of the domestic conflict that divided the country. The substance of nationality continued in development, but the phraseology of politics varied. Since we are concerned with substance as well as formula, consistency of treatment requires respect for historical continuity.

Historical treatment is also required by the very nature of the diplomacy which turns upon national interest. Despite all calls for "a united front" and for the stoppage of politics at the water's edge," American diplomacy, within certain broad limits, reflects party divisions at home, and is party diplomacy. Owing to the inherent characteristics of the American system, government is party government. And it is in historical time that parties succeed one another in control over the machinery and engines of foreign policy. Although some continuity is assured by general considerations, by the bureaucracy of the State Department, and by the permanent technicians of the Navy Department, fluctuations more or less violent have occurred and do occur in the interpretation of national interest. Since this is true, it follows that a wide historical span must be brought under review in a quest for the meaning of national interest.

The first step, therefore, is historical—an inquiry into the things and patterns of conduct covered by the formula, "national interest"—in their development from 1787 to the present moment. Such an inquiry can be objective, factual, and realistic, within the range of empirical scholarship. The things and patterns can be described with fair accuracy, in a manner approaching that of exact science; and typical applications of the formula can be disclosed by historical investigation. When this task has been completed, the way is open for an evaluation of the doctrine, as well as the things and patterns of conduct covered by it, and for an attempt to construct out of the materials a philosophy of national interest, consistent in its several parts, to serve as a guide to policy and an interpretation of history in the process of unfolding. Inasmuch as the second step involves the necessity of choosing and asserting values, it is reserved for a separate volume to follow—to avoid confusing facts with assumptions and predilections.

Although the first step is historical, it does not call for a rewriting of American history. It implies at the outset an exploration of the original conception of national interest under the Constitution, with respect to things and patterns of conduct covered by it. That exploration yields two fundamental relevancies in the field of national interest—territory and commerce, including their connections with domestic affairs. By this disclosure attention is narrowed essentially to nationality, territory, and commerce, in their relation to the conception of interest, as the years of American history unrolled. Since in the study of all human affairs, limitations must be set, these limitations—territory and commerce in relation to national interest—seem to be justified by the nature of the problem before us and by the preliminary findings.

Notes

1. *Annals of the American Academy of Political and Social Science*, Vol. CXI, Supplement, p. 7.
2. *The Problem of Asia*, pp. 97, 187 (italics mine). See also Mahan, *The Interest of America in Sea Power—Present and Future* (1898).
3. Admiral Mahan, *The Interest of America in International Conditions*, quoted in Perla, *What is "National Honor"?* p. xii.
4. *The French Yellow Book*, No. 117.
5. *Ibid.*, No. 129.
6. *Foreign Affairs*, July, 1932, p. 557.
7. "*Interessen* (materialle und ideelle), nicht Ideen, beherrschen unmittelbar das Handeln der Menschen. Aber die 'Weltbilder,' welche durch Ideen geschaffen wurden, haben sehr oft als Weichensteller die Bahnen bestimmt, in denen die Dynamik der Interessen das Handeln fortbewegte." Max Weber, quoted in Marianne Weber, *Max Weber* (1926), pp. 347f.
8. Meinecke, *Die Idee der Staatsräson*, p. 32.
9. Westermarck, *Origin and Development of the Moral Ideas*, Vol. II, p. 179.
10. Westermarck, *op. cit.*, p. 180; the sale of munitions to enemy countries is, of course, not unknown in recent times.
11. F. Meinecke, *Die Idee der Staatsräson*, p. 33.
12. Westermarck, *op. cit.*, Vol. II, p. 181.
13. Owing to the revolution in Germany which tore open the secret archives, it is possible to trace an outline of the affair in German diplomatic documents: *Die Grosse Politik der Europäischen Kabinette, 1871–1914*, Vol. XV, pp. 3–30, upon which the above record is based. What French, English, and Spanish papers may sometime show is a matter for interesting speculation.
14. Meinecke, *op. cit.*, p. 151.
15. Joint resolutions of the American Congress, calling upon the executive for information and reports upon foreign policies, invariably include the phrase "if compatible with the public interest," indicating the modern form into which "state-reason" has passed.
16. The troublesome question of rank and position in diplomatic practice, especially at congresses and conferences, has become less pressing only in recent years as the nations consent to alphabetical arrangements and other abstract standards. The whole code of precedence based upon honor and degrees of eminence has not, of course, been completely obliterated; it has merely become less important.
17. Bishop, *Theodore Roosevelt and His Time*, Vol. I, p. 77.
18. Perla, *What is "National Honor"?* p. 36.

19. The assertion that a particular question is a matter "solely of domestic concern" illustrates one of the modern forms into which the original conception of honor is passing.

20. Thus, Senator McCumber, when questioning Secretary of State Robert Lansing concerning the power given to a "commission of inquiry" by certain labor provisions of the Treaty of Peace with Germany, signed June 28, 1919, asked: "But do you think it an appropriate thing for a great government to put itself in a position in which it should submit itself in honor or in any other way to be hauled up before a commission of this kind to answer as to what it should do with reference to its own labor?" Clearly indicating the insignificance of this aspect of the "honor" formula, Mr. Lansing replied: "I do not think there is anything out of the way about that at all." *Senate Doc.* 106, 66th Congress, Vol. 10, p. 178.

21. Modern diplomatic negotiation frequently appeals to national honor, as for example in connection with the "sanctity" of treaties; but it does so only in support of a position taken rather than as a position per se—"honor" as an independent pivot of diplomacy. The most frequent modern use of the national honor formula is that by which internal, national action is influenced *vis-à-vis* international relationships. It was so used to bring about the repeal of the clause in the Panama Canal Act of August 24, 1912, which exempted American vessels engaged in the coastwise trade from the payment of tolls. Similarly, the "national honor" concept was employed in the debate concerning the devaluation of the gold dollar (Senator R. C. Patterson, *Cong. Record*, 73rd Cong. 1st Sess., April 25, 1933, p. 2339); and again, in connection with the debate on the "joint resolution (H. J. Res. 192) to assure uniform value to the coins and currencies of the United States" (bearing upon the "gold clause" in financial obligations). (See Senator David A. Reed, *Cong. Record*. 73rd Cong., 1st Sess., June 3, 1933, p. 4996.) The number of instances of this kind is almost unlimited, especially when legislation on domestic affairs is likely to have repercussions outside American borders. This is one of the new ways of applying the old "national honor" formula.

22. Although the power of dictatorships is often strong and absolute, the will of the dictator does not have the same moral sanction as the will of the prince once had.

23. Meinecke, *op. cit.*, p. 188.

24. When William Penn was threatened with the loss of his proprietary rights, he wrote to Robert Harley: "It is pretended the King's service, but I hope reason of state shall never be one to violate property." August 27, 1701. *Portland Mss.*, Vol. IV, pp. 19ff.

25. Schmoller, *Jahrbuch*, 1894, p. 1241; citation of W. J. Ashley's writings.

26. With a view to overcoming the resistance of local interests—"the interests of private landowners being often opposed to that of the public"—certain cases were transferred from local courts to the Admiralty courts. *Acts of the Privy Council of England; Colonial Series*; Vol. I, p. 194. A British admiral, stationed in the waters of the West Indies, complained of difficulties placed in his way by the authorities of Jamaica in 1702: "Private interest is what they aim at without regard to the King's order or security of this island, whose interest here will be either lost or ruined if left in their hands." *State Papers: Domestic. Anne*, Vol. I, p. 147.

Stephen B. Jones

Global strategic views

The seaman studies the same globe as the landsman.[1]

IN A PRECEDING PAPER we discussed certain views of the political world stemming from facts of physical and human geography.[2] The last of these facts was circulation—the movement of men and things on the face of the earth. The next step brings us to the present paper, for movement is the essence of strategy. This is true even though strategy is not confined to military art: the implementation of every political decision requires movement. It may be messages that move, or men, or money, or munitions. "Strategy" in the broad sense can be defined as the art of using power. "Global Strategy" implies this art viewed in relation to the whole world. The "global strategic views" of our title are geographical patterns related to global strategic ideas.

We do not attempt encyclopedic coverage. The focus is on certain major ideas about the world, their relationships and their consequences. We begin with one of the first men to write of strategy in global terms, Mahan.

Mahan's view

THE name of Mahan immediately evokes images of gray ships and blue water. However, as all students of his works know, he was concerned not so much with naval operations (though he described many battles) as with sea power, and sea power is as much of the land as of the sea. In his most famous book[3] Mahan listed six fundamental factors affecting the development of sea power: geographical position, physical conformation, extent of territory, number of population, national character, and governmental character. Merely to read this list is to understand the importance of the land base.

Mahan devoted most of his attention to European and North Atlantic naval history, including offshoot campaigns in the Indian Ocean. However, in one of his less well-known books we find a global view, somewhat crudely outlined, that adumbrates the views of Mackinder, Fairgrieve, and Spykman. Here Mahan describes Russia in terms that fit Mackinder's Heartland—a "vast, uninterrupted mass" whose "centre cannot be broken."[4] He emphasizes Russia's landlocked position and its dominance in Central Asia. He points to the latitudinal belt of 30° to 40° N. in Asia as the unstable zone between British sea power and Russian land power.[5] This resembles, roughly, the Asiatic part of Fairgrieve's "crush zone."[6] Mahan also adumbrates Fairgrieve's "northern belt of settlement and movement," pointing out that Suez and Panama would mark the southern limit of most active commerce and politics.[7]

Mahan thought that Russian expansion in Asia could be opposed by sea-transported power—a sort of containment policy. Somewhat surprisingly, he advocated giving Russia access to the sea through China[8]—a premonition of Yalta, one might say. He believed this would satisfy Russian aspirations for warm-water ports, though it is hard to see how that could be the case with the bulk of the Russian population in Europe.[9] Mahan also predicted that Britain, Germany, Japan and the United States would find a common interest in containing Russia and controlling China.[10] This prediction is less startling in 1955 than it seemed 10 years ago, when the present writer first read it. Like Mackinder after him, Mahan probably overestimated the influence of navigable rivers. He refers repeatedly to the navigability of the Yangtze. During the years of China's weakness, when foreign gunboats patrolled the river, it did serve as an avenue for sea power. But adequate land or air forces could make the Yangtze

Reprinted with permission from the *Geographical Review*, Vol. 45, 1955, pp. 492–508.

untenable for foreign ships, as happened when the Japanese bombed the *Panay* and the Chinese Communists attacked the *Amethyst*.

Looking back, one may question whether "sea power" was a really happy phrase. It emphasized one medium of power transmission, rather than the whole picture of national power and the places and purposes of its use. A lingering effect of a too literal interpretation of the sea-power doctrine is an American belief that might be called "naval isolationism." This is to be distinguished from "continental isolationism," which would defend America at its shores. Naval isolationism is the belief that superior sea power can keep an enemy off the oceans and hence that American shores are safe without sending armies to lands overseas. The basic thesis is doubtful in this age of the airplane and the submarine, and the need to maintain a balance of power in Eurasia is ignored. Mahan's own views on Asia do not support the naval isolationist position, and Mackinder and Spykman, to whom we now turn, regarded it as definitely unsound.

Mackinder's view

IT is not surprising that the United States, painfully land-minded since the opening of the West and the decline of sailing ships, should have produced Mahan, while Britain, most maritime of great powers, should have produced Mackinder. Prophets traditionally are voices crying in the wilderness. However, as we have already indicated, the basic views of Mahan and Mackinder are not as far apart as is commonly believed. Mahan outlined in a rough way the Heartland concept. Both men understood that sea power is land-based and that the size, population, and productivity of the land base have much to do with the magnitude of the resulting sea power. Mahan recognized the peculiar virtues of Britain's position, a large island off the European shore, and one of Mackinder's most scholarly works is called "Britain and the British Seas."[11] It was in their forecasts that they drew apart. Mahan continued to believe in the greater capacity and flexibility of movement by sea; Mackinder thought the great improvements in land transportation put the shoe on the other foot.

In his famous paper of 1904,[12] Mackinder designated as the "Pivot Area" that part of Eurasia which has interior drainage or drains to the icebound Arctic. The word "heart-land" appears only once in this paper, but in the 1919

book[13] it is capitalized and dehyphenated and supersedes "Pivot Area." The rest of Eurasia was called by Mackinder in 1904 "the Inner or Marginal Crescent." In 1919 parts of this crescent were called Coastlands. (Spykman later coined the felicitous term "rimland" for the Inner Crescent.) The Americas, Africa south of the Sahara, Australia, and the large islands off the Eurasian shores, such as the British Isles and Japan, were called in 1904 "the Outer or Insular Crescent." In 1919, Eurasia and Africa together were named the "World Island," Africa south of the Sahara "the Southern Heartland," and the other lands of the Outer Crescent "satellites" of the World Island.[14]

Mackinder's recognition of central Eurasia as the source of powerful forces that have affected Europe, South Asia, and the Far East was of course soundly based and was a needed corrective to the egocentricity of maritime Europe. But the original definition of the Pivot Area was the extreme of hydrographic literalness. It assumed that maritime states could move their forces up rivers—though current would favor the continental power—but would be unable to cross divides, however low. Actually, most transport systems work both ways. This statement applies not only to rivers but to the modern means of land transport that Mackinder especially stressed. In 1940 the Germans pushed the British off the continent. In 1945 the armies of the maritime powers swept into Germany along *Autobahnen* built to serve German troops. It is really a question of which side has the most power and makes the best use of it. It is true that improvements in land and air transportation have increased the burdens of the maritime states. But their burdens are increased primarily because they can no longer put so many of their eggs in the naval basket and because they must advance their strategic frontier as deeply into the Rimland as possible, not because the rivers of central Eurasia fail to reach an open sea.

In "Democratic Ideals and Reality" Mackinder made some alterations in the boundaries of the Heartland. "The Heartland, for the purposes of strategical thinking, includes the Baltic Sea, the navigable Middle and Lower Danube, the Black Sea, Asia Minor, Armenia, Persia, Tibet, and Mongolia."[15] Thus Mackinder now thought that the Baltic and Black Seas were closed to the maritime powers, as they had been during the First World War. This again seems a highly literal view. If land-based forces can close the Danish and Turkish straits, they can also keep them open to friendly ships. It is a question of who has the power, the initiative, the speed, and of who is allied to whom.

On a small-scale map the central position of the Heartland, or of the Soviet Union, in Eurasia looks terrifying. The Rimland seems such a narrow margin that it might be overwhelmed in a night. It is true that the Soviet position is strong, and that improvements in land and air transportation make it easier to exploit its advantages. Mahan believed that the sea lanes around Eurasia were really the interior lines, strategically.[16] This may no longer be true. But the speed and size of ships have greatly increased since Mahan's day. A modern freighter can cover as great a distance in a day as a truck convoy, carrying far more cargo, and is fueled for thousands of miles. Fast ships are worthy rivals of railway trains. Only the airplane is clearly superior in speed. We shall see below that this does not necessarily give the Heartland an overwhelming positional advantage. The great advantages of the Soviet Union have been political, especially its ability to follow a planned strategy persistently. The shift of China from the non-Communist to the Communist side was not so much a victory of land power over sea power as of a persistent, planned strategy over an inconsistent and blundering one.

Haushofer and his school adopted the main features of the Mackinder global view as part of the mélange of Geopolitik. They hoped that the first term of the famous dictum could be brought about by a partnership of Germany and the Soviet Union,[17] a hope which proved as illusory as Hitler's belief that Britain would agree to his terms.

Spykman's view

SPYKMAN adopted Mackinder's basic geography but gave it a different interpretation. He rejected the apparent fatalism of the land-power doctrine and offered his own formula: "Who controls the rimland rules Eurasia; who rules Eurasia controls the destinies of the world."[18] Spykman hoped that the Soviet Union, the United Kingdom, and the United States would realize their common stake in controlling the Rimland. He knew, however, that "it may be that the pressure of Russia outward toward the rimland will constitute one important aspect of the post-war settlement."[19]

Mackinder's view has often been twisted into a fatalistic doctrine of "Herzland über alles."[20] Spykman seems to imply such a doctrine when he says that Mackinder emphasized "an inevitable historical opposition between Russian land power and British sea power." But, says Spykman, "there has never really been a simple land power-sea power opposition. The historical alignment has always been in terms of some members of the rimland with Great Britain against some members of the rimland with Russia, or Great Britain and Russia together against a dominating rimland power."[21] Actually Mackinder knew this, and said so. The Heartland, in its limited sense of the interior and Arctic drainage area, menaced the maritime states only in conjunction with part of the Rimland. In the 1904 paper Mackinder[22] spoke of the peril to the marginal lands if Germany were to ally itself with Russia and of the possibility that China, organized by Japan, might conquer the Russian Empire. In the 1919 book it was the domination of the Heartland by East Europe that would lead to command of the world.

Looked at broadly, the Mahan, Mackinder, and Spykman strategic geographies have much in common. They also have much in common with Kennan's containment policy,[23] which was conceived independently.[24] Containment primarily means preventing extensions of Soviet control in the Rimland. Kennan, it might be noted, does not speak of either land power or sea power, avoiding the confusion that those terms are likely to engender. . . .

The wide blue yonder

WHEN Mackinder's "The Geographical Pivot of History" was printed in the *Geographical Journal*, the comments made by members of the audience were, according to the usual practice, printed also. Many readers have noted that one auditor, Amery, called attention to the airplane as possibly upsetting the assumptions on which Mackinder's theory was based[25]—this in 1904, only a few weeks after the Wright brothers had made their first flight.

Mackinder, we have seen, wrote of the seaman's and the landsman's points of view. The basic pattern of the physical world was of course the same for both, but the strategic forecast hinged on the belief that land transportation was overtaking sea transportation as a vehicle of power. We have also seen that putting, or seeming to put, seaman and landsman in strong contrast may have been a disservice to clear thinking. Now we have the airman. Must we add the airman's point of view? Or would that only increase the confusion?

For one thing, there is a wide range of thought about air power. Experience with air power is limited, and the pace of technological change has been extraordinary. We find variation from the "all-out" school, exemplified by such men as Douhet and Seversky, through moderate but firmly "air-first" men to the conservatives who hold that the main function of air power is to assist surface operations.

The conservative group holds that the surface battlefield remains the locus of decision. Sea power is vital to the supply of the battle front. Air power is vital to the security of sea routes, for observation and rapid transportation, and as long-range artillery to interdict enemy movements. Strategic bombardment, to this group, should be related to surface operations. Such a view of air power leads to no very new view of the globe. A third dimension has been added to the Mahan or Mackinder world, but its surface features have not been erased, and the travel-time scale has not been greatly altered, since surface movement dominates.

For an example of the air-first moderates, we may take Slessor, who holds that the strategic air force, with nuclear bombs, is "the Great Deterrent" which may prevent another general war.[26] But local wars are still possible, with ground forces bearing much of the load. Slessor sees a need for armies and navies and even for a special "semi-static" force or militia for local and civil defense. Slessor does not describe his global view, as we use that term here, but manifestly it must combine something like the Rimland—the locus of local wars— with a disbelief in heartlands. His views on heartlands seem like an echo of Amery's, amplified by half a century of aeronautical development:

Meanwhile do not let us be distracted by geopolitical talk about heartlands, which was all very well in Mackinder's day but ceased to be relevant with the advent of the long-range bomber. Russia's central position has some tactical advantages, vis-à-vis her neighbours, but in a world air war she would be at a decisive disadvantage. Air power has turned the vast spaces that were her prime defence against Napoleon and Hindenburg and Hitler into a source of weakness. In these days of near-sonic speeds, the depth of penetration necessary to reach some of her vital centres is offset by the size of the area to

be defended and the fact that it can be attacked from almost all round the compass.[27]

In Slessor's view, the virtues of the Heartland— size, centrality, and inaccessibility—have become either of no advantage or disadvantageous. Have *Raum und Lage* gone into reverse, so to speak, in the air age?

In order that the Soviet power base be penetrable "from almost all round the compass," it is essential that the non-Communist powers maintain a strong position in the Rimland and in what Spykman called the "off-shore islands" of Great Britain, Japan, Africa, and Australia.[28] If these areas come under Communist domination, it will be the Americas that are penetrable "from almost all round the compass."

Whether centrality in Eurasia gives the Soviet Union a commanding position or only a strong one has been discussed above. The relative value of land power and sea power in the Rimland was held undecided. What of air power? It is incomparably fast, of increasing capacity, and less and less restricted by weather and surface features. But the very speed of the airplane may offset some of the advantages of position. At near-sonic speeds, to fly, say, from Tashkent to Delhi would take less than two hours. But from Singapore to Delhi would take only four. Would the difference be critical? Would not what Whittlesey calls "pace"[29]— the average tempo of operations—and timing be more important than the velocity of flight, at such speeds? Fuel remains a great problem until atomic energy is adapted to aircraft, but could not Singapore be supplied as readily as Tashkent? If one is ready and resolute, need one be despondent over geographical position? For that matter, may not the Battle of the Rimland be decided by politics rather than by war? Was Vietminh lost by war, or by French delay in freeing and arming Vietnam and American unwillingness to enter the fray?

How do nuclear weapons affect these matters? One may readily agree that in an all-out nuclear war, with cities blasted from the face of the earth and even the countryside polluted with radioactive fall-out, "Heartland," "Rimland," "land power," and "sea power" are words with little significance. But we hear much of the tactical use of nuclear weapons. Just what "tactical use" means is not clear. Should it be stretched to include use against docks, bridges, and freight yards, it comes perilously close to "strategic bombardment," involving or inviting the destruction of cities. If, however, it is possible to confine nuclear weapons to tactical uses,

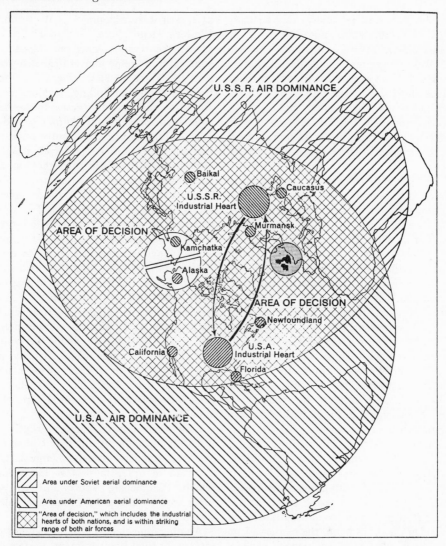

Figure 1. The power equation between the American and Eurasian continents. Map by Alexander P. de Seversky, reproduced in black and white from colored insert map in his book "Air Power: Key to Survival," Simon and Schuster, New York, 1950. facing p. 312. An adaptation of this map also accompanied an article by Major de Seversky in This Week *magazine, February 13, 1949. The dotted circle "denotes the British Isles, our only tenable overseas base. . . . The white circle embraces Alaska and Kamchatka, where land-sea-air teams will have valid application in an attempt at mutual neutralization as strategic bases."*

it is not certain that either land power or sea power is favored or that the Heartland-Rimland relationship is altered. Much depends on the relative improvement in methods of attack and defense and on the alertness of the belligerents and the astuteness of their commanders.

Seversky's view

IF there is a unique "airman's global view," it probably is essentially that of Seversky, and the azimuthal equidistant projection centered on the North Pole is its cartographic expression (Fig. 1).[30] The popularity of North Polar projections has been a valuable corrective to the overuse of the Mercator. The equidistant form, however, has the serious defect of stretching the latitudinal scale in the Southern Hemisphere, and this in turn has the visual effect of greatly exaggerating the width of the southern oceans.

Seversky definitely subordinates the army and

navy to the air force. He believes that virtually complete air supremacy, not just local or temporary air superiority, is possible. The side that obtains air supremacy holds the other at its mercy. He does not expect this to come without enormous effort and losses, but he feels that a country such as the United States, with advanced technology but limited manpower, can better pay the price of air supremacy than that of superiority in three media.[31] Since he wishes the United States to avoid surface, and particularly ground, combat, he regards overseas bases as undesirable, probably untenable, and in an age of intercontinental flight, unnecessary. Besides the Soviet Union and the United States, Britain alone has the potentialities of great air power. Only in the vicinity of Bering Strait does orthodox warfare seem justified.[32] Latin America, within the circle of American air dominance, becomes the main reserve of American industry. Much of Africa and all of Southeast Asia are within the ellipse of Soviet air dominance. The overlap of the American circle and the Soviet ellipse is the "area of decision," where Seversky thinks the mastery of the air will be decided. Seversky's global view thus swings us back to the concept of Western Hemisphere defense, with a north-south rather than an east-west emphasis.

A number of American habits of mind favor acceptance of "the airman's view." A sort of "air isolationism" appears possible, the Western Hemisphere is revived, faith in machines and in American know-how is a string touched, the all-out air strategy seems economical in dollars and men. On the other hand, the conservatism of the Army and Navy and their civilian supporters is aroused. Dislike or disregard for "the frozen north" and habitual east-west thinking are strong. "The suggestive map" that speaks to most Americans is still likely to have the equator across the middle.

The choice among the conservative, moderate, and all-out air views is one of the most critical in the American future. The decision will determine the allocation of manpower and resources, the location of bases, policies toward Rimland countries and Latin America, and many other matters. It is beyond the reach of this paper to settle such weighty affairs. All we can do is to propound a few questions that bear on the evaluation of "the airman's view."

The first question concerns the reality of the Western Hemisphere and its self-sufficiency and defensibility. A report of a Senate subcommittee on strategic and critical materials says, as if it were axiomatic, "We belong in the Western Hemisphere."[33] The report demonstrates the present American dependence on sources of strategic and critical materials outside the Western Hemisphere but maintains that through stockpiling, exploration, subsidization, and scientific research the Americas could be made self-sufficient for a period of war. It is held that sea lanes to South America could hug the shore and be protected from enemy aircraft or submarines. "In the last analysis land transportation can be improved."[34] If we grant, if only for the sake of the argument, that the Americas could be made self-sufficient for a period of war, we must still question their complete defensibility by the strategy envisioned. Soviet planes in Central or even East Africa, beyond the circle of American air dominance, would be approximately as near the most vital parts of South America as planes based on Florida. South American cities, and particularly the influential metropolises of Brazil and Argentina, would be vulnerable unless their defenses were virtually perfect. American ability to retaliate, or to "neutralize" African airfields after a blow had fallen, would offer little solace. If substantial parts of Africa should come under Soviet control, it is not certain that Latin America would remain steadfast in support of the United States. We may thus have to defend large parts of the Rimland in order to protect Latin America, which the Senate subcommittee, possibly influenced by the polar projection, calls "our own backyard."[35]

Another question is that of defense against intercontinental bombardment. Perfect defense on both sides would cancel out the offense. In that case, intercontinental bombardment would not even be "the Great Deterrent." True, perfect defense is improbable, but if defense is less than perfect, retaliation is to be expected, and thus to launch an intercontinental air attack entails great risks. Nevertheless, if a nation places all its defensive bets on this strategy, it must be prepared to use it.

The foregoing questions can be reduced to one: When, and under what circumstances, does a nation that adopts the all-out intercontinental strategy launch its aircraft? One choice would be preventive war, a choice that the United States is unlikely to make. Another would be to use the intercontinental air force in the event of any further aggression across the Iron Curtain. This would be containment by intercontinental means. It might succeed—

even the threat might be enough—but it would require unlimited fortitude for an American commander in chief to stand ready to give the signal, risking retaliatory destruction of American cities, to halt, for example, Communist expansion in some country of southern Asia. Third, there is "air isolationism." A defensive perimeter, to use that unhappy term, might be drawn around the Americas, perhaps including some overseas areas considered particularly important. Intercontinental air war would be used or threatened only if this perimeter were crossed. Such a stand would require as much fortitude as the other. In fact, we have seen that large parts of the Rimland might have to be included within the defensive perimeter if Latin America were to be secure. Thus "air isolationism" approaches "containment."

The nub of the matter is that strategy and foreign policy are complementary and inseparable. This is particularly true of the key question of when to resort to armed defense.[36] Moreover, they are continuing processes and cannot be redirected overnight. If a state adopts a rigid strategy keyed to a single kind of war, its foreign policy is made rigid in major ways. This is not necessarily evil if the rigid view is sound, but history does not encourage the belief that man can foresee the precise course of future events. Some flexibility in strategic view seems wise. "Flexibility" should be forward-looking, however, not patterned on the past.

Recipe for a composite view

WE have examined, in this and a preceding article, a series of global views of politics and strategy. None of them, taken singly, is an adequate picture of the world. None can unhesitatingly be called "the best" or even "the best yet." There is no simple system of political geography, no single thought filter through which to strain all geographical information. We need a series of filters, a composite or an eclectic global view.

Many of the men whose writings we have studied have in fact held composite views. For ease of analysis and comparison we have selected single items. Whittlesey's "exploitable world," though shrinking now, is a harmonious part of his historical approach. Taylor's maps and graphs show many environmental factors. Spykman discussed and mapped location, landforms, climate, economic production, and population before he proceeded to modify

Mackinder's world.[37] There is, however, no virtue in the composite or eclectic process per se. Haushofer's views were eclectic. Even if one chooses good ingredients, there is the problem of relative weight. Huntington, in his last book,[38] held climate, kith, and diet to be mainsprings of civilization, but in a given case, which is the main spring?

There is no easy road out of these difficulties. The "recipe for a composite view" that we give here makes no pretense to completeness or finality, nor does it contain anything that a geographer does not already know. It is merely an attempt to list the elements of a global view based on the concept of national power. No map of it is presented. This may be cowardice, engendered by our own warning, in the first article, that mapping an idea is likely to reveal its fuzziness. But much of the material in our list is already on maps, and for other items data are incomplete.

National power, as has been elaborated elsewhere,[39] has two components that may be called "inventory" and "strategy." The former is what one has, the latter what one does with it. The inventory component can largely be subsumed, we believe, under Mackinder's old term "man settling," the strategic component largely under his "man traveling."[40]

I. Man Settling	II. Man Traveling
A. Population	A. The Atmosphere
B. Culture	B. Oceans and Islands
C. Material Base	C. Continental Interiors and Peripheries
	D. The Northern Region

This list probably needs little explanation. What is left out may be more surprising than what is included. For example, climate, landforms, and mineral resources are not specifically mentioned. They are, however, implied under other headings and would appear in the higher orders of subdivision.

No one is likely to question the place of population or material base in a global view of national power. Population has been mapped many times, and its elements have been carefully outlined by Trewartha.[41] Among the more significant subdivisions are trends, in relation to total numbers and age groups, and urbanization. Urbanization is an indication of the kind of economy and of the tempting targets for nuclear bombs. The material base of course includes sources of food, energy, and essential raw materials. Although maps of such items have been attempted, adequate and commensurable data for recent years are hard to find.[42]

The inclusion of culture as a major heading in a list based on the concept of national power may require some defense. But one element of culture is government, and the common political map is therefore a cultural map. The political interpretation of general culture is difficult and still in the experimental stage; thus it is perhaps faith that leads us to give culture so prominent a place. Culture has been placed between population and the material base because it is through culture that men make the material base economic, turn sources into resources, so to speak.

In subdividing "Man Traveling" our guiding principle has been that, for the immediate future at least, air, land, and sea movement are all of importance as means of projecting power. This is especially true because "projecting power" includes economic as well as military action. The relative importance of the three media varies for different kinds of action and in different parts of the world. The atmosphere, because of its global spread, its vertical extent, and the speed of the vehicles that use it, is of first and increasing importance. This is true whether or not "heartland operations" by strategic air forces are the pattern of future conflict. Every globe and relatively undistorted map gives an airman's view, but it takes imagination to see on them the useful and fearful canopy of air, so that emphasis is justified.

With the oceans we include the islands found in them. Every island is moated to a certain extent, and the defense of Britain in the Second World War and the delay the Formosa Strait imposed on the Chinese Communists show that the moating is still of some significance. But air power, and not just ships or water, is needed to make the moat effective. Not all islands or parts of the oceans are of equal importance. The islands and narrow seas off the Eurasian coast are of first importance today, those off the North American coast of second.

It is hardly news that the peripheries of continents differ from the interiors in ease of maritime access. In the age of nuclear weapons, peripheral location carries increased vulnerability from sabotage, ship- or submarine-launched missiles, and underwater explosion. It usually means a greater dependence on seaborne supplies. But it also means wider economic contacts by the most capacious and economical of carriers. Only in Eurasia does the division into interior and periphery have great political significance, as Mackinder showed long ago. In the Americas the interior has been absorbed by the coastal states, with minor exceptions. Nearly all of Africa today is controlled from the shores, though its future political pattern is obscure.

The final item of our composite view is "the northern region," based on the nature of the Arctic Sea and the northern parts of North America and Eurasia and their relation to the greater centers of power that are certain, for a long time at least, to lie in the Northern Hemisphere. In the northern region surface movement meets resistance for much or all of the year whereas air movement is relatively easy. The northern region may be, as we have said, an aerial "pivot area." There are other parts of the world where air movement is much easier than surface movement, such as the rain forests and the deserts, but these either are smaller than the northlands or offer less serious obstacles. The deserts, for instance, are traversed more easily than the northlands by conventional vehicles, and the Amazon and Congo basins have their immense, never-frozen rivers.

The global view just outlined is merely what the mythical German scientist is supposed to have written, *eine Einführung in das Leben des Elephanten*, though measurable in pages rather than in volumes. The whole elephant is too big for us to see in detail, but we are not blind, only myopic, and we can discern its outlines. And we can and do pursue it, though the path of our safari is beset by pitfalls. On one side is the flood of unfiltered information that rushes endlessly. On the other are the quicksands of oversimplification. To remain still is to be stung by the scholar's conscience. But hazards and discomforts are inevitable accompaniments of adventure, and the pursuit of the global view is the geographer's intellectual adventure.

Notes

This paper was prepared as part of a study of national power sponsored by Yale University and the Office of Naval Research. Reproduction in whole or in part is permitted for any purpose of the United States Government. All opinions expressed are the responsibility of the author, not of the sponsors. Thanks are given to Professors Derwent Whittlesey and Saul B. Cohen for their many helpful comments.

1. G. H. Miller: "Must We Live in Fear?" *U.S. Naval Inst. Proc.*, Vol. 79, 1953, pp. 759–766; reference on p. 763.

2. S. B. Jones: "Views of the Political World," *Geogr. Rev.*, Vol. 45, 1955, pp. 309–326. The introductory paragraphs are applicable to the present paper.

3. A. T. Mahan: *The Influence of Sea Power upon History, 1660–1783* (Boston, 1890), Chap. I.

4. *Idem: The Problem of Asia* (Boston, 1900), pp. 24 and 26.

5. *Ibid.*, pp. 21 ff.

6. James Fairgrieve: *Geography and World Power* (8th edit., New York, 1941), p. 334.

7. Mahan, *The Problem of Asia*, pp. 84–86.

8. *Ibid.*, pp. 117–120.

9. For an interesting related discussion, see J. A. Morrison; "Russia and Warm" Water, *U.S. Naval Inst. Proc.*, Vol. 78, 1952, pp. 1169–1179.

10. Mahan. *The Problem of Asia*, pp. 63–65.

11. H. J. Mackinder: *Britain and the British Seas* (Oxford, 1902).

12. *Idem:* "The Geographical Pivot of History," *Geogr. Journ.*, Vol. 23, 1904, 421–444.

13. *Idem: Democratic Ideals and Reality* (New York, 1919 and 1942).

14. *Ibid.*, pp. 79–82 and 98–99 (1919 edit.).

15. *Ibid.*, pp. 135–136 (1919 edit.). The headwaters of the great Indian and Chinese rivers were also included in the Heartland in 1919 (map on p. 94).

16. Mahan, *The Problem of Asia*, pp. 124 ff.

17. Derwent Whittlesey: "Haushofer: The Geopoliticians" in *Makers of Modern Strategy*, edited by E. M. Earle (Princeton, 1943), pp. 388–411, reference on p. 405.

18. N. J. Spykman: *The Geography of the Peace* (New York, 1944), p. 43.

19. *Ibid.*, p. 53.

20. J. D. Hayes discusses this in his comments on Miller's "Must We Live in Fear?" *U.S. Naval Inst. Proc.*, Vol. 80, 1954, pp. 91–93.

21. Spykman, *op. cit.*, "Always," in this quotation, means considerably less than that.

22. "The Geographical Pivot of History," pp. 436–437.

23. X [G. F. Kennan]: "The Sources of Soviet Conduct," *Foreign Affairs*, Vol. 25, 1946–1947. pp. 566–582. Reprinted in G. F. Kennan: *American Diplomacy, 1900–1950* (Chicago, 1951), pp. 107–128.

24. Personal communication from Mr. Kennan.

25. "The Geographical Pivot of History," p. 441.

26. John Slessor: *Strategy for the West* (New York, 1954), especially Chapters 3 and 4.

27. *Ibid.*, p. 34.

28. Spykman, *op. cit.*, p. 38.

29. Derwent Whittlesey: "The Horizon of Geography," *Annals Assn. of Amer. Geogrs.*, Vol. 35, 1945, pp. 1–36; reference on p. 24.

30. A. P. de Seversky: *Air Power: Key to Survival* (New York, 1950).

31. *Ibid.*, p. 11.

32. *Ibid.*, map facing p. 312.

33. "Report of the Minerals, Materials, and Fuels Economic Subcommittee of the Committee on Interior and Insular Affairs," *83rd Congr.*, *2nd Sess.*, *Senate Rept. No. 1627*, 1954, p. 12.

34. *Ibid.*, p. 28.

35. *Ibid.*, p. 23.

36. Cf. W. W. Kaufmann: "The Requirements of Deterrence," *Princeton Univ. Center of Internatl. Studies Memorandum No. 7*, 1954.

37. Spykman, *op. cit.*, pp. 19–34.

38. Ellsworth Huntington: *Mainsprings of Civilization* (New York and London, 1945).

39. S. B. Jones: "The Power Inventory and National Strategy," *World Politics*, Vol. 6, 1953–1954, pp. 421–452.

40. H. J. Mackinder: "The Physical Basis of Political Geography, *Scottish Geogr. Mag.*, Vol. 6, 1890, pp. 78–84.

41. G. T. Trewartha: "A Case for Population Geography," *Annals Assn. of Amer. Geogrs.*, Vol. 43, 1953, pp. 71–97; reference on pp. 88–89.

42. M. K. Bennett, in his book *The World's Food* (New York, 1954, Chapters 12 and 13), subjects published data on national diets to considerable criticism. Excellent maps of energy production, consumption (1937, with estimates for 1948), and reserves accompany the study of "Energy Resources of the World" prepared under the direction of N. B. Guyol for the Department of State (*U.S. Dept. of State Publ. 3428*, 1949). The energy data in the *Statistical Yearbook* of the United Nations unfortunately do not include major Communist countries. The pending importance of atomic energy in industry further complicates the picture. Rapid strides in the beneficiation of lean iron ores make unreliable many published studies of the distribution of this basic metal.

Hans J. Morgenthau

Another "great debate": the national interest of the United States

THE CONTROVERSY which has arisen on the occasion of Ambassador Kennan's and my recent publications differs from the great historical debates on American foreign policy in two significant respects. It raises an issue more fundamental to the understanding of American foreign policy and of all politics than those with which the previous "great debates" were concerned, and it deals with the issue largely in terms which are not conducive to understanding.

The great debates of the past, such as the one over intervention vs. neutrality in 1793, expansion vs. the status quo before the Mexican and after the Spanish-American War, international cooperation vs. isolation in the 'twenties, intervention vs. abstention in the late 'thirties—all evolved around clear-cut issues of foreign policy. In 1793 you were in favor of going to war on the side of France or of remaining neutral. In the 1840's you approved of the annexation of Texas or you did not. At the turn of the century you supported overseas expansion or you were against it. In the 'twenties you advocated joining the League of Nations or staying out of it. In the late 'thirties you wanted to oppose the Axis Powers by all means short of war or you wanted to abstain from intervening. What separates the "utopian" from the "realist" position cannot be so sharply expressed in terms of alternative foreign policies. The very same policies can be and are being supported by both schools of thought. What sets them apart is not necessarily a matter of practical judgment, but of philosophies and standards of thought.

The issue which the present debate raises concerns the nature of all politics and, more particularly, of the American tradition in foreign policy. The history of modern political thought is the story of a contest between two schools which differ fundamentally in their conception of the nature of man, society, and politics. One believes that a rational and moral political order, derived from universally valid abstract principles, can be achieved here and now. It assumes the essential goodness and infinite malleability of human nature and attributes the failure of the social order to measure up to the rational standards to lack of knowledge and understanding, obsolescent social institutions, or the depravity of certain isolated individuals or groups. It trusts in education, reform, and the sporadic use of force to remedy these deficiencies.[1]

The other school believes that the world, imperfect as it is from the rational point of view, is the result of forces which are inherent in human nature. To improve the world one must work with those forces, not against them. This being inherently a world of opposing interests and of conflict among them, moral principles can never be fully realized, but at best approximated through the ever temporary balancing of interests and the every precarious settlement of conflicts. This school, then, sees in a system of checks and balances a universal principle for all pluralist societies.[2] It appeals to historic precedent rather than to abstract principles, and aims at achievement of the lesser evil rather than of the absolute good.

This conflict between two basic conceptions of man and politics is at the bottom of the present controversy. It is the same conflict

---

Reprinted from *The American Political Science Review*, Vol. 46, No. 4, December 1952, pp. 961–988.

which found its classic expression in the polemic of Burke against the philosophy of the French Revolution. Given the sad state of political thought in our time, it would be vain to expect the spokesmen of political realism to speak with the voice of Burke and the defenders of political utopianism to measure up to the standards of Condorcet and Rousseau. Yet one has a right to expect that scholars discuss the issue without resort to invective and with proper regard for established facts.[3]

I

IN order to refute a theory which pretends to be scientific, it is first necessary to understand what a scientific theory is. A scientific theory is an attempt to bring order and meaning to a mass of phenomena which without it would remain disconnected and unintelligible. Anyone who disputes the scientific character of such a theory either must produce a theory superior in these scientific functions to the one attacked or must, at the very least, demonstrate that the facts as they actually are do not lend themselves to the interpretation which the theory has put upon them. When a historian tells us that the balance of power is not a universal principle of politics, domestic and international, that it was practiced in Europe only for a limited period and never by the United States, that it ruined the states that practiced it,[4] it is incumbent upon him to tell us how we can dispose by means of theory of the historic data by which, for instance, David Hume demonstrated the universality of the balance of power and Paul Scott Mowrer[5] and Alfred Vagts[6] its practice by the United States; what Kautilya was writing about in the fourth century B.C. when he summarized the theoretical and practical tradition of Indian statecraft in terms of the balance of power; what the Greek city states, the Roman republic, and the medieval emperors and popes were doing if they did not apply the principles of the balance of power; and how the nations which either neglected these principles or applied them wrongly suffered political and military defeat and even extinction, while the nation which applied these principles most consistently and consciously, that is, Great Britain, enjoyed unrivalled power for an unparalleled length of time.

The historian who wishes to replace the balance of power as the guiding principle of American foreign policy with the "humanitarian and pacific traditions" of the "coördinate state"[7] must first of all explain how it has come about that the thirteen original states expanded into the full breadth and a good deal of the length of a continent, until today the strategic frontiers of the United States run parallel to the coastline of Asia and along the River Elbe. If such are the results of policies based upon "humanitarian and pacific traditions," never in the history of the world has virtue been more bountifully rewarded! Yet our historian must explain not only the great sweep of American expansion but also the specific foreign policies which in their historic succession make up that sweep. Is it easier to explain the successive shifts of American support from Great Britain to France and back again from the beginning of King George's War in 1744 to the War of 1812 in terms of the "coördinate state" than in terms of the balance of power? The same question might be asked about the postponement of the recognition of the independence of the Spanish colonies until 1822, when the Floridas had been acquired from Spain and Spain had thereby been deprived of the ability to challenge the United States from within the hemisphere. The same question might be asked about the Monroe Doctrine itself, about Lincoln's policies toward Great Britain and France, and about our successive policies with regard to Mexico and the Caribbean. One could go on and pick out at random any foreign policy pursued by the United States from the beginning to 1919 and one would hardly find a policy, with the exception perhaps of the War of 1812, which could not be made intelligible by reference to the national interest defined in terms of power—political, military, and economic—rather than by reference to the principle of the "coördinate state." This inevitable outcome of such an inquiry is well summarized in these words:

Ease and prosperity have made us wish the whole world to be as happy and well to do as ourselves; and we have supposed that institutions and principles like our own were the simple prescription for making them so. And yet, when issues of our own interest arose, we have not been unselfish. We have shown ourselves kin to all the world, when it came to pushing an advantage. Our action against Spain in the Floridas, and against Mexico on the coasts of the Pacific; our attitude toward first the Spaniards, and then the French, with regard to the control of the Mississippi; the unpitying force with which we thrust the Indians to the wall wherever they stood in our way, have suited our professions of peacefulness and justice and liberality no better than the aggressions of other nations that were strong and not to be gainsaid. Even Mr. Jefferson, philanthropist and champion of peaceable and modest government though he was, exemplified this double temper of the people he ruled. "Peace is our passion," he had declared; but the passion abated when he saw the mouth of the Mississippi about to pass into the hands of France. Though he had loved France and hated England, he did not hesitate then what language to hold. "There is on the globe," he wrote to Mr. Livingston at Paris, "one single spot the possessor of which is our natural and habitual enemy. The day that France takes possession of New Orleans seals the union of two nations, who, in conjunction, can maintain exclusive possession of the sea. From that moment we must marry ourselves to the British fleet and nation." Our interests much march forward, altruists though we are; other nations must see to it that they stand off, and do not seek to stay us.

This realist appraisal of the American tradition in foreign policy was published in 1901 in the *Atlantic Monthly.* Its author was a professor of jurisprudence and political economy at Princeton by the name of Woodrow Wilson.[8]

Nothing more needs to be said to demonstrate that facts do not support a revision of American diplomatic history which tries to substitute "humanitarian and pacifist traditions" and the "coördinate state" for power politics and the balance of power as the guiding principle of American foreign policy. What, then, does support it? Three things: the way American statesmen have spoken about American foreign policy; the legal fiction of the "coördinate state"; finally, and foremost, an emotional urge to justify American foreign policy in humanitarian, pacifist terms.

It is elementary that the character of a foreign policy can be ascertained only through the examination of the political acts performed and of the foreseeable consequences of these acts. Thus we can find out what statesmen have actually done, and from the foreseeable consequences of their acts we can surmise what their objectives might have been. Yet examination of the facts is not enough. To give meaning to the factual raw material of history, we must approach historical reality with a kind of rational outline, a map which suggests to us the possible meanings of history. In other words, we put ourselves in the position of a statesman

who must meet a certain problem of foreign policy under certain circumstances and ask ourselves, what are the rational alternatives from which a statesman may choose who must meet this problem under these circumstances, presuming always that he acts in a rational manner, and which of these rational alternatives was this particular statesman, acting under these circumstances, likely to choose? It is the testing of this rational hypothesis against the actual facts and their consequences which gives meaning to the facts of history and makes the scientific writing of political history possible.

In the process of writing the history of foreign policy the interpretations by statesmen of their own acts, especially if they are made for public consumption, must needs have a strictly subsidiary place. The public self-interpretation by actors on the political scene is itself, of course, a political act which seeks to present a certain policy to its presumed supporters in terms of their moral and political folklore and to those against which it is directed in terms which intend to embarrass and deceive. Such declarations may indeed shed light upon the character and objectives of the policy pursued if they are considered in conjunction with, and in subordination to, rational hypotheses, actions, and likely consequences. Yet it is quite a different matter to interpret the American tradition of foreign policy in the light of a collection of official statements which, like most such statements, present humanitarian and pacifist justifications for the policies pursued. If anybody should be bold enough to write a history of world politics with so uncritical a method he would easily and well-nigh inevitably be driven to the conclusion that from Timur to Hitler and Stalin the foreign policies of all nations were inspired by the ideals of humanitarianism and pacifism. The absurdity of the result is commensurate with the defects of the method.

It is only from a method which accepts the declarations of statesmen as evidence of the character of the policies pursued that the principle of the "coördinate state" receives a semblance of plausibility. Statesmen and international lawyers have been wont to speak of the "equal dignity" of all states, regardless of "wealth, power, size, population or culture,"[9] which I take the principle of the "coördinate state" to mean. It is also referred to as the principle of "federalism in international relations."[10] As its prime examples are cited the relations amongst the states of the Union, the states of the American system, the members of the Commonwealth of Nations, and the members of the Swiss Confederation. If the whole world were organized in accordance with this principle, as are already these four political entities, it is assumed that the freedom, dignity, and peace of all nations would then be assured.

There is no need to examine the theoretical merits of the principle of the "coördinate state," because for none of the four political entities mentioned does the idea of the "coördinate state" provide the principle of political organization. The equality of the states as the political foundation of the United States became obsolescent when Chief Justice Marshall's Supreme Court resolved the ambiguity of the Constitution in favor of the federal government, and it became obsolete when the Civil War proved Chief Justice Marshall's point. The equality of the states survives today only in the shadow and by virtue of the federal government's political supremacy, and without the cohesive force of that supremacy there would be no union of equal states to begin with. That these powers of the federal government are limited and qualified by the principle of federalism, that is, by the constitutionally granted powers of the states, is quite a different matter; it concerns the distribution of powers between federal government and states within a general system of checks and balances, but has nothing to do with the equality of the states as the alleged political foundation of the American system of government. With the exception of the equality of senatorial representation, the principle of the equality of the states is today, as it has been for almost a century, devoid of political content. It serves only as a principle of regional organization, of administrative decentralization, and, above all, of constitutional rhetoric. What it really signifies was pointed out more than fifty years ago by W. A. Dunning when he summarized his answer to the question "Are the states equal under the Constitution?" by saying that "the theory of equal states falls to the ground."[11]

Similarly, the federalism of Switzerland is the result of a long series of civil wars, the last one fought a little more than a century ago, which established the predominance of the German-speaking cantons within the confederation. Here too, it is the existence of predominant power, located in one segment of the federal system, which makes federalism possible in the first place.

By the same token, the unchallengeable supremacy of the United States within the Western Hemisphere has throughout been the backbone of the system of American states. As long as this supremacy is secure, there is, on the one hand, no need for the United States to assert it in the political and military sphere, and, taking it for granted, the United States can well afford to pursue a policy of the Good Neighbor; and there is, on the other hand, no opportunity for the other members of the system to challenge that supremacy effectively. This is what the principle of the "coördinate state" amounts to in the Western Hemisphere. Consequently, whenever there was even a remote possibility that the supremacy of the United States might be challenged, generally through instigation from outside the hemisphere, the United States asserted its superior power within the hemisphere and acted as all states must act under similar conditions.

Whatever possibility for common political action there remains among the members of the Commonwealth of Nations is the result of the interests which these members may have in common. In other words, the member states may work together or each of them may work with other nations, as their interests dictate. Their membership in the Commonwealth, as the examples of India, South Africa, Australia, and New Zealand clearly show, has no influence upon this decision; that membership is but a faint remembrance of the times when Great Britain could secure cooperation among the member states on its terms by virtue of its superior power.

What, then, have these four examples of the "coördinate state" in common which would establish them as a distinct type of interstate relationship, and what conclusions can be drawn from them for the organization of the world? The only thing that these four examples seem to have really in common is the legal stipulation of the equality of the members of the respective systems and this characteristic is not peculiar to them, but a general principle of international law applicable to all sovereign states. In the political sphere they seem to have nothing in common at all. What they tend to show, however, is the decisive importance of the distribution of political power for the operation of federal and egalitarian relations among states. The political cohesion of a federal system is the result of superior power located in some part of it. It is by virtue of its superior power that the predominant part can afford to grant the other members of the federal system a measure of equality in the non-political sphere. These observations bring us back to power politics and the balance of power to which the principle of the "coördinate state" was supposed to be the alternative.

In truth, it is not the disinterested consideration of facts which has given birth to the theory of the "coördinate state." That theory is rather the response to an emotional urge, and since this emotion is not peculiar to a particular author but typical of a popular reaction to the new role which the United States must play in world affairs, it deserves a brief analysis.

One of the great experiences of our time which have impressed themselves upon the American mind is the emergence of the United States as a nation among other nations, exposed to the same opportunities, temptations, risks, and liabilities to which other nations have been traditionally exposed. This experience becomes the more shocking if it is compared with the expectation with which we fought the Second World War. We expected from that war a reaffirmation of the secure, detached, and independent position in world affairs which we had inherited from the Founding Fathers and which we had been successful in preserving at least to the First World War. By avoiding what we thought had been Wilson's mistakes, we expected to emerge from that war if not more independent, certainly more secure than we were when we entered it. In fact, probably not even in the early days of the Republic were we more exposed to danger from abroad than we are today, and never had we less freedom of action in taking care of our interests than we have today.

It is naturally shocking to recognize that a happy chapter in the history of the nation and in one's own way of life has come to an end. There are those who reconcile themselves to the inevitable, albeit with sorrow rather than with glee, and try to apply the lessons of the past to the tasks at hand. There are others who try to escape from a disappointing and threatening reality into the realm of fantasy. Three such escapist fantasies have arisen in our midst in response to the challenge of American world leadership and power: the fantasy of needless American participation in war, the fantasy of American treason, and the fantasy of American innocence.

The first of these fantasies presumes that the present predicament is a result not of necessity but of folly, the folly of American statesmen who needlessly intervened in two world wars. The second of these fantasies attributes the present predicament to treason in high places whereby the fruits of victory were handed to the enemy. The third of these fantasies denies that the predicament is real and prefers to think of it as an intellectual fraud perpetrated upon the American people. To support this fictional denial of the actualities of the present, it draws upon a fictional account of the past. The United States does not need to bear at present the intellectual, moral, and political burdens which go with involvement in power politics and the maintenance of the balance of power; for it has never borne them in the past, never having been thus involved. The golden age of past political innocence sheds its glow upon a but seemingly less innocent present and promises a future in which all the world will follow the example of America, forswear power politics and the balance of power, and accept the principle of the "coördinate state." Our rearmament program, as exemplified in the Atlantic Security Pact, we are told, has nothing to do with the balance of power but aims at the "organization of as much of the world as we can upon the basis of the coördinate state. . . . It may prove impossible under present conditions to build such a system without having to fight a war with Russia, but then at least we will be fighting, as we did before, for the thing we consider worth defending with our lives and treasure."[12] Thus a fictional account of the American past, begun as an act of uncalled-for patriotic piety, issues in an ideology for a third world war. Escape we must from the unfamiliar, unpleasant, and dangerous present, first into the political innocence of the past and from there into the immediate future of a third world war, beyond which the revived and universalized innocence of the more distant future will surely lie.

We have said that to present the American tradition in foreign policy as having been free from concern with power politics and the balance of power is not warranted by the facts of American history. Yet it might still be argued and it is actually being argued, that, regardless of the evidence of history, the American people will not be reconciled to power politics and the balance of power and will support only policies based upon abstract moral principles. While in the past the United States might have pursued balance of power policies and while it might be a good thing if it did do so again, the American people will not stand for it. Here the emotional appeal to patriotic piety is joined by calculations of political expediency. Yet the case for misrepresenting American history has nothing to gain from either.

There is a strong tendency in all historiography to glorify the national past, and in popular presentations that tendency takes on the aspects of the jingoist whitewash. Even so penetrating a mind as John Stuart Mill's could deliver himself of an essay in which he proved, no doubt to the satisfaction of many of his English readers but certainly of few others, that Great Britain had never interfered in the affairs of European nations and had interfered in those of the Indian states only for their own good.[13] Yet it is the measure of a nation's maturity to be able to recognize its past for what it actually is. Why should we not admit that American foreign policy has been generally hardheaded and practical and at times ruthless? Why should we deny Jefferson's cunning, say, in the Puget Sound affair, the cruelty with which the Indians were treated, and the faithlessness with which the treaties with the Indians were cast aside? We know that this is the way all nations are when their interests are at stake—so cruel, so faithless, so cunning. We know that the United States has refrained from seeking dominions beyond the seas not because it is more virtuous than other nations, but because it had the better part of a continent to colonize.

As has been pointed out elsewhere at great length, the man in the street, unsophisticated as he is and uninformed as he may be, has a surer grasp of the essentials of foreign policy and a more mature judgment of its basic issues than many of the intellectuals and politicians who pretend to speak for him and cater to what they imagine his prejudices to be. During the recent war the ideologues of the Atlantic Charter, the Four Freedoms, and the United Nations were constantly complaining that the American soldier did not know what he was fighting for. Indeed, if he was fighting for some utopian ideal, divorced from the concrete experiences and interests of the country, then the complaint was well grounded. However, if he was fighting for the territorial integrity of the nation and for its survival as a free country where he could live, think, and act as he pleased, then he had never any doubt about what he was fighting for. Ideological rationalizations and justifications are indeed the indispensable concomitants of all political action. Yet there is something unhealthy in a craving for ideological intoxication and in the inability to act and to see merit in action except under the stimulant of gran-

diose ideas and far-fetched schemes. Have our intellectuals become, like Hamlet, too much beset by doubt to act and, unlike Hamlet, compelled to still their doubts by renouncing their sense of what is real? The man in the street has no such doubts. It is true that ideologues and demagogues can sway him by appealing to his emotions. But it is also true, as American history shows in abundance and as the popular success of Ambassador Kennan's book demonstrates, that responsible statesmen can guide him by awakening his latent understanding of the national interest.

II

YET what is the national interest? How can we define it and give it the content which will make it a guide for action? This is one of the relevant questions to which the current debate has given rise.

It has been frequently argued against the realist conception of foreign policy that its key concept, the national interest, does not provide an acceptable standard for political action. This argument is in the main based upon two grounds: the elusiveness of the concept and its susceptibility to interpretations, such as limitless imperialism and narrow nationalism, which are not in keeping with the American tradition in foreign policy. The argument has substance as far as it goes, but it does not invalidate the usefulness of the concept.

The concept of the national interest is similar in two respects to the "great generalities" of the Constitution, such as the general welfare and due process. It contains a residual meaning which is inherent in the concept itself, but beyond these minimum requirements its content can run the whole gamut of meanings which are logically compatible with it. That content is determined by the political traditions and the total cultural context within which a nation formulates its foreign policy. The concept of the national interest, then, contains two elements, one that is logically required and in that sense necessary, and one that is variable and determined by circumstances.

Any foreign policy which operates under the standard of the national interest must obviously have some reference to the physical, political, and cultural entity which we call a nation. In a world where a number of sovereign nations compete with and oppose each other for power, the foreign policies of all nations must necessarily refer to their survival as their minimum requirements. Thus all nations do what they cannot help but do: protect their physical, political, and cultural identity against encroachments by other nations.

It has been suggested that this reasoning erects the national state into the last word in politics and the national interest into an absolute standard for political action. This, however, is not quite the case. The idea of interest is indeed of the essence of politics and, as such, unaffected by the circumstances of time and place. Thucydides' statement, born of the experiences of ancient Greece, that "identity of interest is the surest of bonds whether between states or individuals" was taken up in the nineteenth century by Lord Salisbury's remark that "the only bond of union that endures" among nations is "the absence of all clashing interests." The perennial issue between the realist and utopian schools of thought over the nature of politics, to which we have referred before, might well be formulated in terms of concrete interests vs. abstract principles. Yet while the concern of politics with interest is perennial, the connection between interest and the national state is a product of history.

The national state itself is obviously a product of history and as such destined to yield in time to different modes of political organization. As long as the world is politically organized into nations, the national interest is indeed the last word in world politics. When the national state will have been replaced by another mode of organization, foreign policy must then protect the interest in survival of that new organization. For the benefit of those who insist upon discarding the national state and constructing supranational organizations by constitutional fiat, it must be pointed out that these new organizational forms will either come into being through conquest or else through consent based upon the mutual recognition of the national interests of the nations concerned; for no nation will forego its freedom of action if it has no reason to expect proportionate benefits in compensation for that loss. This is true of treaties concerning commerce or fisheries as it is true of the great compacts, such as the European Coal and Steel Community, through which nations try to create supranational forms of organization. Thus, by an apparent paradox, what is historically relative in the idea of the national interest can be overcome only through the promotion in concert of the national interest of a number of nations.

The survival of a political unit, such as a nation, in its identity is the irreducible minimum, the necessary element of its interests vis-à-vis other units. Taken in isolation, the determination of its content in a concrete situation is relatively simple; for it encompasses the integrity of the nation's territory, of its political institutions, and of its culture. Thus bipartisanship in foreign policy, especially in times of war, has been most easily achieved in the promotion of these minimum requirements of the national interest. The situation is different with respect to the variable elements of the national interest. All the cross currents of personalities, public opinion, sectional interests, partisan politics, and political and moral folkways are brought to bear upon their determination. In consequence, the contribution which science can make to this field, as to all fields of policy formation, is limited. It can identify the different agencies of the government which contribute to the determination of the variable elements of the national interest and assess their relative weight. It can separate the long-range objectives of foreign policy from the short-term ones which are the means for the achievement of the former and can tentatively establish their rational relations. Finally, it can analyze the variable elements of the national interest in terms of their legitimacy and their compatibility with other national values and with the national interest of other nations. We shall address ourselves briefly to the typical problems with which this analysis must deal.

The legitimacy of the national interest must be determined in the face of possible usurpation by subnational, other-national, and supranational interests. On the subnational level we find group interests, represented particularly by ethnic and economic groups, who tend to identify themselves with the national interest. Charles A. Beard has emphasized, however one-sidedly, the extent to which the economic interests of certain groups have been presented as those of the United States.[14] Group interests exert, of course, constant pressure upon the conduct of our foreign policy, claiming their identity with the national interest. It is, however, doubtful that, with the exception of a few spectacular cases, they have been successful in determining the course of American foreign policy. It is much more likely, given the nature of American domestic politics, that American foreign policy, insofar as it is the object of pressures by sectional interests, will normally be a compromise between divergent sectional interests. The concept of the national interest, as it emerges from this contest as the actual guide for foreign policy, may well fall short of what would be rationally required by the over-all interests of the United States. Yet the concept of the national interest which emerges from this contest of conflicting sectional interests is also more than any particular sectional interest or their sum total. It is, as it were, the lowest common denominator where sectional interests and the national interest meet in an uneasy compromise which may leave much to be desired in view of all the interests concerned.

The national interest can be unsurped by other-national interests in two typical ways. The case of treason by individuals, either out of conviction or for pay, needs only to be mentioned here; for insofar as treason is committed on behalf of a foreign government rather than a supranational principle, it is significant for psychology, sociology, and criminology, but not for the theory of politics. The other case, however, is important not only for the theory of politics but also for its practice, especially in the United States.

National minorities in European countries, ethnic groups in the United States, ideological minorities anywhere may identify themselves, either spontaneously or under the direction of the agents of a foreign government, with the interests of that foreign government and may promote these interests under the guise of the national interest of the country whose citizens they happen to be. The activities of the German-American Bund in the United States in the 'thirties and of Communists everywhere are cases in point. Yet the issue of the national interest vs. other-national interests masquerading as the national interest has arisen constantly in the United States in a less clear-cut fashion.

A country which had been settled by consecutive waves of "foreigners" was bound to find it particularly difficult to identify its own national interest against alleged, seeming, or actual other-national interests represented by certain groups among its own citizens. Since virtually all citizens of the United States are, as it were, "more or less" foreign-born, those who were "less" so have frequently not resisted the temptation to use this distinction as a polemic weapon against latecomers who happened to differ from them in their conception of the national interest of the United States. Frequently, this rationalization has been dis-

pensed with and a conception of foreign policy with which a writer happened to disagree has been attributed outright to foreign sympathy or influence or worse. British influence and interests have served as standard arguments in debates on American foreign policy. Madison, in his polemic against Hamilton on the occasion of Washington's Neutrality Proclamation of 1793, identified the Federalist position with that of "the foreigners and degenerate citizens among us, who hate our republican government, and the French revolution,"[15] and the accusation met with a favorable response in a majority of Congress and of public opinion. However, these traditional attempts to discredit dissenting opinion as being influenced by foreign interests should not obscure the real issue, which is the peculiar vulnerability of the national interest of the United States to usurpation by the interests of other nations.

The usurpation of the national interest by supranational interests can derive in our time from two sources: religious bodies and international organizations. The competition between church and state for determination of certain interests and policies, domestic and international, has been an intermittent issue throughout the history of the national state. Here, too, the legitimate defense of the national interest against usurpation has frequently, especially in the United States, degenerated into the demagogic stigmatization of dissenting views as being inspired by Rome and, hence, being incompatible with the national interest. Yet here, too, the misuse of the issue for demagogic purposes must be considered apart from the legitimacy of the issue itself.

The more acute problem arises at the present time from the importance which the public and government officials, at least in their public utterances, attribute to the values represented and the policies pursued by international organizations either as alternatives or supplements to the values and policies for which the national government stands. It is frequently asserted that the foreign policy of the United States pursues no objectives apart from those of the United Nations, that, in other words, the foreign policy of the United States is actually identical with the policy of the United Nations. This assertion cannot refer to anything real in actual politics to support it. For the constitutional structure of international organizations, such as the United Nations, and their procedural practices make it impossible for them to pursue interests apart from those of the member-states which dominate their policy-forming bodies. The identity between the interests of the United Nations and the United States can only refer to the successful policies of the United States within the United Nations through which the support of the United Nations is being secured for the policies of the United States.[16] The assertion, then, is mere polemic, different from the one discussed previously in that the identification of a certain policy with a supranational interest does not seek to reflect discredit upon the former, but to bestow upon it a dignity which the national interest pure and simple is supposed to lack.

The real issue in view of the problem that concerns us here is not whether the so-called interests of the United Nations, which do not exist apart from the interests of its most influential members, have superseded the national interest of the United States, but for what kind of interests the United States has secured United Nations support. While these interests cannot be United Nations interests, they do not need to be national interests either. Here we are in the presence of that modern phenomenon which has been variously described as "utopianism," "sentimentalism," "moralism," the "legalistic-moralistic approach." The common denominator of all these tendencies in modern political thought is the substitution for the national interest of a supranational standard of action which is generally identified with an international organization, such as the United Nations. The national interest is here not being unsurped by sub- or supranational interests which, however inferior in worth to the national interest, are nevertheless real and worthy of consideration within their proper sphere. What challenges the national interest here is a mere figment of the imagination, a product of wishful thinking, which is postulated as a valid norm for international conduct, without being valid either there or anywhere else. At this point we touch the core of the present controversy between utopianism and realism in international affairs; we shall return to it later in this paper.

The national interest as such must be defended against usurpation by non-national interests. Yet once that task is accomplished, a rational order must be established among the values which make up the national interest and among the resources to be committed to them. While the interests which a nation may pursue in its relation with other nations are of infinite variety and magnitude, the resources which are available for the pursuit of such interests are necessarily limited in quantity and kind. No nation has the resources to promote all desirable objectives with equal vigor; all nations must therefore allocate their scarce resources as rationally as possible. The indispensable precondition of such rational allocation is a clear understanding of the distinction between the necessary and variable elements of the national interest. Given the contentious manner in which in democracies the variable elements of the national interest are generally determined, the advocates of an extensive conception of the national interest will inevitably present certain variable elements of the national interest as though their attainment were necessary for the nation's survival. In other words, the necessary elements of the national interest have a tendency to swallow up the variable elements so that in the end all kinds of objectives, actual or potential, are justified in terms of national survival. Such arguments have been advanced, for instance, in support of the rearmament of Western Germany and of the defense of Formosa. They must be subjected to rational scrutiny which will determine, however tentatively, their approximate place in the scale of national values.

The same problem presents itself in its extreme form when a nation pursues, or is asked to pursue, objectives which are not only unnecessary for its survival but tend to jeopardize it. Second-rate nations which dream of playing the role of great powers, such as Italy and Poland in the interwar period, illustrate this point. So do great powers which dream of remaking the world in their own image and embark upon world-wide crusades, thus straining their resources to exhaustion. Here scientific analysis has the urgent task of pruning down national objectives to the measure of available resources in order to make their pursuit compatible with national survival.

Finally, the national interest of a nation which is conscious not only of its own interests but also of that of other nations must be defined in terms compatible with the latter. In a multinational world this is a requirement of political morality; in an age of total war it is also one of the conditions for survival.

In connection with this problem two mutually exclusive arguments have been advanced. On the one hand, it has been argued against the theory of international politics here presented that the concept of the national interest revives the eighteenth-century concept of enlightened self-interest, presuming that the uniformly enlightened pursuit of their self-interest by all individuals, as by all nations, will of itself be conducive to a peaceful and harmonious society. On the other hand, the point has been made that the pursuit of their national interest by all nations makes war the permanent arbiter of conflicts among them. Neither argument is well taken.

The concept of the national interest presupposes neither a naturally harmonious, peaceful world nor the inevitability of war as a consequence of the pursuit by all nations of their national interest. Quite to the contrary, it assumes continuous conflict and threat of war, to be minimized through the continuous adjustment of conflicting interests by diplomatic action. No such assumption would be warranted if all nations at all times conceived of their national interest only in terms of their survival and, in turn, defined their interest in survival in restrictive and rational terms. As it is, their conception of the national interest is subject to all the hazards of misinterpretation, usurpation, and misjudgment to which reference has been made above. To minimize these hazards is the first task of a foreign policy which seeks the defense of the national interest by peaceful means. Its second task is the defense of the national interest, restrictively and rationally defined, against the national interests of other nations which may or may not be thus defined. If they are not, it becomes the task of armed diplomacy to convince the nations concerned that their legitimate interests have nothing to fear from a restrictive and rational foreign policy and that their illegitimate interests have nothing to gain in the face of armed might rationally employed

III

WE have said before the utopian and realist positions in international affairs do not necessarily differ in the policies they advocate, but that they part company over their general philosophies of politics and their way of thinking about matters political. It does not follow that the present debate is only of academic interest and without practical significance. Both camps, it is true, may support the same policy for different reasons. Yet if the reasons are unsound, the soundness of the policies supported by them is a mere coincidence, and these very same reasons may be, and inevitably are, invoked on other occasions in support of unsound policies. The nefarious consequences of false philosophies and wrong ways of thinking may for the time being be concealed by the apparent success of policies derived from them. You may go to war, justified by your nation's interests, for a moral purpose and in disregard of considerations of power; and military victory seems to satisfy both your moral aspirations and your nation's interests. Yet the manner in which you waged the war, achieved victory, and settled the peace cannot help reflecting your philosophy of politics and your way of thinking about political problems. If these are in error, you may win victory on the field of battle and still assist in the defeat of both your moral principles and the national interest of your country.

Any number of examples could illustrate the real yet subtle practical consequences which follow from the different positions taken. We have chosen two: collective security in Korea and the liberation of the nations that are captives of Communism. A case for both policies can be made from both the utopian and realist positions, but with significant differences in the emphasis and substance of the policies pursued.

Collective security as an abstract principle of utopian politics requires that all nations come to the aid of a victim of aggression by resisting the aggressor with all means necessary to frustrate his aims. Once the case of aggression is established, the duty to act is unequivocal. Its extent may be affected by concern for the nation's survival; obviously no nation will commit outright suicide in the service of collective security. But beyond that elemental limitation no consideration of interest or power, either with regard to the aggressor or his victim or the nation acting in the latter's defense, can qualify the obligation to act under the principle of collective security. Thus high officials of our government have declared that we intervened in Korea not for any narrow interest of ours but in support of the moral principle of collective security.

Collective security as a concrete principle of realist policy is the age-old maxim, "Hang together or hang separately," in modern dress. It recognizes the need for nation A under certain circumstances to defend nation B against attack by nation C. That need is determined, first, by the interest which A has in the territorial integrity of B and by the relation of that interest to all the other interests of A as well as to the resources available for the support of all those interests.

Furthermore, A must take into account the power which is at the disposal of aggressor C for fighting A and B as over against the power available to A and B for fighting C. The same calculation must be carried on concerning the power of the likely allies of C as over against those of A and B. Before going to war for the defense of South Korea in the name of collective security, an American adherent of political realism would have demanded an answer to the following four questions: First, what is our interest in the preservation of the independence of South Korea; second, what is our power to defend that independence against North Korea; third, what is our power to defend that independence against China and the Soviet Union; and fourth, what are the chances for preventing China and the Soviet Union from entering the Korean War?

In view of the principle of collective security, interpreted in utopian terms, our intervention in Korea was a foregone conclusion. The interpretation of this principle in realist terms might or might not, depending upon the concrete circumstances of interest and power, have led us to the same conclusion. In the execution of the policy of collective security the utopian had to be indifferent to the possibility of Chinese and Russian intervention, except for his resolution to apply the principle of collective security to anybody who would intervene on the side of the aggressor. The realist could not help weighing the possibility of the intervention of a great power on the side of the aggressor in terms of the interests engaged and the power available on the other side.[17]

The Truman administration could not bring itself to taking resolutely the utopian or the realist position. It resolved to intervene in good measure on utopian grounds and in spite of military advice to the contrary; it allowed the military commander to advance to the Yalu River in disregard of the risk of the intervention of a great power against which collective security could be carried out only by means of a general war, and then refused to pursue the war with full effectiveness on the realist grounds of the risk of a third world war. Thus Mr. Truman in 1952 is caught in the same dilemma from which Mr. Baldwin could extricate himself in 1936 on the occasion of the League of Nations sanctions against Italy's attack upon Ethiopia only at an enormous loss to British prestige. Collective security as a defense of the status quo short of a general war can be effective only against second-rate powers. Applied against a major power, it is a contradiction in terms, for it means necessarily a major war. Of this self-defeating contradiction Mr. Baldwin was as unaware in the 'thirties as Mr. Truman seemed to be in 1952. Mr. Churchill put Mr. Baldwin's dilemma in these cogent terms: "First, the Prime Minister had declared that sanctions meant war; secondly, he was resolved that there must be no war; and thirdly, he decided upon sanctions. It was evidently impossible to comply with these three conditions." Similarly Mr. Truman had declared that the effective prosecution of the Korean War meant the possibility of a third world war; he resolved that there must be no third world war; and he decided upon intervention in the Korean War. Here, too, it is impossible to comply with these three conditions.

Similar contradictions are inherent in the proposals which would substitute for the current policy of containment one of the liberation of the nations presently the captives of Russian Communism. This objective can be compatible with the utopian or realist position, but the policies designed to secure it will be fundamentally different according to whether they are based upon one or the other position. The clearest case to date for the utopian justification of such policies has been made by Representative Charles J. Kersten of Wisconsin who pointed to these four "basic defects" of the "negative policy of containment and negotiated coexistence";

> It would be immoral and unchristian to negotiate a permanent agreement with forces which by every religious creed and moral precept are evil. It abandons nearly one-half of humanity and the once free nations of Poland, Czechoslovakia, Hungary, Rumania, Bulgaria, Albania, Lithuania, Latvia, Esthonia and China to enslavement of the Communist police state.
>
> It is un-American because it violates the principle of the American Declaration of Independence, which proclaims the rights of all people to freedom and their right and duty to throw off tyranny.
>
> It will lead to all-out World War III because it aligns all the forces of the non-Communist world in military opposition to and against all the forces of the Communist world, including the 800,000,000 peoples behind the Iron Curtain.
>
> The policy of mere containment is uneconomic and will lead to national bankruptcy.[18]

This statement is interesting for its straight-forwardnesss and because it combines in a rather typical fashion considerations of abstract morality and of expediency. The captive nations must be liberated not only because their captivity is immoral, unchristian, and un-American, but also because its continuation will lead to a third world war and to national bankruptcy. To what extent, however, these considerations of expediency are invalidated by their utopian setting will become obvious from a comparison between the utopian and the realist positions.

From the utopian point of view there can be no difference between the liberation of Esthonia or Czechoslovakia, of Poland or China; the captivity of any nation, large or small, close or far away, is a moral outrage which cannot be tolerated. The realist, too, seeks the liberation of all captive nations because he realizes that the presence of the Russian armies in the heart of Europe and their cooperation with the Chinese armies constitute the two main sources of the imbalance of power which threatens our security. Yet before he formulates a program of liberation, he will seek answers to a number of questions such as these: While the United States has a general interest in the liberation of all captive nations, what is the hierachy of interests it has in the liberation, say, of China, Esthonia, and Hungary? And while the Soviet Union has a general interest in keeping all captive nations in that state, what is the hierarchy of its interests in keeping, say, Poland, Eastern Germany, and Bulgaria captive? If we assume, as we must on the historic evidence of two centuries, that Russia would never give up control over Poland without being compelled by force of arms, would the objective of the liberation of Poland justify the ruin of western civilization, that of Poland included, which would be the certain result of a third world war? What resources does the United States have at its disposal for the liberation of all captive nations or some of them? What resources does the Soviet Union have at its disposal to keep in captivity all captive nations or some of them? Are we more likely to avoid national bankruptcy by embarking upon a policy of indiscriminate liberation with the concomitant certainty of war or by continuing the present policy of containment?

It might be that in a particular instance the policies suggested by the answers to these questions will coincide with Representative Kersten's proposals, but there can be no doubt that in its over-all character, substance, emphasis, and likely consequences a utopian policy of liberation differs fundamentally from a realist one.

The issue between liberation as a utopian principle of abstract morality vs. the realist evaluation of the consequences which a policy of liberation would have for the survival of the nation has arisen before in American history. Abraham Lincoln was faced with a dilemma similar to that which confronts us today. Should he make the liberation of the slaves the ultimate standard of his policy even at the risk of destroying the Union, as many urged him to do, or should he subordinate the moral principle of universal freedom to considerations of the national interest? The answer Lincoln gave to Horace Greeley, a spokesman for the utopian moralists, is timeless in its eloquent wisdom. "If there be those," he wrote on August 22, 1862,

> who would not save the Union unless they could at the same time save slavery, I do not agree with them. If there be those who would not save the Union unless they could at the same time destroy slavery, I do not agree with them. My paramount object in this struggle *is* to save the Union, and is *not* either to save or to destroy slavery. If I could save the Union without freeing *any* slave I would do it, and if I could save it by freeing *all* the slaves, I would do it; and I could save it by freeing some and leaving others alone I would also do that. What I do about slavery, and the colored race, I do because I believe it helps to save the Union; and what I forbear, I forbear because I do *not* believe it would help to save the Union. I shall do *less* whenever I shall believe what I am doing hurts the cause, and I shall do more whenever I shall believe doing more will help the cause. I shall try to correct errors when shown to be errors; and I shall adopt new views so fast as they shall appear to be true views.
>
> I have here stated my purpose according to my view of *official* duty; and I intend no modification of my oft-expressed *personal* wish that all men everywhere could be free.

IV

THE foregoing discussion ought to shed additional light, if this is still needed, upon the moral merits of the utopian and realist positions. This question, more than any other, seems to have agitated the critics of realism in international affairs. Disregarding the voluminous evidence, some of them have picked a few words out of their context to prove that realism in international affairs is unprincipled and contemptuous of morality. To mention but one example, one eminent critic summarizes my position, which he supposes to deny the possibility of judging the conduct of states by moral criteria, in these words: "And one spokesman finds 'a profound and neglected truth,' to use his words, in the dictum of Hobbes that 'there is neither morality nor law outside the state.'"[19] These are indeed my words, but not all of them. What I actually said was this:

> There is a profound and neglected truth hidden in Hobbes's extreme dictum that the state creates morality as well as law and that there is neither morality nor law outside the state. Universal moral principles, such as justice or equality, are capable of guiding political action only to the extent that they have been given concrete content and have been related to political situations by society.[20]

It must be obvious from this passage and from all my other writings on the subject[21] that my position is the exact opposite from what this critic makes it out to be. I have always maintained that the actions of states are subject to universal moral principles and I have been careful to differentiate my position in this respect from that of Hobbes. Five points basic to my position may need to be emphasized again.

The first point is what one might call the requirement of cosmic humility with regard to the moral evaluation of the actions of states. To know that states are subject to the moral law is one thing; to pretend to know what is morally required of states in a particular situation is quite another. The human mind tends naturally to identify the particular interests of states, as of individuals, with the moral purposes of the universe. The statesman in the defense of the nation's interests may, and at times even must, yield to that tendency; the scholar must resist it at every turn. For the light-hearted assumption that what one's own nation aims at and does is morally good and that those who oppose that nation's policies are evil is morally indefensible and intellectually untenable and leads in practice to that distortion of judgment, born of the blindness of crusading frenzy, which has been the curse of nations from the beginning of time.

The second point which obviously needs to be made again concerns the effectiveness of the restraints which morality imposes upon the actions of states.

A discussion of international morality must guard against the two extremes either of overrating the influence of ethics upon international politics or else of denying that statesmen and diplomats are moved by anything else but considerations of material power.

On the one hand, there is the dual error of confounding the moral rules which people actually observe with those they pretend to observe as well as with those which writers declare they ought to observe. . . .

On the other hand, there is the misconception, usually associated with the general depreciation and moral condemnation of power politics, discussed above, that international politics is so thoroughly evil that it is no use looking for ethical limitations of the aspirations for power on the international scene. Yet if we ask ourselves what statesmen and diplomats are capable of doing to further the power objectives of their respective nations and what they actually do, we realize that they do less than they probably could and less than they actually did in other periods of history. They refuse to consider certain ends and to use certain means, either altogether or under certain conditions, not because in the light of expediency they appear impractical or unwise, but because certain moral rules interpose an absolute barrier. Moral rules do not permit certain policies to be considered at all from the point of view of expediency. Such ethical inhibitions operate in our time on different levels with different effectiveness. Their restraining function is most obvious and most effective in affirming the sacredness of human life in times of peace.[22]

In connection with this passage we have given a number of historic examples showing the influence of moral principles upon the conduct of foreign policy. An example taken from contemporary history will illustrate the same point. There can be little doubt that the Soviet Union could have achieved the objectives of its foreign policy at the end of the Second World War without antagonizing the nations of the West into that encircling coalition which has been the nightmare of Bolshevist foreign policy since 1917. It could have mitigated cunning for its own sake and the use of force with persuasion, conciliation, and a trust derived from the awareness of a partial community of interests and would thereby have minimized the dangers to itself and the rest of the world which are inherent in the objectives of its policies. Yet the Soviet Union was precluded from relying upon these traditional methods of diplomacy by its general conception of human nature, politics, and morality. In the general philosophy of Bolshevism there is no room for honest dissent, the recognition of the intrinsic worth of divergent interests, and genuine conciliation between such interests. On all levels of social interaction opposition must be destroyed by cunning and violence, since it has no right to exist, rather than be met half way in view of its intrinsic legitimacy. This being the general conception of the political morality of Bolshevism, the foreign policy of the Soviet Union is limited to a much more narrow choice of means than the foreign policies of other nations.

The United States, for instance, has been able, in its relations with the nations of Latin America, to replace military intervention and dollar diplomacy with the policy of the Good Neighbor. That drastic change was made possible by the general conception of political morality which has been prevalent in the United States from its very inception. The United States is a pluralist society which presupposes the continuing existence and legitimacy of divergent interests. The interests are locked in a continuing struggle for supremacy to be decided by force only as a last resort, but normally through a multitude of institutional agencies which are so devised as to allow one or the other interest a temporary advantage but none a permanent supremacy at the price of the destruction of the others. This morality of pluralism allows the United States, once it is secure in that minimum of vital interests to which we have referred above, to transfer those principles of political morality to the international scene and to deal with divergent interests there with the same methods of genuine compromise and conciliation which are a permanent element of its domestic political life.

The third point concerns the relations between universal moral principles and political action. I have always maintained that these universal moral principles cannot be applied to the actions of states in their abstract universal formulation, but that they must be, as it were, filtered through the concrete circumstances of time and place. The individual may say for himself: *"Fiat justitia, pereat mundus"*; the state has no right to say so in the name of those who are in its care. Both individual and state must judge political action by universal moral principles, such as that of liberty. Yet while the individual has a moral right to sacri-

fice himself in defense of such a moral principle, the state has no moral right to let its moral disapprobation of the infringement of liberty get in the way of successful political action, itself inspired by the moral principle of national survival. There can be no political morality without prudence, that is, without consideration of the political consequences of seemingly moral action. Classical and medieval philosophy knew this and so did Lincoln when he said: "I do the very best I know how, the very best I can, and I mean to keep doing so until the end. If the end brings me out all right, what is said against me won't amount to anything. If the end brings me out wrong, ten angels swearing I was right would make no difference." The issue between utopianism and realism, as it bears on this point, has been put most succinctly by Edmund Burke, and what he has to say in the following passage about revolution, that is, civil war, may well be applied *mutatis mutandis* to all war.

Nothing universal can be rationally affirmed on any moral or any political subject. Pure metaphysical abstraction does not belong to these matters. The lines of morality are not like the ideal lines of mathematics. They are broad and deep as well as long. They admit of exceptions; they demand modifications. These exceptions and modifications are not made by the process of logic, but by the rules of prudence. Prudence is not only the first in rank of the virtues political and moral, but she is the director, the regulator, the standard of them all. Metaphysics cannot live without definition; but Prudence is cautious how she defines. Our courts cannot be more fearful in suffering fictitious cases to be brought before them for eliciting their determination on a point of law than prudent moralists are in putting extreme and harzardous cases of conscience upon emergencies not existing. Without attempting, therefore, to define, what never can be defined, the case of a revolution in government, this, I think, may be safely affirmed—that a sore and pressing evil is to be removed, and that a good, great in its amount and unequivocal in its nature, must be probable almost to a certainty, before the inestimable price of our own morals and the well-being of a number of our fellow-citizens is paid for a revolution. If ever we ought to be economists even to parsimony, it is in the voluntary production of evil. Every revolution contains in it something of evil.[23]

Fourth, the realist recognizes that a moral decision, especially in the political sphere, does not imply a simple choice between a moral principle and a standard of action which is morally irrelevant or even outright immoral. A moral decision implies always a choice among different moral principles, one of which is given precedence over others. To say that a political action has no moral purpose is absurd; for political action can be defined as an attempt to realize moral values through the medium of politics, that is, power. The relevant moral question concerns the choice among different moral values, and it is at this point that the realist and the utopian part company again. If an American statesman must choose between the promotion of universal liberty, which is a moral good, at the risk of American security and, hence, of liberty in the United States, and the promotion of American security and of liberty in the United States, which is another moral good, to the detriment of the promotion of universal liberty, which choice ought he to make? The utopian will not face the issue squarely and will deceive himself into believing that he can achieve both goods at the same time. The realist will choose the national interest on both moral and pragmatic grounds; for it he does not take care of the national interest nobody else will, and if he puts American security and liberty in jeopardy the cause of liberty everywhere will be impaired.

Finally, the political realist distinguishes between his moral sympathies and the political interests which he must defend. He will distinguish with Lincoln between his "*official* duty" which is to protect the national interest and his "*personal* wish" which is to see universal moral values realized throughout the world.

The issue has been admirably put by Father Wilfred Parsons of Catholic University in defending Ambassador Kennan's position:

> Mr. Kennan did not say state behavior is not a fit subject for moral judgment, but only that it should not sway our realization of the realities with which we have to deal. Msgr. Koenig continues: "Should we accept power realities and aspirations without feeling the obligation of moral judgment?" And he appeals to the present writer and other political scientists to say whether this doctrine agrees with Pope Pius XII's messages on peace.
>
> I am sure that most political scientists, and

also Mr. Kennan, would agree with the Monsignor that we should not accept those realities "without feeling the obligation of moral judgment." But there is a difference between *feeling* this obligation (and even expressing it) and allowing this feeling to sway our actions in concrete negotiations that deal with the national or world common good. We can still feel and yet deal.

> To make my meaning clearer, I understood Mr. Kennan to hold that we went off the beam with Woodrow Wilson, when we began to make our moral disapprobation an *essential part* of our foreign relations, even sometimes at the expense of our own and the world's common good. Logically, such an attitude would inhibit our dealing with Britain, France and a host of countries. Pius XI, speaking of Mussolini after the Lateran Treaty, said he would deal with the devil himself if he must. Here was moral disapprobation, but it was not "carried over into the affairs of states."
>
> This relative position, and not the absolute one of Msgr. Koenig (with which in itself I agree), is, I think, the issue raised by Mr. Kennan, and it is worth debating on that basis.[24]

The contest between utopianism and realism is not tantamount to a contest between principle and expediency, morality and immorality, although some spokesmen for the former would like to have it that way. The contest is rather between one type of political morality and another type of political morality, one taking as its standard universal moral principles abstractly formulated, the other weighing these principles against the moral requirements of concrete political action, their relative merits to be decided by a prudent evaluation of the political consequences to which they are likely to lead.[25]

These points are re-emphasized by the foregoing discussion. Which attitude with regard to collective security and to the liberation of the captive nations, the utopian or the realist, is more likely to safeguard the survival of the United States in its territorial, political, and cultural identity and at the same time to contribute the most to the security and liberty of other nations? This is the ultimate test—political and moral—by which utopianism and realism must be judged.

Notes

1. This is the ideal type of the utopian position rather than the empirical description of any particular historic type. In actuality, and this is true particularly of the present, the utopian position in international affairs is not always consistent with its philosophic premises.

2. It ought not to need special emphasis that a principle of social conduct, in contrast to a law of nature, allows of, and even presupposes, conduct in violation of the principle. Robert W. Tucker, in "Professor Morgenthau's Theory of Political 'Realism'," *American Political Science Review*, Vol. 46, pp. 214-224 (March, 1952), has missed this and many other points in his zeal to find contradictions where there are none.

3. "This [the realist] doctrine," writes one historian—Frank Tannenbaum, "The Balance of Power versus the Coördinate State," *Political Science Quarterly*, Vol. 67, p. 173 (June, 1952) —"is confessedly, nay gleefully, amoral. It prides itself upon being realistic and takes Machiavelli as its great teacher. It is contemptuous of the simple beliefs of honest men, jeers at the sentimentalism of those who believe that men may strive for peace among nations, and looks upon democracy as a hindrance to skilled diplomacy. It looks with a certain derisive superiority upon the great leaders of this nation from Jefferson and John Quincy Adams to Woodrow Wilson and Franklin Delano Roosevelt and describes them as moralistic and sentimental, and suggests that our models ought to be Richelieu, Clemenceau and Bismarck. Its adherents believe that international wars instead of being made by men and supported by institutions humanely contrived have their origin in the nature of man himself and are inevitable."

Another historian, Arthur Schlesinger, Jr., in "Policy and National Interest," *Partisan Review*, Vol. 18, p. 709 (Nov.–Dec., 1951), however, gives Ambassador Kennan a clean bill of moral health. "But what differentiates," he writes, "the Kennan approach from that of, for example, the followers of Professor Hans J. Morgenthau is that he takes the revelations of international amorality in his stride; more than that, he comprehends them in his understanding of the tragedy of history. Mr. Kennan, in other words, is deeply moral, rather than moralistic, like Judge Hull, or immoral, like the boys who have just discovered that politics involve power."

"This dreadful doctrine," we are told (by Tannenbaum, pp. 173-174), "has now won wide acceptance by teachers and scholars in the field of international relations and has, in fact, become the leading theme in such circles in many of our largest universities. It has be-

come the *science* of international relations— and who would quarrel with science, especially when it comes packaged in good clear English and from high sources? But it is not science. It is, in fact, only poor logic based upon false premises, and its claim to be a science is only a bit of unholy conceit."

It may be remarked in passing that to dispose of a scientific theory as "fashionable" or a "fad," as some do with regard to political realism, may reveal something about the state of mind of the writer, but reveals nothing at all about the scientific value of the theory.

4. Tannenbaum, in the article cited above, and in "The American Tradition in Foreign Relations," *Foreign Affairs*, Vol. 30, pp. 31-50 (Oct., 1951).

5. *Our Foreign Affairs* (New York, 1924), pp. 246 ff.

6. "The United States and the Balance of Power," *The Journal of Politics*, Vol. 3, pp. 401-449 (Nov., 1941).

7. Tannenbaum, "The Balance of Power versus The Coördinate State," cited above, note 3, p. 173.

8. "Democracy and Efficiency," *Atlantic Monthly*, Vol. 87, pp. 293-294 (March, 1901).

9. Tannenbaum, p. 177.

10. *Ibid.*

11. William Archibald Dunning, *Essays on the Civil War and Reconstruction and Related Topics* (New York, 1931), p. 351.

12. Tannenbaum, pp. 195-196.

13. "A Few Words on Non-Intervention," *Dissertations and Discussions: Political, Philosophical, and Historical* (London, 1875), pp. 153-178.

14. *The Idea of National Interest: An Analytical Study in American Foreign Policy* (New York, 1934).

15. "Helvidius, in Answer to Pacificus, on President Washington's Proclamation of Neutrality," in *Letters and other Writings of James Madison* (Philadelphia, 1867), Vol. 1, p. 611.

16. See, on this point, Hans J. Morgenthau, "International Organizations and Foreign Policy," in *Foundations of World Organization: A Political and Cultural Appraisal*, Eleventh Symposium of the Conference on Science, Philosophy and Religion, edited by Lyman Bryson, Louis Finkelstein, Harold D. Lasswell, R. M. MacIver (New York, 1952), pp. 377-383.

17. The difference in these two attitudes is well illustrated by the following passage from a Moon Mullins cartoon. An elderly representative of the utopian school asks little Kayo: "Remember the golden rule. Now, supposing that boy slapped you on the right cheek, what would you do?" Whereupon Kayo replies

realistically: "Jest how big a boy are you supposin'?"

18. *New York Times*, August 14, 1952, p. 1.

19. A. H. Feller, "In Defense of International Law and Morality," *The Annals of the American Academy of Political and Social Science*, Vol. 282, p. 80 (July, 1952).

20. *In Defense of the National Interest: A Critical Examination of American Foreign Policy* (New York, 1951), p. 34.

21. See, for instance, "The Machiavellian Utopia," *Ethics*, Vol. 55, pp. 145–147 (Jan., 1945); "Ethics and Politics," in *Approaches to Group Understanding*, Sixth Symposium of the Conference on Science, Philosophy and Religion, edited by Bryson, Finkelstein, and MacIver (New York, 1947), pp. 319–341; "The Escape from Power in the Western World," in *Conflicts of Power in Modern Culture*, Seventh Symposium of the Conference on Science, Philosophy and Religion, edited by Bryson, Finkelstein, and MacIver, pp. 1–12; *Scientific Man vs. Power Politics* (Chicago, 1946), Chaps. 7, 8; "Views of Nuremberg: Further Analysis of the Trial and Its Importance," *America*, Vol. 76, pp. 266–267 (Dec. 7, 1946); "The Twilight of International Morality," *Ethics*, Vol. 58, pp. 79–99 (Jan., 1948); "The Political Science of E. H. Carr," *World Politics*, Vol. 1, pp. 127–134 (Oct., 1948); *Politics Among Nations* (New York, 1948), Ch. 14; "National Interest and Moral Principles in Foreign Policy: The Primacy of the National Interest," *The American Scholar*, Vol. 18, pp. 207–212 (Spring, 1949); "The Pathology of Power," *American Perspective*, Vol. 4, pp. 6–10 (Winter, 1950); "The Moral Dilemma in Foreign Policy," in *The Year Book of World Affairs, 1951* (London, 1951), pp. 12–36.

22. Morgenthau, *Politics Among Nations*, pp. 174–175.

23. *The Works of The Right Honorable Edmund Burke*, 4th ed. (Boston, 1871), Vol. 4, pp. 80–81. Cf. also Burke, "Speech on A Bill for Shortening the Duration of Parliaments," May 8, 1780, in *Works*, Vol. 7, p. 73: "I must see, to satisfy me, the remedies; I must see, from their operation in the cure of the old evil, and in the cure of those new evils which are inseparable from all remedies, how they balance each other, and what is the total result. The excellence of mathematics and metaphysics is, to have but one thing before you; but he forms the best judgment in all moral disquisitions who has the greatest number and variety of considerations in one view before him, and can take them in with the best possible consideration of the middle results of all."

24. *America*, Vol. 86, p. 700 (March 29, 1952). See also Algernon Cecil, "The Foreign Office," in *The Cambridge History of British Foreign Policy, 1783–1919* (New York, 1923), Vol. 3, p. 605, concerning Lord Salisbury: "Always, however, the motive of his policy was to be found in the political interests as opposed to the political sympathies of Great Britain; and in this way his treatment of Foreign Affairs is at the opposite policy from that of Palmerston or Gladstone." Cf. also the general remarks in Alexander H. Leighton, *Human Relations in a Changing World* (New York, 1949), pp. 155 ff.

25. See, on this point, Shirley R. Letwin, "Rationalism, Principles, and Politics," *The Review of Politics*, Vol. 14, pp. 367–393 (July, 1952); L. Susan Stebbing, *Ideals and Illusions* (London, 1941); Vernon H. Holloway, *Religious Ethics and the Politics of Power* (New York, 1951); and Dorothy Fosdick, "Ethical Standards and Political Strategies," *Political Science Quarterly*, Vol. 57, pp. 214 ff. (1942).

Arnold Wolfers

"National security" as an ambiguous symbol

STATESMEN, PUBLICISTS AND SCHOLARS who wish to be considered realists, as many do today, are inclined to insist that the foreign policy they advocate is dictated by the national interest, more specifically by the national security interest. It is not suprising that this should be so. Today any reference to the pursuit of security is likely to ring a sympathetic chord.

However, when political formulas such as "national interest" or "national security" gain popularity they need to be scrutinized with particular care. They may not mean the same thing to different people. They may not have any precise meaning at all. Thus, while appearing to offer guidance and a basis for broad consensus they may be permitting everyone to label whatever policy he favors with an attractive and possibly deceptive name.

In a very vague and general way "national interest" does suggest a direction of policy which can be distinguished from several others which may present themselves as alternatives. It indicates that the policy is designed to promote demands which are ascribed to the nation rather than to individuals, sub-national groups or mankind as a whole. It emphasizes that the policy subordinates other interests to those of the nation. But beyond this it has very little meaning.

When Charles Beard's study of *The Idea of National Interest* was published in the early years of the New Deal and under the impact of the Great Depression, the lines were drawn differently than they are today. The question at that time was whether American foreign policy, then largely economic in scope and motivation, was aimed not at promoting the welfare interests of the nation as a whole but instead at satisfying the material interests of powerful sub-national interest or pressure groups. While it was found hard to define what was in the interest of national welfare or to discover standards by which to measure it, there could be no doubt as to what people had in mind: they desired to see national policy makers rise above the narrow and special economic interests of parts of the nation to focus their attention on the more inclusive interests of the whole.

Today, the alternative to a policy of the national interest to which people refer is of a different character. They fear policy makers may be unduly concerned with the "interests of all of mankind." They see them sacrificing the less inclusive national community to the wider but in their opinion chimeric world community. The issue, then, is not one of transcending narrow group selfishness, as it was at the time of Beard's discussion, but rather one of according more exclusive devotion to the narrower cause of the national self.

There is another difference between the current and the earlier debate. While it would be wrong to say that the economic interest has ceased to attract attention, it is overshadowed today by the national security interest. Even in the recent debates on the St. Lawrence Seaway, clearly in the first instance an economic enterprise, the defenders of project, when seeking to impress their listeners with the "national interest" involved, spoke mainly of the value of the Seaway for military defense in wartime while some opponents stressed its vulnerability to attack.

The change from a welfare to a security interpretation of the symbol "national interest" is understandable. Today we are living under the impact of cold war and threats of external

Reprinted from the *Political Science Quarterly*, Vol. 67, No. 4, December 1952, pp. 481–502.

aggression rather than of depression and social reform. As a result, the formula of the national interest has come to be practically synonymous with the formula of national security. Unless explicitly denied, spokesmen for a policy which would take the national interest as its guide can be assumed to mean that priority shall be given to measures of security, a term to be analyzed.[1] The question is raised, therefore, whether this seemingly more precise formula of national security offers statesmen a meaningful guide for action. Can they be expected to know what it means? Can policies be distinguished and judged on the ground that they do or do not serve this interest?

The term national security, like national interest, is well enough established in the political discourse of international relations to designate an objective of policy distinguishable from others. We know roughly what people have in mind if they complain that their government is neglecting national security or demanding excessive sacrifices for the sake of enhancing it. Usually those who raise the cry for a policy oriented exclusively toward this interest are afraid their country underestimates the external dangers facing it or is being diverted into idealistic channels unmindful of these dangers. Moreover, the symbol suggests protection through power and therefore figures more frequently in the speech of those who believe in reliance on national power than of those who place their confidence in model behavior, international cooperation, or the United Nations to carry their country safely through the tempests of international conflict. For these reasons it would be an exaggeration to claim that the symbol of national security is nothing but a stimulus to semantic confusion, though closer analysis will show that if used without specifications it leaves room for more confusion than sound political counsel or scientific usage can afford.

The demand for a policy of national security is primarily normative in character. It is supposed to indicate what the policy of a nation should be in order to be either expedient—a rational means toward an accepted end—or moral, the best or least evil course of action. The value judgments implicit in these normative exhortations will be discussed.

Before doing so, attention should be drawn to an assertion of fact which is implicit if not explicit in most appeals for a policy guided by national security. Such appeals usually assume that nations in fact have made security their

goal except when idealism or utopianism of their leaders has led them to stray from the traditional path. If such conformity of behavior actually existed, it would be proper to infer that a country deviating from the established pattern of conduct would risk being penalized. This would greatly strengthen the normative arguments. The trouble with the contention of fact, however, is that the term "security" covers a range of goals so wide that highly divergent policies can be interpreted as policies of security.

Security points to some degree of protection of values previously acquired. In Walter Lippmann's words, a nation is secure to the extent to which it is not in danger of having to sacrifice core values, if it wishes to avoid war, and is able, if challenged, to maintain them by victory in such a war.[2] What this definition implies is that security rises and falls with the ability of a nation to deter an attack, or to defeat it. This is in accord with common usage of the term.

Security is a value, then, of which a nation can have more or less and which it can aspire to have in greater or lesser measure.[3] It has much in common, in this respect, with power or wealth, two other values of great importance in international affairs. But while wealth measures the amount of a nation's material possessions, and power its ability to control the actions of others, security, in an objective sense, measures the absence of threats to acquired values, in a subjective sense, the absence of fear that such values will be attacked. In both respects a nation's security can run a wide gamut from almost complete insecurity or sense of insecurity at one pole, to almost complete security or absence of fear at the other.[4]

The possible discrepancy between the objective and subjective connotation of the term is significant in international relations despite the fact that the chance of future attack never can be measured "objectively"; it must always remain a matter of subjective evaluation and speculation. However, when the French after World War I insisted that they were entitled to additional guarantees of security because of the exceptionally dangerous situation which France was said to be facing, other Powers in the League expressed the view that rather than to submit to what might be French hysterical apprehension the relative security of France should be objectively evaluated. It is a well-known fact that nations, and groups within nations, differ widely in their reaction to one and the same external situation. Some tend to exaggerate the danger while others under-estimate it. With hindsight it is sometimes possible to tell exactly how far they deviated from a rational reaction to the actual or objective state of danger existing at the time. Even if for no other reasons, this difference in the reaction to similar threats suffices to make it probable that nations will differ in their efforts to obtain more security. Some may find the danger to which they are exposed entirely normal and in line with their modest security expectations while others consider it unbearable to live with these same dangers. Although this is not the place to set up hypotheses on the factors which account for one or the other attitude, investigation might confirm the hunch that those nations tend to be most sensitive to threats which have either experienced attacks in the recent past or, having passed through a prolonged period of an exceptionally high degree of security, suddenly find themselves thrust into a situation of danger.[5] Probably national efforts to achieve greater security would also prove, in part at least, to be a function of the power and opportunity which nations possess of reducing danger by their own efforts.[6]

Another and even stronger reason why nations must be expected not to act uniformly is that they are not all or constantly faced with the same degree of danger. For purposes of a working hypothesis, theorists may find it useful at times to postulate conditions wherein all states are enemies—provided they are not allied against others—and wherein all, therefore, are equally in danger of attack.[7] But, while it may be true in the living world, too, that no sovereign nation can be absolutely safe from future attack, nobody can reasonably contend that Canada, for example, is threatened today to the same extent as countries like Iran or Yugoslavia, or that the British had as much reason to be concerned about the French air force in the twenties as about Hitler's *Luftwaffe* in the thirties.

This point, however, should not be over-stressed. There can be no quarrel with the generalization that most nations, most of the time—the great Powers particularly—have shown, and had reason to show, an active concern about some lack of security and have been prepared to make sacrifices for its enhancement. Danger and the awareness of it have been, and continue to be, sufficiently widespread to guarantee some uniformity in this respect. But a generalization which leaves room both for

the frantic kind of struggle for more security which characterized French policy at times and for the neglect of security apparent in American foreign policy after the close of both World Wars throws little light on the behavior of nations. The demand for conformity would have meaning only if it could be said—as it could under the conditions postulated in the working hypothesis of pure power politics—that nations normally subordinate all other values to the maximization of their security, which, however, is obviously not the case.

There have been many instances of struggles for more security taking the form of an un-restrained race for armaments, alliances, strategic boundaries and the like; but one need only recall the many heated parliamentary debates on arms appropriations to realize how uncertain has been the extent to which people will consent to sacrifice for additional increments of security. Even when there has been no question that armaments would mean more security, the cost in taxes, the reduction in social benefits or the sheer discomfort involved has militated effectively against further effort. It may be worth noting in this connection that there seems to be no case in history in which a country started a preventive war on the grounds of security—unless Hitler's wanton attack on his neighbors be allowed to qualify as such—although there must have been circumstances where additional security could have been obtained by war and although so many wars have been launched for the enhancement of other values. Of course, where security serves only as a cloak for other more enticing demands, nations or ambitious leaders may consider no price for it too high. This is one of the reasons why very high security aspirations tend to make a nation suspect of hiding more aggressive aims.

Instead of expecting a uniform drive for enhanced or maximum security, a different hypothesis may offer a more promising lead. Efforts for security are bound to be experienced as a burden; security after all is nothing but the absence of the evil of insecurity, a negative value so to speak. As a consequence, nations will be inclined to minimize these efforts, keeping them at the lowest level which will provide them with what they consider adequate protection. This level will often be lower than what states-men, military leaders or other particularly security-minded participants in the decision-making process believe it should be. In any case, together with the extent of the external threats, numerous domestic factors such as national character, tradition, preferences and prejudices will influence the level of security which a nation chooses to make its target.

It might be objected that in the long run nations are not so free to choose the amount of effort they will put into security. Are they not under a kind of compulsion to spare no effort provided they wish to survive? This objection again would make sense only if the hypothesis of pure power politics were a realistic image of actual world affairs. In fact, however, a glance at history will suffice to show that survival has only exceptionally been at stake, particularly for the major Powers. If nations were not concerned with the protection of values other than their survival as independent states, most of them, most of the time, would not have had to be seriously worried about their security, despite what manipulators of public opinion engaged in mustering greater security efforts may have said to the contrary. What "compulsion" there is, then, is a function not merely of the will of others, real or imagined, to destroy the nation's independence but of national desires and ambitions to retain a wealth of other values such as rank, respect, material possessions and special privileges. It would seem to be a fair guess that the efforts for security by a particular nation will tend to vary, other things being equal, with the range of values for which protection is being sought.

In respect to this range there may seem to exist a considerable degree of uniformity. All over the world today peoples are making sacrifices to protect and preserve what to them appear as the minimum national core values, national independence and territorial integrity. But there is deviation in two directions. Some nations seek protection for more marginal values as well. There was a time when United States policy could afford to be concerned mainly with the protection of the foreign investments or markets of its nationals, its "core values" being out of danger, or when Britain was extending its national self to include large and only vaguely circumscribed "regions of special interest." It is a well-known and portentous phenomenon that bases, security zones and the like may be demanded and acquired for the purpose of protecting values acquired earlier; and they then become new national values requiring protection themselves. Pushed to its logical conclusion, such spatial extension of the range of values does not stop short of world domination.

A deviation in the opposite direction of a compression of the range of core values is hardly exceptional in our days either. There is little indication that Britain is bolstering the security of Hong Kong although colonies were once considered part of the national territory. The Czechs lifted no finger to protect their independence against the Soviet Union and many West Europeans are arguing today that rearmament has become too destructive of values they cherish to be justified even when national independence is obviously at stake.

The lack of uniformity does not end here. A policy is not characterized by its goal, in this case security, alone. In order to become imitable, the means by which the goal is pursued must be taken into account as well. Thus, if two nations were both endeavoring to maximize their security but one were placing all its reliance on armaments and alliances, the other on meticulous neutrality, a policy maker seeking to emulate their behavior would be at a loss where to turn. Those who call for a policy guided by national security are not likely to be unaware of this fact, but they take for granted that they will be understood to mean a security policy based on power, and on military power at that. Were it not so, they would be hard put to prove that their government was not already doing its best for security, though it was seeking to enhance it by such means as international cooperation or by the negotiation of compromise agreements—means which in one instance may be totally ineffective or utopian but which in others may have considerable protective value.

It is understandable why it should so readily be assumed that a quest for security must necessarily translate itself into a quest for coercive power. In view of the fact that security is being sought against external violence—coupled perhaps with internal subversive violence—it seems plausible at first sight that the response should consist in an accumulation of the same kind of force for the purpose of resisting an attack or of deterring a would-be attacker. The most casual reading of history and of contemporary experience, moreover, suffices to confirm the view that such resort to "power of resistance" has been the rule with nations grappling with serious threats to their security, however much the specific form of this power and its extent may differ. Why otherwise would so many nations which have no acquisitive designs maintain costly armaments? Why did Denmark with her state of complete disarmament remain an exception even among the small Powers?

But again, the generalization that nations seeking security usually place great reliance on coercive power does not carry one far. The issue is not whether there is regularly some such reliance but whether there are no significant differences between nations concerning their over-all choice of the means upon which they place their trust. The controversies concerning the best road to future security that are so typical of coalition partners at the close of victorious wars throw light on this question. France in 1919 and all the Allies in 1945 believed that protection against another German attack could be gained only by means of continued military superiority based on German military impotence. President Wilson in 1919 and many observers in 1945 were equally convinced, however, that more hope for security lay in a conciliatory and fair treatment of the defeated enemy, which would rob him of future incentives to renew his attack. While this is not the place to decide which side was right, one cannot help drawing the conclusion that, in the matter of means, the roads which are open may lead in diametrically opposed directions.[8] The choice in every instance will depend on a multitude of variables. including ideological and moral convictions, expectations concerning the psychological and political developments in the camp of the opponent, and inclinations of individual policy makers.[9]

After all that has been said little is left of the sweeping generalization that in actual practice nations, guided by their national security interest, tend to pursue a uniform and therefore imitable policy of security. Instead, there are numerous reasons why they should differ widely in this respect, with some standing close to the pole of complete indifference to security or complete reliance on nonmilitary means, others close to the pole of insistence on absolute security or of complete reliance on coercive power. It should be added that there exists still another category of nations which cannot be placed within the continuum connecting these poles because they regard security of any degree as an insufficient goal; instead they seek to acquire new values even at the price of greater insecurity. In this category must be placed not only the "mad Caesars," who are out for conquest and glory at any price, but also idealistic statesmen who would plunge their country into war for the sake of spreading the benefits of their ideology, for example, of liberating enslaved peoples.

The actual behavior of nations, past and present, does not affect the normative proposition, to which we shall now turn our attention. According to this proposition nations are called upon to give priority to national security and thus to consent to any sacrifice of value which will provide an additional increment of security. It may be expedient, moral or both for nations to do so even if they should have failed to heed such advice in the past and for the most part are not living up to it today.

The first question, then, is whether some definable security policy can be said to be generally expedient. Because the choice of goals is not a matter of expediency, it would seem to make no sense to ask whether it is expedient for nations to be concerned with the goal of security itself; only the means used to this end, so it would seem, can be judged as to their fitness—their instrumental rationality—to promote security. Yet, this is not so. Security, like other aims, may be an intermediate rather than an ultimate goal, in which case it can be judged as a means to these more ultimate ends.

Traditionally, the protection and preservation of national core values have been considered ends in themselves, at least by those who followed in the footsteps of Machiavelli or, for other reasons of political philosophy, placed the prince, state or nation at the pinnacle of their hierarchy of values. Those who do so today will be shocked at the mere suggestion that national security should have to be justified in terms of higher values which it is expected to serve. But there is a large and perhaps growing current of opinion—as a matter of fact influential in this country for a long time—which adheres to this idea. We condemn Nazis and Communists for defending their own totalitarian countries instead of helping to free their people from tyranny; we enlist support for armaments, here and in Allied countries, not so much on the grounds that they will protect national security but that by enhancing such security they will serve to protect ultimate human values like individual liberty. Again, opposition in Europe and Asia to military security measures is based in part on the contention that it would help little to make national core values secure, if in the process the liberties and the social welfare of the people had to be sacrificed; the prevention of Russian conquest, some insist, is useless, if in the course of a war of defense a large part of the people were to be exterminated and most cities destroyed.[10]

While excellent arguments can be made to support the thesis that the preservation of the national independence of this country is worth almost any price as long as no alternative community is available which could assure the same degree of order, justice, peace or individual liberty, it becomes necessary to provide such arguments whenever national security as a value in itself is being questioned. The answer cannot be taken for granted.

But turning away now from the expediency of security as an intermediate goal we must ask whether, aside from any moral considerations which will be discussed later, a specific level of security and specific means of attaining it can claim to be generally expedient.

When one sets out to define in terms of expediency the level of security to which a nation should aspire, one might be tempted to assume that the sky is the limit. Is not insecurity of any kind an evil from which any rational policy maker would want to rescue his country? Yet, there are obvious reasons why this is not so.

In the first place, every increment of security must be paid by additional sacrifices of other values usually of a kind more exacting than the mere expenditure of precious time on the part of policy makers. At a certain point, then, by something like the economic law of diminishing returns, the gain in security no longer compensates for the added costs of attaining it. As in the case of economic value comparisons and preferences, there is frequently disagreement among different layers of policy makers as to where the line should be drawn. This is true particularly because absolute security is out of the question unless a country is capable of world domination, in which case, however, the insecurities and fears would be "internalized" and probably magnified. Because nations must "live dangerously," then, to some extent, whatever they consent to do about it, a modicum of additional but only relative security may easily become unattractive to those who have to bear the chief burden. Nothing renders the task of statesmen in a democracy more difficult than the reluctance of the people to follow them very far along the road to high and costly security levels.

In the second place, national security policies when based on the accumulation of power have a way of defeating themselves if the target level is set too high. This is due to the fact that "power of resistance" cannot be unmistakably distinguished from "power of aggression." What a country does to bolster its own security through power can be interpreted by others, therefore, as a threat to their security. If this occurs, the vicious circle of what John Herz has described as the "security dilemma" sets in: the efforts of one side provoke countermeasures by the other which in turn tend to wipe out the gains of the first. Theoretically there seems to be no escape from this frustrating consequence; in practice, however, there are ways to convince those who might feel threatened that the accumulation of power is not intended and will never be used for attack.[11] The chief way is that of keeping the target level within moderate bounds and of avoiding placing oneself in a position where it has to be raised suddenly and drastically. The desire to escape from this vicious circle presupposes a security policy of much self-restraint and moderation, especially in the choice of the target level.[12] It can never be expedient to pursue a security policy which by the fact of provocation or incentive to others fails to increase the nation's relative power position and capability of resistance.

The question of what means are expedient for the purpose of enhancing security raises even more thorny problems. Policy makers must decide how to distribute their reliance on whatever means are available to them and, particularly, how far to push the accumulation of coercive power. No attempt can be made here to decide what the choice should be in order to be expedient. Obviously, there can be no general answer which would meet the requirements of every case. The answer depends on the circumstances. A week country may have no better means at its disposal than to prove to stronger neighbors that its strict neutrality can be trusted. Potentially strong countries may have a chance to deter an aggressor by creating "positions of strength." In some instances they may have no other way of saving themselves; while in others even they may find it more expedient to supplement such a policy, if not to replace it, by a policy intended to negotiate their opponent out of his aggressive designs.

The reason why "power of resistance" is not the general panacea which some believe it to be lies in the nature of security itself. If security, in the objective sense of the term at least, rises and falls with the presence or absence of aggressive intentions on the part of others, the attitude and behavior of those from whom the threat emanates are of prime importance. Such attitude and behavior need not be beyond the realm of influence by the country seeking to bolster its security. Whenever they do not lie beyond this realm the most effective and least costly security policy consists in inducing the opponent to give up his aggressive intentions.

While there is no easy way to determine when means can and should be used which are directed not at resistance but at the prevention of the desire of others to attack, it will clarify the issue to sketch the type of hypotheses which would link specific security policies, as expedient, to some of the most typical political constellations. One can think of nations lined up between the two poles of maximum and minimum "attack propensity," with those unalterably committed to attack, provided it promises success, at one pole and those whom no amount of opportunity for successful attack could induce to undertake it at the other. While security in respect to the first group can come exclusively as a result of "positions of strength" sufficient to deter or defeat attack, nothing could do more to undermine security in respect to the second group than to start accumulating power of a kind which would provoke fear and countermoves.

Unfortunately it can never be known with certainty, in practice, what position within the continuum one's opponent actually occupies. Statesmen cannot be blamed, moreover, if caution and suspicion lead them to assume a closer proximity to the first pole than hindsight proves to have been justified. We believe we have ample proof that the Soviet Union today is at or very close to the first pole, while Canadian policy makers probably place the United States in its intentions toward Canada at the second pole.

It is fair to assume that, wherever the issue of security becomes a matter of serious concern, statesmen will usually be dealing with potential opponents who occupy a position somewhere between but much closer to the first of the two poles. This means, then, that an attack must be feared as a possibility, even though the intention to launch it cannot be considered to have crystallized to the point where nothing could change it. If this be true, a security policy in order to be expedient cannot avoid accumulating power of resistance and yet cannot let it go at that. Efforts have to be made simultaneously toward the goal of removing the incentives to attack. This is only another way of saying that security policy must seek to bring opponents to occupy a position as close to the second pole as conditions and capabilities permit.

Such a twofold policy presents the greatest dilemmas because efforts to change the intentions of an opponent may run counter to the efforts to build up strength against him. The dangers of any policy of concessions, symbolized by "Munich," cannot be underestimated. The paradox of this situation must be faced, however, if security policy is to be expedient. It implies that national security policy, except when directed against a country unalterably committed to attack, is the more rational the more it succeeds in taking the interests, including the security interests, of the other side into consideration. Only in doing so can it hope to minimize the willingness of the other to resort to violence. Rather than to insist, then, that under all conditions security be sought by reliance on nothing but defensive power and be pushed in a spirit of national selfishness toward the highest targets, it should be stressed that in most instances efforts to satisfy legitimate demands of others are likely to promise better results in terms of security.[13] That is probably what George Kennan had in mind when he advised policy makers to use self-restraint in the pursuit of the national interest. While in the face of a would-be world conqueror who is beyond the pale of external influence it is dangerous to be diverted from the accumulation of sheer defensive power, any mistake about his true state of mind or any neglect of opportunities to influence his designs, where it has a chance of being successful, violates the rules of expediency. It should always be kept in mind that the ideal security policy is one which would lead to a distribution of values so satisfactory to all nations that the intention to attack and with it the problem of security would be minimized. While this is a utopian goal, policy makers and particularly peacemakers would do well to remember that there are occasions when greater approximation to such a goal can be effected.

We can now focus our attention on the moral issue, if such there be.[14] Those who advocate a policy devoted to national security are not always aware of the fact—if they do not explicitly deny it—that they are passing moral judgment when they advise a nation to pursue the goal of national security or when they insist that such means as the accumulation of coercive power—or its use—should be employed for this purpose.[15]

Nations like individuals or other groups may value things not because they consider them good or less evil than their alternative; they may value them because they satisfy their pride, heighten their sense of self-esteem or reduce their fears. However, no policy, or human act in general, can escape becoming a subject for moral judgment—whether by the conscience of the actor himself or by others —which calls for the sacrifice of other values, as any security policy is bound to do. Here it becomes a matter of comparing and weighing values in order to decide which of them are deemed sufficiently good to justify the evil of sacrificing others. If someone insists that his country should do more to build up its strength, he is implying, knowingly or not, that more security is sufficiently desirable to warrant such evils as the cut in much-needed social welfare benefits or as the extension of the period of military service.[16]

Many vivid examples of the moral dilemma are being supplied by current controversies concerning American security policy. Is a "deal with fascist Spain" morally justified, provided it added an increment to our security though principles valued highly by some were being sacrificed? Should we engage in subversive activities and risk the lives of our agents if additional security can be attained thereby? Should we perhaps go so far as to start a preventive war, when ready, with the enormous evils it would carry with it, if we should become convinced that no adequate security can be obtained except by the defeat of the Soviet Union? In this last case, would not the exponents of amoralism have some moral qualms, at least to the point of rationalizing a decision favoring such a war by claiming that it would serve to satisfy not primarily an egotistical national demand for security but an altruistic desire to liberate enslaved peoples? It is easier to argue for the amorality of politics if one does not have to bear the responsibility of choice and decision!

Far be it from a political scientist to claim any particular competence in deciding what efforts for national security are or are not morally justified. What he can contribute here is to point to the ambiguities of any general normative demand that security be bought at whatever price it may cost. He may also be able to make it more difficult for advisers or executors of policy to hide from themselves or others the moral value judgments and preferences which underlie whatever security policy they choose to recommend or conduct.

The moral issue will be resolved in one of several ways depending on the ethical code upon which the decision is based. From one extreme point of view it is argued that every sacrifice, especially if imposed on other nations, is justified provided it contributes in any way to national security. Clearly this implies a position that places national security at the apex of the value pyramid and assumes it to constitute an absolute good to which all other values must be subordinated. Few will be found to take this position because if they subscribed to a nationalistic ethics of this extreme type they would probably go beyond security— the mere preservation of values—and insist that the nation is justified in conquering whatever it can use as *Lebensraum* or otherwise. At the opposite extreme are the absolute pacifists who consider the use of coercive power an absolute evil and condemn any security policy, therefore, which places reliance on such power.

For anyone who does not share these extreme views the moral issue raised by the quest for national security is anything but clear-cut and simple. He should have no doubts about the right of a nation to protect and preserve values to which it has a legitimate title or even about its moral duty to pursue a policy meant to serve such preservation. But he cannot consider security the supreme law as Machiavelli would have the statesman regard the *ragione di stato*. Somewhere a line is drawn, which in every instance he must seek to discover, that divides the realm of neglect, the "too-little," from the realm of excess, the "too-much." Even Hans Morgenthau who extols the moral duty of self-preservation seems to take it for granted that naked force shall be used for security in reaction only to violent attack, not for preventive war.

Decision makers are faced with the moral problem, then, of choosing first the values which deserve protection, with national independence ranking high not merely for its own sake but for the guarantee it may offer to values like liberty, justice and peace. He must further decide which level of security to make his target. This will frequently be his most difficult moral task though terms such as adequacy or fair share indicate the kind of standards that may guide him. Finally, he must choose the means and thus by scrupulous computation of values compare the sacrifices, which his choice of means implies, with the security they promise to provide.

It follows that policies of national security,

far from being all good or all evil, may be morally praiseworthy or condemnable depending on their specific character and the particular circumstances of the case. They may be praised for their self-restraint and the consideration which this implies for values other than security; they may instead be condemned for being inadequate to protect national values. Again, they may be praised in one instance for the consideration given to the interests of others, particularly of weaker nations, or condemned in another because of the recklessness with which national values are risked on the altar of some chimera. The target level falls under moral judgment for being too ambitious, egotistical and provocative or for being inadequate; the means employed for being unnecessarily costly in other values or for being ineffective. This wide range of variety which arises out of the multitude of variables affecting the value computation would make it impossible, and in fact meaningless, to pass moral judgment, positive or negative, on "national security policy in general."

It is this lack of moral homogeneity which in matters of security policy justifies attacks on so-called moralism, though not on moral evaluation. The "moralistic approach" is taken to mean a wholesale condemnation either of any concern with national security—as being an expression of national egotism—or of a security policy relying on coercive and therefore evil power. The exponent of such "moralism" is assumed to believe that security for all peoples can be had today by the exclusive use of such "good" and altruistic means as model behavior and persuasion, a spirit of conciliation, inter-

national organization or world government. If there are any utopians who cling to this notion, and have influence on policy, it makes sense to continue to disabuse them of what can surely be proved to be dangerous illusions.

It is worth emphasizing, however, that the opposite line of argument, which without regard for the special circumstances would praise everything done for national security or more particularly everything done for the enhancement of national power of resistance, is no less guilty of applying simple and abstract moral principles and of failing to judge each case realistically on its merits.

In conclusion, it can be said, then, that normative admonitions to conduct a foreign policy guided by the national security interest are no less ambiguous and misleading than the statement of fact concerning part behavior which was discussed earlier. In order to be meaningful such admonitions would have to specify the degree of security which a nation shall aspire to attain and the means by which it is to be attained in a given situation. It may be good advice in one instance to appeal for greater effort and more armaments; it may be no less expedient and morally advisable in another instance to call for moderation and for greater reliance on means other than coercive power. Because the pendulum of public opinion swings so easily from extreme complacency to extreme apprehension, from utopian reliance on "good will" to disillusioned faith in naked force only, it is particularly important to be wary of any simple panacea, even of one that parades in the realist garb of a policy guided solely by the national security interest.

Notes

1. Hans Morgenthau's *In Defense of the National Interest* (New York, 1951) is the most explicit and impassioned recent plea for an American foreign policy which shall follow "but one guiding star—the National Interest." While Morgenthau is not equally explicit in regard to the meaning he attaches to the symbol "national interest," it becomes clear in the few pages devoted to an exposition of this "perennial" interest that the author is thinking in terms of the national security interest, and specifically of security based on power. The United States, he says, is interested in three things: a unique position as a predominant Power without rival in the Western Hemisphere and the maintenance of the balance of power in Europe as well as in Asia,

demands which make sense only in the context of a quest for security through power.

2. Walter Lippmann, *U.S. Foreign Policy* (Boston, 1943), p. 51.

3. This explains why some nations which would seem to fall into the category of *status quo* Powers *par excellence* may nevertheless be dissatisfied and act very much like "imperialist" Powers, as Morgenthau calls nations with acquisitive goals. They are dissatisfied with the degree of security which they enjoy under the *status quo* and are out to enhance it. France's occupation of the Ruhr in 1923 illustrates this type of behavior. Because the demand for more security may induce a *status quo* Power even to resort to the use of violence as a means of attaining more security,

there is reason to beware of the easy and often self-righteous assumption that nations which desire to preserve the *status quo* are necessarily "peace-loving."

4. Security and power would be synonymous terms if security could be attained only through the accumulation of power, which will be shown not to be the case. The fear of attack—security in the subjective sense—is also not proportionate to the relative power position of a nation. Why, otherwise, would some weak and exposed nations consider themselves more secure today than does the United States?

Harold D. Lasswell and Abraham Kaplan, *Power and Society* (New Haven, 1950), defining security as "high value expectancy" stress the subjective and speculative character of security by using the term "expectancy"; the use of the term "high," while indicating no definite level, would seem to imply that the security-seeker aims at a position in which the events he expects—here the continued unmolested enjoyment of his possessions—have considerably more than an even chance of materializing.

5. The United States offers a good illustration and may be typical in this respect. For a long time this country was beyond the reach of any enemy attack that could be considered probable. During that period, then, it could afford to dismiss any serious preoccupation with security. Events proved that it was no worse off for having done so. However, after this happy condition had ceased to exist, government and people alike showed a lag in their awareness of the change. When Nicholas J. Spykman raised his voice in the years before World War II to advocate a broader security outlook than was indicated by the symbol "Western Hemisphere Defense" and a greater appreciation of the rôle of defensive military power, he was dealing with this lag and with the dangers implied in it. If Hans Morgenthau and others raise their warning voices today, seemingly treading in Spykman's footsteps, they are addressing a nation which after a new relapse into wishful thinking in 1945 has been radically disillusioned and may now be swinging toward excessive security apprehensions.

6. Terms such as "degree" or "level" of security are not intended to indicate merely quantitative differences. Nations may also differ in respect to the breadth of their security perspective as when American leaders at Yalta were so preoccupied with security against the then enemy countries of the United States that they failed or refused to consider future American security vis-à-vis the Soviet Union. The differences may apply, instead, to the time range for which security is sought as

when the British at Versailles were ready to offer France short-run security guarantees while the French with more foresight insisted that the "German danger" would not become acute for some ten years.

7. For a discussion of this working hypothesis—as part of the "pure power" hypothesis—see my article on "The Pole of Power and the Pole of Indifference" in *World Politics*, Vol. IV, No. 1, October 1951.

8. Myres S. McDougal ("Law and Peace" in the *American Journal of International Law*, vol. 46, No. 1, January 1952, pp. 102 *et seq.*) rightly criticizes Hans Morgenthau (and George Kennan for what Kennan himself wrongly believes to be his own point of view in the matter; see note 15 *infra*) for his failure to appreciate the rôle which non-power methods, such as legal procedures and moral appeals, may at times successfully play in the pursuit of security. But it is surprising how little aware McDougal appears to be of the disappointing modesty of the contributions which these "other means" have actually made to the enhancement of security and the quite insignificant contributions they have made to the promotion of changes of the *status quo*. This latter failure signifies that they have been unable to remove the main causes of the attacks which security-minded peoples rightly fear.

9. On the problem of security policy (*Sicherheitspolitik*) with special reference to "collective security" see the comprehensive and illuminating study of Heinrich Rogge, "Kollektivsicherheit Buendnispolitik Voelkerbund." *Theorie der nationalen und internationalen Sicherheit* (Berlin, 1937), which deserves attention despite the fact that it was written and published in Nazi Germany and bears a distinctly "revisionist" slant.

10. Raymond Dennett goes further in making the generalization that, "if economic pressures become great enough, almost any government, when put to the final test, will moderate or abandon a political association" (such as the alliance system of the United States with its usefulness to national security) "if only an alteration of policy seems to offer the possibility of maintaining or achieving living standards adequate enough to permit the regime to survive." "Danger Spots in the Pattern of American Security," in *World Politics*, Vol. IV, No. 4, July 1952, p. 449.

11. Not everyone agrees that this can be done. Jeremy Bentham wrote that "measures of mere defense are naturally taken for projects of aggression" with the result that "each makes haste to begin for fear of being forestalled." *Principles of International Law*, Essay IV.

12. The Quakers, in a book on *The United States*

and the Soviet Union: Some Quaker Proposals for Peace (New Haven, 1949), p. 14, state that "it is highly questionable whether security can be achieved in the modern world through and attempt to establish an overwhelming preponderance of military power." This can be read to mean that a less ambitious military target than overwhelming preponderance might be a means of achieving security.

13. As A. D. Lindsay puts it, "The search for perfect security . . . defeats its own ends. Playing for safety is the most dangerous way to live." Introduction to Thomas Hobbes, *Leviathan*, p. xxii.

14. On the moral problem in international relations see my article on "Statesmanship and Moral Choice" in *World Politics*, Vol. I, No. 2, January 1949, 176 *et seq.*, especially p. 185. In one of his most recent statements on the subject, Reinhold Niebuhr, *The Irony of American History* (New York, 1945), points specifically to the moral problem involved in security policy—"no imperiled nation," he writes, "is morally able to dispense with weapons which might insure its survival" (p. 39).

15. It is not without irony that of the two authors who have recently come out for a policy of the national interest, the one, George F. Kennan, who called for a policy of national self-restraint and humility, usually identified with morality, should deny "that state behavior is a fit subject for moral judgment" (*American Diplomacy, 1900–1950*, Chicago, 1952, p. 100), while the other, Hans Morgenthau (*op. cit,*), calling for a policy of unadulterated national egotism, claims to speak in the name of morality.

16. It would be unrealistic to assume that policy makers divide their attention strictly between ends and means and only after having chosen a specific target level as being morally justified decide whether the means by which it can be attained are morally acceptable. Moral judgment is more likely to be passed on the totality of a course of action which embraces both the desired end and the means which lead to it.

Morton A. Kaplan

The national interest and other interests

A DEBATE has raged concerning whether the national interest is objective. Those who regard the national interest as objective usually regard national interests as permanent, unchanging, and related to power. Those who regard the national interest as subjective usually affirm that it includes values other than power. They also cite disagreement between individuals and groups of individuals concerning the national interest as proof that it is subjective. Objectivists reply by making a distinction between interests and passions or between interests and opinions.

The interest of a system is to obtain the valuable. The interest of a nation is to satisfy national needs. Thus national interests are objective, and there are as many national interests as national needs.

Reprinted from Morton Kaplan, *System and Process in International Politics*, New York, John Wiley & Sons, Inc., 1957, 151–165.

However, what lies behind the distinction between "passion" and "interest" which historically has been commonplace in discussions of statecraft? Does a sharp distinction between analytic levels of action permit a more precise analysis of the problem of the national interest?

Passions and interests

NATIONAL interests have been identified as objective although related to the national level of action and to the structure of the system of action at the national level. However, this does not account for the historic distinction between "interest" and "passion." Does this distinction reflect simply a dispute concerning the national interest? Or is some more basic issue involved?

Many times policies have been opposed as based on passion or sentiment rather than on interest. Somehow this use of "passion" and "interest" implies that some objectives are more ephemeral or less real than other objectives. Although the distinction between "passion" and "interest" rarely is precisely explained, it appears to rest upon the belief that national actors are concrete physical entities. Somehow this physical substratum appears to be the most important element in national life. Therefore national power is the supreme goal of national action. National power is both the means and the objective of statecraft. The more power a nation has, the more secure its life. Other objectives are regarded as ephemeral, or even as dangerous to the life of the nation.

This position has been argued as if it constituted an eternal law of nature rather than a prescription for action within a particular international system of action. The "interest" formulation constitutes both a description of what has occurred and a prescription for national policy.

The "interest" doctrine is a reasonably adequate description of the "balance of power" international system, although, at times, sentiment or "passion" did seem to outweigh "interest," for example, Palmerston's support for Greece and British neutrality in the American Civil War after Lincoln's Emancipation Proclamation.

As a prescription for action, the "interest" doctrine accords reasonably well with the essential rules of the "balance of power" international system, although it does not take proper account of the possible dangers arising from deviant national actors. As interest is understood in this volume, Palmerston may have been wise in running some risks to encourage non-directive national actors. Such action may have had long-term value for stabilizing the "balance of power" system by inhibiting deviancy.

The "interest" doctrine also neglects the consideration that external policy has the function of maintaining a given social structure within the national system as well as the function of preserving the security of the national system against potential enemies. If there really were a sharp segregation between domestic and foreign policy, conditions in the international system would be inconsequential for the internal life of the national system—provided only that the system were secure against enemies.

However, efforts to protect national systems externally affect the internal life of the national system. Things like the draft, industrial mobilization, and problems of security affect the national system. In an age when small professional armies waged war, when conscription affected only the poor and the rootless, these consequences may have been obscure.

The policy best adapted to maintaining external security may not be the best policy from the standpoint of maintaining internal values. Likewise, an external policy that would be best if supported internally may be poor if it arouses opposition within the nation or if it creates economic hardships which lead to apathy and indifference.

If the "interest" doctrine, based upon the concept of national power, is correct, it should be confirmed by the permanency of national policy regardless of changes in government within national actors. Proponents of the "interest" doctrine long have used the striking continuity of foreign policy and the abandonment by incoming governments of positions on foreign affairs taken while out of office as confirmation that the national interest rests on solid realities rather than on "ideas," "opinions," or "passions."

In part, the proof is an artifact. In non-directive systems governments usually rest upon center-based majorities. The majority is usually provided by the great "middle mass" of citizens. A radical break with past policy most often would condemn a party to the status of a permanent minority. Therefore, from a political point of view alone, great changes in foreign policy cannot often be expected simply because one party rather than another comes to office.

However, it must be admitted, some parties out of power, particularly socialist parties, have miscalculated the extent to which foreign policy can be independent of the instrumental means of implementation. At times, popular policies are espoused out of office only to be forsaken when office is attained.

National actors in a "balance of power" or bipolar system require for their defense and also for the effectiveness of policy allies, bases, access to raw materials, and so forth. These needs, although they may be implemented in different ways, cannot well be eliminated by changing office holders.

Moreover, a number of factors may reinforce the specific objectives or means of implementation chosen by preceding governments. In the first place, enunciated objectives tend to become imbedded in the information states of the decision makers who choose them and also in the information states of those decision makers who come to office later. In the second place, once an objective or means of implementation is pursued, the investment in that objective is lost if a change is made. Other actors have already pledged their cooperation. Claims have publicly been made. Reversals would cloud the entire issue and make policies appear arbitrary. Besides, time, money, and personnel have already been expended. Moreover, the organization is structured to scan for information which seems consonant with the given objective and to ignore information which appears to conflict. This is particularly true at non-political levels in the administration. Furthermore, these levels in the administration brief political appointees and play a large role in directing their attention toward given courses of action and away from other equally plausible courses of action.

Alliances and blocs in particular represent large investments of effort and resources. New administrations may intend to make changes, but it is difficult to make changes at a single point without touching off a ramified series of consequences. It is much easier to maintain existing agreements than to negotiate new sets of agreements.

The Republican administration in 1953— even had it wanted to—was in a poor position to renegotiate the role of national forces in NATO or to take a position quite different from the position of the Truman administration with respect to German rearmament. The Republican administration was free to suggest minor modifications, but it would have raised the wrath of its treaty partners had it claimed that it was not bound or committed by the government that was its predecessor. Indeed, such a position would have set a most undesirable precedent. Would even a more conservative Republican group have been willing to pay the cost of reassessment each time the French, Italian, or Belgian cabinet changed?

Generally, only when internal changes within a national system lead to radical changes in the political system of that nation may a change of alignment become a matter of necessity rather than convenience. Obviously, if Italy were to acquire a Communist government, both the United States and Italy would desire to examine the role of Italy in NATO.

Logistic considerations also predispose nations to some objectives rather than others which— apart from logistic considerations—may be equally desirable. Thus air fields in Patagonia may serve as well to service bombing missions as those in Libya except that they are farther from potential targets. Raw materials may be as cheap to acquire in one place as another, except that the transportation route may be safer, and so on.

For these reasons, and perhaps for some others also, it is rare that the foreign policy objectives of a national system change radically. If the Communists, for instance, were to take over Italy, the foreign objectives of Italy would change radically. But most governmental changes are not that sweeping. Particularly in non-directive national systems, the changes rest upon a framework of national consensus.

The replacement of a Labour government in Great Britain by a Conservative government may change national values somewhat. But the place to look for the consequences of the change is not in a vast and sweeping replacement of previous national policies. Rather changes in the priorities accorded alternative objectives or the speed or willingness with which given policies are carried out may characterize the change in governmental policy. The Labour government probably gave India and Burma their freedom faster than a Conservative government would have. But a Conservative government almost surely would have granted independence eventually.

Nevertheless, these differences in priority are not lacking in importance. Indeed, India might not have remained within the Commonwealth had not the grant been made when it was. France finally accorded independence to Viet Nam. But it might have been much better for France if Mendes-France had come to office a year earlier.

Distinctions between the interests of different system levels

THE distinction between the interests of different system levels rests upon the consideration that systems of action are analytic rather than concrete entities. This does not signify that they are unreal but only that classes of actions with relatively permanent characteristics are segregated and treated as independent systems. Indeed, a system may be dominant over the actors within it.

National systems of action, like other systems, are organized to satisfy system needs. Their essential rules represent their adjustment to their environments in terms of the relations of the actors within the system rather than in terms of specific instrumental goal objects.

For instance, curbs were placed on the movement of labor and capital in wartime England. When, however, the external environment became favorable, that is, when the war was won, it became possible to implement the values and thus to satisfy the needs of the national system better by removing some of the wartime curbs.

A national system cannot continue to regulate itself well unless it can satisfy at least some of the needs of at least some of its subsystems. Therefore, the national interest will include the satisfaction of at least some of these subsystem needs. However, even when the national system is not regulating pathologically, there may be conflicts between the interests of the national actor and interests of subsystems of the national actor system.

For instance, it may be in the interest of the political system to send an espionage agent on a dangerous mission or to nationalize an industry. Except for some peculiar conditions, these decisions will not be in the interests of the espionage agent or the industry or the owners of the industry. Although the industry may resist nationalization in the name of the national interest—and although in some cases it may be correct in this claim—the claim, theoretically at least, can be determined independently.

Analytically, the interests of individuals, subnational systems, national systems, supranational systems, and the international system stand on an equal footing. There is no natural order of priority such that one system level ought to defer to another.

There may be occasions when various system interests coincide. Although taxes in general are burdensome, taxpayers may, in keeping with their interests and those of the national actor, vote additional tax monies for defense purposes. Military appropriations may be directly valuable to the national actor and indirectly valuable to citizens whose interests are defended by the national actor.

On other occasions, the national actor may make a decision contrary to the interests of some individual, but it may nevertheless be in the interest of the individual to comply with the decision. Nationalization of industry may be a case in point. The decision may be contrary to the interests of the stockholders but—once taken—the penalty for attempted noncompliance may be sufficiently great to contraindicate that course of action.

On still other occasions, the decisions of the national actor may be so contrary to the interests of individuals that resistance is indicated regardless of the chances of success. Jews being herded into Hitler's gas chambers had no good reason to comply with the decisions of the national government.

There may be still other occasions on which the interests of the government are so opposed to those of the body of citizens that the government will collapse and be replaced by another form of government. The French and Russian revolutions illustrate this point. Reform was no longer possible within the old institutions. The attempt to defend these institutions was doomed to failure. Yet there was no reason from the point of view of the governmental subsystem why the attempt should not have been made.

National systems may be so in conflict with the interests of individual citizens and groupings of citizens that they may be merged within supranational or international political entities. Efforts to forge a United States of Europe rest upon the claim that existing organizational entities are outmoded. Yet the interests of the national actors may lie in resisting such efforts though the interests of subsystems of the national system possibly may sanction attempts to alter or to destroy national institutions. Only if such an integrative merger is the only way left to preserve some of the values of the national system, will the interests of the national actor and of its subsystems prove parallel. Even here, however, there may be conflicts with respect to speed and degree of integration.

There is in nature no inherent priority for the national actor system over any subsystem of that system or over supranational or international systems. As far as individual citizens are concerned, the interests of the national actor within which they hold citizenship have no natural priority over the interests of other national actor systems.

Should the anti-Nazi German have aided loyally in the defense of the Hitlerite regime, or should he have cooperated with the enemies of the regime? It was, in fact, to the interest of the anti-Nazi to cooperate with the Western powers and to the interest of the Nazi regime to discourage and to punish such treasonable and subversive activities.

Should decision makers within a small democracy sacrifice that democracy to give larger and more powerful democracies time to prepare against a totalitarian national actor? Individuals, after all, have no biological ties to the nation. They need not be destroyed with it nor need their values perish with the values of the national actor. Indeed, the destruction of the national actor may facilitate the preservation of individual values. In the first place, citizens may be able to flee and thus to escape the fate of the national actor. In the second place, if the national actor is sacrificed, other democratic or non-directive actors may be given time to destroy the directive national actor.

If the sacrifice is made, the nation may later be reorganized, or it may be absorbed within a supranational non-directive system. If, however, an accommodation is reached with the directive national actor, the national system may survive in a form contrary to the interests of the individual citizens.

Obviously, it is difficult to generalize in the absence of a concrete case. Nevertheless, the distinction between the interests of different system levels is compelling. Interests are objective, but what the national actor ought to do may differ from or conflict with what an individual or subsystem of the national system ought to do.

Some disagreements concerning the national interest may only represent errors in judgment. However, some disagreements may represent clashes between different subsystems concerning their interests but may be phrased as if those interests were the national interest.

Moreover, some disagreements may represent attempts to change the national interest, that is, to change the form and structure of the national system, to change its essential rules and

its needs, and to change the relations of dominance within the system. In this sense, disagreement would concern not what the national interest *is* but what the national interest *ought to be* from the standpoint of or according to the interests of the subsystem making the claim.

Decision makers and the national interest

THE sharp distinction between the interests of different system levels raises a specter. What if decision makers make decisions which implement their interests rather than those of the national actor system?

To some extent, fear, that this may happen lies behind the democratic distrust of foreign policy officials. Within any system the agency dealing with a given sphere of activity will have some degree of subsystem dominance over that particular range of activity. Those who make the decisions scan for information which accords with their expectations. They are attentive to the problems which seem important within the communicative frameworks which structure their activities. They are responsive to their individual interests and to the interests of the subsystems to which they belong, whether by birth or by selection.

In general, no objection can be made to this state of affairs except in terms of different subsystem interests. Any substitution among the decision-making personnel would only change the values and subsystem interests to which attention was given. In terms of national essential rules, a different segment of the nation would become dominant over foreign policy.

There may, however, be cases in which foreign policy decision makers act contrary to the national interest because their subsystem interests conflict with the national interest. Decision makers, like other individuals, respond to their multiple roles. Their role in some other subsystem of the national system may conflict with and dominate their role in the foreign policy subsystem. There are a number of systems in which foreign-policy makers may hold roles which conflict with their foreign-policy-making role.

Political parties with international organizational ties may have interests opposed to the national interest, that is, opposed to the preservation of the nation as an entity with distinctive territorial bounds, or possibly, opposed to the preservation of the national political system except insofar as it adheres to essential rules consonant with the interests of the international party.

Religious, economic, and fraternal groups may have interests which are either consonant with those of some supranational system or independent of national interests insofar as their pursuit is not dependent upon the existence or nonexistence of the national actor system.

To some extent, however, differences concerning the national interest may reflect differences concerning the external environment or concerning the consequences of given actions. Quisling activities represented to some extent interests at variance with the national interest. However, probably some who joined these movements believed that only in this way could they accommodate to Nazi victory and conserve any of the values of the national system.

The situation of decision makers at lower ranks who believe that the national interest is being violated by those in superior positions either through ignorance or contrary interests, is poignant. Should such decision makers carry out policies they believe wrong or even disastrous? Or should they oppose such policies and brave the consequences?

The statement of this problem may stir the fear that anarchy will result if each decision maker, regardless of level in the administrative apparatus, implements the policies he thinks correct and fails to implement policies determined at higher national levels. If proper distinctions are made, such fears lack foundation. It would of course be anarchic if different policies were substituted at each hierarchic level in the administrative apparatus by decision makers who rejected the decisions of those above them in the hierarchy. However, common sense demonstrates that those lower in the hierarchy—regardless of their disagreements with those higher in the administrative hierarchy—are not likely to sabotage policy in this manner.

Many policies which *would* be better if adopted at higher administrative levels are worse if substituted at lower levels. Those lower in the administrative hierarchy—apart from lacking the information upon which the decision was based at the highest levels—are faced with different problems.

Lower ranking officials no longer have the problem of deciding high national policy; they have the problem of implementing that policy and of adjusting it to local conditions.

Their very freedom not to apply that policy if it fails to satisfy local conditions maintains the flexibility of the administrative apparatus.

If the interest of lower ranking officials is consonant with the national interest, administrative flexibility in the implementation of decisions will raise no difficult problems. If officials are incompetent, they may overlook their paucity of information or the consequences for the national interest if they substitute their private judgment for that of their superiors.

But this becomes a matter of choosing competent officials. It would be equally bad to have officials who blindly applied policies regardless of local conditions or who were unable to make local adjustment without referring everything back to their superiors. During the war, for instance, one official without proper authority ordered a captain of a ship in port to unload a cargo of rotten potatoes which was causing the boat to sink. This was in violation of a directive to carry the potatoes to England. But common sense prevailed over red tape.

Suppose a higher ranking official is pathological. Suppose an American officer in charge of occupying a Japanese village had ordered his troops to burn it to the ground although the natives were cooperating with the occupying authorities. It is at least plausible that the national interest would be better served if the troops arrested their officer, ignored the order, and appealed to still higher authority to intercede. It is possible that the order might have been based upon secret information and that the troops therefore might have acted unwisely. But no rules for action are likely to apply to every possible contingency.

On the other hand, the interests of a decision maker may conflict with the interests of the nation. Although the previous examples illustrate cases in which national needs are best satisfied if orders from above are disobeyed, there may be cases when, rather than exercising discretion in implementing policy, a decision maker may be acting contrary to the national interest. Consider a German officer who refused to carry out Hitler's order to devastate a French village and to kill its inhabitants. Refusal to use terror might possibly injure the German war effort. Yet some officers might prefer to injure the war effort—or even to lose the war—rather than to engage in inhumane activity.

National actors have an interest in preventing decision makers from acting contrary to the national interest and in punishing those who do. National actors even have an interest in exaggerating the bad consequences of such actions or of convincing decision makers that such actions are morally wrong. But there is no good reason—except *perhaps* fear of personal consequences—why an administrator who views national values with abhorrence should not sabotage the implementation of those values. Indeed, the myth that administrators have no responsibility except to carry out legally prescribed national policy has been responsible for some of the most sordid violations of individual values in the history of mankind.

From the point of view of the political system, human beings are instrumental for maintaining the existence and interests of the political system. However, from the point of view of individual human beings, the political system has value only as an instrument for implementing human values. There is no reason in logic or theory why individual needs should be subordinated by human agents to the good of the political system.

The good and the just

THE national interest, since it satisfies system needs, is the good for a national actor, just as values or objectives which satisfy individual needs constitute the good for the individual. However, is there also a community of interest in the international system so that a concept of the just also may have relevance?

Analogies between human individuals and national actors are bound to founder with respect to some very important conditions. A nation rarely is dependent for its survival upon paternalistic national actors. There is no immediate and direct dependency between national actors likely to create bonds of solidarity nor is there any inherited biological characteristic which facilitates high affective valuation of the needs of other national actors.

The essential national actor is able to satisfy most of its system needs within its own national boundaries. It has no biological or psychological needs for intercourse with other national actors. There is no reason to believe that an isolated nation will become pathological as will an individual isolated from social and physical stimulation. The nation is able to develop a satisfactory image of the self through the interaction of individuals and groups within the nation. In fact, the national image is an image in the minds of men which expresses itself in national patterns of behavior.

National actors have no inherent constitutional need to communicate with other national actors. They may have a derived need to communicate with other national actors because their actions will affect these actors. If there is no communication, the consequences of actions for other national actors and the probable responses of these national actors to the actions will be misjudged. Thus lack of communication will lead to pathological international-actor behavior. However, it is possible, initially at least, to view these communicative needs from an instrumental standpoint.

Therefore, at least with respect to "balance of power" and bipolar international systems, relations between national actors are primarily instrumental. Yet to some extent this description is inadequate even with respect to the "balance of power" and bipolar international systems. American relations with Great Britain sometimes rise above the purely instrumental. At times aid is given or risks are run when other alternatives would be chosen if *only* instrumental considerations were involved.

Perhaps some of the hesitancy Asiatic nations have concerning the United States arises from the belief that aid has purely instrumental objectives, that they cannot count on American support unless that support is also instrumental to immediate American objectives.

The difficulty with instrumental aid is that it lacks dependability. It ceases as soon as the occasion which called it forth passes. Particularly within universal organizations, national policies cannot be expressed in purely instrumental terms and gain sufficient support to be adopted.

If such support becomes so important from an instrumental point of view that an instrumental attitude can no longer be taken toward it with safety, a solidary international community may arise. The channels of communication may block out information concerning the instrumental character of cooperative action. In other words, the necessity for cooperation may lead to a repression of information concerning the instrumental character of cooperation. But this fact itself may cause cooperative action to become intrinsically valuable at the level of individual actions.

Such considerations lie behind the formation of bloc actors. Blocs are so important to the member actors that maintaining them is more important than possible non-optimal consequences with respect to specific individual actions. For example, France may not like

German rearmament, but that is a price France will pay to remain within NATO.

The level of instrumentality is the all-important consideration. It is important instrumentally to maintain the bloc or association. However, individual actions within the bloc or association are no longer considered on a purely instrumental level, although instrumental considerations may play a role with respect to some aspects of individual decisions.

The hypotheses concerning integration receive a more adequate explanation when these considerations are taken into account. To some extent, the cooperative structure, for instance, the supranational bloc actor, operates to channel information conforming with its purposes and to exclude information inconsistent with those purposes or objectives.

Moreover, discussion within the bloc stresses non-instrumental considerations, although instrumental considerations are not ignored at the level of implementation or adoption by the member actors.

Exclusive concern with instrumental considerations would undermine cooperative behavior. Therefore decision makers who participate in block activity will tend even to repress knowledge of the instrumental reasons for their cooperation. Block objectives will be considered as autonomous and as intrinsically important.

If national system needs increase the incidence of cooperative activity among national actors, cooperative objectives will gain an autonomous status. They will become intrinsic goals or values of national systems. In this event, the good will be supplemented by the just, that is, by the concept that other national states also have a right to satisfy certain system needs.

In this case, national action will represent some weighting of the good and of the just, that is, of the needs of a particular nation, given its specific environment, and of the needs of a supranational or international community.

If the essential rules characterizing any system of action are regarded as important by the actors in that system, these national actors will weigh possible gains from individual actions or decisions against the consequences of the action or decision for the set of essential rules. This is the insight behind the complaint that ends do not justify the means. In any precise sense, ends must always justify the means.[1] However, some actions, although gaining desirable immediate objectives, also undermine more important modes of inter-actor behavior, as expressed in the essential rules of the system.

For instance, one may lie to his wife in order to have some fun, but, if this lie is discovered, the marriage relationship may be injured. There is, therefore, a clear distinction between relationships between actors, that is, the essential rules of the system, and specific goal-oriented actions.

The essential rules of the "balance of power" and bipolar international systems are of less importance to national actors than the essential rules of national systems and therefore will be subordinated to them in case of conflict. Nevertheless, there are limited areas, even in the "balance of power" and bipolar systems, in which the relations among some sets of actors acquire sufficient importance to subordinate gains in specific situations to maintaining the relationship among the actors. This is particularly the case in block arrangements in the loose and tight bipolar systems.

In the universal and hierarchical international systems, the essential rules of the international system will acquire even more importance than the essential rules of the bloc actors in the bipolar international systems.

Finally, cooperative or integrated action may be implemented by institutions or social structures in which large investments have been made. Failure to use these institutions may involve costs which are so large that they cannot be considered. In this case, the cost of maintaining the structure becomes a necessary cost for satisfying the needs of the actors within the system.

Yet, if the system is to be maintained, the cooperation of all actors within the system is necessary. Therefore, within the system the needs of the various actors must be recognized and appeals must be made to them as members of a common system in which the needs of all members are recognized as having intrinsic importance.

The national interest

THE national interest is the interest which a national actor has in implementing the needs of the national system of action. Some of these needs arise inside the national system, and others stem from factors in the environment.

Internal system needs include economic needs for raw materials and other material capabilities. But internal needs also include the need to maintain the essential rules of the system or to satisfy the wants which subsystems have or which the personality systems of human actors demand. To illustrate, a nation may be able to increase its material capabilities by mobilizing its economy and drafting its manhood, by eliminating political dissent and removing legal rights of citizens. Thus mobilized, it may be able to conquer other nations and to protect itself against any combination of external foes. Such action, however, may do violence to its most intense domestic needs. The nation may prefer strongly to endure some external risks rather than to repress its internal needs. Such preferences are in harmony with its national interest.

Environmental needs include defense needs. Such needs depend upon the structure of the international community and upon the presence or absence of dangerous foes. These needs do not vary directly with changes in internal structure. From this fact emerges the opinion that the national interest is unchanging and permanent. However, though these needs do not change directly with internal structure, the weights attributed to them in determining the national interest may change with changes in the needs of domestic institutions.

Internal national changes may make the nation either more or less susceptible to attack. For instance, the economic policy of a new government may work so well that allies or foreign sources of material supplies become less important to its defense. But also, the installation of a government dedicated to non-directive or democratic values may increase the cost of military ventures. Such ventures may weaken democratic institutions. Therefore, as the cost of external aggressive action is raised, it becomes less desirable even though it still satisfies some external needs.

Finally, external needs include cooperative needs, for few, if any, national actors are so well situated that they are safe without allies or bloc partners. Thus the national interest, in some circumstances, may place great importance upon maintaining the essential rules of the cooperative relationship. In this event, the national interest may subordinate gains from individual actions to the desirability of maintaining the alliance or bloc.

The national interest is objective but not independent of the circumstances and of the specific characteristics of the individual national actor. The self-centered interests of the national actor in the "balance of power," bipolar, and unit veto international systems are in part the product of the social structure of those international systems.

However, even in those international systems different national actors have different national interests which function with their values and internal system needs as well as with their international needs. Some national actors place greater value upon supranational and international interests in the "balance of power" and bipolar systems than other actors.

Moreover, in the universal and especially in the hierarchical international system, the international interest becomes an autonomous and intrinsic value for the actors within the system. In the hierarchical system national actors, and consequently national interests, cease to function.

Note

1. The utility of an action is a weighted product of the utilities of the alternate consequences.

Part Two

National security and international conflict: a zero-sum game

Introductory note

The selections included in this part share the basic assumption that national security must be sought primarily through the maximization of national power within international conflict situations. The quest for security is therefore viewed basically as a zero-sum game in which each nation's objective is the improvement of its relative power position. These contributions essentially attempt to develop optimum criteria and methods for mobilizing the power resources of a nation in such conflict situations. Our subdivisions reflect the general tendency of writings in this area to emphasize either the military or the economic or the political ingredients of national security.

SECTION A views national security primarily from the military point of view, and deals with such problems as developing an optimum strategy for future total wars (Rowen), the best methods of deterring nuclear attacks (Brodie), and the place of limited (Osgood) and unconventional (Knorr) warfare in general strategy.

SECTION B emphasizes economic considerations and economic approaches to the problem of national security. Two world wars have clearly demonstrated that the industrial potential and economic resources of a nation are at the heart of its ability to wage war. Knorr's selection examines in detail the elements that make up a nation's economic potential for war, and the effects of the nuclear era, with its new technology, upon the concept of economic potential for war. Hitch and McKean discuss the all-important problem of creating objective criteria by which alternative programs of security can be selected. How to apply such criteria in a rational evaluation of strategic programs in the Department of Defense is discussed by Enthoven. Finally, Barnett analyzes the competing claims of the military and nonmilitary sectors of the economy upon a nation's scarce resources.

SECTION C is, in general, concerned with the demands made by national security upon political institutions. Huntington focuses on the clash between strategic needs

and political interests in the policy-making process. Price analyzes the role that
the administrative bureaucracy should play in the making and executing of national
security policy, and the present weaknesses of American organization. Schilling
discusses the most effective way a nation can use its scientists and their technological
expertise and the implications of the increasingly important role that scientists play
in the policy-making process. Riker discusses the problems of political alliances and
coalitions made acute by the increasing interdependence of the security of nations.
Basing his conclusions on a game-theoretical analysis, he describes the characteristics
of the present-day system of alliances and coalitions ("the age of equalization")
which is ending, and predicts the future development of the new system ("the age of
maneuver"), which has just begun. Almond deals with the difficulty of mobilizing
public opinion to support national security policy, which is, by its nature, delicate, secret,
and highly technical. Lasswell is concerned with the growing pervasiveness of all these
national security concerns, and, bringing his garrison-state hypothesis up to date,
he concludes that the domination of politics by "specialists on violence" will
characterize the future of our epoch.

a. The military problem

Henry S. Rowen

The future of general war

IT IS CONVENIENT to distinguish five different views toward general thermonuclear war:

1. World annihilation.
2. Mutual suicide.
3. Deterrence-plus-insurance.
4. Extended deterrence.
5. Massive retaliation.

The boundaries of these categories are not sharp, and it is possible to classify views on the problem of general war in other ways. Finally, one position has not been included, the preventive war view. There are few today who would argue that the United States should end the uneasy balance of terror by aggression.[1]

The world annihilation view

NOT everyone agrees that deterrence through the threat of nuclear retaliation is rational. Many distinguished people, both here and abroad, regard a general thermonuclear war as the ultimate catastrophe, the destruction of civilization, the endangering of the human race itself:

It is impossible to know with any precision what the outcome of a nuclear war would be. Some think that half the population of the world would survive, some think only a quarter, and some think none. It is not necessary, in considering policy, to decide among such possibilities. What is quite certain is that the world which would emerge

from a nuclear war would not be such as is desired by either Moscow or Washington. On the most favourable hypothesis, it would consist of destitute populations, maddened by hunger, debilitated by disease, deprived of the support of modern industry and means of transport, incapable of supporting educational institutions, and rapidly sinking to the level of ignorant savages. This, I repeat, is the most optimistic forecast which is in any degree plausible.[2]

There is a real possibility that a great nuclear war would change the nature of the pool of human germ plasm in such a way that the human species, as we know it, would not survive.[3]

It follows from these beliefs that thermonuclear war cannot conceivably be a deliberate instrument of national policy, that this type of war must be abolished. And if the world has not quite reached this situation, others argue that it will soon, and we should now behave as though war were no longer a rational alternative to peace.[4]

Although this view is partly based on the image of a general nuclear war in which the bomb stockpiles of the nations would be hurled indiscriminately at major cities of the world in an orgy of destruction, the grim prophecies quoted are based mostly on the genetic and somatic effects of nuclear radiation from fallout.

The amount of worldwide radiation produced by a thermonuclear war could be sizable in

Reprinted from Henry Rowen, *National Security and the American Economy in the 1960's*, 86th Congress, 2nd Session, Joint Economic Committee, Study Paper No. 18, January 30, 1960, pp. 26–45.

comparison to normal background levels, and any amount of radiation is believed to be harmful genetically. The magnitude of these worldwide effects depends on the total yield of bombs detonated, the proportion of the yield produced by nuclear fission, and the height of burst of the bombs. With ground bursts, about 20 per cent of the radioactive material is spread beyond the local fallout area. If we leave aside for the moment the situation in the countries directly attacked and their immediate downwind neighbors that might receive local fallout, the average worldwide radiation received over a generation from a general war that might be fought in the next 5 years or even much later is likely to be about 1 roentgen, with rather more than this in the Northern and less in the Southern Hemisphere.[5] This result, which assumes ground bursts, is based on a war in which 5,000 megatons are detonated worldwide, with 2,500 megatons coming from fission. This, in thermonuclear terms, is neither an exceptionally small nor exceptionally large war. A war of this scale would probably increase the proportion of seriously abnormal births in the first generation after the war by about one-tenth of 1 per cent; that is, an increase from the present level of about 4 per cent to about 4.004 per cent, with somewhat smaller increases tapering off over many later generations. In addition to this relatively immediate genetic effect (produced mostly by the fission product cesium 137), there might be a comparable increase in the absolute number of defective births from carbon 14 spread out over thousands of years (carbon 14 has a half life of 5,600 years).

In addition to worldwide genetic problems, there are somatic ones to take into account; for instance, the life-shortening effect of whole-body radiation. On the basis of present knowledge it appears that such a war might shorten life by something like 10 days or less on the average for the population outside of the countries attacked, though the lives of many people would suffer a much greater shortening than this. (Both the genetic and life-shortening effects of this war would be substantially less than those now produced by natural background radiation.) There are other effects: the average concentration of strontium 90 produced by a war of the size mentioned might come to about one-fourth the level now regarded as tolerable for large populations.

This is a high price to pay for any war. To be sure, these percentage increases for any single genration, including the generation alive at the time of the war, seem small if compared to the usual hazards of life. But these small percentages, multiplied by the large world population, yield over the years an impressive number of people likely to be seriously affected by such a war. For example, a war of this scale might produce one-quarter of a million additional abnormalities in the first postwar generation.

But how can these fallout effects be reasonably regarded as annihilation? The first post-war generation would number over 3 billion births. The great majority of the people in the world would not even notice this aspect of the conflict. This does not mean that there is no problem. On the contrary, governments have an urgent obligation to take this external damage into account in their plans for the weapons systems they buy and in their plans for the conduct of a war just as they have the obligation to weigh the prospective damage to the population of their own countries, their allies, and their enemies.[6] Furthermore, these casualty estimates are not certain. There is always a possibility that some new and more serious worldwide effects of a large nuclear war will be discovered.

It is important to consider very much larger wars than the one illustrated for they may become possible.[7] A war with, say 20 times the fission yield and with all air bursts (increasing worldwide fallout while reducing local) would have worldwide effects about 100 times as great as in the war described. This amount of radiation, about 30 times that from natural sources, is an enormous dose, with really grave, if not annihilating, consequences for mankind. But this does not mean that such an immense war is likely within the next decade. *There is little support for the view that the nuclear powers are now planning to procure weapon delivery systems that will inevitably lead to greater and greater worldwide fallout damage.* On the contrary, delivery systems now in development in the United States should lead to a substantial reduction in the worldwide fallout threat. The trend toward small air, ground, and sea mobile systems means that we will be procuring mostly smaller, not larger, warheads in the future. It may well be that the total yield that U.S. forces could deliver with an undamaged strategic force will be very substantially smaller by the mid-1960's than that deliverable at the present time.

On the other hand, we cannot be confident

that much more devastating weapons will not be developed within the decade. Man's ingenuity in thinking up still more powerful weapons is impressive. The implications of further advances in bomb technology in the direction of weapons that produce the widespread annihilating effects feared and, even without further technological advances, the diffusion of the existing types of nuclear weapons through the world argues for an urgent and systematic search for international measures of control. However, examination of the known effects of a war and current military trends does not support the argument that a general nuclear war in the 1960's would be the ultimate catastrophe. Terrible as the worldwide consequences of a nuclear war would be, it is unwise to assume that governments would be deterred from starting a nuclear war primarily because of these worldwide effects.[8] As we shall see below, their calculations may be dominated by even more pressing considerations—including the threat of much greater damage than the worldwide damage discussed in this section. What about the direct consequences of a war for the participants? Are they of a magnitude to rule out war?

The mutual suicide view

THE prevailing opinion is that general nuclear war, if it does not destroy the world, will certainly destroy the participants. The list of those who have held this view is a long and distinguished one.[9] Some believe that for this reason general nuclear war has been effectively abolished, while others believe that deliberate war has been eliminated and worry only about the chance of an unintended or "accidental" war. They all hold that rational governments would never deliberately choose nuclear war, that it will not be especially difficult to deter a general war. They also do not distinguish levels of damage—damage would be total.

Just what is meant by "suicide" deserves careful attention. There is little question that some extreme level of damage would warrant our use of the word. Retaliation that would inflict 150 million or more fatalities to either the Soviet Union or the United States would certainly qualify. Would 50 million, or 20 million, or 1 million? These would be disasters so far beyond our experience that they might at first glance seem equivalent to total destruction. But most people on reflection would agree that they are not. In the mid-1960's,

50 million fatalities in the United States would mean 150 million survivors. And probably a substantial economic base would survive as well. In addition to grave economic loss, the Soviet Union suffered well over 20 million fatalities during World War II. Judging by the recovery of the Soviet Union since World War II, one cannot say that level of damage was fatal. This does not mean that this experience was one that the Russians would care to repeat. Far from it. It does mean, however, that we must be careful to distinguish between those levels of damage that are a disaster and those that are lethal to a country. This distinction has important implications for our defense policies.

What intensities of attack would produce these different levels of damage? An attack delivering roughly 4,000 megatons could inflict damage in the lethal range if not moderated by civil defense. (The delivery of this weight of attack might require the launching of a much greater weight and, for the side striking second, the possession of even greater forces.) It would probably kill about 120 million people from blast and fallout if they failed to take much advantage of the shielding provided by existing buildings, and at the present public level of understanding of how to behave if we are attacked, this seems to be a reasonable assumption. A very much smaller attack than this could do great, if not necessarily lethal, damage; 50 high-yield bombs totaling about 500 megatons delivered on our largest cities might cause about 30 million fatalities if the populations had not evacuated or sheltered.[10] A larger attack could kill practically our entire population.

The vulnerability of the Soviet Union population to a large attack is roughly comparable to that of the United States. Assuming again that there is no civil defense—a much more dubious assumption with regard to Russia —the damage from, say, a 4,000-megaton attack would be comparable to that in the United States. However, damage from a 50-city attack would be substantially less, for Russian industry and urban population is less concentrated than ours.

What level of attack might be expected? It is essential to distinguish between the situation of the aggressor and that of the defender. The aggressor has the advantage of attacking with an undamaged force and possibly by surprise. If his attack were to destroy a large proportion of the defender's force and possibly disrupt the remainder, and if his active defenses were to exact further attrition of the surviving force, then the actual weight of attack delivered by the defender might be small. And much of it might be delivered against the wrong targets. The weight of attack against civil targets might be significantly less than the smaller of the attacks illustrated. Finally, the effect of the defender's delivered attack would depend very much on the aggressor's use of civil defenses. The aggressor can use civil defense to especially good advantage for, in addition to planning on receiving a deduced weight of attack, his population may be able to evacuate cities and seek fallout shelter well before most of the defender's retaliatory attack arrives. It is somewhat disquieting in this connection to observe that the Soviet Union has been carrying out an extensive civil defense training program in which all adults are supposed to have received over 20 hours of instruction.

The risk to the defender's civil society is much greater. It is threatened initially by the aggressor's undamaged strategic force. The aggressor could inflict lethal damage especially if the defender had little civil defense. However, this does not mean that he would necessarily want to do so or that his attack would be unconstrained. If he wished to take his enemy by surprise and if he wished to retain forces in being, his initial strike might have to be quite limited in size. And it would have to be sent largely against the defender's military forces if damage were to be reduced to his own cities and remaining military forces. The weight of attack sent directly at the defender's population centers might be only a small part of the total, and the aggressor might choose not to attack population directly at all. Where military forces and populations are close together, a purely military attack against an unprepared population would almost certainly do great civilian damage.[11]

Even for the defender, population damage could be drastically reduced over a wide range of attacks by civil defense. Relatively cheap measures (well under a billion dollars a year) could make a big difference. The difference between having an unprepared population and one trained to use available structures as fallout shelter, equipped with radiation meters, provided with emergency food supplies, and trained in decontamination techniques, could reduce fatalities by perhaps 50 million. With special fallout shelters it might be possible to reduce fatalities from a large attack by perhaps

a comparable amount in addition. Beyond this, we might build blast shelters, arrange for the evacuation of the population of cities to rural shelter areas in a crisis, plan on the use of nonurban industry and adopt other measures to promote postwar recovery. A large-scale program of civil defense might be as large as $5 to $10 billion or more a year, a tremendous amount compared with present civil defense expenditures but not, it should be noted, compared to our defense budget nor even to the amount we are now spending on our general war objectives.

Even allowing for civil defense preparations, the long-term radiation effects discussed above would be greatly intensified in any heavily attacked country if ground bursts were used. The survivors of the war might average a long-term radiation dose of 200 or 300 roentgens, and many would receive much more. This is 50 to 100 times as much as they would get from natural sources. It would increase the proportion of seriously defective children born from about 4 per cent to about 5 per cent of the total, and the resulting concentration of strontium 90 in bones would produce a large increase in the incidence of leukemia and cancer. The lives of the survivors might be shortened by an average of 5 to 10 years. And there would be other serious medical and environmental problems as well.

In spite of such unprecedented problems, this does not mean that economic recovery is impossible even following a heavy attack. If a large population were to survive through protective measures, with the economic resources surviving outside of major cities, and with careful pre-attack planning to help us get through the initial period of disruption, recovery would seem to be possible. About one-third of the population of the United States and about half of the manufacturing capital of the United States is located in our 50 largest metropolitan areas. This is much of the United States, and most people think of the survival of the United States in terms of what might happen to these metropolitan areas. Conversely, two-thirds of the population and about half of the manufacturing industry of the country lie outside of these areas. (The comparable figures for the Soviet Union are about four-fifths of the population and six-tenths of manufacturing industry outside of the 50 largest cities.) Half of our population and one-third of manufacturing are outside of the 150 largest urban areas. According to one informed optimistic estimate it might even be possible to restore something like the prewar consumption standard for the survivors in 10 years or so after an attack which had destroyed our 50 largest metropolitan areas.[13]

In sum: (1) An attack delivered on the 50 largest cities of the United States, in the absence of civil defenses, and if the population of these cities were to be found there at the time of the attack, would kill perhaps 30 to 40 million people. (2) This damage, while indeed catastrophic, would not be lethal—the Nation could in time recover, especially if plans for getting through the initial period of disruption had been made. (3) If the population of these cities were to be evacuated and sheltered they would be much less vulnerable, but an attack on the cities would still do great material damage. (4) A larger attack of, say, several thousand megatons, could kill over half of an unprotected population mostly from radioactive fallout (damage almost as great would result from a purely military attack against airbases). (5) This scale of attack need not be lethal if modest civil defense preparations (fallout protection and recovery) have been made; though larger attacks are possible so are larger civil defense programs. (6) The vulnerability of the Soviet Union to a given weight of attack delivered on target is somewhat lower than that of the United States but roughly of the same order of magnitude. However, the combination of a civil defense program combined with the threat that the Soviet Union might strike first could give that country an advantage we would do well not to depreciate.

Suicide, in the literal sense, is not the automatic consequence of a nuclear war. What does all this tell us about the problem of deterring general war? Presumably the assurance of damage substantially less than lethal would deter a nation from choosing war rather than peace. The amount of damage that might be risked in order to achieve certain gains or avoid losses is highly uncertain. Against a rational opponent the amount of damage one need threaten depends on the alternatives open to him. The risk of losing even a few cities, even if their inhabitants had been evacuated, might serve to deter general war in all crisis situations arising in the next decade. If competitive coexistence continues to offer a hopeful prospect for the Soviet Union, the threat of relatively little damage should deter its first strike. However, if its prospects turn out at some point to be grim, the threatened damage

necessary may be quite high. Since we cannot be very sure of the Soviet assessment of the alternatives, we want to be capable of threatening heavy damage, say, large in comparison to that suffered in World War II, for however traumatic that war was for the Russian people, the Communist state survived and has gone on to new heights of power and influence. (A major difference between World War II and World War III would be in the length of time during which the damage accumulated. Damage to Russia in World War II occurred over a 4-year span. A future general nuclear war is more likely to see damage occurring over that many days or weeks. The shock and disruptive effect, and the deterrent effect of comparable absolute levels of damage is often believed to be greater in the time-compressed situation.) Finally, the threat of quite heavy damage might not be enough to deter a dictator as irrational as Hitler, if one were to come into power and have access to nuclear weapons. In any case, the options both sides face will be more complicated than the simple choice between war and peace. Most importantly, it includes the threat of being hit first. However awful the consequences of starting a general nuclear war, the consequences of being hit first are even worse.

One view on this question can be summarily disposed of. It is that a nation would be deterred from an attack by the consequences of its own fallout coming back to its own territory, the "lashback" effect. If it is believed likely to deter the Soviet Union from an attack on so distant a country as the United States, the relevant fallout effects are those common to midlatitudes in the Northern Hemisphere. But these effects are certain to be swamped by the direct effect of even a small nuclear retaliation against the initiating country. If advocates of the "lashback" view of deterrence hold that there will be no retaliation and that the only damage the aggressor would receive is fallout from his own bombs, then they have an exceptionally gloomy view of the strike-second ability of strategic forces and an optimistic view of the deterrent effect of low levels of radiation. As for "lashback" from an attack on closer neighbors, for example, a Russian attack on Western Europe, local fallout could be reduced by airbursts, and in any case most of the local fallout produced would land short of the Soviet Union.

The mutual-suicide view implies a policy position on general war which can be described as deterrence only, for if all possible war outcomes are indistinguishably the ultimate catastrophe, there can be no other objective than deterrence. The possibility of limiting damage is denied.

There is much about American attitudes toward general war and even about our defense posture that suggests, in spite of our expenditures, for example, on air defense, that the deterrence only doctrine is the prevailing one in this country. This hypothesis finds support to choose two examples, in the absence of a serious civil defense program and in the practically universal tendency in public discussion of defense, in scholarly writings on military affairs, and in testimony before the Congress, to avoid reference to the possible conduct of a general war and to its outcome.

Britain, whose position is more exposed than ours, has officially adopted the deterrence only position:

> It must be frankly recognized that there is at present no means of providing adequate protection for the people of this country against the consequences of an attack with nuclear weapons. . . .
> This makes it more than ever clear that the overriding consideration in all military planning must be to prevent war rather than to prepare for it.[14]

Consistent with this policy, Britain has abandoned air defense, except for the protection of its bomber bases, and has not adopted a civil defense program.

While everyone must agree that the prevention of all-out war is a task of the most urgent and crucial importance, the belief that "the overriding consideration . . . must be to prevent war rather than to prepare for it" has some important ramifications: First, as in Britain, it would seem that we could save money on damage-limiting forces such as air defense. Next, it suggests that we need not really "prepare" for war. It is enough to look threatening, to put up a convincing façade—but the façade must really be convincing. Third, to some it suggests that we should not only have a formidable strategic power but also that we should foreclose alternatives to all-out retaliation, i.e., that we should put ourselves in the position where our power to vacillate or to back out in a crisis would be limited. We might do this by being prepared effectively for only one kind of all-out war, or by expecting that the commitment of forces to battle would, after a certain point in a crisis, prove inexorable. Fourth, it suggests the adoption of terror

weapons, for example, the delivery of massive amounts of radioactive fallout in the hope—that might be unfounded—that they might combine cheapness with great effectiveness. To repeat, all this in the belief that these weapons would not have to be used.

Adherence to the deterrence only doctrine tells nothing in itself of the level of damage believed adequate to deter or the forces needed to assure that level. Opinion on these questions range from those who hold that the possession of a few bombs is enough (they neglect the problem of delivering them) to those who believe that the delivery of a lethal weight of attack is needed.

One variant of the deterrence only view is of particular interest.[15] It has come to be known as finite or minimum deterrence. There are two senses in which the concept of "minimum" deterrence is used. One refers to the almost universal view that we should not put more resources into deterring general war than seems to be needed, allowing for uncertainty and possible surprises. The other is a position on force composition and strategy. It holds that we should unilaterally reduce our general war capability: Reduce our active defenses, continue not spending money on civil defense, and limit our strategic offensive force to a level large enough to assure only the destruction of some number, possibly fairly small, of enemy cities.[15] We should not prepare to strike back at the enemy's offensive force (attack military targets), in part because that force would already have been launched by the time our counterattack could arrive; and in part because preparations for counterforce attack, along with preparations for active and civil defense, make war more likely. This is so because we would be more tempted to attack in a crisis and the Soviets would, as a result, be more tempted to strike us. Moreover, this more modest posture would help to save money that might be better spent on limited-war forces.

The minimum-deterrence theorists recognize two very important truths: First, that it is not necessary to promise total destruction of a country in order to deter it from aggressive acts. Beyond a certain level of threatened destruction there is little additional deterrent value to additional damage increments. Second, that the strategic balance is not a stable one—that it is important to try to stabilize it by our policy choices.

While these truths are important and should receive urgent consideration in our defense planning, there are some important limitations to this doctrine. It would be highly risky for us to assume that levels of damage from which recovery might be rapid would be enough. The damage levels proposed by some minimum-deterrence advocates are not large compared to historic levels of damage from which rapid recovery has occurred. Above all, it is important to recognize the great effect of an enemy initial thermonuclear assault and the difficulty of delivering a retaliatory blow. The damage a minimum-deterrence force might actually manage could turn out to be much less than expected in advance.

Next, would we really have no military targets to hit if we were to strike second? This is by no means certain. The enemy probably would not send all or necessarily a majority of his forces in an initial attack, for to do so would not only increase the chance of our getting warning, but it would mean using up all of his military force. He would surely want to reserve part of it for the conduct of the war, short as it might be, and to end the war. Both during the war and at the end he would have to consider his military position vis-à-vis the rest of the world. Moreover, his attack might be badly executed, and a badly executed attack would give us the opportunity not only to save more of our own force but also to damage more of his.

Third, our threat of initiating general war in the defense of vital areas has been and remains an important element in their defense, and its reduction or effective elimination would make their defense more difficult, possibly very much more so. This does not mean that we need continue to depend so much on this type of defense, but the implications of its abandonment must be understood.

Finally, there is the deepest objection to this position and to the entire mutual-suicide set of views. They are essentially based on the idea that both sides will inevitably direct a great weight of attack against civil targets in a general war, that if the United States is attacked, our cities will be destroyed, and we in turn will retaliate heavily against enemy cities. The minimum-deterrence advocates go further and insist that we should try to design our forces for use only against cities. But what would the execution of this threat accomplish? What U.S. national objective would be advanced? It might serve as a lesson to future aggressors or provide a horrible example to shock the world into total disarmament. But the chance of this hardly seems worth enough

to warrant the sacrificing of much of the United States and possibly all of it. The dilemma of a policy of large-scale retaliation against enemy cities is that what it makes sense to threaten is not necessarily the best policy actually to execute. Representative Holifield expressed this dilemma as follows:

> When 72 million people are killed, when 71 cities are wiped out, when that terrible havoc hits the Nation, I will ask you, what could we do to retaliate and what good would it be? . . . a policy of massive retaliation after attack is a completely fallacious doctrine.[17]

Just how inevitable is it that a general war would in fact be conducted in this manner? Almost certainly the primary purpose of the side that strikes first would be to destroy the military power of the other. Our strategic force is the target of highest priority at the outset of such a war. How much of the aggressor's force would be available for use against our cities would depend on the ability of our strategic force to "soak up" his attack. We plan on having a well-protected force and such a force, by definition, is able to withstand the entire weight of the enemy assault and survive. The aggressor might save little for use against cities. Might not both sides have an incentive to avoid cities? The aggressor might attempt to minimize the defender's civil damage in order to hold his cities as hostage and to force a quick end to the war. How about the side that strikes second? Suppose its cities are not attacked initially? If it carries out a policy of only city attack with its surviving forces, it may be condemning its own cities to destruction. Moreover, it is feasible to avoid most cities. Clean weapons can be used instead of dirty ones, airbursts against soft targets rather than ground bursts, relatively small-yield weapons rather than very large. If the surviving force were a minimum-deterrence force designed to be just large enough to assure unacceptable civil damage to the enemy, how credible would its deterrent strength look in this situation. If the war were to begin in a favorable way for the defender, if it managed to have a large part of its force available, a policy of hitting only civil targets would give up the prospect of a favorable military outcome. And the prospect of civil damage is not the only deterrent. The aggressor is not as likely to start a war if it appears he stands a good chance of losing it —as well as receiving some civil damage.

At best, general nuclear war seems to offer a terrible prospect—a prospect so awful that the common view that it is no longer a rational instrument of policy seems warranted. But even if the mutual suicide outcome were to be generally accepted, this acceptance would not necessarily rule out the continued use of the general war threat in support of diplomatic positions, for if there were to remain even a small probability of so large a catastrophe, this threat might have a major influence on foreign policy. Moreover, the mutual suicide view is usually based on particular beliefs about the actual conduct and outcome of a war which are crucial and which cannot be assumed a priori. It is necessary to consider the actual forces, circumstances of war outbreak, the information (and misinformation) likely to be available to political and military leaders, and the performance of weapons, including those that might be revealed for the first time on the day of the war. While sensible policies may reduce the likelihood of general war to a quite low value, it seems unlikely that its probability can be reduced to anything like zero. This is so because there may be some residual possibility of a deliberate attack, and; perhaps more importantly, because we must always continue to fear an irrational attack. These considerations argue for something more than minimum deterrence and for more than a policy of deterrence only.

The deterrence-plus-insurance view

THIS view is that a good deterrent posture against all-out war is difficult to attain, that it is possible to distinguish among different possible outcomes of a general war and, in particular, that it is not inevitable that a general nuclear war would lethally damage any of the participants. It holds also that the actual outcome would depend very much on the preparations of the contenders, circumstances of the outbreak of war, their war objectives, and the actual conduct of the war; that deterrence should not be measured only by the threatened civil damage to the enemy, but also by the prospective military outcome. On the other hand, it should be distinguished from the following views described in this section: It does not place primary reliance for the defense of any very large part of the world on the threat of general war. Rather it advocates the building up of more limited capabilities for that objective.

It recognizes that a war might begin other than with a well-designed surprise attack, but hastily, or in a badly executed way, or after a period of warning, or by a gradual escalation from a limited war. And although a general nuclear war would be extremely short, it would undoubtedly consist of more than the exchange of intercontinental missiles in one or a few salvos. Finally, it recognizes that while a sensibly designed program to deter war can very likely reduce its probability to a quite low value, it cannot reduce it to zero.

For all these reasons, it includes insurance as well as deterrence capabilities, insurance in the form of such damage-limiting measures as active and passive defense and forces designed to attack the enemy's military forces. And, especially, insurance in the form of the capability to fight a nuclear war in a controlled fashion. Carrying out this last objective presents a great opportunity and a risk. It presents the opportunity of an enormous reduction in our losses in the event of war. The risks stem from the possibility that in an attempt to fight a carefully controlled campaign we might waste much of our force on targets of little value. It also suggests another type of preparation—the ability to communicate with the enemy during the campaign.[18] Whether this could actually be done in a general nuclear war is quite uncertain.

It might seem that this view is excessively concerned over the problem of retaliation given the fact that so few delivered bombs would do such great damage and given the uncertainties and risk in the execution of a successful first strike. If the choice were the simple one of war or peace, eliminating war might not seem to be exceptionally difficult. As long as the issue is one of comparing what happens to a country's interests if it does not defend them by attacking, with what happens if it does, then the elements in the comparison are the stake in third areas (for geographic reasons our interests likely to be threatened are abroad) versus the risk of population, industrial, and military losses associated with general war. The same choice would be faced by the other side. Even if both sides were to have strong strategic forces, would this comparison always lead rationally to the election of the nonwar alternative? Not necessarily. This choice would depend on the value attached to the stakes at issue versus the expected war outcome. Communist leaders would do well to proceed cautiously in any plan of aggression against Western Europe since this clearly is an area of the most vital interest to the United States, economically, militarily, and culturally.

And we should not assume that the Soviet Union would always prefer to accept any defeat rather than attack the United States.[19] Nevertheless, each side might aim at assuring its opponent of a level of civil damage in retaliation great enough to exceed in disutility the most serious external setback foreseeable—by threatening, say 20 cities or 50 cities; 5 million or 20 million fatalities. There would seem to be few external interests of the nuclear powers worth this much damage. Actually, achieving high levels of damage in retaliation is far from certain, however, although there are many options open to both sides for helping to assure it.

The problem is not this simple however. There is a third possibility, beyond striking first or accepting the loss to one's interests: Being hit first by the enemy and receiving an attack lethal to the Nation. If faced with the Hobson's choice of striking first or striking second, in a crisis the decision might be made to attack.[20] If there is a significant advantage to striking first and if I think that he might strike me, and if he thinks that I think that he might attack, then I had better attack.... In short, a general war might occur without either party to it preferring war to peace, but through the explosive interaction of expectations. This phenomenon lies behind most of the fear of the war that occurs through "miscalculation," and is a part of the motivation of the advocates of minimum deterrence for our trying to reduce our ability to strike first, and also reducing our ability to limit damage in general. That there is a substantial advantage in striking first with surprise in a nuclear war can hardly be doubted. But will this condition continue? Is it simply a matter of a few years until it vanishes as the result of the introduction of more advanced missiles, of sheltered and of sea and airmobile systems? The expected elimination of the first strike advantage is often expressed in terms of the number of missiles it will take striking first to destroy a single enemy missile. It views a war exclusively as a long-range duel between the ballistic missiles of the two sides, and moreover, a duel in which missiles shoot only at missiles and not at the opposing systems of control and communications of the two sides. While some long-range missiles would undoubtedly be launched at some other missiles in a war, the interplay of forces would undoubtedly be much more complex than this. Strategic capabilites in the 1960's are not likely to be measured very

satisfactorily by simply matching missiles salvos against each other.

We must be wary of predicting the course of technology and the actual weapons choice that might be made by both sides. There are some exceptionally difficult problems in assuring a retaliatory capability. Some tasks will very probably get easier, for example, the preservation of several types of mobile vehicle systems such as the Polaris submarine and its missiles, continually airborne missiles, or constantly moving train-borne missiles. However, other tasks may get more difficult, in particular that of preserving a protected, reliable system of control and communications. We simply cannot say what, on balance, will be the outcome.

The instability caused by the advantage of the first strike is one of the principal reasons why the minimum-deterrence advocates would have us reduce our damage-limiting capabilities, both offensive and defensive, unilaterally if necessary, since our reducing this capability will lessen the enemy's fear of our attack and therefore lessen his motivation to attack us. On this argument, we want to reduce our countermilitary attack capability while preserving a countercivil attack capability. This view assumes that we can distinguish neatly between countermilitary and countercivil capabilities. There is no doubt that we can do this to some degree, but it is not easy. Most of our offensive weapons are useful against both military forces and cities. A ballistic missile in a submarine, for example, is not only an efficient instrument for attacking cities, it is admirably designed to strike against many military targets; it is efficient in a sudden first strike and in a retaliatory second strike. In short, if we were, in accordance with the minimum-deterrence doctrine, to attempt in any simple fashion to reduce our ability to strike against military targets, we would reduce our ability to strike against civil targets, possibly to a dangerous degree. And some civil targets (e.g., a sheltered population) might be more difficult to hit than some military targets (e.g., unsheltered airbases). However, it is possible to partially compensate for this. Leaving our population entirely unprotected effectively weakens our ability to counter enemy military power, just as would a reduction in our active defense force or our offensive missile force. But the possibilities of compensation work both ways. Just as we can unilaterally reduce our first-strike, countermilitary capabilities, we can increase our strike-second, countercity capabilities by building up our protected retaliatory power. If some U.S. damage-limiting measure appeared to raise appreciably the chance that we might look as though we would be more likely to strike, the compensatory action of an increase in our retaliatory capability should dampen our opponent's incentive to strike us first.

However, the main reason we should not regard damage-limiting measures as seriously destabilizing is that they are not likely to be so successful that they will make very much difference to our behavior. Even with these measures, the prospect of many of our major metropolitan areas destroyed and millions of casualties is a catastrophe so large that our preference for nonwar should be evident to everyone, including the Russians.[22]

The deterrence-plus-insurance position has three main objectives: (1) It gives great emphasis to the importance and the difficulty of having a secure retaliatory capability and argues that doing this in the 1960's might take more of our resources rather than less. We have not only the problem of protecting our vehicles but also the task of protecting our command and control functions from surprise attack in the face of a growing missile threat and with the promise of still newer weapons coming along. And we must design our future systems so that decision makers will have the right kind of information at critical times. It does not measure deterrence solely in terms of civil damage threatened but holds that the ability to promise both possible military defeat and great civil damage is a better basis for deterrence. (2) It is concerned about the stability of the balance of terror, the danger of a crisis exploding into general war. It argues for weapons systems that do not have to react quickly to ambiguous signs of a possible attack, and for the operation of our forces under protected, or centralized control, with "fail safe" procedures. It recognizes that a situation of stability may come about unilaterally through the development of less vulnerable retaliatory weapons, or through international agreement aimed at this goal. However, it regards a very low level of forces as likely to be less stable than moderately high levels. (3) It favors insurance. It does so because it believes that while the probability of general war can be reduced, it cannot be reduced to zero. It distinguishes between 50 and 150 million possible American deaths. This view calls for insurance in the form of a combination of active and passive

defenses and a countermilitary offensive capabilities, and in the form of preparations to fight a general nuclear war in a controlled way that might give the Nation some chance of surviving. To actually fight a general nuclear war in a discriminating fashion would put a great burden on the planning, the equipment, and the emotions of both sides. It is by no means certain that a controlled war could, in fact, be fought.

The extended-deterrence view[23]

WE have not limited the threat of nuclear retaliation against the Soviet Union solely to an attack on the United States. Our preparations for the defense of Europe have consistently been based on attacking Russia even in the face of nonnuclear aggression. We have, in effect, drawn a line around a substantial part of the world outside of the United States and have said that attack across this line will result in nuclear retaliation just as it would if U.S. territory were to be violated. To be sure, this line has not always been a sharp one. We have not always said that nuclear retaliation would be certain, but that it is possible. We have often tried to face Soviet planners with the risk of general nuclear war if they engage in a certain class of peripheral and possibly nonnuclear aggression. Finally we have followed this policy during a period in which the vulnerability of the American people and economy has been growing steadily. Our overt policy has been poorly matched by real capabilities.

The extended-deterrence theory holds that the general war threat against some kinds of aggression short of an attack on the United States is an important bulwark of our defense, in fact, that it is essential; that some parts of the world, Europe especially, are so vital to the United States that we should risk general war in their defense, and that it may not be possible to defend Europe unless we use the threat of general war; that the growth of Russian nuclear capabilities is eroding our deterrence threat and we should work hard at strengthening it by adopting a comprehensive program of civil defense and by strengthening our active defenses and our ability to destroy enemy military targets; finally, that we have to draw the line somewhere, for if we do not, our entire position could be eroded away. Our threat to strike can be made more credible if we plan on using the warning provided by the crisis abroad to evacuate cities and to have our population seek blast and fallout shelters. With a major civil defense program and parallel active defense and offensive measures, fatalities to this country if we were to launch the first nuclear strike (in response to aggression abroad) might be held to several million people even in the face of a large nuclear retaliatory attack (although material damage would remain great). To these direct defenses should be added the indirect ones mentioned, such as the ability of a well-defended strategic force to attract enemy bombs away from our cities. And just as our inventives to carry out a program of pure city retaliation once deterrence has failed may be weak, so may the enemy's. He, like ourselves, may be most interested in limiting damage. Finally, we do not have to commit ourselves with certainty to carry out our threat of general war, we only make it likely enough to dissuade Communist action.[24]

The question of resolution in the face of threats is central to the concept of nuclear deterrence and especially to its extension to third areas. Both sides threaten to inflict great damage on the other, damage so severe that neither, if rational, would seem to prefer war to peace. Yet threats of attack are not empty, for even a small chance of so large a catastrophe is of great concern. And the advantage of the first strike, which could lead to the explosive interactions of expectations discussed, may make the probability of war in a crisis uncomfortably high. The side able to move closer to the brink, able to make its threats more convincing, perhaps through feigning irrationality (or actually being irrational), letting things get a little bit out of control, may reap a considerable reward—although at the risk of disaster.[25]

The Communist powers have several important advantages in such brinkmanship. Apart from the military advantage of the Iron Curtain and their somewhat higher state of civil defense preparation, they have the even greater advantage of totalitarian governments. They can threaten the use of force in a way that is difficult for Western statesmen who have as an audience not only Communist opponents but their constituents and allies. If the will of the West, its leader, or popular support, gives way in the face of pressure, then the Communist powers will make great gains.

The following questions are crucial to this view: Could a program aimed at strengthening our general war posture significantly increase the credibility of our resolve to carry out a threat of general war? Would such a program greatly destabilize the strategic balance? Is a program of the scale envisaged feasible? What alternatives have we for the defense of third areas in any case?

There are serious uncertainties about the effectiveness of such a program. First, the extent to which we might be able to limit the size of the enemy's retaliation would depend on the relative military postures. Here we must face the uncertainty in surmounting the barriers to retaliation discussed earlier, now viewed from the other side. Our ability to put barriers in the way of the enemy's retaliation is formidable, but just as we have, if we work at it, a good prospect of assuring a powerful retaliatory blow, so has he. This is not to say that it is certain that he will in fact adopt the necessary measures. Future technology contains enough surprises to eliminate certainty, quite apart from other obstacles. The actual damage we would receive is uncertain. If he could manage even a modest retaliation against our cities, much damage would be done for they, if not their inhabitants, must remain at risk. Second, the effects of a large nuclear war are not completely understood. The rate at which new medical effects, for example, have been discovered in recent years suggests that there may be others yet to be discovered that will make the problem of civil defense and recovery more difficult than it now appears.[26] Third, our program might stimulate the Soviet Union to develop a really massive retaliatory capability that otherwise might not exist. Fourth, even if we were able to protect the United States to a high degree, what would happen to our allies whom we are trying to defend if general war were to occur? It is much more difficult to protect the civil populations abroad, close to the Soviet Union, that would be endangered than it is to protect the American population. If the consequence of a general war were the destruction of our ally, would he be willing for us to use this threat in a crisis? Finally, would such a program be destabilizing? The answer is "Yes." How destabilizing would depend on how massive and successful a program we have. If it appeared that it would leave us able to launch a first strike and get off with little damage, the enemy would have a substantially greater incentive to strike us first. He might feel an overwhelming urge to do so if we were to begin to evacuate the population of our cities to rural shelters in a crisis. But as has been suggested, almost any feasible civil defense program and combinations of forces on both sides is likely to leave us with the prospect of damage so great that we would not feel very ready to initiate thermonuclear war. Even so, extra compensating actions to strengthen our own retaliatory power would undoubtedly be needed to offset the destabilizing effect of a sizable extended deterrence program.

It seems that on balance such a program would increase somewhat the credibility of our present policy. The appearance of resolution that a large-scale civil and military program would create would probably give the Russians pause.[27] It would slow down the rate at which our extended deterrent threat is dwindling. This is not to say that such a program is better than alternative ones, however. It offers little promise of enabling us to hold the line, nor can it turn the clock back even to so recent a period as the early 1950's when the United States could hardly be damaged.

The feasibility of a large civil defense program and expanded active defense and offense programs is not in question. We could support such programs with an increase in tax rates to about the level during the Korean war. However, it is very doubtful that primary reliance for the defense of even vital areas abroad should be placed on this treat. At best a general nuclear war would be a disaster— if not necessarily the ultimate one—not only for ourselves, but also for the Western Europeans we would be attempting to defend. The hazards of general war are so great that we must work hard at interposing defense barriers short of the threat of general war. But to say that we must not use this threat as the primary method of defending third areas is not to say that we can entirely dispense with it. The general war threat is essential if we are to deter attack on the United States; it applies with gradually weakening force as we move outward from our borders. It acts as the sanction to back up our direct defense abroad and to keep limited wars limited, to help put a bound to the erosion of the Western position.

What difference is there between the deterrence-plus-insurance measures and extended-deterrence measures? Both include broadly the same kinds of capabilities, civil and active defense and countermilitary capabilities. It is mainly the point of view that differs and possibly the scale of effort. The deterrence-plus-insurance view focuses on the possibility that war may occur in spite of our best attempts to avoid it and aims at alleviating the catastrophe.

The extended deterrence doctrine focuses on strengthening our ability to respond to grave provocation by threatening general war. There is an important difference here. Limiting fatalities, say, from 150 million to 50 million means not only 100 million lives saved but the difference between having a United States afterward and not having it. On the other hand, being able to limit damage to the much lower levels needed to make a strike-first threat adequately credible would be much more difficult, costly, and uncertain · and risky.

The massive retaliation view

"Massive retaliation" is a loosely used expression.[28] In its origin, it was the doctrine of responding to a wide range of Communist aggressions by threat of nuclear attack. It was announced by Secretary Dulles in a notable speech in January 1954, in which he said that the administration had decided "to depend primarily upon a great capacity to retaliate instantly by means and at places of our own choosing." Shortly afterward, Dulles backed off from his position a bit, and there have been many statements since then to indicate that we would not use this threat indiscriminately. Moreover, we soon gave evidence of our caution by our restrained behavior in the Indochinese crisis in the spring of 1954. Nevertheless, the fact that our military capability to defend ourselves locally has been reduced, especially our nonnuclear capabilities, suggests that this doctrine retains much support.

This doctrine looks for support in the belief that the West is unable to stand up against Communist ground strength, that we must depend on the large-scale use of nuclear weapons against the Soviet Union or China in defense of most of our allies around the periphery. If by massive retaliation we mean large-scale nuclear attack on the Chinese or Soviet Union homeland, then this means launching a general nuclear war. If we mean a limited nuclear attack, this means that we are near to all-out war and, for some time to come, the best way to enter such a war if it seems imminent is to launch a strong attack on enemy military forces first, to strike a strong first blow, and not to attack other targets while the enemy prepares to hit us in return.[29] But this threat raises the same set of problems just discussed. This is the problem of the stability of the balance of terror once again.[30]

The limitations of this doctrine are those of

the extended-deterrence view already discussed, intensified by the application of the general war threat to the defense of less vital areas. These limitations have been pointed out by many writers on military affairs.[31] The essential point is that the threat to use nuclear weapons is not one-sided and has not been for some time. It may not be credible that we would risk all-out war for many peripheral areas with all that that implies for the survival of the United States. If we depend too exclusively on this threat, the Communists will have great freedom of operation in the large area below the threshold of our general war response. While we could increase the credibility of our massive retaliation threat somewhat by adopting the extended-deterrence measures described and by clearly showing resolution, that this policy would work to stop all peripheral aggression is doubtful in the extreme. And if every peripheral challenge beyond the smallest were to raise the threat of general war in any serious way, the cumulative probability of the big war happening could reach intolerable proportions in the next decade.[32] In sum, if our general war threat retains some validity in the defense of so vital an area as Europe, it retains much less for other regions of the world, and the direction in which the power balance is shifting clearly works to diminish it throughout.

Notes

1. For a discussion of the doctrine of preventive war and its demise see Bernard Brodie, *Strategy in the Missile Age*, ch. 7, Princeton University Press, 1959.
2. Bertrand Russell, *Common Sense and Nuclear Warfare*, Simon & Schuster, 1959, p. 42.
3. Linus Pauling, *No More War*, Dodd, Mead & Co., 1958, p. 149.
4. Eugene Rabinowitch, "Status Quo With a Quid Pro Quo," *Bulletin of the Atomic Scientists*, September 1959.
5. Joint Committee on Atomic Energy, "Summary Analyses of Hearings on the Biological and Environmental Effects of Nuclear War," August 1959, p. 29.
6. Governments have an obligation to take radiation damage from peacetime bomb testing into effect also. Two points should be made: first, that while the worldwide radiation from past tests is small in comparison to the war described, it is not trivially so. About 50 megatons of fission products have been distributed widely as compared with the 500 that would be in the illustrative war. Second, that it is possible to eliminate contamination from tests altogether by detonating bombs deep underground or in outer space.
7. *Report on a Study of Non-military Defense*, July 1, 1958, R322-RC, treats an attack on the United States with 20,000 megatons of fission products. Pauling, *op. cit.*, considers a war with 50,000 megatons of fission products. The total energy yield in these two cases would be very much greater. It is worth noting that large estimates of the total yield detonated are often a consequence of assuming roughly equivalent amounts detonated in North America, Europe, and the Soviet Union. This assumes something almost certainly contrary to fact; that the side that strikes first cannot drastically reduce the total yield delivered by its opponents. A well-executed surprise attack might leave the defender with a quite small megatonnage able to surmount the barriers to retaliation unless retaliatory forces are well protected. Even if they are well protected, symmetrical damage is not to be expected.

8. For a discussion of these matters see Herman Kahn, *Three Lectures on Thermonuclear War*, to be published by the Princeton University Press.
9. For a discussion and criticism of this set of opinions see Albert Wohlstetter, "The Delicate Balance of Terror," *Foreign Affairs*, January 1959. A significant number of those who have held this position, once almost universal in the West, have altered it during the past year.

   Much of the material in this section and in the following one on deterrence-plus-insurance is based on unpublished material of Albert Wohlstetter and will be discussed at greater length in his forthcoming book for the Council on Foreign Relations.
10. The destruction of our 50 largest metropolitan areas by an attack of this scale would leave the bulk of our population surviving and a sizable and relatively well-balanced economic base. In the absence of civil defense preparations, including detailed plans for reorganizing and controlling the economy in the immediate postwar period, disruption to that had survived the immediate efforts of the nuclear attack. Arranging for the distribution of food is an obviously critical task whose accomplishment calls for extensive pre-attack planning.
11. A comparative study of the vulnerability of the United States and the Soviet Union population to fallout showed that if these populations had no civil defense preparations, an attack using ground bursts only on military

airbases could cause a very high casualty level; for example, a 4,000-megaton attack might kill 40 per cent or more of the population of either country. "The Distribution and Effect of Fallout in Large Nuclear-Weapons Campaigns," Hugh Everett III and George E. Pugh, "Operations Research," Vol. 7, No. 2, March–April 1959. However, most of the essential elements on an airbase are soft and soft targets are more easily destroyed with air bursts. The same attack using air bursts would probably kill perhaps 2 or 3 per cent of the population of either country. Even with ground bursts, fallout fatalities could be greatly reduced by intelligent use of existing structures by a trained population. The article referred to does not take this into account.

12. Herman Kahn, "How Many Can Be Saved," *Bulletin of the Atomic Scientists*, January 1959.

13. See R322-RC, *op. cit.*

14. "Defense: Outline of Future Policy," "White Paper on Defense," London, April 1957.

15. For a critique of the minimum-deterrence view see the forthcoming Wohlstetter book, *op. cit.*

16. The most lucid presentation of the minimum-deterrence doctrine is to be found in George Rathgen's "Deterrence and Defense," *Bulletin of the Atomic Scientists*, Vol. XIV, No. 6, June 1958, and in "NATO Strategy: Total War," published in *NATO and American Security*, Princeton University Press, 1959. See also, "Finite Deterrence, Controlled Retaliation," by Comdr. P. H. Backus, USN, in "United States Naval Institute Proceedings," March 1959.

17. The Congressional Record, July 15, 1959, p. 12304.

18. See T. C. Schelling, "Surprise Attack and Disarmament," published in *NATO and American Security*, Princeton University Press, 1959.

19. There is an important asymmetry between the Soviet Union and the U.S. first-strike threats. The former may be able to launch an attack between crises when a state of "normalcy" exists. For the United States an actual attack decision would almost certainly have to come in response to some immediate and grave provocation such as the invasion of Western Europe.

20. The choices facing the contenders are not quite as simple as this discussion implies. Even if there does not seem to be the threat of an attack against oneself now, there may be later on. And a significant loss in a third area might seem to bring the threat of a later attack somewhat closer.

21. T. C. Schelling, "The Reciprocal Fear of Surprise Attack," The Rand Corp., paper P-1342, May 28, 1958.

22. Earlier in this paper it was suggested that Soviet civil defences could significantly increase the threat of a surprise attack, while here it seems that U.S. civil defense is not so likely to. There are two asymmetries which support this argument: First, a U.S. first-strike almost certainly would have to come in a crisis in which our allies or the United States itself were threatened. This means that Soviet forces would be on a high state of alert. On the other hand, a Soviet first-strike would not seem to be as constrained in its timing. Second, Communist leaders might be willing to risk much greater damage than Western ones.

23. Extended deterrence is short for deterring aggression against the United States and vital areas abroad through the threat of general war. Herman Kahn's corresponding terms, type I and type II deterrence, have the merit of brevity but not of descriptiveness. Some writers refer to the deterrence of attack on one's homeland as passive deterrence and the deterrence of the attack on other areas as active deterrence, the two types of deterrence corresponding to having a second-strike and second-plus-first-strike capability, respectively. However, the term "passive" hardly seems to do justice to the actively complex job of deterring attack on the United States.

24. See Herman Kahn, *op. cit.*; also "The Nature and Feasibility of War and Deterrence," Stanford Research Institute Journal, Fourth Quarter, 1959.

25. For a fascinating discussion of the profitable uses of madness, see Daniel Ellsberg's Lowell Lectures, "The Art of Coercion: A Study of Threat in Economic Conflict and War." Lowell Institute, Boston, March 1959.

26. This is only one aspect of our advancing understanding. Another is that scientists are discovering means of reducing known damaging effects of radiation.

27. It might also give our citizenry and that of our allies pause if they were to interpret such a program as increasing the probability of war.

28. It is often used to describe the kind of retaliation we would inflict on the Soviet Union if the United States were to be attacked directly, or if there were to be a major attack in Europe. However, as a label for a doctrine, it is most clearly associated with the view that we would use the direct threat of general war, or if any military response which would carry with it a substantial likelihood of general war, in defense of a wide range of peripheral areas. This is the use of the form here. It is by no means clear that many users of this term have had in mind the initiation of a general nuclear war. Secretary Dulles referred at times to a limited nuclear attack against selected industrial targets in China.

29. It might seem unlikely that a nuclear attack on China would lead to a Soviet retaliation, but the United States might look quite dangerous to the Soviet Union at that point, and the consequences of a Soviet decision not to stand by China would be grave. One possibility is the sharing of bombs and delivery systems with China.

30. If both sides have well-protected forces able to retaliate with high confidence, the stategic balance may be stable enough to allow levels of violence that would today seem highly likely to set off general war. It might even be possible to hit homelands without triggering an all-out response. This would really have to be a controlled war. See Morton A. Kaplan, "The Strategy of Limited Retalliation," Policy Memorandum No. 19 of the Center of International Studies, Princeton, 1959.

31. Perhaps the most telling critics have seen Bernard Brodie, "Unlimited Weapons and Limited War," *The Reporter*, Nov. 18, 1954. Brodie has also discussed this aspect in his book, *Strategy in the Missile Age, op. cit.*, Also William Kaufmann, "The Requirements of Deterrence," in *Military Policy and National Security*. W. W. Kaufmann, ed., Princeton University Press, 1956; and Henry Kissinger, *Nuclear Weapons and Foreign Policy*, Harpers, 1957.

32. A counterargument deserves mention. It holds that actual conflict at the periphery of limited war carries with it a significant probability of turning into a big war. A policy which could lead to a series of limited wars might, it is argued, have a higher over-all cumulative probability of a big war than the policy which aims at deterring all wars through the general war threat.

Bernard Brodie

The anatomy of deterrence*

FROM THE AMERICAN POINT OF VIEW, the strategy of deterrence, and the related principle of limiting to tolerable proportions whatever conflicts become inevitable, tend to spring from the premise that the favorable results of a total war can never be sufficient to justify its cost. Such a war, according to that conception, would be too big, too all-consuming, to permit the survival even of those final values, like personal freedom, for which alone one could think of waging it. It need not be certain

* This article is part of a larger study under preparation by the author as a staff member of The RAND Corporation.

that it would turn out so badly; it is enough that there is a large chance that it would.

The conceptions of deterrence and of limited war also take account of the fact that the United States is, and has long been, a *status quo* power. It is uninterested in acquiring new territories or areas of influence or in accepting great hazard in order to rescue or reform those areas of the world which now have political systems radically different from our own. On the other hand, as a *status quo* power it is also determined to keep what it has, including existence in a world of which half or more is friendly or at least not sharply and perennially hostile. In other words,

Reprinted from *World Politics*, Vol. XI, No. 4, January 1959, pp. 13–28.

the minimum security objectives for the United States must include not only its own national independence but also that of other countries which presently have and cherish such independence, especially those which enjoy democratic political institutions comparable to our own. Among the latter are numbered those nations with which we have a special cultural affinity, that is, the countries of Western Europe.

The policy which seeks to protect all we have has been called the policy or strategy of "containment." The conception of containment has been abused by those who would presumably do more rather than less, but the policy of doing more seems quite unable to generate any real dynamism behind it. The reason is that the moment something specific is suggested, one has to take account of attendant risks. Such awareness is pleasantly blanked out so long as talk about "liberation" or "rollback" remains general and abstract.

The philosophy of deterrence also takes account of the enormous American cultural resistances to hitting first in a period of threatened total war. This is not to say that it is out of the question that we should do so. It is possible that we will build so much automaticity and sensitivity into our retaliatory response that it could be triggered by an "indication of hostile intent" rather than a hostile act. Such a development would probably be attributable more to absent-mindedness on the part of our political leaders than to design, but such absent-mindedness is commonplace in peacetime in the area of strategic decision. Also, we must not forget that there is likely to be a threshold of "intolerable provocation" short of direct attack upon us, even though we cannot determine before the event where that threshold is or ought to be.

Nevertheless, it remains unlikely that our government will ever deliberately initiate a total war for the sake of securing for ourselves the military advantage of the first blow, however considerable that advantage may be. The operational corollary of this point is that we must do what we can to reduce the advantage that might accrue to the enemy if he hit first. In other words, our rejection of the idea of "preventive war" has committed us completely and inevitably to the policy and strategy of deterrence, and it is now up to us to pay the price, to make deterrence work. That price includes doctrinal adjustment (e.g., de-emphasis of offensive as against defensive doctrines) as well as a fairly heavy outlay of resources on measures to enhance the security of our retaliatory force.

Deterrence old and new

DETERRENCE as an element in national strategy or diplomacy is certainly nothing new under the sun. However, since the development of nuclear weapons, the term has acquired not only a special emphasis but also a distinctive connotation. It is usually the new and distinctive connotation that we have in mind when we speak nowadays of the "strategy of deterrence."

The threat of war, open or implied, has always been an instrument of diplomacy by which one state deterred another from doing something of a military or political nature which the former did not wish the latter to do. Frequently the threat was completely latent—that is, the position of the monitoring state was so obvious and so strong that no one thought of challenging it. Governments, like men generally, usually have been aware of the hazards involved in provoking powerful neighbors, and have governed themselves accordingly. Because avoidance not only of wars but even of crises hardly makes good copy for historians, we may infer that the past successes of some nations in deterring unwanted action by other nations add up to much more than one would gather from a casual reading of history. Nevertheless, the very large number of wars that have occurred in modern times proves that the threat to use force, even what sometimes looked like superior force, has often failed to deter.

We should, however, notice the positive function served by the failures. The very frequency with which wars occurred contributed importantly to the credibility inherent in any threat. In diplomatic correspondence, the statement that a specified kind of conduct would be deemed "an unfriendly act" was regarded as tantamount to an ultimatum and to be taken without question as seriously intended.

Bluffing, in the sense of deliberately trying to sound more determined or bellicose than one actually felt, was by no means as common a phenomenon in diplomacy as latter-day journalistic interpretations of events would have one believe. In any case, it tended to be confined to the more implicit kinds of threat. In short, the operation of deterrence was dynamic; it acquired relevance and strength from its failures as well as its successes.

However, the policy of deterrence we are

talking about today is markedly different in several respects. For one thing, it uses a kind of threat which we feel must be *absolutely* effective, allowing for no breakdowns whatever. The sanction is, to say the least, not designed for repeating action. One use of it will be fatally too many.

We thus have the anomaly that deterrence is meaningful as a strategic policy only when we are fairly confident that the retaliatory instrument upon which it relies will not be called upon to function at all. And that instrument, if we are to be sure of its not being used, has to have its capacity to function maintained at a very high level and constantly refined—which can be done only at great cost to the community and great dedication on the part of the personnel directly involved. We are, in other words, expecting the system to be constantly perfected while going permanently unused. Surely we must concede that there is something unreal about it all.

The problem of credibility

EVEN SO, the unreality is minimal when we are talking about what we shall henceforward call "basic deterrence"—that is, deterrence of direct, strategic, nuclear attack upon targets within the home territories of the United States. In that instance there is little or no problem of credibility as concerns our reactions. The enemy has little reason to doubt that if he strikes us, we will certainly try to hit back.

But the great and terrible apparatus which we must set up to fulfill our needs for "basic deterrence," and the state of readiness at which we have to maintain it, create a condition of almost embarrassing availability of huge power. The problem of fitting this power into a reasonable conception of its utility has thus far proved a considerable strain. It was responsible at one time for our espousal of the doctrine of "massive retaliation," which we have since rejected in theory but not entirely in commitment. One of the first things wrong with the doctrine of massive retaliation, where it has been meant as a response to less than massive aggression, is that the enemy with a nuclear capability of his own cannot believe that we mean it.

On the other hand, it would be tactically and factually wrong to assure the enemy in advance (as we tend to do by constantly assuring ourselves) that we would in no case take off against him until we had already felt some

bombs on our cities and airfields. We have, for one thing, treaty obligations which forbid so far-reaching a commitment to restraint. It is also impossible for us to predict with absolute assurance our own behaviour in extremely tense and provocative circumstances. If we make a wrong prediction about ourselves, we also encourage the enemy to make a wrong prediction about us. The outbreak of war in Korea in 1950 followed that pattern. The wrong kind of prediction in the future could precipitate that total war which too many persons have lightly concluded is now impossible.

Deterrence strategy versus win-the-war strategies: the sliding scale of deterrence

BUT to return now to the simpler problem of basic deterrence. The capacity to deter is usually confused with the capacity to win a war. Assuming always that "to win" has some useful meaning in a modern total war, we may be sure that it requires either a decisive and effective superiority in strategic air power (by "effective" we mean mostly "available when needed," which may be after an enemy attack) or, more likely, some striking success of initiative. Inasmuch as effective superiority is always a good thing to have anyway if one can afford it, one sees that the confusion between deterring and winning has some method in it. But deterrence effect as such does not depend on superiority.

Prior to the nuclear age, a force which was clearly inferior to a rival's might or might not have some real deterrence value. Surely it is reasonable to surmise that if Stalin had had in late 1939 a better estimate of the capability of the Finns to defend themselves, he would have been much less ready to attack them. If we can deduce his incentive in attacking from the peace terms he ultimately laid down, it seems not to have been so much a desire to conquer and absorb some extra territories, let alone the whole Finnish nation, as it was the wish to administer to the Finns and to others a sharp "lesson." That object was compromised by the successes of the Finnish resistance, despite the country's final defeat. What we wish to emphasize by this example is that deterrence has always suggested something relative, not absolute, and that its effectiveness must be measured not only by the amount of power that it holds in check, but also by the incentives to aggression residing behind that power. We can easily see how truistic this point is when we recall that neither Mexico nor Canada needs military power to defend itself from the United States; but, truistic or not, the point is implicitly denied by those who equate "deterrence" with "capacity to win."

Now that we are in a nuclear age, the potential deterrence value of an admittedly inferior force may be sharply greater that it has ever been before. Let us assume that a menaced small nation could threaten the Soviet Union with only a single thermonuclear bomb, which, however, it could certainly deliver on Moscow if attacked. This retaliatory capability would be sufficient to give the Soviet government much pause. Certainly the Russians would not invoke the destruction of Moscow wantonly, that is, for trivial gains. If we think of five or ten H-bombs delivered on as many of the largest Soviet cities, the deterrence would no doubt be significantly greater—though we would still be far from talking about a force which is either superior to that of the Soviet Union or capable of decisive results.

If we attempt to plot a curve denoting "deterrence effect" as a function of the numbers of thermonuclear weapons expected to fall on the aggressor's cities—with "deterrence effect" as ordinates and numbers of bombs as abscissas—we can surmise that the curve begins at a rather high level of deterrence for the first such bomb, and that while it moves significantly higher as the number of bombs increases beyond one, it does so at a decreasing rate. At a relatively modest number (probably well short of a hundred), the curve is closely approaching the horizontal. The asymptote representing *maximum possible deterrence* which it is possible to reach with this kind of threat would very likely require something acknowledged to be "decisive superiority" over the enemy, but it is likely also that very considerably less force would be only trivially less deterrence.

This is not to say that for that reason we have no interest in "win the war" capabilities and strategies. So long as there is a finite chance of war, we have to be interested in outcomes; and although practically all outcomes would be bad, some would be much worse than others. Also, if we could imagine a conspicuous capability of winning wars which was able to survive even a surprise attack by the enemy, we should have to acknowledge the ultimate in deterrence.[1] But we have to be ready to recognize that deterrence philosophies and win-the-war philo-

sophies may diverge in important respects. We can say in advance that they must diverge in terms of priority. The objective of erecting a high degree of deterrence takes a higher priority that the objective of assuring ourselves of a winning capability, if for no other reason than that there is bound to be a considerable difference between the two in feasibility and in costs. We are also likely to feel a divergence between the two philosophies when it comes to considering alternative military policies in terms of comparative degrees of provocativeness. For the sake of deterrence we want always to choose the less provocative of two policies, even if it may mean some sacrifice of efficiency. But if we were in fact interested primarily in winning and only secondarily in deterrence, we should be extremely loath to make any such sacrifices.

Let us be quite clear that the curve described in the penultimate paragraph above does *not* represent how decision-makers would react to a situation. It is most unlikely that a particular point in the scale of estimated counterblows would represent for them, in any firm, objective way, the dividing line between a "go" and "no-go" decision. Human beings, differing widely as they do in temperamental and psychic makeup, simply do not make difficult and momentous decisions on that basis. Much more is left to what we have to call "intuition." Nevertheless, the curve described above is useful for communicating the intelligence climate in which the decision is made.

We must notice also that when we talked about ultimate deterrence probably depending on "decisive superiority," we were implying, for the first time in the discussion, a *comparison* of damage likely to be suffered by each side. Prior to this point we were talking of deterrence as something resulting from a *unilateral* consideration of damage—that is, an estimate of the damage likely to be suffered by oneself. This is the issue that seems to provoke so much confusion about deterrence. It is a truistic statement that by deterrence we mean obliging the opponent to consider, in an environment of great uncertainty, the probable cost to him of attacking us against the expected gain thereof. It is only a shade less obvious that the cost has to be measured in terms of damage to himself. But what seems very difficult to grasp is that his gain cannot be measured simply in terms of damage to us, or vice versa, even though such damage may indeed provoke an act or condition (i.e., surrender or military obliteration) which he legitimately considers a great gain because it terminates a threat. But damage to an opponent, however large, which for one reason or another fails to have such an effect is no strategic gain at all.

To be willing to accept enormous destruction only for the sake of inflicting greater destruction on the enemy (which may be all that some mean by "winning") argues a kind of desperation at the moment of decision which rules out reason. We may have to expect that at certain extreme conditions of provocation (e.g., conviction that an enemy attack upon oneself is imminent) the deterrent posture will tend to collapse or be discarded without much regard to estimates of damage or gain to either side. But all that means is that the rationality upon which deterrence must be based is ultimately frangible—a conclusion of which history has already given us ample indication.

Another attitude that gets in the way of understanding deterrence is the one which alleges that the Soviet leaders, when faced with issues of peace and war, would be indifferent to the loss of individual cities and certainly of the populations (as distinguished from the production capital) within those cities. The implication of this view is that a government or leadership imbued with that kind of indifference can be deterred not by considerations of loss in any graduated sense of the term, but only by the prospect of *losing a war*. This is hardly the place to attempt to weigh the evidence for and against such an attribution of indifference. But, as this writer see it, the view just described grossly distorts and exaggerates some undeniable and important differences between the Soviet system and our own.

Certainly insensibility to human suffering among subject populations, especially when it can be rationalized as a necessary price for alleged future benefits, is much more characteristic of the Soviet system than of our own. This fact probably affects significantly the dynamics of deterrence as described in preceding paragraphs. But it is not enough to subvert those dynamics. The Soviet leaders might be appreciably less shocked and distressed than our own leaders would be in comparable circumstances by the loss through nuclear bombing of one or more of their large cities, but they certainly would not be indifferent to it—either on humanitarian or on prestige grounds.

Of course, we have to remember that the Soviets have a very high incentive for destroying us, or at least our military power, if they can do

so—at minimum, the incentive of eliminating what is to them a great threat. As we emphasized earlier, the question of incentive is decidedly relevant to the issue of deterrence. In fact, deterrence is simply the effort to erect appropriate disincentives to counteract the incentives which the opponent feels for our destruction, disincentives which not only guarantee him pain if he attempts to attack us, but also heighten his uncertainty about the immediate results of his contemplated attack.

To return to our conception of a "deterrence effect" curve—for which we cannot, of course, fill in specific values—we may now consider how it assists us in formulating our strategic problems.

First, it should be obvious that what counts in basic deterrence is not so much the size and efficiency of one's striking force before it is hit as the size and condition to which the enemy thinks he can reduce it by a surprise attack—as well as his confidence in the correctness of his predictions.[2] However, to many who are in one way or another charged with military planning, that point is not at all obvious. The reasons for their rejecting it may vary. Some are simply unused to thinking in terms of the enemy having the initiative, preferring always to think in terms of our having it. This is an age-old addiction of official war planners. Others, more sophisticated, apparently feel that a force that lets itself take the first blow will not be strong enough to win a war, regardless of what it has done to protect itself, and they are by training, tradition, and often temperament interested only in strategies that can win. They are preoccupied with getting the offensive force launched against the enemy while it is still able to win—i.e., *before* it is hit. They are either not interested in a predominantly deterrent strategy, or they are convinced that a force not strong enough to win is not strong enough to deter. Underlying this view is also the conviction that money spent on protecting the retaliatory force might otherwise have been spent on expanding it.

The latter conviction is certainly correct. The same kind of problem—deciding how much it is worth paying to design protection into an offensive force—has been faced many times before, notably in the history of warship development. Armor on warships has always been expensive and has also absorbed a great deal of the weight-carrying capacity of the ship. So has antiaircraft armament. The initial bias of the users was usually against "sacrificing offensive for defensive armament" (to quote a slogan of the U.S. Navy prior to our entry into World War II), but battle experience would finally intervene to force the necessary adjustment. Each new category of weapons seems to require the same kind of adjustment through the same kind of contact with experience. Perhaps the fact that thermonuclear weapons have made it possible, for the first time, to conceive of having more offensive power than we really need will make it easier to shift emphasis from buying more and better bombers and missiles to buying more and better protection for bombers and missiles. In any case, the overriding considerations should be that *the nation is committed primarily to a deterrence policy*, and that such a commitment dictates concern with the survival of a retaliatory force of reasonable size following surprise attack.

If it were possible to guarantee the survival of a hard-core retaliatory force of reasonable size by protecting massively in individual shelters, even at a very high unit cost, a preselected portion of one's entire retaliatory force, that would be the way to go about it. The rest of the force could conceivably do with less massive protection on the grounds that the worst imaginable contingencies are not the only likely ones, and may not even be the most probable ones. However, it is not likely that shelters can be made strong enough to resist direct hits with thermonuclear weapons; and direct hits can probably be delivered with aircraft, even if not with missiles. Obviously, a much larger proportion of one's total striking force, and preferably the whole of it, has to be given a high level of protection—as well as dispersion and concealment—to make it likely that a reasonable proportion of it will survive. Such a procedure also ensures that the enemy, if he comes at all, has to come with large forces of aircraft, which greatly diminishes his chances for surprise.

The principle of a sliding scale of protection could conceivably be applied in other ways. One way would be to have a proportion of the total force always in flight, fully armed, with tankers in attendance, and another portion kept in very advanced readiness. The U.S. Air Force has indicated, in numerous public pronouncements, its interest in dealing with the problem of vulnerability by such means. But such a system is exceedingly expensive; it is more provocative to the opponent; and as far as concerns the advanced-readiness contingent on the ground, it has considerable value against

manned aircraft attacks, but little or none against missile attacks. Above all, such a system is not intrinsically capable of being applied to more than a minor portion of one's total force.

From the security point of view, there is also value in diversification for the hard-core survival forces. For example, the use of nuclear-powered submarines as a means of hurling nuclear missiles of the Polaris type against strategic targets would seem to be a desirable supplement to a well-protected, land-based force, even if it proved to be (which is not presently established) a costlier and otherwise less satisfactory method measured by effects achieved at targets. The submarine is free of that main defect which characterizes the aircraft-carrier: the latter's relatively easy detectability by air-borne radar combined with high vulnerability to atomic attack.

Deterrence and the choice of bombing vehicles: missiles versus aircraft

WE have thus far stressed the necessity, for deterrence purposes, of providing for a retaliatory force which will survive surprise attack. But the surviving force must also appear to have a good chance of penetrating fully alerted enemy defenses even if launched in relatively small numbers. This requirement affects the choice of vehicles for the hard "deterrence core" of the retaliatory striking force. It undoubtedly upgrades, for example, the value of the long-range ballistic missile as compared with the manned aircraft.

If the ballistic missile is compared with the manned aircraft on any grounds other than penetration capability, the latter appears able easily to hold its own for some time into the future. The airplane can carry heavier and therefore (for the present) more powerful thermonuclear weapons, and it can deliver them more accurately than the missile. It can be protected on the ground through the use of a heavy shelter at least as easily as can the larger and more delicately constructed missile. The aircraft which takes to the air frequently can be more reliably depended upon to do so at the moment of need, and, for those held in advanced readiness, probably with a shorter preparation and check-out time, than the never-previously-flown missile. In addition, the aircraft has the special factor of "recallability," the capability of being sent out at inconclusive warning of enemy attack—thus getting it off the ground into the safer air—subject to being recalled within a reasonable period of time if the warning turns out to be false. This factor of "recallability" has been considered especially valuable to the advanced-readiness force. If one did not have to think about enemy active air defenses, the aircraft would probably also be a cheaper way of assuring a given amount of target destruction, especially where the targets are other than cities and where accurate aiming is required.

However, the speed of the missile not only denies the victim appreciable warning time, but also makes the problem of coping with it through active defenses extraordinarily difficult, even if not altogether hopeless. An anti-missile missile is probably feasible, but to design into it the requisite sensitivity and quickness of re-action, and at the same time immunity to deceptive signals, is going to be anything but easy. As something to be mounted and main-tained during peacetime, an anti-missile missile defense poses problems which are probably as severe on the political as on the technological side. Active anti-missile defense probably makes no sense unless it is highly sensitive and fully automatic, and it is precisely these character-istics which are politically objectionable in peacetime, especially for any system which utilizes nuclear weapons. The problem of destroying missiles in flight is incomparably more difficult than that of destroying aircraft, and we are very far yet from being in an era when it is a simple matter to do the latter—at least to do it well enough to protect our cities and air bases.

The conclusion is unavoidable that, for some time to come, the ideal strategic bombing force will be a mixed missile and manned-aircraft force. But because of the penetration problem, which is bound to be much more difficult in a counterattack than in a surprise initial attack and which will go up disproportionately in difficulty as the number of attacking vehicles diminishes (except where the numbers are kept small in an initial attack for the sake of surprise), one should expect that the missile will be fa-vored in the "hard core" of the retaliatory force.

The problem of target choice in retaliation

THE U.S. Air Force has thoroughly acquainted the public with the information that our individual SAC crews are thoroughly briefed on specific primary and alternative targets for their initial D-day strike. It has also made clear in recent years, since the Soviets have achieved a nuclear bombing capability, that while the ultimate strategic target remains the enemy's "war economy" (whatever that means under thermonuclear conditions, where the so-called "war potential" of the state may be of little or no military value), first priority has to be given to his strategic air force.

But such a priority applies clearly only to an attack in which we hit first. All the major condi-tions governing target selection may change if the enemy strikes us first and ours is a retaliatory mission. In the first place, our retaliatory force is smaller by some unknown, though very likely substantial, factor than the original offensive force. This smaller force, which is probably much disorganized, will now have to attempt to penetrate fully alerted defenses. The enemy air force (including missiles) is no longer at rest at its bases, ready to be struck by us to maximum effect. Its attractiveness as a strategic target had begun to decline sharply from the moment is began to be air-borne. Moreover, depending on the degree of surprise it achieved, it has already done a good part of its total work, almost certainly the major part so far as one's own air force is concerned.

What then happens to the priority of the counter-air mission? The enemy's air force has ceased to be anything like so profitable a target as it was prior to hostilities, and at the same time our capabilities for hitting it have been reduced markedly. They may have been reduced below the critical limits at which we can no longer injure significantly his surviving air power. We can probably prevent some enemy planes from flying second and third missions even if we have been too late to stop the first. That opportunity is not to be dismissed lightly. But it may not seem like a meaningful way to use up our surviving strike capability, especially if that capability is considerably reduced from the original.

What then? Perhaps we will have succeeded in putting enough target flexibility into our system so that surviving units do not simply go charging off against originally assigned targets. Even if it were a rational decision not to change the identity of the top-priority target *system*, certainly a substantial loss of planes, and hence reduction in the number making a counter-attack, argues that individual targets must be reassigned to avoid serious lacunae. But we also have to reconsider the whole system.

If we consider the problem strictly from the point of view of achieving *before* hostilities the maximum deterrent effect for our retaliatory force, the answer seems to be simple. We assign to the hard-core elements in our retaliatory force the enemy's major cities, provide for the maximum automaticity as well as certainty of response, and lose no opportunity to let the enemy know that we have done these things. The enemy therefore has reason to calculate that even a very great success against our air force in a surprise attack will, so long as it is short of 100 per cent success, result in his losing a number of his largest cities. Certainly he cares intrinsically more than those cities than he does for his airfields, especially after the latter have already done their offensive work.

Such an arrangement must surely maximize the deterrent effort of our retaliatory force. We assure the enemy, though assuring ourselves, that we will not reconsider the matter in the event he attacks us. We will hit back with all our surviving power at his cities, and, especially if that surviving power contains a fair number of missiles, he can count on losing those cities. It ought not be too difficult to assure him that, come what may, he will lose fifty or more of his largest cities.

The rub comes from the fact that what appears like the most rational *deterrence* policy involves commitment to a strategy of response which, if we ever had to execute it, might then look very foolish. And the strategy of deterrence ought always to envisage the possibility of deterrence failing.

Suppose, for illustration, we imagine a kind of enemy attack that is far from implausible—in fact, one that has already been publicly proposed as a strategy that we might adopt for ourselves if we ever initiated the attack.[3] Suppose the enemy attacked our retaliatory forces with great power but took scrupulous care to avoid major war injury to our cities. He might indeed understand that, in a thermonuclear war, the *ability* to destroy cities confers more military advantage as a threat than the actual destruction of them is likely to have. If his attack is to any serious degree successful, we should then be left with a severely truncated retaliatory force while his force remained relatively intact. That would hardly seem like a propitious set of circumstances for us to *initiate* an exchange of city destruction, which under such circumstances becomes mere suicidal vindictiveness.

Thus it is easy to imagine a situation where it is useless to attack the enemy's airfields and disastrous as well as futile to attack his cities. Perhaps we would in our rage and helplessness strike blindly at enemy cities, and perhaps also the enemy's anticipation of such "irrational" behavior would help deter him from precipitating such a situation. Perhaps for the sake of maximizing deterrence it is wise deliberately to reject the Napoleonic maxim, *"On s'engage; puis on voit"*—which after all applied to a state of affairs where one had far greater control of events after engaging than would be true of modern total war. If that is the conclusion, then the response ought to be not only automatic but sensibly so—that is, automatic against the things whose loss hurts the enemy the most: cities rather than airfields.

But a reasonable opposing view is that, however difficult it may be to retain control of events in nuclear total war, one ought never to abandon control deliberately. If so, how should we cope with an enemy offensive which exercised the kind of discriminating restraint described above? Clearly one cannot dismiss such restraint on the ground that it represents an unwise strategy. The contrary is probably true. The question is whether men who have been reared in the tradition which holds that extra damage from a delivered bomb is always a "bonus"—a tradition which is probably as strong on the Soviet side of the military fence as it is on our own—are likely to approach the problem in so dangerously fresh a manner.

Choice of weapons for maximum deterrence

THE first underwater shot of a nuclear weapon, the Baker shot at Bikini in 1946, revealed the appalling extent of radioactive debris which resulted from the explosion of a nuclear weapon, even one which by present standards was quite small. For a while it was possible to ignore this result because succeeding shots were set off, as a rule, from atop towers more than 200 feet high. However, the Bravo shot in the CASTLE series on March 1, 1954, involved a large thermonuclear weapon set off at ground level—putting so powerful a weapon atop the usual tower would have made little difference because of the size of the fireball—and the enormous reach of the fallout on that occasion confirmed the existence of a tremendous lethal by-product.

It is fair to say the military would have been happy to do without this radioactive by-product. Not only is its fall not subject to control in the general region of the target, but in wartime some of it is bound to fall on neutral or friendly countries and even to drift back to the territories of the users of the bomb. That is especially true of the long-lived, invidious soil contaminent, Strontium 90.

For those reasons a great deal of research has gone into producing a so-called "clean" bomb that is, a thermonuclear weapon which, relative to its explosive force in blast and thermal effects, will produce only a slight amount of radioactive fallout. It has, of course, been well known that the opposite course was also feasible—that by adding various chemicals one could produce a weapon which released a much greater amount of radioactive fallout for its size than the already quite dirty thermonuclear weapon of the CASTLE-Bravo type. However, development of such super-dirty weapons was bound to be retarded by the feeling that they had little or no military utility and hence could not be morally justified.

But when we consider the special requirements of deterrence in the minimal or basic sense of deterring a direct attack upon oneself, it is possible that one can see some utility in the super-dirty bomb. Since the emphasis has to be on making certain that the enemy fears even the smallest number of bombs that might be sent in retaliation, one wants these bombs to be—and thus to appear before the event—as horrendous as possible. This objective is advanced by making the bomb super-dirty, as well as large, which incidentally also makes accuracy of delivery relatively unimportant. No doubt it will also prove feasible by the appropriate selection of chemicals to augment close fallout without increasing the output of those radioactive elements that are characteristically carried to a great distance.

Deterrence and civil defense[4]

WE have observed that minimal or basic deterrence as we have defined it—that is, retaliation in direct reply to attack upon ourselves—involves little or no strain on credibility. The enemy knows that if he hits our cities, we will hit him back if we can. The question is one of feasibility, not intention. We suspect also that such a statement holds good without regard to the state of our civil defenses at the time.

However, we have already noticed one case where, even in the event of direct attack upon our own territories, the character and spontaneity of our response may become slightly

more doubtful. This is the case where the enemy hits hard at our air and missile bases but takes care to minimize injury to our cities. It may be plausible to argue that in that moment of catastrophe we will be too insensitive to the discrimination he is practicing to let our responses be affected by it, but at present we cannot be certain of that. This uncertainty permits the consideration that perhaps our response will be affected by whether or not we have some shelters to put our people into.

The moment we think of deterrence in somewhat bolder terms—that is, as something to be practiced concerning territories beyond our shores—the issue of whether or not we have provided reasonable protection to our population may become all-important. We may be quite sure we will hit back directly ourselves, but will we do so if any of our chief allies is attacked or threatened with attack? We are, to be sure, legally committed to respond with all our power and our leaders may presently be convinced that if occasion should arise they would honor that commitment. But surely they would on such an occasion be much affected by the consideration—assuming no radical change from the present situation—that our people are hopelessly exposed to enemy counterattack.

We cannot predict for any specific instance that having the appropriate shelters would make a great difference in our behaviour. We could be cowardly with shelters and bold (or reckless?) without them; but surely if they existed at the moment of crisis, their effect would tend to favor courageous rather than craven decision. We should note that in the kind of crisis situation we are hypothetically posing, the question of whether or not there will be enough warning to get people to the shelters in time does not greatly disturb us; we are assuming that our government sends them there as a result not of enemy attack but of its own resolution to act. We do not have to assume that in the event of war the enemy will certainly hit us first in a surprise attack, and that all important population centers will be included as targets in the first wave of the attack. That is a possible and perhaps highly probable contingency, but there are other contingencies, too, that should be taken into account.

It has been pointed out also that an adequate civil defense program may prove an indispensable factor in keeping wars limited. The maintenance by the enemy of limitations acceptable to us depends on our willingness to retaliate in kind and in greater degree in the event of gross enemy violation—going as far as the full use of SAC if need be. The enemy must also believe that we are ready to do so. Surely it would help to develop in ourselves the requisite willingness, and in the enemy the necessary credibility, if we had meanwhile provided some cover for our population.

We are describing an area of crisis and of decision which may seem to be utterly improbable for the future. But most of the billions we are spending on the total-war aspect of national defense envisage situations which are, we hope, at least equally improbable. All our efforts are directed, at least we intend for them to be directed—toward making such situations still more improbable. This is what national defense is all about in the thermonuclear age.

One does not, naturally, accord to civil defense the same level of priority that one accords to comparable measures for the defense of SAC. A *secure* retaliatory force is not only the *sine qua non* of deterrence and of national defense generally, but the one instrument which could conceivably make all other instruments designed for defense unnecessary. But prudence tells us that we need some backstops even to a secure SAC, and a well-designed shelter program for civil defense appears to fill such a need.

One school of thought holds that it is necessary and feasible to protect not only our people but also the tools and materials required for national economic recovery within a reasonable period after the war. This view suggests that a nuclear war is not necessarily the end of the world for us, let alone all humanity, and that we need not settle for anything less than the capacity to protect and preserve under attack the economic basis for our great-power status. The sums required to purchase this capacity over a five- to ten-year period are, allegedly, not outlandishly huge. It is possible to purchase relatively cheaply, in caves and unused mines, a great deal of floor space for the storage or actual operation of essential production capital. Some of this space is held to be already competitive, on an economic basis, with comparable space above ground. Whether or not this apparently optimistic appraisal is true cannot be determined without a careful and detailed technical survey, such as we cannot pretend to carry on here. All we can argue now is that the whole subject deserves careful study, that at the very least protection of population must be seriously provided for, and that such protection can be

reasonably justified on political and strategic as well as on humanitarian grounds.

Individuals may in fact reject this kind of thinking on the ground that they would rather take their chances with a hazardous future without seeing holes dug into the ground around them to provide, at best, a marginal kind of safety. The usual observation on the subject includes some reference to the general undesirability of life anyway following a thermonuclear war. Individuals are entitled to adopt such attitudes for themselves, and perhaps even for their children as well, though they may be deceiving themselves about their feelings in a future crisis. Governments, on the other hand, have no moral right whatever to adopt cavalier attitudes about the value of invidual survival.

Deterrence and armaments control

WE come finally to the question of the political environment favoring the functioning of a deterrence strategy, especially with respect to the much abused and labored subject of international control of armaments. There is a long and dismal history of confusion and frustration on this subject. Those who have been most passionate in urging disarmament have often refused to look unpleasant facts in the face; and on the other hand, the government officials responsible for actual negotiations have usually been extremely rigid in their attitudes, tending to become more preoccupied with winning marginal and ephemeral advantages from the negotiations than in making real progress toward the presumed objective. There has also been a confusion concerning both the objective and the degree of risk warranted by that objective.

Here we can take up only the last point. One must first ask what degree of arms control is a reasonable or sensible objective. It seems by now abundantly clear that total nuclear disarmament is not a reasonable objective. Violation would be too easy, and the risks presented to the non-violator enormous. But it should also be obvious that the kind of bitter, relentless nuclear and missile armaments race that has been going on since the end of World War II has its own intrinsic dangers. We could not view it with equanimity even if we remained confident (as we have not been since the first Sputnik) of our ability to keep ahead technologically for an indefinite period. Inasmuch as this race itself imposes the gravest risks, we ought not to look askance at measures for slowing or otherwise alleviating it simply because those measures themselves involve certain finite risks. In each case the risk has to be measured and weighed against the gain.

The kind of measures in which we ought to be especially interested are those which could seriously reduce on all sides the chances of achieving complete surprise in a strategic attack. Such a policy would be entirely compatible with our basic national commitment to a strategy of deterrence. The kinds of measures one thinks of first in this connection refer to such mutual inspection schemes as would enhance the chances of getting "strategic warning" (as opposed to the "tactical warning" derived from radar screens and the like)—that is, warning of measures being taken that could be a prelude to attack.

It is important to stress that a measure may be valuable even if it is a low-confidence one. This point is generally overlooked in the pursuit of ideal but attainable ironclad guarantees. By a low-confidence measure we do *not* mean one with loopholes which the opponent may exploit without fear of detection. Such a measure

warrants no confidence at all. A system which presents, say, a 10 per cent probability that the opponent's preparations to launch surprise attack will be detected, but which the enemy cannot manipulate to reduce the probabiliy still further, is a low-confidence measure. And a 10 per cent chance of detection may well be utterly unacceptable to an aggressor who feels that surprise is essential to his schemes.

Technological progress is pushing us rapidly and inexorably toward a position of almost intolerable mutual menace. Unless something is done politically to alter the environment, both sides will before many years have numerous missiles accurately pointed at each other's hearts are ready to be fired literally at a moment's notice. Even before that time arrives, aircraft depending for their safety on being in the air in time will be operating more and more provocatively according to so-called "air-borne alert" and "fail safe" patterns. Nothing which has any promise of obviating or alleviating the tensions of such situations should be overlooked.

Notes

1. Provided it was coupled also with the threat of very large damage. Historically it has *not* been true that nations have always regarded ultimate military defeat as more serious than very heavy damage. Defeat has often been accepted in order to avoid such damage, even where victory was far from hopeless. If that were not so, there would be very little hope for limiting war.

2. The pre-hostilities size of one's retaliatory force does have a distinctive and possibly important deterrence effect because of the enemy's concern with what it will mean for him if his attempt to destroy it by surprise attack

should fail utterly. Of course, he may grossly misestimate, in either direction, the chance of failure.

3. See especially Colonel Richard S. Leghorn, "No Need to Bomb Cities to Win War," *U.S. News and World Report*, XXXVIII (January 28, 1955), pp. 79–94.

4. For most of the ideas in this section, I am indebted to my RAND colleague, Mr. Herman Kahn. See the booklet prepared under his direction and published by The Rand Corporation under the title, *Report on a Study of Non-military Defense*, July 1, 1958, Report R322-RC.

Robert E. Osgood

The theory of limited war

The principle of political primacy

IN PRACTICE, the limitation of war is morally and emotionally repugnant to the American people. Yet is is in accord with America's own best principles. The explanation of this paradox lies partly in the fact that Americans have not understood the relation between military force and national policy, and so they have misconceived the real moral and practical implications of national conduct. Therefore, it is imperative at the beginning of this study to develop a sound conception of the relation between force and policy as the first step in examining the requirements of an American strategy of limited war.

The justification of limited war arises, in the most fundamental sense, from the principle that military power should be subordinate to national policy, that the only legitimate purpose of military force is to serve the nation's political objectives. This principle of political primacy is basic to all forms and all uses of military power, whether employed overtly, covertly, or only tacitly. It is as applicable to the formulation of military policies and military strategy as to the actual waging of war. In this principle morality and expediency are joined.

The principle of political primacy is essential to the nation's self-interest because military power is of no practical use as a thing in itself but is useful only insofar as it serves some national purpose. It is useful because it is a prerequisite of national security and because upon security all other national goals depend. Coercion is an indispensable feature of all human relations in which basic security and order cannot be guaranteed by the innate sympathy, reasonableness, and morality of men. The essential role of coercion is especially large in international relations, where institutional organization is anarchical or rudimentary and the bonds of law, custom, and sentiment are relatively impotent as against the intense ties of loyalty binding men to their separate and sovereign national groups.

The practical necessity of military power is obvious to Americans today, but it is not always so obvious that military power does not automatically translate itself into national security. Military power may actually be translated into national insecurity when it is employed without a proper regard for its non-military objectives and consequences. Without intelligent and vigilant political control even the most effective use of military force, by purely military standards, will not necessarily bring comparably satisfactory political results. A capricious, impulsive, or irresponsible use of military power cannot be expedient; for when military policy and strategy lack the guideposts of limited and attainable objectives and become, in effect, ends in themselves, they cease to be controllable and predictable instruments of national policy.

The individual soldier, even the commander of a battle, may sometimes promote the national interest by the kind of boldness that does not calculate the results of military action too closely, but it would be a dangerous error to apply to the whole complex problem of harmonizing military policy with national policy in accordance with an over-all strategic plan the far simpler imperatives of the battlefield. In the field of national strategy, uncalculating heroism is mere self-indulgence at the expense of national survival.

In order that military power may serve as a controllable and predictable instrument of national policy, it must be subjected to an exacting political discipline. This discipline depends upon the existence of controlling political objectives that bear a practical and discernible relation to specific policy goals. These

Reprinted with permission from Robert E. Osgood, *Limited War: The Challenge to American Strategy*, Chicago, The University of Chicago Press, 1957, pp. 13–28.

kinds of objectives are, pre-eminently, those that envision specific configurations of power supporting the nation's security. A treaty recognizing specific international relationships; the control or protection of a certain geographical area; the establishment, recognition, or security of a particular regime; access to certain material resources—these are the kinds of objectives that must form the hard core of politically disciplined power.

One must add, because the rule is so frequently violated in practice, that the controlling political objectives in the use of military power must be not merely desirable but also attainable. Otherwise, there will be no practical and discernible relationships between ends and means. Of course, there are an indefinite number of possible objectives towards which nations may direct military power. One can easily establish a whole hierarchy of interdependent objectives, leading from the most insignificant to the most desirable objective imaginable. However, only a very limited number of these objectives will ever be closely enough related to available national power to serve as a controlling political discipline. Unless the nation's objectives pertain to specific and attainable situations of fact, they will remain in the realm of aspiration, not in the realm of policy; and, consequently, the essential condition for the primacy of politics over force will not exist. Therefore, one can describe the principle of political primacy in terms of the following rule: In the nation's utilization of military power, military means should be subordinated to the ends of national policy through an objective calculation of the most effective methods of attaining concrete, limited, and attainable security objectives.

The principle of political primacy described in this rule is as cogent on moral grounds as on grounds of national self-interest. At the outset, before examining the moral basis of the principle, one must recognize that the primacy of policy over power can be moral only if the political ends toward which military power is directed are themselves moral—or, at least, as consistent with universal principles as the ambiguities of international relations permit. But even if one assumes that this is the case (as I shall for the purposes of this book), one can hardly judge the moral validity of either political ends or military means aside from their interrelationship. The following discussion focuses upon this interrelationship, which is only one aspect of the broader problem of reconciling national policy with liberal, humane ideals that transcend purely national purposes.[1] The principle of political primacy does not embrace all the moral problems that arise in the use of military power. It does not, for example, deal with the question of when or under what circumstances a nation should employ force. However, it is of vital relevance to the question of how and for what purpose a nation should employ force.

The moral basis of political primacy is also its practical basis: the principle that armed force ought to be treated as a means and not an end. Force gains moral justification only by virtue of its relation to some valid purpose beyond its own immediate effect. Furthermore, even when it is a means to a worthy end, armed force must be morally suspect—not only because it is inhumane but because, like all forms of coercion, it is subject to the corruption that accompanies man's exercise of power over man. In Lord Acton's words, "Among all the causes which degrade and demoralize man, power is the most constant and the most active." Certainly, the exercise of military power holds extraordinary opportunities for the degradation of its user and the abuse of those against whom it is used.

But the problem of force is not so easily dismissed. Once we admit that it is morally suspect, we are involved in a moral dilemma. On the one hand, in an ideal world men would dispense with all forms of coercion and settle their conflicts by impartial reference to reason and morality; or, at least, they would channel coercion in social directions by legal controls, which receive the consent of the community. Yet, on the other hand, we know that in the real world men are not sufficiently unselfish or rational to make this ideal practicable. The abolition of force in society would lead either to the anarchy of unrestrained egoism or else to the tyranny of unrestrained despotism. Because of the imperfection of man, force is a moral necessity, an indispensable instrument of justice. Therefore, men are confronted with the fact that their own imperfection makes both force and restraint of force equally imperative from a moral standpoint. There is no way to escape this dilemma. Men can only mitigate its effects. The aim should be, not to abolish force in society, but to moderate it and control it so as to promote social purposes in a manner most compatible with ideal standards of human conduct. How can we translate this principle into the use of military power?

We commonly assume that force is least objectionable morally, as well as most effective practically, when it is exercised with a minimum of violence—preferably, as in the case of police power, when it is implied rather than directly exercised—and when it is exercised legitimately, that is, in accordance with the general consent and approval of society. This assumption suffices for the conduct of everyday affairs within the national community, because the conditions which make it practicable are present— primarily, the conditions that permit force to be exercised in accordance with the orderly procedures of law and government. These legitimate restraints not only moderate force and channel it in social directions; they also provide the individual members of a nation with the basic security they need in order to feel safe in voluntarily subordinating their self-interest to the general welfare.

However, the same procedures for moderating, controlling, and channeling force in socially sanctioned directions do not exist among nations, where the bonds of law, custom, and sympathy are frail and rudimentary. In this age national egoism has such a compelling hold over men's minds that each nation must look to its own independent exercise of power merely in order to survive. The exercise of military power among nations is subject to few of the formal and informal restraints that permit altruism to operate among individuals and groups within nations.

This situation makes a vast difference between what is justifiable in the exercise of force in national society and what is justifiable in international society. It means that among nations military force becomes an indispensable means for promoting national self-interest but a thoroughly ineffective means for attaining the great universal moral goals that transcend national self-interest. This is true, in the first place, because every exercise of military power must be tainted with self-interest and, secondly, because the imperatives of national power and security do not closely conform to the dictates of universal morality.

But military force is not only ineffective as an instrument for attaining transcendent moral goals; it is morally dangerous as well. It is dangerous because the exercise of force for such grandiose goals tends to become an end in itself, subject neither to moral nor practical restraints but only to the intoxication of abstract ideals. The explanation for this tendency lies in the nature of supranational goals. Aside

from the powerful tendency of national egoism to corrupt idealistic pretensions, supranational goals are too remote and too nebulous to discipline a nation's use of force. When the determining objective of force is an ideological goal, there is no way of knowing precisely when force has achieved its purpose, since the tangible results of force have no clear relation to the intangible tests by which the attainment of such goals must be measured. What a conflict of wills is put to the test of force, the final restraint and control of force must be the resolution of the conflict by accommodation, unless it is to continue until one party obtains complete acquiescence or both parties become impotent. But differences of principle, unlike conflicts of interest, by their very nature resist accommodation. Rather, they tend to arouse passions that can be satisfied only by the unconditional surrender of the adversary. Therefore, in effect, the great idealistic goals, once put to the test of force, become the rationalization of purely military objectives, governed only by the blind impulse of destruction.

That is not to say that moral principles are unjustifiable or irrelevant in a nation's use of military power or that the exercise of force, either overtly or tacitly, cannot indirectly promote ideal ends. The point is simply that universal principles must be translated into practical courses of action, directed toward achieving specific situations of fact appropriate to the nature of force, in order to constitute truly moral and rational guides for the exercise of military power. Only if the realization of these principles is conceived as the by-product of attaining concrete limited objectives can they exert a civilizing influence upon national egoism. The great idealistic goals that have traditionally provided the dynamism and inspiration of American foreign policy, insofar as they can be attained at all by military means, must be attained through a series of moderate steps toward intermediate objectives, defined in terms of national power and interest.

An important corollary of the principle of political primacy may be called the economy of force. It prescribes that in the use of armed force as an instrument of national policy no greater force should be employed than is necessary to achieve the objectives toward which it is directed; or, stated another way, the dimensions of military force should be proportionate to the value of the objectives at stake.

Clearly, this is an expedient rule; for unless

a nation has a large surplus of available military power in relation to its policy objectives, one can hardly conceive of the effective use of power without the efficient use as well. Moreover, as an examination of the interaction between military means and political ends will show, the proportionate use of force is a necessary condition for the limitation and effective control of war.

The moral implications of an economy of force are no less significant. For, as we have acknowledged, the violence and destruction that accompany the use of force are an obvious, though sometimes necessary, evil. Therefore, it is morally incumbent to use force deliberately and scrupulously and as sparingly as is consistent with the attainment of the national objectives at stake.

In applying the principle of political primacy we must make allowances for the legitimate claims of military considerations upon national policy as well as the other way around. The relationship between military means and political ends should be understood as a two-way relationship, such that the ends are kept within range of the means as well as the means made adequate to attain the ends. Common sense tells us that a nation must decide what it ought to do in light of what it is able to do; that it should establish policy objectives in the light of military capabilities. Otherwise, military power will be no more effective or politically responsible than if it were employed as an end in itself.

Moreover, we must recognize the fact that, however scrupulously we may seek to impose political discipline upon military power, military power will remain an imperfect instrument of politics. To a disturbing extent it bears its own unpredictable effects, which create, alter, or preclude the objective for which it can feasibly be employed.

However, this does not obviate the necessity of determining the claims of military means upon political ends—so far as conscious control permits—within the general framework of national strategy; for in the absence of such a framework there can be no clear criterion for judging the validity of any claims. In other words, if military power is to serve as a rational instrument of policy, the entire process of balancing ends and means, coordinating military with non-military means, must be subordinated to the controlling purpose of pursuing national policy objectives according to the most effective strategic plan.

War as an instrument of national policy

THE principles of political primacy and the economy of force apply to the whole spectrum of military power in its various uses, not just to its active use in warfare; but this book is concerned primarily with their application to war itself. There is a good reason for stressing this aspect of military power: In all uses of military power, whether overt, covert, or tacit; in all accumulation, allocation, and distribution of military power; and in all military planning there is at least an implicit assumption that the basic measure of a nation's power is its ability to wage war in defense of its interests. In the struggle for power among nations, the ability to wage war has something of the status of a common currency by which nations can roughly measure their capacity to achieve certain basic needs and desires—ultimately, if necessary, by violence.

However, the ability to wage war cannot be measured in purely quantitative terms of military power. A nation can be adequately prepared to wage one kind of war under one set of circumstances and inadequately prepared to wage another kind of war under a different set of circumstances. The utility of a nation's military power, either in diplomacy or in war itself, will depend not merely upon the size and firepower of the military establishment but also upon its suitability for countering the specific kind of military threats impinging upon the nation's interests and objectives. Thus the effectiveness of military power depends upon the nature of the military threat, the nation's estimate of that threat, and its ability to fight the kind of war that will successfully meet the threat. It depends, equally, upon the nation's will to wage war; the way in which it combines force with diplomacy; how it enters war, how it terminates war, and how it conducts policy after a war. In other words, the effectiveness of military power depends not only upon a nation's physical and technical command of the means of warfare but, just as much, upon the whole conception of war—especially, the relation of war to international politics. And this conception of war in reflected throughout the whole spectrum of military power—in defense policies and the formulation of military strategy as well as in the actual conduct of war. Therefore, since a nation's military power depends upon its conception of war, it behooves us to act upon a conception of war that is compatible with the use of military power as a rational instrument of national policy. That conception must be based upon the principle of political primacy.

But, first, let us be clear what we mean by "war." War can be defined most simply as an organized clash of arms between sovereign states seeking to assert their wills against one another. However, it would be a mistake to regard war as a single, simple, uniform entity or as an independent thing it itself, to which one applies a wholly different set of rules and considerations that properly apply to other forms of international conflict. It is more realistic in the light of the complex and multifarious nature of international conflict to regard war as the upper extremity of a whole scale of international conflict of ascending intensity and scope. All along this scale one may think of sovereign nations asserting their wills in conflict with other nations by a variety of military and non-military means of coercion, but no definition can determine precisely at what point on the scale conflict becomes "war." In this sense, war is a matter of degree, which itself contains different degrees of intensity and scope.

Accepting this description of war, we must see how the principle of political primacy applies to the conduct of war. The primacy of politics in war means, simply, that military operations should be conducted so as to achieve concrete, limited, and attainable security objectives, in order that war's destruction and violence may be rationally directed toward legitimate ends of national policy.

On the face of it, the validity of this principle seems clear enough; and yet in its practical implications it does not meet with ready or universal acceptance. In fact, quite contrary principles of war have commonly received the applause of democratic peoples. For example, in the Kellogg-Briand Pact of 1928 the United States and fourteen other nations promised to "renounce war as an instrument of national policy in their relations with one another," thereby expressing in treaty form a widespread conviction that is still congenial to the American outlook. The principle is valid, of course, if it is interpreted merely as a proscription against unprovoked aggression; but insofar as it implies the divorce of war from the ends of national interest, it is valid neither practically nor ideally. In this sense, nations might better renounce the use of war as an instrument of *anything but* national policy.

Karl von Clausewitz, the famous German military theorist of the nineteenth century, expounded the principle of political primacy with an unsurpassed cogency. In his famous work *On War* he concluded his comprehensive analysis of the mass of factors comprising war by singling out their unifying characteristic. This, he believed, was the essential basis for apprehending all war's complexities and contradictions from a single standpoint, without which one could not form consistent judgments. He described that characteristic in the following words:

> Now this unity is the conception that war is only a part of political intercourse, therefore by no means an independent thing in itself. We know, of course, that war is only caused through the political intercourse of governments and nations; but in general it is supposed that such intercourse is broken off by war, and that a totally different state of things ensues, subject to no laws but its own. We maintain, on the contrary, that war is nothing but a continuation of political intercourse with an admixture of other means. . . . Accordingly, war can never be separated from political intercourse, and if, in the consideration of the matter, this occurs anywhere, all the threads of the different relations are, in a certain sense, broken, and we have before us a senseless thing without an object.[2]

As a description of the actual nature of war, Clausewitz' dictum that war continues political intercourse is by no means universally true; but as a statement of what war should be, it is the only view in accord with universal moral principles and national self-interest, for it is the only view consistent with the use of force as a means rather than an end. If we find this view as repugnant as the sentiment of the Kellogg-Briand Pact is congenial, then we have not fully grasped the practical and moral necessity of disciplining mass violence. On the other hand, many who can agree with Clausewitz' dictum in the abstract find it difficult in practice to accept the corollary that victory is not an end in itself. Nevertheless, the corollary is logically inseparable from the principle of political primacy. For if war is not an end in itself, but only a means to some political objective, then military victory cannot rightly be a self-sufficient end. If war is a continuation of political intercourse, then success in war can be properly measured only in political terms and not purely in terms of crushing the enemy. To be sure, a measure of military success is the necessary condition for achieving the political objectives of war; but the most effective military measures for overcoming the enemy's resistance are not necessarily the most effective measures for securing the continuing ends of national policy in the aftermath of war.

Therefore, one of the most important practical implications of the principle of political primacy is this: The whole conduct of warfare —its strategy, its tactics, its termination—must be governed by the nature of a nation's political objectives and not by independent standards of military success or glory. Statesmen, far from suspending diplomacy during war, must make every effort to keep diplomacy alive throughout the hostilities, to the end that war may be as nearly a continuation of political intercourse as possible rather than "a senseless thing without an object."

The dimensions of war

THE practical requirements of maintaining the primacy of politics in the conduct of war are not so clear as the general principle, for the general principle must be qualified in the light of the actual conditions of war. The most serious qualification results from the difficulty of controlling the consequences of war as the dimensions of violence and destruction increase. This difficulty emphasizes the importance of striving for an economy of force.

Despite the theoretical validity of the principle of political primacy, in practice we must recognize that war is not a delicate instrument for achieving precise political ends. It is a crude instrument of coercion and persuasion. The violence and destruction of war set off a chain of consequences than can be neither perfectly controlled nor perfectly anticipated and that may, therefore, contravene the best laid plans for achieving specific configurations of power and particular political relations among nations.

At the same time, the legitimate claims of military means upon political ends are particularly strong when national conflict reaches the extremity of war. The sheer physical circumstances of the military struggle may narrowly restrict the choice of military means that nations can safely employ. To subordinate military operations to political considerations might mean sacrificing the military success indispensable for the attainment of any worthwhile national purpose at all. Therefore, in practice, military necessities and the fortunes of war may determine the nature of the feasible political choices, and the subordination of certain political considerations to military requirements may be the necessary condition for avoiding defeat.

However the need for compromising political objectives in the light of immediate military necessities only qualifies, it does not negate, the applicability of the principle of political primacy; because the wisdom of such compromises must still be judged by their relation to some superior political objective if purely military objectives are not to become ends in themselves. Clausewitz acknowledged this very qualification and reconciled it with his view of war as a continuation of political intercourse in words that are compelling today. While recognizing that the political object of war could not regulate every aspect of war, he nevertheless maintained that war would be sheer uncontrolled violence without this unifying factor.

Now if we reflect that war has its origin in a political object, we see that this first motive, which called it into existence, naturally remains the first and highest consideration to be regarded in its conduct. But the political object is not on that account a despotic lawgiver; it must adapt itself to the nature of the means at its disposal and is often thereby completely changed, but it must always be the first thing to be considered. Policy, therefore, will permeate the whole action of war and exercise a continual influence upon it, so far as the nature of the explosive forces in it allow. . . . What now still remains peculiar to war relates merely to the peculiar character of the means it uses. The art of war in general and the commander in each particular case can demand that the tendencies and designs of policy shall be not incompatible with these means, and the claim is certainly no trifling one. But however powerfully it may react on political designs in particular cases, still it must always be regarded only as a modification of them; for the political design is the object, while war is the means, and the means can never be thought of apart from the object.[3]

If, then, the principle of political primacy holds good despite the considerable claims of military necessity the task of statesmen is to minimize the difficulties and maximize the potentialities of political control. There are three closely related rules of general application that would greatly facilitate this purpose:

1. Statesmen should scrupulously limit the controlling political objectives of war and clearly communicate the limited nature of these objectives to the enemy. The reason for this is

that nations tend to observe a rough proportion between the scope of their objectives and the scale of the military effort; that is, they tend to exert a degree of force proportionate to the value they ascribe to the objectives at stake. Therefore, the more ambitious the objectives of one belligerent, the more important it is to the other belligerent to deny those objectives and the greater the scale of force both belligerents will undertake in order to gain their own objectives and frustrate the enemy's. In this manner a spiral of expanding objectives and mounting force may drive warfare beyond the bounds of political control.

2. Statesmen should make every effort to maintain an active diplomatic intercourse toward the end of terminating the war by a negotiated settlement on the basis of limited objectives. This rule rests on the following considerations. War is a contest between national wills. The final resolution of this contest must be some sort of political settlement, or war will lack any object except the purely military object of overcoming the enemy. To the extent that statesmen keep political intercourse active during hostilities, war becomes a political contest rather than a purely military contest. The immediate object of political intercourse must be a negotiated settlement, but a negotiated settlement is impossible among belligerents of roughly equal power unless their political objectives are limited. This consideration becomes especially important in the light of the fact that even a small nation that possessed an arsenal of nuclear weapons might, in desperation, inflict devastating destruction upon a larger power rather than accept humiliating terms.

3. Statesmen should try to restrict the physical dimensions of war as stringently as compatible with the attainment of the objectives at stake, since the opportunities for the political control of war—especially under the conditions of modern war, with its tremendous potentialities of destruction—tend to decrease as the dimensions of war increase and tend to increase as the dimensions of war decrease. This proportion between the dimensions of war and its susceptibility to political control is neither universally true nor mathematically exact; but as a rough generalization it finds important verification in the history of war. Three underlying reasons for this fact are especially germane to the warfare of this century:

a. The greater the scale and scope of war, the more likely the war will result in extreme changes in the configurations of national power.

These extreme changes are not amenable to control; they result more from the internal logic of the military operations than from the designs of statesmen. At the same time, they tend to create vast new political problems which confound the expectations and plans of the victor and the vanquished alike. Moreover, modern war can change the configurations of power not only through the massive destruction of material and human resources but also by disrupting the whole social, economic, and political fabric of existence. On the other hand, when the destructiveness and the resulting disturbance of the configurations of power are moderate, the chances of anticipating and controlling its political effects are proportionately greater; and the whole character of warfare, in proportion as it is removed from the domination of military events, becomes more clearly a continuation of political intercourse.

b. The magnitude of a war's threat to national survival is likely to be proportionate to the scale and the scope of hostilities. But in proportion as the belligerents' very survival is threatened, they must logically place a higher priority upon immediate military considerations as compared to political considerations. For when war reaches extremities, a belligerent must calculate that even the slightest inference with the destruction of the enemy in the most effective manner possible for the sake of some uncertain political maneuver will involve an exorbitant risk of the enemy destroying that belligerent first. Military victory, no matter how it comes about, at least provides a nation with the opportunity to solve its political problems later; whereas the dubious attempt to manipulate the vast and unpredictable forces of war in precise political ways may end by placing this postwar opportunity at the disposal of the enemy. When immediate military considerations are at such a premium, political control must obviously suffer accordingly; but, by the same reasoning, when the scale and scope of war impose no such immediate threat of total defeat, the primacy of politics can more readily be asserted.

c. As the dimensions of violence and destruction increase, war tends to arouse passionate fears and hatreds, which, regardless of the dictates of cold reason, become the determining motives in the conduct of war. These passions find their outlet in the blind, unreasoning destruction of the enemy. They are antithetical to the political control of war, because political control would restrict the use of force. Thus the greater the scale of violence, the greater the suffering and sacrifice, and the greater the suffering and sacrifice, the less the inclination either to fight or to make peace for limited, prosaic ends. Instead, nations will seek compensation in extreme demands upon the enemy or in elevating the war into an ideological crusade. Unlimited aims will, in turn, demand unlimited force. Thus, in effect, the scale of war and the passions of war, interacting, will create a purely military phenomenon beyond effective political guidance.

In the light of this proportion between the dimensions of warfare and its susceptibility to political control, the importance of preserving an economy of force is apparent. For if modern warfare tends to exceed the bounds of political control as it increases in magnitude, then it is essential to limit force to a scale that is no greater then necessary to achieve the objectives at stake. By the same token, if war becomes more susceptible to political control in proportion as its dimensions are moderated, then the economy of force is an essential condition of the primacy of politics in war.

The rationale of limited war

IF this analysis is sound, the principal justification of limited war lies in the fact that it maximizes the opportunities for the effective use of military force as a rational instrument of national policy. In accordance with this rationale, limited war would be equally desirable if nuclear weapons had never been invented. However, the existence of these and other weapons of mass destruction clearly adds great urgency to limitation. Before nations possessed nuclear weapons, they might fain worthwhile objectives consonant with the sacrifices of war even in a war fought with their total resources. But now the stupendous destruction accompanying all-out nuclear war makes it hard to conceive of such a war serving any rational purpose except the continued existence of the nation as a political unit—and, perhaps, the salvage of the remnants of civilization—in the midst of the wreckage. Only by carefully limiting the dimensions of warfare can nations minimize the risk of war becoming an intolerable disaster.

Beyond this general reason for limiting war, which applies to all nations equally, there are special reasons why democratic nations should prefer limited war. Obviously, limited war is more compatible with a respect for human life and an aversion to violence. But apart from humanitarian considerations, we should recognize that liberal institutions and values do not thrive amid the social, economic and political dislocations that inevitably follow in the wake of unlimited war. The liberal and humane spirit needs an environment conducive to compromise and moderation. Only tyranny is likely to profit from the festering hatreds and resentments that accompany sudden and violent upheavals in the relations among governments and peoples. The aftermath of the two total wars of this century amply demonstrates this fact.

The external interests of democratic powers are not necessarily identified with the status quo in all respects, nor do they require that the rest of the world be democratic. Clearly, neither condition is feasible. However, they do require that the inevitable adjustments and accommodations among governments and peoples should be sufficiently moderate and gradual to permit orderly change. Long-run interests as well as immediate interests of democratic nations lie in preserving an external environment conducive to relative stability and security in the world.

The mitigation of sudden and violent change becomes all the more important in a period like the present, when the most resourceful tyranny in the modern world strives to capture an indigenous revolution among colonial and formerly colonial peoples who yearn to acquire the Western blessings of national independence and economic power but who are fearfully impatient with the evolutionary processes by which the West acquired them. In these areas peace may be too much to expect, but we can anticipate revolutionary chaos or Communist domination if the world is seized by the convulsions of unlimited war.

Finally, we must add to these considerations one of even broader significance. As long as the necessary international political conditions for the limitation of armaments do not exist, the best assurance that armaments will not destroy civilization lies in the limitation of their use.

Notes

1. I have grappled with this broader problem in *Ideals and Self-Interest in America's Foreign Relations* (Chicago: University of Chicago Press, 1953). See especially the Introduction.
2. Karl von Clausewitz, *On War*, trans. by O. J. Matthijs Jolles (Washington, D.C.: Combat Forces Press, 1953), p. 596.
3. *Ibid.*, p. 16.

Klaus Knorr

Unconventional warfare: strategy and tactics in internal political strife

IN INTERNAL WAR, the population can be classified as follows:[1] (A) Insurgents, (B) Giving some support to the insurgents, (C) Supporting neither the insurgents nor the incumbents, (D) Giving some support to the incumbents, (E) Incumbents.

A complete developmental construct of full-fledged internal war would distinguish three possible stages of violence, in which terrorism, guerrilla operations, and regular warfare, respectively, predominate. These stages were reached successively, for example, during the war in French Indo-China.[2] How to manage the transition from one stage to another is an important problem for insurgent leaders.[3] This paper, however, is concerned only with the second stage, in which irregular warfare is the predominant mode of military action.

The middle stage

THE general theory of war applies, of course, to irregular warfare,[4] and the strategy of irregular war is largely an adaptation of the general principles of military strategy.[5] The modern theory of military strategy and tactics[6] in irregular warfare was largely developed by Clausewitz in the chapter of *On War* entitled "Arming the Nation" and somewhat refined by subsequent writers, especially Mao. The following brief presentation of the military aspects of irregular warfare draws largely on the writings of Clausewitz and Mao.[7]

In the middle stage, the crucial problem for the insurgents is to compensate for their inferiority in regular military forces and gain time until either (1) the extension of their political influence, relative to that of the incumbents, causes the latter's authority to collapse or yield to the insurgents' demands, or (2) insurgent military strength expands sufficiently, relative to that of the incumbents, to seek a military decision in regular warfare.

WAR OF ATTRITION

The war in the middle stage, then, is one of attrition—attrition of men, supplies, the will to fight—in short, of all the elements that make up military power. In order to compensate for their inferiority in regular military strength, the insurgents may draw on any one of several factors in which they may be superior—leadership, morale, discipline, intelligence, mobility, concealment—and they may force the opponent to battle in a theater of war in which physical features—such as mountains, jungle, swamp, deserts—and poor means of communication make it difficult for regular forces to capitalize on their superior numbers and equipment. It will be insurgent strategy not to accept positional warfare and head-on major battles but to induce the opponent to disperse his forces, to diffuse his strength over space, so that, though these forces are superior *in toto*, they will be small and vulnerable enough in many localities to permit confident attack by insurgent troops. In such local combat the insurgents seek to exploit terrain, surprise, and possibly larger forces,[8] and they will disengage themselves as soon as the incumbent command pulls in reinforcements.

As Clausewitz says: "There is always still time to die."[9] And as Mao observes, the suc-

Reprinted from *The Annals of the American Academy of Political and Social Science*, Vol. 341, May 1962, pp. 53–64.

cessful rule is the " . . . swift attack and withdrawal, swift concentration and dispersal";[10] and "quick decisions" are at a premium in protracted war.[11] Or, in Mao's famous formula, " . . . enemy advances, we retreat; enemy halts, we harass; enemy tires, we attack; enemy retreats, we pursue."[12] In luring the enemy's troops into traps, in preying on his lines of communication, ambushing his columns, and raiding his isolated garrisons, although the over-all strategy is defensive, tactical operations are aggressive whenever and wherever circumstances permit.

This strategy, based on surprise and, hence, on mobility and deception, makes Clausewitz liken the insurgent's irregular forces to a nebulous "vapory essence," a "mist" which never condenses in a large solid body, but only sufficiently and transiently in order to permit attack, under favorable circumstances, here or there. Similarly, T. E. Lawrence speaks of them as if they were a "gas," and concludes that making war upon a rebellion is "like eating soup with a knife."[13]

In conducting his kind of irregular war, the insurgents will exploit whatever weakness the incumbent forces may exhibit. Being regular forces, the latter may lack doctrine, training, and equipment for fighting guerrillas, their leadership may be hidebound, and their morale weak. They may depend upon a large logistical tail and be roadbound and clumsy in maneuver. They are likely to be easily visible and noisy,[14] and, above all, the special obligations upon the incumbent authority to protect the population, to display its power everywhere, will induce it to scatter troops over many local posts. Thus, if the balance of power is right, and adroitly exploited, a small irregular force can match or even paralyze one ten or more times larger.[15] The protracted, irregular war is like "a slow, gradual fire"[16] which eats away at the incumbents, and the successful insurgents will be able eventually to shift to an offensive war of movement, wresting control of territory from the opponent, and finally defeating him in major battle.

SABOTAGE AND TERRORISM

Two kinds of actions, which may be the sole form of insurgent resort to physical violence during the initial phase of rebellion, are of subsidiary importance in the middle stage. These are sabotage, which is directed against things, and terrorism, which is directed against persons. The main functions of sabotage are to make the theater of war more favorable to guerrilla operations by blowing up bridges, rail lines, and the like, and to increase attrition of the opponent's resources by destroying arsenals, power stations, and all kinds of economic assets, especially those of importance to the incumbents' war effort. Sabotage may also serve the purpose of demonstrating to the public at large the inability of the incumbent government to protect the country and, by inciting the incumbents to initiate sharp and perhaps indiscriminate measures of repression or reprisal, thus weakening the public's identification with the incumbents.[17]

The employment of terror is more controversial. There is general agreement that the insurgents' resort to it tends to be most successful when it is discriminate, because it thus runs less risk of alienating the public. Practitioners and theorists approve of its discriminatory use (1) against persons conspicuously identified with the cause of the incumbents in order to put pressure on members of categories D and E (see introductory paragraph); and (2) to punish traitors and informers in categories A, B, and C in order to safeguard the security of insurgent forces and operations. Insurgents have employed terror more generally, notably against members of category C, in order to secure intelligence and supplies on the basis of fear.[18] But such use of terror is rejected by most rebel leaders and theorists on the ground that, for ultimate success, the insurgents require increasing voluntary identification with their cause,[19] although even indiscriminate terror may shake the public's confidence in the incumbent government and its ability to maintain security.[20] From a theoretical point of view, incidentally, the concept of terrorism, as generally used, is very fuzzy. It is not clear whether indiscriminate practice is not of the essence of terrorism; if it is, then what is commonly referred to as discriminatory terrorism is either acts of war against the incumbents or the administration of justice based on the penal code of the insurgent counter-authorities.

Assets and utilization

I HAVE already identified the main military assets —such as military manpower, morale, security —which, if sufficient in the aggregate, will enable the insurgents to assert themselves in the strategic situation just described. I also pointed out that there is a degree of substitutability among the assets, though only a degree.

Obviously, even the best leadership and the highest morale can only within limits make up for a lack of numbers or supplies, and so on. It is not profitable, however, to generalize about thresholds of substitutability or about optimum combinations of military assets, for these matters, as Mao never tired of reiterating, depend upon the circumstances of time and place. Above all, they depend on the structure and magnitude of the military assets available to the incumbents and on the prevailing balance of political influence.

SOURCES

It is worthwhile, however, to raise certain general questions about the sources of these military assets and about certain general conditions governing their proper utilization. For military manpower, intelligence about and security from the opponent, and food and similar supplies, the insurgents are likely to depend heavily upon support from people in categories A and B—and, of course, on expanding these groups by recruitment from categories C through E. Weapons and other military supplies are likely to be manufactured by the insurgents, captured from the incumbents, and imported from abroad. Indeed, the procurement of some kinds of military assets from abroad can be substituted for domestic procurement.

But one suspects that there are also definite political limits to this kind of substitution. Are these limits more severe for the recruitment of combatants than for the receipt of equipment, supplies, diplomatic support, and military instruction? Will the employment of foreign soldiers by either insurgents or incumbents be resented by the rest of the population and induce it to give more support to the other party? How much does this effect tend to vary with the nationality of foreign soldiery? For example, would the use of foreign Arabs in the internal war of an Arab country arouse as much resentment —if it were resented at all—as the employment of non-Arabs? How do other characteristics of foreign soldiers—color, culture, comportment, and the like—affect this response? What are the consequences if both insurgents and incumbents make conspicuous use of foreign combatants? At what point, as the employment of foreign military assets rises, does the war cease to be internal and become international?

BASE AREAS

The transformation of military assets into military outputs demands organization and a process of production. This requires space as well as time—a problem beyond the purview of this paper, which assumes that the transition to the middle phase has been managed. From this arises, as already mentioned, the importance of base areas or redoubts for which, again, foreign sanctuaries can act as substitutes, as in the internal wars of Laos and Vietnam.

There is general agreement that, against an opponent who is greatly superior in regular strength, the insurgents' ability to establish, maintain, and replace base areas depends on one or more of three special conditions: (1) physically difficult terrain; (2) a low level of economic development and, hence, of means of transportation; and (3), to a lesser extent, the size of the country involved. The first two factors tend to reduce the mobility and effectiveness of regular armies; the third will tend to scatter the incumbents' regular forces, if their strength, though great in relation to the insurgents', is small relative to the size of the country—for example, China.

It is indeed plausible that the classic type of guerrilla war will, by itself, only occur in the setting of an essentially underdeveloped area in which natural obstacles have not been overcome by modern techniques of communication.[21] In an industrial area, internal war is more likely to take the forms of *coups d'état*, brief uprisings,[22] terrorism and—provided the armed forces are politically split—regular warfare.[23]

The desirable properties of a base area vary with the insurgents' requirements which, be it noted, may well make conflicting demands. A base in terrain which is geographically difficult, provided with inadequate lines of communication, and, hence, is economically relatively poor and sparsely populated may constitute a net advantage to weak insurgent forces which are on the defensive. However, from the viewpoint of manpower, supplies,[24] and political communication and prestige, a populous area with presumably better means of communication is an obvious advantage. The inclination of insurgents to trade off one set of advantages for the other will obviously depend on the balance of military capability between insurgents and incumbents.

USE OF REGULARS

The three special conditions for the maintenance of insurgent base areas can obviously be relaxed if the war is not purely one of guerrilla operations but becomes mixed because the military assets of the insurgents are sufficient to permit them to oppose the incumbents' army, at least in some areas and at some times, in regular though fluid warfare. Thus, Tito's partisans were eventually able to challenge the Axis troops in open and populous parts of Yugoslavia—for example, Slovenia.

In that event, the insurgent forces will be composed not only of the usual full-time and part-time guerrillas,[25] but also of fairly large units capable of regular combat. Even when the Communist fortunes ran low, after 1928, Mao had units manned by thousands of men, vaguely referred to as armies or divisions, and the Vietminh had regular divisions as early as 1950.[26] On the other hand, it is sometimes claimed that, without some support from regular troops, guerrillas are not very effective against regular forces, may be unable to maintain bases, and may be forced to shift to highly dispersed operations in which acts of sabotage and terrorism predominate.[27] Pye cites this absence of some regular force as a decisive weakness of the Communist insurrection in Malaya.[28]

An interesting, because it is ambiguous, example is furnished by the present organization of the Viet Cong in South Vietnam. Their total number of combatants was estimated at from 12,000 to 14,000 in 1961, in addition to part-time guerrillas and sympathizers in the village "cells." The full-time guerrillas were grouped in twenty-seven "regular" battalions operating from fairly well-defined bases in jungle or marsh land and in forty-three regional companies of "local troops at the district level" which were "true guerrillas" who supported the "regulars" in the battalions but were always on the move from village to village. Upon the approach of strong government columns, these battalions do not defend their bases, but melt into the jungle or retreat across the country's boundary and re-establish bases where and when conditions permit.[29] Castro did not command large units of regular forces in his struggle with Batista. On this matter, no general conclusion can be derived from either theory or historical experience. The essentiality of a regular military component obviously depends upon many variable factors, notably on the strength of the incumbents' forces.

Political confrontation

THERE is far less focused theory about the political, as distinct from the military, confrontation between insurgents and incumbents in the type of internal war under discussion. It is generally recognized that the military assets and strength of both sides depend heavily on their political influence in the community; and it is generally agreed that—directly as well as indirectly—the outcome of the internal struggle depends heavily on the relative success of the two opponents in their competition for political influence. But, from these general observations, the literature jumps immediately to a set of specific, tactical prescriptions for waging the political struggle.

The general problem is clear enough. If internal war breaks out and progresses to the stage of prolonged but predominantly irregular warfare, the incumbent authorities have obviously frustrated, or appeared to frustrate, irreducible expectations of goal achievement, not necessarily on the part of the majority of the population, but—as a minimum—on the part of groups sufficient in number, skill, ambition, and influence to set themselves up as a rival authority. The incumbents may have brought about this critical degree of political disunity because they appeared to be grossly unresponsive to the goal aspirations of the rebels, their supporters, and possibly the population in category C or because, though not thus unresponsive, they appeared to be grossly inefficient in managing the community's goal achievement.[30]

Except when the insurgents are out for independence on a high degree of autonomy, they will wage the political struggle by impressing the community (1) with the inefficiency, corruption, and injustice of the incumbents and, hence, with the ultimate illegitimacy of their claim to authority, and (2) with the expectation that a government formed, or a constitution prepared, by the rebels would lead to an enlarged output, and a just distribution, of such values as income, security, respect, and political influence. The insurgent claim may be expressed in an ideology or social myth sharply conflicting with that of the incumbents or manipulate relatively simple symbols such as land and bread.[31] Contrariwise, the incumbent government may try to discredit the rebel claims and try to impress the community with the legitimacy of its claim to government and with the basic efficiency and justice of its policies.

ASYMMETRIES

There are several aspects of this political confrontation which have not been studied or not studied sufficiently. It may, of course, be assumed, and turn out upon further study, that everything else about this situation depends so much on the concrete circumstances of each case that it is an infertile field for generalization. But the assumption is not obviously true and merits testing. For example, are there not important asymmetries in the rival political postures which may hold for a large number of actual cases? Will not the incumbent authorities tend to command large advantages in terms of administrative and economic, as well as military, capabilities, and in terms of legal or traditional legitimacy and hence, in the reluctance of large parts of the population to defy the incumbent authorities or to withhold support from them?

On the other hand, once an internal war has been precipitated and has progressed to the stage under discussion—which could rarely happen without, at least apparently, serious deficiencies in the performance of the incumbent government—will the latter not enter the political struggle with an essentially defensive posture? Will it not be difficult for the incumbents, in making their counterclaims, to proceed to an offensive political posture, since any promises of reform may be suspected of being inspired by tactical opportunism rather than a genuine commitment to change? Will the promises of the insurgents be more readily believed than those of the incumbents? In the political component of internal war, are there other asymmetries resulting from the fact that a legitimate government is making war on a proportion of its own people?

COMMUNICATIONS

The means available to both sides for defining the issue in one's favor and for establishing political claims and counterclaims fall into three groups: (1) verbal communications through various media; (2) other symbolic acts to demonstrate the virtues of one's side; and (3) actions designed to incite the opponent to discreditable behavior. The general availability of these means is recognized in the literature. But again, little attempt has been made to inquire systematically into the conditions of their use and their effectiveness in internal war and into the asymmetries in the ability of each side to employ them.

If internal wars of the kind under discussion are likely to occur only in countries which are relatively underdeveloped economically, then the problems of propaganda, psychological warfare, and political warfare[32] will have to be studied within the context not only of internal rather than external conflict but also of a primarily agrarian rather than industrial setting. Regarding the latter contrast, due allowance will have to be made for striking disparities in literacy, in the development of mass media of communication, and in basic political structures and processes.[33] For instance, how is the political component of internal war affected if, compared with industrial societies, the country at war is economically underdeveloped and highly deficient in ethnic, cultural, and political integration and, hence, exhibits sharp discontinuities in political communication? In such a setting, what are the target characteristics of urban workers, the armed services, bureaucratic personnel, the peasantry? To what extent do discontinuities in political communication make it likely that sizable sections of the population—especially when organized on a communal basis—will, in effect, "sit out" the internal war?

MOTIVATIONS

Indeed, one would like to see more systematic study of the factors conditioning the reactions of people in categories B, C, and D. Instead of only formulating a participant structure on the basis of behavior, one would then want to proceed to a structure of relevant motivations which lie behind behavior in categories A to E. Thus, people in categories B and D—and even in A and E—may support the insurgents or incumbents because they sympathize with them and their cause or because, speculating on the outcome of the internal war, they want to derive benefits from being identified with the winning side or at least to avoid penalties for having supported the loser.

Again, the population in C may fall into three subcategories: (1) those who, though aware of the political aims of the contenders, are politically neutral toward them;[34] (2) those who have political preferences for one side or the other but do not want to run the risk of being identified with the loser; and (3) those who are politically ignorant of, or apathetic toward, the internal conflict. It is precisely in relatively underdeveloped countries that this third group may be very large and that the internal war may be conducted by relatively small minorities. Clearly, the way the political war is waged, and its outcome, depend heavily on the structure of motivation and political engagement; and, clearly, the support which the contestants can derive for their military effort depends on the structure of motivation—for example, on the extent to which people are prepared to run the risk of overt or covert support. The structure of motivations, and its manipulability, thus circumscribe the internal war potential of insurgents and incumbents.

ISSUES

It has also been recognized that the means employed to wage the political struggle must be related to the specific issues over which the internal war is fought. If the insurgents are relatively weak politically, the incumbents may win by treating the rebellion as a mere matter of restoring legitimate law and order. On the other hand, if the insurgents are politically strong and not foredoomed to military defeat, the incumbents will be under pressure to go beyond this position and respond positively to the political as well as the military challenge. Mere propaganda and limited reforms may then not suffice, and the incumbents face a dilemma which calls for more serious study than it has received.

Once internal war has reached a serious pitch, to what extent, and under what conditions, will incumbents be able to offer the population a better future than the *status quo ante* or even to identify themselves with revolutionary demands?[35] In the case of wars of secession, this is obviously difficult (for example, French Indo-China, Algeria), though not impossible (for example, British Malaya). But it should also be difficult in other cases of internal strife, if only in terms of accepting the cost and of preserving unity among the incumbents and their supporters. Batista was unable to do so in Cuba, and it is widely believed that, despite a strong military superiority, the government of South Vietnam has found it impossible to defeat the Viet Cong because it has no political hold over a large part of the peasant population. This problem also raises the further question of the circumstances under which major accommodation to rebel demands will tend to give victory to the insurgent rather than the incumbent side.

Insurgent tactics

THROUGHOUT his writings on the subject, Mao stresses that political mobilization is "the most important problem"[36] in internal war. The primacy of political penetration and conquest over military actions was emphasized by General Giap, the Vietminh military commander.[37] The strategy of fighting the political war must be organized and formulated in a set of appropriate tactical precepts. The insurgents require base areas for this purpose as well as for sustaining the military contest; their rival authority is reinforced if it commands a territory over which it holds sway; and—as pointed out in the foregoing—physically difficult and economically underdeveloped areas are a drawback from the political point of view. From this point of view also, a foreign base, even though militarily convenient, is an incomplete substitute for a domestic base or bases. However, even though not needed on military grounds, a foreign base may be desirable because it facilitates the internationalization of the internal war—for example, generates diplomatic support which may be of value to the insurgents, especially when they are fighting for independence. However, the question arises to what extent, and under which conditions, the availability of foreign bases is also a disadvantage because it is, or is suspected of being, purchased in exchange for political concessions to a foreign power.

Usually, insurgent organization shows a close integration of political and military leadership, features the appointment of political officers or commissars,[38] and requires the guerrilla soldier to be a political as well as a military fighter.[39] From this conception it follows that the rebel guerrilla must adhere to rigid discipline, conduct himself scrupulously in his dealings with the civilian population, pay for food and other goods (if only in IOU's), help the peasant population at harvest time, and treat captured enemy soldiers with leniency in order to encourage desertion from the incumbents' ranks. For the same reason, the insurgent fighters are given political and ideological as well as military training, the civil administration in rebel-occupied territory is sensitive to the goals and preferences of the population, and—in waging war—short-term military advantages are not rarely foregone in order to reap political gain.[40]

Conclusion

BY way of conclusion, it may be said that, for the internal war in the middle stage to be in equilibrium (neither side winning), the distribution of some of the main factors is likely to be as follows:

Advantage (X) on the side of:

	Insurgents	Incumbents
Regular military strength		X
Military logistics		X
Other supplies		X
Military intelligence	X	
Military morale and discipline	X	
Skill in guerrilla warfare	X	
Integration of political and military leadership	X	
Civilian support	X	
Foreign support	?	?

There should be no argument about the likelihood—in terms of a number of cases of prolonged guerrilla war—that the incumbents have the advantage in regular military strength, logistics, and other supplies and that the insurgents have the edge in military intelligence and guerrilla skill. The insurgents are also likely to excel in military morale because most of their soldiers are self-recruited and join on the basis of political convictions and with a willingness to run severe risks, whereas, on the incumbent side, most conscripts and professionals are probably deficient in these determinants of morale. As the war proceeds, military success or failure will, of course, act as another and possibly countervailing and decisive factor in comparative morale.

Military discipline may be high among the incumbents' professional soldiers, though probably less so among conscripts. But, as the cases of China, Vietnam, Cuba, and Algeria have shown, insurgent guerrillas are able to put up with tight discipline—often a requisite of survival—under extraordinarily exacting conditions. The incumbents may be able to achieve close integration of political and military leadership—as Britain eventually did in Malaya and Cyprus and Magsaysay in the Philippines—and insurgent leadership is not seldom rent by factional squabbles. Still, insurgency is political in origin, whereas the military leaders of the incumbents are usually professional specialists and, hence, not trained in political skills. There is, therefore, at least some probability that the insurgents will have better integration of political and military leadership.

As already pointed out, in order to wage prolonged guerrilla war, the insurgents require considerable support from the population which will, at least in part, offset their inferiority in regular military strength. The magnitude of such support, however, must be measured against that received by the incumbents. It may appreciably exceed the latter's, even though a majority of the population occupies category C. Enjoyment of greater civilian support is, however, only a likely, not a necessary, condition of prolonged irregular warfare. It would be unnecessary if the insurgents' inferiority in regular military forces were slight and could be compensated by a superiority in other factors listed in the table. Furthermore, should the insurgents represent a distinct, geographically concentrated group of the population, their enjoyment of superior civilian support may, and need, be only local.

The outcome of the kind of internal war under discussion also is governed, of course, by the degree of superiority in all of the factors listed in the table, and, depending thereon, the situation could still be stabilized even if one or another of the advantages were on the other side. Depending somewhat on degrees of superiority in the other factors, one may also infer that the insurgents are likely to win if they achieve great superiority in civilian and/or foreign support and then reduce their inferiority in capability for regular warfare.

Notes

1. I noted a similar classification for the first time in an unpublished memorandum by M. W. Royse.
2. Cf. Brian Crozier, *The Rebels* (London, 1960), pp. 127, 149 ff. Actual internal wars may, of course, skip the first stage, or never pass beyond the first or second, or relapse from the second to the first, and so on.
3. *E.g.*, Mao was preoccupied with the planning and timing of passage from the second to the third stage. He criticized, on the one hand, the "adventurist" "left opportunists" who pressed for a premature all-out challenge to the Kuomintang and, on the other hand, those given to "localism" and "guerrillaism" who resisted the advance to large-scale warfare. Cf. Mao's *Problems of War and Strategy* (Peking, 1954), pp. 20 ff. and his *Strategic Problems of China's Revolutionary War* (Peking, 1954), pp. 47–55.
4. Mao, *Strategic Problems of China's Revolutionary War*, pp. 2–3.

5. For a brief summary of these principles, see B. H. Liddell-Hart, *Strategy: The Indirect Approach* (London, 1941), pp. 336 ff.

6. According to Clausewitz, " . . . tactics teaches the use of armed forces in engagements, and strategy the use of engagements to obtain the object of the war." Karl von Clausewitz, *On War* (Washington, D.C., 1950), p. 62. In the following, however, I will focus on strategy, since tactics, more than strategy, must be adapted to the peculiar conditions of each case of war, and I will make no consistent attempt to distinguish between strategy and tactics, two categories which, despite Clausewitz' dictum, are difficult to separate. Cf. Liddell-Hart, *op. cit.*, p. 335.

7. For an excellent analytical survey, see Peter Paret and John W. Shy, *Guerillas in the 1960's* (New York, 1962).

8. "We defeat the many with the few. . . . Yet we also defeat the few with the many. . . . " Mao, *Stategic Problems of China's Revolutionary War*, p. 114.

9. *On War*, p. 461.

10. Mao Tse-Tung, *On the Protracted War* (Peking, 1954), p. 12.

11. *Strategic Problems of China's Revolutionary War*, pp. 123 ff.

12. *Ibid.*, p. 69.

13. "The Evolution of a Revolt," *Oriental Assembly* (London, 1937), pp. 112 ff. Incidentally, Lawrence also remarked that " . . . analogy is fudge. . . . " *Ibid.*

14. For which reason, as Lawrence remarks, it may be easier in some ways " . . . to defend a range of hills against nine or ten thousand men than against nine or ten." *Ibid.*, p. 105.

15. According to Rostow, between 10 and 20 soldiers are required "to control one guerilla in an organized operation." W. W. Rostow, "Countering Guerrilla Warfare," *The New Leader*, Vol. 44, No. 29 (July 31–August 7, 1961), p. 14.

16. Clausewitz, *On War*, p. 458.

17. "Things" may be destroyed by terrorist acts as well as by acts of sabotage, but the object remains that of terrorizing people rather than of modifying the military balance directly.

18. For example, such practices have allegedly been employed by the Viet Cong in South Vietnam and by the rebel forces in Portuguese Angola. Cf. Rostow, *op. cit.*, p. 14; and Agricola, "Der Krieg in Angola," *Wehrkunde*, Vol. 10 (October 1961), pp. 530–533.

19. This is the opinion of Mao as formulated in his famous "Three Disciplinary Rules" and "Eight Points of Attention." Cf. S. M. Chiu, *Chinese Communist Revolutionary Strategy, 1945–1949: Extracts from Volume IV of*

Mao Tse-tung's "Selected Works" (Research Monograph No. 13; Princeton, N.J.: Center of International Studies, Princeton University, 1961), pp. 45–46. See also Che Guevara, *On Guerrilla Warfare* (New York, 1961), p. 17.

20. Cf. Lucian W. Pye, *Lessons from the Malayan Struggle Against Communism* (Cambridge, Mass.: Center for International Studies, Massachusetts Institute of Technology, n.d.), pp. 25 ff.

21. Disguised guerrillas, however, can fight in the cities controlled by the incumbents—*e.g.* in the Algerian cities and in the outskirts of Saigon. Cf. George K. Tanham, *Communist Revolutionary Warfare*, (New York, 1961), p. 25.

22. This does not mean that uprisings and *coups d'état* may not also occur less often in highly industrialized than in relatively underdeveloped countries.

23. In economically developed countries, Mao argues, the correct insurgent strategy is first to seize the cities, and then to advance on the countryside. Cf. *Problems of War and Strategy*, pp. 2–3.

24. Cf. Guevara, *On Guerrilla Warfare*, p. 22.

25. Part-time guerrillas are members of local civilian populations and, hence, are concealed combatants who are used intermittently, chiefly for acts of sabotage, terrorism, and intelligence Cf. Vincent Ney, "Guerrilla War and Modern Strategy," *Orbis*, Vol. 2 (1958), pp. 77–78. Part-time guerrillas are sometimes grouped in local militia-type units. Cf. Tanham, *op. cit.*, pp. 45–46.

26. *Ibid.*, pp. 41–43.

27. Ney, *op. cit.*, pp. 80–81.

28. Pye, *op. cit.*, pp. 52–53.

29. "Vietnam War Moves to New Climax," *The Times* (London), September 27, 1961, p. 13.

30. Appearance and reality may, of course, differ. A government may be relatively responsive to the long-run goal-striving of the population and relatively efficient, yet appear to be unresponsive and inefficient because the country suffers from adversities beyond the government's control (*e.g.*, a series of crop failures or attack by a militarily superior country) or because it is the target of an effective propaganda and subversive attack directed from the outside.

31. In order to maximize popular support, the insurgents may not, however, reveal their goals if these would elicit opposition in categories B and C. Thus, the Chinese Communists acted as land reformers. And Guevara wrote of the model guerrilla: "At first, he will not stress social reform, acting more like a big brother to the poor farmer. . . . " *On Guerrilla Warfare*, p. 31, Similarly, parts of the civilian population may support the insurgents not because they sympathize with their goals, but simply

because they sympathize even less with those of the incumbents.

32. For definitions of these terms, see William E. Dougherty and Morris Janowitz (eds.), *A Psychological Warfare Casebook* (Baltimore, Md., 1958), chaps. 1–2.

33. Cf. Gabriel A. Almond and James S. Coleman (eds.), *The Politics of the Developing Areas* (Princeton, N.J., 1960), especially the Introduction and Conclusion.

34. This need not mean that they are also indifferent toward the fact of internal war, which is obviously a burden on any community in which it takes place. Except for groups which can isolate themselves from these effects, or in one way or another profit from them, it is hard to imagine people who are neutral to the fact of war even though they have no political preferences for either opponent.

35. Whether the incumbents are pressed to follow one line rather than the other depends, of course, on whether a large proportion of the population supports the insurgents, or fails to support the incumbents, and acts more out of hostility to the latter than out of sympathy with the former.

36. *Strategic Problems of China's Revolutionary War*, p. 61.

37. Tanham, *op. cit.*, pp. 27, 142.

38. *E.g., ibid.*, chap. 2; Paret and Shy, op. cit., pp. 21 ff.

39. Guevara, *op. cit.*, pp. 7 ff.

40. Paret and Shy, *op. cit.*, p. 21; Tanham, *op. cit.*, pp. 32, 140.

b. The economic problem

Klaus Knorr

The concept of economic potential for war*

TOWARD THE END OF THE SECOND WORLD WAR, Field Marshal Rommel confided to his diary that, once the German U-boats were beaten in the Battle of the Atlantic, and the swelling stream of American soldiers and supplies could reach Europe, Germany "was doomed to inevitable defeat at any place which was accessible to the Anglo-American transport fleets."[1] Not everyone will agree with this assertion of the prominent roles played by sheer masses of military manpower and matériel in deciding the outcome of World War II. It is suggestive, however, that the fortunes of that war turned in close association with the changing ratio of munitions production by the Axis powers and the United Nations.[2] Indeed, the evidence of the last two world wars gave rise to the widespread impression that, in any large-scale modern war, it was not military forces, mobilized in peacetime, that were likely to determine the outcome, but war potential, i.e., the ultimate capacity of belligerent nations to produce combat power. Economic war potential in particular came to be valued highly. Although the first atomic bombs had been dropped on an enemy, by the end of the war long-range defense planning in the United States was largely based on the concept of economic war potential or, as it was often called, "the mobilization base." Economic capability for war was to be enhanced by means

of stockpiling strategic raw materials and by using government protection or subsidies in order to maintain certain critical industries at a desirable output capacity. Under the impression derived from the two world wars, Detroit and Pittsburgh had become the chief symbols of American military power.

But this orientation, though not some of the economic policies justified by it, was to be short-lived. No sooner had the lessons of the two world wars been learned than the validity of those lessons was called into question by the swift advent of nuclear airpower. This abrupt and revolutionary change in weapons seemed to imply that wars of the World War II type were definitely passé, that future wars would be either all-out nuclear conflicts, with the economic mobilization base reduced to a shambles within a matter of days, or engagements in the "Gray Areas," which would be limited in area, target selection, time, objectives, and possibly in the application of weapons, and which would likewise require mobilized forces —"fire brigades" to extinguish "brushfires." In the age of thermonuclear bombs, it appeared to many that only mobilized strength counted; economic capability was irrelevant and economic war potential had ceased to exist.

Persuasive as this conclusion may seem at first, it appears to be rash on second thought. It is the main purpose of this article to demonstrate that the concept of economic war potential remains a useful tool of analysis. To be

* This article is a revised version of a lecture delivered at the Industrial War College, Washington D.C., on March 19, 1957.

Reprinted from *World Politics*, Vol. X, No. 1, October 1957, pp. 49–61.

useful, the concept must be applicable in two ways. It must assist us to evaluate the military power which various countries are able to produce. This is its predictive use. And it must assist us to choose policies by means of which we can increase the military power that we are able to produce. This is its manipulative use.

I

IN the traditional view, economic war potential was properly defined as the capacity to produce military forces and supplies in time of war and thus to add substantially to, and often to multiply, the amount of combat power maintained in peacetime. In this sense, economic war potential was seen to be determined by a nation's existing manpower, farms, factories, and other economic resources that could be diverted from other employment or idleness to the production of military power. Since a nation must subsist and carry on most of its peacetime activities even in time of war, though on a reduced scale, obviously not all of this economic capacity would be available for military purposes. But whatever military power could and would be mobilized had to come from this complex of resources, and their kind and quantity were therefore regarded as a prime condition of a nation's military strength.

Now, economic war potential in this sense seemed to be of crucial importance to the outcome of the last two world wars (and also of the American Civil War) because these were essentially wars of attrition. Among the conditions that made them wars of attrition, the following were prominent; there was no decisive imbalance of military strength during their opening phases; there was no gross imbalance between the technical efficiency and defensive weapons; the effective transmission of firepower over space was costly in terms of resources and time; and the war aims of the coalitions threatened the defeated with extreme deprivations. Since for these reasons these wars were of long duration, there was plenty of time to mobilize potential military strength.

The inclination to scrap the concept of economic war potential is predicated on the expectation that future wars will not be wars of attrition. In the case of all-out war, the new military technology not only has produced arms of unprecedented destructive power, but has also given offensive arms a striking and seemingly abiding edge over defensive arms; and it has drastically cut down the protective function of space and distance. In unlimited thermonuclear war, the decisive blows are expected to fall at the very outset. In strict logic, it may be said that attrition will not be absent, but that it will be consummated in a matter of days or weeks. In the case of brush-fires, the dominant assumption is that military forces will be required at once and that the test of arms will be limited; the burden will fall overwhelmingly, if not entirely, on mobilized forces, and little need is foreseen for potential military strength.

The trouble with this thesis is that it rests both on highly uncertain predictions regarding the complexion of future hostilities and on a failure to adapt the concept of war potential to current conditions.

Do current predictions about the nature of future warfare exhaust not all possible, but all likely, contingencies? It can be granted that a long drawn-out and massive war conducted with conventional (i.e., modernized but non-atomic) weapons is so unlikely to occur that it may be safely neglected as a contingency. There definitely is no future for World War II.[3] It can also be granted that, once unlimited thermonuclear war has broken out, there is no economic war potential to be mobilized for its conduct. Even an ensuing broken-backed war would have to be fought with munitions on hand at the start of the hostilities. However, nations will differ in their ability to absorb and recover from nuclear attack. While there may be little diversion of rehabilitation potential to sustaining any broken-backed war, the capacity to recuperate is in a real sense part of a nation's defence capacity (for it is part of the nature of the target presented to the enemy), and the estimate of recovery potential may well influence the decision to participate in all-out nuclear war or in the prewar bluffing game. Thus, at the point where power to retaliate fails to deter an aggressor, awareness of a very low recovery potential may induce a threatened country to give in, and eventually to capitulate, rather than continue its counter-threat (whose sole purpose lay in deterrence) or follow through by taking retaliatory action.

Limited war is far less capable of predictive definition than unlimited nuclear war. Envisaged as a contingency, it may vary greatly in geographic location, in the number and power of belligerents, in the use of weapons, in the nature of war aims, in scale and duration. Given the thermonuclear stalemate between the United States and Soviet Russia, we cannot be certain that the fear that a limited war will degenerate into unlimited hostilities will deter limited operations altogether, or will confine their magnitude and duration. A nation with nuclear airpower may hesitate, in some circumstances, to unleash this power against an opponent who has only non-nuclear arms at his disposal or who, though in possession of nuclear weapons, restricts himself to the employment of non-nuclear arms. In sheer logic, it is possible that a stalemate in thermonuclear airpower will encourage an aggressor to start limited operations because he is fairly sure that the opponent will not lightly choose to retaliate by starting unlimited nuclear war. Furthermore, it should not be assumed that limited wars will necessarily be cheap. That modern arms technology permits military manpower to be reduced owing to an increase in firepower per man does not at all mean a reduction in the real resources that sustain up-to-date fighting units. In short, it is unrealistic to assume that engagements in limited wars may not call for some mobilization of war potential following the precipitation of hostilities. Of course, the need for recourse to potential would become greatly intensified if participation in limited war were accompanied —as it is likely to be in any limited war involving major nuclear powers—by a stepping-up of defensive preparations for unlimited war. Finally, the outbreak of unlimited conflict may be preceded by a build-up period during which additional military strength is mobilized.

However, the disposition to discard war potential as a relevant concept in the nuclear age is, in addition and primarily, based on a rigid and unimaginative tradition governing its application. In a time without secure and presumably durable peace, the distinction between formal peace and war loses much of its operational significance when it comes to the maintenance and use of military power. This is especially true at present, when the militarily important countries are putting themselves, year after year, under a heavy strain in order to maintain large military establishments in so-called peacetime. It is conceivable that this condition will be of long duration and that some countries, unable or unwilling to bear the burden, will quit the race and be "defeated" without a single shot being fired or a single bomb dropped. If we simply dismiss the term "war potential" and substitute "military potential," or "defense potential," it becomes immediately apparent that the concept applies meaningfully to a wide spectrum of military effort, ranging from peacetime military establishments, through various types of police action and limited wars to unlimited nuclear conflict. Since such a long-term, though possibly fluctuating, commitment of military effort puts any society to heavy exertion, the factor of attrition obviously re-enters the picture. Psychological factors— the will to provide for military power—will be predominant in this kind of attrition. But if the military sector persistently receives resources at the expense of investment, economic attrition may also occur. Clearly, the capacity of a nation to provide for its external security inder these circumstances depends on its military potential. Military potential, then, is the ability of a nation to divert resources to defense in both formal peace and war.

Economc (including technological) capacity is, of course, one constituent of military potential in this sense. But before concentrating on this particular factor, its relation to other major constituents must be clarified. The production of military power demands an input of manpower and other productive resources which would otherwise be directed to non-military output or, marginally, remain idle. But at no time, not even when engaged in total war, can a nation allocate all resources to the production of combat power. The proportion which can and will be diverted to this purpose depends (a) on the structure and productivity of these resources and (b) on the nation's will to provide for military power, i.e., to pay the price for military strength. This price is to be paid not only financially but in terms of foregoing the satisfaction of a wide range of interests—consumption, leisure, comfort, safety, etc.—that conflict with the commitment of resources to the production of military power. The will to provide for military power is therefore another constituent of a nation's defense potential.

Furthermore, given any degree of willingness to pay this price (including the discipline with which the population supports government measures), the output of military power depends upon the efficiency with which the diverted resources are employed. Hence, organizational ability and especially administrative competence represent a third major constituent of military potential.[4] To illustrate, the amount of military power maintained by the United States at any one time is not only a function of the country's productive capacity. It also depends on the size of the defense budget (which permits a proportion of this capacity to be allotted to the output of combat power, and which is contingent upon a political decision reflecting the price the American people are willing to pay for defense), and on the efficiency with which every defense dollar— and, indeed, every non-defense dollar—is spent. As will appear in the following, any realistic analysis of economic and technological potential for defense must pay heed to these interrelationships.

II

WHILE it is useful to theorize on the general meaning of military potential and on the general ways in which this concept can be put to predictive and manipulative use, practical application calls for an immediate descent from the general to the particular. In real life, a nation has no such thing as *a* military potential or *an* economic defense potential which is the same for all possible situations calling for the use of military power in formal peace or war. At present, for example, there are countries which have a relatively high potential for fighting with non-atomic weapons on their own territory or in nearby theaters of war; but they have a very low potential for conducting war with non-atomic arms in distant theaters of operations and a still lower, or zero, potential for waging thermonuclear war. It cannot be stressed too strongly that the analysis of the war potential of any particular country or alliance must begin with specific assumptions about the kind of situation demanding the use of military power. If we are interested in military potential, we must relate our analysis to the likely situations that require, or will require, a military effort. At the present time, and using the United States as an example in the following analysis, it is reasonable to concentrate on three such situations: (1) the long-run maintenance of an adequate defense establishment (which, in fact, it is hoped will deter aggression without jeopardy to vital American interests abroad); (2) involvement in limited wars; and (3) the outbreak of unlimited war. For illustrative purposes, we may furthermore assume that the first two situations demand a diversion of resources from the civilian to the military sector of the economy amounting to from 8 to 12 per cent and from 14 to 18 per cent of the Gross National Product (GNP) respectively.[5]

Obviously, the basic factors governing *economic* defense potential are the same for the two first situations, in the sense that a nation endowed with a high economic defense potential for fighting limited war usually also enjoys a high potential for maintaining a strong military posture in the absence of formal war. The main conditions that make up *economic* defense potential for limited war are:

1. *The volume of the GNP.* The absolute volume is patently significant, since the economic effort for defense will be measured as a proportion of total capacity for producing goods and services. The volume of GNP per capita, or per head of the labor force, is a rough index of the productivity of labor and helps in estimating how much civilian consumption can be compressed in an emergency in order to release productive factors for the defense section. Clearly, it makes a difference whether the GNP per capita is the equivalent of $2,000, $800, or $100 per year.

2. *The rate of growth of the GNP.* This datum will help in estimating changes in economic defense potential over time. Growth will result chiefly from increases in the labor force, from the rate of savings and investment, and from technological innovation. These three factors each have their own bearing on economic defense potential—e.g., a country with a high rate of savings and investment may be able to sustain the conduct of limited war by temporarily switching resources to the military sector entirely or largely from investment, rather than from consumption.

3. *The structure of output.* The most relevant condition is the degree to which the normal product mix approaches the output mix required for waging limited war. This includes the value of industrial as against agricultural, mining, and service production; of heavy as against light industrial production; within these categories, of production of the many goods of special importance to defense such as arms, aircraft, electronics, and fuels; and the growth rate for all of these key products.

4. *The flexibility of output.* It is important to know the relative ease and speed with which output patterns can be modified and, especially, the output of key military supplies be expanded. To the extent that this depends on the flexibility of an economy rather than on government policy, the main factors are the organizational ability of management, the mobility of labor, and the state of such industries as construction, transportation, and machine tools which facilitate the conversion of plant from one output mix to another or the shift of labour from one plant or locality to another.

5. *Science and technology.* The current pace

of technological innovation in weapons production is unprecedented in history and is indeed so swift that a nation's endowment in scientists and technicians, the rates and quality of their training, the distribution of this precious personnel over various research fields, and its division between pure and applied research have become major constituents of economic defense potential.

6. *Size and structure of the defense budget.* This factor will in large measure determine a country's ready capacity for producing military supplies and skills required in limited war.

7. *The size and structure of the tax burden.* Both the magnitude of tax revenues in relation to the national income and the tax pattern affect the ease with which the financial instrument can be used in an emergency for allocating additional resources to defense production.

It should be noted that the degree of national self-sufficiency, as against dependence on foreign supplies, is considered as part of the "structure of output." For industrial nations, this problem is chiefly one of foodstuffs and primary commodities. Normally, there should be no problem so far as the long-range maintenance of defense forces in time of formal peace is concerned. But as the Suez Canal crisis and the sharp rises of raw materials prices during the Korean War showed, dependence on foreign supplies may be a very serious handicap in time of limited war. Yet, since most primary materials are storable, and since participation in international trade tends to raise labor productivity and the GNP—another determinant of economic defense potential—self-sufficiency achieved by a deliberate cutback of foreign trade is distinctively less of an asset than when it is the natural outcome of comparative production advantages.

In view of the number of main conditions affecting the economic war potential of nations, it is immediately apparent that there is no magic key to the estimation of war potential. An estimate of any one condition cannot be expected to yield more than partial results. For instance, a mere comparison of the GNP of two countries —although it offers valuable information—is not only difficult technically but also of narrowly limited value by itself.

When the conditions of economic defense potential are discussed, reference is often made to conditions that are not actually economic, but constituents of administrative capacity or of the nation's will to provide for military power. Thus, how large an input of productive resources is needed to generate a given amount of military strength depends in large measure on the administrative efficiency with which defense dollars are spent. The flexibility of the output mix depends on administrative competence, which is a considerable element in lead-times, whenever new admixtures of military end-items are urgently required.

The maintenance of a large-scale defense effort in time of formal peace must, in the long run, rest on a commensurate degree of taxation, so that there are no consumption and investment dollars in excess of what can be spent on consumption and investment goods at current prices. If the defense effort is not put on a pay-as-you-go basis whenever full employment prevails, inflationary pressures will result and, if strong and prolonged, they will have various debilitating consequences. Whether the defense effort will or will not be mounted on a pay-as-you-go basis is not, of course, an economic but a political and psychological problem (and, since public attitudes are subject to government leadership, it is an administrative problem as well). This crucial factor of the will to provide for defense is frequently slighted in American discussion of how large a defense budget the "economy" can stand. What the "economy" can stand is something quite different from, though not unrelated to, what the electorate will stand. Provided the electorate agrees to be taxed for a defense effort requiring year after year, say, 12 per cent of the GNP, the question of whether or not this tax load (in addition to taxes for the civilian purposes of government) will undermine the "soundness" of the economy. The economy might suffer if high taxes engendered a fall in the rate of savings and investment (public as well as private) and, in a private enterprise economy, weakened the incentive to work, innovate, and employ productive resources efficiently. Such ill consequences would slow down the rate of economic growth in, and reduce the flexibility of, the economy and thereby diminish economic defense potential over time.

Contrary to the assurance with which such deleterious effects are frequently predicted, we know unfortunately little about the circumstances under which they would represent a serious risk. We do know that the high tax rates levied in the United States since the outbreak of the Korean War have not prevented a very high rate of economic growth; that the effects on the incentives and the savings of high-income groups as a whole have been minor;[6] that harmful effects of severe taxation depend on the structure of taxation as well as on its level; and that, in democratic communities, the slackening of the electorate's will to provide for defense in peacetime is likely to keep taxes from reaching the level at which these subversive risks to the economy would become serious.[7]

During the Korean War, when United States expenditures on national security rose from $18.5 billion in 1950 to $51.5 billion in 1953, or from 6.4 to 14.2 per cent of the GNP, additional resources were allocated to the military sector by means of cutting the rate of investment somewhat[8] and by preventing consumption from rising as fast as the GNP. This diversion of productive capacity was effected primarily by hiking income taxes and by a relatively mild rise in prices. It is probably that the burden of any limited war, claiming from 14 to 18 per cent of the GNP, will be borne roughly in this way—i.e., the additional resources needed in the defense sector will come largely from a reduction in non-defense investment[9] and from any current growth in productive capacity; and this transfer of resources will be financed in part by an increase in taxation and in part by inflationary methods. This makes the level and structure of existing taxes and the choice of new taxes (i.e., administrative competence for war) a matter of considerable importance, lest taxpayers respond to new taxes or to inflation by slackening their productive efforts or by reducing their savings.

The will to provide for military power and the administrative capacity for doing so are also important in that the waging of limited war may well lead to a special scarcity of key materials and facilities, and this strain may require government allocation in order to keep the entire defense effort from being hampered by a few specific bottlenecks. As the first year of the Korean War demonstrated, there is also the danger that the public will anticipate shortages of greater spread and severity than are warranted by the objective situation, and that the resulting scare-buying will add materially to inflationary pressures. In that event, more comprehensive price and rationing controls may be advisable; and the choice, timing, and administration of such measures will again put a premium on administrative competence and the public will to provide for defense.

III

BECAUSE the predictive uses of the concept of military potential should be obvious from the foregoing, it may suffice to make some general observations on its manipulative use. For either the maintenance of a large peacetime defense establishment or the conduct of limited war, the following conditions are favorable to economic defense potential and can be promoted by public policy.

1. The more rapidly and steadily the GNP grows, the more easily will a high but fixed budget be borne over time, since it will claim a progressively smaller share of the GNP; and the easier it will be—economically, politically, and administratively—to increase the defense budget by allowing it to rise short of, equal to, or somewhat in excess of the rise in the GNP. Again, the faster economic growth proceeds, the greater will be the opportunity to bear the burden of limited war without depressing consumption or investment, or without depressing them severely.

Appropriate policies for fostering the rapid growth of the GNP, and for avoiding or moderating its temporary shrinkage as a result of business depression, are therefore desirable for defense as well as other reasons. In addition to proper fiscal, monetary, and trade policies, the government is in a position to further growth by public investment of various kinds, notably for the purpose of augmenting human resources.

2. The maintenance of a large defense budget will, in an industrial country, automatically stimulate over a wide range precisely those industries which are of key importance to military power. Adroit public subsidies can be used for the purpose of maintaining reserve output capacity in a few selected industries, such as aircraft. Stockpiles of critical raw materials can be set up in order to minimize inconvenient shortages in time of limited war.

3. Special efforts, financed from public as well as private funds, can be made to guarantee a sufficient supply of competent scientists and technicians, and to direct research into areas which, because of the long-range or uncertain nature of probable pay-offs, are likely to be neglected by private industry and the defense department.

4. The administrative capability for conducting limited war can be improved by preparing in advance emergency programs for taxation and both selective and comprehensive price control and rationing.

Defense potential for unlimited thermonuclear war is far more of a conundrum than potential power for activation in peacetime or in limited conflicts. As observed above, there is no direct military potential to be mobilized for the waging of all-out war. Even under the assumption of a lingering, broken-backed war, economic defense potential after all makes up much of the back that has been broken. As also pointed out, however, the capacity of nations to recover from thermonuclear devastation is indirectly part of their military power, no matter whether recovery permits some diversion of resources to the conduct of broken-backed war or whether the recuperation potential affects the decision of a would-be aggressor to precipitate, and of his opponent to accept, unlimited hostilities or threats based thereon.

But what can be said about recovery potential? Despite obvious differences among countries in size and location of territory, and in density and layout of population and industries, any prediction of the productive capacity that might escape destruction and remain effective is so speculative as to be worthless, in view of current and imminent technological developments in nuclear weapons systems. This situation is bound to continue unless a breakthrough in active defense robs these offensive weapons of their decisive technical superiority.

One point, however, is quite apparent and merits emphasis. The very way societies are physically organized—economically, politically, indeed, for the pursuit of nearly all the peacetime interests of their members—makes them extremely vulnerable in unlimited war. They present a natural target for thermonuclear weapons. Recovery potential, therefore, must reside principally in deliberate measures designed to alter the target, to render it less vulnerable to destruction. To do so to a degree highly protective of physical assets is, of course, prohibitive in cost economically and in terms of all that makes life worth living.

At the present and now foreseeable stage of weapons development, however, the cost of protective measures (especially adequate emergency shelters) for substantially reducing civilian casualties is not excessive for a wealthy nation such as the United States, in the event that the will to provide for military strength and administrative competence can be made to extend to these matters. A nation which thus supplies the means to protect human life in thermonuclear war is protecting human resources, the most valuable economic asset of any economically developed country. Yet if a society takes this course, it and its recovery potential will suffer all the more keenly from a lack of complementary resources—that is, capital goods—which are destroyed in unlimited war and whose protection is not feasible to any substantial extent. What is feasible, however, are preparations which will maintain the surviving population and shorten appreciably the time needed for the repair, recombination, and reproduction of non-human resources. Among such measures would be the stockpiling of food and other essential supplies for civilian subsistence, the storage of key repair resources and, of course, preparations for the functioning of government under conditions of nuclear disaster.

To conclude: in view of the various roles which military power must be expected to play in the future, and given a refocusing of the concepts of war potential and economic war potential, these concepts retain demonstrable usefulness for predictive and manipulative purposes. Once the focus has been redirected, the main determinants of war potential for fighting the Second World War are found to determine military potential in the nuclear age; and much of what has been learned from an analysis of war potential under the conditions prevailing a decade or even a few decades ago can be adapted to present conditions. While there is no future for World War II, there seems to be a future for the concept of military potential. What remains to be done, but cannot be done within the confines of a brief article, is to develop its application in progressively greater detail.

To do so will by no means be easy. As various techniques of analysis are employed—whether GNP analysis, input-output analysis, process analysis, or others—it would soon become apparent that they can take us only part way toward complete knowledge, either because of the nature of the techniques or because of a paucity of data. In the end, when all we are able to learn is summed up, there will be disconcerting gaps in our knowledge and an obvious need to rely on "judgment." But such imperfection should be no cause for abandoning the effort to learn. The fact is that political and military leaders cannot escape the necessity of constantly estimating military power, of which potential power is still a part. Surely, it is better to learn as much as we can than to rely entirely on intuition.

Notes

1. B. H. Liddell Hart, ed., *The Rommel Papers*, New York, 1953, p. 507.
2. U.S. War Production Board, Bureau of Planning and Statistics, *World Munitions Production, 1938–1944*, Document No. 21 (mimeographed), Washington, D.C., July 15, 1944, p. 33.
3. Cf. Brigadier General S. F. Giffin, USAF, "A New Future for World War II?" *World Politics*, IX, No. 2 (January 1957), pp. 280–86.
4. For an extensive discussion of this conceptual problem, see Klaus Knorr, *The War Potential of Nations*, Princeton, N.J., 1956, pp. 40–47 and *passim*.
5. Since the Korean War ended, United States expenditures on defense have hovered around 10 per cent of the GNP. The figure selected for limited war is more arbitrary. At the height of the Korean War, American expenditures on external security were about 14 per cent of the GNP. While it is possible that a very limited military action might be fought without any boost in the defense budget, it is also possible that a prolonged limited war on a large scale might claim more than 18 per cent of the GNP. At the height of the Second World War, the major industrial belligerents devoted from 40 to 50 per cent of their GNP to warfare.
6. Thus, in the United States, the main effect of high taxes on executive behavior has been observed in the methods of executive compensation (deferred compensation plans, stock options, untaxable fringe benefits and per-

quisites, etc.). These loopholes in the tax system has protected incentives and preserved the ability and effort to save. G. J. Keith Butters, "Taxation, Incentives, and Financial Capacity," *American Economic Review, Papers and Proceedings*, XLIV (May 1954), pp. 504–19.
7. However, there is considerable evidence that high and steeply progressive income taxes are entailing harmful long-run effects in Great Britain. Although there, too, business executives have found legal ways of evading stringent tax rates, these loopholes have not offered relief, and hence protection of incentives, to other highly skilled occupations. The difficulties encountered in recruiting personnel for high civil service positions and the continuous emigration of highly trained technicians indicate the productivity losses which British taxes inflict on the economy.
8. This cutback was achieved by keeping investment in durable equipment and residential construction stable and by a sharp decline in business inventories.
9. The aftereffects of a reduced investment rate on economic growth will be relatively minor as long as the cut falls primarily on inventories and residential building. And even if the growth of the GNP is slowed down temporarily, this need not entail a *relative* decline of economic defense potential so long as the main adversary in limited war is the main adversary in any conceivable war and is likewise forced to accept a cut in investment.

Charles J. Hitch and Roland Neeley McKean

The criterion problem

PREVIOUSLY WE STATED that the selection of an appropriate criterion is frequently the central problem in the design of an economic analysis intended to improve military decision. Whatever the particular problem, military or civilian, it is fairly obvious that, in choosing among alternative means to our ends, we need to scan the ends themselves with a critical eye. New techniques of types of equipment may be extremely efficient in achieving certain aims, but these aims may be the wrong ones—aims that are selected almost unconsciously or at least without sufficient critical thought.

But to say that we should scrutinize our ultimate ends carefully in deciding upon the best course of action is much too vague. Suppose we wish to choose among various motorcars. Merely to name and list the things we ultimately value (such as growth, approval, security, freedom, leisure, goods) is not very helpful in solving the problem. It is wise to think about such a list, for it may prevent us from making some absurd choice that does not contribute to *any* of these things, but in most situations the list provides little counsel. One reason it fails to do so is the tremendous gap between gas consumption, wheel base, and new seat covers, on the one hand, and leisure, security, and approval, on the other. This gap has to be at least partially bridged in order to reach any conclusions about policies. Another reason is the necessity of trading part of one desideratum for some of another, sacrificing faster "pick-up" for improved fuel consumption or giving up some comforts for a little more leisure.

Similarly, the mere enumeration of objectives in choosing among weapon systems, while it may be pertinent, does not serve as a guide to specific action. The objectives may include target destruction potential, invulnerability to enemy attack, strengthening of alliances, and reliability—all to be achieved "as soon as possible." All of these things would indeed be nice to have. But while good intentions are sometimes reputed to be excellent paving materials, in themselves they do not pave the way to preferred action. In practical problems of military (or other) choice there are always constraints which prevent us from simultaneously achieving all our objectives.

Criteria

HENCE, in choosing among alternatives, we do more than to list things which it would be nice to have. Explicitly or implicitly we adopt criteria or tests of preferredness. One essential step in the analysis is predicting the consequences of alternative actions or systems—a step which, as indicated earlier, involves the use of sets of relationships called models. Another vital step is distinguishing preferred combinations of consequences from less desirable ones; this step entails the use of criteria. Thus, after having the features of different cars spelled out, the chooser has to decide what is the best combination of features. He may want the car that has maximum acceleration while meeting specific constraints on other aspects in performance and on cost. If so, that is his criterion. Or he may compare the features (including cost implications) of different cars subjectively and reach his decision. If so, the criterion is never made explicit, but is presumably the maximization of some function constrained by the chooser's limited resources.

There are times when the term "criterion"

Reprinted from Charles J. Hitch and Roland N. McKean, *The Economics of Defense in the Nuclear Age*, Cambridge, Harvard University Press, Copyright 1960, by The Rand Corporation, pp. 158–181.

appears to be a misnomer. For, on occasion, as we have seen, analysis can unravel only *some* of the consequences of alternative actions and exhibit these consequences to decision-makers after the usual manner of consumers' research.[1] (By this term we mean the kind of research that is often done to help consumers choose an item such as an automobile or a refrigerator.) Insofar as this is the case, a partial criterion (comparison in terms of selected consequences) may be used. There is then no problem of devising a definitive test, but there is the closely related problem of deciding *what* consequences the decision-maker should know about. In other situations, however, the analyst may be able (or may try) to trace out all the significant effects and learn enough about the decision-maker's preferences to evaluate those effects. In these instances, quantitative analysis *per se* may be used to pick out and recommend preferred courses of action. Insofar as this is the case, a definitive test of preferredness is necessary, and the criterion problem is the devising of that test. Most of the discussion that follows will relate directly to the criterion problem faced in the latter situations, but much of it will pertain, at least indirectly, to the selection of partial criteria, that is, of selected effects that are relevant to the comparison of alternative actions.

THE NECESSITY FOR USING "PROXIMATE" CRITERIA

Ideally we should choose that course of action which, with available resources, maximizes something like the "satisfaction" of an individual, the profits of a firm, the "military worth" of the military establishment, or the "well-being" of a group. If possible, we should like to ascertain the total amount of these magnitudes under each of various alternative policies. Then we would pick the policy that promised to yield the most satisfaction, the most profits, the most military worth, or the most well-being, depending on the identity of the person or organization whose choice we were advising. But this prescription usually helps little more than saying that we want the best. Nobody knows precisely how satisfaction and military worth are related to the observable outcomes of various courses of action. We do not have the ability to translate outcomes into such terms. In practical problem-solving, therefore, we have to look at some "proximate" criterion which serves to reflect what is happening to satisfaction or military worth. Actual criteria

are the practicable substitutes for the maximization of whatever we would ultimately like to maximize.

In comparisons of military operations or equipment, what is desired is the course of action that would contribute most to "winning" or deterring some kind (or kinds) of war, or even more generally, to achieving national security. Since it will usually be impossible to measure achievements in any of these terms, it is necessary to adopt indirect but workable criteria that appear to be consistent with ultimate aims.

SUB-OPTIMIZATION AND CRITERIA

The need to use proximate rather than ultimate tests opens the door to the selection of incorrect criteria. But the door is really swung wide open—in fact one might say that the welcome mat is put out—by another fact of life stressed previously: the fact that problems of choice must be broken down into component pieces or sub-problems.

Let us examine this difficulty in somewhat greater detail. A military service (or government department or large corporation) cannot possibly have one man or one committee examine *all* its problems of choice simultaneously and pick each course of action in the light of all other decisions. It is inevitable that decision-making be broken into pieces. The division is almost necessarily along hierarchical lines, some of the broader policy choices being made by high level officials or groups, others being delegated to lower levels.[2]

Similarly, analyses may be piecemeal, since it is impossible for a single analysis to cover all problems of choice simultaneously in a large organization. Thus comparisons of alternative courses of action always pertain to a part of the government's (or corporation's) problem. Other parts of the over-all problem are temporarily put aside, possible decisions about some matters being ignored, specific decisions about others being taken for granted. The resulting analyses are intended to provide assistance in finding optimal, or at least good, solutions to sub-problems: in the jargon of systems analysis and operations research, they are sub-optimizations.

Note again, however, that the scope of analysis does not have to, and indeed usually should not, coincide with the scope of authority in decision-making. Take the case of military decisions within the government. Analysis of a problem in antisubmarine warfare may have to be made in the context of a global war involving all services and the national economy, even though it is relevant to decisions within one bureau of the Navy Department. Fortunately no single authority runs the whole executive-legislative-judicial process in the United States government, but this does not mean that individual departments and subordinate units should not, on occasion, take a broad national point of view ("context" and criterion) in making decisions for which it is responsible in the hierarchy. The situation in a private corporation is precisely analogous. The individual division or department of the corporation, in making certain decisions delegated to it, will be expected to take a corporation-wide point of view, tracing the full consequences of its actions on all operations of the firm.[3] The sales department is not expected to choose actions which maximize sales, or sales minus selling costs, but the total profits of the corporation—sales and other receipts minus all costs in all departments.

Piecemeal analysis and decision-making have great advantages, some of which have already been stated. Small problems tend to be more "manageable" in a number of senses. As problems are broken down into smaller chunks, more detail can be taken into account by both researchers and decision-makers. In large firms a degree of decentralization greater than that which is inevitable is usually believed to be desirable so that the "man on the spot" can decide about many matters—and be held responsible for them.[4] In analysis, somewhat similarly, considerable breakdown of the problems of a corporation or a government department may be desirable so that the models used in estimating outcomes can be "on the spot," that is, less aggregative and more precise in their predictions than global or firm-wide models would be.

Finally, better hedging against uncertainty *may* result from breaking big problems into smaller ones. The difficulties that stem from inherent uncertainties will be discussed mostly in the next chapter, but a few words are in order here. If decision-making is decentralized to a considerable extent, it may help against the possibility of getting stuck with lop-sided views at the top. In civil government it has long been widely recognized that some separation of powers and dispersal of authority are important, partly as a hedging device. And in analysis, a degree of sub-optimization *may* mean, for some problems, less risk of tying all analytical results

to a "bad" criterion, for instance, one involving a spuriously specific objective in which uncertainty is neglected.

On the other hand, there is a real danger in piecemeal analysis, one whose importance must be re-emphasized because it is probably not as widely appreciated as are the difficulties inherent in biting off too big a chunk of the problem. The danger is that the criteria adopted in lower level problems may be unrelated to and inconsistent with higher level criteria. As mentioned before, proximate criteria have to be used in any case; but since problems must be considered one piece at a time, a whole hierarchy of proximate criteria comes into play, and potential inconsistencies are abundant.

As an example from the military sphere, suppose that the military establishes a requirement for 90 per cent reliability in the functioning of its weapon systems. Bows and arrows may pass such a test with flying colors, yet hand grenades may accomplish much more at the same cost, even if half of them are duds. Perhaps 90 per cent or 50 or 99 per cent has some intuitive appeal, but this gives little assurance that it is a sensible "requirement," criterion, or test. The point is that even plausible criteria for choosing lower level policies may not harmonize with higher level tests, that is, may not be in agreement with what we really want to do. Earlier we criticized the widespread practice in government of setting "requirements" without looking explicitly at costs. Because problems must be taken up piecemeal, there is danger that requirements will be set without looking critically at payoffs either. And the achievement of a blindly selected "requirement" (even at minimum cost)[5] is likely to be inconsistent with higher level aims.

In a free enterprise economy we have a price mechanism and a system of incentives which, imperfectly but pervasively, enforce some measure of consistency between the lower level criteria used by individuals and firms in making their economic decisions and certain higher level criteria appropriate to the economy. A whole branch of economic theory, rather unfortunately labeled "welfare economics," is concerned with relations between high and low level economic criteria.[6] Under certain circumstances (the most important being absence of monopoly, free movement of factors of production, "full employment," and no external economies or diseconomies), the maximization of their own preference functions by individuals and of their own profits by firms will lead to an "efficient" use of resources in the economy—in the precisely defined senses that it will be impossible to produce more of any one good or service without producing less of some other *and* that it will be impossible to improve the satisfaction of any one individual without reducing that of another.[7] Since, in general, firms do try to maximize profits and individuals do try to maximize preference functions, there will be a tendency for resources to be efficiently used in the economy to the extent that the assumed circumstances are approximated.

This is an interesting and, within limits, a useful conclusion. It might be regarded as equally plausible, or even more plausible, that the higher level economic criterion would require firms to minimize cost per unit of output (the ratio of cost to output) or to maximize productivity per head or per man-hour (the ratio of output to some one input) instead of maximizing profits (receipts minus costs). In fact, both these criteria have been widely used— in some cases appropriately, in others not— as indexes of efficiency in comparisons between firms and countries. But it can be demonstrated that maximizing either of the ratios by firms in choosing methods of production, scale of operations, and so on, would result in an inefficient use of resources in the economy.

Some criterion errors

IN the military (and indeed in the government generally) there is no comparable mechanism that tends to insure consistency between high level and low level criteria.[8] Since piecemeal analysis (sub-optimization) and therefore the use of low level criteria cannot be avoided, the prevention of even gross errors in the selection of criteria requires hard thought. In a very general sense all criterion errors involve inconsistency between the tests that are selected in analyzing lower level problems and the tests that are applicable at higher levels. However, some of the mistakes that occur most frequently have special characteristics and can be put into categories.

MAXIMIZING GAIN WHILE MINIMIZING COST

The consequences of an action fall into two types—(1) those positive gains which we like to increase, or the achievement of objectives, and (2) those negative effects which we like to decrease, or the incurrence of costs. Neither type by itself can serve as an adequate criterion: the

maximizing of gains without regard to cost or resource limitation is hardly a helpful test, and the minimizing of cost regardless of other consequences of the alternative actions is nonsense. Hence both gains and costs must appear in criteria but, as will be seen, they can make their appearance in various ways.

One ubiquitous source of confusion is the attempt to maximize gain while minimizing cost or, as a variant, the attempt to maximize two types of gain at once. Such efforts are made, or at least talked about, in connection with all manner of problems. It is sometimes said, for example, that we should choose new weapons "on a 'maximum effectiveness at minimum cost' basis."[9] Or consider the following criterion, which allegedly guided one military operation: "The Germans' triumphant campaign . . . was inspired by the idea of . . . achieving the unexpected in direction, time, and method, preceded by the fullest possible distraction and followed by the quickest possible exploitation along the line of least resistance to the deepest possible range."[10] In connection with civil-government choices (in India), even the London *Economist* slips. "Above all, in choosing between possible schemes, the Indian planners never admit to using the simple test: which will be more profitable? Which, in other words, will give the maximum increase in the national income for the minimum use of real resources?"[11]

Actually, of course, it is impossible to choose that policy which simultaneously maximizes gain and minimizes cost, because there is no such policy. To be sure, in a comparison of policies A and B, it may turn out occasionally that A yields greater gain, yet costs less, than B. But A will not also yield more and cost less than all other policies C through Z; and A will therefore not maximize yield while minimizing cost. Maximum gain is infinitely large, and minimum cost is zero. Seek the policy which has that outcome, and you will not find it.

It may seem that proposals to use such tests are harmless, since it is impossible to use such a criterion when the analyst buckles down to the comparison of specific alternatives. Nonetheless, this type of criterion error should be taken seriously, for it can lead to some wild compromise criteria. If a person approaches a problem with the intention of using such a criterion, he is confused to begin with; then, when he finds that it will not work, he may fasten upon *any* sort of constraint on gain or cost that converts this impossible test into a feasible one.

OVERLOOKING ABSOLUTE SIZE OF GAIN OR COST

One common procedure is to pick that policy which has the highest ratio of "effectiveness," or achievement-of-objective, to cost. In that case, the maximizing of this ratio is the criterion. Note that the terms "effectiveness" and "achievement of objectives" means positive gains, or the achievement of tasks that it is desirable to carry out. To examine this criterion, let us look at the comparison of alternative military weapons. These could be anything from various antitank weapons to different bombers, but suppose it is the latter. Let the ability to destroy targets, in the relevant circumstances, be the measure of effectiveness. Suppose next that a B-29 system, already on hand and relatively easy to maintain, would be able to destroy 10 targets and would entail extra costs of $1 billion—a ratio of 10 to 1 —while System X would destroy 200 targets and cost $50 billion—a ratio of 4 to 1. Does it follow that we should choose the B-29 system, the one with the higher ratio? The answer is surely No, for it might merely be a system that would invite and lose a war inexpensively. To maximize the *ratio* of effectiveness to cost may be a plausible criterion at first glance, but it allows the absolute magnitude of the achievement or the cost to roam at will. Surely it would be a mistake to tempt the decision-maker to ignore the absolute amount of damage that the bombing system could do.

Without constraints on either total level of effectiveness or total budget, the ratio of the two may point to extreme solutions, to nearly-zero or to almost infinite effectiveness and cost. Of course, common sense and empty pocketbooks prevent us from paying attention to such a ratio at the extremes. But what is its significance in the middle-ground that is not ruled out by common sense? Does the ratio take on meaning in these circumstances? The absurdity of the choice to which the ratio might lead is then bounded, and perhaps the chances that its prescription will coincide with the "correct" choice are increased, simply because the ratio is partly penned up. But still the ratio does not take on real meaning. In fact, the only way to know what such a ratio really means is to tighten the constraint until either a single budget or particular degree of effectiveness is specified. And at that juncture, the ratio reduces itself to a test of maximum effectiveness for a given budget, or a specified effectiveness at minimum cost, and might better have been put that way at the outset.

Of course, if the ratios did not alter with changes in the scale of achievement (or cost), the higher ratio would indicate the preferred system, no matter what the scale. That is, if the ratio of achievement to cost were 10 to 1 for the B-29 system and 4 to 1 for System X at *all* levels of achievement, then the B-29 system would be "dominant." For it would destroy 500 targets at the $50 billion level of cost, clearly a better performance than that of System X. But to assume that such ratios are constant is inadmissible some of the time and hazardous the rest. In the bomber illustration the assumption of constant ratios would obviously be wrong, because with larger scales of activity it would be necessary to buy more B-29's instead of merely using the ones on hand. Moreover, whatever one's belief about the constancy of the ratio, the straightforward test of maximum effectiveness for a given budget (or, alternatively, minimum cost of achieving a specified level of effectiveness) reveals just as much as the ratio—and seems much less likely to mislead the unwary.[12]

It might be observed that ratios are sometimes handy devices for ranking a list of possible actions when (1) the scale of activity is fixed, and (2) the actions are not interdependent (more on this point later). Thus the rate of return on stocks and bonds (the ratio of annual net return to the cost of the investment) is a convenient aid in ranking securities. Then, *with a fixed investment fund*, the set of securities that yields the greatest return for that fund can be quickly determined. Note, however, the limited conditions under which this procedure can be used.

SETTING WRONG SIZE OF GAIN OR COST

As just suggested, a criterion in which the budget or level of effectiveness is specified has the virtue of being aboveboard. The test's limitation, the fact that it relates to a particular level of cost or achievement, is perceivable with the naked eye. The fact indicates, though, that while avoidance of ratio tests is a step in the right direction, our troubles are not over. For if an incorrect or irrelevant scale of gain or cost is taken as given, the test is unlikely to result in good policy decisions.

In choosing the bombing system, let us suppose that the test is minimum cost of achieving the ability to destroy 10 targets. In these circumstances, the hypothetical B-29 system is better than System X. On the other hand, if the criterion is minimum cost of achieving an ability to destroy 200 targets, System X is better.

Clearly it makes a difference which scale of gain (that is, effectiveness) is stipulated, and it would be possible to fix upon the wrong scale.

If the analyst has been instructed to specify a particular level of effectiveness, then someone else has, in effect, chosen this aspect of his criterion for him—for better or worse. If he has leeway, however, and chooses the scale uncritically, he is using what was described earlier as the requirements approach.[13] In other words, he is picking the desired task or level of achievement without inquiry into the sacrifices of other achievements that would be entailed. What he can do to choose the right scale will be discussed a little later. The thing to be noted here is that this sort of criterion error is always a threat in piecemeal analysis.

There is precisely the same danger if the cost (or budget, or resources) is to be stipulated instead of the task. Of course, if the budget is already definitely set by higher level decision, the analysis has to take the predetermined amount as given. But budgets for future years are never "definitely set" in a democracy, and if the analysis is concerned with development or procurement, it is usually the magnitude of future budgets that is relevant. Wherever the budget is subject to change, perhaps on the advice of the analyst, his test should not take as given a budget that is uncritically assumed or stipulated.

NEGLECTING SPILLOVERS

In economics, impacts of one firm's action upon other firms' gains or costs are referred to as "external economies and diseconomies."[14] For example, an oil well that forces brine into the underground water supply may reduce the fertility of adjacent farmlands. Within firms or governmental units, similarly, the action of one department may affect the gains or costs of operations in other departments. (This would be the case, for instance, if the oil-producing firm owned the farmlands.) The term "spillovers"[15] will be used here, chiefly because it is short, as a general title covering all such effects.

In comparing alternative military policies, it is easy to adopt a criterion that leads to the neglect of spillover effects. For example, a classic piece of military operations research may have ignored some impacts on activities other than the one that was directly under examination. In the frequently cited example of successful analysis, alternative arrangements for washing and rinsing mess-kits were compared.

As his test of preferredness, the analyst used the minimization of the number of man-hours required to do the job, given a total of four tubs. The optimal arrangement, according to this test, turned out to be the use of three tubs for washing and one tub for rinsing. A hypothetical reaction of the mess sergeant has been reported as follows:

> Yeah, I remember that guy. He had some screwball idea that the mission of the Army was to eliminate waiting lines. Actually I had it all figured out that two was the right number of rinse tubs. With everyone rinsing in one tub the bacteria count would get way past the critical level. But we switched to one rinse tub while he was around because the old man says he's an important scientist or something and we got to humor him. Had damn near a third of the outfit out with the bellyache before we got the character off the reservation. Then we quick switched to three rinse tubs and really made a nice line. "Nothing like a good line to get the men's legs in condition," the old man says.[16]

The purpose of this example is not to disparage this particular piece of analysis, which may have been quite useful. The point is simply to suggest how easy it is, in the comparison of *any* policies, to neglect spillover effects.

USING WRONG CONCEPTS OF COST OR GAIN

The manner in which cost and gain may seem to be a matter of measurement. These definitions are pertinent in a discussion of criterion errors, however, because wrong concepts of cost and gain may grow out of, or be inextricably bound up with, the adoption of incorrect criteria.

Probably the most important cause of error of this sort is the exclusion of relevant costs from the computation. As we have emphasized previously, the costs to be compared are the full system costs of each alternative—all the costs directly or indirectly stemming from the decision. Thus, if we are trying to decide between a missile and an aircraft to accomplish a given mission, it can be completely misleading to compare the manufacturing costs of the competing major equipments. We must also count the costs (except where they are already "sunk") of all the auxiliary equipment, of the ground-handling and support equipment, of the training of personnel, and of operation for some appropriate period of time.

Our major emphasis in this volume is on peacetime preparations for war and on deterring war. This means that we are interested *mainly* in peacetime, not wartime costs. We are trying to make the most of the resources available for national security in peacetime. In principle, the wartime costs are relevant. In practice, we can frequently ignore them. For in the case of general nuclear war, we expect the war to be fought with the forces in being at its outbreak. The major economic problem is to maximize the capability of these forces by using resources efficiently before the war starts—so efficiently that we hope an enemy will never dare start it. In the case of limited war there may well be significant production of weapons and expenditure of resources after the limited war begins (as in the case of Korea), but occasional wars for limited objectives will cost little compared with the year-in year-out costs of peacetime preparedness. It is estimated that the "cost of United States forces in Korea over and above the normal cost of such forces if no action was taking place" was approximately five billion dollars in the fiscal year 1951/52, about 11 per cent of total United States expenditures for major national security programs that year.[17]

Right and wrong concepts of cost and gain can, however, be illustrated by either wartime or peacetime studies. For example, in a World War II study of alternative ways to destroy enemy shipping, the criterion adopted was the ratio of enemy ships sunk (the gain) to allied man-years of effort (the cost).[18] Now our concern in this section is not with the hazards of such a ratio test,[19] but rather with the nature of these concepts of gain and cost.

Neglect of higher level gain. First, "ships sunk" as a measure of gain may have been an unfortunate choice (whether made by the analysts or by "higher authority"), for shipping could be effectively destroyed by actions such as minelaying without necessarily sinking many ships. The criterion adopted would have prejudiced the case against such measures.

Neglect of valuable inputs. Next, let us examine the costs of these ship-sinking operations. Costs are the consequences that have negative values, or in other words they are the sacrifices that have to be made in order to conduct the operation. In the above-mentioned study, man-years of effort—which included those used in construction of vessels and equipment, training, operations, and replacements—appear to be a somewhat dubious measure of these sacrifices. One reason is that man-years, while important in wartime (and in peacetime), were

not the only items given up. Thus a method of destroying enemy shipping that used comparatively little manpower, even though it required extremely valuable equipment and skills, had a spurious advantage over a method that utilized relatively worthless equipment and much labor. In effect the test ignored inputs other than man-years as if they were free.

In extreme cases, this sort of procedure may be the correct one. Since the cost of one course of action is whatever has to be sacrificed, that cost depends upon what alternatives are genuinely possible. If, for example, the only courses of action that can be considered are different ways for unskilled laborers to use given equipment to carry out a specified task, the only input that has other uses is the labor. The analysis becomes a time-and-motion study, and a suitable test is the achievement of the specified task with the minimum expenditure of man-hours.

In general, however, the use of man-hours, a "critical material," or any other single input to represent cost is likely to be wrong. Other valuable inputs are usually involved. To ignore these other inputs is to pretend that their use involves no sacrifice, whatever the quantity employed. Another plausible procedure—putting a specific constraint on the amount of each input that is to be used—is in most cases equally misleading. Such a constraint pretends that we do not have the choice of acquiring extra amounts of the input. Sometimes the choices open to us are limited in this fashion, but placing specific constraints on all inputs usually shortens the list of alternatives that is truly admissible; hence it distorts the sacrifices entailed by taking the actions that are in fact examined.

What then, is the right way to measure cost? The answer, in principle, is that the measures in any particular problem should approximate the value of the alternative that must be sacrificed. In long-run problems (most development and many procurement choices) the almost unlimited possibilities of substitution in the economy make dollar costs—the dollars representing general resources—a satisfactory measure in most cases, and far superior to such practical alternatives as man-hours. Dollars do, even if imperfectly, take account of the value in other uses of different skills and of factors of production other than labor. In short-run and intermediate-run problems the difficulties are greater, and one must usually impose cost or resource constraints of several kinds. In the extreme case of a field commander who has to prepare for an imminent battle with what he has on hand, the amount of each specific resource (men, tanks, ammunition, and so on) he has is fixed,[20] and no more of any one can be secured at any price. In this case each resource must be taken as a constraint on his tactics. In less extreme cases some resources will be fixed and others variable—the latter frequently at "increasing costs" reflecting either higher incremental production costs in the short run or the withdrawal of the additional resources from increasingly valuable uses elsewhere.

The Navy, for example, may have a certain number of warships readily available for an operation in the Mediterranean (those on station there). In a very short-run problem, no more could be made available from anywhere. In an intermediate-run problem, additional ships could be obtained, but only by the very expensive method of "de-mothballing" or by transferring to the Mediterranean ships whose "outputs" are valuable in other areas (increasingly valuable the more are transferred). In a long-run problem, of course, additional ships could be procured for more dollars. Finding satisfactory cost measures and resource constraints in the intermediate-run problems will frequently tax the ingenuity of the analyst. He must try to avoid treating as free those resources that have value in other uses, or as fixed those resources that, at some cost, are variable. (Also, of course, he should avoid the opposite errors.) While perfection is unattainable, the avoidance of the grosser fallacies is not.

"Sunk" costs and salvage values. Consider once again the costs counted in the search for the best way to destroy enemy shipping. These costs included man-years of effort used in the construction of ships, equipment, and submarines—many of which were already built and on hand. Yet the sacrifice entailed by the use of existing equipment was really its value in other operations,[21] not the original or historical cost of constructing it. Only future sacrifices are relevant—not past. In an economic calculus "bygones are forever bygones."

This point was critical in the comparison that we made above of B-29 and X bombing systems, where the B-29's had already been produced and the X-bombers had not. Should the Air Force "be fair" to System X and insist upon costing each bomber from scratch? Never could considerations of equity be more misplaced. Any real cost associated with the production of the B-29's had already been incurred and is un-

affected by what is done with them; if they have no alternative use and no scrap value, then the cost of incorporating them into the bombing system is zero. If they have a scrap value or a value in alternative uses that is sacrificed, then that value is the relevant cost. It is only the extra or incremental cost, not historical or "from scratch" cost, entailed by each alternative system that is relevant to the comparison. The analogy with a business firm's view of cost is complete: in deciding whether to replace an old machine with a new one, the production cost or purchase price of the new machine enters into the calculus, but only the scrap value (or alternative use value) of the old machine, however unfair this may appear to be to the new machine.[22] Considerations of fairness, which might be appropriate in courts of equity, are an undependable basis for choosing production methods or weapon systems.

Frequently in comparing the costs and gains from alternative weapon systems during some relevant period, it will be apparent that some of the systems will be worth more than others at the end of the period. An estimate of the worth of the system at the end of the period—its probable contribution to security in following periods—is commonly referred to as the system's "salvage value." If salvage values are substantial and vary significantly from system to system, they should be subtracted from system costs (or added to system gains). If these values are small or appear to be similar for all systems, of course they can be ignored.

ALLOCATION OF JOINT COSTS

In sub-optimizing, the analyst is frequently confronted with the necessity of computing the cost of X, when some or all of the costs of X are also costs of Y and Z. Suppose, for example, that the construction of an airbase is being considered for joint tenancy by three fighter squadrons and various Military Air Transport Service (MATS) facilities and services. Suppose that the total cost of the base is 100, of which 50 is the cost of basic or common facilities, 30 the cost of facilities required by MATS only (these might include, for example, costs of extending or strengthening runways for heavier MATS planes), and 20 the cost of facilities required by the fighter squadrons. If the base were used only by MATS its cost would be 80; if only by fighters, 70.

One way to approach the problem (it turns out to be a treacherous way) is to ask: How should the common costs be allocated among the various uses? One cabinet officer attempted to answer the question in this manner: "The Department believes that the costs of multiple-purpose . . . projects should be allocated on a basis which properly recognizes the added costs of including each separable function and a *fair*[23] share of the joint costs."[24] Again we have the unwarranted intrusion of ethical concepts into an economic calculus. In the Twentieth Century, it appears, we must be fair not only to people, but to weapon systems, machinery, and airbases.

If we keep firmly in mind the principle that only the *incremental* costs for which a system is responsible should be counted, problems of the type presented by the airbase offer no great difficulty. Of course which costs *are* incremental depends upon the breadth of context and the precise definition of the system. If the problem is whether to construct the airbase, and if so, whether for joint tenancy, for MATS only, or for the fighters only, we have to cost the base in three alternative systems. In the first (joint tenancy), the cost is 100; in the second (MATS only), 80; in the third (fighters only), 70. The base should be constructed if its value to MATS exceeds 80, if its value to the fighter command exceeds 70, *or if its value to both exceeds 100*. If its value to both combined exceeds 100, the base should be constructed for joint tenancy as long as its value to MATS exceeds 30 and its value to the fighter command 20. A business-man launching a multiproduct investment would think along precisely these same lines in maximizing his profits.[25] As long as the use values can be calculated,[26] the analyst can find a unique solution to his problem without allocating, "fairly" or otherwise, the common costs. The question simply doesn't arise.

If a formula for allocating total costs among uses is intended to show how costs respond when one use is eliminated, it can serve a very useful purpose; it is then an attempt to get better estimates of incremental costs. But a formula that is supposed to hand out "fair shares" of joint costs, the shares exactly exhaust-ing the total, is not needed for good decisions and can lead to bad ones. Inability to allocate *all* costs meaningfully among joint products is often a fact of life, not a disgrace or a sign of laziness. The extra cost of adding on a function or a feature can be calculated, or the total cost of the combination of features—but not a meaningful total cost for one feature when undertaken jointly with the others.

Appropriate criteria

So much for potential errors in the devising of tests for preferred policies. What of a con-structive nature can be said about the selection of criteria? Clearly, there is no all-purpose criterion, for the appropriate test depends upon what alternatives are open to the decision-maker, upon what aspects of the situation must be taken as given, and even upon what kind of measurements are feasible. Nonetheless a few general observations about suitable criterion-forms can be made.

MAXIMUM GAINS-MINUS-COSTS

If gains and costs can be measured in the same unit, then to maximize gains-minus-costs is certainly an acceptable criterion-form—the equi-valent of making the most out of whatever ac-tions can be taken. Suppose the possible courses of action are to put available resources to one of three uses, to be called A, B, and C. Now the gains that could have been obtained by using the resources in B and C are what have to be given up when we use the resources in A. These sacrifices are the *costs* of devoting the inputs to use A, the cost of obtaining the gains from A. When costs are viewed in this way (that is, as gains that must be given up), it is easy to see that maximizing gains-minus-costs is the same as maximizing total gains. If A yields 100 units of gain, B yields 75 units, and C 50 units, A is the use that maximizes gains-minus-costs (100 minus 75), and it is the use that yields the great-est total gain in the circumstances. Note again that this sort of test is possible only when gains and costs are commensurable. It can be used in the comparison of the actions of business firms and certain government measures but only exceptionally in the analysis of military activities.

EITHER GAIN OR COST FIXED

In any situation there are constraints. The decision-maker can borrow additional funds only at higher rates of interest, only a limited number of practical actions are open to him, and there are only twenty-fours hours in his day. In many analyses, one constraint is that a particular scale of gain or cost is fixed. This constraint may be imposed when gain and cost are commensur-able, as in the case of a firm comparing different ways to use a given investment budget. And it should be imposed, as a rule, for analysis in which costs and gains are incommensurable. In the latter case, naturally it is impossible to maximize gains-minus-costs; what would be the meaning of the ability to destroy ten targets minus one billion dollars? The next-best procedure[27] is to "set" either the costs or gains, seeking the way to get the most for a given cost, or to achieve a specified objective at least cost.

These two criterion-forms are equivalent, if the size of either gain or cost is the same in the two tests. If the test of maximum gain for a $5 budget points to the policy which yields a gain of 10 units, then the test of minimum cost to achieve a fixed gain of 10 will point to the same policy—the one which achieves the gain of 10 at a cost of $5. The two tests also yield equivalent information if calculations are carried out for many different scales of cost and gain. The choice between these two criteria depends largely upon convenience of analysis and upon whether it is gain or cost that can be fixed with the greater degree of "correctness." In some cases it will be immediately apparent which way round the criterion should be stated and the analysis made. For example, the field commander (or his operations analyst), preparing for an imminent battle with a multiplicity of fixed specific resources, will obviously fix the level of resource constraints and attempt to maximize his chances of winning, rather than set some arbitrary chance of winning and calculate the combinations of resources necessary to achieve it. In other cases the preferred way round will not be apparent, and it may indeed make little difference from any point of view which is selected. For example, we can either choose some index of strategic capability we think we might be able to achieve, and calculate the necessary budget, or assume some practical budget and calculate the corresponding index of capability.

This leads us to the big question: How does one determine the right achievement or budget? If the achievement or budget is set uncritically, the procedure degenerates into the "requirements approach." What can be done to improve upon this approach?

As a starter, several tasks or scale of effectiveness can be tried, and several budget-sizes can be assumed. If the same system is preferred for all tasks or budgets, that system is dominant. In the bombing-system example, the best bomber (though not the right scale or capability) is then determined.[28] If the same course of action is not dominant, the use of several tasks or budgets is nevertheless an essential step,

because it provides vital information to the decision-maker.

Note, however, that the decision-maker, if he is making a quantitative decision or if the qualitative answers vary in the scale, must then himself select the scale of the task or budget. He is presumably helped in reaching this decision by the information about the cost of achieving different tasks or the potential achievements with different budgets. But he has to draw on further information in order to set the right task or budget. He has to ask what task or budget, as the case may be, is consistent with higher-level criteria. Is a capability of destroying ten thousand targets too much or too little in view of the over-all aims of the defense program?

Clearly the analyst will be more helpful if he can answer these questions than if he merely estimates the results for a variety of budgets or tasks. As a matter of fact, he must try to answer these questions approximately if he is even to hit upon a reasonable range of tasks or budgets. He cannot experiment with all possible scales of achievement or cost, as the computations would be too expensive and voluminous to provide any net assistance. Hence the analyst can and should do more than try several tasks or budgets (the procedure which was labeled a "starter"). He should make some inquiry into higher level criteria and into their relationship to possible lower level tests. He may even convert the analysis into a higher sub-optimization. At *some* higher level, of course, the criterion must be taken as given—that is, to carry out the high level task at minimum cost, or to get most out of the high level budget. But this acceptance of a task or budget as given at some high level is skies apart from setting "requirements" uncritically all the way up and down the line.

THE CRITERION FOR CHOOSING A MILITARY AIR TRANSPORT FLEET

In the hypothetical example in a preceding chapter the criterion selected was the minimum cost of maintaining a specified airlift capability over the years 1958–1967. This criterion avoids some of the elementary pitfalls of criterion selection that we have discussed. It does not try to achieve a maximum capability at minimum cost. Nor does it employ a crude ratio—like minimum cost per ton-mile—irrespective of the scale of the job to be done (the distances to be traveled and the volume of cargo to be carried). It uses system costs, omitting sunk costs and, at least in principle, allowing for the salvage value of what is left over in 1967.

It concentrates on minimizing the cost of achieving a given objective instead of maximizing the objective for a given cost, because in this particular case it seems to be easier to select a "reasonable" level for the objective than for the budget. Providing airlift is a small proportion of the total cost of preparing to fight peripheral wars, and a small part of the total cost of operating the peacetime Air Force and military establishment. To choose some arbitrary budget level for airlift and adjust all other plans to it would be to make the tail wag the dog.

The level of the objective to be achieved was not chosen arbitrarily: it was based on certain plans for fighting peripheral wars if they occur, and for supporting a planned peacetime military establishment with rapid transport. It was an objective that had to be described in considerable detail—the war had to be fought in a certain geographical location and to be of a certain magnitude, and the peacetime support had to be provided using an established network of bases involving routes of diverse specific lengths. The degree of detail in defining the objective may appear excessive (it would certainly prove to be wrong as a specific forecast). This detail was intended to illustrate representative tasks, however, and it was believed that a change in the geographical location of the war, or in the pattern of available peacetime bases, would not greatly alter the mix of short- and long-legged vehicles needed. It would be desirable, in a more complete analysis, to test this belief by trying the various fleets in achieving different tasks.

A very important side calculation was made which (assuming it to be correct) determined that any fleet that could meet the requirements of the assumed limited war and peacetime re-supply could *a fortiori* meet the requirement for air transport in a general all-out war.

Nevertheless, some doubts remain regarding this particular criterion. The calculation was a low level sub-optimization, and some of the conclusions (especially regarding the size of the task and of the fleet) might be upset by a good economic analysis at a higher level. In limited wars expensive airlift is a substitute for other expensive things we can buy, such as pre-positioned supplies, tactical air forces and troops stationed overseas, and allied military forces sustained by United States military aid. Since the study in a previous chapter did not explore for the optimal mix of these elements, the ob-

jective chosen may have been too large or too small, perhaps influencing the composition of the optimal fleet.

There are other interdependencies (spillovers) and intangibles and uncertainties that could conceivably upset some of the assumptions or conclusions or both. For example, purchasing the more advanced types might help to promote the general state of the art of American transport aviation. A fleet which used fewer crews might make it easier for SAC to obtain the crews it needs to improve its alert status and thereby its deterrent capability. A fleet with a more flexible capability would help us deal with a variety of contingencies not included in the study—like a new Berlin airlift.

There are also complications associated with time and development uncertainties that affect the validity of the criterion. We will postpone a consideration of these; but in general it would be indefensible to compare expenditures incurred in different years, as this example does, without applying appropriate discount rates. The advanced types require heavier expenditures now, lower expenditures in the future, compared to the types in inventory. If a sensitivity test had not shown that discount rates as high as 25 per cent failed to upset the ranking of the fleets, we would have grave doubts about the relevance of the conclusions. Since even high rates do not alter the ranking, and since many of the other omitted factors tend to reinforce the preference for the advanced types, we can safely conclude from the study that *if the projections of performance are correct*, the procurement of one of the newer fleets would be economical. It is interesting that the economic criterion in this instance calls for the acquisition of new, more expensive equipment even though no direct competition in performance with the enemy is involved. Of course similar economic criteria frequently lead business men to precisely the same sort of conclusion.

CRITERIA FOR DETERRENCE

Suppose that our problem (in 1959) is the design of a strategic offensive force for the middle 1960's to deter prospective enemies from attacking us. Deterrence of World War III is a frequently stated national objective. Our strategic offense force, while not the only force important for deterrence, is generally recognized to be the principal one. But "deterrence" is an elusive and qualitative concept, not too far removed from "military worth" itself. To calculate the relative contributions of alternative weapon systems, base locations, and strategies to deterrence, we require a much more precise and objective proximate criterion. What is a good criterion—one that avoids the pitfalls we have outlined and is consistent with the high level national objective of deterrence? Let us consider some possibilities (all of which have been used in similar studies), beginning with some that, while avoiding the crudest fallacies, are still clearly unsatisfactory.

a. *Numbers or weight of offense weapons (for a given budget)*. Criteria of this general type are used in a surprisingly large number of cases by military correspondents, columnists, and other "experts" who should know better. Our deterrent force is held to be effective because we have more (or bigger) bombers than the Russians; or thought not to be effective because the Russians allegedly are building more long-range missiles than we. Little thought is required to dismiss such crude counting devices. What matters is not the number of aircraft or missiles on either side, or any other physical measure of their size, but in some sense the damage they are able to inflict. A missile that can carry a small bomb and deliver it within 10 miles of its target presents nothing like the deterrent threat of a missile that can carry a large bomb and deliver it within two miles.

b. *The number or value of enemy targets that can be destroyed (for a given budget)*. This is a criterion that makes a little more sense. It takes into account not only the numbers of our offense bombers and missiles, but also their operational effectiveness, the yield of the bombs they can carry, their ability to penetrate enemy defenses, and the accuracy with which their bombs can be delivered. It is still, of course, an ambiguous criterion, and requires more precise definition. For example, what target system—population, industry, or military bases—should we use to keep score on alternative United States strategic forces? In principle, the one whose prospective destruction would be most likely to deter the Russians from striking. If we are not sure which target system would have this characteristic, we might have to try several, to see whether the same strategic force performed best (or well) against all. Similarly, what kind of air defenses should we assume the Russians will have in the mid-sixties? Here we will almost certainly have to assume several kinds and quantities to test the alternative forces, giving the Russians some opportunity in each instance to adjust their defenses to the composition and basing of our force. But there remains another ambiguity in this criterion —one of crucial importance. Should we count the destruction potential of the entire force (the customary procedure) or the potential of that part of the force that survives an enemy attack? In other words, are we interested in a "strike-first" or a "strike-second" capability? Which is consistent with the national objective of deterrence?

To the extent that we are concerned with deterring a direct Russian assault on us, the essence of deterrence is a strike-second capability. The Russians will be deterred, not by the damage we can do if they refrain from attacking, but by the damage we can do if and after they attack. An American force that can make a devastating first strike but is easily destroyed on the ground is more likely to invite direct attack than to deter it. (It may, however, have some utility in deterring lesser aggression, for example, against third parties.)

c. *The value of enemy targets that can be destroyed (for a given budget) after an enemy first strike*. This is much closer to what we want. It requires us, in allocating our given budget, to reduce the vulnerability of our force whenever money spent on reducing vulnerability (say, on dispersal, on increased alertness, or on underground construction) will increase our strike-second capability more than the same money spent on additional bombers or missiles and the personnel to operate them. In general, this is what deterrence demands. This criterion is probably good enough to justify extensive quantitative comparisons of our capabilities with different kinds of weapons (bombers and missiles), different base systems (continental United States *versus* overseas *versus* on or under the seas; fixed *versus* mobile), and different modes of protection (such as ground alert, airborne alert, dispersal, and underground construction). In making the comparisons we must consider a range of possible Russian attacks, with special emphasis on those that look most dangerous to us, and are therefore most likely to be preferred by the Russians.

But we should be under no illusions that this good, workable criterion is good enough to yield definitive answers. It too ignores several vital elements of this exceedingly difficult and complex problem. For example, it ignores the danger that World War III might break out as the result of an accident or misunderstanding; it would do us little good to deter a rational enemy from attacking only to stumble into hostilities by accident (and some weapons and modes of operating them are more "accident prone" than others). This criterion partly neglects the objective of deterring "minor" aggressions, such as enemy attacks on United States or free-world positions in the NATO area or the Middle East. A strike-second capability would also have a strike-first potential, but it is not obvious that the measures that are optimal for deterring a direct attack are also optimal for deterring an indirect one. This test also ignores a good many interdependencies among different military capabilities: can our strategic offensive forces be designed in such a way as to contribute to our ability to fight limited, local wars or to facilitate the task of air defense? Can it even be assumed that the best force for deterring World War III is also best for fighting it—in the event that deterrence fails?

There is, moreover, the problem of what size the "given" budget should be. The optimal mix of weapons, bases, and protective measures may or may not be similar at different budget levels (this could be tested by trying a number of different levels). But even if the mixes are similar, it is tremendously important to get the absolute level somewhere near right—to have a deterrent force that is good enough, not merely the best achievable on a budget too low to provide deterrence, or one so good that we over-deter World War III and have little left over for other vital capabilities. The fixing of this level, requires, of course, a higher level study that focuses on the size of the national security budget and its allocation among the major military claimants—for strategic offense, strategic defense, limited war, and cold war. We have indicated that while rigorous maximization at this level is silly, hard straight thinking in an economic framework can help, and can be helped by quantitative calculations. The size of the budget for the strategic offensive force must not be accepted *uncritically* as "given"; its determination is one of the most important national security decisions.

Notes

1. Consumers' research publications sometimes recommend a single "best buy," using a criterion which may or may not be acceptable to a particular subscriber. But usually they content themselves with describing features and analyzing certain consequences, letting the subscriber supply (a total or final) evaluation and make the choice.

2. We must again stress that no connotation of greater or lesser significance should be associated with these terms "higher" and "lower" levels. The lower level decisions may in some circumstances be the more important ones. Choosing the best bomber-missile systems and the means of protecting them, for example, may do more to enhance our deterrent force than allocating more funds to the Air Force to buy inferior systems.

3. The exceptions in which individual divisions (e.g., those of General Motors and U.S. Steel), are instructed to act autonomously and ignore the possible repercussions of their actions on the profits of other divisions of the corporation, are instructive. In these cases the corporation has deliberately decided that the "spillover" effects on other divisions are less important in the long run than the advantages of fixing responsibility and providing strong, clear-cut incentives. There is probably also a fear that the use of corporation-wide criteria in analysis may inevitably lead to an undesirable centralization of decision-making itself—a sort of "spillover" effect of a different kind. In any event, these exceptions are usually limited to certain kinds of decisions. Divisions of General Motors are supposed to be completely autonomous in buying and selling, but not in financing and therefore not in decisions requiring major capital expenditures. There are useful analogies in all this for the military.

4. This not only takes advantage of the man-on-the-spot's familiarity with the details of a problem but also constitutes a more desirable decision-making process anyway, getting more persons in the habit of using ingenuity and taking responsibility. Indeed this is of major importance for the functioning of the economy, and probably of equal importance in the military services.

5. Admittedly, if the requirement *has* to be taken as given, it is better to achieve it at minimum cost than at higher cost. Even a "bad" sub-optimization may be better than none at all. It may not make sense in the total context to raise the reliability of hand grenades to a magic 90 per cent, but if it has to be so raised the fewer resources we use in doing so the more will be available for sensible products.

6. The classic work in this field in A. C. Pigou, *The Economics of Welfare*, 1st ed., Macmillan and Co., London, 1920. For an introductory and somewhat more modern exposition, see J. E. Meade and C. J. Hitch, *Introduction to Economic Analysis and Policy*, Oxford University Press, New York, 1938, especially

Part II. For development in, and qualifications to, the theory of welfare economics, see Paul A. Samuelson, *Foundations of Economic Analysis*, Harvard University Press, Cambridge, Mass., 1948, pp. 203–253; Kenneth J. Arrow, *Social Choice and Individual Values*, John Wiley and Sons, New York, 1951; and R. C. Lipsey and K. Lancaster, "The General Theory of Second Best," *Review of Economic Studies*, 1956–57, pp. 11–32.

7. Of course efficiency in this sense does not imply an "optimal" distribution of income from anyone's point of view or an "optimal" rate of growth. Efficiency is not a sufficient condition for an optimum, but it does enable us to identify improvements in many situations.

8. There are administrative devices—committees, special staffs at high levels, etc.—which attempt, through cooperation and "coordination," to mitigate the consequences of the absence of such a mechanism.

9. "Organizing for Technological War," a staff study, *Air Force*, December 1957, p. 44.

10. B. H. Liddell Hart, *Strategy*, Frederick A. Praeger, Inc., New York, 1954, p. 240.

11. *The Economist*, July 30, 1955, p. 400.

12. For examples of ratios used as criteria, see Charles Kittel, "The Nature and Development of Operations Research," *Science*, February 7, 1947, pp. 152–53. For more on the hazards of using ratios as criteria, see Charles Hitch, "Suboptimization in Operations Problems," *Journal of the Operations Research Society of America*, May 1953, pp. 94–95 and *passim*. See also Charles Hitch, "Economics and Military Operations Research," *Review of Economics and Statistics*, August 1958, pp. 199–209.

13. Of course, he will presumably minimize the cost of satisfying the requirement—which is, as we have seen, better than choosing uncritically both the task and the method of accomplishing it (the "pure" requirements approach, undefiled by any cost considerations).

14. Or sometimes "divergences between private and social product or cost."

15. The term "spillover costs" and a helpful discussion of those that arise from congestion are contained in J. M. Buchanan's article, "The Pricing of Highway Services," *National Tax Journal*, June 1952, pp. 97–106.

16. From A. M. Mood's review of P. M. Morse and C. E. Kimball, *Methods of Operations Research*, in the *Journal of the Operations Research Society of America*, November 1953, p. 307.

17. *Mutual Security Acts of 1952*, Hearings before the Committee on Foreign Affairs, House of Representatives, 82nd Congress, 2nd Session, U.S. Government Printing Office, Washington, D.C., 1952, p. 359.

18. Kittel, p. 152.

19. The operation that maximized the *ratio* of ships sunk to allied effort might be a trivial operation sinking one ship or a gigantic effort destroying vast quantities of shipping and requiring the bulk of our resources. There is little assurance that the operation picked solely on the basis of this *ratio* would contribute the most toward victory.

20. Though even here some of his resources may have value for later battles—a relevant alternative use.

21. This may well be hard to measure quantitatively, but better the roughest approximation of the relevant magnitude than the most precise measure of the irrelevant.

22. For examples in which business management formally compares alternative policies in terms of incremental costs and gains, see Horace C. Levinson, "Experiences in Commercial Operations Research," *Journal of the Operations Research Society of America*, August 1953, pp. 220–239.

23. Italics ours.

24. Former Secretary of Agriculture Brannan in *Study of Civil Works*, Part 2, Hearings before the Subcommittee to Study Civil Works of the Committee on Public Works, House of Representatives, 82nd Congress, 2nd Session, U.S Government Printing Office, Washington, 1952, p. 198.

25. George J. Stigler, *The Theory of Price*, Macmillan Co., New York, 1946, p. 307.

26. Of course if the use values can't be calculated, the analyst may have a difficult problem on his hands and may have to be content with a "good" or "better" rather than a unique optimal solution. But allocating the common costs won't help him in this case. His fundamental difficulty is his inability to measure military worth.

27. Equivalent to maximizing gains-minus-costs in the special case where gains and costs are commensurate and the right level of gains or costs is fixed.

28. This may be the decision-maker's current problem—*which* bomber to develop or procure. The decision regarding numbers may be made (and re-made) much later.

Alain C. Enthoven

Economic analysis and defense policy*

Introduction

TRADITIONALLY, the economics of national defense has meant the study of economic war potential and the problems of mobilizing it to produce armaments. During the fifties, the range of national security problems treated by economists was broadened to include many topics quite unrelated to fiscal policy and monetary theory. The economics of national defense now includes studies of the organization and management of the Defense Establishment and the armaments industries, and it includes economic analysis of the requirements for weapon systems and forces; that is, the central issues of defense policy and programming. Although much of the research on these problems has been classified, enough outstanding unclassified examples have appeared to provide the economics profession in general with a good survey of the range of topics being studied.[1]

In 1961, a group of economists who had been specializing in this field joined the Department of Defense in positions which gave them the opportunity to take the initiative in applying the results of their research to the practical problems of policy planning and financial management in the Department. This paper is a progress report on some of their work.

Of course, let me emphasize, the principal military advisers to the Secretary of Defense are the Joint Chiefs of Staff. Military planning is the responsibility of the Joint Staff and the planning organizations of the military departments. However, the Secretary of Defense has

* I would like to thank my colleagues Wm. Niskanen, M. J. Peck, and J. A. Stockfisch for their helpful suggestions in the preparation of this paper.

the responsibility to see to it that the plans and programs of the Department of Defense are selected with proper attention to considerations of economy and efficiency, and in this he is assisted by, among others, the economists on his staff. Although this paper is about the work of economists, I do not want to suggest that we think we are doing the whole job ourselves.

I believe that it is fair to say that the economists in the Defence Department have been successful in making economic analysis an effective contributor to the efficiency of the Department's program. Such basic concepts as marginal products and marginal costs have made it possible for the economists to summarize and integrate a great deal of critical program data and other diverse kinds of information for the few key officials who must make the major decisions on resource allocation. Moreover, although we have learned much from the experience, I believe that our earlier research has stood up well under the practical tests of realism and relevance.

Economic analysis within the Department of Defense is now as diverse as economics itself. It covers many areas. We have, for example, problems of industrial organization in administering the $10 billion weapons industry which the Department of Defense has created. Determining rates of military compensation raises all the traditional problems of the labor market. The Defense Department must consider the substantial impact of its expenditures on the U.S. balance of payments. Rather than cataloguing all of the activities in which economics, or more accurately economists, have proved useful, I have chosen to focus in this paper upon the problems of determining

Reprinted from "Defense and Disarmament: Economic Analysis in the Department of Defense," *American Economic Review*, Vol. 53, No. 2, May 1963, pp. 413–422.

requirements for weapon systems and forces; that is, the allocation of the defense budget. While this application of economics is relatively novel, I hope to make clear that economic analysis here is simply traditional marginal analysis, compounded, however, by real life uncertainties, data problems, problems of complex interactions between many diverse elements, and the continuing dialogue with the politically and legally responsible decision-makers.

The programming system

BEFORE economic analysis could be applied systematically to the problem of allocating the defense budget, it was necessary to install a financial management system that provided the right kind of information for top-level decision making. The system we found did not do this. It had several important defects, perhaps the most important of which was the almost complete separation between planning and decision making on weapon systems and forces, on the one hand, and budgeting on the other. What Arthur Smithies found in 1954 was still true six years later. To use his words: "Planning and programming precede budgeting and programs provide the basis on which budgets are prepared. Programs, however, are prepared in terms of military concepts and not in terms of dollars. When a program is completed, the cost in dollars is not known."[2] In other words, the long-range plans for weapon systems, forces, and all of their supporting elements were made by the services on the basis of their estimates of the forces required to assure our national security. Generally speaking, costs were not introduced systematically, either to test the feasibility of the whole program or for purposes of evaluating the efficiency of allocation.

Budgeting, on the other hand, had as its point of departure the guideline dollar totals laid down by the Administration and based on estimates of the burden the economy could or should bear. The result was a gap. The "required forces" always cost much more than the Administration and the Congress were willing to pay. The process by which the conflicting interests were resolved was unsystematic and wasteful because it led to unbalanced programs.

Furthermore, the Secretary of Defense did not receive adequate cost data. The budgetary system identified costs by object classes—Procurement, Military Personnel, Installations,

etc.—the inputs to the Defence Department, rather than by weapon systems and forces, such as B-52 wings and Army divisions which are the tangible outputs of the Department. The identification by object classes is suitable for purposes of appropriations and for management of a program already decided upon, and we have retained it for those purposes, but it is not suitable for top-level decision making on such questions as the proper mix between B-52 wings and Army divisions. Moreover, cost data were presented and financial management was conducted at the Defense Department level on a year-at-a-time basis. The full time-phased costs of the proposed forces were not presented to the Secretary of Defense. Because the costs of most programs are small in their first years, this led to the starting of many programs that could not be completed at anything like existing budget levels. Although a certain amount of this is a desirable hedge against uncertainty, it is clear that there were a great many wasteful stretch-outs and cancellations of programs that would not have been started if the costs of all of the approved programs had been anticipated.

Another problem was that the cost data that were presented when a program was being "sold" to the Secretary of Defense were not related in any systematic way to the costs used for budgeting. This meant that the services had a very powerful incentive to understate the costs, without the offsetting incentive of knowing that they would be held accountable for the same estimates when it came to budget preparation. Still another problem with the cost data was that the estimates that were made of the marginal costs of the various programs were incomplete and generally very low. For example, in 1961 the Congress appropriated a half billion dollars to buy another wing of B-52's, apparently in the belief that that appropriation would "pay for" the wing. As the Secretary of Defense pointed out in his announcement of his decision not to procure the extra bombers, the half billion represented only procurement costs. The total cost to buy and operate the bombers and their associated equipment for a period of five years would be three times that much. The understatement of marginal costs has a sort of "Duesenberry effect"; it makes increases appear to be relatively attractive and it makes program reduction appear to be unrewarding in terms of savings.

There were other problems also. Program decisions were made largely unilaterally on a single-service basis. For example, the Navy and the Air Force decided on their long-range ballistic missile programs largely independently of each other. To the extent that there was interaction, it was more competitive than cooperative.

Finally, the system did not provide data on marginal utilities or marginal products. The traditional military requirements study was typically a calculation of the forces required to achieve a single hypothesized objective. To give an oversimplified example, suppose that the objective were to achieve an expectation of destroying 97 per cent of 100 targets, using missiles having a 50 per cent single-shot kill probability. The requirements study would conclude that 500 missiles were required, without pointing out that the last 100 missiles only added an expectation of killing about 3 extra targets. We are now finding that it is just the latter kind of information that is required to close the gap I referred to earlier.

To correct these deficiencies, we established the Programming System. Reduced to simplest terms, the Programming System consists of a five-year projection of all forces, weapon systems, and other activities described in physical (or nonfinancial) terms, together with their costs, all as approved by the Secretary of Defense, plus a set of regular procedures for modifying the plan.

The key to the Programming System is decision making by program elements and major programs; that is, by the outputs of the Department rather than by the inputs. A program element is an integrated activity combining men, equipment, and installations whose effectiveness can be related to our national security policy objectives. The list includes B-52 wings, infantry battalions, and combatant ships, taken together with all the equipment, men, installations, and supplies required to make them effective military forces. The program elements are assembled into major programs which contain interrelated elements which closely complement each other or are close substitutes for each other and which must therefore be considered together in arriving at top-level decisions. The entire defense program is now divided into major programs as follows: (1) Strategic Retaliatory Forces, (2) Continental Air and Missile Defense Forces, (3) General Purpose Forces (primarily intended for the nonnuclear defense of overseas theaters), (4) Airlift and Sealift Forces, (5) Reserve and Guard Forces, (6) Research and Development, (7) General Support, (8) Civil Defense, and (9) Military Assistance.

The key point about a program element is that it has both costs and benefits associated with it. The benefits are the ways in which it helps us to achieve broad national security objectives. The costs are primarily the appropriations in all categories that will be required for its execution, not only in the current year, but throughout the lifetime of the program.

The Programming System has made it possible to unify program decisions and budget decisions. Budgets are still prepared annually in much the same way as before. However, the Five-Year Force Structure and Financial Plan is used as guidance to the military departments for the preparation of their budgets. During the annual budget review, the approved five-year plan is translated into requests for appropriations, by object classes, and there is a detailed review of the cost estimates and the manner in which the approved program is being carried out.

The programming approach is based on an over-all Department of Defense look at national security requirements, not a single service approach. Decisions about Polaris and Minuteman, Army divisions and tactical fighters, and other closely related programs supported by different services are made by the Secretary of Defense. This has made possible better balanced forces for the Department as a whole.

The Programming System frees the Department from year-at-a-time decision making, and forces us to look systematically at our plans and programs over a longer period of time. For defense planning, a year is arbitrary and short. The leadtime for most weapon systems is at least several years. The decisions that were made in 1961 about the fiscal 1963 budget will not have their full impact on our military posture until the period 1965 to 1967. We need an economically realistic plan for the future, so that long-lead decisions on program components will have a reasonable chance of turning out to be right.

Finally, and perhaps most important, the Programming System has formed the foundation for a systematic approach to the problem of reconciling "military requirements" and "reasonable budget levels." In the Programming System, costs and benefits are looked at together at the same time and by the same people rather than at different times and by different people. What is required militarily is looked at in the light of its costs, and estimates of what the country can or should afford to pay are considered in the light of the requirements of national security. Estimates of marginal costs and marginal products are provided for the Secretary of Defense, so that he and his principal advisers can concentrate their attention not so much on such questions as whether we need a capability to destroy 97 per cent of the 100 targets, with the alternatives unspecified, as on such questions as whether the capability to raise expected target destruction from 94 to 97 per cent is worth the cost of 100 extra missiles. Of course, data on marginal costs and marginal products do not imply mathematically what the number should be. We have no equivalent to the point at which marginal cost equals marginal revenue. A complex judgment still has to be made. But data of this kind contribute a great deal to making that judgment an informed one.

The economics of our posture for thermonuclear war

THE U.S. military posture for thermonuclear war includes our Strategic Retaliatory Forces, Continental Air and Missile Defense Forces, our Civil Defense Program, parts of our theater-based forces, plus research and development and weapon production programs to support them. An economic theory is required to allocate resources among these components.

By 1961, a great deal of progress had been made in the development of an economic theory for our posture for thermonuclear war. Many possible objectives had been explored, the important criteria had been clarified, and a reasonably good understanding had been developed of how the various elements of the program are related to the objectives.[3] It should be emphasized, however, that although the analytical methods were developed to a point of high sophistication, the theory rests on very little empirical data, and hopefully will remain so. There is no lack of awareness of this point among top-level policy-makers in our government.

Briefly stated, the objectives sought for our posture for thermonuclear war are twofold: First, we seek to make war unlikely; and, second, if despite our best efforts a war should occur, we seek to limit the damage caused to U.S. and Allied population and industry and to put ourselves in a position to achieve a speedy and favorable termination of the war. For the most part, these objectives can be translated into the quantitative criteria of damage to U.S., Allied, and Sino-Soviet population and industry and the balance of surviving military forces

occurring under various different circumstances of outbreak and conduct of the war.

Although there is obviously much more to the problem of thermonuclear war than economic analysis of efficient and inefficient postures, I will comment here only on two lines of advance that we have made in the past two years in the economics of the problem. First, we have made a great deal of progress in the translation of our broad objectives into specific quantitative criteria that can be applied in a systematic and practical way to the evaluation of alternative proposed forces and postures. This has been a matter of translating research results into practical operating procedures.

Second, prior to 1961, very little was done on the questions of budget level and total requirements. Economic research was limited almost entirely to questions of allocation within existing budgets and force levels. Although the problem of determining the budget level cannot be separated altogether from the efficiency of allocation, it was easier for economists to assume a given budget level and address exclusively the question of efficiency of allocation. However, when the Secretary of Defense made it clear that he was not going to begin with a predetermined budget level, but rather was going to address the problems of requirements directly, it became necessary to change somewhat the focus of the analysis. Instead of working in terms of marginal rates of transformation and substitution, in effect we switched to marginal products and marginal costs. This allowed the Secretary to make his own judgments as to the point at which the various marginal products were no longer large enough to justify the incurring of extra costs.

Conventional force requirements

ALTHOUGH the determination of conventional (i.e., nonnuclear) force requirements, in the sense of forces required to do a particular well defined task, has traditionally received thorough study by the military profession, the broader problems of relating alternative conventional force levels to national security objectives and of determining the over-all U.S. conventional force levels had not received much systematic treatment. Of course, as in the case of our nuclear forces, nonmilitary considerations such as those of foreign policy and domestic economic policy and political factors must enter into the decision.

There are several factors that make the

economic analysis of conventional force requirements a very different kind of problem from the economics of our posture for thermonuclear war. First, the uncertainties appear to be much greater and intangibles play a larger part in the case of conventional forces. I say "appear" to be "much greater" because it is altogether possible that our ability to put quantitative limits on the effects of nuclear weapons is based on ignorance of some crucial aspects of the problem. On the other hand, the United States has fought many nonnuclear wars. From the study of these and many other wars, the military profession has developed empirical generalization about the effects of various force ratios, weapons, terrain, and other factors. But, as they are quick to point out, the averages are surrounded by very wide variances. The uncertainties are large because of the critical importance of such factors as morale, leadership, surprise, etc., and the fact that the outcomes of conventional land-air battles are the product of very large numbers of complex interacting elements.

Another important difference is that the specific objectives sought by conventional forces lend themselves much less easily to quantitative treatment than do the objectives of our posture for nuclear war. The economic theory of our posture for nuclear war can be described in terms very similar to the economic theory of a multiproduct firm. There are smooth continuous rates of transformation and substitution and almost ubiquitous diminishing marginal returns. The objectives for conventional forces must generally be defined in terms of seizing or holding specific pieces of terrain in or for specified periods of time against specified enemy forces.

The approach we have adopted has been to formulate, in collaboration with the military planners, a range of carefully defined limited war problems in each of the various theaters in which our security requires a capability for major military operations. The questions are of the form, "What is the minimum amount of forces that would be required to hold, with high probability, for X weeks (perhaps indefinitely) at the Y line against an attack by Z forces?" After examining limited wars in each theater, mixes of wars in two or more theaters are examined. Then alternative forces, together with their required logistic support, are assembled to deal with the various assumed limited wars, their costs estimated, and the results presented to the Secretary of Defense. Although much remains to be done, these military-economic studies have given the civilian leadership a much clearer picture than they had before of over-all force requirements to implement the desired strategic objectives.

Practical ways of dealing with uncertainty

I HAVE referred several times to the numerous and major uncertainties present in this kind of work. There are good ways and bad ways of dealing with the problems of decision making under uncertainty. Economists have the advantage of familiarity with an extensive and sophisticated literature on the subject. I would like to outline here some of the practical quantitative methods we have adopted to deal with uncertainties in our work.

One encounters many different kinds of uncertainties in empirical studies of weapon systems and defense policy. Most of them fall into the following categories. There are uncertainties about operational factors such as the accuracy and reliability of missile systems, the hardness of targets, or the range of future aircraft. These are closely related to uncertainties about the time and cost to develop weapon systems. There are uncertainties about enemy behavior, his weapon systems and forces, and the behavior of other countries. How many ICBM's will the Soviet Union have in 1968? Will country X continue to grant us base rights in 1967? There are also conceptual uncertainties. How will the weapon systems we are buying now for the late sixties be related to our national security objectives then? If past experience is a reliable guide, it is almost certain that our strategy will change between now and then. If we fail to anticipate the change and allow for it now, our weapon systems may be quite inappropriately designed for the strategy of 1968, and the deficiency may have to be remedied at great cost later on.

Without attempting to give a complete catalogue of the tricks of this trade, let me indicate some of the methods and rules we follow.

First, there seems to be a widespread belief that the safe thing to do, in cases of doubt, is to overestimate one's opponent and underestimate one's own capabilities. If uncertain about the reliability of the enemy's missiles and ours, so this belief would have it, one should pick from the high end of the range of uncertainty for the opponent's and from the low end for our missiles.

In fact, we have learned that it is just as dangerous to overestimate the enemy's capabilities relative to our own as it is to underestimate them. Overestimates do not necessarily lead to insurance and safety. They are just as likely to lead to despair, to pricing of important policy objectives out of the market, and to strategies of desperation.

Next, we have found that in cases of uncertainty, it is often useful to carry three sets of factors through the calculations: an "Optimistic" and a "Pessimistic" estimate that bracket the range of uncertainty and a "Best Estimate" that has the highest likelihood. These terms are not very rigorous. A subjective judgment is required. But it is surprising how often reasonable men studying the same evidence can agree on three numbers where they cannot agree on one. In fact, one of the great benefits of this approach has been to eliminate much senseless quibbling over minor variations in numerical estimates of very uncertain magnitudes.

I pointed out earlier that the relationship of marginal products to marginal costs is usually of central importance in determining force levels. Interestingly enough, we have found that it is frequently the case that although there are major uncertainties about total products and costs, the marginal products and costs will be much less sensitive to variations in the factors.

In the case of uncertainties about enemy behavior, we have often found it useful to play a simple two-person game in which the enemy is permitted to adjust to variations in our posture, in order to evaluate our own alternatives. Of course, thinking through the enemy's countermove is a time-honored part of military procedure. The trick, in the long-range planning business, is to apply realistic technical, budgetary, lead-time, bureaucratic and other constraints to the enemy's hypothesized freedom to react. A frequent error here is to allow him too much freedom to adjust; the consequences are those of over-estimating the opponent, described earlier.

With respect to conceptual uncertainties and uncertainties about strategic context, another error to be avoided is becoming locked in tightly by current strategic concepts and assumptions. We therefore make a conscious effort to evaluate alternative postures under a wide range of different hypothetical future circumstances and policies. Although this procedure doubtless is not nearly as good as actually knowing the future, it does help our decision-makers to build into our posture a certain amount of flexibility that might not otherwise be included.

Conclusions

I WOULD like to conclude with three general observations.

First, the tools of analysis that we use are the simplest, most fundamental concepts of economic theory, combined with the simplest quantitative methods. The requirements for success in this line of work are a thorough understanding of and, if you like, belief in the relevance of such concepts as marginal products and marginal costs, and an ability to discover the marginal products and costs in complex situations, combined with a good quantitative sense. The advanced mathematical techniques of econometrics and operations research have not proved to be particularly useful in dealing with the problems I have described. Although a good grasp of this kind of mathematics is very valuable as intellectual formation, we are not applying linear programming, formal game theory, queuing theory, multiple regression theory, nonlinear programming under uncertainty, or anything like it. The economic theory we are using is the theory most of us learned as sophomores. The reason Ph.D.'s are required is that many economists do not believe what they have learned until they have gone through graduate school and acquired a vested interest in marginal analysis.

Second, I observed earlier that economic analysis cannot determine the optimum allocation or size of the defense budget. It stops with informing the legally constituted officials who have to make the critical judgments. Because the range of possible alternatives is so great, economic analysis in the Office of the Secretary of Defense has become a continuing dialogue between policy-makers and economists, in which the policy-makers ask for alternative solutions to their problems, make decisions to exclude some in order to focus attention on the most interesting candidates, and make value judgments and policy decisions, while the economist attempts to clarify the conceptual framework in which decisions must be made, to define alternative possible objectives and criteria, and to explore in as clear terms as possible (and quantitatively) the cost and effectiveness of alternative courses of action.

Finally, the range of interesting and important problems urgently requiring the attention of economists is very great. As well as the many unsolved problems remaining in the area of weapon systems and force requirements, we have problems of personnel compensation, requirements and utilization, problems of internal organization and pricing, inventory management, contracting for research and development and procurement, and many others. For economists interested in the field of national security, the Defense Department offers excellent and exciting opportunities for public service.

Notes

1. See, for example, C. J. Hitch and R. N. McKean, *The Economics of Defense in the Nuclear Age* (Cambridge 1960). Henry S. Rowen, *National Security and the American Economy in the 1960's* (G.P.O., Washington, 1960). M. J. Peck and F. M. Scherer, *The Weapons Acquisition Process: An Economic Analysis* (Boston, 1962). J. A. Stockfisch, ed., *Planning and Forecasting in the Defense Industries* (Belmont, Calif., 1962).

2. *The Budgetary Process in the United States* (New York, 1955), p. 241.
3. See, for example, A. J. Wohlstetter, "The Delicate Balance of Terror," *Foreign Affairs*, Jan. 1959; H. S. Rowen, *op. cit.*, and Herman Kahn, *On Thermonuclear War* (Princeton, 1960).

Harold J. Barnett

The changing relation of natural resources to national security*

MY ASSIGNMENT HERE is to convey information—facts and ideas—on the relation of natural resources to national security. This subject matter cannot be neutralized from government policies and behavior, or from social values. At its core, it concerns social goals, international relations, politics, economics, and other fields of social analysis. It is an arena where non-physical variables such as military alliances and other international relations are the major influences, and where value judgments concerning the world and national societies in which we want to live, on such matters as democracy, free enterprise, and durable peace, set our objectives.

With this warning, let us now define our terms rather quickly. By national security we mean long-term security from hostile military behavior. This excludes from our considera-

* I am indebted for advice and criticism to several of my colleagues—R. G. Gustavson, J. L. Fisher, N. Potter, F. T. Christy, and H. Jarrett. The opinions expressed are, however, personal ones and not organizational policies or attitudes.

Reprinted from *Economic Geography*, Vol. 34, No. 3, July, 1958, pp. 189–201.

tion a non-military concept of "security"— the conservationists' and ecologists' concepts of a durable and secure balance between man and nature. By natural resources, we mean both the flow of useful materials from our physical surroundings, and the spatial relationship which this environment provides. By the relationship between our two variables, we mean both the direct and indirect influence of natural resources upon national security.

A few sentences will suffice to tell my outline. I first discuss *lebensraum*, a philosophy of world growth in which resources are held to be a major cause of war. This is the most general and widely held public view concerning the relation of resources to war. In the next part I survey and comment on three more specific, narrower, but also accepted views on resources and war. The heading "Materials for War" validly describes that these views are concerned with resources as an instrument for the prosecution of war. The views are not inconsistent with the *lebensraum* doctrine, and, in fact, in some respects derive from its more general principles. In the final part, I turn to United States policies concerning the resources-security relationship, present some assumptions and evidence, and derive therefrom some tentative conclusions.

Lebensraum

ONE major aspect of the *lebensraum* doctrine emphasizes the importance of space, position, topography, weather, and the like (which for convenience I call spatial relationships), as determinants of military security. This relationship operates at several levels. It is subsumed in international policies where it operates (other things equal) to minimize frictions and prevent war, as for example, by putting great distance between Western hemisphere nations and Asiatic ones; or to facilitate war, as for example, between Egypt and Israel, or France and Germany. At another level, the space relationship influences military strategy. For example the Channel protects Britain from invasion; the oceans invite submarine warfare against the United States and inhibit ground attack; and the fact of relationship of space and security prompted Russian utilization of vast and frigid space to defeat the Napoleonic and Hitler invasions, and neutralized the historic conquests of China. Finally, space is a dominant influence upon military tactics, as we remember

from our World War training and action, or from reading Major Eliot.

It is inevitable that the space factor will always have some importance for differential national security. Yet it is becoming less of a differentiating factor with the advance of technology which shrinks the world, and in this sense becoming less important. We no longer depend upon space to prevent conflict between the United States and Russia, not to reduce significantly the mutual hurt which conflict would bring. And this is because the space between formerly distant countries has shrunk to a matter of hours, no less than because of weapon technology advance.

In addition to the fact that space is becoming less capable of *differentially* influencing national security of the several nations, the shrinkage of space is also weakening absolutely the security of all nations and of mankind in a revolutionary way. One of the functions of space is that it provides capacity to absorb pressures and tensions among nations. While some of the forces of growth in recent world history have been of the type which reduce international pressures and tensions, most of the forces have operated to increase these. The pressure-increasing forces include, among others, sheer numbers and weights of aspiring national groups; increased dependence upon international trade and other intercourse; and the thrust of civil and military technology. And this trend of increased pressures and tensions has coincided with a loss of space in two meanings—its reduction in terms of time intervals between nations; and the merging into a single world unit of what were formerly distinct and separate national atmospheres, and formerly unused "satellite space."[1]

It is tempting to give physical analogies of the importance of space as a cushion and shielding device, and of the dangers from its shrinkage. The most apt analogy, I think, is the simple electrical one of short-circuit. Space may be used to insulate a wire carrying an electrical load. Let the charge build up or the space decrease, and the threat of short-circuit increases. At sufficiently high charge or small enough space, the malfunction is continuous and the design, which depended upon space for insulation, obsolete. "The great globe itself is in a rapidly maturing crisis—a crisis attributable to the fact that the environment in which technological progress must occur has become undersized . . . literally and figuratively, we are running out of room. . . . Thus the crisis does not arise from accidental events or human errors. It is inherent in technology's relation to geography on the one hand, to political organization on the other."[2]

RAW MATERIALS PRESSURES

The second aspect of the *lebensraum* doctrine might be called "raw materials pressures." The view is that growth of populations and levels of living press upon limited natural resources and thus generate international tensions and war. Much public belief and scholarly research subscribes to this opinion of the relation of natural resources to war. In support of the view its proponents parade the list of modern wars. They point to colonialism of the eighteenth and nineteenth centuries and the several major and numerous minor wars which created the colonial empires of the European nations. In the twentieth century, they point to the expansionary efforts of Japan, which produced the Russo-Japanese War, the Japanese invasion of China in the 30's, and the Japanese declaration of war in 1941; the empire quests of the German Kaiser and of Hitler and the consequent two World Wars; the Italian invasion of Ethiopia; and perhaps the current scramble for Middle East oil.

But the case for this relationship of natural resources to war is not as conclusive as this. A first possible criticism has to do with the evidence. The list of wars allegedly due to drive for raw materials claims too much. In most of the cases just given, it is the nations with high and improving levels of output per capita which incite the war—the Western European nations in the colonial period, and Germany, Japan, and Italy in this century. It is nations able to procure raw materials from indigenous sources, from technological substitutions, from international trade. Yet the hypothesis is that they were driven to war to get raw materials. Is there not inconsistency here? On the other hand, one can think of cases of major nations with a high ratio of population to developed resources who have not started wars to get materials, for example, India and China. Finally, even if belief in need for raw materials by conquest is one influence leading to war, was it the dominant or even a main one? What of the hypotheses that wars are generated by need for markets to dispose of industrial goods, as has been charged against Germany; or by national ambitions, as charged against Italy and Japan; or by envy deriving from relative economic welfare or relative political power as

compared with, say, the United States; or by the personal drives for power of dictators, such as Hitler, Mussolini, and Stalin? Does it not appear, perhaps, that not only is it difficult to establish shortage as a sufficient or necessary condition for war, but that it is even difficult to be sure that it is a very major influence in generating war?

The second criticism that might be made is of the validity of the Malthusian-type doctrine upon which this raw materials shortage view rests. Is it clear that high ratios of population to developed resources inevitably bring lower standards of living and thereby incite nations to war? What of the role of technological advance and capital formation in permitting improved welfare simultaneous with population increase? What of the role of international trade as an efficient provider of materials for developed nations, and capital and know-how for less developed ones? And is there not some evidence of retardation of birth-rates over the long term as incomes rise and knowledge of birth control increases?

I find this question quite complex, and understand it only partially and imperfectly. I would argue against elevating the raw materials element of the *lebensraum* doctrine to something equivalent to natural law. But I would not deny that public belief in it has been significant in generating international tensions. For it is not enough to observe that per capita incomes have been increasing the world over if aspirations in low income nations generate emotional heat, as is presently the case in the Middle East. And it is not enough to say that international trade, foreign investment, and technical assistance are possible, if international tensions and uncertainties are such that the world has not come to believe these to be dependable as foundations for national welfare. If the United States at times betrays anxieties over dependence upon Malaya and Indonesia for tin and rubber, how much more anxious might France be over reliance on Middle East oil, or Brazil and Cuba over dependence upon foreign purchases of their coffee and sugar, respectively.

International trade seems capable of a Dr. Jekyll and Mr. Hyde role. That in general it is to mutual advantage is demonstrated in the chapter on the principle of comparative advantage in any elementary international trade text. After all, economic development of raw material producing nations is limited by their ability to market products on a sustained basis. And developed nations have equivalent reciprocal need to market fabricated products. In theory, the principal is similar to that of regional and urban-rural interdependence in the United States. The difficulty is that the mutual dependencies build up may not be symmetrical and in the international arena of independent, sovereign nations, this may properly generate anxieties primarily on one side. Although the ratio of imports to gross national product in the United States is only about 4 per cent, the similar ratio is 10 per cent in Japan; 20 per cent in Britain; 30 per cent in Belgium, Cuba, and Iceland; and 50 per cent in Venezuela. Thus a nation like the United States that is not very dependent on foreign trade may have much leverage over nations like Cuba or Japan, which are heavily dependent on it and do not have good alternative markets for buying or selling.

The case of Japan is illustrative. Japanese population grew about 15 per cent from 1912 to 1925. National income and industrial output increased several times as much, and Japan became dependent on imports for two-thirds of her petroleum, and over 90 per cent of her iron ore, phosphates, and raw cotton. Simultaneously, she developed a large silk trade, which in the 1920's constituted one-third of her total exports. Between 1926 and 1934 the price of silk exports dropped 65 per cent, as a result of world-wide depression and the introduction of rayon. This drop in price reduced the revenue by an equal percentage, since export quantities changed comparatively little. And thus her purchasing power for imports of grains, cotton, petroleum, etc., was cut by about 15 per cent, in the face of needs that were rapidly increasing as a result of industrialization and rising population.

In our discussion of space as a military parameter, above, I suggested that possibly it was becoming less influential as a differentiating factor. What about the future role of population growth and quest for raw materials as an influence on war? In one sense, this also may be becoming less important. Technological advance in materials substitution, for example atomic energy, plastics, and light metals, has been extremely rapid. Atomic energy, particularly, promises to reduce tensions from growing energy needs. Rises in income per capita are more world-wide than ever. Capital formation is at high rates. Birth rates in advanced countries are less than a century ago. The world's two major contesting powers, the United States and the Soviet Union, are both well endowed with natural resources. On the other hand, as I have

just pointed out, the problem may go beyond "need" in the physical sense, to that of "desire." And the number of nationally-conscious, nationally-inspiring countries is now larger than before the two World Wars, as the present Middle East crises show.

Materials for war

IT is generally believed that war and preparations for war call for enormous increases in raw materials consumption over peacetime levels. (This, in turn, leads to the worry that such level of consumption might quickly exhaust the nation's natural resource wealth.) I am not sure how the view of enormous increases has become popular; but that it is in part erroneous is suggested by the fact that present and recent annual levels of fuel and minerals consumption

TABLE I—U.S. CONSUMPTION OF SELECTED RAW MATERIALS

1935–39 = 100

Commodity	Average 1935–39	1943	1946	1949	1954	1955
Lumber	100	159	143	153	169	184
Cotton	100	160	146	117	125	133
Pig Iron	100	200	149	177	194	256
Copper	100	258	239	183	212	229
Zinc	100	151	148	131	163	199
Aluminium	100	664	436	482	1,286	1,323
Fertilizer	100	156	203	224	282	278
Cement	100	120	159	194	258	280
Petroleum	100	127	154	173	226	242
Natural Gas	100	162	183	258	460	502
Bituminous Coal	100	156	131	117	95	111

Source: Data are preliminary, from Resources for the Future worksheets of research now underway by F. T. Christy. Based upon published data of U.S. Departments of Commerce, Agriculture and Interior: *American Metal Market*; and American Bureau of Metal Statistics.

exceed those of World War II (see Table I, last five columns).

The view may derive from public knowledge of very large increases in World War II consumption of raw materials over the levels of the immediately preceding peacetime years—compare the first two columns of Table I. But the 30's were years of substantial unemployment, of relative depression, particularly in such activities as construction and equipment production. One out of each six people in the civilian labor force during 1935–1939 was unemployed. And thus outputs of many raw materials in the 30's, particularly minerals, were relatively low, due to low economic activity as compared with the all-out employment levels we achieved in World War II, or the full employment levels since its close. In general, the excess of war-time output over peacetime full employment might be of the order of 20 per cent for a war of World War II type. (The case of thermo-nuclear war is discussed in a later section).

Perhaps the view of enormously enlarged materials requirements embodies the premise that war and war preparation are peculiarly *intensive* in their requirements for raw materials. And, thus, even if the over-all level of national product rose only moderately, nevertheless the demand for raw materials could rise immoder-ately. This is undoubtedly true for some materi-als—e.g., uranium, titanium, steel armor plate and others. But, in general and in the aggregate we find that demands for industrial raw materials per unit of national product for a wartime "product mix" are not markedly different from those of peacetime. This is illustrated in Table II. The reason is that many of the luxuries we give up in preparations for war or in wartime because labor is the major scarcity—new auto-mobiles, unlimited travel, new housing con-struction, new household appliances, etc.—are just as materials-intensive as the war goods which we produce instead.

MILITARY STRENGTH AS A FUNCTION OF NATURAL RESOURCE WEALTH

Our discussion of raw material requirements for war just now has in part implicitly discussed the concept of military strength being a function of natural resource wealth. But a few words directly focused on it are desirable. The view is that military potential depends on natural resource wealth, because economic war potential depends on natural resource condition—e.g. that the military strengths of the United States and the Soviet Union are determined by their natural resource riches.

The dependence of military strength upon natural resource riches has, perhaps, been over-stated. It is true that the United States and the Soviet Union, the most powerful military na-tions in the world, are richly endowed with natural resources. But observe that there are other nations as rich or richer in this endow-ment who are not militarily strong—Brazil, India, Canada, large areas of Africa. Apparent-ly, then, natural resource riches are not a sufficient condition for military strength. Now observe that until the rise of the United States and the Soviet Union to dominant positions after the last war, Germany, England. and France were also first-class military powers, on

a par with the United States and Soviet Union. Apparently, then, further, since these West European countries are less well-endowed than many militarily weak ones, natural resource riches were not a necessary condition of mili-tary strength.

There is of course no paradox here, but oversimplification. Military strength does de-pend on natural resources. But provided the resources are available, they need not be indi-genous. Further, military strength requires an advanced industrial society, with all that this implies for technology, education, labor skills, capital investment and so forth. And contem-poraneously it places a premium on military forces in being upon outbreak of war. Finally, military strength up to recently, at least, has required relatively large population size.

TABLE II—U.S. CONSUMPTION OF SELECTED RAW MATERIALS PER UNIT OF REAL GROSS NATIONAL PRODUCT

1935–39 = 100

Commodity	Average 1935–39	1943	1946	1949	1954	1955
Lumber	100	94	89	93	82	84
Cotton	100	94	92	71	61	60
Pig Iron	100	117	93	107	95	116
Copper	100	152	150	112	104	104
Zinc	100	88	92	79	79	90
Aluminium	100	393	275	294	630	606
Fertilizer	100	91	126	135	137	126
Cement	100	71	100	118	126	127
Petroleum	100	75	96	104	110	110
Natural Gas	100	95	114	156	223	228
Bituminous Coal	100	91	82	71	46	50

Source: Materials consumption from Table I. GNP from U.S. Department of Commerce.

The proposition that luxurious United States standards of living and resource use are exhausting its natural wealth and thereby propelling it toward the status of a second-rate military power within the next century or so is even more serious over-simplification. It stems from viewing resource wealth as a bank account or reservoir from which only with-drawals take place, to reduce the balance. But withdrawal is not the only thing that occurs with the passage of time. New resources are con-stantly being discovered, made usable, and added to our wealth—uranium, oil shale, magnesium from the sea, aluminium from clay, oil from the ocean bed, steel from taconite and so forth. Other technological changes reduce the amount of resource we need to get a unit of product, as for example, in the increased efficiency in combustion of fuels in electric power production and railroad transport; or the amount of steel needed to carry a transmission line. And still other economic change occurs. This whole question is, I suggest, far more complex than the simple notion of a fixed stock being drawn upon.

U.S. PRODUCTION SELF-SUFFICIENCY

Finally, there is a widely held belief that if war occurs we may find ourselves cut off from foreign sources of essential raw material supply outside the nation. It has been vigorously argued that the nation must undertake to assure national production self-sufficiency for all those requirements of war for which this is physically possible, irrespective of the cost or of the international repercussions. Further, it is the full level of wartime materials requirements for which domestic capacity must be in being. Since in some cases the costs would be very high, strenuous government interventions are necessary and desirable—protective tariffs high enough to exclude foreign supplies; government price and other guarantees; government loans; and other subsidies.

The production self-sufficiency thesis is, in my view, basically erroneous. It damages the free world military alliances; it is excessively costly; it tends to damage our free-enterprise economy; and it seeks to buy excessive insurance against yesterday's type of war at the expense of insurance against today's hazards. These points are elaborated somewhat in the next part of my paper.

Suggestions concerning natural resources policy for national security

MY first suggestion is that it is impossible to avoid casting the topic as one of high governmental policy and behavior concerning natural resources and national security, with all that this implies concerning assumptions and goals. After all, private persons do not make decisions in this sphere. Further, once the problem is thus posed, a most useful implication appears: The solution needs to be consistent with United States economic policy and international policy. These constitute a large body of national objectives and behavior in which natural resources and national security are but components. It becomes clear that the wisdom of governmental natural resources policy proposed as improvement of our defense must be

economically sensible, in terms of the benefit exceeding the cost, and the efficiency of the preferred policy as compared with others. It becomes clear, also, that current decisions must be made without certainty of whether there will be war, of when there might be war, or of what kind of war the next one might be. It becomes relevant to observe that there is plentiful availability of weapons in the multi-megaton sizes, and no presently foreseeable progress in defensive weapons sufficient to prevent delivery of hundreds of these to target areas in the several nations. And finally, it seems clear that we can no longer hope for anything approaching absolute national security—that the increased defense we can procure in this age will fall extremely far short of being security in the sense of certainty.

The national income of even the United States is not large enough to support advance preparations for all conceivable contingencies in this shrunken world. And still less abundantly adequate is the portion of national income which our democratically-controlled country is willing to devote to such purposes before war.[3] We have just seen military budgets cut to avoid raising the national debt limit. Just as the task for military policy is to arrive at some combination of forces that is sensibly related to the probabilities, so natural resource and other economic policy must also be based on consideration of specific probabilities, individually and in combination. Ultimately, both military and economic policies must be closely related to the war plans they are designed to support. How can it be possible for sensible economic measures aimed at improving our military security not to be related to actual war plans and foreign policies?

PREMISES CONCERNING TYPES OF WAR AND PROBABILITIES

If rational decisions are to be made, we must visualize four kinds of possible war and the likelihood of each. The four are: (1) prevention of war, and thus no war; (2) peripheral wars; (3) major world war without thermonuclear bombardment of cities; (4) unlimited thermonuclear war. I shall discuss each, in turn, after which I shall point to the implication for natural resources.

1. *Prevention of war. No war.* The United States and Russia (and soon other nations) have the capability of literally destroying each other's —or anybody's—urban and industrial societies.

Hence I think that all nations will strenuously try to avoid major wars; and there is a possibility that they will be successful. With respect to this possibility, I quote the President (as reported in the *New York Times*, February 7, 1957):

> The vulnerability of any nation is probably greater than it ever was, because one bomb today can do the damage of probably all that we dropped on Germany in World War II.... Of course anything is possible in this world in which we live.... But I say this: The likelihood of any nation possessing these great weapons of massive destruction using them in an attack grows less, I think, every year. I believe as their understanding of them grows, then the less the chance that they would go on an adventure that brought these things into play, because, as I see it, any such operation today is just another way of committing suicide.

As a way of avoiding war, the United States seeks to create a strong free world alliance to stop Soviet political and economic expansion into Western Europe, the Middle East, and Asia. An appropriate question, then, with respect to any contemplated economic measure concerns its contribution to this United States strategy of preventing war: would the measure weaken or improve free world unity? If it would damage relations with other free nations, what is supposed to be the offsetting advantage? This question is not trivial—it is possible to believe that our free world alliances and relations with neutrals are of the same order of importance in containing Russia and preventing war as the United States military strength *per se*. And, to a major degree, therefore, government policies must be designed to strengthen these alliances and our comity with neutrals.

2. *Peripheral wars.* Consider now the second possibility, that Soviet expansionary adventurism will engage us in Korea-type wars at one or more points. This also is not a far-fetched assumption. For proof, examine the composition of the nation's military forces and the public statements of their leaders. Or think over the history of the past dozen years and the crises in Greece, Turkey, Iran, Yugoslavia, Indonesia, Korea, Indo-China, Formosa, Malaya, the Middle East, and Hungary. Or recall that we have as national policy the determination to risk or engage in localized wars, if necessary to deter Soviet expansion and major war.

What economic measures should we take to prepare for this contingency? Our need in this case—in which the battleground could be as varied as the Middle East, Indo-China, the Balkans, or a Polar area—is first, to have flexible military forces and munitions properly positioned to contain such thrusts. Second, we need reservists and military supplies in readiness and strategically located, in the United States and elsewhere, to be able to supplement such forces in days and weeks. Third, we need help from other countries—both those attacked and other allies. We need their economic and military strength as well as the benefit of common aims.

3. *World War II-Type hostilities.* The third possibility is a large-scale, long World War II kind of action in (say) Europe, in which both sides abstain from thermonuclear bombardment of home territories. It is really quite difficult to believe that this could happen, and from a reading of public statements it does not appear that the military are preparing to fight World War II all over again. One reason is that tactical use of nuclear weapons in populated areas would quickly develop into nuclear strikes against home territories. A second is that our whole deterrence program rests upon Soviet and our belief that the Soviet Union will experience swift retaliation by the Strategic Air Command if, for example, she invades Western Europe. A third is that in any lengthy large-scale war in which both sides have thermonuclear capabilities but have refrained from using them, only a stalemate outcome could induce continued abstention of their use. If Hitler had thermonuclear warheads, would he have refrained from their use in the V-1's and V-2's which showered England and Belgium in 1944 and 1945? And, finally, even if both sides try to confine use of thermonuclear weapons to military targets, such as the opposing strategic airbases, ports, rail centers, etc., the numbers of weapons involved and their lethal areas of radioactivity would make the effects on civil population hardly distinguishable from attacks on cities proper. Please note that I am not saying that any war between the United States and the Soviet Union must be a thermonuclear one. We just discussed such a situation under the heading "peripheral wars." I am saying that any war begun as, or developing into, a massive, long one of the World War II type would with high probability become a thermonuclear war, and thereby a short one.

If it is a new type of war, with modern weapons, that we visualize, then massive conversion of the economy following outbreak of war and estimates of materials required in such mobilization along World War II lines have dubious relevance.

But there is a strong human tendency to look ahead in terms of the recent past. Despite the intellectual awareness that the next large war—if there should be one—will be different, much of the economic planning and discussion of economic policy seems to be in terms of a conflict much like World War II. To the extent that preparation for such a war is desired, it must rest upon detailed plans for converting the economy to war output following outbreak of war. In such plans, it will become possible to identify specific bottlenecks and shortages which, if not prepared for, would delay the mobilization schedule. It is only on the basis of identification of specific bottlenecks that economic preparations can be justified; for otherwise the measure, such as particular industry assistance or a stockpile, might merely generate some fat in the economy not closely related to anything. Further, mere identification of bottlenecks does not by itself specify the most sensible measure from the large variety of alternatives. There still remains the task of intelligent choice.

4. *Major thermonuclear war.* Finally, despite efforts to avoid war, to restrict war to small scale, and at least to restrict war to the non-suicidal form, there is the fourth possibility—that a war involving thermonuclear bombing of cities and correlative radioactive "fallout" on most of the country will take place. Sensible prewar economic preparations for this contingency are not likely to be similar to those required to avoid bottlenecks in the World War II type conversions just discussed. There will be little time or occasion for World War II type military output if an atomic war devastates the whole economy at its outbreak. Such a war involves the prospect of millions, perhaps tens of millions, of mortalities, and equivalent numbers of wounded and sick. At the same time there will be wholesale destruction of essential water, food, medical, communication, transport, housing and other services. I am sure that the military services have adequate plans for continued supply, from remaining munitions stocks, of such military forces as survive. But what the United States needs in addition are passive defense measures.

These are desirable for two reasons. First, the effectiveness of our deterrence policy requires belief by our leaders and by the enemy that the deterrence force can be used against him if he incites a major war. Second, such measures are needed, should deterrence fail, to reduce casualties and to reconstitute a viable society out of the remnants of population and economic resources that survive. As to the instruments of passive defense, the list is a long one—country-wide shelters against radioactivity and urban ones against blast; warning time; dispersal and evacuation; stocks of subsistence goods, survival and recuperation plans. While the possible combinations are quite complex, shelter protection of the entire population against radioactive fallout and of urban populations against blast, in addition, are central to any solution.

From our examination of four types of war, we can highlight several points:

a. Because of the advance in military technology, the dangers to national security and the costs to offset them are so high that we must be selective in our defense efforts.

b. The possibility of preventing large-scale thermonuclear war (by a strong deterrent force, by free world alliances and by risking small peripheral war) is so desirable, the probability of success is so high, and the cost is so clearly manageable, that this is obviously our major objective. This requires among other things, fidelity to principles in international cooperation; and emphasis on substantial flexible military forces in being and readiness.

c. The small likelihood that a large-scale, long war could occur without thermonuclear bombing of the United States, the disorganization and destruction of United States industry which would take place if subjected to thermonuclear bombing, the fact of economic superiority of the United States over the Soviet Union if both sides refrain from thermonuclear bombing—all these argue against diversion of large efforts from direct military preparedness for the purpose of achieving self-sufficiency in production capacities, particularly if at the expense of international trade with the free world.

d. Finally, it is desirable to give more serious and effective attention than heretofore to protection of the civilian population against thermonuclear attack. Because offensive capability (against home economies) has completely outpaced the development of defensive measures since World War II, there should be no illusions that such protection is cheap or that it can be secured beyond a moderate degree at all. The February 14, 1957, *New York Times,* for example, reports that the White House is considering a plan for atomic shelters, estimated to cost $20 to $40 billions.

The following quotations are interesting and relevant as summary statements of the military probabilities:

> Should a nuclear war come, I think its duration is likely to be inversely proportional to its size. I do have the feeling that a big nuclear war will never come. But if it comes, the period in which such a war will be most devastating will be very short, indeed. It will be measured in hours, possibly in fractions of hours. The period in which the decision is made as to who wins the war, on the other hand, will be long, such as ten years preceding the time of the war. The actual fighting will be, I think, a matter of days or weeks. (Physicist Edward Teller in the Washington *Sunday Star*, January 13, 1957, p. A-28.)

> Destructive power has now become so cheap that wars can be won or economies destroyed before there is time for mobilization. In allout thermonuclear war the superior economic war potential of the United States is important only to the extent that it has been effectively diverted to security purposes before the war starts. (Economist Charles Hitch in *Defence Essentiality and Foreign Economic Policy* in Case Study: The Watch Industry and Precision Skills; Hearing before the Subcommittee on Foreign Economic Policy of the Joint Economic Committee, 84th Congress, 2nd Session; Washington, GPO, 1956; page 20.)

> The nostalgic idea that our industrial strength is our greatest military asset could ruin our military planning. (Former Secretary for Air Thomas Finletter in *Power and Policy* [New York: Harcourt, Brace & Company, 1954], p. 256.)

IMPLICATION FOR NATURAL RESOURCES POLICY

What are the implications for natural resources policies and behavior?

The first one, I think, is the opportunity afforded by raw materials for cementing and making strong the free world bulwark against Soviet and Chinese expansion. Unlike ourselves, whose economic welfare does not depend heavily on foreign trade, most other nations must export to continue their present lesser standards of living, let alone advance them:

a. Exports account for 20 per cent or more of national income in such countries as Australia Cuba, Egypt, Iceland, Norway, Peru, United Kingdom, and Venezuela; and more than 10 per cent in, for example, Bolivia, Brazil, Colombia, Indonesia, Japan, Mexico, Philippine Islands, Portugal, and Thailand.

b. The importance of the United States-Canadian market to almost all exporting nations is large—for example, more than half the total export market of Bolivia, Colombia, Cuba, and Mexico; between one-fourth and one-half of all exports of Brazil, Chile, Peru, Venezuela, Japan, and Philippines, and Thailand; and more than 10 per cent of the exports of Norway, Portugal, Turkey, the United Kingdom, Iceland, India, Indonesia, and Israel.

c. Many nations depend primarily upon raw material exports. For example, three-fourths of Bolivia's exports are tin and tungsten; three-fourths of Chile's are copper and nitrates; four-fifths of Cuba's are sugar; one-fifth of Mexico's is lead, zinc and copper; two-fifth's of Peru's are minerals; three-fourths of Indonesia's are rubber, petroleum, and tin; nine-tenths of Venezuela's total are petroleum; and so forth.

If we accept the opportunity of foreign trade, we not only benefit ourselves economically but also militarily. For we become partners in the economic growth of other nations. Despite some regrettable exceptions, in such partnership with underdeveloped nations there is stimulus to political development along democratic avenues. There is frequently a merging of interest to the point of military alliance, and thereby opportunity for advantageous location of military bases. If we reject international partnership, we may lose more than merely opportunity for gain. Internal economic distress from inability to trade with us may foster growth of undemocratic political parties and institutions, and reduced military establishments for the common defense against Communism. The pressure to export may impel the foreign nation beyond arm's length trade with the Communist countries (which in itself is not objectionable) to political and military relations or even dependence. The recent Iceland case, when the free world export markets for its fish (more than 90 per cent of its total exports) collapsed, is relevant. Russia magnanimously offered to buy the fish instead, and Iceland gave notice (since fortunately rescinded) that she was cancelling the United States air base leases there. Finally, except as the free world is welded together economically, the line of demarcation we have drawn to contain Communist expansion becomes blurred, and the area becomes subject to Soviet adventurism, and possible peripheral war.

We might add that in most of the world, United States foreign trade behavior goes beyond immediate economic importance. It is watched as the sign of United States belief in collective defense, and as an earnest of our dedication to the goal of international peace.

The second implication for natural resources has to do with protection against the effects of interdiction of foreign materials supply in the event of recurrence of drawn-out, massive World War II type hostilities. We bypass the questions of likelihood of such war, of diversion of effort to such protection at the expense of other protection, foreign military and political repercussions, of whether arguments for essentiality and prospective shortage of particular commodities are merely convenient rationalizations for private economic interest. To the extent we need protection for this contingency, how should we insure against war-time interdiction of ocean raw materials transport? There are three principles for appropriate behavior here—

(1) maximizing the protection we can get from whatever preparatory costs we decide to incur;

(2) minimizing peacetime interference with the efficiency of the price allocation mechanism of the free enterprise system;

(3) reliance upon ability to ration short goods, particularly luxuries, in wartime.

These argue, in general, in favor of gradual accumulation of raw material stockpiles limited to clearly essential levels, from least cost (usually foreign) sources, in preference to a combination of tariffs or quotas and subsidized domestic raw material production capacity. We get more protection for the dollars we allocate, and without raising market prices to the whole domestic economy. There are, however, two evils that a stockpile program must resist. One is the possibility that its national security purpose will be distorted by political pressures into price support subsidy of particular producers, with consequent damage to the national security program. The second is that unwillingness to contemplate sharply reduced civilian consumption during wartime will result in too lavish estimates of stockpile needs.

There may be a few specific cases in which stockpiles are not an efficient instrument and in which domestic production capacity must be expanded or maintained. There is still considerable choice on principles of least cost and

least interference before deciding upon import quotas, tariffs, and wide-spread supports and other subsidies. In general, maintenance of standby facilities at government expense or subsidy payments to marginal producers only are preferable to over-all price supports; and direct measures explicitly covered in the defense budget are preferable to indirect assistance through taxes, tariffs and quotas. But, I repeat, not too much effort or funds should be allocated for insurance against this kind of war.

Why have I emphasized preparations for the World War II contingency, which I think to be unlikely? I have done so because it is for this aspect of national security that government natural resource activities have been most wide-spread and costly. For example, more than $20 billions of tax amortization certificates, a significant portion in the materials industries, have been granted by the government in the past half dozen years in order to induce expansion in domestic industry capacities believed to be necessary for national security reasons. About $6 billions of materials were stored in strategic stockpiles in June, 1956, and the rate of addition at that time was several hundred million dollars per year. The General Services Administration estimated the loss on its inventories of domestically produced manganese and tungsten due to excess of prices paid to encourage domestic production over free market prices, at about $150 millions. And the United States Government is legally obligated to purchase several hundred million dollars of aluminium, which (as of mid-1957) is does not want.

The third implication for natural resources materials has to do with reducing casualties in the event of thermonuclear bombardment of this country. The prevention of mortalities by appropriate combinations of active defense, warning time, dispersal and shelters is not directly related to materials. But survival of the population which escapes death in such attack would be directly related to appropriately located and shielded stocks of food, medicines, water purifying chemicals, fuel, and other materials, which would permit at least primitive survival levels while society undertakes the climb back to civilization. The thought I should like to leave is the possibility that we can afford greater analysis of the materials requirements for post-attack survival; and the possibility that we can afford the accumulation, at protected and appropriate places, of survival stocks.

Notes

1. I use the atmosphere and satellite examples because of the widely publicized radioactive fallout threat and the first satellite excursion this year. According to the late John von Neuman, the threats and promises of world climate control and ice-cap melting are no less significant. See his "Can We Survive Technology?" in *The Fabulous Future* (New York: E. P. Dutton & Co., 1955–56), pp. 39–42.

2. *Ibid.*, pp. 33–35.

3. As of date of writing in mid-1957.

c. The political problem

Samuel P. Huntington

Strategic planning and the political process

FOR A DECADE OR MORE statesmen and scholars have been unhappy about American methods of making decisions on strategic programs—that is, decisions on the over-all size of the military effort, the scope and character of military programs (continental defense, antisubmarine warfare), the composition of the military forces (force levels), and the number and nature of their weapons. The most common criticisms have been:

1. National security policy lacks unity and coherence. Decisions are made on an ad hoc basis, unguided by an over-all purpose.

2. National security policies are stated largely in terms of compromises and generalities. The real issues are not brought to the highest level for decision.

3. Delay and slowness characterize the policy-making process.

4. The principal organs of policy-making, particularly the National Security Council, are ineffective vehicles for the development of new ideas and approaches. They tend to routinize the old rather than stimulate the new.

5. Policy-making procedures tend to magnify the obstacles and difficulties facing any proposed course of action.

6. These deficiencies are primarily the product of government by committee, especially when the committee members must represent the interests of particular departments and services.

Few persons familiar with the processes by which strategic programs are determined would challenge the general accuracy of these allegations. The persistence of the criticism since World War II, moreover, suggests that the defects are not incidental phenomena easily remedied by exhortations to high-mindedness, assertions of executive authority, or changes in personnel or Administration. Instead, it suggests the necessity of viewing the defects in the context of the political system of which they are a part, and of analyzing the functions which they serve in that system and the underlying causes which have brought them into existence.

In domestic legislation, it is often said, the Executive proposes and Congress disposes. Except when a presidential veto seems likely to be involved, the political processes of arousing support or opposition for bills are directed toward the Congress. In determining strategic programs, on the other hand, the effective power of decision rests not with Congress and its committees but with the President and his advisors.

Congressional incapacity to determine force levels and strategic programs is often attributed to the lack of proper information and technical competence. This is indeed a factor, but it is only a contributory one. Congressmen often tend to consider broad questions of general military policy as technical while at the same time they do not hesitate to probe thoroughly

Reprinted from *Foreign Affairs*, Vol. 38, No. 2, January 1960, copyright by the Council on Foreign Relations, Inc., New York, pp. 285–299.

and to render judgments about highly specialized and detailed questions of military administration. The inability of Congress to act effectively on strategic programs derives primarily not from its technical failings but from its political ones.

The initiation and elimination of programs and the apportionment of resources among them are highly political decisions involving conflicting interests and groups. They can be made only by bodies in which all the conflicting interests can be brought in focus. The principal groups concerned with the determination of strategic programs are the armed services, the Office of the Secretary of Defense, the State Department, the Treasury, the Budget Bureau, plus a few other governmental departments. The military programs have to be weighed against each other, against conflicting interpretations of the security threats and military requirements, against domestic needs and non-military foreign policy programs, and against probable tax revenues and the demands of fiscal policy. No congressional committee is competent to do this, not because it lacks the technical knowledge, but because it lacks the legal authority and political capability to bring together all these conflicting interests, balance off one against another, and arrive at some sort of compromise or decision. Congress cannot effectively determine strategic programs because the interests which are primarily concerned with those programs are not adequately represented in any single congressional body. The armed services, appropriations, finance, foreign relations, space and atomic energy committees are all, in one way or another, involved in the process. No one of them can have more than a partial view of the interests involved in the determination of any single major strategic program. Every congressional action in military affairs is to some extent *ex parte*.

Congressional bodies may become advocates of particular programs, but they lack sufficient political competence to determine an over-all program. After World War II, except when confronted by similar competing programs, Congress *never* vetoed directly a major strategic program, a force-level recommendation or a major weapons system proposed by the Administration in power. Nor did Congress ever achieve this result, with one partial exception (the Navy's second nuclear carrier), through the failure to appropriate funds recommended by the Executive. The relative inviolability of the military requests was striking when compared with those for domestic or foreign-aid appropriations. Almost regularly, of course, Congress reduced the *total* military request, but it virtually never did this in a manner which seriously affected a major strategic program. Quite properly, Congressmen generally feel that they are ill-equipped to be responsible for the security of the country, and they have, by and large, recognized and accepted the decisive role of the Executive in formulating strategic programs. "God help the American people," Senator Russell once remarked, "if Congress starts legislating military strategy."

The inability and unwillingness of Congress to choose and decide does not mean that congressional groups play no role in the formulation of strategic programs. On the contrary, with respect to strategy, Congress has, like Bagehot's queen, "the right to be consulted, the right to encourage, the right to warn." The most prominent congressional role is that of prodder or goad of the Executive on behalf of specific programs or activities. With the Executive as the decision-maker, Congress has become the lobbyist. Congressional groups engage in sustained campaigns of pressure and persuasion to produce the desired strategic decisions on the part of the Executive, just as in other areas the Administration uses pressure and persuasion to move its legislation through Congress.

In lobbying with the Executive, Congress employs three major techniques. First, congressional groups may attempt, through letters, speeches, investigations and threats of retaliation in other fields, to bring continuing pressure upon the Administration to construct certain types of weapons. The Joint Committee on Atomic Energy, for instance, has been an active lobby on behalf of nuclear weapons: its members played important roles in prompting executive decisions on the hydrogen bomb, the nuclear powered submarine, the intermediate-range ballistic missiles. On the other hand, no lobby ever scores 100 per cent, and the Committee was somewhat less successful with the Polaris speed-up and the nuclear-powered airplane.

Second, congressional groups may establish force-level minimums for their favored services or appropriate more money for the services than the Administration requested. In these cases, Congress attempts to use its ancient powers of authorization and appropriation for the positive purpose of establishing *floors*, whereas these powers were designed originally for the negative purpose of establishing *ceilings* to prevent a tyrannical executive from maintaining military forces without the consent of the people. Such actions undoubtedly influence the Administration in planning future force levels, and in two cases involving the National Guard and the Marine Corps, the Administration formally complied with congressional wishes. In the final analysis, however, no way has yet been evolved of compelling an Administration to maintain forces it does not wish to maintain or to spend money it does not wish to spend.

Third, Congress can bring pressure upon the Executive through investigation and debate. Although it is generally held that Congress' power to investigate rests upon its power to legislate, in actual fact Congress investigates, in the grand manner, matters which it cannot legislate. The activities of Senators McCarthy and Kefauver are obvious examples, but more reputable and worthwhile ones are furnished by the great investigations of strategy: the 1949 inquiry into "Unification and Strategy," the 1951 MacArthur investigation, the 1956 Symington airpower hearings, and the Johnson missile investigation of 1957–1958. None of these directly produced legislation but they did compel the Administration to make a public defense of its policies, enabled Congress to bring pressure to bear on the Executive and helped to educate the attentive public on strategic issues.

Strategic programs are thus decided upon in the Executive rather than in Congress. The process of decision within the Executive, however, bears many striking resemblances to the process of decision in Congress. It retains a peculiarly legislative flavor. Legislative and executive *processes* of policy-making do not necessarily correspond to the legislative and executive *branches* of government. A policy-making process is legislative in character to the extent that (1) the units participating in the process are relatively equal in power (and consequently must bargain with each other), (2) important disagreements exist concerning the goals of policy, and (3) there are many possible alternatives. A process is executive in character to the extent that (1) the participating units differ in power (i.e., are hierarchically arranged), (2) fundamental goals and values are not at issue, and (3) the range of possible choice is limited.

Strategic programs, like other major policies,

are not the product of expert planners rationally determining the actions necessary to achieve desired goals. Rather, they are the product of controversy, negotiation and bargaining among different groups with different interests and perspectives. The conflicts between budgeteers and security spokesmen, between the defenders of military and non-military programs, among the four services, and among the partisans of massive retaliation, continental defense and limited war, are as real and as sharp as most conflicts of group interests in Congress. The location of the groups within the executive branch makes their differences no less difficult to resolve. The variety and importance of the interests, the intensity of the conflicting claims, the significance of the values at stake, all compel recourse to the complex processes of legislation. The inability of Congress to legislate strategic programs does not eliminate the necessity to proceed through a legislative process. It simply concentrates it in the executive branch.

To be sure, the specific techniques for innovating proposals, mobilizing support, distracting and dissuading opponents, and timing decisions may differ in the executive "legislative" process from those in the congressional "legislative" process. None the less, in its broad outlines the development of a major strategic program, such as continental air defense, lacks none of the phases involved in the passage of a major piece of domestic legislation through Congress. The need for the program is recognized by an executive agency or some skill group (nuclear physicists) or consulting group close to the executive branch. The agency or group develops policy proposals to deal with the problem and arouses support for them among other executive agencies, congressional committees and, possibly, some non-governmental groups. Opposition develops. Alternative solutions to the problem are proposed. Coalitions pro and con are organized. The proposals are referred from committee to committee. Consultants and advisory groups lend their prestige to one side or another. The policies are bargained over and compromised. Eventually a decision, or more accurately, an agreement is hammered out among the interested agencies, probably through the mechanisms of the Joint Chiefs of Staff and the National Security Council, and is approved by the President. The locus of decision is executive; the process of decision is primarily legislative.

The building of a consensus for a particular strategic program is as complex and subtle as it is for either domestic policy or foreign policy. At a minimum, within the Executive, it involves complicated interlocking patterns of vertical bargaining along the executive hierarchy and horizontal bargaining through a conciliar structure. In almost no executive hierarchy is the exercise of power all in one direction: the actual authority—even the influence—of administrative superiors over their subordinates is hedged around by a variety of inhibiting considerations. Underlying the hierarchy is a set of bargaining relationships, explicit or implicit. The dispersion of power in American society and the separation of powers in government tend to reinforce this tendency. Agencies and officials in subordinate positions often are substantially independent of their administrative superiors. At best the superior may be able to persuade; at worst the may be openly defied.

Vertical bargaining is exemplified in the efforts of the Administration to secure the concurrence of the Joint Chiefs of Staff, individually and collectively, in its budgetary and force-level decisions. On the one hand, each Chief presses for what he believes is essential for his service; on the other, the Administration attempts to cut back and fit service demands into its strategic plan and budgetary goals. Each side has to balance the risks involved in alienating the other against the benefits gained in shaping the final decision. The interlarding of hierarchical and bargaining roles inevitably enhances the possibilities for ambiguity and confusion. As subordinates the Chiefs would be expected to accept but not necessarily to approve decisions made by their administrative superiors. "I'd be worried," Secretary Wilson once declared, "if Ridgway didn't believe in the good old Army."[1] On the other hand, the semi-autonomous position of the Chiefs enhances the value of their approval to their superiors. An administrative decision derives legitimacy (as well as effectiveness) in part from its acceptance and support by the subordinate officials and agencies affected by it. Consequently, great efforts are made to secure the Chiefs' concurrence. "The pressure brought on me to make my military judgment conform to the views of higher authority," General Ridgway declared, "was sometimes subtly, sometimes crudely, applied."[2] The intensity of the pressure applied was tribute to the value of the approval sought.

While vertical bargaining plays a crucial role in strategic decision-making, horizontal bargaining is probably even more widespread and important. Theoretically, of course, authority to determine strategic programs rests with the President and the Secretary of Defense. Actually, the compromising and balancing of interests tends to focus about the two most important committees in the executive branch of the national government: the J.C.S. and the N.S.C. On the surface, it seems strange that two committees should play such important roles in the formulation of military policy and national security. These are areas where one might expect clear-cut lines of authority and executive decision-making. Within the executive branch, few committees of comparable stature exist in domestic areas of policy-making. The J.C.S. and the N.S.C. are significant, however, precisely because they do perform essentially legislative rather than executive functions. They have what Congress lacks: the political capability to legislate strategy. Just as agricultural policy is the product of conflict, bargaining and compromise among the interested groups represented in Congress, military strategy is the product of conflict, bargaining and compromise among the interested groups represented in the J.C.S. and the N.S.C. Hence, the same criticisms are now leveled at these committees which have long been leveled at Congress: logrolling prevails; over-all objectives get lost in the mechanism; a premium is put upon agreement rather than decision. Just as Congress often wrote tariff legislation by giving each industry the protection it wanted, the N.S.C. and the Joint Chiefs make decisions on weapons by giving each service what it desires. The individual members of these bodies suffer the classic conflict known to members of all legislatures: on the the one hand, they must represent the interests of their departments or constituencies; on the other, their decisions are expected to be in the national interest.

In strategy, as elsewhere, effective policy requires some measure of both content and consensus. Strategic programs, like statutes or treaties, are both prescriptions for future action and ratifications of existing power relationships. A strategy which is so vague or contradictory that it provides no prescription for action is no strategy. So too, a strategy whose prescriptions are so unacceptable that they are ignored is no strategy. Consensus is a cost to each participant but a prerequisite of effective policy.

In strategy-making, as in congressional legislating, one means of avoiding disagreement is to postpone decision. The proliferation of committees serves the useful political end of facilitating and, in some cases, legitimizing the avoidance of decision. Issues can be referred from committee to committee, up and down the hierarchy. Normally the same service and departmental interests are represented on all the committees; agreement in one is just as unlikely as agreement in any other. Controversial decisions may also be removed entirely from the jurisdiction of the N.S.C. or the Joint Chiefs and devolved back upon the interested agencies; the "decision" is that each will pursue its own policy. Disagreement on major issues also may be avoided simply by devoting more time to minor ones. The J.C.S. "dips into matters it should avoid," Vannevar Bush complained in 1952, "it fails to bring well considered resolution to our most important military problems, and it fritters away its energy on minutiae."[3] The Joint Chiefs, however, were treading a classic legislative path. In almost identical terms, political scientists for years have accused Congress of refusing to grapple with major issues of public policy and of wasting time and energy on minor matters of administrative detail.

Where stringent limits are imposed from the outside, the decision-makers are especially prone to compromise. As the $14 and $13 billion ceilings firmly succeeded each other in the late 1940s, the tendency to divide the funds equally among the three services became more and more pronounced. On the other hand, if the limits permitted by superior executive authority are relatively undefined or broad, logrolling enables each agency to obtain what it considers most important. The result is "Operation Paperclip," in which Army, Navy and Air Force proposals are added together and called a joint plan. Duplication in weapons systems—Thor and Jupiter, Nike and Bomarc— is simply the price of harmony. It is hardly surprising that the J.C.S. should be referred to as "a trading post." This, after all, is the traditional legislative means of achieving agreement among conflicting interests. As one Congressman remarked to his colleagues:

> If you are concerned, you politicians, with getting unanimity of action, I refer you to the Joint Chiefs of Staff. There is a classic example of unanimity of action on anything:

You scratch my back and I will scratch yours. "Give me atomic carriers," says the Navy, "and you can have your B-52s in the Air Force." I do not know why General Taylor is going along, because I have never been able to find anything that the Army is getting out of the deal.[4]

The political and legislative character of the strategy-making process also casts a different light on the argument that the N.S.C. and J.C.S. have failed to initiate new policy proposals. As many observers of the domestic legislative process have pointed out, relatively few statutes actually originate within a legislative assembly. They are first developed by interest groups or executive agencies. It is therefore not surprising that relatively few strategic programs originally come to life in the committees or staffs of the N.S.C. or J.C.S. The latter necessarily serve as negotiating bodies; the responsibility for innovation lies with the participating agencies.

Just as much of the early criticism of Congress stemmed from a failure to appreciate the political roles of that body, so much of the criticism of the N.S.C. and J.C.S. stems from the application to these bodies of nonpolitical standards. At times in the past, it has been assumed that through investigation and debate all members of a legislative body should arrive at similar conclusions as to where the public interest lay. More recently, conflict within a legislature has been viewed as normal, and policy thought of as the result, not of a collective process of rational inquiry, but of a mutual process of political give and take. Congress is seldom criticized today because of conflicts and disagreements among its members. To a considerable extent, however, the J.C.S. and the N.S.C. are judged by the former theory: in them disagreement is still considered inherently evil. As one naval officer wryly commented: "How curious it is that the Congress *debates*, the Supreme Court *deliberates*, but for some reason or other the Joint Chiefs of Staff just *bicker!*"[5]

Significantly, the Joint Chiefs have also been criticized for employing precisely those mechanisms designed for reaching agreement: delay, devolution, referral, platitudinous policies, compromise, logrolling. On the one hand, the Chiefs are criticized because they cannot resolve major issues; on the other hand, they are criticized because they do resolve them through the classic means of politics.

Much criticism of strategic decision-making

has failed to appreciate the tenuous and limited character of hierarchical authority in American government. Reacting against the prevalence of horizontal bargaining, the critics have advocated the abolition of committees and the strengthening of executive controls. In brief periods of emergency, presidential coordination may partially replace the normal bargaining processes. But no presidential laying on of hands can accomplish this on a permanent basis. Decisions on strategic programs are simply too important to be fitted into a symmetrical and immaculate model of executive decision-making. Clarifications of the chain of command and legal assertions of formal authority may reduce bargaining, but they can never eliminate it. Each of the three reorganizations of the military establishment since 1947 has purported to give the Secretary of Defense full legal authority to control is department and yet each succeeding Secretary found his control circumscribed if not frustrated. The existence of counterparts to the N.S.C. and J.C.S. in virtually every other modern state suggests that the causes which have brought them into existence may be pervasive and inherent in the problems with which they deal.

The problem of legislating strategic programs is thus the dual one of producing both content and consensus. On the one hand, little is gained by assuming that effective policy can be achieved without compromise, or that the political problems of strategy-making can be eliminated by strengthening the executive chain of command. On the other hand, it is also impossible to accept what emerges from the bargaining processes as ipso facto in the national interest. Too often, this has blatantly not been the case, and national purposes have been lost in bureaucratic feuding and compromise. The road to reform begins with recognition of the inherently complex political and legislative character of strategic decision-making. The need is for methods which will, at best, contribute both to the substance and the acceptance of policy, or, failing that, at least contribute more to the improvement of one than to the impairment of the other.

When the strategy-making process is viewed as essentially legislative in nature, the critical points appear to be not the prevalence of bargaining but rather the weakness of legislative leadership and the limited scope of the strategic consensus.

In the traditional legislative process, interest groups and executive agencies originate proposals, the President integrates them into a coherent legislative program, Congress debates, amends and decides. In the strategy-making process, executive agencies and related groups originate proposals, the N.S.C., the J.C.S., the President and Secretary of Defense debate, amend and decide upon them. But who plays the role of the legislative leader? Who winnows out the various ideas in the light of an over-all set of priorities or grand strategy and integrates these proposals into general programs which can then be discussed, amended and ratified? In the decade after World War II no clear concept developed as to which official or agency had the responsibility for leading the J.C.S. and the N.S.C. in their deliberations. In actual practice, leadership tended to rest with the Chairman in the J.C.S. and with the Department of State in the N.S.C. However, the case was frequently made for expanding the N.S.C. staff in the Executive Office of the President and for strengthening the Special Assistant for National Security Affairs. Similarly, it was often urged that the Secretary of Defense be provided with a mixed civilian-military policy staff which would, at the least, give him an independent source of advice, and, at most, enable him to play a stronger role in making strategic decisions. Other suggestions[6] include the creation outside the executive hierarchy of a council of elder statesmen, a "supreme court" for foreign and military policy, or an "academy of political affairs" (modeled on the National Academy of Sciences) which could study national security problems, issue reports and advise the President directly.

It seems likely that either the leadership functions of the Secretary of State and the Chairman of the Joint Chiefs will become more fully recognized and clarified, or the Special Assistant and Secretary of Defense will develop the staff facilities necessary to perform these functions, or new organs of policy recommendation will come into existence. Such developments not only would facilitate consensus but also would probably improve the content of strategic decisions. The form in which issues are presented for decision often drastically affects the nature of the decision. The problem in the Executive today resides not in the presence of bargaining but rather at the point at which bargaining begins. The development of more effective leadership organs in the N.S.C. and J.C.S. would permit bargaining to be more limited and focused. The starting point would become not three separate proposals advanced by three separate departments but rather one set of proposals advanced by the legislative leader. The requirements of consensus might still cause those proposals to be torn apart tooth and limb, but, at the very least, the clear visibility of the mutilation would have certain restraining effects. It has had them in Congress.

A related and perhaps more important problem concerns the relatively limited scope of the strategic consensus. The strategy-making process goes on largely within the Executive, and the consensus arrived at, if any, is primarily an executive one. As a result, it tends to be both tenuous and tentative. Although the effective power of decision rests with the executive branch, the possibility always exists that it may be upset by forces from the outside. Consequently the activity of the Administration is largely devoted to defending a policy which has been decided upon rather than advocating a policy which has yet to be adopted.

In the traditional legislative process, an issue is debated first within the Executive and then publicly within and about Congress. All the debate, however, contributes directly or indirectly to shaping the final product; to pushing the legislation through without change, amending it in one direction or another, or defeating it entirely. When the President signs the bill, the policy-making process is over, and the debate stops—or at least lessens—for a while. In strategy-making, debate among the various executive agencies and related groups also contributes directly to shaping the measure. Once the decision is made, this debate subsides, but as soon as the decision becomes known to non-executive agencies and groups, the public debate begins. The likelihood of such debate may have had its effects upon the executive policy-makers before the decision was reached, but their anticipation of public reaction to policy often is, at best, an informed hunch and, at worst, a rationalization that the public will not accept policies which they do not accept themselves. Public debate of a strategic decision may also affect its implementation and may influence subsequent decisions. Coming after the initial decision, however, the debate necessarily loses much of its force and value.

It is striking that both the Truman and Eisenhower Administrations, different as they are otherwise, have been regularly criticized for not exercising "leadership" in national security policy. In each case, it is alleged, the President has failed to take the initiative in bringing strategic issues to the people, in arousing support for foreign and military policy proposals, and in educating the public to its responsibilities in the nuclear age. Such criticism assumes that the President should play the same leadership role in strategic matters that he does in domestic legislation. In the latter, the President must be the source of energy for his program, and it is normally in his interest to dramatize the issue and to broaden the public concerned with it. The concept of presidential leadership is that of Theodore Roosevelt, Wilson, F.D.R. rallying support for a legislative program which he is urging upon a recalcitrant Congress.

In the strategy process, however, the President's role is very different, and the domestic model is inapplicable. Here, the President and his Administration have little reason to desire public debate and many reasons to fear it. The decision has been made; the policy is being implemented. The extension of the public concerned with the policy can only lead to pressure to change it in one respect or another and to the exploitation of the issues by the opposition. The primary role of the Administration has to be defensive: to protect the balance of interests, the policy equilibrium which has been laboriously reached within the Executive, against the impact of profane forces and interests outside the Executive. Mr. Cutler put the matter bluntly when he declared:

There is another seamlessness in our complex world: the fabric of our national defense. Perhaps the most potent argument against public disclosure of secret projects or of short-falls (which inevitably always exist) in any one aspect of our national defense is that such disclosure builds up a Potomac propaganda war to rectify that defect or over-finance that project. But if you devote larger resources to one area of national defense, you are apt to imbalance the rest.[7]

Given the nature of the decision-making process, this concern is a natural one. The cold-war Presidents have evolved a variety of means to limit public interest in strategy, to minimize the concern of external groups with force levels and weapons, and, most particularly, to insulate and protect the executive balance from the disruption of outside interests. Hence the tendency of both Presidents and their

Administrations to reassure the public, to pour on the "soothing syrup" which has so exasperated the Alsops and others, to limit the information available on American deficiencies and Soviet achievements, to discount these achievements and to minimize their significance, to preserve discipline and to suppress leaks, to discourage dissenting and disquieting testimony before congressional committees, and in general to maintain an air of calm assurance, an imperturbable façade. All these actions stem from a fear of the fragility of the executive consensus and of the irrationality and uncontrollability of the external political forces. These are the new "defensive" weapons of presidential leadership, as important to an Administration in the formulation of strategy as the old "offensive" techniques are in the promotion of domestic legislation in Congress.

A striking feature of the past dozen years has been the extent to which expressions of alarm at the decline of presidential leadership have occurred simultaneously with expressions of alarm at the growth of executive power. This apparent paradox simply reflects the fact that the increasing responsibility of the executive branch in making crucial decisions on strategic programs has undermined the ability of the President to lead. The more the President becomes, at least in theory, the judge, the less he can be the advocate. Yet, in practice, even his power to decide strategic issues is difficult to exercise. To be sure, the N.S.C. and the J.C.S. are theoretically only his advisors: no policy exists until he has approved it. But in part this is a myth to preserve the appearance of presidential decision-making. Surely the President does not override united opinion among his top advisors much more often than he vetoes acts of Congress. The theory that the President makes the decisions, in short, serves as a cloak to shield the elaborate processes of executive legislation and bargaining through which the policies are actually hammered out. Consequently, the President may be less influential as a decision-maker than he is as a legislative leader. The latter function is personal to him. The former is one which he shares with a variety of other groups in the executive branch.

Whatever defects may exist in this situation cannot be removed by shifting the point of decision away from the executive branch. The tenuous character of the decisions and the defensive role of the Administration could be modified only by broadening the scope of discussion and concern in the early stages of the policy process—*before* key decisions are made. Once adequate legislative leadership emerges in the executive branch, the debate could focus on the proposals of this leadership, provided they were made public to the fullest extent possible. Greater publicity for and public participation in strategy-making at an earlier stage would tend to restrain some of the more gross forms of "horse trading" in the Executive and should enhance the President's actual power of decision. At present, one way in which issues are brought to the top and forced upon the President for decision is through the lobbying activities of congressional committees. Broader and earlier public discussion of strategic programs would in all probability have a similar effect, and instead of interested guesses we would be provided with concrete evidence of what "the public will support." Certainly, discussion is more useful before decisions are made than afterward. Broadening the scope of the policy consensus could well go hand in hand with improving the quality of the policy content.

Notes

1. Duncan Norton-Taylor, "The Wilson Pentagon," *Fortune*, December 1954, p. 94.
2. General Matthew B. Ridgway, "My Battles in War and Peace," *The Saturday Evening Post*, January 21, 1956, p. 46.
3. "Planning," speech at Mayo Clinic Auditorium, Rochester, Minnesota, September 26, 1952, p. 8.
4. Rep. Daniel J. Flood, *Congressional Record* (85th Congress, 1st Session), May 27, 1957, p. 7733.
5. Vice Admiral H. E. Orem, "Shall We Junk the Joint Chiefs of Staff?" *U.S. Naval Institute Proceedings*, February 1958, p. 57.
6. See Walter Millis, *The Constitution and the Common Defense*, New York: The Fund for the Republic, 1959, pp. 36–46.
7. "The Seamless Web," *Harvard Alumni Bulletin*, June 4, 1955, p. 665.

Don K. Price

Administrative leadership

ONE OF THE CLASSIC ANECDOTES in the apocrypha of Washington tells how the chairman of the board of a great corporation, many years ago, was brought in as a staff member of the White House. When reporters asked how his responsibilities could be distinguished from those of the Secretary of a certain Department, he said, that was easy; unlike the Secretary, he was interested only in policy, not in administration. What, insisted a reporter, was the difference? Well, replied the industrialist, take my company; our board of directors leaves administration to the president; we are interested only in high policy like—well, for example, like the design of a soap wrapper.

This story, of course, is worth cherishing not for its accuracy (not guaranteed) but for its moral. The obvious part of the moral is that men in business often spend their energies on issues less important than those they would deal with in government—which may suggest that the nation could afford to transfer some of their talents to more important public purposes. The less obvious part of the moral is that in government, as in business, high officials may take great satisfaction in dealing efficiently with trivial problems, while the big issues are settled by subordinates, or by accident, or by factional politics, or by default.

For a good many years now we have been informed as to the first of these points. When the Commission on National Goals recently reported to the then President Eisenhower that "the vastly increased demands upon the federal government require at the higher levels more public servants equal in competence and imagination to those in private business and the professions," and suggested that "this involves a drastic increase in their compensation," it was doing little more than repeating what the second Hoover Commission had said soon after Eisen-

hower took office. But in between, a great many things had happened to change our national attitudes; an administration whose backers at the beginning had looked to it mainly to get government out of competition with business ended by proposing to accept responsibility for inducing economic growth at home and abroad, for producing more physics Ph.D.'s than the Russians did, and for exploring the solar system. It may well be that we are now ready to admit that our government cannot do what we expect of it unless it can claim a larger share of the best administrative ability in the nation. "A great empire and little minds go ill together."

If we come to accept this idea, it will not be merely because the government has grown in size. Even more important are two changes in the kind of things it does, and the way it does them. The first is a change in the degree of specialized competence required to deal with public affairs. This is true of the economic and social as well as the technological aspects of government; in the latter it is only the more obvious. With this change, the technological and scientific corps (in and out of uniform) have begun to exert a more powerful influence on policy. (Who would have dreamed a decade or so ago, when we were holding our annual budget down to thirteen billion, that we would so soon take their word for the need to spend more than twice that much to put a man on the moon!) As a result, the politician may now see in the general administrator, not a bureaucrat who threatens to usurp his policy-making function, but an ally without whose professional help he can never comprehend and control the new social forces.

Second, in the most dynamic sectors of our economy and educational system, we are beginning to change the relation between

Reprinted from *Daedalus*, Journal of the American Academy of Arts and Sciences, Vol. 90, No. 4, Fall 1961, pp. 117-127.

government and private institutions in much the same way that we changed the relation between the federal government and the states about a quarter of a century earlier. In place of the grants-in-aid that tied the states to Washington in fields like soil conservation and social security, we now have contracts and grants that link Washington with Du Pont in atomic energy, with General Dynamics in the missile program and with the Massachusetts Institute of Technology and the California Institute of Technology in fields ranging from physics to international affairs. We therefore have no longer a system in which all private institutions look apprehensively at the higher bureaucracy as the motive power for immoral government spending, and try to suppress such spending. Indeed, it may now be clear, even to extreme conservatives, that it will require very great authority and administrative strength at the center of our government either to enforce economy against private demands for government spending or to direct that spending in the national interest.

These two changes call on us not merely to get more capable men into government, so as to manage efficiently the policies that politicians have prefabricated. That could be done quite simply by raising salaries and providing other incentives. But there is no point in merely transferring to government the avarice of the private sector without its enterprise, by giving high salaries to men who will not rise to the challenge of big problems. This brings us to the second half of our moral. For our traditional prejudices have not merely made it difficult to get for government a fair share of the top administrative talent, but they have forced the able men now in government careers to concentrate their talents on the interests of particular bureaus or services. And so we have made it almost impossible for the career service to do its main job—which is to look ahead at the great problems that confront the nation, to devise and recommend policies to meet them, and to see that the various departments are effectively coordinated in carrying out the decisions of responsible political authorities.

Some of the best career men in government know this quite well, and know what should be done about it. But it is hard for them to do their main job well when our system was set up on the assumption that it ought not to be done at all. We are comparatively good at politics, but then we were born free. At the other end of the spectrum, we are very good

indeed at technology and detailed management; no nation is better at getting specific things invented or managed. But the connection between these two aspects of government is weak, and sometimes it is not there at all. This is the crucial blind spot in our political vision.

We hardly notice the gap, perhaps because we have no word for the function that is missing. We have taken the word "administration" from British usage, and it will have to do, but its connotations in Whitehall and in Washington are quite different. The British administrative class hardly manages anything: its job is (under general political control) to make policy and see that the departments are effectively coordinated. Its purpose is to be the corporate custodian of a great tradition, and to adjust it to new political needs.

If we are tempted to comfort ourselves by saying that such a career civil service simply will not fit the American tradition, we ought to forget about the British and look at the career systems we ourselves have created. For, with all their defects—some of which our civil service ought to avoid with the greatest care—the military services and the Foreign Service suggest that, once we decide a career system is worth the cost, we know how to develop it and to train it for the higher functions of policymaking.

We have given up *laissez faire* in any economic issue that we consider of national importance. We are beginning to give it up in education; how many people should be attracted by fellowships into the study of Urdu or microbiology is now acknowledged as a proper matter for Congressional concern. The one field in which we most stubbornly continue our faith in the free play of the market is in the provision of personnel for high administrative positions in government, and this at a time when that type of excellence in government is the key to the success of all our other efforts.

It may be too kind to suggest that this neglect comes from a blind faith in tradition or from absentmindedness. On the face of the matter, it would seem that the system is rigged so that a capable young man, having risen rapidly in government to a position of responsibility for policy, will have to take a private job to protect his family's future.

The main point here is not a very abstruse one. If you talk to a college senior about going into the civil service, you cannot tell him that he will be promoted on the basis of his usefulness to the government as a whole. You are tempted to warn him that, to get ahead, he may have to plan his career in terms of the specialized interest of a single bureau. Happily, there are still men who ignore this counsel of caution, and whose government careers show real dedication to the public service and a breadth of interest that transcends any specialized field in the natural or social sciences or in management. But this like asking our army to rely on individual heroism or on election by the troops, rather than a system of training and promotion, to develop officers for general staff work.

That, of course, is just what we did do until we saw the importance of the problem. We came to see this only gradually. Today the young man who becomes a military officer knows that the people who decide on his next assignment are instructed to think of it as a step in the purposeful development of his career, in which his rewards for developing as a general officer will be greater than those of any speciality.

There are many important differences between military and civilian administration, but in a rough sense the work of the staff planners and the top command in a military service is like that of central administration in the civil service. Today, in our recognition of the importance of this civilian function, we are not far ahead of where we were in military affairs when President Wilson indignantly ordered the General Staff to stop preparing war plans: we are afraid that such work will usurp the proper function of political leadership.

A half-century ago we had just begun to organize our Army General Staff, in the face of dire predictions that it would lead to a military caste or a dictatorship. Today it is evident that it is possible to develop a professional system for military officers without destroying democratic responsibility: the officer corps of the several services are drawn from a wide variety of civilian universities as well as from the service academies, and the Congressional committees (as well as the President) still maintain a control over military policy that has no counterpart in any other major political system. But the main point is that we recognized in time that we not only need to have career system for the officer corps, but that it needed to be headed up in a corporate staff concerned, not with the command of particular divisions or the direction of particular technical services, but with the general policies and strategy of the forces.

It is hard to imagine how we should have survived if we had not developed something like the general staff function in all our military services. The nature of warfare, with its growing complexity, velocity, and lethality, made this function necessary; the new military technology, and the new weapons systems, added immeasurably to the intricacy of military affairs, and to the speed of innovation, and above all to the utterly fatal results of falling behind. If you read the administrative history of the Civil War or the Spanish-American War and compare it with that of the Second World War or the Korean War, the contrast gives a faint idea of the need for general staff work.

Or if your imagination boggles at this comparison, you can try to imagine what the Pentagon would be like if all the staff officers were removed, and their functions were left entirely to part-time consultants from industry, Congressional committee staff members, and political coordinating committees, with a few columnists and commentators taking part occasionally to keep the mixture from being too bureaucratic. This is unthinkable, because everyone understands that the changes in the complexity, velocity, and lethality of our military developments have made a fundamental change in the way in which we must try to keep military matters under democratic control. Political authorities can make decisions on immediate issues only if professional staff officers have worked out acceptable alternative solutions for them, and the most effective use of top political authority may well be to set the professionals to work on issues that have to be faced five or ten years hence—or to develop a system to improve the professional corps so that it can do so.

Political responsibility, in short, depends on having a responsive and well-trained professional corps, and cannot be achieved by keeping it in a state of fragmentation and anarchy. We as a sovereign people are quick to criticize the lack of integration of our military services and their strategic plans, but we would never know of such conflicts if the professional staffs had not prepared the plans and been forced to bring their discrepancies into the open by our civilian political controls. Like any other testy and temperamental sovereign, we resent having our experts bring us hard problems. Perhaps it would be better if they solved them without bothering us. But it would be much worse if they failed to recognize them.

If we are not very worried about the lack of

unification of the civilian departments, perhaps it is because they have not been very good about bringing up the issues that we ought not to duck. In the light of the probable developments over the next decade or two, are our agricultural policies as closely coordinated with that of our Air Force? I doubt it. Does our planning for the use of radio and television wave lengths take into account our future educational needs? Is someone worrying about the way in which our programs of water conservation relate to the future distribution of our population as it will be affected by our transportation and industrial development and housing policies?

I am not proposing that career administrators have any more authority—but only an opportunity to help bring up the issues that political authority must resolve. Nor am I advocating additional governmental controls—I am only asking whether the extensive controls we already have are being used in a rationally related manner. For if their interrelations are ignored, the waste in our civilian economy will be far greater than could be caused by poor business methods. This is the scale of waste involved not in the mismanagement of logistics, but in civil war. I do not think the metaphor is too strong. President after President has seen the fight between the Army Corps of Engineers and the Reclamation Bureau over the development of water resources; advisory committee after advisory committee has pointed to the waste involved in this competition; but the strife between these two agencies, and their supporters throughout the country representing two sets of interests and two conceptions of policy, has not only kept the President and the Congress from putting a rational single policy into effect, but has destroyed a Presidential staff agency which tried to deal with the question, prevented the development of another, and restricted the staff which the Secretary of the Interior could build up to work on the problem.

Similarly, the political battles of the affected interests have kept our transportation policies mainly in the hands of independent commissions, with little relation to each other or to the President or Congress. Here, too, all recent Presidents have seen the issue; I doubt that any would have been permitted by the Congress even to set up a staff to work on the problem. And without some staff work to bring out the issues clearly, there is no grist for the mills of democracy; as a sovereign people, we do not even effectively know the issues exist, though we may blindly, by governmental action, be

determining the economic and social fate of whole industries or regions or metropolitan areas.

If this kind of waste were all that was involved, we could stand it. But there is a graver problem. The basic nature of the relation of military to civilian affairs has changed since World War II. Then, we could still get along with a small peace-time army; then, the term "mobilization" meant that we could wait till after the war began to draft the soldiers and manufacture the munitions. But now, with the possibility of instant long-range destruction, the military cannot be set off in a corner until the shooting starts, when the rest of us can then volunteer for the duration. It has to be interwoven with every aspect of our society, and our future plans. Especially our future plans.

And if the civil government has no future plans of its own, the military will make them. It cannot wait around while civilians squabble about the nature of the regulatory process and government-business relations, when it sees the air space over our major cities cluttered up in a traffic jam of civilian planes that would be fatal in a crisis; it has to become one of the major political stockholders, so to speak, of a new Federal Aviation Agency to replace a Civil Aeronautics Administration. It cannot wait for civilians to settle their arguments about federal control of education or the relation of a potential National Science Foundation to the President; it has to go ahead through military grants to support ninetenths of the physics research in the major universities in the country. It cannot wait for Congressman Rooney to ease up on the diplomatic allowances or the training funds or any of the other costs of a higher-quality career Foreign Service; it can give the military attaché of an embassy or the head of a Military Assistance Advisory Group much more entertainment money than to the ambassador, and the only American official airplanes available in the country, so that the ambassador may entertain and travel by courtesy of his military colleagues.

Any civilian with even a dim sense of our political tradition, when he hears of such cases, is tempted to draw on the mantle of Hampden or Jefferson and wave the banner of civilian supremacy. But this is an irrational reaction. The problem is not caused by any desire of the military to encroach on civilian functions, but by their expansion to fill a vacuum. The vacuum is the absence, on the civilian side, of anything like an adequate career corps to deal with general policies and government-wide interests. In the army, the function of the general staff is to take care of the big general questions; the special staffs and the technical services take care of the specialized and subsidiary and house-keeping problems. On the civilian side, the typical Department head is permitted to have only some special staff units; the real centers of continuing power are in the bureaus, which are the civilian equivalents of the technical services. A civilian general staff would be considered dangerous.

The results are what you would expect. The real old pros are the men who run the bureaus, and a good pro can usually outclass a good amateur. Consequently, the development of civilian policy rather resembles the way I suppose a war would be run if it were left to the technical services and the politicians.

We are still bemused in the United States by the notion that we tolerate the inefficiency of a spoils system because it makes it easier for a new President to come in with a gallant band of amateurs and, at some cost to efficiency, take over the direction of the bureaus. This is wrong on all counts; we do not change many of the real power centers—the leadership of the bureaus—and it would not do any good if we did. The career head of a bureau symbolizes the professional opportunities, and controls the guiding incentives, of his subordinates. Above his post, advancement is possible but risky; there is no system for it, and no chief of a service with a professional interest in developing his men. It is no wonder that the able career people are likely to keep their interests focused on the problems of their own bureaus, and their loyalties engaged in advancing them. This is a sure recipe for seeing to it that the career adminis-trators are interested in the second rather than in the first rank of national problems, or even that they are emotionally engaged in furthering specialized interests at the expense of national interests.

The great failure in our political vision is our not seeing that the main function of the top career administrators is to help develop policy. If the career administrators above the level of the specialized bureaus do not provide strong support for their political superiors in the development of policy, our system of political responsibility suffers. Then the Secretary of a Department can do little but preside over a group of quasi-independent bureaus, while the important potential issues within the Depart-

ment and between it and the rest of the govern-ment will never be brought up for consideration by the President and the Congress. The big issues—at any rate, the biggest—are rarely brought out in the policies which a bureau and its clientele and the related Congressional committees like to put forward for considera-tion. In particular, in the wide range of pro-blems in which both military and civilian considerations are involved, the advantage in initiative and staff work will rest with the bigger staff battalions of the Pentagon.

If we are to cure this blind spot, we have to give up three prejudices that have come to be accepted as American traditions. The first is the traditional prejudice against hierarchy. We like to think we are against ranks and titles. This works mainly, we may note, with respect to the ranks and titles of other people or in fields we consider unimportant; it does not hold down the number of vice presidents in any metropolitan bank, or the importance of pro-fessional rank in any university, or the number of general and flag officers; but it does keep us from giving much in the way of rank or status to civilian administrators with broad interests in policy.

We began, during the Federalist period with a rudimentary but respectable corps of career administrators, but the Jacksonian revolution abolished all that. A half-century later, as we began to build up a civil service that would serve the nation rather than the warring parties, we built it from the bottom up, rather than from the top down, as the British had done; we put large numbers in the lower ranks under the merit system in order to deny mass patron-age to the bosses, rather than reforming the higher ranks in order to create an effective and responsible system of authority for the President and Congress. Then the organized sciences and some of the professions began to demand that their specialities be exempted from patronage. The dogmas of frontier democracy found it impossible to admit that general administra-tion required any talent that the average citizen could not supply, but such ideas yielded to the special mysteries of the professions and sciences. In an effort to protect their standards against corrupt or ignorant politics, the engineers and doctors and scientists pushed their men up the hierarchy into the jobs at the heads of their bureaus.

The dogmas of frontier democracy would not accept the pretension of general administra-tive superiority; if anyone was to be given a government job, he ought to be asked to prove his superior fitness for the specific duties of that job. This was not too troublesome at the lower grades; but at the higher, it had two unhappy effects. The first was that administrators, in order to justify a professional and career status for themselves, were forced to develop various aspects of management into specialized techniques. Personnel administration and budgeting, for example, are normal parts of the functions of an administrator, and he may need some people who specialize in them to help him. But we went far beyond that and made them into technical specialities, emphasizing their peculiar mysteries rather than their utility to the central purpose of administration: the development and execution of policy. And then the top political executives, having hardly any other career administrators at hand, had to put too much reliance on the budget officers for the control of policy.

The second bad effect grew out of the first: those who wanted to strengthen the career service emphasized the management specialties because they could be defended as semiscientific and hence nonpolicy-forming and nonpolitical. Administration became the victim of its own defense mechanism. In the end, this defense was not really persuasive, for the management specialists cannot stay out of policy any more than the admirals or ambassadors can; what is more political than the argument over veterans' preference in personnel administration or over the influence of the budget on military spending? By adopting this defense they perpetuated the dangerous myth that administration is not concerned with policy.

The purpose of a hierarchical pyramid, of course, is to raise to the top the difficult issues that the specialists cannot settle, so that these may be decided by legitimate political authority —in the United States, by the President and the Congress. We still like to think of a President's decision as a lonely act of will at a dramatic instant, just as we like to think of a general's commands as being delivered on horseback, with a wave of the sword. But a decision always requires staff help, to make it and to carry it out, and for that the President cannot rely entirely on any one speciality. On any complex and difficult issue—for example, disarmament—it is impossible for a political executive to make a rational decision merely by taking the well-organized and strongly conflicting positions and programs of different specialized groups and deciding

instantaneously among them. If a President, for example, receives staff papers prepared separately by groups of generals, diplomats, and scientists, he probably cannot take immediate action one way or another; all he can do is to determine some guiding principles, and they will be meaningless unless he organizes a system of staff work, involving or controlling all three groups, to work those principles into a program and see that it is carried out. This requires the help of a career service in which the top ranks are the rewards of ability to deal imaginatively with major policy issues in their broadest context—not one of fixed allegiance to the position of a particular bureau or professional service, and not one of devotion to a particular management speciality.

The second prejudice we need to modify is the prejudice against admitting the corporate nature of an administrative service. That prejudice has a sound core: we should not tolerate a closed bureaucracy; we should do all we can to keep the career service flexible in its policy attitudes by a certain amount of interchange at all levels with private careers. But that does not mean that we should not have a system for the policy level of administration that gives some corporate protection to individual careers. We have been improvising a system, but the structure of our institutions is still against it. As the second Hoover Commission said in the best of its reports, "The Civil Service System emphasizes positions, not people. Jobs are classified, ranked, rated, and their compensation determined on the bland assumption that they can always be filled like so many jugs, merely by turning the tap." In short, at a time when the major business corporations and virtually all other major institutions in society (including universities) have come to put great stress on the planned recruitment and training of top talent and on effective long-term tenure, we force the civil service (though not the military services or the Foreign Service) to ignore the elements of continuity and corporate spirit that are essential in order to retain most of the best men it gets.

This tradition that resists the development of a corporate service above the bureau-chief level misleads us most conspicuously in our efforts to coordinate policy. You can bring an outsider in to analyze a scientific problem for you, or a problem in managerial procedure; both can be defined as separate problems, to be solved by a known form of expertise. But the coordination of policy is fundamentally different. It requires not only some understanding of the main substantive aspects of the policy, but also an appreciation of the subtle interconnections of various parts of the government that can come only from years of experience. More than that, it calls for a professional sympathy, a bond of mutual trust based on a common corporate loyalty, between those working in the several departments concerned. This is why we often make no progress toward coordination either by giving additional authority to a political executive or by legislative elaborate structures of interdepartmental coordination. Structure and procedures do not make an organization. After World War II, when we set up a structure of interdepartmental policy committees (such as the NSC), we were imitating the skeleton of British administration without appreciating the function of its central nervous system.

The myth of the Minute Man dies hard. Those of us who are interested in government like to be called to Washington as consultants, or for brief adventurous periods in emergency administration. We cherish the notion that the real ability is outside the career service. We must simply find better ways of bringing it in for one or two years at a time—perhaps by some scheme for supplementing federal salaries for those who are not willing to sacrifice their private incomes temporarily.

But this will not do the main job (however useful it may be as a supplement), again for the reason that we cannot wait for the outbreak of an emergency to call for volunteers as general staff officers. We are already in the middle of the emergency, in one sense; in the other and more awsome sense, if the emergency comes, everything will be too late that has not been started five or ten years before. And the military problem is only the most easily understandable aspect of the many problems that technology has forced on our society.

This brings us to our third traditional prejudice: that government work must not be made as attractive in material rewards as private careers. This might have seemed plausible at one stage of our history: government was not very important in the production of material goods, and government salaries, like relief payments, had to be kept low so as not to reduce the incentive to go into more productive work. But this way of thinking is obsolete, whether you judge the importance of government in terms of sheer military security, or of

the hope of building a more humane civilization. Such rational considerations might not prevail against traditional prejudice. But if our logic is weak, our sense of humor is fairly strong, and surely we will soon appreciate the absurdity of holding down the salary of an administrator who runs a government program while at the same time he runs it by contracting with corporations who use government funds to pay higher salaries for less important work. No better incentive could be devised to get administrators to avoid the careers in which they would be responsible for promoting the general interest, and to take jobs which require them to lobby for special interests.

Nevertheless, we cannot solve this problem by higher salaries alone, any more than we can make our affluent society more civilized merely by shifting funds to the public sector. We have invented too many ways in recent years to use public funds for private purposes, for such measures to suffice. A great deal will depend on whether the career administrators who spend those funds are made into a disciplined corps responsive to the public interest, or whether they continue to shape national policy according to their various *déformations professionelles*.

Our foreign-aid and technical-assistance missions, realizing that many underdeveloped countries fail to progress in specialized fields because they have not learned the arts of administration, complain of the slowness of traditional societies to adapt their governments to modern needs. When we have taught the Asians and Africans how to abandon their traditional prejudices, perhaps we shall be ready to reconsider our own. After all, the British built up their civil service on the principles they had first tried out in the East India Company. It may not be too late for us to learn from the British example and to improve a system whose shortcomings we did not see until we tried to export it.

If we do so, we must surely do the job differently. We should not try to provide the the same kind of educational basis for a top civil service, for all our sentimental admiration for the Permament Secretary who can write Greek verse. The effective theory of the British service was based not on a reverence for the classics but on a determination to get the most capable men by taking them from any field in which they might be studying. "If astrology were taught at our universities," said Macaulay, "the young man who cast nativities best would generally turn out a superior man." This pragmatic approach would lead us in the direction our Civil Service Commission has generally been going, slowly and within the limits of political tolerance, for the past two decades, in recruiting college graduates for government careers on the basis of a solid general education, as well as from the sciences and professions.

When he is recruited, the administrator's training has only begun. From the outset of his career, he will have to learn a twofold job. Its first phase is to deal with the substance of policy. The sciences have swept away the oversimplified notion of the administrator as a complete generalist who needs to know nothing about the content and substance of the policies he administers. More and more we shall be adding men with training in science to our administrative ranks, and those of us who lack it will have to make desperate and belated efforts to comprehend the nature of the impact of science on government and society. That impact is now so great, and science in turn has come to rely so heavily on government policy, that the scientist turned administrator, like the management specialist, will have to acquire an understanding of the complexities of our constitution system and of the way in which it must bring all techniques into a responsible relation with our basic political values.

The administrator of the future, for all his concern for policy, can never forget the other aspect of his job, which is to organize and co-ordinate a complex and dynamic system to carry out policy decisions that are made by others. We are in no danger of establishing an irresponsible bureaucracy, so long as the administrator is kept under the direction of responsible executives, and called to account by an independent Congress. For we do not really want administrative leadership: we want political leadership, which requires a strong administrative underpinning in order to be effective. The professional administrator must try to bridge the great gap between the way the scientists think and work and that of the politicians. He can never enjoy the luxury of the intellectual pride of the former, or the power of the latter. Through his professional skills, he must try to reconcile our technology with our democratic values. In this effort, the purpose of his profession is to carry, with a higher degree of concentrated responsibility, the moral burden that in a free society must be shared by all citizens.

Warner R. Schilling

Scientists, foreign policy, and politics

. . . we must take, so far as we can, a picture of the world into our minds. Is it not a startling circumstance for one thing that the great discoveries of science, that the quiet study of men in laboratories, that the thoughtful developments which have taken place in quiet lecture rooms, have now been turned to the destruction of civilization? . . . The enemy whom we have just overcome had at its seats of learning some of the principal centres of scientific study and discovery, and used them in order to make destruction sudden and complete; and only the watchful, continuous cooperation of men can see to it that science, as well as armed men, is kept within the harness of civilization.[1]

THESE WORDS WERE SPOKEN in Paris in January 1919 by Woodrow Wilson, addressing the second Plenary Session of the Peace Conference. Wilson believed he had found a watchdog for civilization in the League of Nations. In this he was sadly mistaken. Science and armed men have indeed been harnessed, but in order to promote and maintain the goals of conflicting politics. Whether in the pursuit of these ends the cause of civilization will yet be served remains, we may hope, an open question.

The cooperation of scientists and armed men was not a new relationship, even in Wilson's day. In the United States, for example, the president of the American Association for the Advancement of Science had declared in 1861:

. . . it is easy to see that there are few applications of science which do not bear on the interests of commerce and navigation, naval or military concerns, the customs, the lighthouses, the public lands, post offices or post roads, either directly or remotely. If all examination is refused . . . the Government may lose a most important advantage.[2]

As a result of the interest of a number of American scientists and government officials, the National Academy of Sciences was established in 1863 for the purpose of providing scientific advice to the United States Government. The use made of this Academy by the War Department between 1863 and 1913 bespeaks a bygone era. During those years the Department requested the Academy to constitute scientific committees on exactly five matters:

On the Question of Tests for the Purity of Whiskey; On the Preservation of Paint on Army Knapsacks; On Galvanic Action from Association of Zinc and Iron; On the Exploration of the Yellowstone; On questions of Meteorological Science and its Applications.[3]

It would be unfair to presume from this list that the War Department was uninterested in new weapons systems. Until about the turn of the century, military technology, like industrial technology, generally developed independently of advances in basic scientific knowledge. Thus, in 1915, when Wilson's Secretary of the Navy decided to establish a "Department of Invention and Development" in the hope of securing effective weapons with which to combat that "new and terrible engine of warfare . . . the submarine," it was the inventor, Thomas Edison, who was asked to head the new organization.[4] Although the contributions of university and industrial scientists to the fighting of World War I were marked enough to have caught Wilson's imagination, it was not until a generation later, with the advent of World War II, that the mobilization of scientists brought military results which were of great and in some instances decisive importance to the course of combat.

Reprinted from the *American Political Science Review*, Vol. 56, No. 2, June 1962, pp. 287–300.

What has transformed the relationship between science and war has been the fact that in the twentieth century the development of technology has become increasingly dependent upon advances in basic knowledge about the physical world. Moreover, in the technically advanced nations, both the rate of technological innovation and the growth of new scientific knowledge have been increasing exponentially. As crudely measured by the volume of scientific publication, scientific knowledge has been doubling every ten to fifteen years.[5] In a non-Wilsonian world, the consequences of these conditions for national security policy have been as necessary as they are obvious. As the United States and the Soviet Union throw one weapons system after another into the effort to maintain at least a balance of terror, neither dares fall behind in either the discovery of new physical relationships or in the application of scientific knowledge to military hardware and political-military strategy. Thus, by the end of the first decade of the Cold War, about 50 per cent of the engineers in the United States and 25 per cent of the scientists were employed by the Federal government, either directly or on contract, and about 65 per cent of the scientific research in universities and 57 per cent of that in private industry was government-financed.[6]

Indicative of the new relationship between science and war, figures and graphs comparing the Great Powers in numbers of scientists and engineers have become as familiar as those in the 1930s which compared the Powers in their output of steel, coal, and oil. Nor is it only in the military field that science and technology have become vital to the course of foreign policy. Science has been harnessed to the advancement of foreign policy goals in such diverse fields as the exploration of space, birth and disease control, weather modification, economic development, and global communications.[7]

Present, prospective, and future developments in science and technology are certain to bring a host of problems and opportunities to those responsible for the conduct of foreign policy. In recognition of this fact, the governments of the major Powers have endeavored to find ways to make themselves more alert to such developments and more active in determining the course of science and technology. The United States and the Soviet Union are the most extensively engaged in this effort, but it should not be forgotten that the nations of Western and Central Europe were among the pioneers in cultivating the relationship between science and government. The three elements that have revolutionized current military technology and strategy (electronics, missiles, and nuclear weapons) had their harbingers in the World War II development of British radar, the German V-2, and the American A-bomb, and it is noteworthy that the two European developments were conceived, initiated, and directed by officials and employees of established government organizations. In contrast, the American A-bomb was the result of conceptions and initiatives that came from outside the government—and primarily from exiled Europeans at that.

As an integral part of the efforts of governments to become both more responsive to and responsible for the development of science and technology, scientists have been invited into the highest councils of government, and it is with some of the problems occasioned by the presence of these "new" participants in the making of national policy that the remainder of this article will be concerned. Although some illustrative material will be drawn from the experience of other governments, the paper focuses on problems associated with the participation of scientists in the American policy process.

Needless to say, the problems in policy-making that may arise will vary greatly with the kind of scientists participating (oceanographer, theoretical physicist, specialist in space medicine, industrial chemist), with the nature of the policy issue at stake (weapons development, science education, public health, the exploration of space, the allocation of funds for basic research), and with the manner in which the scientist is involved in the policy process (member of the attentive public, adviser to the President, worker in a government laboratory, official in an executive department or agency). This article will make no attempt to deal systematically with the combinations possible among these three variables (profession, issue, and involvement). The discussion will be confined to a few of the central problems that the layman and the scientist are likely to encounter in working together on national security issues; and the treatment, as will become evident, will be of a very general and suggestive order.

In their general character, the problems occasioned by the participation of scientists in the determination of high policy are not nearly so novel as is generally supposed. The scientist has been brought into the councils of government because he possesses specialized skills and information believed relevant to the identification and resolution of particular policy problems. His relationship to the policy process is therefore a familiar one, that of an expert. Just as Sputnik I precipitated the establishment of a Special Assistant to the President for Science and Technology, so the earlier problems of fighting World War II and insuring postwar employment had brought the Joint Chiefs of Staff and the Council of Economic Advisers into the Offices of the President.

The central problems in policy-making posed by the entry of scientists into the policy process are thus formally no different from those associated with any other expert involved in the determination of national security policy. In particular, four such problems can be noted. (1) Like all experts, scientists will at times disagree, and the non-scientist (be he politician, administrator, or an expert in some other field) will confront the problem of choosing a course of action in the face of conflicting scientific advice. (2) Like all experts, scientists will at times evince certain predispositions toward the resolution of the policy problems on which their advice is sought, and the non-scientist will confront the problem of identifying the policy predilections peculiar to scientists and being on his guard against them. (3) The non-scientist and scientist will confront one problem in common, and that is how to organize themselves to maximize the contribution that science can make to the government's programs, opportunities, and choices. Finally, (4) the scientist will confront a problem common to all experts who participate in the American policy process, and that is how to engage in politics without debasing the coinage of his own expertise.

The difficulties the non-scientist confronts in choosing a course of action in the face of conflicting scientific advice seem inherently no more formidable than those a non-expert would face in deciding what to do in the event of conflicting advice from economists, soldiers, or specialists on Soviet foreign policy. There are at least seven procedures that the non-expert can follow in such circumstances, singly or in combination, and they appear to have about the same promise, for better or for worse, regardless of the kind of experts involved.[8]

The first step the non-scientist can take is to make certain that it is really conflicting *scien-*

tific advice he is receiving. In the fall of 1949 President Truman asked Secretary Acheson to look into the disputes then current within the Atomic Energy Commisson and elsewhere about the consequences of undertaking an intensive effort to make an H-bomb. Upon investigation the Secretary of State concluded that the scientists involved were not really very far apart except on the foreign policy issues that were his and Truman's responsibility to decide.[9]

Procedures two and three are simple: the non-scientist may be guided by quantitative or qualitative features of the division (he can side with the majority, or with that side whose past record is the more confidence-inspiring). Failing these, there is, four, the "principle of least harm" and, five, the "principle of minimal choice." In the former, one chooses that course of action which appears to involve the least cost if the technical premise on which it is based proves to be wrong. Thus in World War II, given the American belief that the Germans were hard at work on an A-bomb, it seemed more sensible to spend $2 billion on the assumption that the bomb could be made than to do little or nothing on the assumption that it could not. In the case of the "principle of minimal choice," one chooses that course of action which seems to close off the least number of future alternatives. This was the character of President Truman's first decision on the H-bomb. He decided to go ahead in the effort to explore the feasibility of an H-bomb, but nothing was decided about technical steps of a greater political or military consequence (for example, testing a device if one were fabricated, or preparing to produce the materials that would be required for weapons production in the event of a successful test).[10]

In the case of procedure six the non-scientist can make his choice among conflicting scientists on the basis of whichever technical estimate is most in accord with policy on which he was already intent. (In contrast to the first procedure, where the non-scientist endeavors to factor out of the conflict the policy preferences of the scientists, here he is factoring into the conflict his own policy preferences.) In the spring of 1942, the British scientists Henry Tizard and F. A. Lindemann (Lord Cherwell) diverged greatly in their estimates of the destruction that could be accomplished by an intensive bombing of the homes of the German working class. There was general agreement among the soldiers and politicians involved that if the lower estimate were correct there were better military uses for the resources the bombing campaign would require, but in the end the campaign was made in the expectation that the higher estimate would prove to be the more accurate (which it did not). This choice was clearly influenced by Churchill's interest in presenting the Russians with a dramatically visible contribution to the war against Germany and by the fact that British air doctrine had long presumed the efficacy of strategic bombing.[11]

In procedure seven the non-scientist is guided by his own sense for the scientific and technical problems involved. In the 1949 H-bomb debate, some of the politicians involved were little deterred by the fact that the scientists were by no means confident that they could make such a weapon and the by the possibility that an all-out but failing effort might entail very high costs for the A-bomb program. These politicians were willing to press ahead in part because of their belief that the scientists were not really aware of their own potential. Similarly, when the German soldiers, scientists, and engineers engaged in the development of the V-2 divided on the question of whether it should be launched from mobile or fixed batteries, Hitler's own technical enthusiasm for large, hardened bunkers led him, unwisely as it turned out, to decide on behalf of the latter.[12]

In concluding this survey of the problem of conflicting advice, it should be noted that one of the more likely outcomes is that the actions of the contending scientists may prove much more influential than the procedures followed by the non-scientist. Divided experts will not always be equal in their physical or personal access to the decision-maker, in the persistence with which they state their case, or in the force and clarity of their arguments. Thus, in the H-bomb debate, there were instances where equally qualified scientists differed greatly in the time and energy they spent circulating their views of the technical (and political) prospects, and such differences were by no means without consequence for the judgments of others.[13]

The discussion of the policy predispositions displayed by scientists must be entered with considerable caution. The major theoretical premise involved is that all experts will evidence certain predilections with regard to policy and policy-making which are the result of the character of their expertise: their skills, knowledge, and experience. Since experts differ in the skills, knowledge, and experience they command (or in the responsibilities with which they are charged), they will differ in the biases they characteristically exhibit. Thus scientists, soldiers, and diplomats jointly concerned with a policy problem are likely to approach the question of how and in what manner it should be resolved with rather dissimilar predispositions.

These points, however, are easier stated than demonstrated. To begin with, it should be clear that, insofar as policy is concerned, "the scientific mind" is as much a chimera as "the military mind." Scientists, like soldiers and the rest of us, differ greatly in the ideas they have about the political world and the things that will (or ought to) happen in it, and their views on foreign policy matters are far more likely to be reflective of their differences than conditioned by their common professional skills and interests. Moreover, even if differences in expertise or responsibility were the only factors determining the views of policy-makers (and they certainly are not), one would still have to take account of the fact that scientists are as varied in their professional skills and pursuits as soldiers. The perspectives of a theoretical physicist engaged in basic research are no more to be equated with those of an organic chemist engaged in applying extant knowledge to the improvement of an industrial product than is the outlook of a staff officer in Washington drafting a war plan to be considered identical with that of a general in charge of a theatre of operations.

In addition to these difficulties, analysis must also contend with the fact that it is directed toward a moving target. The policy perspectives that a physicist may have developed as a result of two decades in a university laboratory are unlikely to endure without change after a few years on a Washington advisory committee. Many American scientists are well along the same route that transformed the policy perspectives of large numbers of the American military profession during the war and immediate postwar years. As a result of new problems and new responsibilities, these soldiers acquired new skills, knowledge, and experience. In consequence, with regard to their approach to foreign policy, some are, for all practical purposes, interchangeable between the Pentagon and the State Department, and one could wish that there were more diplomats equally well equipped to work on both sides of the Potomac.

With these reservations in mind, six policy perspectives will be presented here which seem moderately characteristic of many scientists, most of them physicists, who have participated in national security policy in recent times. Most of these predispositions were first evidenced during their work with the military during World War II, and the extent and manner in which they have been later operative in reference to larger foreign policy issues is not always easy to document, since most of the sources are still classified. Needless to say, in outlining these predispositions, one is presenting a cross between a caricature and a Weberian ideal type, not describing real people. In discussing these predispositions, the present writer does not mean to convey the impression that they are either "good" or "bad" from the point of view of policy or policy-making or that one or another of these predispositions may not also be evidenced by groups other than scientists. The point to this discussion is that if certain orders of scientists are indeed prone to these or other policy predispositions, the non-scientist will be wise to be alert to them, even if in the event he should conclude that they are all for the good.

Naive utopianism or naive belligerency. C.P. Snow has described the scientist as an impatient optimist in his approach to social wrongs; he is quick to search for something to do and inclined to expect favorable results.[14] Certainly, the scientist's profession inclines him to look at problems in terms of searching for a solution to them. When this perspective is turned to problems of international politics, however, the scientist's approach often appears open to the characterization of "naive utopianism or naive belligerency."[15] His approach to international relations appears simplistic and mechanistic. It is almost as if he conceives of policy being made primarily by forward-looking, solution-oriented, rational-thinking types like himself.

In these perspectives the scientist is likely to find little in common with the diplomat (who is inclined to believe that most of his problems have no solution, and who is in any event too busy with the crises of the day to plan for tomorrow), or with the politician (whose approach to problems is so spasmodic as to seem neither analytical nor rational, and whose policy positions are anyway soon blurred by his efforts to accommodate to the positions of others), or with the professional student of international politics (who, when the opportunity permits, lectures the scientist on the elegant complexity of the political process, but who never seems, to the scientist at least, to have any really good ideas about what to do). It is perhaps these differences in perspective that lead the scientist on occasion to seem "intellectually arrogant"; it is as if he concludes that those who have no promising solutions or are not seeking them cannot be very bright. In his predisposition toward action and solutions, the scientist comes closest to sharing the predilection of the soldier for decision, which may be one reason why their partnership has been so spectacularly successful.

The whole problem approach. The first grant made by the United States Government for experimental research was in 1832 to the Franklin Institute. The scientists were asked to investigate the reasons for explosions in steamboat boilers. They reported back not only with a technical explanation but with a draft bill to provide for Federal regulation of steamboats.[16] In this they evidenced the scientists' predilection for the "whole problem approach." The reluctance of scientists to apply their expertise to mere fragments of the total problem, especially under conditions where those who prescribe the fragments do not reveal the whole of which they are a part, was evident in the work of both British and American scientists during World War II. Military officials initially approached the scientists with requests for the development of particular weapons and devices without revealing the military problems or reasoning responsible for their requests. The scientists objected to this procedure, and they were eventually able to persuade the soldiers to inform them of the general military problems involved in order that the scientists might reach their own conclusions about the kinds of weapons and devices the military would need to meet those problems.[17]

In 1952, in connection with an Air Force project on air defense, a group of American scientists were asked to review the prospects for improving the nation's continental air defense. The scientists concluded that some new and promising systems were possible, and they submitted an estimate of what the developments might cost. They also recommended that the money be spent. The Air Force did not approve the recommendation, and as is customary in Washington the disputants on both sides began to search for allies and to leak their cases to the press. Certain Air Force officials, who feared that additional funds for air defense would come at the expense of dollars otherwise available for the Strategic Air Command and who were convinced that this would be militarily undesirable, charged that the scientists by entering into matters of military strategy and budget policy had exceeded both their assignment and their expertise. Commenting on this charge, one of the scientists involved later explained that he would have little interest in working on a study project that did not have the potential for leading into the question of whether the conclusions should be acted upon.[18]

The predisposition to want to be told and to deal with the whole problem no doubt has its base in the professional experience of scientists (and one of the central credos of science) that good ideas on a problem may come from the most unexpected quarters and that the widest possible dissemination of information about a problem will significantly enhance its chances for an early solution.[19] Still, there are problems and problems; some are open to determinate solutions, and others can be resolved only through the exercise of political power. The point about the "whole problem approach," as the air defense example illustrates, is that it not only helps propel the scientists from an advisory to a political role but it serves to make the scientist somewhat blind to the fact that he is so moving. In its most extreme form, the "whole problem approach" coupled with the "intellectual arrogance" perspective can lead to such instances as when, on one high-level advisory committee concerned with several areas of national security policy, a scientist whose formal claim to participation was a knowledge of infra-red ray phenomena was reportedly quite free with his proposals for what political policies should be adopted with regard to the United Nations.

Quantum jumps versus improvements. A number of scientists have advanced the proposition that the military tend to be more interested in improving existing weapons than in developing radically new ones, and they have urged that a separate civilian agency be established to undertake such development. Both scientists and soldiers have explained this difference in their approach to military research and development, "quantum jumps versus improvements," with the hypothesis that the soldier's interest in developing entirely new weapons must always be inhibited by his concern for the possibility that war may come in the near future, since in this event his interests are best served by improving existing weapons. It has

also been suggested that military leaders, who must be prepared at any time to ask others to take up the weapons at hand and fight with them, cannot afford to let themselves or others become too impressed with the deficiencies of those weapons as compared with others that might have been had.[20]

An explanation less flattering to the military for this difference is the occasional assertion by scientists that theirs is a profession which stimulates original and creative thought, while that of the military tends to develop minds which accept the existing situation without too much question. As indicated in the discussion of the first predilection, this is a judgment which the scientist may extend to the diplomat and the politician as well. The structure of both the domestic and the international political process is normally such as to make "quantum jumps" in policy infeasible. Diplomats and politicians are accustomed to seeing the same old policy problems come around year after year, and they are generally intent on policies which promise only slow and modest change. Scientists, on the other hand, have been demanding and searching for quantum jumps in foreign policy ever since the end of World War II. It is symptomatic that the first proposal developed by the Advisory Committee on Science and Technology to the Democratic National Advisory Council, established in 1959, was for the creation of a new scientific agency, independent of the State and Defense Departments, whose function would be "to face all the problems of disarmament."[21]

Technology for its own sweet sake. In the summer of 1945, after the A-bomb had been tested but before the first drop on Japan, the Director of the Los Alamos Laboratory. J. Robert Oppenheimer, suggested to his superior, General Leslie Groves, that if some improvements were made in the design of the bomb it would be more effective. Groves decided against the improvements because he did not want to incur any delay in the use of the bomb, which he expected would end the war with Japan. In the summer of 1943, after the Director of the German V-2 project, General Dornberger, had finally secured a first-class priority for the use of the weapon, those responsible for producing it in quantity were increasingly handicapped by the scientists and engineers who kept improving but changing its design. Dornberger was finally obliged to issue a flat order against any further improvements.[22]

There was nothing irresponsible in these

scientists' actions. Charged with the technical development of weapons, they would have been remiss in their responsibilities if they had failed to call attention to the prospects for improvement. The point to the examples is that scientists and engineers, in the pursuit of their own responsibilities and interests, may easily lose sight of those of the policy maker.

The scientists on the General Advisory Committee to the Atomic Energy Commission who recommended against the development of an H-bomb in 1949 did so in part because of their concern for the foreign-policy consequences of introducing a weapon of such destructive power into the world. Oppenheimer, the Chairman of the Committee, later stated that the thermonuclear design developed by Edward Teller in 1951 was "technically so sweet" that, if it had been available in 1949, the Committee would probably not have made the recommendation that it did. Since, with a technically more promising design at hand, one might suppose that the Committee's foreign-policy concerns would have been all the greater, some observers have concluded that in the pursuit of his technical interests the scientist can also easily lose sight of his own policy concerns.[23]

Such a judgment ignores the complexity of the Committee's position. For example, one of the reasons why the Committee thought the United States should take the initiative in renouncing the H-bomb was precisely because the device then in view seemed likely to be both difficult to make and of dubious military value. It was thought that for this reason the Russians might be willing to follow the American example and that, if they did not, the United States would not have risked much by the delay. These were considerations which obviously would have been changed if a technically more promising design had been available in 1949.[24] Still, the comments of several scientists close to these events are not without relevance. It is their feeling that there are times when the technician does take over, that when the scientist is faced with an interesting and challenging problem his inclination is to get to work on it, and that under these circumstances he should not be the first person to be expected to keep larger policy considerations in balance. This predisposition, "technology for its own sweet sake," appears to have its roots in two more of science's central credos: the belief in the value of pursuing knowledge for its own sake, and the belief that the best motivation for the direction of research is the strength and character of individual curiosities. But the direction and strength of scientific interests and curiosities is not necessarily coincident with the requirements of military or foreign policy. One of the most recent examples of the scientist's capacity to get caught up in a challenging problem (assigned, to be sure, by policymakers) is afforded by the ingenious techniques scientists conceived for evading nuclear-test detection systems and for the design of new systems to meet those evasions. In the light of the later course of negotiations, an American statesman who believed there was considerable foreign-policy gain in a test-ban treaty and who believed that the Russians were at one time seriously interested in such a treaty might well conclude that the formula developed by Watson-Watt, the scientist who fathered radar, with reference to the problem of meeting wartime military requirements was not without its implications for meeting peacetime foreign policy requirements: "Give them the third best to go with; the second comes too late, the best never comes."[25] This observation is not intended as an argument that the interests of the United States would have been better served by a test-ban treaty with a "third best" detection system than by no treaty at all. The point is that the policy maker must be sensitive to the prospect that, because of the constant advance of technology, his only real choices may be of this order.

The sense for paradise lost. This predisposition is likely to be more characteristic of the scientists who had their graduate training and early professional experience in the years before World War II than of those who have known only war or Cold War conditions.[26] The prewar scientists took it as an article of faith that certain conditions were essential for the progress of science, in particular that scientists be free to select their research problems and that both scientists and scientific information be free to move among as well as within nations.[27] All of these conditions were violated during World War II, and as a result of the Cold War they were never fully re-established. The nuclear physicists had had perhaps the most highly developed sense of international community. They were relatively few in number, had intimate personal relationships at home and abroad, and had been experiencing an exciting exchange of discoveries since Rutherford identified the nucleus in 1911. They also lost the most, for theirs was militarily the most sensitive knowledge, and the pages of the

Bulletin of the Atomic Scientists offer eloquent testimony to their ideological disturbance.

The result is that the senior scientists tend to be especially sensitive to possibilities which hold some promise for restoring the former order. They may usually be found on the side (or in front) of those urging freer exchange of scientific and military information with allied governments, less secrecy in the circulation of scientific (and sometimes military) information, and more extensive cultural, and especially scientific, exchanges with the Soviet Union. Similarly, the major activities of the Foreign Policy Panel of the President's Science Advisory Committee and of the Office of the Science Adviser to the Secretary of State have been in connection with the Science Attaché program, the facilitation of international scientific programs and conferences, and the exchange of scientists with the Soviet Union.[28]

Science serves mankind. For at least 300 years the western scientific tradition has assumed that the unrestricted generation of new knowledge about the world was a social good. Over these years science in its purest form (the discovery of the facts of nature for knowledge's sake alone) became increasingly an autonomous social institution; research scientists were largely disassociated from the practical applications of their discoveries, but they took it for granted that these discoveries would ultimately benefit mankind.[29] The advent of nuclear and bacteriological weapons systems which have the potential of destroying so much of mankind and his works has called this faith sharply into question. It does not take much imagination to wonder if man, in view of his apparent inability to escape from the order of conflicts which have historically resulted in war, would not be better off in a world where the knowledge that has made the new weapons possible did not exist. For some of the senior nuclear physicists this is more than a philosophical question. They are unable to avoid a sense of real personal responsibility; they reason from the premise that they were few, and if they had acted differently weapons development might not have taken the turn it did.

In the immediate postwar years, the apparent contradiction between the good of science and the evil of war was resolved by the expectation that the very destructiveness of the new weapons would lead man to renounce at last the folly of war. The course of foreign policy in later years has weakened these expectations but not destroyed them, as the recent flurry of arms-control proposals premised on the rational self-interest of both sides in avoiding mutual destruction testifies.

The need to preserve their sense of service to mankind led some American scientists to refuse to work on weapons. Similarly, there are reports that several Russian scientists were imprisoned, exiled, or placed under surveillance for refusing to participate in weapons work between 1945 and 1953, and in 1957 a number of Germany's elite physicists announced that they would have no part in nuclear weapons work.[30] Such cases are dramatic, but nowhere have they prevented the development of weapons on which governments were determined. The more consequential resolutions have been those in which scientists have simply identified the good of mankind with the strength of their nation or have endeavored to develop new weapons systems which would be as effective as the old in promoting national policy but which would result in less slaughter if used. This was part of the rationale behind the recommendation made by a group of American scientists in 1951 that the government undertake the development and production of a large number of A-bombs for tactical use in the ground defense of Western Europe. Their hope was that such an innovation would relieve the United States of the burden of having to rely solely on the threat of strategic bombing to contain the Red Army.[31]

The failure of the United States to orbit a satellite before the Soviet Union did was the result of the State Department's insensitivity to the political implications of the event and the decision of the President and the Secretary of Defense not to let a satellite program interfere with military missile programs. A small part of the story, however, is to be found in the reluctance of some of the American scientists involved in the programming of the International Geophysical Year to see an American IGY satellite propelled by an operational military weapon. Their preference for the less developed but non-military Vanguard over the Army's Redstone appears to have reflected a combination of the "sense for paradise lost" and the "science serves mankind" predispositions, in this case an interest in showing the world the peaceful side of science and in demonstrating that the scientists of the world could cooperate in the interests of knowledge as well as compete in the interests of nations.[32]

With regard to the two remaining problems

to be discussed—how to organize relations between science and government, and how the scientist can participate in policy-making and still keep his expert standing—four points seem deserving of special emphasis: (A) the problem of organization, especially in the area of foreign policy, is still very much in the research and development stage, and so it may long remain, considering the precedent set by the problem of how to relate military experts and foreign policy; (B) in many areas of policy it will never be possible to specify what constitutes "the best" organization; the way in which policy-makers are organized is not without influence on the kind of policies they will produce, and so long as there are differences over policy there will be no agreement about organization; (C) in the American political system, at least, the science expert at the high-policy level has no real hope of keeping out of politics; his only choice is in the character of his political style; and finally, (D) it should not be forgotten that organization and policy-making are not the same as policy; successful instances of foreign policy capitalizing on or guiding developments in science and technology will not automatically follow just because scientists have been liberally injected into the policy-making process.

Organization. Current American organization in the area of science and foreign policy still reflects the emergency responses to the Russian ICBM and Sputnik I. One effect of these events was that scientists were rushed to the most important single center of power, the Office of the President, by means of the creation of the Special Assistant to the President for Science and Technology and the President's Science Advisory Committee.

The President certainly needs men around him sensitive to the areas of interaction between science and foreign policy. But a case can be made for the proposition that the center of gravity for the input of scientific advice into the policy-making process should be at a lower level than the White House. The President's political interests lie in keeping the staff about him small and generalized. Well-developed plans and programs will have a better chance of maturing in the larger and more diversified facilities that departments and agencies can provide. Secondly, as C. P. Snow concludes in his account of the differences between Tizard and Lindemann, there are risks in having a single science adviser sitting next to the center of political power. Although it should be noted

that Churchill fared better with a single science adviser than Hitler did with none ("The Führer has dreamed," Dornberger was told, "that no [V-2] will ever reach England"), Snow's point has merit and it holds for institutions as well as for individuals.[33] The President will generally find his choices facilitated by the existence of multiple and independent sources of scientific advice.

This is a condition that already prevails in the case of many of the departments and agencies whose actions have significant foreign policy consequences, especially in the use of scientists by the Department of Defense, the Atomic Energy Commission, and the National Aeronautics and Space Administration. It is, however, a condition notably absent in the case of the Department of State. As it now stands, the President has more scientists to advise him on the scientific and technical aspects of various foreign policy issues, particularly in the national security field, than has the Secretary of State.

Excluding the science attachés overseas, the Department of State's Office of the Science Adviser numbers six people of whom three, including the director, are professional scientists. There are no scientists, full or part-time, in the Department's offices for policy planning, space and atomic energy, or political-military affairs. As might be inferred from these arrangements, many of the policy-makers concerned believe that their needs for scientific advice are adequately met through formal and informal communication with scientists employed in the operating agencies and departments and with the President's own Science Advisory Committee. (It should also be noted that in at least one office the need for additional political personnel is clearly more urgent than the need for scientists.) The Department's Science Adviser, who participates in the work of both the President's Committee and the Federal Council on Science and Technology, serves to facilitate such communication; otherwise both the demands placed on the Office and its own interests have limited its activity, as previously noted, to a relatively narrow range of foreign policy problems.[34]

Whether the interests of the Department of State would be better served by a larger "in-house" scientific competence is a question that an outside observer cannot easily answer. Much depends on the validity of the expectations that the Department can rely on the scientists of the operating agencies to alert it to developments and information relevant to foreign policy. Even more depends on how determined the Department is to play an active and influential part in shaping the scientific and technical programs of the government to conform to its own conception of national needs and priorities.[35] Should this determination be high, it is difficult to avoid the hypothesis that if the President has found it useful to have a relatively large science advisory body to help him monitor and direct the course of science and technology as they affect foreign and domestic policy, so too might the Secretary of State in the area of his own more limited but still extensive responsibilities.

Organization and purpose. Since administrative organizations exist for the purpose of serving policy goals and implementing policy programs, it is to be expected that those who differ on the goals and programs of policy will differ about the proper design of administrative organizations. The desire of many scientists in 1945 to see atomic energy used for peaceful rather than military purposes was one of the reasons for their political campaign to place the postwar atomic energy program in the hands of a civilian commission instead of the War Department. Similarly, more recent differences about how to organize the government's space effort reflect, in part, policy differences about whether space will or should be an area for major military operations.

The same point can be seen in the proposal to create a Department of Science and Technology which would include the variety of "little" science programs now scattered throughout the Executive structure (for example, those of the Weather Bureau, National Bureau of Standards, the Antarctic Office) but would exclude those of the Department of Defense, the Atomic Energy Commission, and the Space Administration. The hope behind this proposal is that, combined together, the "little" programs would be able to compete more effectively in the struggle for government dollars with the "big" science programs of the military, atomic energy, and space organizations.[36]

The question of the "best" science organization is thus inescapably tied to the question of what is the "best" science policy. But who can demonstrate whether science and foreign policy would be better served by allocating dollars to a program to control weather or to a program to explore Mars? There are no determinate solutions to problems of this order. Neither, for that matter, is there any "one

right amount" of the nation's scientific resources that should be allocated to basic as compared to applied research. Differences on policy questions such as these are unavoidable among scientists and non-scientists alike, and they can be resolved in but one manner: through the interplay of power and interest in a political arena.

This condition, plus the increasing dependence of scientific programs and research on government funds, plus the increasing consequences of the choices the government makes in allocating those funds, all promise to put the politicians and the scientists under increasing pressure. As the opportunities for further development in each of a thousand different scientific fields mushroom with the acceleration of scientific knowledge, whatever the government decides to support, it will be deciding *not* to support more. Indeed, it is not too difficult to see the scientists becoming practiced advocates and lobbyists for the government's support of their cherished fields and projects, or to imagine the day when the politicians start to complain about "interscience rivalry" and begin to fancy that, if only there were a single Chief of Science, competition and duplication could be ended and the nation could have an integrated science policy.

Scientists in politics. The American political system is not one that insulates its experts from the politics of choice.[37] The scientist involved in high-policy matters is likely to find himself propelled into the political arena, either by a push from behind or by his own interest in seeing that the "right" choices are made. Some of the incentives the scientist may have, to follow up his advice with an effort to see that it is accepted (and to take a hand in a few other matters while he is at it), were outlined and illustrated in the preceding section. It is equally important to recognize that the scientist may find himself on the political firing line, placed there by a politician interested in using the scientist's prestige as an "expert" to disarm the critics of his (the politician's) choices.

Thus, prior to the moratorium on nuclear tests, the Eisenhower administration appeared to be using scientists and their scientific facts on fall-out as a means of justifying and defending a policy that was obviously compounded of a variety of considerations besides that of the radiological hazard. The comparison with Truman's use of the prestige of the Joint Chiefs of Staff to defend his choices in the

Korean War comes easily to mind. So, too, do the statements of various Republican leaders that they had lost confidence in the Joint Chiefs and their determination, when they came to power, to get rid of the "Democratic" Chiefs and to appoint Chiefs in sympathy with Republican policies.

The scientist, in short, is not likely to orbit the centres of political power emitting upon request "beeps" of purely technical information. He will inevitably be pulled into the political arena. If his participation there is to be either productive or personally satisfying, both the scientist and the non-scientist need to be highly conscious of the character of their activity and the problems involved. The scientist (and many a non-scientist) must learn that the making of foreign policy is not a quest for the "right" answers to the problems of our time. There are only hard choices, the consequences of which will be uncertain and the making of which will often seem interminable in time and irrational in procedure.

The debate and disagreement over these choices will be heated and confused under the best of circumstances, but emotion and misunderstanding can be eased if scientists and non-scientists are both alert to the limits as well as the potential of the scientist's contribution. On the scientist's part, there is the obvious need to exercise the utmost care in making clear to himself and to others the areas where he speaks as a concerned citizen and those where he speaks as a professional expert. More difficult will be the task of learning how and to whom to address himself in each of these capacities when he is dissatisfied with the outcome of a policy decision in which he has participated. There is, as Don Price has pointed out, no clear code in Washington to govern the conduct of dissenting experts, only a "flexible" set of possible relationships with one's immediate superiors and those whose authority competes with or exceeds that of one's superiors. In contrast to the soldier, who can find some although not complete guidance in the doctrine of "civilian control," the very nature of the scientist's intellectual habits and many of his policy predispositions may make especially difficult his task in determining the limits to which he can stretch his dissent.[38]

On their part, the non-scientists need to recognize that scientists can hardly be expected to remain politically indifferent or inactive about the policy issues with which they are involved (especially when no one else in Washington practices such restraint). It was the naïveté of this expectation that was so appalling in the conclusion of the Gray Board that Oppenheimer was a security risk because (among other reasons) "he may have departed his role as scientific adviser to exercise highly persuasive influence in matters in which his convictions were not necessarily a reflection of technical judgment, and also not necessarily related to the protection of the strongest offensive military interests of the country."[39] It is unlikely that "civil-scientist" relations will ever get any worse than this. With time and experience one can expect many of these problems to be eased, but it would be unrealistic to expect them to disappear. Military experts have participated in the making of foreign policy far longer than scientists, and the question of how they can best do so is still the subject of more than a little disagreement.

Policy processes and policy. In closing this discussion of scientists and the problems of their organizational and political relationships to others engaged in the determination of foreign policy, it is important to remember that the policy process can bring minds together but it cannot make them think. It is worth noting that, in the political and administrative structure of the Soviet Union, no scientist is as institutionally close to the Premier as is the Special Assistant for Science and Technology to the President of the United States and that there is no equivalent of the Science Advisory Office in the Russian Ministry of Foreign Affairs.[40] Yet one would not say that the foreign policy of the Soviet Union has appeared either ineffectual or insensitive in its response to developments in science and technology.

The circumstances attendant on the development of radar by the British from 1935 to 1940 provide a useful insight into both the potential and the limits of effective organization. Essential, obviously, were the scientific and technical ideas that Watson-Watt and his colleagues had in mind in 1935, ideas which in turn were the result of the earlier years of research they had been free to conduct in the facilities of a government laboratory. Certainly, it was important that there were administrative scientists in the Air Ministry who were so alert to the military problems of the Air Force that they could see on their own initiative the need to establish a special scientific committee for the study of air defense (the Tizard Committee) and who were so alert to the work of the scientific community that they made their first request for information to Watson-Watt.[41] Of consequence, too, was the fact that the personal and political relations of the members of the Tizard committee with the members of the military, administrative, and political hierarchies whose interest and cooperation were vital for the subsequent progress of the research and development program were relations characterized by mutual ease, respect, and understanding.

But these conditions would not have led from the formation of the Tizard Committee in 1935 to a chain of operational radar stations by 1940 and a Fighter Command practiced in their use if it had not been for the military ideas of members of the Royal Air Force. It was they who first thought of the formation of a committee to look specifically into the problem of detection, they who recommend more funds than those first proposed by the Tizard Committee for the development of an electromagnetic detection system, and they who were responsible for the decision to start constructing the stations and training the personnel while the equipment was still under development.[42] The explanation for this interest and support is to be found in their theories about the next World War. They believed the Germans were planning to engage in the strategic bombing of Great Britain, and they wished to be prepared for it.[43]

The point is obvious but important. British scientists and science organization were in the final measure but ready tools. They were good tools, but the use to which they were put was the result of the kind of ideas the military men had about war. The same will hold in the other areas in which science may affect foreign policy. The contributions that science and technology will bring to international politics will largely turn, not so much on the particular arrangements of scientists in the policy-making process, but on the purposes of statesmen and the theories they have about the political world in which they live.

Notes

An earlier version of this paper was prepared for discussion at the Fifth Congress of the International Political Science Association in Paris, September 1961. The points made in it owe much to the comment and counsel of William T. R. Fox.

1. U.S. Department of State, *Papers Relating to the Foreign Relations of the United States, The Peace Conference*, 13 vols. (Washington, 1942–1947), vol. 3, p. 179.
2. Quoted in *Science and Technology Act of 1958* Staff Study of the Senate Committee on Government Operations, 85th Cong., 2d sess., Washington, 1958, p. 110.
3. *Ibid.*, p. 115.
4. See Daniels' letter to Edison, in Josephus Daniels, *The Wilson Era: Years of Peace, 1910–1917* (Chapel Hill: The University of North Carolina Press, 1944), p. 491.
5. Ellis A. Johnson, "The Crisis in Science and Technology and its Effect on Military Development," *Operations Research*, January–February 1958, pp. 14–15.
6. See Lee A. DuBridge, "The American Scientist: 1955," *Yale Review*, Spring 1955, p. 13, and the *Bulletin of the Atomic Scientists*, March 1957, p. 82, and May–June 1961, p. 254. The figure for private industry is for the year 1959; the others are for the year 1955.
7. For a more detailed treatment of some of the points in the preceding paragraphs and a general discussion of the effect of science on international relations, see the present writer's "Science, Technology, and Foreign Policy," *Journal of International Affairs*, Fall 1959, pp. 7–18.
8. *Cf.* the implication in the following remarks of Glenn T. Seaborg, the Chairman of the Atomic Energy Commission: "Scientists don't necessarily have to make the final political decisions, but it might be easier to let a capable scientist learn political reality than to teach a politician science." Quoted in the *Bulletin of the Atomic Scientists*, February 1961, p. 79.
9. In this and subsequent undocumented references the present writer has drawn upon personal interviews during 1956–1958 with participants in the H-bomb decision.
10. For the "principle of least harm," see Bernard Brodie, "Strategy as a Science." *World Politics*, July 1949, p. 479n. On the H-bomb choice, see the present writer's "The H-Bomb Decision: How To Decide Without Actually Choosing," *Political Science Quarterly*, March 1961, pp. 37–38.
11. See C. P. Snow, *Science and Government* (Cambridge: Harvard University Press, 1961), pp. 47–51, the review of this book by P. M. S. Blackett in *Scientific American*, April 1961, pp. 192–194, and Winston S. Churchill, *The Second World War: The Hinge of Fate* (Boston: Houghton Mifflin Company, 1950), p. 281. For British air doctrine see also Herbert S.

Dinnerstein, "The Impact of Air Power on the International Scene, 1933–1940," *Military Affairs*, Summer 1955, pp. 67–68.

12. Maj. Gen. Walter Dornberger, *V-2* (New York: Ballantine Books, 1954), pp. 97, 158–160, and Lt. Gen. James M. Gavin, *War and Peace in the Space Age* (New York, 1958), pp. 76–77.

13. Note should also be taken of the problem the policy-maker faces when all his experts are *agreed*. The present writer is unable to suggest a useful procedure here (other than variations on numbers five, six, and seven above); but that the problem is a real one can be seen in the conclusion of the German physicists that it would be infeasible for any Power to develop an atomic bomb during World War II. Some of the German scientists later stated that political considerations were partly responsible for their advice and for the fact that they made so little progress themselves on an A-bomb (*cf*, procedure one).

The German work on the A-bomb during World War II is described in Samuel A. Goudsmit, *Alsos* (New York: Henry Schuman, Inc., 1947). For various appraisals of the influence exercised by political considerations, see Robert Jungk, *Brighter than a Thousand Suns* (New York: Harcourt, Brace and Company, 1958), pp. 88–104, Hans Bethe in the *Bulletin of the Atomic Scientists*, December 1958, p. 427, and William L. Laurence, *Men and Atoms* (New York: Simon and Schuster, 1959), pp. 90–93.

14. C. P. Snow, *The Two Cultures and the Scientific Revolution* (New York: Cambridge University Press, 1959), pp. 9–11.

15. I am indebted to Hans Speier for the phrasing of this point.

16. Don K. Price, *Government and Science* (New York: New York University Press, 1954), pp. 10–11.

17. This persuasion was largely accomplished through demonstrations of the military utility of the scientists' taking such an approach, although in the early history of the M.I.T. Radiation Laboratory a certain amount of polite bargaining was apparently practiced. One scientist involved, whenever told that the reason for a request was a problem for Washington, not him, to worry about, adopted the practice of working on something else until he was given a description of the problem involved. For a brief summary of the British experience, see Alexander Haddow, "The Scientist as Citizen," *Bulletin of the Atomic Scientists*, September 1956, p. 247.

18. *Cf.* the following exchange between Gordon Gray and Jerrold Zacharias during the Oppenheimer hearing. Gray: "If you were directing a study which had to do with electronics, a pretty clearly defined field, and it started to come up with recommendations with respect to foreign policy, would you feel that an official of the Defense Department who urged that you stick to electronics was acting with impropriety?" Zacharias: "I think I would not direct a project that was as restrictive as that, sir, as to be restricted only to electronics." U.S. Atomic Energy Commission, *In the Matter of J. Robert Oppenheimer, Transcript of Hearing before Personnel Security Board*, Washington, 1954, p. 930.

For some of the issues involved in the 1952 air defense study, see *ibid.*, pp. 598–99, 749–50, 763–65, 923–24, 930–31, 935, 938, and also the account in Price, *Government and Science*, pp. 136–38.

19. General Leslie Groves, who directed the Manhattan project, was especially sensitive to the scientists' tendency to take on the whole problem. (Some even advised him on how the garbage should be collected at Los Alamos, an act which may possibly have reflected self- rather than scientific interest). One reason for his effort to compartmentalize the work scientists were doing was his fear that "if I brought them into the whole project, they would never do their own job. There was just too much of scientific interest, and they would just be frittering from one thing to another." *Oppenheimer Transcript*, p. 164.

20. See, for example, Lloyd V. Berkner, "Science and National Strength," *Bulletin of the Atomic Scientists*, June 1953, pp. 155, 180.

21. See the *Bulletin of the Atomic Scientists*, December 1959, p. 412.

22. *Oppenheimer Transcript*, p. 33, and Dornberger, *V-2*, pp. 134–137.

23. *Oppenheimer Transcript*, p. 251. For an extreme judgment, see Jungk, *Brighter Than a Thousand Suns*, p. 296.

24. See Oppenheimer's statements in *Oppenheimer Transcript*, pp. 81, 251, 897, and "The H-bomb Decision: How to Decide Without Actually Choosing," *loc. cit.*, pp. 30–36.

25. Sir Robert Watson-Watt, *Three Steps to Victory* (London: Odhams, 1957), p. 74.

26. In 1955 slightly more than half of the active research physicists in the United States were under forty years of age and had received their doctorates after December 7, 1941. Lee A. DuBridge, "The American Scientist: 1955," *Yale Review*, September 1955, p. 1.

27. These assumptions are excellently set forth in Margret Smith Stahl, "Splits and Schisms: Nuclear and Social," unpublished doctoral dissertation, University of Wisconsin, 1946, ch. 4.

28. For the activities of the Panel and the Office, see James R. Killian, "Science and Public Policy," Address to the American Association

for the Advancement of Science, December 29, 1958, as printed in *Science Program—86th Congress*, Report of the Senate Committee on Government Operations, 86th Cong., 1st sess. (1959), pp. 12–13, and *The Science Adviser of the Department of State*, Department of State Publication 7056 (Washington, 1960).

29. See Stahl, *op. cit.*, ch. 4.

30. See Arnold Kramish, *Atomic Energy in the Soviet Union* (Stanford: Stanford University Press, 1959), p. 105. Kramish states that it is not certain whether the objections of the Russian scientists were technical or political. For the declaration of the German physicists, see the *Bulletin of the Atomic Scientists*, June 1957, p. 228.

31. *Oppenheimer Transcript*, pp. 584, 594–95, 891–94.

32. See Walter Sullivan, *Assault on the Unknown* (New York: McGraw-Hill, 1961), pp. 79–81.

33. Snow, *Science and Government*, pp. 66–68, and Dornberger, *V-2*, p. 87.

34. There are eighteen scientists on the President's Science Advisory Committee; its working panels also contain participants from outside the committee. In December 1958 the Committee and the Office of the Special Assistant for Science and Technology had together some 75 scientists and engineers serving part time. See Killian, "Science and Public Policy," *loc. cit.*, p. 8. The work of the Committee and the Office are additionally described and appraised in *Science Organization and the President's Office*, Staff Study of the Subcommittee on National Policy Machinery, Senate Committee on Government Operations, 87th Cong., 1st sess. (1961).

The information presented about the Department of State is based on U.S. Department of State, *The Science adviser of the Department of State*, and interviews with several Department officials in February 1962. Needless to say, the description and interpretation made above are entirely the present writer's responsibility.

35. These two conditions are not unrelated. The more influence the Department exercises in determining the goals and programs of other agencies, the more confident it can be that scientists in those agencies will call the Department's attention to goals and programs which they believe to be receiving too much or too little attention.

36. See Lloyd V. Berkner, "National Science Policy and the Future," Address at Johns Hopkins University, December 16, 1958, as printed in *Science Program—86th Congress*, pp. 116–18.

37. This point, especially as it relates to science experts, is discussed in Price, *Government and Science*, pp. 61–62, and in Herman Finer,

"Government and the Expert," *Bulletin of the Atomic Scientists*, November 1956, pp. 331–32.

38. See the discussion in Price, *Government and Science*, pp. 131, 133, 138–42. The point about the scientists' lacking a tradition of "civilian control" was suggested by William T. R. Fox.

39. U.S. Atomic Energy Commission, *In the Matter of J. Robert Oppenheimer, Texts of Principal Documents and Letters* (Washington, 1954), pp. 19–20. Note the policy predisposition in the phrase "strongest offensive military interests."

It should not be comfortable for an American to reflect on the career of Peter Kapitsa, a Soviet physicist who was a student of Rutherford and who worked in England from 1922 to 1934 and then returned to the Soviet Union. Kapitsa was placed under house arrest in 1947 and remained there until after Stalin's death. Kapitsa has told western scientists and newsmen that his arrest was the result of his refusal to work on nuclear energy for military purposes. Kramish believes that his arrest was due to the government's dissatisfaction with his advice on certain technical approaches to weapons development. In either event, it is noteworthy that Kapitsa is believed to have recently been, on an informal basis, one of Khrushchev's main science advisers.

On the matter of his arrest, see the report by Harrison Salisbury in the *New York Times*, July 11, 1956; the *Bulletin of the Atomic Scientists*, January 1957, p. 38; and Kramish, *Atomic Energy in the Soviet Union*, pp. 109–110. The information on his recent activity was supplied by the staff of the Subcommittee on National Policy Machinery, Senate Committee on Government Operations.

40. On Soviet government and science organization, see *National Policy Machinery in the Soviet Union*, Report of the Subcommittee on National Policy Machinery, Senate Committee on Government Operations, 86th Cong., 2d sess. (Washington, 1949, pp. 24–35, 59–62, and Nicholas DeWitt, "Reorganization of Science and Research in the U.S.S.R.," *Science*, June 23, 1961, pp. 1981–91. The points made above were additionally confirmed by the staff of the Subcommittee on National Policy Machinery.

41. The circumstances provide an interesting variation of the "whole problem approach." The Tizard Committee was initially interested in techniques for destroying aircraft or their crews, and Watson-Watt was asked in 1935 to investigate the possibility of using electromagnetic radiation for this purpose. He reported that such a use was apparently infeasible. In any event, he went on to note, the aircraft would first have to be located,

and if anyone was interested electromagnetic radiation might be useful for this. Watson-Watt, *Three Steps to Victory*, pp. 81–83.

42. For the development of radar, see *ibid.*, pp. 108–09; C. P. Snow, *Science and Government*, pp. 24–38, 60–61, 74–75; P. M. S. Blackett, "Tizard and the Science of War," *Nature*, March 5, 1960, pp. 648–49; and Basil Collier, *The Defense of the United Kingdom* (London: H.M.S.O., 1957), pp. 33, 36–39.

43. Ironically, the British were mistaken in their theory. The German Air Force had no such strategy in mind, and in 1940 when it tried to improvise a strategic bombing campaign it had neither the equipment nor the doctrine with which to conduct the campaign effectively. See Herbert Dinnerstein, "The Impact of Air Power on the International Scene: 1933–1940," *Military Affairs*, Summer 1955, pp. 65–71; Telford Taylor, *The March of Conquest* (New York: Simon and Schuster, 1958), pp. 24–30; and Adolf Galland, *The First and the Last* (New York: Ballantine Books, 1954), chs. 2–5.

William H. Riker

Politics in the age of maneuver

SO FAR THREE MAIN PROPOSITIONS about political coalitions have been developed from the model of *n*-person games:

1. *The size principle.* This is the assertion that, with complete and perfect information, winning coalitions tend toward the minimal winning size.

2. *The strategic principle.* This is the assertion that, in systems or bodies in which the size principle is operative, participants in the final stages of coalition-formation should and do move toward a minimal winning coalition.

3. *The disequilibrium principle.* This is the assertion, that, in systems or bodies where the size and strategic principles are operative, the systems or bodies are themselves unstable. That is, they contain forces leading toward decision regardless of stakes and hence toward the elimination of participants.

The first principle was deduced from the model and the latter who were deduced both from the model and the first principle. Some empirical evidence was offered from the size principle, though of course it needs much more detailed verification from less partial hands than mine before it can be generally accepted. Insofar as the size principle is verified, however, its two corollaries are somewhat verified also.

In one sense it is proper to end at this point for the theory from the model has now been carried as far as I am at present prepared to carry it. Nevertheless, the model was constructed in order to study the real world and, because of that purpose, it seems appropriate to conclude by inquiring further into the significance of the principles for reality. Assuming, then, that the three principles are validly deduced and either verified or verifiable empirically, what do they imply about the state of world politics?. . .

Reprinted from Willian Riker, *The Theory of Political Coalitions*, New Haven, Yale University Press, 1962, pp. 215–243.

The place of the United States in the world

SINCE 1945 at least consciously and since 1941 in retrospective consciousness, the United States has been the leader of a world-dominating coalition. It has been challenged, of course, by the Soviet Union, but at least as late as 1957 the challenger acknowledged a subordinate position for itself. In the course of an interview on on 24 July 1957 in which Prime Minister Khrushchev was advocating a greater degree of exchange of persons between the U.S. and the U.S.S.R., he spoke quite incidentally of the power relationships between the two countries, calling his own nation "the second greatest power in the world." Considering the incidental and accidental nature of the utterance, this statement probably represented his actual intuitive judgment at the time.[1] Whether the subsequent Soviet success in the technology of rockets and missiles has altered his judgment, one cannot say. Yet the tone of his remarks during his visit to the United States in 1960 (e.g., his references to passing the United States in the next decade) indicates, I believe, that he still holds his pre-Sputnik opinion. If the main opponent of United States leadership regards the United States as its superior to be emulated, there can be little doubt, I believe, that this country has, at least from 1945 to 1957 and probably still today, been the leader of a world-dominating coalition.

American citizens have on the whole been loath to recognize and accept this national role. The prevailing isolationist sentiment among politicans of all persuasions during the 1920s and 1930s effectively prevented our assumption of the role of world leader in that period, although probably this role was ours for the asking even then. Still today, in the face of the objective fact of our leadership, we are isolationists enough in sentiment to try to close our eyes to our real position. Our national reluctance to play the role of world leader in Korea—a reluctance demonstrated by Eisenhower's overwhelming victory in 1952—was undoubtedly a reflection of this isolationist temper. In short, most Americans would prefer that their government be a follower rather than a leader so that, freed from the responsibilities of leadership, the citizens can go quietly about their business.

This political isolationism has been socially intertwined with a kind of cultural timidity and deference. Despite our cultural chauvinism on

a popular level—a chauvinism that may well have had its roots in a repressed sense of inferiority—our intellectuals have generally been acustomed to defer to the taste and intellectual standards of Europeans. We have sent our best students to study painting in France, philosophy in England, medicine in Austria, chemistry in Germany, music in Italy, and mathematics all over Europe. Such action was objectively justified up to the time of the First World War for indeed the world centers of learning were in European cities. Since then, and especially since the Second World War, the export of students has been justifiable only on political or sentimental grounds—not on intellectual grounds, especially since the cream of European scholarship has gradually migrated to the United States. But despite the change, the export of students continues—a kind of intellectual deference that expresses our deep-felt hesitation about the role of world leadership, even on the intellectual level.

As a consequence of our isolation and our reluctance to lead or to acknowledge leadership even in areas of action quite peripheral to politics, we have been quite unable to formulate a political position appropriate to our role. While many of our international difficulties of the past score of years have been an inescapable function of circumstances beyond our control, part of our difficulty does stem, it seems to me, from our reluctance to recognize the role we actually now play. Hence, one of the first steps toward the construction of an adequate posture in world affairs is the self-recognition of our leadership. The next step is to discover the content and possibilities for action in this role.

The conditions of leadership

PROBABLY the essential fact about the role of leader in a world-dominating coalition is that the actor who once occupies this role cannot resign from it without unpleasant consequences. Many Americans, harking back to a joyful and carefree golden age of national adolescence in the nineteenth century, would perhaps prefer to resign from the role rather than accept its incessant crises, its worrisome calculations, and its perpetual sense of high stakes on a hair trigger. But such sentimental preference for resignation—which is probably the main emotion driving such diverse groups as peace-marchers and McCarthyites, both of whom prefer domestic conflict to combating the external enemy—is almost invariably expressed in ignorance or scorn of the actual consequences of resignation. In order to demonstrate, therefore, how fully committed we are to (some would say "trapped in") the role of leadership, let us consider some of the putative consequences of resigning from the role.

Most Americans fancy that their commanding position has been achieved without forceful mistreatment of other peoples. Compared with other empires of the past, compared even with so liberal and guilt-stricken an empire as the British, American leadership has been milder still. But mild as it has probably been, it does not follow that our dependents have felt kindly toward us. The discovery that Castro expresses the deep hostility of the Cuban—and indeed the Latin American—middle class toward the United States, has been a shock to many North Americans. But we have used force, mostly economic, but occasionally military, to control Latin America. It should be no surprise, therefore, that the persons so controlled have regarded the controller as a tyrant. To the degree that some dependent nations have regarded our leadership as tyrannical, we can expect retribution if we relinquish the leadership role. Initially such retribution might be no more than the seizure of our investment in Latin America and a restriction of trade. (This may or may not be negligible: About one-third of our income from foreign investments and about one-third of our imports originate there. About one-fifth of our exports are destined for there. If one assumes that foreign trade has a multiplier effect, then this loss alone might have serious repercussions on our economy). But in the course of time surely the effects of the loss of leadership would be greater than this. It is not too fanciful to suggest that the ultimate effects would even include a reopening of the territorial settlement after the Mexican War.

Our leadership elsewhere in the world has involved less use of force than in Latin America and hence the loss of the role would doubtless involve less retribution. But political loss would surely involve also the loss of many commercial advantages and a drastic reduction in foreign trade. It would be an interesting enterprise in economic prediction to calculate the effect of these potential losses on our gross national product. Although I cannot make such a calculation in detail, a reasonable guess seems to me that we would return initially to about the level of our preleadership position,

adjusted for the loss of income from Latin America. This would mean an average family income about like that of the early 1930s. Eventually, of course, one would expect the income to slide much lower.

Entirely apart from economic losses, which would undoubtedly be very great were the United States to abandon its leadership, other potential losses seem to me to be greater still. As a function of our leadership we have developed a really large intellectual class, perhaps the largest the world has seen. The mathematicians, physicists, biologists, psychologists, and social scientists necessary to maintain our military position vis-à-vis the Soviet Union are a remarkable collection just now beginning to establish an intellectual tradition which holds great promise of creativity. American intellectual life was once dominated by a kind of utilitarianism or pragmatism that produced much of immediate value but little new knowledge in the absolute sense. The postwar generation of intellectuals is, however, gradually overcoming the pragmatism of its ancestors and hence stands on the threshold of magnificent intellectual achievements. Should the United States abandon its role of leadership, most of this class would no longer be necessary and indeed too expensive to support. The loss of leadership would then mean also a heavy sacrifice of potential intellectual creativity.

It can be expected also that the loss of leadership—even though in our present imaginary examination it would occur by voluntary resignation—would, very probably, also involve a loss of self-confidence in all other areas of life, as well as the intellectual. American self-confidence, which often unfortunately appears to be brashness to other peoples, is, in my opinion, one of the most attractive of our national traits of character. Its replacement with either a chastened humility or a querulous debility would, I believe, be an incalculable personal loss.

Finally, resignation of leadership would involve the systematic betrayal of many peoples who have believed in us. A foretaste of what might happen can be observed in the results of the abortive Hungarian revolution of 1956. That revolution, which was partly predicated on an expectation of American aid, resulted in the slaughter of a large number of people, especially of idealistic and trusting adolescents. They did not understand that the foreign policy of "liberation" was announced by Secretary Dulles mostly for domestic consumption as an incident for the struggle for votes in the era of McCarthyism. Nor did they realize that Radio Free Europe, again inspired by McCarthyism, represented purely the private opinion of persons who would doubtless have liked to make American policy but in fact did not. The United States was culpable, of course, to the degree that it did not indicate that the slogan of "liberation" did not mean what it might appear to mean and that Radio Free Europe did not represent the United States. But to how much greater a degree would it be culpable if it abandoned the smaller nations of NATO, CENTO, and SEATO to Soviet imperialism after binding them into formal defensive alliances. The guilt of betrayal would be almost insurmountable.

In short, the loss of or resignation from leadership would involve, at the very least, unpleasant consequences for economic life, for intellectual creativity, for national character, and for the national conscience. The isolationists of the last generation may well have been wiser than they knew in seeking to avoid the leader's role. But once we are in it, we cannot abandon it without substantial sacrifice. This is indeed a larger sacrifice than most citizens are, I believe, willing to make. Hence, we probably cannot voluntarily abandon our position of leadership. This is the first and essential fact about our present occupancy of the leader's role.

The present balance of coalitions in world politics

IN 1945 the United States stood at what has turned out to be the apex of its world leadership. Its previous enemies—Germany, Italy, and Japan—had been reduced to insignificance and the way was prepared to bring them back into the world society under the aegis of American leadership. Its most immediate allies —England, France, and China—were so crippled by the war that they had no choice but to look to the United States for leadership. Most of Latin America, while perhaps covertly hostile to the United States (and, in the case of the Peronist Argentine, openly hostile), was nonetheless willing to accept American leadership in affairs outside the hemisphere. The only conceivable threat to world leadership by the United States lay in the Soviet Union which, somewhat like the United States, had been physically strengthened by its very participation in the war. Yet the Soviet Union could not then defend itself against nuclear

weapons so that it too had reason to accept American leadership.

Five years later, however, American hegemony was a thing entirely of the past. The United States was opposed by a fairly strong minority coalition which could check many American actions and might even reasonably aspire to defeat it. How did this change come about?

In 1945 and for a few years thereafter, the United States had an opportunity to consolidate its position as world leader and to impose, perhaps, an imperial order on the whole world. There were some among us, indeed, who urged that we do so (e.g., Henry Luce, whose notion of the American century apparently meant an imperial *pax Americana*). But with characteristic reluctance to lead, with characteristic hesitation to tell other people what to do, the United States chose not to maintain the commanding position. (Although it is doubtless immodest for an American to say so, there stands no finer tribute to the essential modesty of the American character than the fact that, during the brief period of our exclusive possession of atomic weapons, the nation as a whole rejected as preposterous the temptation to establish world empire. It does not, I think, detract seriously from the humaneness of this decision that we subsequently executed the traitors Rosenberg who were in some part responsible for removing this temptation from our consciousness.)

Having chosen not to maintain indefinitely the status quo of 1945, something which could have been done only by the imposition of world empire, the United States necessarily also condemned itself to a long (?) period of attrition in which, by the operation of the size principle, the scope of its leadership would be reduced. Since it refused the imperial technique (the only feasible technique) of preventing change and since it was in an almost world-dominating position, its decision to allow change meant that most change that might occur would be to its disadvantage.

This is, of course, what happened. First, without serious opposition the Soviet Union was allowed to solidify its influence in all those nations whose territory it physically occupied in 1945. Presumably the ejection of the Red Army from those places was a task beyond our energy. That is to say, having accepted the international world not as something to govern but as something in which to play an *n*-person (probably zero-sum) game, the United States decided that the allegiance of Poland, Hungary, Bulgaria, Romania, Czechoslovakia, Eastern Germany, and Yugoslavia was not worth expending energy for, inasmuch as it could control the main things it desired to control without them. Put another way, the U.S. decided to rehabilitate Western Europe, but not to go to the expense and trouble of rehabilitating Eastern Europe. Very shortly thereafter, however, the United States decided to expend considerable energy in preventing further Soviet expansion in Greece and Turkey, an action which doubtless informed Tito that when Yugoslavia defected from the Soviet bloc it could count on sympathy from the United States. In Eastern Europe, then, the United States, after initially losing those Soviet satellites which it had initially expected to return to their prewar status of independence, successfully contained its opponent and even weaned partially away one of its opponent's hitherto wholly dependent allies. Almost all American energy was spent on maintaining this portion of its coalition, however. Consequently, elsewhere in the world its opponent was able to make serious inroads on the American coalition.

In concentrating on the rehabilitation of its European allies, the United States in effect decided that it would not pay very much to keep China, which perhaps seemed relatively worthless in military potential and indeed would have been an extremely expensive ally to maintain. It seems fairly clear also that the Soviet Union devoted relatively little energy to winning China, but when, suddenly, the Chinese Communists were successful, naturally the Soviet Union expended considerable energy in helping them consolidate their power. The important point is that here the size principle operated in terms of American policymakers' judgments of where to spend their working capital on side-payments. Having chosen Europe and the Near East, the United States allowed its relatively unsupported ally in the Far East, beset with internal strife, to be taken over by the other side. At the time most Americans did not even regard China as a serious loss.

While the United States chose to expend considerable energy on maintaining its European alliance, it made no effort to maintain its allies' empires. Indeed, for ideological reasons, it usually approved the dismemberment of them, doubtless hoping that if it covertly aided the revolutionaries, they would

as leaders of free governments ally themselves with the United States. Unfortunately for the United States, however, it has not always turned out that way. To ally with the United States has often meant that the ex-colonies ally with the ex-colonial powers and this has often been an unpalatable contract. Furthermore, each of the new participants in world affairs (whether ex-colonies or hitherto neglected states) has been the object of courtship by the opposing coalition. In selected instances it has bid the price of alliance up to the point that the United States has believed it not worthwhile, either in terms of the price itself or in terms of internal strains within the coalition led by the United States. Thus, in the case of Egypt, the price has become much military equipment, much purchasing of cotton, and perhaps the financing of the Aswan Dam. But military subsidies are not only costly; they are also deeply offensive to Israel, one of our few firm allies in the Near East. As for cotton, we already have too much of it. And the Aswan Dam is not only extremely expensive and a doubtful financial risk, but also is opposed by the Sudan, which might well turn out to be as valuable an ally as Egypt. And so, in accordance with the size principle, we have not paid for an ally which is not, at the moment at least, necessary for winning interim decisions. Similar considerations have led us to bid only half-heartedly for Afghanistan, which the Soviet Union has successfully integrated into its own economy. Not only is Afghanistan hard to defend, directly exposed as it is to the Soviet Union, but also to arm it is offensive to our firm ally, Pakistan. Furthermore, Afghanistan's oil, which presently the West does not need, is with little expense exported to the Soviet Union, while to export it to the West would require a very large capital investment. And so we have in effect allowed the Soviet Union to integrate the Afghan economy with its own.

In other areas, where substantial economic or military penetration has not been feasible for either side, the curious phenomenon of neutralism has appeared. By judicious management of the neutralist position, numerous Asian and African governments have been able to wring some side-payments from each coalition for temporary support (as on a vote in the United Nations) without firmly committing themselves to either side. In a sense, both Africa south of the Sahara and many states of north Africa and the Near East have managed to avoid both coalitions, thus reducing the significance of each, and to deploy their mobile diplomacy to their own greatest advantage.

Thus, in accordance with the size principle, the coalition led by the United States has been whittled down in size fairly continuously since the end of the Second World War. Where once it controlled most of the world, it now has certain control only of Western Europe, the Americas, some of the maritime portions of Eastern Asia and scattered portions of the Near East. Its opponent controls Eastern Europe and two-thirds of Asia. The remainder of the world is in balance between them, although it appears that the United States has at the moment closer ties with India and other Southeast Asian neutrals (except Indonesia) and with most of the new states of Africa than does the Soviet Union.

A question of great import for the future of West is whether or not this gradual whittling down of Western strength in accordance with the size principle is a now completed process. I do not believe that it is, for it seems to me that the West is still sufficiently confident of its winning strength to allow further losses of allies. The occurrences in Cuba are instructive in this respect. While the Cuban revolution was probably home-grown, still the revolutionaries have turned to the Soviet Union for protection. If the Soviet Union has not yet gained a firm ally, the United States has lost one. Will the United States attempt to regain it? To regain probably means fostering and financing another revolution, as we seem to have done on a much smaller scale in Guatemala. Whether or not we will pay such a relatively high price remains to be seen. If we do not, then we can, I assume, expect further such defections, even in the Americas. And outside the Americas further defections seem more likely still, especially if we should fail to maintain the status quo in Laos. The rest of the Indo-Chinese peninsula as well as Thailand and Burma seem likely candidates for defection. And if they should go, Indonesia, already aggressively neutral, may well prefer to plump openly for the other side. So it seems likely that the Soviet Union will continue to gain allies, both neutrals and former allies of the West, until in the world's opinion the two great coalitions are roughly equal in size.

In the journalism of the West the dominant interpretation of the events in the world society during the last fifteen years is that of an aggressive imperial power (i.e., the Soviet Union) constantly upsetting the status quo. In this theory, the main propulsion of change is the evil motive of the Communist leaders. In the interpretation offered here, on the other hand, a rational (rather than evil) motive is ascribed to the leaders of both sides. The changes in the relative strength of coalitions is viewed as a normal political process. In both theories, the Soviet Union is interpreted as aggressive while the Western bloc is seen as a defender of the status quo. The difference between the theories is that, from the journalistic theory, one might infer that, were Communists to be replaced by liberals or democrats or aristocrats or kings, the aggression would cease. In the interpretation offered here, however, the aggression is a function of the total situation and would not be affected by a change of Eastern rulers except perhaps that kings might be less efficient aggressors than Communists.

Politics in an age of maneuver

THE fifteen years since the Second World War may well be called the Age of Equalization. This is the period in which, in accordance with the size principle, the Western coalition has diminished and the Communist one expanded. How long this age may be expected to continue is not entirely clear. The United States has lost much power relative to the Soviet Union which suggests that the age may be nearly over; but since the two coalitions do not yet seem to be roughly equal, one can expect the equalization process to continue for an indefinite time.

It is possible, however, to suggest a standard by which one may know when the Age of Equalization has come to an end. The standard is an inference from the United States policy of "containment." The basic form of the political problem for the United States in the Age of Equalization has been to determine what final coalition to seek to hold. While few, if any, policymakers in the United States have had a broad enough view of the political process to realize that this was what they were doing, still, in building the NATO, CENTO, and SEATO alliances, they were in effect deciding where to draw the line of their future coalition, what to attempt to retain, and what to abandon. In the period in which both the policy of containment (which, though the policymakers ordinarily did not realize it, contained both the United States and the Soviet Union) and the actual alliances were constructed, the main kind of political event was border warfare, or what the Communists euphemistically call "wars of national liberation." Such warfare was in effect a probe by the Communist alliance to find weak spots in the Western coalition (i.e., allies the West would not pay or fight to hold on to). The Korean action was the main instance of such border warfare, but the guerrilla wars in Vietnam, Laos, Burma, Iran, and Greece, as well as the political strikes in Italy and France were also instances of the same kind of border probing. The number of places where such probing may now continue is limited. A probe is worthwhile only if it is reasonably close to the borders of the Soviet bloc so that the guerrillas et al., can be adequately supplied. Since the West has now made firm alliances and commitments over most of the border territories, the occasion for border warfare has substantially disappeared. Of course, the probing is still going on in various parts of the Indo-Chinese peninsula and the position of India, especially Kashmir, is perhaps vague enough to occasion some probing. Further, the exact position of Afghanistan and Finland and even Sweden is somewhat ambiguous, although the United States acts as if it expects the first two to be absorbed ultimately into a Soviet alliance. Still unless the Communists reopen border warfare in places in which it has been effectively settled, there are not very many places left for probing. When the few remaining ambiguities of border territory have been clarified, the Age of Equalization will be over.

At that point the character of world politics will change rather abruptly. We will pass from the Age of Equalization to the Age of Maneuver. And there will then be an entirely different tone to world politics.

The main features of the Age of Maneuver will, I submit, be the following:

1. The price asked by neutrals or marginal members for their allegiance to one side or the other will rise steadily.
2. The tone of politics will become more intense in the sense that each decision will seem to involve the entire future of each coalition.
3. As a result of the previous effect, the danger of general warfare will increase.
4. Finally, as a result of all three previous effects, the two main opposing powers will exhaust their resources in maintaining their alliances and other nations will come to the fore as world leaders.

Let us examine each of these effects in some detail.

The price asked by neutrals can hardly fail to rise as the border territories are worked into a tight set of alliances. That is, a reduction in the supply of neutrals will raise their individual prices, probably to the point that, for each side, the total bill for allegiance will be considerably greater than it is now. Up to the present time this rise in the price of side-payments has been obscured by the systematic dismemberment of the colonial holdings of the United States, Italy, Britain, France, Netherlands, and Belgium. Only the Portuguese empire remains for dismemberment, something which (judging from the events in Goa and the Congo) can be expected to occur fairly soon. In effect, there has been a constant increase in the supply of neutrals over the last fifteen years. But now the source of neutrals in the system is about exhausted. From now on the supply may be expected to contract gradually as some neutrals are firmly drawn into one orbit or the other. Entirely apart from this kind of restriction on supply is another and essentially independent restriction, namely, the prospective tendency of ex-colonial nations to federate with each other. The boundaries of most of the new nations of Africa, the Near East, and Southeast Asia were drawn originally by the colonial powers for administrative or military convenience. No effort was made to ensure the viability of any particular colony inasmuch as viability was felt to be a feature not of the parts but of the colonial system as a whole. As a result, when, as often happened, the empires were dismembered in accord with the colonial boundaries, many new states were not large enough to develop either military or economic strength. Undoubtedly this result was intended by the colonial powers, for it permits a kind of sub rosa economic imperialism to flourish long after the political imperialism ostensibly ends. But in the long run the economic disadvantages for the too-small states of Africa and the Near East and Southeast Asia will probably be unsupportable. If so, then consolidation will occur on the pattern of the Canadian absorption of Newfoundland. In this way also, then, the supply of neutrals will probably contract.

On the other hand, the supply of neutrals may well be increased by occasional flurries of Titoism. The process can be visualized thus: Dependent members of each alliance, resentful of the fact that their foreign policies are actually made in either Washington or Moscow, and resentful also of the fact that the pattern of their domestic lives is deeply influenced by the foreign-made foreign policy, may declare themselves neutral. Often such declarations will fail (as in Hungary or Guatemala, for example); but often they will succeed (as in Yugoslavia or, provisionally at least, Cuba). As the possession of the technology of nuclear warfare spreads, such defections may well become more frequent. Thus, in the last few years, France, gaining confidence with each Saharan explosion and resenting more and more rabidly the part played by the United States in the dismemberment of the French empire, has become a less and less reliable member of NATO and the Western alliance generally. It is not too fanciful to suggest that France may neutralize itself, not by means of a Communist revolt—the French Communist party seems to be decreasingly effective—but rather by an independent rapprochement with the Soviet Union, a rapprochement reminiscent of numerous Franco-Russian treaties of friendship over the past several hundred years.

Titoist defections of this sort can, however, hardly be expected to occur frequently or in large numbers. Hence, the supply of neutrals may be expected to decline.

Along with the prospective decline in the supply of neutrals, an effect which alone will raise their price, an entirely independent force will probably operate on the demand for allies in such fashion as to raise the price from the demand side. If, as I shall try to show in subsequent paragraphs, the tone of world politics becomes more intense in the Age of Maneuver than it has been in the Age of Equalization, then allies will be more desperately needed than they are now. If the fate of world leaders is believed to hang on every decision, however minor, then allies must be acquired at any price in order to assure victory.

Anticipating, then, a shorter supply of prospective new allies and a greater demand for those available, one can also anticipate that the price will go up. In an auction in which the ultimate outcome determines life or death, it is unreasonable to suppose that there will be table stakes. Hence one can further anticipate that the total bill for allies will also increase for both sides. Not only will they have to continue to maintain the allegiance of already attracted ex-neutrals, but also they will have to pay inflated prices for new ones. In the United States there has been much resentment (which

seems to me to have grown in recent years) of the large expenditure on allies in the Age of Equalization. If, as I suggest, the expenditures already made will appear minute in comparison with those needed in the Age of Maneuver, one of the great political problems of the Western alliance will be the persuasion of its own citizens to pay the necessary costs of leadership. Indeed, it may well be that a failure of the United States and Western Europe to solve that elementary problem within a democratic framework will result in either the abandonment of democracy or a total defeat for the West.

The second previously listed feature of the Age of Maneuver is a putative intensification of the tone of politics. It may seem to some who have lived through the recurrent crises of the Cold War in the Age of Equalization that the sense of crisis cannot be deepened. Yet, I suggest, exactly such deepening will occur. In the similar phases of equalization and maneuver in American politics of the last century and three-quarters the atmosphere of politics has been much more heated in ages of maneuver than in ages of equalization. The ages of maneuver have been those in which the two parties are approximately equal in voting strength, namely, the late 1790s, the 1840s, the late 1870s and the 1880s, the late 1930s and early 1940s and, possibly, the period we are entering now. Assuming that the participation of a large proportion of eligible voters is evidence of an intensity of emotion in politics, then the ages of maneuver are also the ages of greatest intensity of emotion. The proportion of eligible voters participating was at a high point for a generation on either side in the Presidential elections of 1840, 1888, and 1940. While we have no adequate record of voting in the 1790s, it seems likely from scattered evidence that the turnout in the election of 1800 was exceptionally high for its era. Even without the evidence from the amount of voting, however, there is much evidence that political life in the ages of maneuver was more vituperative than at other times. And excessive vituperation seems to me evidence of intensity of emotion. In the age of Jefferson the pattern of extreme vituperation was established by such journalists as Freneau, Bache, and Cobbett. It was revived in Jackson's day by Isaac Hill, Duff Green, and Nicholas Biddle. In the 1870s and 1880s one kind of vituperation was so common it acquired a special name, "waving the bloody shirt." And those who remember the late 1930s know well the vituperative emotions aroused by Franklin Roosevelt.

And so, arguing from the analogy of the ages of maneuver in American politics, I suggest that the coming age of maneuver in world politics will generate its own new levels of intensity of emotion. Nor, on reflection, is this surprising. If each side has a chance to win on even the interim decisions, then the energy that each side puts into trying to win will probably be much greater than the energy either has put into decisions likely to be won by the much weightier side. And the mutual expenditure of energy will undoubtedly generate intense emotion.

The third feature of the Age of Maneuver is that, owing to the increase of tension, the danger of general war becomes much greater. As emotions become more intense on each decision, as, increasingly, both sides believe that every decision, however trivial objectively, determines the pattern of the future, then the temptation to deploy all resources on a particular decision is seductive indeed. In previous ages, when the technology of warfare was simpler, governments could succumb to this temptation without serious consequences to the species. The total wars both of antiquity and modern times have been total only in the sense of involving all governments. But the total war of the forthcoming age of maneuver will involve, if it occurs, every complex living thing. Out of fear of this prospect reasonable men on both sides have sought for some way to control atomic weapons. But, unfortunately, safety for the species cannot be obtained by as simple an expedient as arms control. The dilemma is this: If men know about nuclear weapons and if they believe that their entire future is at stake, then they may use them regardless of all the elaborate plans for nuclear disarmament and the like. Hence, no matter how much reasonable men may wish to avoid the obliteration of mammals, they still may do so. If a government comes to believe that it may use nuclear weapons without totally destructive retaliation, then in the prospective tension of the Age of Maneuver, when emotions will probably run so much higher than they do now, the temptation to use these weapons may be irresistible. If the belief is correct that complete retaliation is impossible, then the species may survive; but if the belief is false (as it may well be) then the species will be obliterated—and probably not in as pleasantly romantic a fashion as depicted by Mr. Nevil Shute.

This is the main horror of the forthcoming Age of Maneuver. But there is another horror, not nearly so terrifying to all mankind, but unpleasant enough for people in the United States and the Soviet Union. This lesser horror is the prospect of systematic overpayment of allies or, alternatively, mutual self-destruction so that at the end of the age both nations are thoroughly enfeebled. If and when this comes about—and it is the fourth listed feature of politics in the Age of Maneuver—the United States and the Soviet Union will have been reduced to dismembered followers and other more vigorous peoples will take up the leadership of the world.

This lesser horror for the citizens of the two world-dominating nations is almost certain to come about. Assuming that the tone of world politics becomes increasingly intense and that the price of the allegiance of neutrals becomes greatly inflated, then both leading nations will feel compelled to pay the anticipated high prices for allies. Entirely apart from side-payments to allies, both the major powers will be required to continue to expend vast sums on armaments. Even if they can come to an agreement to restrict the production of nuclear weapons and even if they can agree on a practical and efficient system of inspection to enforce the agreement, they will still need to spend large amounts of money on both the technology of space travel and conventional military devices. Bases on natural or artificial satellites will unquestionably be of great military significance throughout the Age of Maneuver. It does not seem fanciful to suppose, should the emotions of this age concentrate competition on a race for space, that both nations might spend a quarter of their national income in the competition. And all this without reference to nuclear weapons. On a more mundane level, military equipment of the conventional sort will continue to be necessary in large quantities in order to fight such occasional limited wars as may arise and in order to keep one's allies properly awed. A curious phenomenon: One of the chief kinds of side-payments presently desired by neutrals and marginal allies is a supply of conventional arms. In most instances these are desired in order to awe or even to fight another neutral. But as the supply of them increases, each of the two main powers must increase its own supply simply in order to police those whom it has armed. And, of course, rapid technological change and obsolescence of conventional weapons is a necessary part of offering acceptable side-payments. So the supply of conventional weapons alone can be expected to be inordinately expensive.

Even if no wars occur, therefore, allies and armaments will undoubtedly be a heavy drain on the resources of both leading powers. Their dependents, freed to some degree from these costs, may then be expected to grow rich and powerful at the expense of their leaders. If wars occur, either limited or total, it is, of course, the two leading powers that much bear the greater portion of the expense both in money and men. The leaders have most at stake and hence will be expected to stand most of the cost. And this will, in the long run, also favor the marginal allies at the expense of the leaders.

In the beginning of this chapter the fall of empires was attributed both to the size principle and to systematic overestimation by leaders of the objective value of decisions. In the Age of Equalization, it is the size principle that contributes most to the decline, but in the Age of Maneuver it will doubtless be the overpayment of followers and the excessive expenditure of energy on the maintenance of leadership. The end-product of both processes in both ages is, of course, the decline of the leaders. And that is what the United States and the Soviet Union have to look forward to toward the end of the Age of Maneuver.

Strategy in the age of maneuver

IN the Age of Maneuver, for both the United States and the Soviet Union, the main strategic goal—albeit perhaps a goal unrecognized by one or both governments—is the prolongation of the age for the greatest possible duration. Inasmuch as the end of this age is likely also to be the end of the leadership of both powers, it is in the objective interests of both to forestall the end.

For the achievement of this goal, there are several obvious strategic policies.

First and foremost, each ought to take every possible precaution to avoid nuclear war or even total war without nuclear weapons. If either such war occurs, neither of the leading powers can possibly be the winner, even though the wars are zero-sum. The winner will of course win the power that the loser loses. But soon after the war is over it will appear that marginal members of both sides are stronger than the original leaders. I do not know how

such wars are to be avoided, except by the conscious intention of both powers. Indeed, both must recognize that they are playing not only a zero-sum game against each other but also are playing a sub rosa zero-sum game in which they are allies against the rest of the world. The main challenge to the diplomacy of both powers is to keep the other forever cognizant of the sub rosa game even when the tensions of the Age of Maneuver are at their most intense. Like parliamentary leaders who at heart have greater sympathy with the leaders of the parliamentary opposition than they have with their own back benchers, these two powers can only at their deepest peril forget that leadership itself is as much a value as winning.

In order to remember this point, both governments need institutional reminders. This is the chief role that the United Nations can play. Since the beginning of the Korean Conflict the U.N. General Assembly has been something of a covert American agent. But with the projection into it of African neutrals, it seems likely that the U.N. as a whole will revert to its intended function as a world parliament. As such it may be able to transmute military hostilities into verbal ones. If it is able to do so, then it may be a genuine institutional damper on the war-inducing tensions of the Age of Maneuver. Every institutional change that strengthens the U.N.—e.g., giving it responsibilities for, initially, controlling nuclear testing; giving it, subsequently, responsibility for arms control; giving it, ultimately, some of the powers of a genuine world government—will increase its effectiveness as a damper. Hence, it is in the best interests of both the United States and the Soviet Union now to strengthen the U.N. in preparation for the Age of Maneuver. Of course, in many daily ways, a strengthened U.N. appears to be a threat to both powers, especially when it is strengthened somewhat at the expense of one of them, as occurred in 1950 and as will occur when Red China gets its seat on the Security Council. But daily threats are, I think, less significant than the ultimate potentiality of this institution to dampen the tensions that may induce military action. Hence, it seems to me strategically correct, from the point of view of prolonging the Age of Maneuver, to strengthen the U.N. as much as possible.

A second obvious and basic strategy for the Age of Maneuver is to control in some way the prices paid for allies. If the free market price is allowed to prevail, it will, as I have earlier suggested, be extraordinarily high. There is no reason, however, why clever men cannot rig these prices just as prices of all other commodities have in one way or another been controlled to advantage. The Soviet Union has made most of its conquests in the Age of Equalization at a remarkably low price, that is, by infusing home-grown guerrillas with the Communist ideology and perhaps by supplying a rather small quantity of equipment for guerrilla warfare. It has been able to do this in so-called underdeveloped societies because the statist technique of modernization and industrialization, invented by Lenin and demonstrated to be practicable for a rural society by Stalin, has proved extraordinarily attractive to the intelligentsia of underdeveloped societies. By contrast, the liberal ideology of the West, which depends for its economic effectiveness on the existence of a large class of literate and cosmopolitan entrepreneurs, has seemed economically irrelevant in places where most of the people are illiterate peasants or tribesmen. On the other hand, the United States has retained some of its most secure allies at little cost simply because it was the main exponent of the liberal ideology of freedom. Freedom may be a somewhat defective ideal, for it is difficult to imagine the commitment the human psyche craves directed at so instrumental and morally empty a goal as freedom. Yet for those who do not have a bit of it, freedom can become an absolute. Those who remember a past tyranny have rejoicingly identified with the American standard of freedom, simply because it is freedom and regardless of its economic significance. Thus in two contrasting ways during the Age of Equalization the two main antagonists have bought allies with ideology, which costs very little. Doubtless they will continue to be able to do so.

But as the possibilities of the neutralist role are more thoroughly grasped and exploited, it may well happen that ideology is not enough to hold even thoroughly convinced allies. In the case of Yugoslavia, for example, neither devotion to Marxism nor gratitude for Soviet assistance were sufficient to maintain the alliance in the face of Stalinist tyranny. It seems likely that such Titoist behavior will be more common in the future than in the past and will involve defections from both sides. And it is at this point that the problem of price control becomes most pressing.

For the United States, presumably the leader of the leading coalition and presumably desirous of maintaining its lead, this poses an extraordinarily important strategic problem. Will it meet the price that neutrals and marginal and recalcitrant members of its coalition demand? If it meets every price asked, it may well squander its resources. So the strategic problem will necessarily be the establishment of the policy for dealing with high prices. Control of prices is, it seems to me, possible on the basis of a fine sense of necessity. In a world in which ultimate victory or defeat is controlled by the possession of nuclear warheads in intercontinental missiles, the allegiance of recalcitrant allies is neither desirable nor negotiable. Those allies attracted by our ideology—which, I believe, is more attractive than the Communist one to nations on what Rostow has called the "take off" level of development—and those attracted by a simple fear of Soviet imperialism should of course be welcomed. But those who must be coerced or heavily bribed need not be paid for at all, especially if they find the Soviet ideology deeply unpalatable (e.g., Spain). All this calls for very delicate calculations. The United States must pay heavily, but not too heavily.

In making these calculations, the most important consideration, it seems to me, is that the United States not be mesmerized by the need to maintain a weightier alliance than the Soviet Union. Let us suppose—what is not essentially unreasonable—that to win a nuclear or non-nuclear total war a leader must have a coalition comprising two-thirds the weight of the world. If so, the consistent maintenance of an alliance of considerably over half but somewhat less than two-thirds the weight of the world is overly expensive. Yet this is precisely what the United States is now doing. Without endangering its position it could allow the Soviet alliance to grow to a weight greater than half. Indeed, such action, if gradually and consciously but secretly taken, would tend to prolong the Age of Maneuver and at the same time to increase the costs of leadership for the Soviet Union while reducing them for the United States. This is, however, a difficult policy to follow and one requiring both delicacy and political maturity on the part of both government and citizenry. A democracy bedeviled by a McCarthyite demagoguery, for example, would probably be entirely unable to follow such a policy and would, therefore, be expected to exhaust itself in overpayments quite quickly. But if the American democracy can learn to transcend demagoguery of this and other sorts, it may actually be able to follow such a policy for a long period of years.

If it can establish a policy involving relatively little overpayment and if it can avoid great wars, then the Age of Maneuver may be prolonged indefinitely.

Note

1. For the sake of conveying the full flavor of the judgment, a larger quotation from the interview follows:

Even Soviet cooks are not allowed in the United States because the U.S. is afraid they will shake the foundations of its way of life! I met a farmer by the name of Garston who is a specialist on the hybridization of corn. He was very nice and wanted to invite a group of agronomists to the U.S. They were refused entry by your government and when he went to champion their entry he had no luck. How can we improve prospects for peace when we can't even discuss corn.

Question [Mr. Jerome Davis]: We had an exchange of farmers recently, didn't we?

Answer: Yes, but only once, then it stopped. We would like to maintain the exchange. We favor an exchange of engineers since we have ideas of engineering even as you do.

The idea of not letting people into our respective countries is stupid or foolish. I don't know if such words are polite and I don't want to insult but I think so anyway. When people respect or accept a certain idea or system, that depends on their will but you can't ignore the fact that Bulgaria, Roumania, Albania, China, one third of Germany, North Vietnam and Poland exist. When we set up our system we didn't ask Dulles. You hate Communism and we Capitalism but that's not important. We have done wonders in our country and you envy us because *we are the second greatest power in the world* and will, through Communism, soon be the first. We must subdue passion and subordinate it into common-sense. Some politicians are blinded by hate and, like a bull seeing red, they leap forth blindly. Let us exchange scientific information and cooperate with each other.

Report of the American European Seminar on the USSR Including their Interview with Khrushchev in the Kremlin (West Haven, Conn., Promoting Enduring Peace, Inc., no date, presumably 1957), p. 18, emphasis added.

Gabriel A. Almond

Public opinion and national security policy

NATIONAL SECURITY POLICY is that part of a nation's foreign policy which is concerned with the allocation of resources for the production, deployment, and employment of what we might call the coercive facilities which a nation uses in pursuing its interests. These coercive facilities are one among a number of foreign policy instrumentalities. Diplomatic negotiation

Reprinted from the *Public Opinion Quarterly*, Vol. 20, 1956, pp. 371–378.

is another, economic means are another, and mass communication is a fourth. These four means—military, diplomatic, economic, and symbolic—are the four major instruments of foreign policy. The art of foreign policy consists in the selection of foreign policy goals consistent with the interests and values of the people of the nation and capable of achievement at bearable costs in the international arena, and in the utilization of these means in effective combination for the attainment of these goals.

It is obvious from this that we cannot separate national security policy from the goals which it is intended to achieve on the one hand or from the other instruments of foreign policy. One classic illustration of the interdependence of foreign policy means is the Panmunjon negotiations during the "Cease fire" of the Korean war when the Communists won a military victory through the use of diplomacy and when we lost the fruits of a military victory through our failure to appreciate the interdependence of military and diplomatic means in the conduct of foreign policy. If we cannot separate national security policy from the other elements of foreign policy, or separate the making of national security policy from the rest of the foreign policy-making process, there are a few special points which have to be made about the relation of public opinion and national security policy. These have to do with (1) the highly technical nature of most of the issues of security policy, (2) the problem of secrecy in the handling of security policy information, and (3) the enormous risks involved in the making of policies governing the magnitude of the security effort, its composition, its deployment, and its employment. These three characteristics of national security policy taken together create a situation of extraordinary gravity, and put the utmost strain on our capacity to make and maintain a foreign policy which is both democratic and effective.

First, let us examine the highly technical character of the issues of national security policy. It takes a most specialized competence to make intelligent judgments of such questions as how our basic resources shall be allocated among the major military services, or how within these services these resources shall be allocated to the various weapons systems, and how these weapons systems shall be knit together in a common strategic plan. It takes a highly specialized competence to make intelligent judgments of questions relating to the deployment of these facilities—where shall

we have what kinds of bases, how much of a strategic reserve shall we maintain, how shall our efforts be coordinated with those of our allies and the like. Finally, it takes both specialized competence and the most exacting sense of moral responsibility to make intelligent judgments as to the conditions under which we shall employ what kinds of military action—the staffing and training of foreign troops, the employment of conventional armaments, the use of tactical nuclear weapons, and finally the use of strategic nuclear weapons. The problem of making intelligent decisions in these areas is one of extraordinary difficulty and complexity even for those who are highly trained specialists.

I referred secondly to the problem of secrecy, for much of the essential information necessary to appraise national security policy decisions has to be withheld from public knowledge and discussion. Without it public discussion is helpless, or often positively misled by leaks and rumors. These two characteristics of national security policy—the technical nature of the problems and the security of some of the essential information—combine to produce a shallow base for public discussion of security policy issues. And if we take this in conjunction with the third characteristic of national security policy—the gravity of the issues with which it deals—we have stated the difficulties in the relationship between public opinion and national security policy in their full dimensions. For national security policy does deal with the issues of life and death—not of "expendable" proportions of societies and these resources—but in the contemporary world with the very life and death of whole societies and their cultures. The pathos of the man in the street in this connection, therefore, lies in the fact that he is confronted with issues in which the stakes are so high as to be almost meaningless, and so complex as to be beyond his understanding. Stating the problem in this pessimistic way avoids the temptation of easy answers and evangelical optimism which so often enter into discussions of the role of public opinion in the formation of public policy.

The policy process

ANY thoroughgoing analysis of the process by means of which national security policy is made will have to cover five elements—(a) the formal governmental agencies including the Executive and the Congress, (b) the media of communication, (c) interest groups, (d) the attentive public, and (e) the mass public.

Government. Let us start with the first of these, the formal governmental agencies, and treat them insofar as they affect the role of the non-governmental agencies and forces. In this respect the Executive and the Congress play a role of enormous importance in the public discussion of foreign policy and national security policy issues. They are largely responsible for setting the terms of public debate. The Executive initiates public discussion by taking action or by proposing legislation. In so doing it in effect proposes a theory or an hypothesis, that by doing such and such, certain consequences will follow. This ordinarily initiates public debate which involves the exploration of the Executive action or proposal and the examination of other alternatives. Nowhere more than in foreign policy and particularly national security policy is public opinion so dependent on the initiative of the Executive. The classic illustration, of course, is China policy. The Administration in 1947-48-49 chose not only to be inactive, but also largely silent about the collapse of Nationalist China and its consequences. It took the position that no reasonable amount of aid could rescue the Nationalists. It also in effect was taking the position that the fall of China to the Communists did not require any rectification of the American security position. The silence of the administration during these years meant that there was no discussion of these significant issues, and that the mobilization of Chinese military power and the Korean war fell upon American public opinion with an enormous impact. This was a case in which the Executive failed in its responsibility to initiate foreign policy and public discussion. Without such initiative it is usually impossible to utilize our intellectual resources in appraising foreign policy alternatives. At the very time China was collapsing, the military budget was being cut. The Executive failed to lead in a process of examination of the consequences of that policy, particularly the implications for national security policy.

If it is the primary job of the Executive to initiate national security action and legislation, it is the task of the Congress to set the terms of the debate, to explore other alternatives, to modify Executive proposals, and to ratify or to reject them. Contrary to the terms of the Constitution, the Executive initiates legislative action, and the Congress modifies and ratifies. Together they give structure to the issues of national security policy, and thereby facilitate public discussion.

The media. The media of mass communication have the primary function of communicating the foreign policy and security policy issues as formulated by the Executive, and as reformulated by the Congress to different parts of the public. But this function is not simply a matter of neutral communication. It involves selection, interpretation, in other words decisions about the salience of issues, and the importance of information.

Let me say one general thing about the media of communication in this respect and then proceed to some more differentiated comments. Taken by and large and with noteworthy exceptions the mass media in this country, as in others, tend to perpetuate two unfortunate tendencies in mass opinion. They deepen complacency and indifference in the absence of a hot story in the foreign policy field, or when they have a sensational item they play it to the maximum, and hence encourage panic reactions. But this is true primarily of the mass media.

One way of classifying the media of communication from the point of view of national security policy is to distinguish the "quality media"—newspapers like the *New York Times*, the *Herald Tribune*, and the *Christian Science Monitor*, the journals of opinion, the news weeklies, the serious newspaper columnists, radio and TV commentators, and influential publicists—from the mass media of which the tabloids are the best illustration.

The quality media reach the attentive public with foreign policy and security policy debate. They take an active part in the structuring of issues. They participate in foreign policy discussion continually. They reach into the formal governmental agencies and among the non-governmental opinion leaders. They help create a kind of laboratory atmosphere in which foreign policy ideas can be tested out through the use of responsible speculation and imagination. They constitute a "feedback" on the consequences of policy decisions, and furnish the necessary basis for the constant process of modifying and adapting decisions which have already been made.

If a careful study were made, we would probably find that the impact of the quality media has been increasing over the past years, that they are now meeting a much larger demand for continuous and serious information on the issues of foreign and security policy. The trend is moderately encouraging, and the possibilities of a responsible foreign policy discussion are greater today than they were ten years ago.

Interest groups. As you know America is unique in the number and variety of its voluntary organized groups. There are literally thousands of groups in the United States which take an active part in the making of public policy. There are economic interest groups, ethnic groups, religious groups, veterans groups, civic groups, women's groups, young people's groups. There are groups which are active at the national level, the regional level, the state level, and the local level. The U.S. is unique not only in the number and variety of its pressure and interest groups, it is also unique in the number of its *civic* groups. One of the most striking things that comes out of a comparison of French and German interest groups with the American is that the civic general interest group is practically absent on the European continent. They have special interest groups in profusion, but they have no civic reform groups—Parent Teachers Associations, League of Women Voters, Foreign Policy associations and the like. This gradation of public to private is one of the most striking characteristics of the American democratic tradition. Civic responsibility and political involvement extend beyond governmental office into the private citizenry.

Now what is the function of interest groups in the making of foreign policy? We have ceased viewing them as sinister, lobbying organizations engaged in corrupt practices of one kind or another, although some of them continue to operate this way. In their constructive aspect, organized interest groups play the role of translating general policies into their special impacts on particular groups. They constitute a special group of brokers who bargain for modification in policy in exchange for special group support. In doing this they add another useful dimension to the foreign policy-making process. We cannot quarrel with the function they perform, but only with its misuse. Policies do not affect all interests equally. They often impose inequalities in sacrifice. Some mechanism is essential to represent interests, to anticipate such inequalities of impact, and to moderate them to the extent that is possible.

Interest groups do not always enter into the process of making security policy in the same way as the adoption of the North Atlantic Treaty and the Reciprocal Trade Agreements

Act demonstrate. In the first case there was a well-dramatized issue, with considerable public interest. It was the great national organizations which became active in connection with the North Atlantic Treaty. The Chamber of Commerce, the Labor Federations, the national farm organizations and the like took a responsible part in the national debate on the treaty. In contrast whenever the renewal of the reciprocal trade agreements act comes up for consideration the impact of interest groups is fragmentary, local, and special, and hence irrational in its impact on national policy. It is the wheat farmers, the watchmakers, the textile manufacturers and the like who enter into the policy making process and attempt, often with success, to carve out special domains of privilege and protection.

In this respect, much depends on how widespread and active public discussion is. If there is a well-publicized discussion of a security issue, with the Executive and the Congress engaged in an active debate, and if the media of communication bring these issues to the general public, the irrational and special impact of interest groups can be kept within proportions. If there is no live public discussion reaching to the grass roots, special groups working largely without publicity can bring effective pressure to bear on Congressmen in their own constituencies, or on members of the Executive. There is a kind of twilight of public discussion which gives cover to this kind of effort.

Those who have had responsibilities in the field of Congressional liaison and public relations will recognize these differences in the patterns of pressure group activity. There is less to be concerned about when there is a great public issue up for discussion, and when the media of communication are active in publicizing it. The worries begin once a law has been enacted and the administrators have to decide how to place the orders or where to locate the bases. Then the whole machinery of special interest groups becomes activated, working through Congressional and political party contacts, striving for exceptions to general rules, and for special and local advantage.

Opinion and policy

NOW let us turn to public opinion proper. In connection with the media of communication, we discussed the quality media and the mass media, and in connection with interest groups we distinguished between general or civic interest groups and special and local interest groups. These differences in the structure of the media of communication and the interest groups are reflected in the structure of public opinion. It is useful in thinking about public opinion and its impact on national security policy to distingush three elements— the mass public, attention groups, and the attentive public. The mass public, fed by the mass media, is generally uninformed about national security policy issues. It responds to these issues with moods. It looks at headlines in the press, or listen to news over the radio for *cues* for *mood* responses in public discussion of foreign policy. It does not listen to the content of discussion but to its tone. A presidential statement that a crisis exists will ordinarily be registered in the form of apprehension. A reassuring statement will be received with complacency reactions. In both cases the reaction has no depth and no structure. For persons responsible for the making of security policy these *mood* impacts of the mass public have a highly irrational effect. Often public opinion is apathetic when it should be concerned, and panicky when it should be calm. But the problem is even more complicated than this, for these irrational mood impulses are not only general phenomena of public opinion; they enter into policy-making in the specialized form of attention groups. An issue involving Eastern Europe brings Americans of Slavic origin into the policy-making process with a sudden impact as it did in 1952 when the Republicans announced their policy of liberation. An issue involving Israel and the Arab states suddenly creates a special attention group among Jews in the United States. One can go down the line of Italians, Germans, Irish, and the like, to refer only to attention groups which have an ethnic base. There are many other kinds, and their impact on public policy and security policy can be understood in terms of the analogy of loaded pistols which are triggered off by special issues which bring generally inattentive and uninformed groups into a sudden impact on the policy-making process.

These irrational tendencies are, however, counteracted by the attentive public—a stratum of public opinion which is more analytically oriented to problems of public affairs, which is regularly informed on these issues, and which constitutes a critical audience for the discussion of public issues. This group is increasing in size and in discrimination. It is fed by the universities, sustained by the quality media of communication, and organized by the civic interest groups. The forces which can limit the impact of special interest, can contain and overcome indifference and panic, are the attentive public, the universities and colleges which train it, and the quality media which inform it and whose very quality depends on its existence, and to the civic and general interest groups which bring its impact to bear on policy-makers.

Conclusions

IT has been suggested that the issues of national security policy differ from other issues of public policy in three respects—the highly technical character of the issues, the element of secrecy, and the gravity of the stakes and the risks involved. If one examines the American political process from the point of view of its capacity to handle issues of this kind, one has to recognize that it is in respect of these issues that we are weakest. Military policy has long been the special domain of the military specialist. There are only half a dozen places in the country where problems of national security policy are being seriously treated in academic terms today. The media of communication and the interest groups are also weak in this regard. The shortage of this kind of expertness outside of the military establishment itself is attributable to the recency of our military and foreign policy responsibilities. We simply have not had the time to train and develop this kind of interest and competence at the points where it is needed.

A sound program of public opinion development in the field of national security policy would have as its main aim the creation of an attentive public competent to handle the issues of national security policy. This means in very specific terms four lines of action: (1) The introduction of problems of military policy into university curricula and the development of military scholarship in the universities to produce a leadership with a basic competence to understand the issues of security policy. (2) The development of soundly trained military specialists in the media of communication to ensure that the issues of security policy will be rapidly and accurately transmitted throughout the significant strata of the population. (3) The training of specialists in problems of military policy in the major interest groups to ensure more responsible interest group pressures. (4) The development of scholarship in political and military affairs among the military leadership to create a homogeneous leadership capable of organizing and articulating the issues in public debate.

In other words competence to handle military and security problems in their relation to foreign policy and other aspects of public policy must be introduced effectively into the processes of public opinion formation. We have to create depth in the public discussion of security problems. The model of the future toward which we ought to strive is one in which basic military and security issues can be thrashed out in a lively public discussion, with alternative points of view presented before an interested and informed audience. It is only in this way that the strengths of a democratic political process—the interplay of free minds— can be introduced into the making of security policy. Without it, we are as vulnerable in the policy-making sphere as the lack of an essential weapons system might make us in the military sphere.

Harold D. Lasswell

The garrison-state hypothesis today

THE GARRISON-STATE hypothesis was first published about a quarter of a century ago[1]. The object of the present exercise is to consider the significance of the hypothesis in the light of scholarship and of the flow of history to date. The plan of discussion is this: (1) to consider certain points of method and terminology; (2) to examine the prospects for the continuation or discontinuation of the expectation of violence, which is a fundamental factor assumed by the garrison construct; (3) to explore the internal structure of decision within the several nation-states during future years; and (4) to draw implications for the guidance of science and policy.

I

THE simplest version of the garrison-state hypothesis is that the arena of world politics is moving toward the domination of specialists on violence. The hypothesis offers a characterization of significant patterns of the past and future, thereby providing a provisional orientation within the flow of events "from what" "toward what." If we take the mid-nineteenth-century nation-states of European culture as the point of departure, it is meaningful to say that the most important elites were specialized in the exercise of business skills, and skills of symbol management, official administration,

Reprinted from Samuel P. Huntington, ed., *Changing Patterns of Military Politics*, New York, The Free Press of Glencoe, 1962, pp. 51–70.

and party organization. Skills in the management of violence (or, more generally, of extreme coercion) continued to play a prominent role. Nevertheless, their subordination is indicated by the degree to which spokesmen for armies, navies, and police forces justified their appropriations by emphasizing power as a base of wealth, rather than wealth as a base of military-diplomatic power. Post-Napoleonic Europe was progressively absorbed in enrichment through the expansion of industrial society and the further decline of feudal values and institutions. The garrison-state construct proposes a model in which the sequence marches from the relatively mixed elite pattern of the nineteenth century to military-police dominance in the impending future.

With regard to method, the garrison-state fomulation exemplifies one of the five intellectual tasks common to all problem solving and hence to the solution of problems of politics. The five tasks are the clarification of goal, the description of trend in the realization of goal, the analysis of conditioning factors, the projection of future development, and the invention and evaluation of policy alternatives. The garrison-state construct obviously belongs primarily to the third and fourth of the intellectual tasks, since it deals directly with trend and projection.

It is worth noting, perhaps, that the garrison-state conception was originally put forward for the purpose, in part, of emphasizing a methodological position which had been outlined by the writer in *World Politics and Personal Insecurity*.[2] I was underlining the fruitfulness of comprehensive hypotheses about the manifold of future as well as past events—after the manner of Marx and other evolutionists—while rejecting the claim of such comprehensive formulations to be called scientific. A "developmental construct" is not limited to the extrapolation of trend curves, nor does it fail to take into account the available supply of scientific data or generalization. A construct such as the garrison state is a means of orientation *in time* toward the most significant features of the total configuration of events. Although comprehensive propositions about past-future configurations have often been labeled "scientific," as Marx and Engels called their bourgeois-proletariat formulation, it is misleading to do so, since their current degree of confirmation in regard to future events is too low to justify the use of the symbol of "science." Hence the word "construct."

Problems of policy are oriented toward the future, and part of the technique of rational decision is to adopt procedures that expose all assumptions about the future to the discipline of explicit consideration. To formulate or to evaluate a developmental construct is to engage in the use of problem-solving procedures.[3] Among political thinkers the developmental method can be most effectively employed in choosing problems of study, in the clarification of goals, and in the invention and evaluation of policy.[4]

In devising constructs, care must be taken to adhere to the distinction between expectation and preference. The garrison-state hypothesis is put forward as a matter-of-fact statement of expectation. The contingencies referred to, however, are perceived as welcome opportunities by some and as catastrophic challenges by others. In estimating the likelihood of future events, every candid person knows that there is a strong tendency to exaggerate the probability or the improbability of whatever contradicts his conscious or unconscious value orientation. Part of the procedure of problem solving is to search for covert as well as overt preferences and to give explicit consideration to the possibility of bias. In my case this precaution is of no little importance, since my preferred goal is to participate in activities that have promise for the eventual success of a universal order consonant with the requirements of human dignity.[5] Hence I have always regarded the possible coming of a garrisoned world with apprehension. I would like to help prevent this outcome by suitable policies—or, failing this, to encourage policies that humanize the garrison as completely as it can be.

Concerning terminology, a few points are worth mentioning. I use "state" in the conventional sense of jurisprudence and political science to designate a body politic that, when viewed in the context of the world arena, possesses a high degree of formal authority and effective control. Some scholars define terms so that "totalitarian" political systems are not entitled to be regarded as possessing true legal order. To the extent that garrison "states" are totalitarian, on these definitions, the proper terminology, following *Power and Society*, is garrison "rule."[6] I adhere to the earlier label partly because it is well established, and partly because, as presently will be seen, I do not limit the construct so drastically.

Many terms were, and are, available in place of "garrison." Among the considerations that led me to choose "garrison" was that I wanted to include "military" and "police," leaving the two words available as subcategories. Since in common usage "garrison" has strong military connotations, the expression "garrison police state" is sometimes employed to emphasize that all coercive specialists are included.

The present review of the construct must begin with an outline of the equilibrium conditions of a garrison system. Enough knowledge of the past is at hand to enable us to devise at least a rough working model of this kind. We formulate the fundamental conditions of a garrison system as follows: (1) the power elites value power enough to resort to large-scale coercion when they regard such coercive strategies as useful to the maintenance of their ascendancy; and (2) the elites accept the expectation that the retention of power during at least the immediate and middle-range future depends upon capability and willingness to coerce external or internal challengers.

Since the garrison construct is an aggregate hypothesis, it refers to the dominant characteristics of the entire arena of world politics, thereby going beyond the circumstances of a particular body politic. A garrisoned world is a military arena—not a civic arena—in which resort to extreme measures of coercion is regarded as a persisting state of affairs, or as a chronic danger.

We shall work within the frame of reference provided by these abbreviated models despite the disadvantage that they do not include definite specifications concerning the degree to which demands and expectations regarding power are affected by such factors as civilization, class, interest, personality, or level of crisis. To present a detailed model would involve the discussion with many more categories and formulations than we can touch upon within the limits of the present inquiry. We shall first concentrate upon the examination of the variables likely to affect the expectation of violence, the broad factor whose crucial role is stressed in the highly generalized model sketched above.

Note that the garrison-state construct does not stipulate whether the decision process internal to the state is characterized by narrow or wide participation in the making of important decisions. Hence the garrison is not "by definition" nondemocratic. This is left to empirical inquiry. However, my initial concern for the garrison system grew out of

apprehension regarding the future of democracy and of large-scale violence. Although it was not my intention to assert that democracy and military activity are always and everywhere incompatible with one another, I did intend to suggest that in the light of historical and analytic knowledge there were ample grounds for concern about the viability of democracy under conditions of chronic war and threat of war or violent revolution. My concern was heightened by new factors in the environment of democratic systems—namely, the explosive growth of modern science and technology and the connection of these developments with the control of large population and resource basins suitable for huge capital accumulation. It seemed probable that the dynamism of Germany and Russia was largely to be understood in terms of the destructive implication of the introduction of scientific and technological factors into a divided world arena.

The rise of totalitarian or near-totalitarian systems in Russia, Germany, Italy, and Japan was confronting the traditional strongholds of relatively free government and society with challenges of enormous gravity. Regardless of the immediate outcome of the rivalries and conflicts that were in the foreground twenty-five years ago, I was impressed by the cumulative impact of profound transformations in the structure of world societies, transformations that were not likely to be reversed by short-range wins or losses sustained by particular coalitions in the world arena. My hypothesis was that the Marx-Engels construct of universal felicity after an epoch of world war and revolution is dangerously oversanguine, the more probable outcome being a world of ruling castes (or a single caste) learning how to maintain ascendancy against internal challenge by the ruthless exploitation of hitherto unapplied instruments of modern science and technology. My view is the same today, though, as indicated above, I continue to regard it as inadmissible to use the term "inevitable" in referring to comprehensive future developments and regard preventive measures of policy with some confidence.

II

IT is apparent that the garrison-state construct depends in large part upon the assumption that the expectation of violence (of extreme coercion) will continue, either in the form of a divided and mutually apprehensive arena in world politics or, in the case of a universal state, within the internal arena of the new order. We begin, therefore, by examining the prospects for the continuation or discontinuation of the expectation of violence.

Will the possibility of mutual destruction provide sufficiently strong incentive to bring about world unification by consent? If it is more widely recognized that politics as at present organized precipitates coerciveness, will identifications with the nation-state system grow weaker, enabling movements toward world unit to succeed? On balance is it probable that the expectation of violence will increase, decrease, or remain the same?

THE SHADOW OF DESTRUCTION

A recurring ground for hope of world unity and peace among advocates of a voluntarily unified world community is the destructiveness of contemporary weapons. In the last 200 years the appearance of new scientific and technological advances has been accompanied by a fresh round of prediction that war has now at last become so awesome that no thinking man could possibly take the risk of involving his people in a new conflict. Pacifists thought they saw the handwriting on the wall for humanity when balloons soared into the sky, carrying the possibility of a new and overwhelming front against armies, military bases, and cities. In turn, the airplane, long-range artillery, and especially poison gas seemed to hold the key to frightening men into a better world. Today it is commonplace to hear—and to hear from some heads of states—that nuclear war is unthinkable.

No one denies that mankind *can* be destroyed by bombs or gas. But the problems that confront responsible officials are couched in less simple terms. They are not faced with a single button marked "To destroy humanity, push here." The many policy alternatives available at any given moment blur the picture. The following questions serve to indicate the complexity of the "choice map" of top leaders:

Since we and our opponents both recognize the ultimate disaster that can befall us, is it likely that anyone will take the irrevocable step?

Is it not probable that the measures adopted in any immediate crisis will be designed, not for total, but for partial destruction?

Is it not likely that whatever measures are initially launched will be less effective than expected owing to equipment failures and human error, as well as to sabotage and instantaneous counteraction?

If we continue to hold out a little longer in our negotiations to reduce and limit the most destructive categories of weapon and weapon use, is it not likely that we will obtain better terms of agreement, in the sense that the arrangements agreed upon will provide more security, and also that we have a greater voice in inclusive administrative bodies?

If I seem too eager to agree now will it not weaken my power position at home by suggesting I am willing to give too much in return for concessions whose true worth cannot be accurately appraised in advance?

POSSIBLE CHANGES IN IDENTIFICATION

The scope of action available to a political leader at a given time depends in part upon the intensity of identification with the established order that prevails at various levels. Is it likely that identifications will be affected by the perpetual mobilization to a degree that makes it "good politics" for leaders to reorganize the existing structure of the arena of world politics in the direction of a united world order attained by consent rather than by coercion?

Analysts of modern civilization have called attention to a phenomenon that is practically unheard of in folk societies although found in some city-centered civilizations of the past.[7] The phenomenon is alienation, by which is meant nonparticipation in the perspectives and behaviors appropriate to nation-states, and the carrying of nonparticipation to the ultimate of self-destruction. Included among nonparticipation patterns are practices which may be part of traditional culture, as when worldly things are abandoned in order to live the life of a recluse for the purpose of meditating upon transempirical matters.

Many scholars have been impressed by the evidence of alienation in the modern history of Western Europe.[8] A principal factor is alleged to be the breakdown in the ideological unity of Christendom, a breakup traumatically expressed by the willingness of Christian powers to form coalitions with the infidel and by the Protestant Reformation. It is conjectured that an additional factor is the unsettling impact of scientific knowledge upon man's image of himself and the world in which he lives. A "personal" God has dissolved into macrodistances or microphenomena equally alien to the cosmologies of the prescientific age. Mass and energy distributions are not yet integrated with the "subjective events" that seem so near yet so remarkably private and unique in human experience.

Investigators point to a variety of factors connected with social change that confront adults with problems of adaptation with which that are unable to cope by reason of the failure of childhood environments to provide the equipment required to enter the adult world with appropriate problem-solving capabilities. This failure to cope, reflected especially in the phenomenon of suicide, has been the focal point of many researches.[9] Investigators have examined the consequences of geographical mobility, which often fails to provide adults or children with a steady "supporting" configuration. Studies have also directed attention to social mobility, the raise or fall of individuals and groups in the class structure of society. Here again exposure to cross-pressure frequently works havoc with the minimum of stability required for early socialization or later continuation.

It is also recognized that our civilization specializes in the rapid obsolescing of old interests and the rapid rise of new ways of thinking, talking, and doing. Within the same ideological and territorial unit, and at the same class level, individuals are perpetually shifting occupations and leisure-time activities. New scientific and technological innovations draw attention to new sources of raw material and energy, or stimulate the invention of novel goods and services and of modified modes of production, merchandising, and utilization. Or the lead is taken by a new control device that makes it seem advantageous to merge plants, to revamp organizational structures, and to reassign personnel. The point of innovation may be a new accounting technique that alters the tax vulnerability of an organization and favors its survival. In any case, the social environment is complicated by operational networks that confront individuals with new patterns of attention and perspective.

The phenomenon called alienation is an extreme form of response precipitated by the clash of norm with norm or of norm with normlessness. It is possible that the spread of schooling, of travel, and of mass media of communication is having results quite different from that sought by the manipulators of communication as an instrument of policy. For instance, despite great apparent differences in the key symbols, slogans, and doctrines of socialism, Communism, and capitalism, the impression may be gathering strength that in all essentials everybody is talking about the same basic pattern of life.[10] Among articulate spokesmen for contemporary nation-states everyone seems to profess human dignity and freedom as an ultimate goal. Everyone favors peace and security, and everyone fosters the sciences and the technologies of production and destruction. Practically everyone endorses a rising standard of living, including social security against unemployment, accident and illness, old age, and related vicissitudes. Almost everyone seems to endorse the recognition of individual merit and to deplore discriminations based upon caste. Nearly everyone appears to advocate freedom to choose friends and intimates and to found a family. In the face of those overwhelming harmonies of goal, differences seem opportunistic, related to the timing of various stages in meeting the problems that arise in modernizing and industrializing peoples of various degrees of backwardness.

I summarize these points because they indicate why it is to be expected that in some states individuals will withdraw their willingness to fight for the preservation of the traditional autonomy of the nation-states or blocs to which they belong. Is it likely that these developments will be important enough to put an end to world rivalry and in so doing to weaken the forces that foster garrison states?

It is probable that the perspective referred to will be more frequent in the industrial countries of the non-Soviet than the Soviet world. The Soviet world has leaped ahead sensationally in ways that strengthen the way of its central myth. More prosperity in the older countries is welcome, but it is "old hat." It evokes less pride than it once did.

We do not expect "peace at any price" movements to gain influence quickly in the United States in view of the likelihood that most alienated individuals will be recruited from among Americans who are least movitated to join active political programs of pressure-group and party agitation and organization.[11] Furthermore, any new movement will be obstructed by the opposition of established leaders who sense that such movements are potential threats. It is perceived that if "peace at any price" groups were to obtain the support of the Soviet leadership—as they undoubtedly would—Soviet leaders would work with and through them to the disadvantage of other elements.

If in the older industrial nations "peace at any price" movements begin to win significant support, it is safe to predict that police measures will be strengthened against "subversion." The "political vacuum" created by withdrawals of identification may be occupied, therefore, not by anticoercive elements, but rather by persons and programs having a militantly nationalistic coloration. As a means of heightening differentiation from the Soviet-centered world, nationalistic symbols would probably be elaborated and embellished by "religious" symbols (such as "atheistic communism").

It is probable that liberal political leaders would respond to future evidence of general disenchantment by seeking policies capable of firing the imagination of the rising generation at home and abroad. But foreign aid programs, for instance, suffer from the doubts and scruples of liberal regard for autonomy. By raising the cry of foreign interference the established elites of receiving countries are able to obtain exemption from effective supervision. American leaders, for instance, have been embarrassed by this strategy and have tended to leave local cliques of landlords, officers, and officials free to enrich themselves without making a commensurate contribution to economic and social development. By perpetuating sources of discontent that can be exploited by rival world political elements the growth of stable and responsible government is precluded.[12]

The conclusion is that withdrawals of identification with politics, insofar as they gain enough initial strength to threaten the unity of older non-Soviet powers, will provoke policies of the garrison-police-state type.

THE OVER-ALL EXPECTATION OF VIOLENCE

We turn to the future of the over-all expectation of violence, recognizing that some points made in the preceding analysis of alienation are also pertinent here. We begin by replying to the question: By what broad paths of change is it conceivable that the world military arena can be transmuted into a civic arena? (1) By a general war that establishes the supremacy of one of the polar powers without damaging the victor to a degree that leaves him unable to hold the dominant position against a coalition of the remaining powers; (2) by limited wars that expand one of the polar powers without precipitating a general war and that establish such a position of supremacy that the other polar power throws in the sponge and becomes

a satellite; (3) by policies short of active war that expand the effective domain of one polar power with the results outlined in (2) above; (4) by a fusion of the effective elites of the polar powers in order to protect themselves from further weakening their position for the benefit of other powers (the fusion could be effective if implemented by ultimatum and active pressure); and (5) by a fusion of effective elites, recruited from many powers in addition to the polar powers, who who would establish unity largely by consent.

From past experience we know that one limitation of forecasters is their inability to free themselves from the assumption that the conspicuous scientific and technological features of their time are permanent. Recognizing that a major characteristic of science to date is the tremendous advantage of world powers that have great concentrations of capital at their disposal, we now ask whether technology can change so drastically that instruments of production and destruction are likely to be produced with small-scale outlays? Further, will the tremendous advantage of offensive weapons be nullified by the perfecting of defense? At present there are no convincing signs of basic revolutionary innovations.[13]

It is not to be overlooked that the growth of vast administrative networks under centralized and even largely automatized direction may have the seemingly paradoxical result of making top control spots more vulnerable than before to individual and small-group strategies of power seizure.[14] The patterns of control are continually transformed as new activities require more prompt and refined means of linkage with established and emerging operations. The networks of communication and decision become more elaborate—that is, more centered and subcentered. If small platoons are prepared to make simultaneous assaults upon key panels of control, the chances of success are good enough to risk, especially in times of general stress. Far from relaxing garrison-police conditions, such possibilities confirm the importance of eternal vigilance as the price of maintaining established elites in power.

In considering the future, we do not underestimate emerging technologies connected with "brain machines" and with experimental embryology and genetics. Mechanized robots are not only of potential importance as defensive guards or offensive elements. We are on the verge of producing machines that are capable of devising complex strategies of action and possibly—as Norbert Weiner suggests—of relegating mankind to a subordinate role.[15] At present it appears equally likely that a machine-run globe would be divided along present-day lines or that it would achieve unity. The same point applies to advanced forms of life that may be developed by experimental biology. And we do not dismiss as absurd the possibility that living forms which have developed elsewhere impose themselves here and inaugurate the "discipline from without" that mankind has been unable to attain from within.[16]

Can a communications revolution occur in which world elites voluntarily subject themselves to an ethico-political training that motivates the self-regulating, cooperative efforts necessary to actualize a global order of human dignity? Can such a reconstruction begin at the top (or with mid-elite elements) and lay the foundation for voluntary unification of demand, expectation, and identification?[17] Desirable as these developments are, we cannot at present view their chances with much hope.

III

THE preceding examination of the prospects of terrifying the world into voluntary unity, of weakening local identifications for the benefit of an effective universal allegiance, and of weakening the expectations of violence points to one conclusion: the outlook is dim. Hence the precondition of the garrison-state outcome is likely to be fulfilled.

The garrison construct goes further: it characterizes the principal changes in intrastate power that are likely to result from factor combinations that tip the internal equilibrium toward narrow rather than wide power sharing and that favor the self-perpetuation of an elite specialized to the planning and implementation of coercive strategies of power.

Within the Soviet block of totalitarian powers the garrison-police construct is highly approximated, though it cannot yet be said with certainty that the ruling families have as yet consolidated themselves into a self-perpetuating caste. I shall not enter into a detailed discussion of the excellent literature now available for estimating the future course of development within the Soviet bloc as it relates to the wider sharing of effective power. I assert only that the garrison construct is more in harmony with

the dynamics of totalitarian systems than are alternative hypotheses.

More critical for the future is the course of evolution within advanced industrial nations having traditions and customs of popular government. In previous expositions of the garrison conception we have projected the sequence of change that results when emphasis moves from wealth or other values and is placed upon power.

Perpetual apprehension of war keeps the accent upon the consideration of power measured as fighting potential. The common goal of maintaining national freedom from external dictation is perceived as requiring the appraisal of all social values and institutional practices with state-power considerations in view. Economic values and institutions are drawn into the preparation of weapons and thereby subordinated to power. Scientific skill and education are requisitioned for research and development. Public enlightenment is limited in the name of military secrecy. Public health is fostered by programs designed to conserve the human resources that figure in military potential. Family and ecclesiastical institutions are given encouragement so long as they interpose no ideological or behavioral obstacles to national security. Institutions of social class and caste are remodeled to the extent that national vulnerability is believed to be at stake.

THE FUNCTIONAL PHASES OF DECISION

In this connection a distinction is to be drawn between those individuals, groups, and structures that are functionally specialized to violence and those that, at any given time, are conventionally recognized as military or police. The growing accent upon power and the institutions of power that occurs in periods of chronic mobilization typically works to improve the position of the uniformed professionals (when the base line of comparison is the precrisis period). At the same time, the comprehensiveness of the problems relating to modern war and war preparation tends to bring about a different result. Party politicians and other group leaders make themselves felt in the planning and execution of strategy; and scientists, engineers, and managers with non-military backgrounds move into the complex and often high-level activities of state and society. The total decision process is carried on with a shifting balance between old and new elements at every phase. In examining the seven functions, we are guided to some extent by occurrences to date,[18] supplemented by the expectation of high levels of continuing and intermittent crisis that we have justified in the earlier part of the paper. In the final part of the present discussion we shall draw some policy implications from the interpenetration of old and new elements in the decision process.

The *intelligence* function is the obtaining and interpretation of information pertinent to decision. In a mobilized world the specialist on violence is in a preferred position, since he seems professionally more qualified than anybody else to give the estimates required in making the translation of "change in general" into "fighting potential." Laymen can listen with understanding to scientists and engineers who discuss the state of research and development at home and abroad, but for policy purposes this testimony must be fused with knowledge of how these activities and results are integrated with military resources organized in particular ways and affected by specific traditions of strategy. War games and exercises provide the specialist on weapons with a basis for making inferences that must be accepted in the last resort as the equations to be built into computing machines engaged in simulation programs. Also, we must depend upon these specialists to guide the delicate operations by which it is sought to penetrate the enemy's wall of secrecy for the sake of uncovering clues to intention and capability.

Perpetual mobilization makes it plausible to extend the scope of the function of the political police to include more thorough investigations of the present loyalty of personnel and of personnel vulnerability under hypothetical future contingencies. These contingencies include inducements offered by opposing powers and the more subtle effects of deprivations connected with a fluctuating state of tension and combat. The political-police function at home merges with the work of those who are seeking to find vulnerable spots in the personnel of foreign powers.

The intelligence function includes the invention and evaluation of strategic programs in the light of formulated goals and of the available body of trend and scientific knowledge, critically projected into the future. All questions of goal, no matter how seemingly trivial at first glance, can be plausibly shown to have a bearing upon the security position of the community.

The *recommending* (promoting) function in the decision process includes the advocacy of courses of action. Hence it goes beyond the presentation of plans to the bringing of pressure to bear upon critical points of action. In the United States, as in many other countries, specialists on violence are traditionally accepted as professional advisors rather than advocates. Hence in the rough-and-tumble of party and pressure politics specialists tend to be looked upon as special pleaders for high expenditure on behalf of provocative policies from which they obtain special benefits. While world crisis continues, however, this evaluation is likely to be modified, as the community comes to believe that proposals relating to strategy have little weight unless they have some measure of professional support. Hence, party leaders find it wise to align themselves with military figures, who are initially treated as advisors but who gradually intervene in public debate as policy advocates in their own right. Thus the scope of permissible participation by the military increases, and the path is cleared for confidence-inspiring personalities among the violence specialists to become candidates for nomination and election. Since the making of military policy evokes interservice differences, struggling factions reach out for elements in the community at large with which they can join in tacit coalitions to support controverted positions. Party and pressure-group leaders, journalists, scholars, and others will be drawn into these blocs.

Another decision function is *prescription*. At this stage, rules, whether constitutional, statutory, or administrative, are made for the guidance of policy. In Western countries the bodies charged with the prescribing function have been overwhelmingly civilian, subject to the modification that "veterans" are at an advantage after a war has vanished into the distance and the veterans are somewhat obsolete as soldiers. Perpetual crisis now brings older military specialists and newer specialists who are scientists into regular advisory contact with prescribers, and it is safe to say that the deliberations of political bodies are likely to be regarded with some disdain. They have much evidence of time-serving, ignorance, evasion, and general irresponsibility; and this provides a "moral" basis for the possible assumption of authority by the military during moments of severe crisis.

The *invocation* stage of decision is of very direct importance to police specialists, since they are traditionally regarded as the principal agents of the community in performing this function. To invoke is to characterize conduct provisionally as a deviation from prescribed norms. During times of crisis loyalty norms are added to the standards of intercrisis peacetime society. Hence the political-police function flourishes, affording opportunities for specialists in investigation to multiply their numbers and to extend their influence upon personnel selection. The casting of doubt upon the integrity of individuals becomes an instrument by which unscrupulous or credulous members of the political police are often able to rise in power and to appear indispensable to the central elite nucleus.

After invocation comes *application*, which is a final, not a provisional, judgment of conduct. Courts, for example, are organs of government that are highly adapted to the applying function. Whenever police evidence is turned down, courts cause some frustration among the police and often become targets of cumulative resentment. Political-police officials are continually edging toward the pre-emption of judicial functions.

The *appraisal* stage of decision is the conducting of "autopsies" on the connection between policy goals, the means employed, and the results achieved. Those who obtain facts pertinent to appraisal are strategically situated, since they control many of the inferences upon which judgment depends. Since policy groups do not like criticism, they exert continual pressure to insure exemption from adverse appraisal by controlling the appraisers. The point is not only to escape criticism, but to do so by providing a scapegoat. For instance, the effort is often made to show that alleged military failures are not failures by the military but are properly attributable to legislative limitation, civilian administrative confusion, and the like.

Finally, we speak of the *terminating* function, which puts an end to arrangements which apply the prescriptive framework, and also to prescription themselves. Termination is often a matter of freeing individuals from obligation (or refusing to do so) and hence provides many points of leverage in the social process, especially in civilizations rather than folk societies where contract takes the place of custom.

Glancing over the seven functions, it is clear that specialists on violence are already located at strategic phases of intelligence, invocation, and application, providing bases from which they are in a position to edge toward wider spheres of effective control as crisis continues.[19]

POLITICAL SOCIALIZATION

The foregoing examination of the decision process has indicated how crisis accentuation of state power tends to subordinate all social values and institutions to considerations of military potential, and how as a result, military and police specialists are placed in advantageous positions within the decision process. We cannot terminate the analysis without giving more direct attention to the socialization process (the process of political education). Can we foresee any connection between changes in the perspectives entertained by young citizens as they move toward full participation in the body politic and the rise or fall of garrison states?

The idea that the future of politics depends in part upon the success or failure of political education is no novelty among political thinkers.[20] Many of the generalizations put forward by Plato have been confirmed, broadened, or modified by modern social and behavioral sciences. Plato was explicit in assigning the chief role in bringing about altered perspectives to the parental generation. He spoke, for example, of the "exaggeration" of an accepted ideal by the elders and sketched the political cycles that result therefrom. Assume, for instance, a community whose chief preferred value is wealth; Plato's proposition is that exaggerated stress on wealth—as in the encouragement of saving and investment—provokes a demand on the part of youth to enjoy life by greater consumption, leading in turn to self-indulgence in superfluities, and in a later generation to self-indulgence of the antisocial lusts characteristic of unconscious sexuality and aggression. The end of the cycle is tyranny.

In modern civilization specific sequences similar to these have often been described. Families which focus upon material accumulation are confronted by the rebellious potential of the young, which often leads to rejection of the family-wide goal in order to obtain more egocentric gratification in the form of expenditures on immediate enjoyment. Since a life pattern of egocentricity provides no generalizable norm of responsible conduct for the young, the next generation achieves no superego or ego ideal strong enough to enable the individual to "contain" the extremes of sexual and aggressive conduct referred to above.

Affluent "economies" appear to favor expenditures for egocentric enjoyment. Thus, in industrialized societies the family loses many functions connected with the transmission of cultural norms, which are left to such auxiliary institutions as schools, neighborhoods, and the mass media. The communications industry is particularly dominated by economic considerations and encourages consumption expenditure by exploiting the most exciting appeals, which are largely sexual and aggressive. Owing to the growth of economic concentration, these merchandising appeals spread to the local retailer and penetrate deeply into the body politic.

We sum up these tendencies by saying that the passage from group involvement to egocentricity fosters subsequent passage from "superfluous" enjoyment to sexual and assaultive excesses. These trends are furthered by *failure of superego formation* from (1) *absence of models who are group-oriented* toward such goals as accumulation for family wealth, political power, religious eminence, or medical distinction and (2) *conflict of models as a result of geographical and social mobility.* (These factors often support one another.)

Having recognized the strength of the forces working toward ego indulgence, we must not overlook the possible improvement of educational technique when a problem is fully perceived. Many elements are then stirred into intense activity in the direction of restoring a former equilibrium or of bringing a new and more satisfactory state of affairs into existence. It is true that the subdividing, mobile, and affluent civilization which we know in the United States has not mastered the technique of socialization; hence, uncounted millions of young people are as yet ineffectively challenged to lead significant lives that are contributory to the good of the commonwealth. But we have formidable instruments of communication at our disposal, and there are great reservoirs of aspiration and competence in our civilization. Possibly we can reverse trends toward egocentricity and successfully cultivate personality systems in which identifications are effectively oriented to include the larger community.[21]

A danger in such programs is that they will try to rebuild social consciences by encouraging militancy directed against the stranger (the "other"). Undoubtedly the most ancient and successful means of integrating an individual ego into a more comprehensive self-system is by using the traditional syndrome that includes the expectation of violence, the ethical demand to sacrifice for the common good, and identification with a community less comprehensive

than all mankind. Perpetual crisis puts a premium upon acquiring the social discipline symbolized by the folklore that presents the soldier at his best. In this way political power is renewable as a primary social value in rivalry with affection (family), well-being (comfort), skill and enlightenment, and wealth and respect when these values are pursued through the institutional forms of civilian life.

We have recently been reminded, if such reminders are needed, that young people are predisposed toward the submersion of the narrow ego into the larger self of great social movements that foster action and sacrifice.[22] It is also evident from psychiatric and psychological knowledge how deep are the demands to escape from guilt, "self-contempt," feelings of weakness and related deprivations by plunging into social programs of vast scope. But it is never to be forgotten that everyone does not become sexually or aggressively egoindulgent all at once; on the contrary, increases in a countermores direction generate tendencies toward restoration of the mores. With rare exceptions, the completely egocentric personality is not met with in fact. He is a "theoretical limit." No matter how flamboyantly ego-indulgent the individual may be, intimate investigation almost always shows evidence of conflict with less egocentric tendencies within the personality as a whole.[23] These considerations strengthen the chances that movements on behalf of social responsibility will succeed after periods of drift in the opposite direction.

Can the specialist on violence provide the model of social responsibility capable of mobilizing the latent propensities of the young in modern societies? It is already evident that in industrial society the specialist on violence is not condemned to the role of thug as he was in some of the disdainful images perpetuated by the scholars of China. The professional preparation of the military is not frozen in a sacrosanct mold. On the contrary the curriculum of training has been greatly transformed under the pressure of changes that stem from modern science, technology, and ideology.[24] Despite the cleavages generated within the armed services by the rapid tempo of professional renovation, it is possible to point to officers who have attained distinction in their own right as contributors to the new technologies. A far larger number has achieved enough competence to establish easy working relations with outstanding men of science and scholarship.

IV

CIVILIANISM VS. MILITARISM

WE come finally to the point of asking by what policies we can maintain as many as possible of the effective institutions of a free society despite the improbability of moving soon into a world relatively free of the chronic threat of serious coercion. From the point of view of the strategy of human dignity the most promising trends to encourage are "civilianism," the movement that to a degree we can say is developing counter to "militarism." If we understand by "militarism" the permeation of an entire society by the self-serving ideology of the officer and soldier,[25] we can speak of "civilianism" as the absorption of the military by the multivalued orientation of a society in which violent coercion is deglamorized as an end in itself and is perceived as a regrettable concession to the persistence of variables whose magnitudes we have not as yet been able to control without paying what appears to be an excessive cost in terms of such autonomy as is possible under the cloud of chronic peril. As the perspectives of society become adapted to contemporary levels of risk, together with a common acceptance of the fruits of science, can the culture of science itself be more widely understood and applied to problem-solving *procedures* throughout society, including the decision process?[26]

The perception that scientific model building and data processing, when adapted to any recurring set of problems, call for the suspension of final commitment until appropriate assumptions have been explored in disciplined fashion, pertinent data obtained by appropriate methods, and interpretations evaluated by a rigorous procedure—all this indicates the diffusion of the scientific pattern throughout civilization. One implication is that physical scientists, for example, will never betray the culture of science by committing themselves to opinions on political and social matters without having examined the pertinent context with proper discipline.

However Utopian this may be, in the visible future the dynamic equilibrium of politics will work in favor of civilianism to the extent that people—that is, large populations, including the lower classes—continue to be positively valued for military purposes. Hitherto the dependence of arms production upon a huge labor force has been a factor making for a degree of democratization. This trend has gained importance as a result of the modern socialization of risk among all members of the population, whether military or civilian. However, in a technology run by automation the labor force may begin to appear redundant as the disadvantages of a human labor force become more obvious, especially its vulnerability to discontent and hence to the appeal of ideologies counter to the established system of public order. To the extent that mere numbers are perceived as endangering the resource base of a nation-state, demands will be furthered for such policies as effective birth control and the substitution of robots for people.[27]

Up to the present the huge techno-scientific advance in the United States during recent years has greatly retarded the factors making for a police polity of internal repression. It has been possible to supply consumer goods in increasing abundance and to introduce automation at a rate compatible with existing techniques of expansion, re-education, and relocation. In the absence of sudden peaks of crisis the forum providing news and debate has been open to movements to protect civil liberty against disastrous assault or erosion. Despite relevations of the thinness of our subculture of civil liberty,[28] the forces of infringements have been rolled back on some fronts.

The process by which a garrison is civilianized is likely to make rather subtle transformations in the "nucleus elites" of the future. The following questions point toward new elite patterns through a fusion of the skills which are representative of the highly developed specialties of modern civilization:

Is it likely that effective elites will be recruited somewhat outside, though partly inside, the traditional framework of the armed forces? For example, will a new elite emerge that is initially composed of officers, physical scientists and engineers, administrators, party and pressure-group leaders, public relations specialists and lawyers, who gain acceptance as the most realistic and creative individuals in coping with the total decision problem?

Will the traditional services contribute to, while failing to dominate, the new class that emerges in the interstitial positions created within our ever complicating social process?

Will the culmination be a truly civil garrison where anyone resembling the traditional soldier or policeman is as out of date as horse cavalry?

Pertinent to these queries is the evidence brought together in the contemporary study of elites in large-scale industrial societies. The modern decision process appears to function through shifting coalitions composed of formal and tacit representatives of the plurality of groups and persons formed by exposure to and interaction with the complex symbolic and material subdivisions of our civilization. Persons rise to top eliteship who have the personality structure and skill patterns adapted to the task of maintaining internal acceptance within a constituency while engaging in coalitional activities with persons of corresponding aptitude and position. For example, data are now available for distinguishing the "nuclear elite" within the broad elite structure of the armed services of the United States. The problems that arise in operating large-scale organizations in our techno-scientific age tend to converge as one nears the center of formal authority and effective control, and hence to reduce the differences in perspective and operational strategy from one top level to another.[29]

The structure of the elite differs in nations of low industrialization and modernization from the pattern described for the United States; it also diverges in totalitarian polities. In many contemporary nations it is possible to recognize legacies of myth and technique from political systems formed under pre-industrial conditions, such as "oriental despotisms,"[30] in which centralized bureaucracies leaned heavily upon coercive instruments of power. It is also possible to identify political institutions dating from the period in which, under an umbrella of formal centralization, the effective control usually resided with rulers of component territories, who also depended upon coercive means of maintaining their rule against the center and against further dispersion to subcenters.[31] Similarly, we perceive the survival of patterns once current in a feudal society in which rule was not neatly articulated with large contiguous territory, although power relations were fundamental features of the whole society.[32] Furthermore, we sometimes become aware of perspectives persisting from brief or long experience of city-states.[33] In the latter we recognize the close connection between banditry and trade, but we also perceive the strength of the urban sub-division of the social environment as a factor in shaping civilizations in place of folk societies. In peasant villages—and these are spread over a sizable part of the globe—we now see, not a folk society cut off from wider arenas, but social formations resulting from the centraliz-ing consequences of expanding urban-based civilizations.[34] Among the active folk societies of today—in various stages of disorganization and reintegration in civilization—it is rewarding to trace the extremes of emphasis or de-emphasis upon central authority and control.[35]

Wherever we examine the situation thoroughly, we find that a potent influence is the tendency to introject the standards set by the largest and most successful bodies politic in the arena of global politics. Often the focal point of local discontent is among the military, some of whom are pace-setters in comprehending the technology, science, and total culture of the principal powers. In view of the tendency "diffusion by partial incorporation" of the pattern of the top powers, we are justified in saying that it is by no means out of the question that military education may aid in producing a generation of top professional elements who are multivalue-oriented.

Within the Soviet world the elite structure has remained tenaciously in favor of the formal principle of civilian supremacy; hence, the Party continues to be the principal ladder up the authority and control pyramid. Within the Party, of course, it is the specialist upon the political-police function who has an advantage, since central power elements look to the police to protect them from the challenges that arise in a totalitarian system. Established elites in such a system typically consider themselves endangered by decentralization, deconcentration, democratization, pluralization, and de-regimentation. It has been indicated above why it is unlikely that existing top-elite components will regard it as advantageous to put an immediate end to the present divided structure of world politics.[36]

In the light of our previous discussion, we conclude, however reluctantly, that the garrison hypothesis provides a probable image of the past and future of our epoch. We would prefer it to be a self-disconfirming hypothesis. The master challenge of modern politics, therefore, is to civilianize a garrisoning world, thereby cultivating the conditions for its eventual dissolution.[37] The discipline acquired in the process may make it possible for mankind to accomplish what it has never been able to achieve before—namely, to create and perpetuate a universal public order of human dignity. So long as there is a gleam of hope for this culminating outcome of man's history, there is hope for life itself.

Notes

1. My first publications employing the term were in 1937 and 1941. A summary and critique is to be found in Samuel P. Huntington, *The Soldier and the State* (Cambridge, Mass., 1957), pp. 346–350.

2. Harold D. Lasswell, *World Politics and Personal Insecurity* (New York, 1935), ch. 1. For a compendium of my characterizations of the construct, see H. Eulau, "H. D. Lasswell's Developmental Analysis," *Western Political Quarterly*, 11 (June 1958), 229–242.

3. The allusion here is to the distinction between principles of content and of procedure. The first may be illustrated by the proposition that all rational thought requires goal clarification; the latter by the statement that in a problem-solving process it is important to find a place on the agenda for the clarification of goal.

4. See my discussion of "Strategies of Inquiry: The Rational Use of Observation," in Daniel Lerner (ed.), *The Human Meaning of the Social Sciences* (New York, 1959), ch. 4.

5. Compare M. S. McDougal, "Perspectives for an International Law of Human Dignity," *Proceedings American Society of International Law* (1959), 107–132.

6. Consult Carl J. Friedrich and Zbigniew K. Brzezinski, *Totalitarian Dictatorship and Autocracy* (Cambridge, Mass, 1956). For the definition of "rule," see Harold D. Lasswell and Abraham Kaplan, *Power and Society* (New Haven, 1950), p. 208; "regime" is defined at p. 130. The latter refers to formal authority, the former to effective control. "Law" is both authoritative and controlling.

7. V. Gordon Childe emphasizes the fundamental importance of the invention of cities for the emergence of civilization. The invention is tentatively located in a few river valleys about 7,000 years ago. See his *New Light on the Most Ancient East* (London, 1935) and later publications. Also Robert Redfield, *The Primitive World and its Transformations* (Ithaca, 1953).

8. Tomás G. Masaryk, *Der Selbstmord als sociale Massenerscheinung der modernen civilisation* (Vienna, 1881); Emile Durkheim, *Suicide* (Glencoe, Ill., tr. 1951).

9. Andrew F. Henry and James F. Short, *Suicide and Homicide* (Glencoe, Ill., 1954).

10. The impression is supported by such official acts as proposing and ratifying the Universal Declaration of the Rights of Man, and by the results of content analysis of the language of politics. For background see Herschel C. Baker, *The Dignity of Man* (Cambridge, Mass., 1947) and the data reported in the Stanford studies of political symbols by Lasswell, Pool, Lerner and others.

11. Indications of the connection between alienation and political participation are found in Robert E. Lane, *Political Life; Why People Get Involved in Politics* (Glencoe, Ill., 1959). See also William Kornhauser, *The Politics of Mass Society* (Glencoe, Ill., 1959); Eugene Burdick and Arthur J. Brodbeck (eds.), *American Voting Behavior* (Glencoe, Ill., 1959).

12. The complications of economic development are shown in studies such as Berthold F. Hoselitz (ed.), *The Progress of Underdeveloped Areas* (Chicago, 1952); Simon S. Kuznets et al., *Economic Growth: Brazil, India, Japan* (Durham, N. C., 1955); Gunnar Myrdal, *An International Economy: Problems and Prospects* (New York, 1956); Albert O. Hirschman, *The Strategy of Economic Development* (New Haven, 1958).

13. The reference is to more sweeping transformations than the spread of nuclear technology although this gives rise to complications. See *The Nth Country Problem and Arms Control* by the National Planning Association Washington, 1960, which includes a technical annex by W. Davidon and others.

14. A theme that occurs in some writing on strategy; for example, Ferdinand O. Miksche, *Atomic Weapons and Armies* (New York, 1955).

15. The current developments in the science and technology of machines are summarized at intervals in *Science and Scientific American*.

16. See my projections in "Men in Space," *Annals of the New York Academy of Sciences*, 72 (April 1958), 180–194.

17. Attention should be called to new techniques of training that, if used for parochial purposes, may work against more comprehensive perspectives. Consult B. F. Skinner's novel, *Walden Two* (New York, 1948), and his *Science and Human Behavior* (New York, 1953).

18. For indications see: Ralph S. Brown, *Loyalty and Security; Employment Tests in the U.S.* (New Haven, 1958); Comment, "School Boards, School Books, and the Freedom to Learn," *Yale Law Journal*, 59 (April, 1950), 928–954; Note, "Government Exclusion of Foreign Political Propaganda," *Harvard Law Review*, 68 (1955), 1393–1409; Robert K. Carr, *The House Committee on Un-American Activities* (Ithaca, 1952); Walter Gellhorn, *Security, Loyalty and Science* (Ithaca, 1950); Eleanor Bontecou, *The Federal Loyalty-Security Program* (Ithaca, 1953); Edward A. Shils, *The Torment of Secrecy* (Glencoe, Ill., 1956); Charles V. Kidd, *American Universities and Federal Research* (Cambridge, Mass., 1959); Solomon Fabricant, *The Trend of Government Activity in the U.S. Since 1900* (New York, 1952); F. S. Hoffman, "The Economic

Analysis of Defense: Choice Without Markets," *American Economic Review*, 49 (May, 1959), 368, and discussion; James R. Schlesinger, *The Political Economy of National Security* (New York, 1960); Eli Ginzberg and Associates, *The Ineffective Soldier* (New York, 1959), 3 v.; Huntington, *op. cit.*, Part III; National Manpower Council, *A Policy for Scientific and Professional Manpower* (New York, 1953).

19. Existing data concerning participation by coercive specialists in official elites are fragmentary not only in regard to composition but, more importantly, in perspective. The Second *International Yearbook of Political Behavior Research*, edited by H. Eulau and D. Marvick, is devoted to the methods and results of elite research to date.

20. Herbert H. Hyman, *Political Socialization* (Glencoe, Ill., 1959); Lasswell, "Political Constitution and Character," *Psychoanalysis and the Psychoanalytic Review*, 46 (Winter, 1959), 3–18.

21. The systematic study of juvenile delinquency has led to the invention of group as well as individual strategies for dealing with the problems involved—e.g. Fritz Redl and David Wineman, *Children Who Hate* (Glencoe, Ill., 1951)—and the strategies involved in capturing gangs for socially approved activities.

22. Friedrich and Brzezinski, *op. cit.*, ch. 4.

23. Consult *American Handbook of Psychiatry*, especially vol. 1 (New York, 1959).

24. Gene M. Lyons and John W. Masland, *Education and Military Leadership: A Study of the ROTC* (Princeton, 1959).

25. This is the conception employed by Alfred Vagts in *A History of Militarism* (New York, 1937).

26. The task of integrating the scientific outlook with our total civilization appears more urgent and formidable than ever. See C. P. Snow, the physicist-novelist, whose phrase "the two cultures" stirred up lively discussion. Note his "Reply to my critics" in *Encounter*, 14 (February, 1960), 64–68. Also see *Daedalus, Journal of the American Academy of Arts and Sciences*, 89 (Winter, 1959), the issue devoted to "Education in the Age of Science."

27. Lurking in the background is the threat of "Machiavelli, M. D.," to which I referred in *World Politics and Personal Insecurity*. Luckily

the top elite in Nazi Berlin and Communist Moscow was not recruited from individuals possessing enough knowledge of science and technology to discover the more destructive potentials. See also my "Political Science of Science: An Inquiry into the Possible Reconciliation of Mastery and Freedom," *American Political Science Review*, 50 (December, 1956), 961–979.

28. Notably Samuel A. Stouffer, *Communism, Conformity and Civil Liberties* (Garden City, N.Y., 1955).

29. Morris Janowitz, *The Professional Soldier; A Social and Political Portrait* (Glencoe, Ill., 1960), especially ch. 8 and Part VII.

30. Karl A. Wittfogel, *Oriental Despotism: A Comparative Study of Total Power* (New Haven, 1957).

31. Sally F. Moore, *Power and Property in Inca Peru* (New York, 1958). This book corrects the image of Inca society, law, and politics as a supercentralized system. See also Edwin Lieuwen, *Arms and Politics in Latin America* (New York, 1960).

32. Rushton Coulborn (ed.), *Feudalism in History* (Princeton, 1956).

33. Miriam Beard, *History of the Business Man* (New York, 1938) summarizes the data for the Mediterranean world of the fifth century B.C. and of 1500 A.D.

34. Redfield, *op. cit.*

35. Note especially John Middleton and David Tait (eds.), *Tribes Without Rulers; Studies in African Segmentary Systems* (London, 1958).

36. For details see Simon Wolin and Robert M. Slusser (eds.), *The Soviet Secret Police* (New York, 1957); Merle Fainsod, *Smolensk under Soviet Rule* (Cambridge, Mass., 1958); Nathan C. Leites and Elsa Bernaut, *Ritual of Liquidation* (Glencoe, Ill., 1954); Boris Meissner (and John S. Reshetar), *The Communist Party of the Soviet Union* (New York, 1956).

37. See in this context Huntington, *op. cit.*, and in Janowitz, *op. cit.*, the discussion of "the constabulary concept" in the last chapter. There is a legitimate place for professionals who specialize upon sanctioning policy. I view this as a potential fusion of military, police, correctional, judicial and related skills. See Richard Arens and H. D. Lasswell, *In Defense of Public Order; The Emerging Field of Sanction Law* (New York, 1961).

Part Three

National security and international cooperation: a non-zero-sum game

Introductory note

The assumption implicit in all the following contributions is that security as a
national objective must be pursued by minimizing national power and encouraging the
growth of international cooperation, or even international integration. The quest for
national security is turned into a non-zero-sum game in which the security of all
players may be increased simultaneously. The individual sections deal with areas
in which cooperation and integration are sought.

Disarmament and arms control (SECTION A) are, ironically, at one and the
same time the most immediately crucial and the least successful areas of international
cooperation. The urgency of finding solutions in these areas has perhaps obscured
the enormous complexity of the technical and political problems involved. The
selections survey these problems, indicating their scope and magnitude. Blackett
presents an exhaustive and detailed analysis of the technical problems likely to
arise at every stage of disarmament. Deterrence has been one of the most important
concepts in strategic thought, (see Part Two, Section *a*), and Schelling's is one of the
first theoretical attempts to reconcile the goals of deterrence and disarmament, hitherto
considered mutually exclusive. He argues persuasively that the existence of deterrent
force can provide the incentive for nations to abide by the successive stages of
disarmament agreements. In distinction to disarmament, arms control has more limited
objectives: to reduce the likelihood of war (rather than eliminate it entirely), and to
diminish the violence if war should occur (King). The serious problems of the spread of
nuclear weapons to an ever increasing number of countries, and its implication for
disarmament, are discussed by Iklé. If all the above-mentioned problems are
solved and a disarmament program is successfully set in motion, serious economic
problems will have to be met. The report of the United States Disarmament Agency
attempts to outline such problems and indicate ways in which they can be solved.
Finally, the conclusions of a United Nations study on the social and economic

consequences of disarmament present a complementary treatment from an international point of view.

In addition to disarmament, other areas of international cooperation can contribute to the increase of international security. Four such areas are dealt with in SECTION B: tendencies toward regional integration, leading perhaps to world order (Yalem); cooperation in specific technical areas contributing to the improvement of the international political climate (Jessup and Taubenfeld); unilateral actions by major powers, designed to produce similar responses by other nations and so to reduce the level of international tension (Osgood); and long-term fundamental trends toward international economic integration (Myrdal).

In contrast to the limited and temporary objectives described in the previous sections, SECTION C discusses the permanent institutions and processes required for international cooperation and integration. Claude deals with the contribution of the United Nations to the solution of international conflicts by providing the institutional setting within which nations may pursue peaceful methods of political change. Alger describes how participation in United Nations activities makes the participants more internationally minded and hopefully predisposes them toward increasing international cooperation. The article by Henkin discusses the development of international law and the role it can play in the creation of a true sense of international community. Clark carries this approach somewhat further by emphasizing the need for institutional arrangements for world order which would, in effect, constitute a world government.

a. Disarmament and arms control

P. M. S. Blackett

Steps toward disarmament

THE REPRESENTATIVES of 17 nations—the two main nuclear powers, seven nations allied with one or the other of them, and eight uncommitted nations—have convened at Geneva for the third formal, full-dress attempt since the end of World War II to negotiate disarmament. It must be conceded that the circumstances are not entirely favorable to agreement. During 1961 the U.S. and the U.S.S.R. reversed the trend of nearly a decade and increased their military expenditures by something on the order of 25 per cent. The three-year moratorium on the testing of nuclear weapons was terminated by the series of Soviet tests in the fall; on the eve of the Geneva meeting the U.S. announced its intention to move its present series of underground tests into the atmosphere if the U.S.S.R. did not immediately agree to a test ban.

On the other hand, both the Soviet and the Western bloc are committed by categorical public statements to the objective of complete and general disarmament under strict inspection and control. What is more, practical military considerations, arising from the nature of nuclear weapons, commend substantial reduction in armaments to the great powers as a measure that will increase their security in the first step toward disarmament.

In considering possible first steps that would lead to increased security for both sides, partisans of each side should try to understand how the present military situation must look to the other. A military commander, in planning a campaign or a battle, attempts to do this as a matter of course. He has first to find out all he can about the material facts of his opponent's military deployment and secondly to assess the probable intentions of his opponent for its use. This is the process that has been described as "guessing what is happening on the other side of the hill." A similar obligation rests on those who plan a disarmament negotiation. A military planner, it is true, can much more easily put himself mentally in the position of his military opponent than a statesman can think himself into the position of his opposite number, because a statesman must enter imaginatively into the political as well as the military thought processes of his opponent. This is hard to do at a time of acute ideological struggle. It is nonetheless essential that the military and political leaders of both sides do just this. No small part of the present crisis, concerning armaments in general and nuclear weapons in particular, has been due to a tendency in the West to attribute to ideological motives actions by the U.S.S.R. that seem to have been motivated mainly by military considerations. Conversely, much of the West's defense policy appears to have been influenced by political and economic factors.

It may be useful to start by describing the most

---

important elements in the military capabilities of the Soviet bloc and the Western alliance. In recent months there have been significant disclosures about the nuclear weapons and their means of delivery possessed by both sides. On November 12 of last year Robert S. McNamara, Secretary of Defense of the U.S., said that the U.S. nuclear strike force consists of 1,700 intercontinental bombers, including 630 B-52's, 55 B-58's and 1,000 B-47's. He said that the U.S. possesses in addition several dozen operational intercontinental ballistic missiles (ICBM's), some 80 Polaris

therefore we can be confident that the Soviets will not provoke a major conflict." The U.S. stockpile of nuclear weapons is most often estimated as around 30,000 megatons, that is, enough for some 30,000 one-megaton bombs.

Naturally no such precise figures for Soviet strength are available. I have seen no reliable estimates of the U.S.S.R's nuclear stockpile, nor of its possible nuclear-armed submarine strength, nor of its nuclear-armed fighter-bomber strength (the last, of course, would not have sufficient range to contribute to the Soviet strike power against the U.S.). But recent

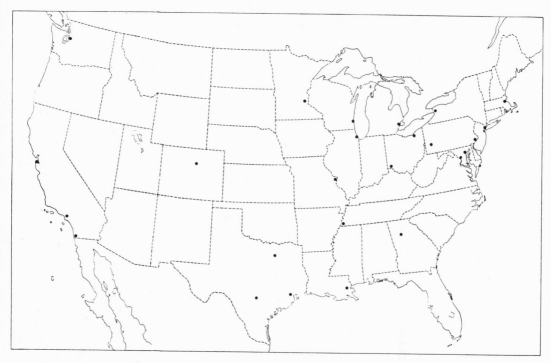

Figure 1. Minimum deterrent strategy of a nuclear opponent of the U.S. could logically be based on an attack on the U.S. population rather than on U.S. airfields and missile bases. The dots on this map represent the 25 largest U.S. cities. In the 1960 census the combined population of the metropolitan areas of these cities was 60.8 million.

missiles in nuclear-powered submarines, about the same number of Thor and Jupiter intermediate-range missiles, some 300 carrier-borne aircraft armed with megaton war heads and nearly 1,000 supersonic land-based fighters with nuclear war heads. According to his deputy, Roswell L. Gilpatric, "the total number of our nuclear delivery vehicles, tactical as well as strategic, is in the tens of thousands, and of course we have more than one war head for each vehicle. . . . We have a second-strike capability that is at least as extensive as what the Soviets can deliver by striking first,

semiofficial estimates from Washington give the U.S.S.R. some 50 ICBM's some 150 intercontinental bombers and some 400 medium-range missiles (the last able to cover Europe but not the U.S.). The same sources indicate that the U.S. may have a small lead over the U.S.S.R. in the number of ICBM's. That such estimates should issue from Washington may seem surprising in view of the role that an alleged "missile gap" played in the 1960 presidential election campaign. That the estimates are realistic, however, is indicated by the statement of Senator Stuart Symington that the U.S. intelligence estimate of the missile force available to the U.S.S.R. at the middle of 1961 was only 3.5 per cent of the number predicted a few years ago. The corresponding estimate of Soviet bomber strength, he revealed, was 19 per cent of the number predicted in 1956 [*see* Figure 6]. Mr. Symington explained that the new figures are predicted on intelligence about Soviet "intentions" as well as "capability" and expressed his own disquiet at "the tentativeness at best of our intelligence estimates." It is one of the purposes of this article to attempt to elucidate some of these Soviet intentions.

At first sight there appears to be a contradiction between Washington's claim of a marked over-all nuclear superiority and the recent statement by Marshal Rodion Y. Malinovsky, the Soviet Minister of Defense, that the U.S.S.R. has the power to destroy all the important industrial, administrative and political centers of the U.S. and "whole countries that have provided their territories for the siting of American war bases." The explanation may be as follows. To carry out such destruction would require not more than 1,000 megatons of nuclear destructive power, say five megatons for each of 100 key targets in the U.S. and another 500 megatons for Western Europe and U.S. bases overseas. At only 100,000 dead per megaton such an attack would kill 100 million people. The U.S. stockpile, estimated at 30,000 megatons, is 30 times greater than the U.S.S.R. would need to carry out the retaliatory blow described by Malinovsky.

There is, of course, the possibility that the new U.S. estimates of Soviet nuclear strength are too low. After all, firm information about Soviet military preparations is notoriously hard to come by. It seems certain, however, that the U.S. Department of Defense must believe the estimates to be roughly correct. It would be politically disastrous for the Administration to be found guilty of underestimating Soviet nuclear strength. But even assuming that the estimates of the relative strength of the two sides are only approximately correct, they show that the possibility of a rationally planned surprise nuclear attack by the U.S.S.R. on the nuclear delivery system of the West must be quite negligible. The question of why the U.S.S.R. has built such a small nuclear delivery system should perhaps be replaced by the question of why the U.S. has built such an enormous striking capacity.

In order to understand the possible motives behind Soviet defense policy, it is necessary to consider the history of the growth of nuclear-weapon power. During the period of monopoly or overwhelming numerical superiority, say from 1947 to 1954, the role of the U.S. Strategic Air Command was to attack and destroy Soviet cities in case of war. This countercity policy, like most traditional military doctrines, had both an offensive and a defensive aspect. From the Western viewpoint, under the doctrine of "massive retaliation," this nuclear striking power was seen to be both a deterrent to the possibility of attack by Soviet land forces and, in the extreme "roll back," or "liberation," statement of the doctrine, an offensive weapon to obtain political concessions by threat of its use. By 1954 the threat was implemented by more than 1,000 intercontinental B-47 bombers, plus larger numbers of short-range vehicles deployed around the U.S.S.R.

From the U.S.S.R.'s point of view, its land forces were the only available counter to the Western nuclear monopoly during this period. The answer to the threat of nuclear attack was the threat of taking over Europe on the ground. In retrospect the military reaction of the U.S.S.R. seems understandable. It started a crash program to produce its own nuclear weapons. It also embarked on a huge air defense program; by 1953 it was credited with an operational fighter strength of some 10,000 aircraft. As Western nuclear strength grew, the U.S.S.R. gradually built up its land forces so as to be able to invade Europe, even after a U.S. nuclear attack. At the political level the U.S.S.R. consolidated its forward military line by the political coup in 1948 in Czechoslovakia and integrated the other satellite countries more closely into the Soviet defense system. Since the main military threat then to the U.S.S.R. was from manned nuclear bombers, the greatest possible depth for air defense was vital. During World War II it was found that the efficacy of a fighter defense system increased steeply with the depth of the defense zone. Finally, the U.S.S.R. maintained strict geographical secrecy over its land area so as to deny target information to the U.S. Strategic Air Command.

The doctrine of massive retaliation became less and less plausible as the Soviet nuclear stockpile grew. It had to be abandoned after 1954, when hydrogen bombs became available to both East and West. When the U.S.S.R. proceeded to build up a fleet of long-range

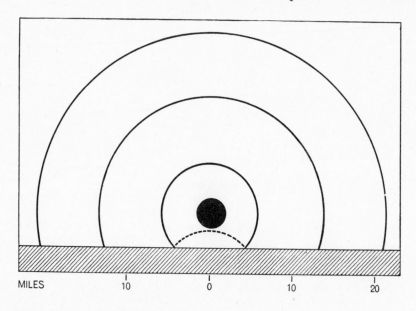

MILES   10   0   10   20

Figure 2. Air burst of a nuclear bomb would maximize its effects on a city, the most widespread of which would be due to heat. This drawing outlines the effects of a 10-megaton bomb set off at 20,000 feet. At 12 miles (middle circle) from "ground zero" the fireball, 3.4 miles in diameter, would deliver 30 calories per square centimeter at a rate sufficient to ignite virtually all flammable building materials. At 20 miles (outer circle) from ground zero the heat would be 12 calories per square centimeter, enough to cause third-degree burns and start many fires. Arc extending upward from ground below the burst is a reflected shock wave that would amplify blast effects of the explosion (see Figure 3).

bombers to deliver its hydrogen bombs, the U.S. became vulnerable to nuclear counterattack. Some form of nuclear stalemate by balance of terror seemed to have arrived.

This balance seemed still further strengthened about 1957, when rapid progress in the technology of nuclear weapons and missiles made is possible to carry multimegaton hydrogen bombs in ICBM's. Because such missiles are most difficult, if not impossible, to destroy in flight, a nuclear aggressor would have to leave no enemy missiles undestroyed if it wanted to keep its own major cities from being wiped out by a retaliatory attack. The advent of long-range missiles therefore made the balance of terror more stable.

Two contrasting systems of military theory evolved in response to this new situation. The first led off from the premise that a rather stable kind of military balance had been reached, in which neither side could make use of its strategic nuclear power without ensuring its own destruction. In other words, the balance of terror was likely to be rather stable against rational action, even though the actual nuclear

strengths of the two sides were markedly different, as indeed they were in the middle 1950's, when the U.S. was already vastly stronger in over-all deployed nuclear strength. This view rested on the assumption that neither side could hope to knock out the other's nuclear system entirely. Since some power to retaliate would survive attack, a rational government would be nearly as much, if not just as much, deterred from a first strike by the expectation that it would suffer, say, 10 million deaths as it would be if the expectation were 100 million.

This view led to the practical conclusion that "enough is enough." In today's jargon this is the policy of the minimum deterrent—that is, the possession of a nuclear force adequate only for a retaliatory attack on enemy cities but incapable of successful attack on the enemy's nuclear delivery system. It is clear that only a small nuclear delivery system is necessary for a minimum deterrent. One big hydrogen bomb dropped on a big city could kill several millions. The small delivery system must, however, be highly invulnerable. Otherwise the enemy might think it possible to bring

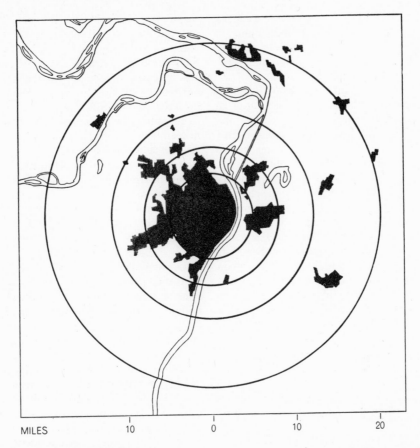

MILES   10   0   10   20

Figure 3. Radii of effects of a 10-megaton air burst are superimposed on a map of St. Louis and the surrounding area. The two outer circles correspond to the similar circles in Figure 2, whereas the two inner circles concern the effects due to blast. At a distance of five miles (inner circle) from ground zero, virtually all buildings would be destroyed. At eight miles (second inner circle), virtually all wooden buildings would be destroyed.

off a successful "counterforce" first strike, aimed at the destruction of the system. Little operational intelligence is needed for such a minimum deterrent policy because this involves attack on cities, whose locations are known, and does not involve surprise attack on nuclear bases, whose locations therefore do not need to be known.

On the political plane, it was thought, the resulting period of relative stability would be favorable for a serious attempt to negotiate a substantial measure of disarmament, both nuclear and conventional. Far-reaching disarmament was seen to be highly desirable, if only because such a balance of terror is stable solely against rational acts of responsible governments. It is not stable against irresponsible actions of individuals or dissident groups

or technical accidents. A few suitably placed individuals—a missile crew or the crew of a nuclear bomber on a routine flight—could kill a few million enemy city dwellers on their own initiative. The best way to reduce this danger is to reduce drastically the number of nuclear weapons on both sides.

The second and quite different doctrine was that the balance of terror was not even stable against rational acts of responsible governments. This was based on the view that a determined nuclear power might be able to launch a surprise counterforce attack on the enemy's nuclear delivery system of such strength that the enemy would not be able to retaliate. The aggressor, without suffering unacceptable casualties, would then have the enemy at its mercy. The practical consequence of this doctrine is to strive for maximum superiority in number of weapons, maximum invulnerability of one's own nuclear delivery system and maximum intelligence about the enemy's nuclear system.

Plainly a successful counterforce attack would require knowledge of the location of all the enemy's nuclear missile and air bases and the power to dispatch several weapons against each, so as to ensure that at least one reached its target. A counterforce strategy thus implies the necessity for a many-fold nuclear superiority over the enemy. Moreover, to have the slightest chance of success such an attack must come as a complete surprise to the enemy: it must be a first strike. This policy has various pseudonyms: maximum deterrent posture, first-counterforce-strike capability, or, in plain English, preparation for nuclear aggression.

Since the possession of nuclear armament raises the possibility that either side could adopt either one of these strategies, both of them must have been discussed in military circles in Moscow and Washington during the years after the explosion of the first hydrogen bombs in 1954. Let us try to find out how the discussions went by studying what shape the nuclear-defense policies of the U.S.S.R. and the U.S. took in the subsequent years.

If the Washington figures for Soviet nuclear strength are valid, it is clear that the U.S.S.R. has planned for a purely retaliatory nuclear role and has definitely not planned for a surprise attack on the U.S. delivery system. As long ago as 1956 the U.S.S.R. was believed to have the capability of making 25 long-range bombers a month. It appears today to have only some 150, compared with the 1,700 U.S. long-range bombers able to reach the U.S.S.R. Even though Soviet medium-range bombers could reach the U.S. on a one-way flight, this is much more than counterbalanced by the 1,500 or so Western fighter bombers, carrier-borne aircraft and medium-range missiles able to reach the U.S.S.R. It is also probable that the U.S.S.R. could have made many more than the 50 or so ICBM's with which it is now credited, since its space program indicates substantial industrial resources for making missiles. The evidence is that the U.S.S.R. has based its safety on the retaliatory power of a small number of missiles and aircraft operating from bases whose exact locations are kept as secret as possible. The deterrent value of its missiles is certainly enhanced by the prestige of its space program.

That the U.S.S.R. believed the danger of a major war, intentionally initiated, had been reduced by the advent of hydrogen bombs seems indicated by the fact that it reduced the total number of men in its armed forces from 5.8 million in 1955 to 3.6 million in 1959. In January, 1960, Premier Khrushchev announced the U.S.S.R.'s intention to reduce this to 2.4 million by the end of 1961. The U.S.S.R. needed fewer troops because it no longer had to rely on a retaliatory land blow in Europe to counter a Western nuclear attack. Its concern about the danger of accidental, irresponsible or escalated war is probably one of the reasons for its strong espousal in 1955 of a drastic measure of comprehensive and general disarmament.

Turning to the history of U.S. defense policy over this period, it is to be noted that the total service manpower fell slowly from 2.9 million in 1955 to 2.6 million in 1960. The development of improved nuclear weapons, missiles and aircraft continued, but not at a great rate, even after the Soviet launching of an artificial satellite in 1957 and much boasting by the U.S.S.R. of its missile prowess. Although subjected to considerable public pressure to engage in a crash program to close the alleged missile gap, President Eisenhower maintained that the existing program was adequate for the safety of the nation. In his last State of the Union Message in January, 1961, he declared: "The 'bomber gap' of several years ago was always a fiction and the 'missile gap' shows every sign of being the same."

As 1954 was the year of the hydrogen bomb, so 1961 was for both sides in the cold war the year of the Great Rearmament. In the U.S.S.R. the decrease of total armed forces to 2.4 million projected for 1961 was deferred and the arms budget was markedly increased. In July the Soviet Government went on the diplomatic offensive to bring about changes in the status of Berlin and to get the division of Germany recognized. In August it began testing nuclear weapons again, in spite of a promise in January, 1960, by Premier Khrushchev that the U.S.S.R. would not be the first to do so. No doubt there were some political motives behind these drastic moves. Possibly heavy pressure was put on Khrushchev from China and from the opposition elements in the U.S.S.R. to admit that this policy of coexistence had not produced political gains commensurate with its possible military risks. But such drastic changes, with the inevitable adverse reaction of much of world opinion, would hardly have been made unless there were strong military reasons for them. To get at these reasons it is necessary to recall in more detail the circumstances in which the changes took place.

In the first place the flights of the U.S. reconnaissance U-2 aircraft must have had decisive importance in shaping the attitudes of Soviet military leaders. Although the over-all nuclear strength of the U.S. is now, and was then, much greater than that of the U.S.S.R. Soviet leaders could reckon that one vital factor would make a U.S. nuclear attack on the U.S.S.R. exceedingly risky: the secrecy as to the location of the Soviet nuclear bases. Obviously one of the main objectives of the U-2 flights was to locate those nuclear bases. The Soviet command knew that the U-2 flights had been going on for some years before the first aircraft was shot down in the spring of 1960; presumably they reacted by greater dispersal and camouflage. What must have disturbed the Soviet military staff was President Eisenhower's justification of the flights as essential for U.S. security. This implied that U.S. security could only be maintained if the U.S. had sufficient information as to the location of Soviet nuclear sites to make possible a successful surprise attack on the Soviet retaliatory force.

If these were the Soviet fears, the rejection by the U.S.S.R. early in 1961 of the British-American draft of a treaty to ban the testing of nuclear weapons finds explanation in the same jealous military concern to protect the country's geographical security. A detailed study of this document makes it clear that the elaborate international inspection system proposed for the prevention of underground tests could conceivably have served to reveal the location of at least some of the Soviet missile sites. It would be hard to convince a military staff officer of any nationality that this possibility was negligible. If the West had been content to monitor only the atmosphere against test violations, a much less comprehensive inspection system would have sufficed and a test-ban treaty might well have been signed. The Soviet fear of inspection may have been the more acute because there was so little in the U.S.S.R. to inspect.

The resumption of testing by the U.S.S.R. in September, 1961, would seem to fall into the same pattern of motivation. Although its timing may have been influenced by the Berlin crisis, which Khrushchev himself brought to a head, the testing of war heads with an explosive force of up to 60 megatons and the simultaneous well-publicized success of putting seven ICBM's on their target in the Pacific at a range of some 7,000 miles was an effective way of re-establishing the U.S.S.R.'s confidence in the few deployed ICBM's that formed its main retaliatory force. Soviet spokesmen were at pains to promote the credibility of the U.S.S.R.'s deterrent by emphasizing to the U.S. the accuracy of its missiles and the possible power of the war heads demonstrated in these tests.

In the redirection of Soviet military policy considerable weight must also have been carried by the fear that if the NATO rearmament continued, the time could not be far distant when West Germany would get *de facto* control of its own nuclear weapons. In Soviet eyes the refusal of the West to take disarmament seriously at the "Committee of Ten" conference in 1960 was evidently decisive. As early as November, 1960, the Russians stated that if the West continued to temporize on disarmament, the U.S.S.R. would be forced into massive rearmament.

Sometime in the latter half of 1960 or early in 1961 it seems probable that the Soviet military staff began to have doubts as to the adequacy of the minimum deterrent posture in relation to the near-maximum deterrent posture of the U.S. It must have been later than January of 1960, for in that month Khrushchev announced a drastic cutback of both long-range bombers and conventional forces. Since the effectiveness of the Soviet minimum deterrent rested so heavily on geographical secrecy, the U.S.S.R. command may have feared that the U.S., by further air or satellite reconnaissance, or by espionage or defections, would ultimately acquire the intelligence necessary to make a successful nuclear attack on Soviet nuclear bases. Probably the main fear of the Soviet Government was that circumstances might arise in which the U.S. Government would be pushed by irresponsible or fanatical groups into reckless action. The Russians certainly noted the doctrine of some civilian analysts that it would be quite rational to make a "preemptive first strike" even at the cost of 10 million deaths to the attacking side, and the doctrine of others that the U.S. should prepare itself mentally and materially to suffer such casualties.

In the U.S. the program for the Great
Rearmament was projected as early as 1959
by the Democratic National Committee. In
preparation for the impending presidential
election the party leadership published a
detailed study of defense problems and recommended a $7 billion increase (16 per cent)
in the $43 billion defense budget proposed by
President Eisenhower. The funds were to go
partly for increased conventional forces and
partly to increase the strength and reduce the
vulnerability of the U.S. nuclear striking power.
In January, 1961, almost immediately after
taking office, the Administration authorized an
increase of $3 billion and later in the year
another $4 billion, thus carrying out the pro-
gram in full. The present plans include the provision of up to 800 ICBM's of the solid-fuel
Minuteman type in underground "hardened"
bases by 1965

The Democratic Party's campaign for increased nuclear armaments was closely linked
with the theoretical doctrine of the instability
of the balance of terror, derived from the
alleged overwhelming advantage accruing to
the nuclear aggressor. This was ably argued by
civilian analysts closely associated with the
U.S. Air Force. The U.S.S.R. was said to have
both the capability and the intention to launch
a surprise nuclear attack on the U.S. In
retrospect, it would seem that these "looking-
glass strategists" endowed the U.S.S.R. with
a capability that it did not have and that the
U.S. had once had and had now lost.

That the Soviet military staff had reason to
take this element in U.S. opinion seriously may
be judged by the fact that President Kennedy
himself found it necessary to launch in the fall
of 1961 a vigorous campaign against all those
in the U.S. who urge "total war and total
victory over communism . . . who seek to find
an American solution for all problems"—
against those who were living in the long-past
era of the U.S. nuclear monopoly. In this
campaign President Kennedy has been vigorously supported by ex-President Eisenhower.
Very possibly the U.S.S.R. may have overestimated the potential influence of the proponents of aggressive nuclear strategy and the
ultra-right-wing groups that yearn "to get it
over with." Nonetheless, the fact that both
Kennedy and Eisenhower have felt it necessary
to combat them must also imply that the
Soviet military planners could not afford to
ignore their existence.

The Kennedy Administration's recent vigo-

rous emphasis on the overwhelming nuclear
superiority of the U.S. over the U.S.S.R., and
the assertion that the U.S. possesses a second
strike that is as strong as the Soviet first strike
might perhaps be held in the U.S.S.R. to
suggest a move by the U.S. Administration
toward a preventive war posture. Undoubtedly
the exact reverse is the case. The Administration's statements are designed to bury officially
the fear of a Soviet first strike, sedulously pro-
pagated by those who believe that the U.S.S.R.
has planned for, and in fact now has, a
first-counterforce capability, and so at a time of
crisis might use it. If this were in truth the
situation, the argument that the U.S. must
forestall the Soviet blow might seem strong.
The Kennedy Administration evidently fore-
saw this danger arising and effectively removed it by denying that the U.S.S.R. has ever
had an effective first-strike capacity; thus
there would be no reason for a forestalling
blow in a crisis. The President, by emphasizing
U.S. nuclear superiority over the U.S.S.R.,
has forestalled the potential forestallers, or, in
the current jargon, has pre-empted the potential pre-empters. At the same time he has
refuted many of the arguments on which the
Democratic Party based much of its election
campaign, and indeed many of the arguments
for his own present rearmament program.

It is, for instance, hard to see the military
justification for the program of up to 800
Minuteman ICBM's in the next few years.
If these are, as claimed, reasonably invulnerable, this number is at least 10 times larger than
is necessary for an effective retaliatory force to
attack Soviet cities.

The only military circumstance that could
justify such a continuous build-up of nuclear
striking force would be that the other party
could adequately protect its cities or succeed
in perfecting an antimissile defense system.
Recently Soviet generals have boasted that "the
complex and important problems of destroying
enemy rockets in flight have been solved."
This must refer to the scientific and technical
problems; these have also been solved in the
U.S. A complete antimissile defense system
that is of any operational significance certainly
does not exist today and, in my view, will not
exist in the foreseeable future. Suppose, however, that I am wrong and that a system can
eventually be constructed capable of destroying,
say, 50 per cent of a retaliatory missile attack
by 50 ICBM's, so reducing the number reaching the target to 25. Even this reduced blow

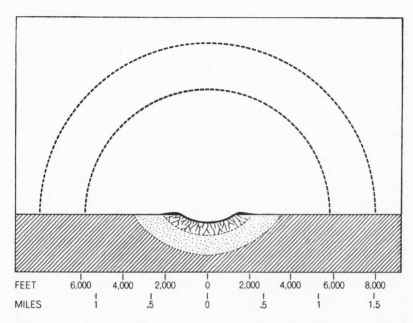

FEET 6,000 4,000 2,000 0 2,000 4,000 6,000 8,000

MILES 1 .5 0 .5 1 1.5

Figure 4. Ground burst of a nuclear bomb would be required to neutralize a "hardened" (i.e., buried) missile site. Diameter of the crater dug by a 10-megaton ground burst in dry soil would be 2,600 feet; the depth of the crater would be 250 feet. Radius of the underground "plastic zone" (outer line below ground) would be 3,250 feet; the radius of the "rupture zone" (inner line below ground) would be 2,000 feet. At a distance of 1.1 miles from ground zero the blast would exert an air pressure of some 300 pounds per square inch (inner circle above ground); at a distance of 1.5 miles (outer circle above ground), 100 pounds per square inch.

would kill tens of millions of people. Moreover, it would only be necessary to increase the strength of the retaliatory force from 50 to 100 missiles to cancel out the antimissile missile. This illustrates the general conclusion that since a purely retaliatory nuclear force can be quite small, any possible defense system, either active or passive, can be canceled out by a small number of additional missiles. The fact that a purely retaliatory posture is little affected by technological innovation, whereas a counterforce posture is very much affected, may prove a vital factor in disarmament negotiations.

It cannot be seriously believed now that the U.S.S.R. has either the capability or the intention of making an all-out attack on U.S. missile sites and bomber bases. Much genuine alarm in the West might have been allayed if the U.S.S.R. had been more successful in making clearer its disbelief in the military possibility of a successful first-counterforce strike and its intention not to plan for such a possibility. After the brutality of Soviet action in Hungary in 1956 and the technological triumph of the artificial satellite the following

year, there may have been legitimate grounds in the West for fearing that the U.S.S.R. might adopt the Western policy of massive retaliation, which, against a nuclear power, requires a counterforce capability. In January, 1960, however, Khrushchev explicitly declared the Soviet commitment to a purely retaliatory strategy. The Soviet second-strike force was strong enough, he said, "to wipe the country or countries which attack us off the face of the earth." To his own rhetorical question, "Will they not, possibly, show perfidy and attack us first . . . and thus have an advantage to achieve victory?" he replied: "No. Contemporary means of waging war do not give any country such advantages." In addition to freeing resources for capital development, the Soviet minimum-deterrent strategy has avoided the greatest military danger: that the U.S. might attack the U.S.S.R. because of a belief that the U.S.S.R. was about to attack the U.S.

If the analysis given here is approximately correct, what are the prospects of progress toward disarmament at the present meeting in

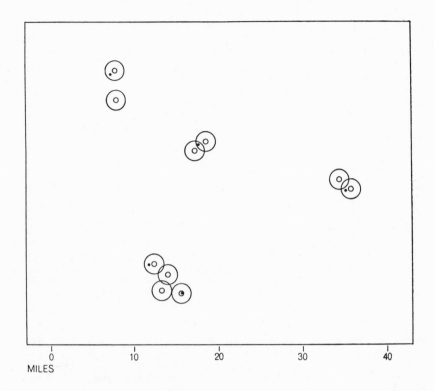

Figure 5. Pattern of ground bursts would be required to neutralize a dispersed group of hardened missile sites. In this schematic drawing a "circle of probable error" of one mile is assumed for each of the attacking missiles; this implies that at least two missiles would be directed at each of the sites. There are five sites, represented by dots. The smaller of each of the 10 pairs of concentric circles represents the 2,600-foot diameter of a 10-megaton bomb crater; the larger of the circles, the 1.1-mile radius at which the air pressure is 300 pounds per square inch. The total weight of the attack on the five bases is 100 megatons.

Geneva? Both blocs are fully committed by official pronouncements to the goal of complete and general disarmament under strict control and inspection—notably by the British Commonwealth Prime Ministers' statement in the spring of 1961, by President Kennedy's speech to the General Assembly of the United Nations and by the Soviet-American Joint Statement of Principles, both in September of 1961. Moreover, both sides are committed to attempting to work out first steps of the disarmament process that do not impair the present strategic balance.

Clearly, conventional and nuclear disarmament must go in parallel. The fear of the West of Soviet superiority in trained and deployed land forces must be met by a drastic reduction during the first stage to low levels such as those suggested by the Anglo-French memorandum of 1954: one million or at most 1.5 million men each for the U.S., the U.S.S.R. and China.

When the correspondingly limited contributions to the land forces of NATO from Great Britain, France and West Germany are taken into account, the armies of the Soviet bloc would not have the capability of overrunning Europe in a surprise land attack.

The number of nuclear weapons in existence on both sides, their explosive power and the diversity of the delivery systems are so overwhelming that no small step in nuclear disarmament can have much significance. In a situation in which the U.S. has 10,000 delivery vehicles and a stockpile of 30,000 megatons of explosive (which is said to be increasing at the fastest rate in its history), a first disarmament step involving only a small percentage reduction is not worth negotiating. To justify the labor of negotiating any agreed reduction, and to offset the undoubted strains and disputes that will inevitably arise from the operation of any inspection and control system, the

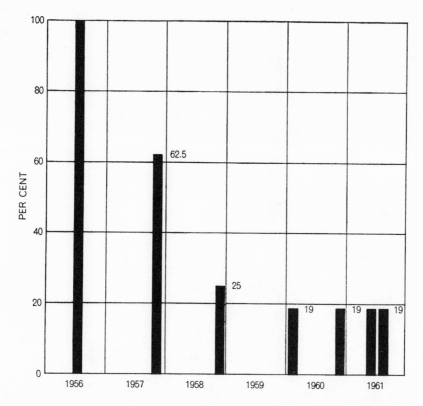

Figure 6. U.S. estimate of Soviet heavy-bomber strength by the middle of 1961, according to an article by Senator Stuart Symington in The Reporter, *decreased by 81 per cent between August, 1956* (bar at left), *and August, 1961* (right). *Senator Symington's figures were given in percentages, rather than absolute numbers, for security reasons.*

negotiated reduction must be a major one; in fact, of such magnitude as to change qualitatively the nature of the relative nuclear postures of the two giant powers.

The simplest big first step, and the one most consistent with realistic military considerations, is that both giant powers should reduce their nuclear forces to a very low and purely retaliatory role. That is, each should retain only enough invulnerable long-range vehicles to attack the other's cities if it is itself attacked, say less than 100 ICBM's with one-megaton war heads. This is still an enormous force, capable of killing tens of millions of people. A reduction to a level of 20 ICBM's or less would be much preferable. Such a reduction would at once prevent nuclear weapons from being used by sane governments as weapons of aggression or coercion. It would not, of course, prevent them from being used by irresponsible groups who do not calculate the cost. It is only at a later stage in disarmament, when nuclear weapons are completely destroyed

that this danger will be excluded. It has always been clear that the ever present danger of accidental or irresponsible war is a cogent reason for big and rapid steps in the disarmament process.

Detailed studies are needed of possible ways in which both the U.S.S.R. and the U.S. could take such an important first step without upsetting the present strategic balance. A major problem is how to phase the building up of a system of general inspection while at the same time making a drastic reduction in nuclear delivery systems by their actual destruction under international verification. Taking military considerations only into account, I believe that a procedure acceptable to both blocs could be devised.

The difference hitherto between the proposed Western and Soviet first steps in relation to nuclear weapons has been often simplified to the statement that the U.S.S.R. wants disarmament without control and the West wants

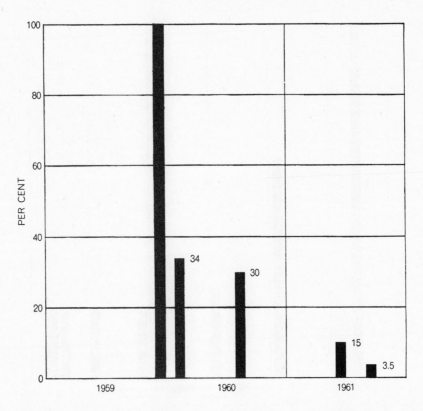

Figure 7. U.S. estimate of Soviet operational ICBM strength similarly decreased, according to Senator Symington, by 96.5 per cent between December, 1959, and September, 1961.

control without disarmament. It would be more accurate to say that the clash is on the phasing of the stages of disarmament and the stages of control.

In its 1960 proposals the U.S.S.R. suggested that, in the first step, international teams should be dispatched to inspect the destruction of all rocket weapons, military aircraft and other carriers of nuclear weapons. It did not propose the inspection or control of those that remain waiting to be destroyed. Full inspection of a country was to be undertaken only when all weapons had been destroyed. It is clear that the U.S.S.R.'s first steps of disarmament are consistent with its presumed military policy of relying for its safety from nuclear attack on a relatively small force of purely retaliatory nuclear weapons in secret sites.

On the other hand, the U.S. proposals in 1960 envisaged widespread inspection in the first stages and no actual disarmament until the second stage. This proposal might make military sense if put by a weak nuclear power to a much stronger one. But when put by a

strong power to a weaker one, rejection must have been expected. If the U.S.S.R. had accepted the proposal, the geographical secrecy of its nuclear sites would have been lost and it would have been vulnerable to nuclear attack from the much stronger West.

Any realistic first stage must start from the fact that the present nuclear balance, such as it is, has a highly asymmetric character: the West's much greater nuclear power is balanced by Soviet geographical secrecy. Since the military balance is asymmetric, so must be any mutually acceptable first step. Concessions must be made by both sides and these must be based on the realities of the military postures of the two blocs.

The U.S.S.R. should accept general inspection not, as in their proposals hitherto, when disarmament is complete but at some intermediate stage on the road to disarmament. Reciprocally, the West should not demand widespread inspection before any disarmament has taken place, as it has done hitherto, but only after substantial destruction of nuclear armaments has taken place under international verification.

In the first stage, therefore, all parties might supply to one another a list of nuclear weapons and their delivery systems, together with research and production facilities. The exact location of sites would not be included at this stage. An agreed number of weapons would then be destroyed and their destruction would be verified by on-site inspection by the international control organization. When this destruction has been verified, a general inspection, using some sampling technique, would begin. The object would then be to verify the correctness of the original declared inventories by checking the numbers remaining after the agreed reductions had been verified, and to proceed to the elimination of the armament remaining.

A word must be said about the place of a test-ban agreement in the stages of a disarmament plan. If this agreement did not involve a type of inspection that might reveal the Soviet nuclear sites, it would be advantageous for it to be included in the first stage, or preferably agreed to at once. If, however, it involved widespread inspection that might reveal these sites, Soviet military planners would certainly advise its rejection. It would then have to wait for the second stage of disarmament, when general inspection starts after the destruction of agreed numbers of nuclear weapons in the first stage.

Some such compromise between Western and Soviet proposals would seem to meet many of the reciprocal criticisms made by the two parties of their respective 1960 proposals without compromising the military security of either. The problem becomes more difficult however, when nonmilitary considerations are taken into account. Since nonmilitary considerations have played a major role in shaping the defense policies of the great powers, they must inevitably also affect their disarmament policies. For example, if it is difficult to find legitimate military reasons for the vast number of U.S. nuclear weapons and delivery vehicles, it is clear that military arguments alone are not likely to be dominant in U.S. discussion of a possible drastic first step toward nuclear disarmament. This is widely admitted in the U.S., where the impediments to disarmament are being seen more and more as economic, political and emotional in origin rather than

as based on operational military considerations. A vital aspect of the problem for the U.S. is the effect that drastic disarmament steps would have not only on the economy as a whole but also on those special sections of high-grade, science-based and highly localized industries that are now so overwhelmingly involved in defense work. A valuble step would be for both the U.S. and Soviet governments to produce and publish detailed and politically realistic economic plans for the transition to a purely retaliatory capacity.

It is fair to conclude that a realistic military basis for an agreed drastic first step in disarmament may not be impossible to find. The urgency of the situation was declared with eloquence by President Kennedy in his speech to the United Nations in September:

"Today, every inhabitant of this planet must contemplate the day when this planet may no longer be habitable. Every man, woman and child lives under a nuclear sword of Damocles, hanging by the slenderest of threads, capable of being cut at any moment by accident or miscalculation or by madness. . . . The risks inherent in disarmament pale in comparison to the risks inherent in an unlimited arms race."

This great goal of disarmament will be achieved only if the real nature of the arguments against disarmament are clearly identified and frankly faced. The problems of disarmament must not be obscured, as they sometimes have been in the past, by ingenious but fallacious military doctrine applied to false intelligence estimates.

The growing power of China, and the evidence of an ideological rift between it and Russia, provide an added reason for urgency in the drive for disarmament. The U.S.S.R. and the U.S. will be wise to limit drastically their nuclear arms before China becomes a major nuclear power. It is to be observed that whatever influence China may now be exerting on the U.S.S.R. to adopt a harder policy with the West certainly arises in part from the failure of Premier Khrushchev's campaign for disarmament. This failure greatly weakens Khrushchev's argument for the feasibility of peaceful coexistence of the Soviet and the Western worlds. It would seem urgently necessary to attempt to bring China into the disarmament negotiations as soon as possible.

Thomas C. Schelling

The role of deterrence in total disarmament

A SHARP DISTINCTION is often drawn between arms control and disarmament. The former seeks to reshape military incentives and capabilities; the latter, it is alleged, eliminates them. But the success of either depends on mutual deterrence. Short of universal brain surgery, nothing can erase the memory of weapons and how to build them. If "total disarmament" is to make war unlikely, it must reduce the incentives. It cannot eliminate the potential for destruction; the most primitive war can be modernized by rearmament as it goes along.

To determine whether and how disarmament might make war less likely we have to look at what the military opportunities, risks, dangers, fears and potential capabilities would be in a disarmed world. If nations now suspect each other of contemplating war, we have to suppose that they might suspect each other of contemplating rearmament. If nations are willing to risk war, or to threaten it, they certainly might risk rearming or the threatening to rearm. Nations though capable now of being panicked into war might be panicked into rearmament. To suppose the contrary is to assume away the problem that disarmament is intended to help solve.

An international military authority is commonly proposed as a part of plans for total disarmament. It does make a difference whether or not we assume the existence of such an authority to police the otherwise disarmed world. But for the visible future it is a little extreme to suppose that an international force could contain or deter the United States and the Soviet Union; more than that, the concept poses problems of deterrence not wholly unlike those that would confront the major powers in a fully disarmed world. So we shall first consider universal disarmament without any international security force. And we shall assume a world disarmed to the levels proposed by those who favor the most drastic "total disarmament."

There are good reasons why this phrase should be set off in quotation marks. An obvious one is that there can be no absolute assurance that some nuclear weapons have not been kept. But, cheating aside, war can be waged with even the most primitive weapons, especially with the help of commercial aircraft, ships, trucks, radios and the other paraphernalia of industrial society. More important, if war breaks out a nation can rearm unless its capacity is destroyed at the outset and kept destroyed. By the standards of 1944, the United States was fairly near to total disarmament when World War II broke out. Virtually all munitions later expended by United States forces were nonexistent in September 1939. "Disarmament" did not preclude U.S. participation; it just slowed it down.

As we eliminate weapons, warning systems, vehicles and bases, we change the criteria of military effectiveness. Airplanes are more important if missiles are banned; complex airplanes are needed less if complex defenses are banned. Since weapons themselves are the most urgent targets in war, to eliminate a weapon eliminates a target and changes the requirements for attack. At some stage in disarmament a donkey becomes a means of delivery, though we assume that "total" disarmament stops short of that.

The difficulty cannot be avoided by banning weapons of attack and keeping those of defense. If nations were large, self-sufficient islands, coast artillery might seem useless for aggres-

Reprinted from *Foreign Affairs*, Vol. 40, No. 3, April 1962. Copyright by the Council on Foreign Relations, Inc., New York, pp. 392–406.

sion and valuable safeguards against war and the fear of war. But they are not; and in the present era, "defensive" weapons often embody equipment or technology that is superbly useful in attack and invasion. Moreover, a prerequisite of successful attack is some ability to defend against retaliation or counterattack. In a disarmed world, whatever lessens the scale of retaliation reduces the risk a nation runs in starting war. Defenses against retaliation thus are close substitutes for offensive power.

General war in a disarmed world

DISARMAMENT would not preclude the eruption of a crisis; war and rearmament could seem imminent. Even without possessing complex weapons, a nation might consider initiating war with whatever resources it had, on grounds that delay would allow an enemy to strike or mobilize first. If a nation believed its opponent might rush to rearm to achieve military preponderance, it might consider "preventive war" to forestall its opponent's dominance. Or, if confidence in the maintenance of disarmament were low and if war later under worse conditions seemed at all likely, there could be motives for "preventive ultimatums," or for winning a short war through coercion with illicitly retained nuclear weapons, or for using force to impose a more durable disarmament arrangement.

The decision to attack might be made reluctantly, motivated not by the prospective gains of victory but by the disadvantages of not seizing the initiative. Motives to undertake preventive or pre-emptive war might be as powerful under disarmament as with today's weapons—perhaps more powerful.

In a disarmed world, as now, the objective would probably be to destroy the enemy's ability to bring war into one's homeland, and to "win" sufficiently to prevent his subsequent build-up as a military menace. The urgent targets would be the enemy's available weapons of mass destruction (if any), his means of delivery, his equipment that could be quickly converted for strategic use, and the components, stand-by facilities and cadres from which he could assemble a capability for strategic warfare.

Suppose both sides have violated the agreement and possess nuclear bombs at least in the scores or hundreds (or suppose the attacker has, and must anticipate that his opponent has). The attacker's first objective is to forestall the delivery of bombs in return. Compared with the present, the disarmed world would offer the attacker both advantages and disadvantages.

An advantage is that the time scale of attack may be more lenient. The victim may have a secret nuclear stockpile; but if he is unprepared it will take time to bring together, say, commercial aircraft, crews and the hidden nuclear weapons, and to improvise fueling arrangements and target plans. To do this in the hostile environment of even small-scale nuclear attack might be difficult. But the attacker would be coordinated rather than surprised and could make effective use of evacuation procedures or of any air defenses he could improvise.

If, instead, each side has plans for the contingency and maintains a "reserve force"—some part, say, of its commercial air fleet and crews—the victim of attack may react quickly. The attacker's own air defenses have been banned by agreement (and air defenses may be hard to conceal); in these conditions a retaliatory force of even low efficiency may be effective if it is large and dispersed.

If the aggressor has nuclear weapons and the victim does not, the latter's response will depend on how rapidly production can be resumed. Standby capacity may be available, or there may be nuclear facilities that can be converted to produce weapons. If these facilities have not been destroyed, the lag may be short, but a matter of days at least. Critically important would be the defenses, the dispersal or the secrecy of the facilities for producing nuclear materials or for assembling nuclear weapons. If the sites are few in number, of known location, above ground and without air defense, they would be destroyed before operations could be resumed. If the production facilities are in secret locations, we may as well assume that nuclear weapons also exist.

A war of nuclear mobilization

IN the event that neither side had nuclear weapons, asymmetrical lead-times in nuclear rearmament could be decisive. Whether it took days or months, the side that believed it could be first to acquire a few dozen megatons through a crash rearmament program would expect to dominate its opponent. This advantage would be greatest if nuclear facilities themselves were vulnerable to nuclear bombardment: the first few weapons produced would be used to spoil the opponent's nuclear rearmament. Even if facilities are deep under the ground, well disguised or highly dispersed, a small difference in the time needed to acquire a few score megatons might make the war unendurable for the side that is behind. If one side appears likely to gain the decisive advantage, it might find "preventive rearmament" coupled with a surrender ultimatum an irresistibly attractive move.

It would not necessarily be essential to possess nuclear weapons in order to destroy nuclear facilities. High explosives, commandos or saboteurs could be effective. "Strategic warfare" might reach a purity not known in this century: like the king in chess, nuclear facilities would be the overriding objective. Their protection would have absolute claim on defense.

In such a war the object would be to preserve one's mobilization base and to destroy the enemy's. To win a war would not require overcoming the enemy's defenses—just winning the rearmament race. If commandos can bypass home defenses and paralyze the adversary's nuclear mobilization base, the jig is up—unless all participants can do this to each other. If they can, the prospect is for a bizarre kind of "broken-backed" war, bizarre because no back is broken, and the struggle to acquire nuclear weapons goes on—hopefully not too fast and too furiously to allow parallel negotiations for an agreed stalemate or a second try at "disarmament."

Another kind of warfare may emerge—"nuclear coercion." If an attacker possesses illicit nuclear weapons that can be dropped on a country that is unable to retaliate promptly, it might force a surrender through the destruction of cities and the threat of destroying more. Or the coercive campaign could combine preclusive destruction of the mobilization base with the demoralizing effects of concurrent civil damage. The expectation would be that, if significant rearmament could be retarded, capitulation would be forthcoming.

Such a war might be less destructive than war under present conditions, not primarily because disarmament had reduced the attacker's capability but because, with the victim unable to respond, the attacker could adopt a more measured pace with allowed time to negotiate a cease-fire before he had reduced his victim to rubble. Victory, of course, might be achieved without violence. If one side appears to have an advantage so convincingly decisive as to make the outcome of the war seem inevitable, it could then deliver an ultimatum instead of weapons.[1]

Disarmament might also cause nuclear weapons to be a greater equalizer among nations than they are now. A future Castro might be in a better position to plague or coerce the great powers by secreting nuclear weapons on his territory. In a world in which such forms of nuclear mischief have replaced the space-age machinery of war and in which the push-button has given way to improvised aerial ferries, the military environment may become less predictable and possibly more unstable.

To sum up: a stable military environment will not result automatically from a ban on weapons and the facilities to make them. The timing of war and rearmament, and the role of speed and initiative, will remain critically important in a world in which the pace of war is initially slowed. War may become more calculable and less fearsome. And there would remain, even in the design of "total disarmament," the difficult choice between minimizing war's destructiveness and minimizing its likelihood. If disarmament is to discourage the initiation of war and to remove the incentives toward pre-emptive and preventive war, it has to be *designed* to do that. Disarmament does not eliminate military potential; it changes it.

Limited war in a disarmed world

WHILE disarmament would eliminate the guns, it would not eliminate the trucks, aircraft, ships, communication equipment and canned food that are required for limited military campaigns. Nations could be expected to have plans for limited-war mobilization, including limited departures from the arms agreement itself.[2]

As important as the direct consequences that disarmament would have for limited war would be the indirect consequences. If disarmament reduces fears of general war—if explosion or escalation into general war seems a less likely prospect, or less disastrous if it should occur—the result may be fewer inhibitions on limited war. There could also be new restraints. If it is perceived that the outbreak of local wars may destroy the agreement itself—either through a sudden breakdown or steady erosion—this may create a determination to preserve what has been achieved and a recognition that to abandon restraints would signal "open season" on military competition. Of course, the more all parties value the climate of disarmament, the more can be gained by threatening to disturb it.

As "limited war" is possible, so is "limited violation" of disarmament. Since limits on hostilities can evidently be observed during war itself, limits on rearmament might be arrived at in similar fashion, even in the course of limited hostilities. The responses of countries not participating in the war would be important— perhaps an important brake, possibly a stimulus, on the resumed armament.

In limited war as in general war under conditions of "total disarmament," timing would be important. Offensive strategy in a limited war is often designed to achieve a *fait accompli*. Defense against this strategy in a disarmed world would depend on the ability of the defender (or protector) to rearm in time to repel or to stalemate the aggression. If we reflect on the critical timing of the North Korean invasion and the shortage of ammunition that plagued us throughout the whole Korean campaign, or the problems of the preemptive landing of Marines in Lebanon or the progress of the Suez campaign, it is evident that logistical considerations can be decisive. The likelihood that limited aggression will be deterred by the threat of limited rearmament may therefore depend on the mobilization speed that can be achieved from a standing start.

The deterrence of rearmament in a disarmed world

MANY concepts that apply to the deterrence of war apply to deterrence of rearmament: "preventive" rearmament, "pre-emptive" rearmament, "escalation" of rearmament, "catalytic" rearmament, and rearmament stimulated by misinformation, misinterpretation, accident, false alarm, unauthorized conspiracy and other processes analogous to those that might trigger "inadvertent war" in an armed world. In addition, there are the possibilities of rearmament bubbling up out of a crisis, occurring in the course of a limited war or being undertaken by cool premeditation.

But despite the parallel, rearmament is not war. The fears, motives and moral attitudes that make initiation of war an opprobrious act do not apply with the same force to rearmament. The question whether to remain disarmed or to initiate limited rearmament could become a legitimate political issue. If the disarmament is so delicately balanced that there is great advantage in being the first to rearm, the mere existence of a political party pledged to abandon the disarmament treaty might disturb the arrangement. And to the extent that the treaty explicitly allows certain weapons or a mobilization base, continuing developments in technology will make armament, as well as disarmament, a proper topic of discussion and continuing negotiation.

The essential requirement is for some stable situation of "rearmament parity." If disarmament is to be durable, it must be apparent that the disadvantages of being behind in case an arms race should resume are not too great and that, in the face of ambiguous evidence of clandestine rearmament or overt evidence of imminent rearmament, nations can react without haste. The straightforward elimination of so-called "military production facilities" might, by sheer coincidence, provide the stability; but stability is more likely if there is a deliberately designed system of "stable equal readiness for rearmament." It is impossible to eliminate the ability to rearm; one can only hope to stretch the time required to reach, from the word "go," any specified level of rearmament. The problem is not *whether* to leave a mobilization base for rearmament, but what kind.

It is not certain that maximizing the time required to rearm is a way to deter it. Lengthening the racecourse does not necessarily lessen the incentive to be first under the wire. But it may reduce the advantage of a small head-start; it may allow time to renegotiate before the race has too much momentum; and it may reduce the confidence of a fast starter that he could win if he called for a race.

If rearmament is undertaken to improve mutual deterrence, not to achieve offensive superiority, it may not matter whether some nations fall behind. The leader will not necessarily race as fast as he can; for if he does, other nations may have to regard his behavior as a declaration of war and to respond accordingly. If a low-grade war of nuclear reprisal is within the capability of some laggard in the rearmament race, he may feel obliged to initiate such a war to disrupt another's rearmament; thus rearmament could lead to pre-emptive action and trigger a war. On the other hand, this prospect may help deter rearmament itself.

The likelihood of war, then, depends on the character of the disarmament. If mobilization potentials are such that a head-start is not decisive and the racecourse is long, preemptive action may be delayed until motives are clear. This, however, presents a dilemma analogous to that of deterring limited war today: the smaller the fear that rearmament will precipitate general war, the smaller the inhibition on rearmament.

Important elements for stability in a disarmed world would be the dispersal and duplication of standby facilities for rearmament and of reserve personnel or cadres around which rearmament can be mobilized. Dispersal is important because of the interaction between rearmament and war itself. If a nation can achieve just enough production of weapons to disrupt its opponent's rearmament, it may gain a decisive advantage. Once the race is on, a few easily-located facilities for producing nuclear weapons might invite a "preventive" and very limited war. If instead there were, say, scores or hundreds of laboratories able to produce unconventional weapons and if their destruction would require substantial military capabilities, there might be less incentive on one side to acquire and exploit a small advantage and less fear on the other of falling a little behind and being taken advantage of.

Nations are now willing to threaten war; in a disarmed world they certainly might threaten rearmament. The agreement itself would certainly have to be renegotiated from time to time, or continuously; and, just as a threat of "no sale" hangs over the head of commercial traders, so will the threat of rearmament hang over the heads of negotiators. The main sanction on the negotiations will be that, in the absence of a satisfactory agreement, nations may take unilateral steps for their own security or take steps to put pressure on others.

Attitudes toward rearmament

THE terms of an agreement must take into account what the attitude toward rearmament would be in the disarmed world. One approach would be that any overt rearmament would be a mortal sin, a total failure of the disarmament process, a contingency that can neither be planned for nor discussed coolly within countries or between governments. Alternatively, rearmament might be viewed as we view war now—as a tragedy and failure of policy, but a tragedy that can occur, that can even occur from motives of self-defense, that can perhaps be limited and contained, and that need not signal the termination of all efforts at settlement and reconciliation.

The first attitude, which would try to insulate rearmament from the cold war and deprecate any planning for the contingency of rearmament, might be preferable if it could promise to create sufficiently strong inhibitions. If, instead, we have to expect—as surely we do—lapses under even the most ideal disarmament scheme, it is better to plan for such contingencies and to create the expectation that occasional lapses need not trigger a real arms race or the full fury of war itself. We cannot have it both ways. For if we recognize "limited rearmament" as a possibility and prepare for "limited responses" against it, we take some of the curse off rearmament, just as plans for limited war seem to legitimize war. This is a genuine dilemma.

Rearmament has other dimensions than speed and volume. We should distinguish between rearmament aimed at stable deterrence and rearmament aimed at brinkmanship or war. In this country we would certainly want to have careful rearmament plans so that, in the event we found ourselves unavoidably drawn into a renewed arms race, our actions would be consistent with deterrence of war and with an effort to slow down the pace of rearmament. The further rearmament goes and the more unstable the environment which it creates, the harder it will be to get back to the business of disarmament if we wish to.

It will also make a difference whether military and strategic planning is permitted and expected or frowned on. The dilemma is that stability will require careful planning of a kind inconsistent with the philosophy that military planning is illegal, immoral and a sign of evil intent. If nations suddenly awoke to rearmament dangers of which they had not been aware, their response might be more undisciplined and more unstable in the absence of military planning than if vigilance had been deliberately maintained.

It should not be expected that reduced tensions will be the natural consequence of a disarmament agreement. Not everyone will be confident that disarmament provides a viable military environment or promises the political atmosphere most conducive to peace and good relations. It is hard to believe that any sober person under any conceivable world arrangement could come to believe with confidence that war had at last been banished from human affairs until there had been at the very least some decades of experience. There will be surprises, rumors and sharp misunderstandings. Even if something that looks like "general and complete disarmament" is achieved, it is not out of the question that responsible governments might decide that international apprehensions would be reduced if they possessed more secure, more diversified and more professionally organized mobilization bases or weapon systems, with more freedom to improve them, drill them and discuss the strategy of their use.

It is even conceivable that a "rearmament agreement" would be negotiated in the interest of reducing tensions, the likelihood of war, the scope for "rearmament blackmail," the Nth-country problem, and perhaps even the economic costs of preparedness. It might be that moderate though expensive modern weapon systems, professionally organized and segregated from the main population centres, would provide less—not more—military interference in everyday life than a "total" disarmament agreement under which every commercial pilot carried emergency mobilization instructions in his briefcase. In any event, a decision on total disarmament, taken jointly by the major powers, would not bring an end to arguments about arms control.

An international military authority

SOME kind of international authority is generally proposed as part of an agreement on total disarmament. If militarily superior to any combination of national forces, an international force implies (or is) some form of world government. To call such an arrangement "disarmament" is about as oblique as to call the Constitution of the United States "a Treaty for Uniform Currency and Interstate Commerce." The authors of the Federalist Papers were under no illusion as to the far-reaching character of the institution they were discussing, and we should not be either. Here, however, we can focus only on those aspects of an International Force that directly affect the military environment.

One concept deserves mention in passing: that the projected police force should aim to control persons rather than nations. Its weapons would be squad cars, tear gas and pistols; its intelligence system would be phone taps, lie detectors and detectives; its mission would be to arrest people, not to threaten war on governments. Here, however, we shall concentrate on the concept of an International Force to police nations—and all nations, not just small ones. The most intriguing questions are those that relate to the Force's technique or strategy for deterring and containing the former nuclear powers.

The mission of the Force would be to police the world against war and rearmament. It might be authorized only to stop war; but some kinds of rearmament would be clear signals of war, obliging the Force to take action. There might be, explicitly or implicitly, a distinction between the kinds of rearmament that call for intervention and the kinds that are not hostile.

The operations of the Force raise a number of questions. Should it try to contain aggression locally, or to invade the aggressor countries (or all parties to the conflict) and to disable them militarily? Should it use long-range strategic weapons to disable the country militarily? Should it rely on the threat of massive punitive retaliation? Should it use the threat or, if necessary, the practice of limited nuclear reprisal as a coercive technique? In the case of rearmament, the choices would include invasion or threats of invasion, strategic warfare, reprisal or the threat of reprisal; "containment" could not forestall rearmament unless the country were vulnerable to blockade.

Is the Force intended to do the job itself or to head a worldwide alliance against transgressors? In case of aggression, is the victim to participate in his own defense? If the Indians take Tibet, or the Chinese encourage armed homesteading in Siberia, the Force would have to possess great manpower unless it was prepared to rely on nuclear weapons. A Force could not be maintained on a scale sufficient to "contain" such excursions by a nation with a large population unless it relied on the sudden mobilization of the rest of the world or on superior weaponry—nuclear weapons if the defense is to be confined to the area of incursion. But the use of such weapons to defend, for example, South Viet Nam against Chinese infiltrators, Western Europe against the Soviet bloc, East Germany against West Germany or Cuba against the United States, would be subject to the ordinary difficulties of employing nuclear weapons in populated areas. A country threatened by invasion might rather capitulate than be defended in that fashion. Moreover, the Force might require logistical facilities, infrastructure and occasional large-scale manoeuvres in areas where it expects to be called upon. Keeping large forces stationed permanently along the Iron Curtain is a possibility, but not one that brings with it all the psychological benefits hoped for from disarmament.

A sizeable intervention of the Force between

major powers is not, of course, something to be expected often in a disarmed world. Nevertheless, if the Force is conceived of as superseding Soviet and American reliance on their own nuclear capabilities, it needs to have some plausible capability to meet large-scale aggression; if it hasn't, the major powers may still be deterred, but it is not the Force that deters them.

A capability for massive or measured nuclear punishment is probably the easiest attribute with which to equip the Force. But it is not evident that the Force could solve the problems of "credibility" or of collective decision any better than can the United States alone or NATO collectively at the present time. This does not mean that it could not solve them— just that they are not automatically solved when a treaty is signed. If the Force is itself stateless, it may have no "homeland" against which counterreprisal could be threatened by a transgressor nation; but if it is at all civilized, it will not be wholly immune to the counter-deterrent threats of a transgressor to create civil damage in other countries. These could be either explicit threats of reprisal or implicit threats of civil destruction collateral to the bombardment of the Force's own mobilization base. (The Force presumably produces or procures its weaponry in the industrial nations, and cannot be entirely housed in Antarctica, on the high seas or in outer space.)

If it should appear technically impossible to police the complete elimination of nuclear weapons, then we should have to assume that at least minimal stockpiles had been retained by the major powers. In that case, the Force might not be a great deal more than one additional deterrent force; it would not enjoy the military monopoly generally envisaged.

One concept needs to be disposed of—that the Force should be strong enough to defeat a coalition of aggressors but not so strong as to impose its will against universal opposition. Even if the world had only the weapons of Napoleon, the attempt to calculate such a delicate power balance would seem impossible. With concepts like pre-emption, retaliation and nuclear blackmail, any arithmetical solution is out of the question.

The knottiest strategic problem for an International Force would be to halt the unilateral rearmament of a major country. The credibility of its threat to employ nuclear weapons whenever some country renounces the agreement and begins to rearm itself would seem to be very low indeed.

The kind of rearmament would make a difference. If a major country openly arrived at a political decision to abandon the agreement and to recover the security it felt it had lost by starting to build a merely retaliatory capability and sizeable home-defense forces, it is hard to envisage a civilized International Force using weapons of mass destruction on a large scale to stop it. Limited nuclear reprisals might be undertaken in an effort to discourage the transgressor from his purpose. But unless the rearmament program is accompanied by some overt aggressive moves, perhaps in limited war, the cool and restrained introduction of nuclear or other unconventional weapons into the country's population centres does not seem plausible, unless non-lethal chemical or biological weapons could be used.

Invasion might offer a more plausible sanction, perhaps with paratroops armed with small nuclear weapons for their own defense; their objective would be to paralyze the transgressor's government and mobilization. But if this should be considered the most feasible technique for preventing rearmament, we have to consider two implications. We have provided the Force a bloodless way of taking over national governments. And a pre-emptive invasion of this kind might require the Force to act with a speed and secrecy inconsistent with political safeguards.

There is also the question of what kinds of rearmament or political activity leading to rearmament should precipitate occupation by the Force. In our country, could the Republicans or Democrats campaign on a rearmament platform, go to the polls and win, wait to be inaugurated, denounce the agreement, and begin orderly rearmament? If the Force intervenes, should it do so after rearmament is begun, or after a party has introduced a rearmament resolution in Congress? The illustration suggests that one function of the Force, or the political body behind it, would be to attempt first to negotiate with a potential rearming country rather than to intervene abruptly at some point in these developments.

Again, the character of rearmament would make a difference. Suppose the President presented a well-designed plan to build an obviously second-strike retaliatory force of poor pre-emptive capability against either the International Force or other countries, but relatively secure from attack. If he justified it on the grounds that the current military environment was susceptible to sudden overturn by technological developments, political upheavals, irrepressible international antagonisms, the impotence of the Force for decisive intervention, the corruption or subversion of the Force, or other such reasons, then the authorization of a drastic intervention by the Force in the United States would be less likely than if the President ordered a crash program to assemble nuclear weapons, trained crews and long-range aircraft. It would make a considerable difference, too, whether rearmament occurred at a time of crisis, perhaps with a war going on, or in calmer times.

The point of all this is simply that even an International Military Authority with an acknowledged sole right in the possession of major weapons will have strategic problems that are not easy. This is, of course, aside from the even more severe problems of political control of the "executive branch" and "military establishment" of the world governing body. If we hope to turn all our international disputes over to a formal procedure of adjudication and to rely on an international military bureaucracy to enforce decisions, we are simply longing for government without politics. We are hoping for the luxury, which most of us enjoy municipally, of turning over our dirtiest jobs— especially those that require strong nerves— to some specialized employees. That works fairly well for burglary, but not so well for school integration, general strikes or Algerian independence. We may achieve it if we create a sufficiently potent and despotic ruling force; but then some of us would have to turn around and start plotting civil war, and the Force's strategic problems would be only beginning.

THIS is not an essay against disarmament, even "total disarmament." It is simply a warning against the notion that there is any once-for-all solution to the problems of world peace and government. It is against the notion that if only disarmament is "total" enough, we can forget about deterrence and all that. It is against the notion that under "total" disarmament there is no military potential to be controlled, balanced or stabilized.

There should be no divorce between deterrence and disarmament. If disarmament is to work, it has got to improve deterrence and to stabilize deterrence. Until a much greater community of interest exists in the world than is likely in this generation, war will have to be made unprofitable. It cannot be made impossible.

It is sometimes argued that to perpetuate military deterrence is to settle for a peace based on fear. But the implied contrast between arms control and total disarmament is not persuasive. What would deter rearmament in a disarmed world, or small wars that may escalate into large ones, must be the apprehension of a resumed arms race and war. The extent of the "fear" involved in any arrangement—total disarmament, negotiated mutual deterrence, or anything else—is a function of confidence. If the consequences of transgression are plainly bad—bad for all parties, and little dependent on who transgresses first—we can take the consequences for granted and call it a "balance of prudence." What keeps us from stepping off a train before it stops is not "fear"; we just know better.

Notes

1. Deterrence being largely a matter of credibility, it might not always be an advantage to have it believed that one is complying with the prohibition on nuclear weapons. At the slightest suspicion that others might be initiating preparations, a government might prefer to hint that it was already prepared. A small nuclear capability might be used to demonstrate a larger professed capability.

2. The Chinese civil war of 1948–49 may illustrate how extensive a war can be fought with poor weaponry and primitive logistical support. Or the American Civil War.

James E. King, Jr.

Arms control and United States security

Purpose and assumptions

THE OBJECTIVE HERE is to present for arms control a possible role consistent with the analysis of the United States security problem developed in the preceding sections. It is first necessary, however, to identify the sense in which the phrase "arms control" will be employed, and to make explicit certain assumptions that will prevail throughout the discussion.

The term "arms control" will be interpreted to mean explicit international agreements based upon a recognized common interest in two purposes: (1) to reduce the likelihood of war, and (2) if that fails, to diminish the violence in any war. It need not be assumed, however, that because there is a community of basic interest the parties to the arms control negotiations will forbear to seek unilateral political and military gains from them. It is even possible that one of them will enter into an agreement with the deliberate intention of evading it later. There can be an acknowledged common interest without full mutual trust. Nevertheless, if the negotiations are to succeed, it is reasonable to suppose that both sides must make concessions.

The possible nature of these concessions was suggested in the last section. It is an assumption (necessary to the case for arms control) that (1) both sides will recognize the improvement in stability as the deterrent strategic forces become less vulnerable, and (2) they will prefer to seek their security in safeguarding that improvement rather than in an attempt to reverse it by reinstating the first strike advantage. But neither side can afford to do this without assurances that the other is doing it too.

Specifically, if the United States is to exercise restraint by not trying to build a decisive counterforce posture, we need more assurance than our current information sources can afford us that the Russians are not taking advantage of our restraint to build a counterforce system that will endanger our deterrent. Presumably the Russians need not be concerned to the same degree about the failure of *their* sources of information to alert them to our actions in time to permit them to take remedial measures. Consequently, the United States' concession to the Soviet Union may be somewhat different from the Soviet concession to the United States.

What is it we have to concede? The answer is that *we can abandon our intention, or hope, of achieving a position of predominance that would enable us to impose stability.* It is well that this be stated bluntly, and without qualification, to avoid misunderstanding. It has been explained that counterforce may be an essential of the stability built upon mutual deterrence. The question where we should or can stop (how much counterforce is enough?) has been described as perhaps the most difficult to answer if we intend to accept and support the fortuitous stability. There will be great pressures to push onward, at the very least to achieve a margin of safety. If we do, we must expect the Russians to follow, compounding the arms race, and hastening the return of a more unstable situation. If we do not, we risk being caught short either by Communist improvement and expansion of which we have not been warned in time, or by some unforeseen technological development. Arms control may give us the requisite assurance to justify these risks.

Why should the Russians accept as a con-

Reprinted from Louis Henkin, ed., *Arms Control: Issues for the Public*, by The American Assembly, Columbia University, N.Y., by permission of Prentice-Hall, Inc., Englewood Cliffs, N.J., 1961, pp. 96–109.

cession this disavowal of our intention, if the openness of our society gives them ready access to all the information they need to assess our intentions? Perhaps they will not. It is always possible, even probable, that they would regard the exchange of inspection rights as no bargain. But it is also possible they will accept.

Despite their sanguine claims regarding their own economic progress, there is little doubt that the Russian leaders are fully aware of the superiority of United States industrial power. Our capacity to produce weapons when fully mobilized, proved in two world wars, must always be prominent in their calculations. At the same time, the chances are that the Kremlin is nearly overwhelmed by the plethora of information, much of it conflicting, that comes from the United States. It must surely be exceedingly difficult for the Russians to assess our intentions or even our capabilities.

For example, testimony before the committees of Congress on defense appropriations is normally contradictory. In and out of government, our own experts arrive at opposite conclusions after reading this testimony, even when they have access to the classified material upon which it is based. Further, as long as we continue to support costly armaments, both the allegations of danger to our security that would follow a reduction of expenditures, and, on the other hand, the awesome threat of our weapons, are sure to receive sensational publicity. That is the way our democracy works. For these reasons, the Soviet Union and its bloc might conceivably welcome more comprehensible information regarding our real intentions. And this they might receive if they were permitted to determine (within limits) what items of information they need, and if there were inspection procedures capable of assuring them they were getting this information.

The first assumption of this examination of arms control, then, is that both sides (all parties) must explicitly abandon the effort to achieve an overwhelming offensive capability for their long-range nuclear strike forces. The second assumption is that it is not possible to abolish nuclear weapons, by agreement or otherwise. The science and technology that builds them cannot be unlearned, and those already built can be too easily hidden.

Arms control incorporates at least three distinct elements. *First*, there is the agreement itself, expressing the intentions of the parties. *Second*, there are procedures to assure each of the parties that the others are complying with the terms of the agreement. *Third*, there are incentives to dispose the parties to comply with the terms of the agreement and sanctions, to deal with violations if they occur, which also have a deterrent effect.

The succeeding sections of this part will be devoted to these three elements in arms control arrangements. Major emphasis will be given to the objects of control in a broad sense—i.e., the intentions of the parties to agreement— because these bear most directly upon the planning of United States security. The problems of inspection, taken up in another chapter will be noted only to the extent necessary to ensure that their importance is recognized. The final section will examine briefly the question of incentives and sanctions.

Accidental war as an object of control

CERTAIN unilateral safeguards against war by technical accident, if matched by the other side, might become tacit agreements. A major return to be expected from the decline in the first-strike advantage is a diminution of the risk of war that may erupt from postures provocative of a preventive or "pre-emptive" war. It would be sensible to use arms control measures to formalize certain of these unilateral measures and tacit agreements (though some of them probably would not lend themselves to incorporation in a formal agreement). Many suggestions have been made that would go beyond this. Most of these involve arrangements to exchange information, or rather assurances, regarding intentions at certain critical moments. Some of these proposals are possibly more ingenious than practical. One such is the idea of direct communications between SAC and the Soviet missile command. The more radical ones, it may be hoped, will seem less attractive as the deterrent force becomes less vulnerable. At any rate, the role of arms control as conceived here will be directed at safeguarding the resulting improvement in stability rather than at preventing the accidents that gross instability makes possible.

Arms control may not be achievable at all unless there is a marked improvement in stability. Measures to "safeguard against surprise attack," when the great adversaries are relying for security on the mutual first-strike threat, are exceedingly difficult to design, let alone implement. This is not to say that such measures are not worth trying to achieve if that is the best we can do. But if the forecast of probable future developments is sound, arms control negotiations starting now would go badly off the track if aimed at the military environment created by the air power "dominance of the offensive" (i.e., preoccupation with surprise attack) rather than with the missile-centered environment in which the deterrent function is more likely to be "dominant." For one thing, it is unlikely the negotiations could be completed before the situation is changed. Also the nature of the problem in the two cases is quite different. In the first case, arms control must, in effect, "harness the winds" to make a contribution. Experience of past negotiations has shown how nearly impossible this is. In the latter case, arms control must be expected merely to reinforce and safeguard basic trends toward a more stable situation. The best hope for arms control is that this latter may not be impossible.

Control of strategic forces: numbers

MEASURES to limit or to reduce the opposed long-range strike forces, as well as measures to control their character and deployments, may help fulfill the designated role for arms control. The level of strategic armaments bears upon the likelihood of war in various circumstances and upon the level of violence in any war that may occur. Nevertheless, there are ample grounds for caution in approaching the problem of numbers. National armaments may be reduced so low that the resulting temptation to evade the controls may heighten the likelihood of war. Thus, dependence on the controls mounts as the strength of the deterrent forces declines. For example, if the level were set at 10 missiles, the addition of 10 or 15 clandestine missiles could give one side an overwhelming advantage, and tempt it to initiate war. At higher levels, because successful evasion is more difficult, perfection need not be asked of the controls. By the same token, of course, the more confidence the controls inspire, the lower the prudent level of the deterrent forces may be. Further, it is obvious that arms reductions must be carefully ordered and phased so that attractive or provocative invitations to start a war do not emerge from the reduction itself.

As Thomas C. Schelling emphasizes, stability is a desideratum at all levels of armament, if the chance of war is to be minimized. Given the existence of nuclear weapons, and of air

and missile technology (not to say, security forces, militia units, and small arms), even so-called "total" disarmament would require a balance of deterrent factors. And unless there is a great transformation of international relations, including virtual liquidation of the cold war, the requirements imposed upon the control system at very low levels of armament would be inordinately exacting.

For these reasons, if it is to be the function of arms control to safeguard the stability based upon mutual deterrence, proposals to *abolish* the "terror" in the "balance of terror" are clearly out of order. It may be appropriate, nevertheless, to seek early agreement to *limit* the number of long-range missiles (and aircraft) on each side, and thereby to diminish the implicit threat of terror.

In principle, the United States and the Soviet Union might agree to retain an *equal* number of equally protected missiles and manned aircraft to be inspected by the control authority. Then, if the protection in the form of hardening or mobility available to the retained forces were such that more than one attacking weapon must be launched to destroy each one in the deterrent, these forces of the parties to the agreement would be in stalemate. The arrangement would not be stable, however, unless there were reliable controls to make certain no other forces were being kept or developed that might in time produce a counterforce capability effective against the deterrent forces. This problem of forces outside those submitted to control suggests that the possibility of instituting controls on the testing and production necessary to create long-range weapons systems should be explored as perhaps the best approach to the problem of numbers.

Controlling missile testing and production

IN connection with this and similar arms control measures, the compliance procedures might be a combination of reporting and verification. The parties, having agreed to limit their missile development programs, for example, would report their missile activities, and the report would be spot-checked by inspectors. The latter could represent either an international control agency, or the other party or parties to the agreement. The procedures would reflect the principle that each party intends to carry out the terms of the agreement and that its purpose in reporting and submitting its activities to inspection by outsiders is to assure that it is doing so. The procedures would not guarantee that every advance and every missile produced would be made known. Nevertheless, they might be sufficient if they gave all parties assurance that each knew the general character and magnitude of the programs of the others. This might suffice because of the size and complexity of the effort required to create either the counterforce or the active defense that could upset the stability of the deterrent.

In time, and, indeed, from the beginning, if agreement is delayed until the major powers have built and deployed hundreds or even thousands of missiles, a *reduction* in numbers as well as a production cutoff might be desired. Both these objectives pose staggering problems for the architects of inspection systems. These may not be beyond solution if the purpose of the inspection is to enable the power being inspected to assure the other parties that it is actually doing what it has reported, and nothing more, and if the elements of stability in the strategic power balance make it difficult to evade the controls successfully.

Little more will be said about the problems of inspection here. However, it should be stated that no inspection system can be expected to work perfectly. Under comparatively favorable circumstances, such as the anticipated improvement in stability, it may be possible to design inspection systems that will operate within acceptable limits of reliability. If this is not possible, then arms control seems a lost cause in today's world. It is a lost cause, too, if the Communist powers (including Red China) are unwilling or unable, for reasons of domestic or international politics, to enter into inspection arrangements that will satisfy the major security demands of the non-Communist parties to the agreement.

Arms control and local stability

IT has been noted that growing Soviet long-range nuclear power began some years ago to diminish the credibility of United States extended nuclear deterrence as a guarantee of our allies' security, and that the advent of a more stable strategic balance seems calculated to reduce it still more. This is a challenge the United States must face with or without arms control. The primary solution is a more persuasive United States capacity to support its allies in local wars. Nevertheless, there is no reason to overlook the possibility of favorable returns from arms control as applied to the problem of local defense. And there is every reason to be alive to any pitfalls that might be encountered in that application.

It should first, however, be pointed out that *there is no local equivalent of the factors that tend to produce a fortuitous mutual deterrence at the center of East-West conflict.* The reason: the very condition that makes the deterrence of war at the center credible is lacking, namely, the fact that the consequences of such a war seem predictable. In local war the political factors dominate the military, and psychology is more significant than engineering. For these reasons, its consequences cannot be so readily predicted, and, as they are far less likely to spell utter disaster, they cannot be counted on to deter military initiatives.

At one time, the commitment of the United States to nuclear weapons in any local conflict in which it found itself was suggested as an equivalent to the strategic deterrent. But later reflection has caused even early proponents to shy away from this idea. The threat to employ nuclear weapons, considering both the local consequences and the chances of spiraling into global nuclear war, is not sufficiently credible as a deterrent to deserve high confidence. Extended nuclear deterrence must still have some effect, but how much and in what circumstances we do not know. For example, it has not prevented the recurrent crises in Southeast Asia from 1953 to the present, though it may have dampened them by discouraging Red China from intervening more massively and more openly.

A proposal to outlaw the *use* of nuclear weapons for any purpose, offensive or defensive, in any armed conflict engaging forces other than the long-range strategic forces of the major nuclear powers would probably gain wide support. Such a proposal would be unreliable, however, unless the great nuclear powers themselves actively enforced it. A ban on the *possession* of nuclear weapons for local use would also be unreliable: nuclear weapons can be hidden. Nevertheless, a general agreement not to employ nuclear weapons in local conflict, to which the great powers were party, might help to discourage some minor powers from seeking nuclear weapons, or from using them once acquired. A reliable test-ban among all nations capable of building nuclear weapons, in combination with a general treaty banning the transfer of nuclear weapons to governments not now possessing them, would offer additional (though less than perfect) guarantees against their use in localized hostilities.

In the remainder of this discussion, the local security problem will be considered primarily in terms of conventional armaments. The context must be kept in mind. It is United States policy to support the United Nations, a world assembly devoted primarily to the airing and peaceful settlement of conflicts between nations, but with power to keep the peace by force, if necessary, vested in the Security Council. Principally because of the great schism of East and West, but perhaps also because of the stresses and strains inevitable in a world of social and economic revolution, the United Nations Organization has not proved fully equal to the responsibility so hopefully given it. Hence, to meet the challenge of Communist expansion, the United States adopted its postwar policy of "containment," based upon a number of collective defense self-agreements, such as were envisaged by Articles 51 and 52 of the Charter ("inside the Charter but outside the veto,' as Senator Vandenberg said in presenting to the Senate the resolution that made NATO possible.)

The primary purpose of these alliances was to deter the Communist powers from direct aggression against a number of weak (or war-weakened) states along the periphery of Communist-dominated territories. In fact, however, "indirect aggression" based upon subversion and other forms of intervention has been a more serious challenge. United States policies of military and economic aid have been aimed at strengthening these smaller countries against both forms of aggression. But the promise of active military support also is present, and the circumstances are such that to carry out its obligations the United States requires certain military freedoms and the capacity to make use of them, which the Communist powers would most certainly desire to restrict by any arms control agreements to which they were parties. The first of these is freedom to intervene formally, with United States regular forces, against Communist indirect aggression—for example, Communist sponsorship of insurrectionary forces—if deemed necessary to preserve the security of an ally. Second, both for this purpose and in the event of open aggression, the United States must have freedom of physical access to the troublespot. Third, the United States needs the forces, and enough of them, to enable it to come to the aid of its allies.

Our overseas troops and bases contribute to the pattern of deterrence which the United States has made the prime military support of its containment policy. It may be that neither of these will be as important for deterrence as the strategic balance becomes more stable. But the right and the power to maintain forces and bases overseas is important to preserve our capacity to intervene promptly to defend our allies, and may be expected to become even more important as the credibility of extended nuclear deterrence is further eroded.

It is therefore possible to state generally that arms control measures that weaken our ability to intervene locally in support of our allies will be unacceptable, unless the restriction is compensated for by substantial gains in local security. The control measures usually proposed include reduction in force levels and in weapons, "qualitative" weapons controls that would outlaw or sharply restrict so-called offensive weapons the establishment of neutral or demilitarized zones between potentially hostile forces, and bans on overseas bases and stationing of forces (proposed by the Communist powers).

The acceptability of quantitative controls in terms of United States security is complex, if only because qualitative factors must be considered simultaneously. For example, at present, and for the future, *in the absence of effective arms controls*, there appears to be a need to improve the equipment of United States forces appropriate to local defense, and to increase their capacity for prompt movement to the point of need. To facilitate this movement there is, moreover, a requirement for strategic air bases to which troops can be lifted (not corresponding, necessarily, to present overseas SAC bases) and for overseas bases on which equipment and supplies can be pre-positioned. There may also be a need to *increase* the strength of Army and Marine units available for ground defense, as well as the strength of supporting naval and tactical air forces appropriate to local defense operations. This need cannot be readily assessed by an outsider, because much depends upon the possibility of reorganizing the present regular forces in such a way as to make more units available for frontline employment, as well as upon broader plans affecting the mobilization base, including the reserves. But, at least, strengthening the forces available for local employment has been widely recommended by observers concerned about the impact of the decline in extended deterrence upon local stability.

How these qualitative and quantitative requirements might be affected by arms control measures has not been thought through. The numbers of ready forces needed to honor our commitments is not a simple function of troop and weapon strength on the other side, because we have a fixed number of commitments each of which might be assumed to contribute a finite amount to the absolute minimum force needed. Nevertheless, sharp reductions of Communist standing forces might justify reductions in United States counterparts, to the extent that such reductions would diminish the threat of the "massive landpower of the Communist world."

Likewise, "qualitative" (i.e., offensive) weapons controls might be acceptable, provided they affected our forces and their prospective enemies equally—although this would have to be carefully examined in view of the United States practice of relying upon advanced weapons and other equipment to replace manpower (as in the Korean War). In some cases, mutual withdrawal of troops from points of confrontation on territorial borders, and the establishment of inspected zones of demilitarization, might be desirable. Such zones can blunt the threat of local surprise attack by affording the defenders some advance warning. This is, of course, not to endorse all of the various "disengagement" proposals that have been made, specifically for Germany. These plans have political implications beyond the limits of this chapter.

The familiar difficulty with all such proposals in past disarmament negotiations has been the problem of defining and contriving the "parity" to obtain among the forces after the controls are imposed, as well as at various stages while the forces are being reduced to the terminal level. For the reasons already given, this difficulty, as applied to conventional weapons and forces in and affecting the local security situation, may be even more formidable than in the past.

The fact is, of course, that the complex and imperfect balance of a variety of military and political elements that characterizes the current (or initial) situation is indefinable in terms of parity. The Communist powers enjoy a potential superiority of ground and tactical air forces immediately available at most points of contact with the free world, while the United States and its allies have an overwhelming superiority in seapower and a considerable marginal advantage in nuclear weapons, together with substantial capability of local reinforcement if time allows it. Moreover, this intricate balance, which can hardly be described as "stable," is in almost continuous flux, as the credibility of the extended deterrent wanes and as local political changes (as in Laos recently) alter the political stability and self-reliance of our allies. The difficulty of designing a move from an indefinable situation of imperfect balance to a defined situation that is at least not disastrously more unstable, when the elements affecting the balance are so variable and so poorly identified, is a major obstacle to arms control as a means of improving local stability.

The obvious hazards ought not to rule out the attempt to negotiate workable arms control arrangements. Unless the effort is made, we have no way of knowing what accommodations the Communist powers might be willing to enter into. It is conceivable they might accept arrangements we could approve, even at the cost of some sacrifice of their capacity to intimidate the minor powers and to intervene in their affairs. But it must be presumed that they will make such concessions only if they want stability at the level of strategic forces badly enough. . . .

Incentives and sanctions

IT is prudent to assume that at least one, probably more than one, of the parties to any significant arms control agreement will be tempted to evade its restrictions. The motive for evasion may be a sense of insecurity, from fear that the other side may gain an advantage by evading the agreement first. Alternatively, there may be a positive inclination to evade the constraints in order to gain an advantage. In either case, as suggested earlier, the temptation to violate the agreement will imperil the control system only if there is opportunity for successful evasion.

To the extent that intrinsic elements of stability are present in the arms balance, the chance of profitable evasion is lessened. Sustained effort of several years would probably be required to engineer the massive military programs that might nullify the opponent's deterrent. These requirements in terms of resources and time increase the probability that the evasion would be discovered before it could be successful. The risk tends to make evasion unattractive because the opportunity to carry it out is questionable. This is one of the main reasons why arms control is more promising with relatively stable military balance.

Moreover, when this is the situation, reservation of the right of the other parties to withdraw from the agreement if they suspect one party of evading its terms may prove a considerable deterrent to evasion. Here again, time and effort are required to make evasion "pay off". This gives the other powers both opportunity to detect and time to catch up with the evader after detection.

As Robert R. Bowie has suggested, the right of abrogation after due notice but without cause is desirable for another reason. It would enable this country to exert unprovocative pressure (the threat of abrogation) to ensure that the control arrangements are kept reasonably fluid so as not to be outdated by technological change. It might also permit escape from the controls with a minimum of shock to stability if that became necessary.

It would be imprudent to rely upon abrogation alone as a deterrent to evasion, however, even in the early stages when the contribution of the arms control arrangements to security may be marginal. In later stages, when many weapons may have been developed but not produced, dependence on the controls will be increased and the temptation of evasion will grow proportionately. The free societies, those having responsible governments, would find it difficult to abrogate, and thereby to generate an international crisis, unless the evidence of evasion were overwhelming; and by then it might be too late. But even if abrogation were possible in time, it might not serve as an effective deterrent to evasion.

As Fred Charles Iklé has pointed out, the sanctions that uphold arms control agreements will be effective only if each party to the agreement is convinced that it will be worse off if caught evading the agreements than if it observed them. If all the evader had to fear in detection was a return to the pre-agreement situation, he might not be deterred. Also, if much time had passed since the agreements went into effect, it might be impossible for the victims

of evasion to take simple restorative measures, because an entirely new stage might have been reached, potentially at least, in military technology.

The problem of sanctions needs more attention than it has yet received. Iklé and others recommend retributive action that goes beyond merely trying to restore the pre-agreement situation. Because of its questionable credibility the threat of punitive military action cannot be relied upon to deter evasion. The provocation would have to be extreme indeed before any government of a free society would impose military reprisals, and this fact would be known to the evader. The most convincing sanction may be the threat of prompt and substantial increases in the defense budgets of the offended parties. This would impose a tangible penalty upon the evader, forcing him to increase his defense effort and confronting him with a more perilous military situation. The expectation of such a penalty could provide a weighty deterrent to evasion.

In our case, before the arms control treaty is ratified, Congress might be asked to vote a substantial addition to defense expenditures to be made available to the President any time he proclaims that there has been a violation of the agreements sufficiently important to warrant it. There are partial precedents for this in the Formosa Resolution of 1954 and the Middle East Resolution of 1958. In both cases, Congress expressed its support in advance if the President should later find it necessary to employ the armed forces. It would admittedly be more difficult for Congress to authorize in advance a substantial addition (say $50 billion) to the current defense budget. Yet, the unprecedented dependence upon arms control for security ought to be sufficient to justify unprecedented action on the part of Congress.

Obviously this contingency-fund device is not a complete guarantee of security. Every device fails if the standards are set too high. But it could be a considerable deterrent, which, added to other incentives and sanctions, might provide a tolerable degree of security. . . .

Fred C. Iklé

Nth countries and disarmament

THE POSSIBILITY that more and more countries might acquire nuclear weapons—often referred to as the "Nth country" problem—has received a great deal of attention in discussions on disarmament. Concern has been expressed lest this diffusion of nuclear capabilities upset international stability and increase the danger of general war. As a result, many people believe that the "Nth country" problem should receive highest priority in our efforts for arms control measures. Indeed, it has been argued that disarmament might turn out to be impossible unless immediate steps are taken to control this problem.[1]

The high priority assigned to controls against "Nth countries" is based, essentially, on three arguments: (1) that the diffusion of nuclear capabilities presents one of the greatest dangers, (2) that it is feasible to stop this diffusion now, and (3) that it will become increasingly more difficult or impossible to control it later. It is our thesis that each of these arguments must be qualified by a number of counterarguments, so that on balance it becomes more doubtful whether "Nth country" controls must figure so prominently in disarmament policies. But this is not to say that we should be disinterested in controlling the spread of nuclear weapons!

Since the above-listed arguments have been developed cogently in a number of thoughtful writings,[2] we can, for the sake of brevity, confine ourselves mainly to the counterarguments.

The dangers from "Nth countries"

THE most important argument that has been advanced against the diffusion of nuclear capabilities is that this diffusion would increase the probability of a global thermonuclear war. Two explanations have been offered for this argument; we might call them the "statistical theory" and the "catalytic war theory."

According to the "statistical theory" the probability of a global thermonuclear war increases as the number of nuclear powers increases, because (a) the larger the number of these powers, the greater the probability that nuclear weapons will be used in some conflict (both because of more opportunities and a greater chance of irresponsibility); and (b) if nuclear weapons are used in a conflict, the risk of its expanding into a global war is greater than if the conflict remained non-nuclear.[3]

The counterargument, which should be weighed against this proposition, is that the diffusion of nuclear capabilities might make the involvement of major powers in local conflicts appear to be more risky and hence render it less likely. In other words, "Nth country" capabilities might either help to deter local aggression altogether or they might help to isolate local conflicts. Intuitively, one would probably give more weight to the "statistical theory" than to this counterargument, but the case is not as clear-cut and well-proven as it might seem at first brush.

The second theory, the "catalytic war" theory, holds that an "Nth country" might start a global war deliberately through the simulation of an attack by one of the major powers against the other. If the major powers maintain some elementary precautions against such an accidental triggering of a war, the technological requirements for such a strategy will be much greater than commonly assumed in this theory. However, even if an "Nth country"

Reprinted with permission from the *Bulletin of the Atomic Scientists*, December 1960, published by the Educational Foundation for Nuclear Science, Inc., Chicago, pp. 391–394.

possessed the requisite capability (including delivery systems, intelligence information, etc.) its possible motives for "catalyzing" a global war would seem to be outweighed by overwhelming risks: (1) the instigating "Nth country" might not survive the central war, (a) because of the repercussions from world-wide fallout, (b) because it might be on the target list of one of the major powers and suffer direct attack. (2) If one of the major powers emerged as a strong winner, the instigating government would fall under its domination instead of gaining opportunities for aggrandizement. (3) The nuclear weapons might fail to trigger a central war and the instigators might subsequently be discovered and eliminated. (4) The operation might be discovered before it was accomplished, with similar results.[4]

These counterarguments both against the "statistical theory" and against the "catalytic war theory" do not deny that the diffusion of nuclear capabilities might make local nuclear disasters more likely, either in an "Nth country" conflict or as a result of irresponsible action. What they question is the notion that such local disasters would necessarily increase the risk of global war. The more critical factors that determine that risk are the reaction time, the decision-making processes, and the vulnerability of the major powers, all of which are more or less independent of "Nth countries."[5]

Can potential "Nth countries" now be stopped?

THE second argument, which we wish to examine, is that it is feasible to stop the diffusion of nuclear weapons at this time through some arms control measures. What measures have been proposed?

The one most prominently mentioned is an international agreement to stop the testing of nuclear weapons. Both those in favor of a test ban and those opposed have rarely analyzed the actual effect of such a ban on the "Nth country" problem—quite a remarkable short-coming of this long intellectual debate! Here we only wish to examine this link; we will *not* deal with a test ban proper and the various arguments for and against it that have been raised.

The effectiveness of test suspension to curb "Nth country" capabilities is subject to four limitations:

1. Important potential "Nth countries" might simply refuse to accede to the treaty—world opinion not withstanding. There exists no legal, or at least politically feasible, international measure by which the United Nations or any other group of powers could force a country to accede.[6] Some potential nuclear powers might try to wrest unacceptable concessions for their accession to the treaty—especially from countries where domestic political forces demand that the treaty be made universal. For example, in the British Parliament statements have been made that France must accede to the treaty, and in the U.S. Senate the importance of China's accession has often been stressed. How high a price will France or China try to exact for their signature to the treaty?

2. Even if most countries did accede to the treaty, certain nuclear weapons could be developed without testing, and perhaps with good reliability. An "Nth country" might feel confident enough about such weapons, and it could try to convince the world by arguing that the *first* weapons test by the other nuclear powers all seemed to have worked.

3. Certain tests of small weapons might not be detectable by the international inspection mechanism, especially in a large, closed country like China. (This limitation has received a great deal of attention—perhaps excessively in relation to the other limitations.)

4. An irresponsible country could expect that there would be no significant sanction, should its violation be detected. (The present draft treaty does not provide for any sanctions!) Would a Hitler be deterred from breaking a treaty by the risk of an unfavorable reaction of world opinion? We must recall here, that it is precisely the irresponsible governments, not the law-abiding ones, that worry us in the "Nth country" problem.

In spite of all these limitations, however, a test ban might have some inhibiting effect on "Nth country" capabilities by slowing down international competition, so that even aggressive and irresponsible countries might move more slowly. We can hope for such an inhibiting effect, but we can't count on it.

Other possible measures to curb "Nth countries" are subject to similar limitations. The more rigorous the controls, the greater is the accession problem; the more palatable —and hence weaker—the controls, the greater the risk of evasion. The reluctance of many countries to submit to international controls is well-illustrated by India's opposition to the rather mild controls of the International

Atomic Energy Agency. Effective measures against "Nth country" capabilities would have to go much further than these IAEA controls.

In theory, the two major powers in co-operation would of course have the military might to prevent any other nation from developing its nuclear weapons. It has often happened that former opponents joined forces to face a new common enemy. In the present-day reality, however, the basic conflict of interests between the United States and the Soviet Union interferes even with very mild common efforts to control "Nth countries." For one thing, the West suffers from a negotiatory weakness. The more exercised Western statesmen and public opinion become about "Nth country" dangers, the more disinterested can the Soviet negotiators pretend to be.[7] Thus, the West may pay an inordinate price to make some small progress on an ostensibly mutual problem.

Furthermore, in those areas where "Nth country" capabilities are a live issue today, the mutuality of interest is tempered by diametrically opposed political objectives. Since the Communist bloc can use military threats to exert political pressures on Western allies (for instance, the military threats used in official statements regarding Berlin and West Germany), nuclear weapons play a different role among our allies than they would, say, among Warsaw pact countries. Similarly, it would seem to be in the Western interest that nuclear assistance becomes a divisive issue between Moscow and Peking, whereas the Russians would probably like this issue to cause trouble between us and the French.

Despite all these qualifications, a case can be made for a *limited* mutuality of interest between us and the Russians in curbing the spread of nuclear capabilities. But this might express itself more effectively in tacit mutual restraint than in explicit arms control measures. For example, it would seem politically infeasible for the Russians to sign an agreement to withhold nuclear assistance from China, in return, say, for a U.S. commitment to do likewise with regards to West Germany or other allies, for this would impose unacceptable strains on Moscow's relations with Peking. But as long as we do not commit ourselves to give, or not to give, nuclear weapons to our Far Eastern allies, the Russians have a double incentive to remain cautious about giving nuclear assistance to China.

"Nth country" controls

THE third argument which we think should be qualified maintains that the only time to control the spread of nuclear weapons is now, before more than three or four powers possess independent capabilities. It may be true that the progressive diffusion of these weapons is hard to reverse. Or to put it more precisely, it seems likely that a country which possessed nuclear weapons would demand more in return for giving up these weapons than a country that did not yet possess them. And if two countries are hostile to each other, the acquisition of nuclear weapons by one will spur the other to follow suit. But this does not mean that undesirable effects from diffused nuclear capabilities would be beyond control. In fact, it may be easier to control the possible dangers from "Nth countries" when they begin to manifest themselves, than to try to prevent the development of indigenous nuclear capabilities. Manifest dangers would stimulate the mutuality of interest among the major powers more strongly than more potential dangers. Hence, the climate for international control with effective sanctions could become far more favorable than it is today.

The negotiatory prospects, too, need not necessarily deteriorate. It is true that more nations would have to participate in the initial negotiations for nuclear arms controls, rather than in the subsequent negotiations concerning the accession to a finished treaty (which might be just as tough!). This would make life harder for the negotiating teams, but it need not make an agreement less likely. Would a test ban have been facilitated if only the United States and the Soviet Union had been involved? The few agreements bearing on arms control which have recently been concluded—such as the IAEA statute and the Antarctica treaty—typically involved many nations.

The argument that the diffusion of nuclear weapons is irreversible is also based partly on the contention that an agreement to abolish nuclear weapons would become more difficult to control with an increasingly larger number of countries in a position to hide finished weapons. It is certainly true that we know of no method to detect hidden nuclear weapons, and that this would constitute an immense problem if the United States and the Soviet Union tried to set up an inspection scheme to make sure that neither one kept any hidden bombs. The comparatively few weapons that other countries might eventually produce would add little to this problem. Furthermore, it must be remembered that it is by no means certain that clandestine diversion of peaceful nuclear energy programs to weapons production could always be detected, although this task is more manageable than the detection of hidden bombs.

Particular concern has been expressed that irresponsible small or medium powers might create serious international problems to the disadvantage of the major powers. If none of the major powers wants to back up such an irresponsible country and become involved in its conflicts, the threat could readily be controlled with the means now available to international organizations. For example, the United Nations Security Council might be a useful organ to enforce restitution of any gain from an act of local nuclear aggression.[8] A historical precedent for such action may be found in the U.N. settlement of the British-French-Israeli attack on Egypt. The Soviet Union, of course, did not openly cooperate with the United States at that time, but in a sense it consented to the settlement sponsored by the United States and Canada. (It abstained on the vote creating the United Nations Emergency Force.)

In an area where the major powers could not agree on joint international action, the threats from a smaller nuclear power might still be controlled by *regional* arrangements. For example, if a Latin American country threatened a neighboring country with nuclear weapons, the United States would probably not wish to see the Soviet Union enter as a "peacemaker," assuming that the American-Russian conflict would still be the dominant problem at such a time. Given some cooperation from the other hemisphere countries, however, the aggressor could be restrained, or if necessary punished, through an effort of the Organization of American States.

In these two examples we have suggested only the use of international bodies that already exist. It seems reasonable to expect that additional arrangements might be developed, or existing arrangements strengthened, if the irresponsibility or aggressiveness of *independent*

nuclear powers became a serious problem, particularly after nuclear weapons had once been used irresponsibly in a local conflict without direct involvement by the major powers. It is quite likely that the possible diffusion of nuclear capabilities in various regions of the world will require a special effort by the major powers influential in these regions to prevent serious threats to peace. This development, however, need not necessarily result in a net loss for international stability.

To re-emphasize, we do not wish to imply that the possible dangers from "Nth countries" are unimportant. The present nuclear powers have good reason to discourage the proliferation of independent nuclear capabilities. One way to slow it down a little, for example, would be not to assist the spreading of reactor technology since this technology inevitably creates local capabilities that could later be misused to manufacture nuclear bombs.[9] A reduction in this kind of assistance appears more tolerable today than it would have some years ago, since the economic urgency of nuclear power has recently become rather doubtful and the enthusiasm for it in underdeveloped countries has waned.

Progress in world peace and arms control, however, does not become impossible if nuclear weapons should spread to more countries. This is not the last chance to control this problem. On the one hand, there seem to be no politically feasible measures to *stop* the spread of nuclear weapons now (although it can be slowed down). On the other hand, it is not impossible to control the dangers from "Nth countries" as they arise; in fact, such controls later might be more feasible than stopping the spread of weapons technology now. Those who argue for the ease of stopping the spread now, as compared with the difficulties of controlling it later, should not forget that even if it were possible to force all non-nuclear countries into an agreement never to manufacture nuclear weapons, the future enforcement of such an agreement against violators would still depend on the cooperation of the major powers. But given this cooperation, the "Nth country" problem will not be out of control!

Notes

1. Hugh Gaitskell, for example, said: "I view the spread of nuclear weapons to the nations of the world as a prospect fraught with the utmost danger. Unless something is done to stop it I believe that within the next ten years this problem is going to dominate the whole international situation," (Speech at Walsall, June 28, 1959.) And Senator Hubert Hum-

phrey wrote: "If decisive action is not taken soon on agreements to control and curb the weapons of mass destruction, so many countries will possess them that control will no longer be a possibility." (*The Progressive*, October 1959.) Similarly, Hans Morgenthau stated: "If the nuclear armaments race cannot be brought under control before any number of nations will have nuclear weapons, only a miracle will save mankind." (Letter to the *Washington Post*, February 23, 1960.)

2. National Planning Association, *The "Nth Country" Problem and Arms Control*, (1959); Arthur Lee Burns, *Power Politics and the Growing Nuclear Club* (Center of International Studies, Princeton University, 1959); Richard S. Leghorn, "The Problem of Accidental War," *Bulletin of the Atomic Scientists*, June 1958; Howard Simons, "World-Wide Capabilities for Production and Control of Nuclear Weapons," *Daedalus*, Summer 1959; and Denis Healy, "H-bombs for Everybody? The Dangers of Nuclear Plenty," *Commentary*, January 1960.

3. Usually, this "statistical theory" is not spelled out in detail, but advanced more as an intuitive proposition that "Nth countries" would increase the "mathematical chances of war."

4. In spite of frequent references to the "catalytic war theory," these hurdles which the catalyzing" country would have to pass, are rarely discussed. Arthur Lee Burn's study, *The Rationale of Catalytic War* (Center of International Studies, Princeton University, 1959)—its title notwithstanding—does not deal with the nationale of the "catalyzing" government or its possible irrational processes. (This does not detract from the usefulness of Burns' analysis of a situation where several, about equally strong, nuclear powers fear a surprise attack from each other.)

5. To the extent that there is a dependence, it might well work in the other direction: the presence of "Nth countries" might stimulate the major powers to institute more cautious reaction and decision processes.

6. It is remarkable that this fundamental limitation has scarcely been mentioned in public discussions. For example, even the very thoughtful studies of the National Planning Association make no mention of the accession problem. (*Establishing International Control of Nuclear Testing*, pp. 9 and 16, and *The "Nth Country" Problem and Arms Control*, pp. xvi–xvii and 33.) Leo Szilard, in his article "To Stop or Not To Stop" (*Bulletin of the Atomic Scientists*, March 1960), however, did point out that a potential "Nth country" might well demand bombs in return for acceding to a test ban.

7. For example, during the United Nations debate on the IAEA the Soviet representative said: "The Soviet delegation considers that the inspection and control of recipient states, that is to say the underdeveloped countries, can only infringe their sovereign rights and retard . . . peaceful atomic industry. . . . The Soviet Union concludes bilateral agreements on atomic cooperation with other countries on the basis of equality and mutual respect. . . . The agreements contain no conditions referring to control and inspection. . . . " (U.N. General Assembly, October 30, 1958.)

Similarly, on November 20, 1959, the U.N. General Assembly adopted with 70 votes the Irish resolution which recommended that the ten-nation disarmament conference study measures to curb the spread of nuclear weapons. The Soviet bloc, however, abstained (as did France).

8. Since only the present four nuclear powers and Nationalist China have a veto power in the Security Council, a small "Nth country" could not obstruct the U.N. machinery.

9. The restrictions of the IAEA or of bilateral agreements cannot apply to the skills and know-how, only to the materials. And even restrictions on materials might later be violated.

U.S. Arms Control and Disarmament Agency

The economic problems of disarmament

Introduction

THE MOTIVATING FORCE behind the efforts of the United States to achieve general and complete disarmament under effective international control is to save present and future generations from the scourge of war, and to attain for them a more certain and beneficent security.

This basic and vital objective completely overshadows any economic calculations of gain or loss connected with disarmament. Actually, the United States can maintain as high or as low a level of defense expenditures as is deemed necessary for its security. At the same time it is clear that a basic change in our methods of achieving security will have distinct effects on our economy. Any examination of the question of disarmament therefore requires study of its economic impact in order to enlarge our understanding of the policies, programs, and actions required to derive the maximum economic and social benefit from it for ourselves and the rest of mankind.

It must be stressed that the allocation of resources to purely military purposes is not an economically creative process, except in an incidental way. It yields relatively few goods or services which contribute to the enrichment of individual lives or to the growth of the national economy. It prevents or retards the satisfacton of many civilian needs. By the same token, if the world should be fortunate enough to be able to rid itself of the burden of national defense efforts, resources would then be released everywhere which could be devoted to the production of those goods and services which advance man's material, cultural, and spiritual state. This is the basic economic interest of the United States in disarmament, and it is an entirely positive one.

This study of the extent to which the defense effort affects the American economy, and of the economic problems and opportunities which would be encountered under a program of general and complete disarmament is in no sense definitive. This is because there are important gaps in our basic knowledge of detailed facts, and because there is as yet no indication as to the timing, phasing, and duration of the disarmament program which may eventually emerge from international negotiations.

Despite these limitations, it is possible to arrive at several significant conclusions.

1. The current national defense effort of the United States takes about one-tenth of our gross national product and employs somewhat less than that portion of our employed labor force. This allocation of human and material resources must be seen against the background of the vast and costly changes which have been taking place in the technology of arms, and of the tremendous enlargement, geographically and otherwise, in the security requirements of the United States as the leading Power in the Free World. As a component of total economic demand defense expeditures are not of such magnitude that the economy is vitally dependent on them. In fact, the American economy proved itself after World War II, to be very resilient to a considerably greater and more rapid reduction in defense expenditures than would be involved under any disarmament program starting at the present level of armaments.

From the U.S. Reply to the Inquiry of the Secretary General of the UN, EC121(13), September 22, 1961, U.S. Arms Control & Disarmament Agency, Washington, D.C., 1962, pp. 740–762.

2. The currently recognized needs of Americans individually and collectively are so extensive that, if translated into economic demand, they would more than offset the loss of demand resulting from an agreed disarmament program. The factors required to effect this translation of civilian needs into economic demand are well understood. Moreover, there are increasingly refined tools available with which to observe, analyze and influence the development of the economy. Advance planning and sensible policies at all levels of government will be essential to the maintenance of over-all economic activity in the face of progressive elimination of defense demand.

3. Unquestionably, any program of disarmament will in the short and intermediate run give rise to problems of adjustment in all factors of production. However, these adjustment problems—of varying intensity depending on the timing, phasing, and duration of any agreed disarmament program—are not novel to the American economy; quite apart from previous successful adjustments to major changes in defense expenditures, the economy is constantly undergoing adjustment in a wide range of industries as a result of changes in technology and economic demand. Concerted effort on the part of government at all levels and of business and labor, to bring to bear numerous available instruments and, if necessary, to create additional ones, can reduce to a minimum any hardship and waste in the adjustment process under a program for general and complete disarmament.

4. The United States has long recognized that general and complete disarmament would present opportunities for enlarged assistance to less developed countries and has sponsored United Nations resolutions in this sense. However, the United States has not waited for disarmament; it has extended foreign economic aid over the past twenty years on a scale unequalled by any other country. The United Nations, recognizing that added impetus needs to be given in the current decade to economic cooperation for development in underdeveloped countries, has designated the 1960's as the International Decade of Development. The United States, as one of the sponsors of this resolution, will do its part. When and as disarmament is achieved, the American people can be expected to face imaginatively the added challenges and opportunities which this development would hold for the welfare of mankind.

5. In the area of international economic relations, the elimination, as a result of disarmament, of U.S. Government defense-related expenditures abroad, and of defense-related imports of raw materials and other commodities, would have a corrective effect on the U.S. balance of payments deficit. There would probably be a noticeably adverse effect in only a few countries; these effects could be overcome with increased external economic assistance and growth and diversification in the respective economies. The elimination of military-oriented production and trade controls under disarmament would permit more international trade to flow on the basis of comparative advantage.

I. The impact of defense on the national economy

SIZE AND COMPOSITION OF DEFENSE EXPENDITURES

ANNUAL expenditures for goods and services for national defense in the 1955–60 period have consistently accounted for about 9–10 per cent of gross national product in current dollars and have constituted about 86 per cent of total Federal purchases of goods and services.

Of total defense spending in 1960 approximately 35 per cent ($16.0 billion) was for purchases of military equipment, somewhat less than that (15.6 billion) was for military and civilian personnel, about 20 per cent ($9.5 billion) was for purchases of non-military goods and services (such as food for the armed services, office equipment, etc.), about 5 per cent ($2.3 billion) was in the atomic energy field, and less than 5 per cent ($2.1 billion) was devoted to all other purposes, among which construction was the principal item. Research and development are included in various of the above categories.

In the period 1955 to 1960, total defense purchases increased from $39 billion to $45.5 billion in current prices, while declining slightly as a per cent of GNP. Within the total, the shares of expenditures for military equipment, "other goods and services," and atomic energy activities have increased, whereas all other items (personnel expenditures, construction, stockpiling and defense facilities, and miscellaneous) have declined relatively.

In the expenditures for military equipment during the same period, there were major increases for missiles and a considerable decline for aircraft, ordinance and vehicles. Procurement expenditures for electronics and communications also increased.

IMPACT ON EMPLOYMENT

Corresponding to the expenditures on defense, more than 6 million persons were employed in all Federal and industrial defense-related activities in 1960. They represent about 9 per cent of all U.S. employment.

A. *Federal defense-related employment.* Active duty military personnel totaled approximately 2.5 million. Slightly more than 1 million civilians were employed in 1960, in Federal defense-related agencies, principally the Department of Defense, but also including the Atomic Energy Commission, the National Aeronautics and Space Administration, and several smaller organizations. Together these employees represented 47 percent of all Federal civilian employment. It is important to note, however, that employment in defense-related activities in the U.S. government has represented a constantly decreasing share of all U.S. employment, both civilian and military, since 1953, when the Korean hostilities ended.

During the Korean War period, a rapid build-up took place. The number of U.S. military personnel increased from less than 1.5 million in 1950 to 3.6 million in 1952, and employment in Federal civilian defense-related activities also expanded sharply. At the peak in 1952 these two groups combined formed 7.7 per cent of total U.S. employment, public and private.

In every year from 1953 to 1960 a decline occurred both in numbers engaged in defense activities of the Federal Government and in their proportion of total employment. The number of military personnel was less than 2.5 million in 1960, down by more than over one million, and the number of civilian personnel in Federal defense-related agencies was down from over 1.3 million in 1952 to about one million in 1960. Together they represented only slightly more than 5 per cent of total U.S. employment in 1960. In the summer and autumn of 1961, the size of the Armed Forces increased slightly to a total of 2.7 million in October.

B. *Industrial defense-related employment.* It has been estimated that in 1960 approximately 2.6 million persons—5 per cent of all non-agricultural employment—were employed directly and indirectly in supplying goods and services, principally (but not exclusively) military equipment, to the Federal defense-related agencies. This includes employment in industries providing materials, supplies and services such as transportation.

DISTRIBUTION OF DEFENSE GEOGRAPHICALLY AND BY INDUSTRY

A principal characteristic of defense spending in the U.S. is its uneven distribution, geographically and by industry. While no detailed nationwide information is available on the geographic impact of national security programs combined, sufficient evidence is at hand to indicate the areas of greatest concentration. For this purpose, good indicators are employment in the four leading defense-related manufacturing industries in relation to over-all employment, and the disbursement of payrolls in these defense-related industries and in Federal defense-related agencies, in relation to total personal incomes in the areas concerned.

All of the employment in the ordnance industry, over 93 per cent of employment in aircraft and missiles construction, 60 per cent of employment in ship and boat building, and 21 per cent of employment in the electrical machinery industry (38 per cent in radio and communications equipment) was attributable to defense procurement.

Employment in these four manufacturing industries which are most dependent upon defense totaled 1,233,000 in the year 1960. At that time the total, which, of course, includes employment on production not related to defense, represented only about $7\frac{1}{2}$ per cent of all manufacturing employment and less than $2\frac{1}{4}$ per cent of total nonagricultural employment.

These major defense manufacturing industries have a high degree of concentration in certain States and cities. The military establishments and civilian government employment connected with defense are also concentrated to a considerable degree. Not infrequently both are located in the same general area.

Among the areas most affected are Alaska and Hawaii; California, and the State of Washington; the Maryland, Virginia, and District of Columbia complex; certain New England States, notably Connecticut and Massachusetts; some of the less populous mountain States like New Mexico and Utah where the government's defense operations loom large, and some of the

Southern States where there are growing military installations, such as Oklahoma, Kansas, Alabama, Georgia, and South Carolina.

A summary of wages and salaries in the four defense-related industries and in the Federal defense-related agencies in the year 1960 shows that their impact is greatest, relatively, in Alaska and Hawaii, where 29 and 22 per cent of these States' personal income, respectively, is from these sources.[2] Next in order is the State of Virginia, with 15 per cent; and then Washington, Maryland, the District of Columbia, and New Mexico, with 11–12 per cent; and California, Kansas, South Carolina, Georgia and Utah, each with 9–10 per cent.

In actual dollars, the payrolls in the above defense-related activities (including pay of military personnel) are greatest in California, where in 1960 they exceeded $4,250 million; in Texas with almost $1,350 million and in Virginia with over $1 billion. Payments were also very substantial in some of the other larger States, such as New York and Pennsylvania, but the impact of defense expenditures on industries is relatively much smaller than in many of the smaller States listed above.

Excluding the Armed Services, which are deployed in many parts of the world, and considering only employment in the four principal defense-related industries and civilian employment in the Federal defense agencies, a similarly concentrated geographic pattern prevails. About 10 per cent of all nonagricultural employment in five States is provided by these civilian activities, namely in Washington, Alaska, Utah, Virginia, and Connecticut. In another eight States 6 to 9 per cent is provided: California, Maryland, Kansas, New Mexico, Alabama, the District of Columbia, Colorado, and Maine. In Oklahoma, Arizona and Massachusetts the ratio is 5 per cent.

The four defense-related industries are especially important in the less populous States where new installations have developed in what were originally agricultural and trading areas. Kansas, New Mexico, Utah, and Arizona are good examples.

Within these States, certain communities have a notably high concentration of defense-connected activities. Examples are the Los Angeles-Long Beach and San Diego areas in California; the Seattle-Takoma area in Washington; Greater Washington, D.C.; Wichita, Kansas; the Boston-Cambridge area in Massachusetts; Huntsville, Alabama, etc. Smaller areas in which military installations and other

defense activities are concentrated include such cities as Newport, Rhode Island; Portsmouth, New Hampshire; Norfolk, Virginia; and New London, Connecticut. In certain small communities the economy is built almost entirely around specialized plants producing defense materiel or around military bases. Some of them are areas with high and persistent unemployment.

IMPACT ON RESEARCH AND DEVELOPMENT (R&D)

In fiscal year 1960/61, 46 per cent of the national R&D effort was financed by the Department of Defense alone, and when the contributions of NASA and the AEC are counted, the R&D spending of defense-related agencies was 56 per cent of the estimated national total of $14 billion. In addition to work done in government laboratories, the defense agencies paid for better than half of the research undertaken in industry-run laboratories, and about 60 per cent of the work performed by universities and other non-profit institutions. In the industries producing aircraft and parts and communications and other electrical equipment, which account for more than 75 per cent of government research funds spent in industries, R&D spending exceeds 10 per cent of sales, while for all other industries together R&D spending does not exceed 3 per cent.

Another significant characteristic of defense R&D is that it employs more equipment, materials and overhead per scientific personnel than does civilian R&D. Finally, it is clear that defense needs have, in recent years, significantly restricted the availability of R&D scientists and engineers for the civilian sector.

IMPACT ON CIVILIAN EXPENDITURES

Any analysis of the economic impact of defense spending cannot leave out of account the fact that the allocation of substantial financial resources to this sector inevitably involves individual and collective self-denial in others. The large national defense budget has decreased the Federal Government's ability to finance many worthwhile and important non-military programs because of pressures against increasing an already large tax burden. High Federal taxes have tended to limit the ability of State and local governments to pay for basic services and public facilities and have retarded local solutions to such problems as urban blight, inadequate educational facilities, and overburdened mass transportation systems. Finally, the current tax burden has prevented individuals and firms from giving freer rein to the satisfaction of their needs for services. consumer goods, and new capital equipment.

With due regard for the incidental benefits which flow from the defense program to the civilian sector (peaceful uses of military technological development, training of personnel, etc.), this continuous self-denial is substantial, and its implications for our current and future economic and social well-being are incalculable. It is here that the real cost of the defense program is expressed.

II. The problems of adjustment to disarmament

IN considering the problems which must be dealt with if, as, and when an agreed disarmament program permits the American people to reallocate the human and material resources now devoted to defense, two important factors must be taken into account.

CONTINUING EXPENDITURES FOR SECURITY

In the first place, it is clear that even in a disarmed or disarming world resources—possibly substantial ones—must be devoted to the maintenance of security. In this connection it is useful to recall the Joint U.S.-USSR Statement of Agreed Principles for Disarmament Negotiations, of September 20, 1961:

> The program for general and complete disarmament shall ensure that States will have at their disposal only those non-nuclear armaments, forces, facilities, and establishments as are agreed to be necessary to maintain internal order and protect the personal security of citizens; and that States shall support and provide agreed manpower for a UN peace force. (Item Two.)

> All disarmament measures should be implemented from beginning to end under such strict and effective international control as would provide firm assurance that all parties are honoring their obligations. During and after the implementation of general and complete disarmament, the most thorough control should be exercised, the nature and extent of such control depending on the requirements for verification and disarmament measures being carried out. (Item Six.)

> . . . during and after the implementation of the program of general and complete disarmament, there should be taken, in accordance with the principles of the United Nations Charter, the necessary measures to maintain international peace and security, including the obligation of States to place at the disposal of the United Nations agreed manpower necessary for an international peace force to be equipped with agreed types of armaments. Arrangements for the use of this force should ensure that the United Nations can effectively deter or suppress any threat or use of arms in violation of the purposes and principles of the United Nations. (Item Seven.)

It is upon these types of measures that security and world peace will depend under a disarmament program. The United States Disarmament Program of September 25, 1961, expands upon these measures. It foresees the establishment, in Stage I, of an International Disarmament Organization and sets forth its duties. The program also provides for arrangements for the establishment, in Stage II, of a UN peace observation group. In later stages the International Disarmament Organization, the Peace Force and the machinery for the settlement of disputes would all be expanded. In Stage III of the U.S. program national forces are to be limited, the UN Peace Force fully functioning, and arms manufacturing prohibited except for agreed types to supply the UN Force.

The logical conclusion from the foregoing is that the achievement of "general and complete disarmament," while setting a new framework for security and resulting in changes in the instruments and methods for safeguarding security, will not relieve the United States and other nations of the necessity to continue to allocate funds and resources for purposes of international peacekeeping. Indeed, the new forms and instruments of security will have first call on human and material resources which would be released by the elimination of our national military program. To the—at this time unknown—extent that this occurs, it would naturally reduce somewhat the scope of the over-all conversion problem.

TIMING, PHASING, AND DURATION OF DISARMAMENT

The second consideration affecting examination of the economic effects of disarmament is that at this time there is no indication when a disarmament agreement might go into effect, how its incidence on particular defense expenditures would be phased, and how long it would be before the entire process has been concluded. Yet these variable factors have profound effect on the problems of economic adjustment. Thus, a disarmament program phased over a considerable number of years and having no sudden and major impact on any one group of defense expenditures would present different problems of adjustment than would, for example, greatly accelerated or concentrated programs. Likewise, the commencement of a disarmament program at a peak in a business cycle would influence the problem of maintaining over-all demand differently than if significant disarmament began in a cyclical trough.

In the absence of specific details on the timing, phasing, and duration of a disarmament program it is therefore not possible to discuss the problems of adjustment except in general terms.

TWO BASIC PROBLEMS OF ADJUSTMENT

It is important to distinguish between two basic problems of adjustment. The first is to maintain aggregate economic demand in the nation despite more or less substantial and progressive declines in demand from the defense sector. The second is to minimize hardships and waste as the human and material resources now devoted to defense find new uses.

These two problems, while different in nature and in the policy instruments suited to deal with them, are interconnected. Thus, if there is general inadequacy of aggregate demand, it will be more difficult, if not impossible, to overcome the structural problems of transition. On the other hand, if the transition from national defense efforts to general and complete disarmament should be characterized by persistent structural maladjustment, the effect of measures to maintain aggregate demand on output and employment would tend to be dissipated in inflation. With advance planning and sensible policies at all levels of government and on the part of business and labor, it should be possible to master both of these problems satisfactorily.

A. Maintaining aggregate demand

THE PROBLEM

IT is clear that, if not offset, significant and progressive declines in defense spending would reduce the growth rate of economic activity and quite possibly bring about an absolute decline. In the absence of compensating factors, total demand would be reduced by significantly more than the reduction in defense spending. Declining defense spending would be reflected in reduced income for employees of the defense industries and of the industries supplying, directly and indirectly, the defense contractors. Decreases in personal income would be moderated, to some extent automatically, by reduced taxes and increased transfer payments, but, with existing legislation, a dollar reduction in defense spending would cause, directly and indirectly, about a dollar reduction in personal consumption. In addition, the decline in aggregate demand would lead to a reduction in capacity and inventory requirements and thus to some fall in the rate of investment.

In the event of disarmament it would be necessary to encourage, stimulate, or create those offsets which would counteract these negative factors to the maximum extent and absorb the slack in the economy. The nature of the required policies is well understood, and historical experience testifies to the ability of the American economy to respond in a healthy way to major reductions in defense expenditures.

[A discussion of the post-World War II and and the post-Korean War experience has been omitted. A good deal of this material is to be found in the United Nations document, "The Economic and Social Consequences of Disarmament," Chapter 3, under the heading, "The post-war conversion."]

MEETING THE PROBLEM OF AGGREGATE DEMAND

The most important factor to bear in mind in meeting the problem of aggregate demand in the event of a sizeable disarmament program getting under way within the decade is that today and in the foreseeable future there are in the United States as well as in other countries very substantial unmet needs and opportunities which could work as a powerful factor on the economy given the necessary conditions. Many of them will be increasingly met as the decade progresses, whether there is a program for general and complete disarmament or not, but they will not be eliminated; moreover, new needs will become apparent with the passage of time.

Reference has been made to the role of dynamic optimism in our society after World

War II as a positive influence on economic development. It would be hard to imagine that the American people would not respond very positively to an agreed and safeguarded program to substitute an international rule of law and order for the present national security efforts, once the full implications of such a change were understood. The beneficent effect of such a development on the economic plans and actions of the American people, acting individually and through their institutions, would be incalculable.

Even without the psychological stimulus that could be expected from the type of disarmament program which it is the object of our policy to obtain, the American economy does not lack dynamism. It is the strength of the free enterprise system that it not only affords large opportunities for the exercise of inventive genius and economic initiative but in fact inspires them on a large scale. These are among the principal forces which have provided the motive power for the growth of the American economy, and they will certainly contribute significantly to maintaining the momentum of the economy in the event of disarmament.

Government policy will have a vital role in dealing with the problem of aggregate demand. Sensitive response to the particular economic facts and forces prevailing prior to and at the commencement of disarmament, and far-sighted action can contribute strongly to the creation of the conditions which will allow the unmet needs of society to be translated into the kind of economic demand that will—potentially—more than take up the slack caused by the progressive decline in national defense spending. Several powerful tools and instruments are available to the Federal Government and, to a more limited extent, to State and local governments, for this purpose.

An important and obvious tool for action to translate civilian needs into economic demand is reduction in Federal tax schedules. Such reductions would, of course, make more funds available to individuals and businesses. Some of the funds would go into investment, others would go into consumption. Federal tax reductions would also leave additional room for State and local taxes to finance new or enlarged public programs and investments in such areas as education, social services, recreational facilities, water supply, waste disposal, and so forth, which in the aggregate, could go far in helping to offset the decline in defense spending. In any case, Federal tax reductions would

stimulate total economic demand, though, depending on the precise measures adopted, in different ways and with different time impacts.

Another significant possibility is to expand public civilian expenditures, which, as noted, have tended to be confined within relatively narrow limits as a result of the major need for funds for the defense effort, to the detriment of numerous areas where our growing population and other factors have intensified the need for increased governmental activity.

The fields of resource development and conservation, civil aviation, education, public health and public works afford numerous possibilities for the Federal Government in this regard. Federal expenditures for civilian atomic energy development and space exploration could also be readily expanded to the benefit of present and future generations.

State and local governments could expand their programs in such fields as urban development, public housing, school and hospital construction, roads and other public works: increased Federal loans and grants to State and local governments for these purposes could have significant beneficial effect.

Undoubtedly there would also be expanded transfer payments by the Federal Government, some of which would occur automatically under existing laws. By supporting income levels, they would have a stabilizing effect on total demand. Included among possibilities under this heading are such measures as unemployment compensation, various types of retirement benefits, mustering-out pay to military personnel, education and training grants and other similar programs discussed in another chapter, in some cases requiring new legislation in order to provide new or improved coverage.

The Federal Government also has direct control of a series of loan programs to individuals and business firms which would be beneficially employed in an integrated economic program to provide offsets to declining military expenditures.

Aid to less developed countries, which is discussed in another chapter, would afford another meaningful opportunity for expansion of Federal civilian expenditures.

In this connection it is pertinent to note that in the post-World War II years the total purchases of non-defense goods and services by government at all levels actually were lower, on a per capita basis and also as a per cent of gross national product, than in 1939.

A third tool is monetary policy. Measures to

lower interest rates, to reduce reserve requirements, to increase liquidity could act as a stimulant to the economy which would be felt particularly in such areas as industrial investment and housing. They would, of course, be taken in the context of our international balance of payments and other factors.

All of these tools were used successfully after World War II and some after the Korean War. There is no reason why they should not be used, with maximum impact, again. In this connection it is of interest to note the President's recent request to Congress for standby authority to accelerate public improvement programs, to implement income tax reductions, and to provide extended unemployment compensation payments in the event of threatening recession. Adoption of this proposal would, of course, be most helpful in dealing with substantial declines in defense spending under a disarmament program.

Determination of the precise combination of measures to support aggregate demand under a disarmament program is in itself a complex process requiring advance planning, continuing evaluation of economic developments and likely economic impacts, and political decision. As noted at the beginning of this chapter, the success of any program of maintaining demand will also be dependent on the success of parallel measures to deal with any structural problems such as regional or local concentration of defense activities, and industry and manpower specialization.

At every step there will be the problem of making choices, of striking the most appropriate balance as between numerous possible courses of action, each of which will have a different impact on the economy. Thus, either an increase in government expenditures for goods and services or a decrease in taxes increases aggregate demand and brings additional resources into employment. Either action has a multiplier effect which is greater than its initial impact. The initial expenditures—increased private consumption or investment in the case of a tax cut, increased school or road construction, for example, in the case of a rise in government outlays—create additional income which, in turn, is spent and re-spent. Thus either tax reduction or increased government spending indirectly stimulates almost all categories of private demand, and, in particular private consumption. But the direct effect of a tax reduction is to employ resources for private consumption or investment, while the direct effect of government spending is to employ resources on production of public goods and services.

The proper balance between tax reduction and increased public civilian expenditures will involve an economic and political evaluation of the relative priorities of the goods and services which would be purchased by households and businesses if their incomes were greater—food, houses, automobiles, medical services, college education, machine tools—as against those of public goods—school construction, highways, resource conservation and development, public health, urban renewal. Similarly, the proper balance between reduced personal and excise taxes on the one hand and reduced profits taxes and a policy of easy money on the other will be governed, generally, by the relative importance accorded respectively to consumption and investment.

An element of uncertainty in a situation involving the systematic elimination of the current pattern of military expenditures over a period of time would be the precise reaction of private consumption, and of private investment in plant and equipment and inventories, to the decline in defense orders and to the compensating policies. What fraction of tax reductions on personal incomes would in fact go into consumption? What lags would be involved? How would inventories and investment develop in different industries? These are some of the imponderables to which the answers will not be readily available. However, the very fact that the timing, phasing and likely duration of a disarmament program would be known well in advance to policymakers places the whole problem of providing for adequate demand offsets on a considerably more certain and favorable basis than is normally available for the development of countercyclical policy. Utilization of this favorable circumstance by the Federal Government and, as appropriate, by State and local governments to prepare in advance the desirable offsetting measures in the fields of taxation, public expenditures, and monetary policy, would have a most beneficial effect on public confidence that the economic and social benefits of disarmament would be realized. This in itself would be a potent factor making for success in the adjustment process.

B. Overcoming structural problems

THE PROBLEM

Any considerable change in the composition of final demand is bound to require some degree of structural adjustment as regards both manpower and physical facilities, and it may entail geographic redistribution of production and related activities. Actually the economy is constantly experiencing structural changes as a result of technological developments, the introduction of new products and services, population developments, and other factors. Taken together, these changes over a period of time are substantial, and while it cannot be said that they have always proceeded with a minimum of hardship and waste, nevertheless it is clear that they have not prevented the attainment of substantial growth in the economy.

Disarmament could, and probably would, seriously add to the problems of structural adjustment. The likely quantitative effect of disarmament is difficult to predict with any precision at this time. Certainly the timing, phasing, and duration of a disarmament program would be important factors—the more gradual the process, the easier the required shift in resources to civilian demand. Another factor is the nature and composition of the civilian demand that will emerge as the financial burden of the national defense program is lifted; if it is such as to be readily satisfied to a large extent by the kinds of resources being released from the defense effort, the problem of adjustment will be minimal.

Although more information is required on the precise composition and distribution of resources now serving defense effort, directly and indirectly, and on the other factors noted above, it is evident that disarmament would require considerable adjustment, geographically occupationally, and as regards actual production. One of the principal characteristics of the current defense effort is the relatively high concentration of its economic impact geographically and by industry. Moreover, a large share of defense work is in the hands of specialized defense contractors whose product and expertise may not be readily adaptable to production for a civilian market. After World War II many firms which had stressed military production during the conflict had little difficulty in reconverting. It is not clear whether the same easy shift would be possible under present conditions on as wide a scale.

Under the circumstances disarmament will require some shifting of manpower to new industries, occupations, and possibly even to new locations. Many plants will have to convert to new lines of production, and to the extent that such conversion on existing sites is not possible or desirable, relocations and in some cases liquidations may be in order; also, it is to be expected that new industries will have to be encouraged to establish themselves in many areas where defense production is now concentrated.

These structural adjustments would be faced in the context of the sizeable increase in the labor force and in automation which is expected to develop over the coming years.

It will be desirable to bend every effort to reduce the friction in the process of adjustment to a minimum, in order to minimize hardship and waste, and as another means of maximizing the benefits of disarmament. There are several significant instruments and factors as well as a growing body of experience which will be helpful in this connection.

AREA REDEVELOPMENT

Increasing attention has been given by government, labor, and business to the problem of depressed areas which is directly relevant to the problem of adjusting to disarmament because of the heavy geographic concentration of the defense effort. Thousands of local communities have over the years established development and promotional agencies to attract business, apart from the State development commissions in virtually every State. Many have organized development loan funds to buy land and erect buildings and to assist potential newcomers in other ways. Increasing awareness of the need for coordinated action to meet specific local problems is evident. Furthermore, in dealing with this problem, as with others, the initiative of American entrepreneurs in our free enterprise system is an invaluable asset.

Recognition that redevelopment of "depressed areas" which already exist in our country was a matter transcending local interest led to the adoption of the Federal Area Redevelopment Act under which the Federal Government seeks to assist local and State groups in the economic development of areas with high and persistent unemployment. In addition to the support of retraining programs which will be discussed below, this aid takes the form of technical assistance for planning economic redevelopment and Federal participation, if needed, in low-rate loans for land and buildings for industrial or commercial enterprises and for needed public facilities. One of the principal achievements of this new legislation has been the encouragement of hundreds of communities to develop Overall Economic Development Plans. These communities are thus better able to cope with any kind of economic adjustment that may be necessary—whether it be due to armament cutbacks, trade impacts, automation, depletion of natural resources, or other causes.

The deactivation of defense installations in the course of a disarmament program will create specific redevelopment situations, which will be of major proportions where the installations are the economic mainstay of particular communities. It will no doubt be found that many of these facilities can be adapted to civilian uses in such fields as education, health, research, recreation and industry. Such adaptation will benefit from adequate and coordinated advance planning by the local communities, the Federal Government, and other interested elements; it could make a real contribution not only to the life of the affected communities, but also in filling some of the over-all needs for plant and equipment which are discussed in another chapter.

In this connection it is pertinent to note that since the beginning of 1961 the Federal Government has concerned itself specifically with the economic adjustment problems attendant upon the deactivation of defense installations—whether in the so-called depressed areas or not—in connection with the changing requirements of our defense programs. Thus, there was established in the Department of Defense a high level position of Economic Adjustment Adviser whose responsibility it is to assist the affected local communities with adjustment measures. Subsequently the President directed the establishment of an interagency committee to advise the Secretary of Defense in this field and bring to bear the experience and instruments available in other parts of the Federal Government. The scope of these arrangements has since been expanded to include economic adjustment to shifts in defense programs.

Experience with area redevelopment to date suggests that solutions are not quick or easy and emphasizes the need for careful appraisal of potential difficulties and for advance planning, as well as coordinated and united action by all elements involved. The practical lessons under the Area Redevelopment Act and the numerous other measures and programs having the same general objective will be invaluable in dealing with such significant local or regional dislocations as may be caused by disarmament.

INDUSTRIAL CONVERSION

In our free enterprise system the task of converting industrial production from defense to civilian uses will in the main rest on the affected firms, responding to the actual and anticipated demands in the market at home and abroad. Here, too, advance planning will go a long way in smoothing and expediting the adjustment process. The problems will not be basically different from those which continually arise in a changing economy. The increasing emphasis which many American firms place on careful analysis of trends and prospects not only in their own markets but in the economy generally, as a basis for their production programs, will be most helpful in meeting the conversion problem in the industrial sector. Many firms will no doubt find it profitable to accelerate their civilian activities in scientific and technical research and development, in some cases readily reallocating facilities and manpower now devoted by them to military work.

Policies and measures which the Federal Government will apply to the termination or cancellation of defense contracts under a progressive disarmament program could be designed with a view to facilitating the adjustment process in the affected firms. There is a considerable body of successful experience in this area in connection with the demobilization at the end of World War II.

The Federal Government could also aid the adjustment process by extending loans and technical assistance to those firms which have a particular need for such support. If the proposed Trade Expansion Act of 1962 is adopted, its provision for loans and technical assistance to businesses adversely affected by imports would provide valuable experience which would be relevant to adjustment problems in industry under disarmament.

ADAPTABILITY OF AMERICAN LABOR

The mobility of the American labor force is one of the nation's assets in adjusting to economic change. This is true whether the need for change arises out of the development of new industrial technology and shifts in civilian demand or whether it is induced by mobilization or disarmament.

Geographically there has been continuous

movement from one area to another in the United States. Many of these moves are to nearby areas, but others are long moves, between States. The increase in population of the three Pacific Coast States from 1940 to 1960 is ample evidence of this shift. California's population rose from 6.9 million to 15.7 million or 128 per cent; and Washington's from 1.7 million to 2.9 million or 64 per cent.

Many American workers also move into and out of the labor force by choice. During the course of a single year, the size of the labor force varies by several million from the seasonal peak in the autumn to the low of employment in the late winter. Most adult men over 25 and under 65, who are able to work, are permanently attached to the labor force. However, millions of adult women, young people, and older people who have retired or can retire from work either do not work or seek work for part of the year. During the course of the year 1960, for example, there were 4,800,000 more people in the labor force in June than in January.

There has also long been substantial movement of workers to higher levels of skill and responsibility, both in the nonagricultural and in the agricultural sector.

Although there are indications that willingness to move has diminished in recent years with the accumulation of a variety of financial assets attached to the community, such as more general homeownership and increased rights to pensions and other benefits associated with seniority in employment in a particular firm, there is still a great deal of shifting both geographically and, to a more limited extent, occupationally. Young people, in particular, are willing to make changes; and the more education they have, the more readily they move.

Analysis of the occupations of the people now engaged directly in the defense effort in the United States—in the armed services, the Federal civilian agencies engaged in national security activities, and the industries producing weapons and other defense material—indicates a relatively high proportion in the professions, and in the skilled occupations. As a group, they are relatively well educated. Moreover, they are generally younger (the median age of male military personnel on active duty was 24.5 years in mid-1960), but still with some experience to count in their favor in finding a job. These characteristics of younger age, higher education, skill and training are assets in readjustment. They should offset to some extent

the problems attendant on the high degree of specialization in much of today's defense effort.

The educational level of military personnel is higher than that of the general population. The Department of Defense has estimated that about two-thirds of the enlisted personnel and more than 99 per cent of the commissioned officers on active duty as of 1960 had a high school education or better. In contrast, only about 60 per cent of the new young workers entering the labor force in the 1950's had completed their high school education. A considerable number of the military personnel receive comprehensive vocational training while in the armed forces. Many enlisted men are trained for occupations for which there is a growing demand in the civilian economy, such as electronics maintenance and repairmen, automotive and aircraft mechanics, construction craftsmen, medical and technical assistants, and draftsmen.

The occupational distribution of employees in defense-related governmental agencies indicates that a considerable number of personnel employed by these agencies is in white-collar occupations, for which the demand is increasing in our economy.

Of the estimated 2.6 million persons employed directly and indirectly in all private industries providing defense goods and services in 1960, it is estimated that over 380,000 were professional and technical workers. Another 545,000 were skilled craftsmen. These proportions are very high relative to the national average, and employment prospects in these occupational fields are expected to expand rapidly over the next decade. On the other hand, over 30 per cent were semi-skilled workers ("operative"), as compared to under 20 per cent for all non-agricultural employment. For this group unemployment rates have been higher than average. Clerical workers, for whom demand is quite good, are in about the same proportion in defense as in all industries, while service workers and laborers—with an even higher rate of unemployment—are relatively less numerous.

OPPORTUNITIES FOR TRAINING AND RETRAINING

Opportunities for training and retraining arise in a variety of ways and from a variety of sources, including industry, local institutions and State and Federal programs. In large part the initiative rests with private individuals and business firms. Individuals voluntarily learn new skills and increase their knowledge by a variety of means; attending school formally or going to special classes in off hours or the evening, taking correspondence courses, learning the job. Private industry has extensive on-the-job training and retraining programs. In fact, most training in the skilled crafts and in many technical occupations is effectively done on the job through apprenticeship and other forms of training. The extent of training programs in industry and the number of people who benefit by them is not known, but some form of induction training is almost universal in large private enterprises, and many have extensive training programs for experienced workers. Thus, a large proportion of the persons now engaged in defense-related activities could expect to be trained or retrained by their new employers.

It has long been a policy of the government of the United States to encourage and help support certain types of vocational education and occupational training. Important among these is the vocational education system in the public high schools largely financed by local and State educational authorities, with assistance from the Federal government. Once directed primarily to young people already in school, attention has turned more recently to vocational training and retraining of out-of-school youth and adults. Increasingly this type of class has been used for training the unemployed. In fiscal year 1960, 43,900 unemployed or underemployed adults and out-of-school youths enrolled in these short-term classes to prepare for entering into employment in new occupational pursuits. Training programs were offered for 62 different occupations, including welding, machine operators, automotive repair, draftsmen, electrical workers and electronics technicians, nursing aides, beauty operators, and food trades workers.

In addition, several States have established their own special programs for retraining the adult unemployed. The State of Pennsylvania, for example, has had such a program for ten years. In 1960–61 it had over 20 local programs in operation teaching a variety of skills, with an enrollment of approximately 500 unemployed persons. The placement record of those enrolled has been particularly high—between 70 and 80 per cent.

The passage of the Area Redevelopment Act in 1961 established additional Federal aid for the training of unemployed workers in areas with long-standing unemployment. The Act provided for financial assistance by the Federal government in qualified "redevelopment areas" in the provision of educational facilities and services, and for benefits for up to 16 weeks at the level of State unemployment compensation to unemployed persons while retraining. The program under present financial limitations in the Act is relatively small, permitting training of less than 20,000 persons per year.

A much broader program, embodied in the Manpower Development and Training Act of 1962, was adopted in March 1962. It provides a nationwide opportunity for occupational training, with priority given to experienced unemployed persons who are heads of families. Training will also be given to employed persons to improve their skills.

This is a 3-year program, with total authorization of $435 million, many times larger than that in the Area Redevelopment Act. It should make possible the training of as many as a million people in 3 years. Its benefits are not confined to areas in which unemployment, has been persistent, as is the Area Redevelopment Act, but are available to any area. The Act provides a program of Federal financial assistance for vocational education and on-the-job training, to be carried out primarily through the existing State vocational education agencies under the general supervision of the Department of Health, Education and Welfare. Training allowances roughly equal to unemployment compensation in each State may be paid to persons in training, for a period of up to 52 weeks. Many courses in skilled and technical occupations can now be provided because of the longer duration of available retraining allowances.

Special provision is made for training of unemployed persons 19–21 years old. The Act also provides for an annual Manpower Report by the Secretary of Labor to the Congress on skill requirements, occupational outlook, job opportunities, labor supply in various skills, and employment trends.

Enactment of the proposed Trade Expansion Act of 1962 would be of further relevance in this context. In addition to the possibility of assistance to industries adversely affected by imports it also foresees the institution, where appropriate, of worker training programs after vocational counselling and testing.

Also before the Congress in 1962 is the Youth Employment Opportunities Bill, which should provide work experience and further occupational training for a limited number of out-of-school youth through a Youth Conservation Corps to work on Federal conservation and recreational facilities, through employment on local public works programs, combined with further education, and through on-the-job training.

Since these measures are directed toward the relief of localized problems of unemployment, they should greatly strengthen the capabilities of the United States to help members of the civilian work force presently engaged in defense-related work to equip themselves for new jobs in the event of disarmament.

At the close of World War II and again at the close of the Korean War the Government undertook massive programs for the education, training and job placement of men and women discharged from the Armed Services. These programs, for which approximately $20 billion was spent, were exceedingly effective not only in restoring millions of individuals fairly promptly to a useful role in the economy of the country but also in providing extensive educational and technical training.

Among the veterans of World War II, 7.8 million had entered training under Public Law 346 through June 1955. Of these 28 per cent attended colleges and universities, 45 per cent schools below college level and approximately 18 per cent engaged in on-the-job training. Following the Korean War more than 2 million Korean veterans—about one-third of those eligible—had entered training under Public Law 550 by June 1958. It is anticipated that before this program is concluded about half of those eligible will have taken advantage of these training opportunities as in the case of World War II veterans.

Both of these programs were on a very large scale, dealing with millions of men—far more than are at present in the armed services. Both were effective. Both have been appraised, and recommendations for their improvement have been made. Experience in their administration provides a basis for planning similar programs to meet future needs.

OTHER MEANS OF EASING THE ADJUSTMENT PROCESS IN THE LABOR FORCE

Programs of training and retraining would need to be complemented by a nationwide system for collecting information on employment opportunities and available manpower to facilitate the matching of men with jobs. Extended unemployment compensation for workers released by defense industries and for veterans,

and relocation grants or loans to help workers move to areas where the employment opportunities are greatest are other possibilities. Here, again, the proposed Trade Expansion Act of 1962, with its provision for financing reasonable costs of relocating families in cases where the head of the household is made unemployed by imports and has a definite job offer elsewhere, could provide valuable practical experience in dealing with disarmament adjustment problems.

THE SPECIAL CASE OF RESEARCH AND DEVELOPMENT

Employment of scientists and engineers is growing at a faster rate than employment of almost any other occupational group. In recent years non-military R&D has grown rapidly and in all likelihood would have grown even faster had more resources been available. The release of scientists and engineers by defense industries should facilitate an acceleration of civilian R&D. Such an increase in R&D manpower could be used with great benefit to society and yield high returns in many industries where presently very little R&D is directed toward improving products or processes. The civilian economy would benefit especially from increased long-range research and experimentation with advanced technological possibilities of the sort that the research teams presently employed by defense industries have conducted so successfully.

It is, however, impossible to predict how much private research support would increase in the event of disarmament. Certainly the increase would be substantial. It is likely, however, that in order to absorb the released R&D resources smoothly and to help guide them to the highest priority uses a positive government program would be required. It could operate with effectiveness in matching personnel becoming available with employment opportunities. A particular problem— possibly more severe than would be encountered in other occupations—might arise in switching scientists and engineers who have spent their careers in one field to other new specializations, and appropriate government assistance to facilitate the adjustment might be in order and yield large benefits.

A disarmament program would provide an unmatched opportunity to review public policies toward non-military R&D. There are in fact urgent needs for more research and development in areas where private incentives and financial capabilities are inadequate or non-existent. Some of the R&D resources freed by disarmament would no doubt be transferred to more substantial civilian atomic energy and space programs. But there are also urgent needs or desirable goals for research and development in such fields as urban transportation, housing, health, education, and exploration and exploitation of the ocean resources.

Released R&D resources could also be used to great advantage to complement an expanded foreign aid program. Efforts here might well focus on such problems as the development of simple teaching machines and related communications equipment, techniques for overcoming aridity, efficient and low cost transportation systems, cheap and reliable power sources, and other equipment and processes specially tailored to the resources and labor availabilities of the less developed countries. Research and engineering personnel released by disarmament might serve as technical consultants on development and planning and in helping to establish new industries on a sound technical basis.

The freeing of R&D resources could be one of the most important economic benefits of disarmament. But here, as in other aspects, advanced planning and coordinated action will minimize the transitional problems and make it possible to profit more extensively from the large opportunities which disarmament affords.

Notes

1. Included in the term "national defense" in this study are those items which the Department of Commerce includes in the National Defense component of Gross National Product, except when otherwise indicated. Specifically included under this heading are: Department of Defense military functions and military assistance, stockpiling, expansion of defense production, and purchases by the Atomic Energy Commission (AEC), National Aeronautics and Space Administration (NASA), Selective Service System, and Federal Civil Defense Administration. Excluded are such items as economic assistance for defense support under the mutual defense assistance program, and the civilian functions of the Army Corps of Engineers. It should be noted that the Department of Commerce classification is not identical with the National Defense category in the Federal budget document. Furthermore, the AEC and NASA components include substantial expenditures for purely civilian purposes which cannot be separated out of the total because of the non-availability of relevant data.

2. For the Armed Services the allocation is to their place of residence.

The economic and social consequences of disarmament: summary and conclusions

THE PRESENT LEVEL OF MILITARY EXPENDITURE not only represents a grave political danger but also imposes a heavy economic and social burden on most countries. It absorbs a large volume of human and material resources of all kinds, which could be used to increase economic and social welfare throughout the world —both in the highly industrialized countries, which at the present time incur the bulk of the world's military expenditures, and in the less developed areas.

Resources devoted to military purposes

THERE appears to be general agreement that the world is spending roughly $120 billion annually on military account at the present time. This corresponds to about one-half of the total gross capital formation throughout the world. It is at least two-thirds of—and according to some estimates, of the same order of magnitude as— the entire national income of all the under-developed countries.

It is important that countries, in preparing to disarm, should take stock of the various resources that disarmament would release for peaceful uses. In the major military powers, military production is highly concentrated in a few industry groups. In those countries that rely upon imports for their supplies of military goods or in which the major part of military expenditure is for the pay and subsistence of the armed forces, rather than for their equipment, the resources devoted to military purposes consist essentially of manpower and foreign exchange.

The peaceful use of released resources

THERE are so many competing claims for usefully employing the resources released by disarmament that the real problem is to establish a scale of priorities. The most urgent of these claims would undoubtedly already have been largely satisfied were it not for the armaments race.

Increased personal consumption might well absorb a large share of the released resources. A substantial portion of them, however, would be used for expansion of productive capacities because only such expansion can provide a firm basis for further increases in consumption. In the less developed countries, the utilization of released resources for capital formation must be considered vitally important.

Social investment is an important alternative both to private consumption and to industrial and agricultural investment. Its claims rest partly upon the clear urgency of the direct need for improved social amenities, and partly upon the fact that growth of industrial and agricultural productivity is dependent upon developments in education, housing, health, and other fields.

The release of scientific and technical manpower would make it possible to encourage programmes of basic scientific research in fields which have hitherto been neglected. Disarmament would also open up possibilities for joint international ventures of an ambitious kind, such as the utilization of atomic energy for peaceful purposes, space research, the exploration of the Arctic and Antarctic for the

From the Report of the Secretary General, E/3593/Rev. 1, UN Department of Economic and Social Affairs, New York, 1962, pp. 832–837.

benefit of mankind and projects to change the climates of large areas of the world.

Thus, though it would take active decisions by Governments in the light of national and international needs to set in motion the necessary programmes for employing the released resources, it seems abundantly clear that no country need fear a lack of useful employment opportunities for the resources that would become available to it through disarmament.

Impact on national production and employment

DISARMAMENT would raise both general problems of maintaining the over-all level of economic activity and employment and specific problems in so far as manpower or productive capacity might require adaptation to non-military needs. In the economic life of all countries, shifts in the pattern of demand and in the allocation of productive resources are continually occurring. The reallocation of productive resources which would accompany disarmament is in many respects merely a special case of the phenomenon of economic growth.

The post-war conversion was a much larger one and involved a more rapid transfer of resources than total disarmament would require at present. Nevertheless, huge armies were quickly demobilized without a significant rise in unemployment in most countries. The pace of recovery, particularly of industrial output, was impressively rapid. During the post-war conversion, however, the major concern of economic policy was to restrain, rather than to maintain, over-all demand.

Much attention has already been given in the industrialized private enterprise economies to the methods by which total effective demand can be maintained. Monetary and fiscal policy could be used to offset the effect of a shortfall in total demand that might result from a decline in military expenditure to the extent that it were not offset by a rise in civil government expenditure. Bearing in mind that a substantial part of military expenditure would probably be replaced by other government expenditure in most countries, it may be concluded that the maintenance of effective demand in the face of disarmament should not prove difficult.

For many under-developed countries, the effect of disarmament upon the industrial countries' demands for primary products, and

thus on the export earnings of the primary producing countries, would be of great importance. So would the methods of dealing with the liquidation of strategic stockpiles.

In the centrally planned economies, the maintenance of effective demand while reducing military expenditure would be simply a matter of the efficiency of planning techniques. In consequence, effective demand could be readily maintained, and the principal problems of conversion would concern the physical adaptation of plants producing armaments to the production of goods for civilian use.

Structural problems of conversion

EVEN with the successful maintenance of total effective demand during a period of disarmament, significant problems of adjustment would remain in specific sectors and areas of the economy. The resources now supplying military requirements could be adapted to peace-time needs partly by shifts within industries and plants. This might be a relatively easy procedure, in many cases involving little more than changes in designs, retooling, and minor adaptations of skills, particularly in plants and enterprises which already produce both military and civilian goods. Shifts between industries would necessitate new investment and acquisition of different types of skill by the working force. In the longer run disarmament would allow each country to raise the rate of investment and to adapt productive capacity more adequately to the needs of the population and to the requirements of economic growth, both in the private enterprise and the centrally planned economies.

Hypothetical studies on the assumption that military expenditure is replaced wholly by increases in expenditure on other kinds of goods and services suggest that in the event of very rapid disarmament some 6 or 7 per cent (including the armed forces) of the total labour force in the United States and $3\frac{1}{2}$ to 4 per cent in the United Kingdom would have to find civilian instead of military employment or change their employment from one industry group to another. These shifts would be small if spread out over a number of years and would be greatly facilitated by the normal process of turnover. The higher the rate of growth of the economy, the easier the process of adaptation.

Under-developed countries generally have

been meeting their requirements for military goods and services by imports, so that their disarmament would release foreign exchange rather than industrial workers. It would also free members of the forces, many with useful skills and training. Some of these would be usefully employed in the development of social capital. In some of the semi-industrialized countries, newly started basic industries could concentrate, without any transitional difficulty, on the manufacture of capital goods.

In the centrally planned economies, where productive capacity is usually fully utilized, it would be necessary to convert plants producing military equipment to production of durable consumer goods and of such investment goods as can be produced in them with only minor retooling. This could be done rapidly.

Some special problems would arise with regard to re-employment and training of manpower and reorientation of scientific research. While most members of the armed forces have received training that would fit them easily for civilian life, a special effort would have to be made to find suitable employment for the rest. The demobilization of the non-professional members of the armed forces would imply only that the number of new entrants for that period would be augmented by this special factor.

In industries depending heavily on military orders, many of the employees possess a level of skill that should find gainful employment in other brances of production, so long as over-all effective demand is rising. Even so, there might be some special cases which would require special assistance to encourage the adaptation of skills to new jobs. The uneven geographical distribution of the activity based on military expenditure would give rise to a need for various forms of public and other assistance to facilitate readjustment.

The task of shifting scientific and technical personnel to non-military fields of research in some countries would be considerable. No reduction in the actual employment of scientific and technical personnel need be feared, however, because the demand for civilian research would increase rapidly.

Impact on international economic relations

DISARMAMENT would be bound to have favourable effects on the development of international relations. The political *détente* that would accompany an international disarmament programme would in itself imply that nations were willing to reconsider their economic relations with one another. The relaxation of international tensions would provide a sound basis for reduction of trade barriers and for modification of existing trade agreements and trading practices. An important consequence of this would be a substantial increase in trade between the centrally planned economies and the rest of the world.

Since disarmament may be expected to result in an acceleration of economic growth, it should stimulate the growth of demand for primary production in general. Accelerated economic growth would be still more powerful in increasing total demand for manufactures. The over-all impact of disarmament on the trade of under-developed countries is likely to be favourable, not only because of the acceleration of economic growth but also because of the greatly expanded aid to be expected from the more advanced countries.

Some exports of primary products, such as petroleum, rubber and most metallic ores, depend significantly at present on direct and indirect demand generated by military purchases. Provided, however, that miliary expenditure were fully replaced by public and private non-military spending, the impact on over-all demand for these commodities would be only minor. There might, however, be instances in which declines in demand for particular commodities would cause appreciable difficulties. In these cases consideration should be given to special aid for the countries concerned, in the same way as for particular industries or areas within the principal disarming countries. For most other primary commodities, the reallocation of military expenditure to civilian use would probably bring about a net increase in demand.

During the conversion period changes in the level of aggregate economic activity associated with disarmament in the major industrial countries would be a major determinant of the level of international trade. It is believed that significant fluctuations in the general level of international trade could be avoided, but it should nevertheless be realized that any failure to achieve this goal could have serious consequences. Regardless of the technique employed, no country should be allowed to suffer a disruption to its economic life, even temporarily, as a result of disarmament.

Effects on the volume and framework of aid for economic development

NATIONAL efforts and international co-operation in the development of the underdeveloped countries have so far not brought about the desired acceleration of economic growth. A much larger volume of resources could be allocated to investment for productive development in these countries even if only a fraction of the resources currently devoted to military purposes were used in this way. Disarmament could thus bring about a marked increase in the rate of growth of real income in the poorer parts of the world.

Bilateral and multilateral programmes of aid each have their own particular advantages and disadvantages, but in so far as political circumstances have had any weight in determining the direction and form of aid, effective disarmament and the related lessening of international tensions should improve the prospects for more co-operative international action. Since repayment of loans granted on commercial terms may impose heavy burdens on the balances of payments of the under-developed countries, as large a proportion of economic aid as possible should take the form of grants or "soft" loans.

Because the competing claims in developed countries are also urgent there is a serious possiblity that the financial resources released by disarmament might be rapidly absorbed by purely national aims. It is therefore desirable that an appropriate proportion of these resources should be allocated to international aid in its various forms simultaneously with their use for domestic purposes.

Foreign aid, however, can play only a supplementary role in the development of these countries and the responsibility for initiation and intensification of development efforts would continue to lie entirely with the Governments and peoples concerned.

Some social consequences

IN a disarmed world, a general improvement could be expected in the level of living, including an increase in leisure. With the end of the armaments race, Governments would accord social objectives a higher priority. The psychological, moral and material evils of compulsory military service and of stationing troops away from their homes would be avoided; so would the danger that security considerations and the armed forces might play an extensive role in forming the values of the community. Scientific co-operation and the arts would benefit from an extension of international exchanges.

Conclusion

THE Consultative Group is unanimously of the opinion that all the problems and difficulties of transition connected with disarmament could be met by appropriate national and international measures. There should thus be no doubt that the diversion to peaceful purposes of the resources now in military use could be accomplished to the benefit of all countries and lead to the improvement of world economic and social conditions. The achievement of general and complete disarmament would be an unqualified blessing to all mankind.

b. Limited cooperation

Ronald J. Yalem

Regionalism and world order

THE PROLIFERATION OF REGIONAL ORGANIZA-
tions since 1945 is one of the most significant
developments of contemporary international
relations. Certainly it was not foreseen by the
framers of the United Nations' Charter who
believed that regionalism must be subordinated
to the universal approach to peace and security.
What then is the relationship between such
organizations and the United Nations in terms
of the maintenance of peace and security?
Is regionalism a symptom or a cause of international disorder? Assuming the continued
growth of regional organizations, what possibilities are there of eventually promoting world
order? Do regional organizations reflect a
movement away from exclusive reliance on the
nation-state as the basic unit in international
relations?

These questions are suggested by the increasing prominence of regional groups in world
affairs today. This article attempts to suggest
tentative answers by examining the reasons for
the growth of contemporary regionalism, the
lines of compatibility and conflict between
regional and universal forms of international
organization, and the relationship between
regionalism and the concept of a world order;
and these answers are based on the assumption
that the growth of regionalism has been more
a pragmatic response to the changing dynamics
of international politics than the outcome of a
conviction that regionalism was theoretically
superior to universalism as a form of international cooperation.

Regionalism as an institutional form of
international cooperation is often identified
with the number of security agencies that have
developed since 1945 such as NATO, SEATO,
and the Warsaw Pact. But there are numerous
examples of regional economic and social
organizations, especially in Western Europe.
The European Economic Community, European Coal and Steel Community and the
Organization for Economic Cooperation and
Development are important regional agencies.
In the Latin American area a new Inter-
American Development Bank has recently been
formed as well as a Free Trade Association
between nine of the republics.[1] In South Asia
the Colombo Plan organization, comprising
both economically advanced and underdeveloped States, serves to channel important
economic aid and technical assistance into the
area. It seems likely that as the newly independent States of Africa gain political maturity,
regional organizations to promote the economic
and social well-being of that continent may be
developed. Already a customs union involving
seven former dependencies of French West
Africa has been formed.[2]

The development of such organizations is
certainly a phenomenon of the years since the
second World War. However, it is possible to
look back to the inter-war period to find precedents for regional cooperation although these,
such as the Little Entente, were mainly of a
defensive nature. While the League of Nations
represented the first attempt to universalize

Reprinted from *International Affairs*, Vol. 38, No. 4, October 1962, pp.
460–471.

peace and security, Article 21 of the Covenant provided that regional understandings for securing peace were legitimate. This article, inserted at the request of President Wilson to safeguard the integrity of the Monroe Doctrine, could be interpreted as implicit recognition of the principle of regionalism. Even so there were many statesmen who opposed it for fear that it would jeopardize the operations of the League by undermining universalism.

The experience of the inter-war period, however, revealed little if any direct antagonism between the various regional arrangements of the time and the League of Nations. The eventual collapse of the universal approach to peace and security was attributable much more to the unwillingness of the leading members of the League to accept the demands of collective security than to the existence of regional organizations. In fact these were formed largely to supplement what were thought to be the inadequate security guarantees of the Covenant.

When the San Francisco Conference met in 1945 to draft a charter for a new international organization for the maintenance of peace and security, the prevailing sentiment again favored the universal rather than the regional approach to the problem, and this view was reflected in those articles of the U.N. Charter giving to the Security Council the dominant responsibility for enforcing peace and security. On the other hand, the Charter contained more explicit recognition of regionalism than had the Covenant, for Chapter VIII was devoted to provisions governing the relationship between so called regional arrangements and the United Nations. These provisions were inserted at the insistence of certain Latin American and Middle Eastern delegations whose countries had just concluded regional agreements in the form of the Act of Chapultepec and the Arab League. Article 33 of the Charter also implicitly recognized regionalism by exhorting member States to resort first to regional agencies in seeking the peaceful settlement of disputes before submitting them to the United Nations, while Article 51 legalized the right of collective self-defense against armed aggression.

Nevertheless, Articles 52, 53, and 54 of the Charter definitely establish the subordination of regional arrangements to the United Nations. Article 52 establishes the legality of such arrangements if consistent with the purposes and principles of the United Nations. Article 53 stipulates that regional enforcement action is subject to the prior approval of the Security Council except in cases involving enemy States of the Second World War. Article 54 obliges regional arrangements to keep the Security Council informed of any action they may contemplate for the maintenance of peace and security.

The subordinate position thus clearly relegated to regional security agencies in the Charter is in sharp contrast to their actual relationship with the United Nations today. To the great disappointment of many ardent supporters of universalism, regional security agencies have assumed a significance that overshadows the United Nations. Although this development is primarily the result of political factors for the most part unforeseen in 1945, the existence of such agencies in increasing numbers has been morally justified on the ground that they are consistent with the purposes and principles of the United Nations. Indeed, it is asserted that these purposes and principles are identical in that regional security agencies, like the United Nations, are designed to keep the peace.

This view is based on Article 51 of the Charter which permits the right of individual or collective self-defense "... if an armed attack occurs against a Member of the United Nations, until the Security Council has taken the measures necessary to maintain international peace and security." While the Western Powers have maintained that NATO, SEATO, and the Rio Treaty do not conflict with the paramount position of the United Nations as regards the enforcement of peace, it could be argued that Article 51 was designed to permit the *ad hoc* organization of collective force to meet specific situations rather than as the basis for the establishment of permanent security organizations, for which provision is made in Chapter VIII of the Charter in respect of regional arrangements. The fact that these agencies are based on Article 51 means that they have escaped regulation and control by the Security Council. Although such control would have obviously interfered with the efficacy of these agencies because of the veto power of the Soviet Union, this does not alter the view that they fall more properly under Chapter VIII rather than under Article 51 of the Charter.

Since the legal relationship of such agencies to the United Nations has not been clarified by an advisory opinion from the International Court of Justice, it seems likely that in the event of future military action they will be required only to inform the Security Council or the General Assembly of action taken; and as both the super-Powers on the Council have a right of veto over any enforcement action by the Council, it would be virtually impossible for the United Nations to act even though such action is provided for under Article 51. The net effect of this situation has been to exempt both the Western and Soviet regional security systems from effective control by the United Nations.

Basic to any assessment of regionalism and world order is an examination of the major causes for the disproportionate influence of regionalism in contemporary world politics. Such an examination must not be limited solely to political factors but must also take account of the fact that regionalism is a response to what Professor John Herz has called "the decline of the territorial State" in which changing technological conditions have rendered the State more penetrable and less secure than at any other period in modern history.[3] First, therefore, I will examine some political explanations for the emergence of regional security organizations and I will then examine regionalism as a response to the possible obsolescence of the nation-State.

It is a truism to assert that hopes for the restoration of a stable world order after the Second World War rested on the continuation of wartime cooperation among the major Powers. Yet a recognition of this fact is a necessary prerequisite to an awareness of the steady disintegration of universalism since 1945 and the consequent rise of regionalism. Given the extent and nature of the disparity of power between States in the modern world, peace must always rest on some minimum degree of consensus among the most powerful States. Such a consensus pervaded the era of *Pax Britannica* in the nineteenth century. However, it must be admitted that the prospects for such consensus and stability were much less in 1945 than in 1815. In the earlier period the existence of a complex balance of power involving several States of approximately equal strength, and the stabilizing factor of Great Britain as the "balancer," contributed to political order. But by 1945 the structure of the balance of power had so altered that peace no longer depended on a consensus among several Powers but only on the United States and the Soviet Union. While the change in the balance of power must thus be adduced as a reason for

the failure to restore an effective universalism, perhaps the most important cause for the failure lay in the increasing ideological conflict between the United States and the Soviet Union manifested in and out of the United Nations. Amicable relations even between two States that shared a common ideology would have been subject to severe strain. The bipolar structure of power would have made them potential if not actual competitors since no third State was powerful enough to act as a "balancer" in any conflict that might arise. Nevertheless, it was assumed that the United States and the Soviet Union would be able to cooperate to maintain the peace, and this assumption rested in turn on another: that they shared a common view of what was to be defended or what constituted the territorial *status quo*. When it soon appeared that there were divergent interpretations of the *status quo* revealed by Soviet aggrandizement in Eastern Europe and attempts to engulf Western Europe as well, all hopes for a universal order under the aegis of the United Nations began to fade. It became apparent that international organization for peace and security could not be divorced from the dynamics of international politics which began to set limits on the possibilities that the United Nations could achieve.

The repeated use of the veto by the Soviet Union in the Security Council, her menacing attitude toward Iran, and generally uncooperative behavior in negotiating the various European peace treaties, prompted the United States and her allies to search for alternatives to a system of universal peace and security. In 1949 the North Atlantic Treaty Organization was created to deter further Soviet expansion, particularly in Europe. In 1954 the Southeast Asia Treaty Organization was formed to block Soviet, and especially Communist Chinese influence in that area. The United States also concluded numerous bilateral treaties involving American commitment to protect such allies as Nationalist China, South Korea, Japan and the Philippines in the event of these States being attacked by Communist aggressors.

Although it may be argued that the United States-sponsored Uniting for Peace Resolution of 1950 constituted evidence of a willingness to endorse universal collective security, possible action under this resolution is limited by the nature of the obligation that it imposes on members of the United Nations—in contrast to the various regional commitments which involve heavier obligations. Under this Resolution the General Assembly can only recommend military or non-military sanctions against an aggressor. It is therefore doubtful if, in the event of Communist armed aggression, the General Assembly could bring about resistance to the extent that would be achieved by either NATO or SEATO which are directly designed for such a purpose.

The Suez crisis of 1956 provides an interesting example of the limitations of the Uniting for Peace Resolution. The General Assembly responded to the vacuum created in the Security Council by the vetoes of Britain and France by passing a resolution calling for a cease-fire and the withdrawal of British, French and Israeli forces from the Suez Canal. But there was no recommendation that military sanctions should be imposed. The General Assembly resolution constituted an effective expression of world public opinion condemnatory of Britain and France, but it in no sense amounted to a collective security action. In fact it was influences exerted outside the United Nations, in the shape of diplomatic pressures from the United States and the Soviet Union that helped to bring about a cessation of hostilities.

It is customary to attribute the growth of regionalism since 1945 to the disintegration of the universal security system of the United Nations. Yet this does not adequately explain the reasons for the growth of non-military regional agencies reflecting the desires of various States to raise standards of living and accelerate industrial development. The tremendous regionalization of Western Europe evidenced in the European Economic Community, the European Coal and Steel Community, the European Atomic Community and the Council of Europe is only partially explained by the threat of Soviet expansion and the decline of Western Europe as a center of world power. It would be naïve to underrate these facts for they have been important influences in the creation of these groupings. A greater degree of unity in Europe has been necessary as a protection against Soviet penetration through divisive tactics. Many Europeans also believe that greater unity will provide compensation for the weakness of individual European States and so make it possible for the continent to exert more influence in world politics than would otherwise be possible.

In the same way the newly independent States of Africa and Asia could be more immune to Soviet subversion, and could exert more power in world politics, through regional unity. The fact that such unity is not forthcoming in those areas suggests that circumstances within nation-states must be considered no less than external factors if the dynamics of regional integration are to be understood. What are these circumstances and what do they reveal regarding the adequacy of the nation-State to satisfy the changing needs and demands of its citizens?

Part of the answer may lie in the "decline of the territorial State" as a result of technological developments that have created a situation in areas such as Western Europe where nations can no longer function effectively as self-contained military, economic or political units but must seek wider cooperation to solve common problems. If this growth of regionalism has been faster there it has been due not only to the Soviet threat but also because the area, artificially fragmented economically, in reality constitutes a natural economic unity in terms of the exchange of goods and services.

The growth of regionalism in Western Europe was also hastened by the recognition by Europe's leading statesmen that they could avoid permanent dependence on the United States, and regain their full economic potential and independence, by a form of economic union that might also provide a basis for political union. Underlying this view was a certain disillusionment with the excessive nationalism of the past, and the feeling that this must be ended if Western Europe was to regain a semblance of its former importance in world affairs. This could only mean that nationalism must yield to internationalism.

Such awareness presupposes, however, a degree of political maturity and stability missing in most of the States that have gained their independence from colonial rule since 1945. These nations are still too intoxicated with the emotion of freedom and self-determination to be willing to subordinate aspects of their newly-acquired national sovereignty to trans-national control. We must conclude, therefore, that regionalism as an approach to world order is not automatically transferable from one geographical area to another, but is contingent for its success on a complex of internal factors as well as external conditions.

This is not to imply that the movement away from the nation-State is a one-way process.

Regional integration depends upon a certain degree of shared economic, political, and ideological interests before it can be successfully launched. Yet the impact of regional institutions upon the evolving process of unification should not be minimized. For example, while the Council of Europe in no way possesses the substantive powers of a European parliament or European executive, it has provided an institutional setting for discussion by European statesmen of various integration schemes. Similarly, the Assembly that serves the three functional Communities of continental Europe acts as a permanent organization structure for continuous contact among the member States as well as an important symbol of a rapidly evolving regional unity.

While the preceding discussion may have implied the inevitability of political integration among the States of continental Europe, it would be imprudent to predict such a development without qualification. The process of unification beyond the nation-State is apt to be marked by setbacks as well as by progress, as the stillborn European Defence Community revealed.

We are now in a position to raise some important questions regarding regionalism and the United Nations. To what extent have regional security agencies served as successful replacements for the disintegrated United Nations security system? Have they brought the world any closer to peace and order? Does the creation of non-military regional agencies complement or conflict with the economic and social functions of the United Nations and its specialized agencies? Finally, to what extent do regional agencies constitute genuine departures from a system of international relations based on the nation-State, and what are the prospects that regionalism will continue to flourish in the future as an alternative to global cooperation? These are difficult questions to answer, but the task must be attempted so that a preliminary assessment of the relationship between regional and universal approaches to peace and security may be made.

Proponents of regional security organizations argue that such arrangements have not only filled in the gap caused by the weakness of the United Nations but that, in Europe, they have prevented the Soviet Union from achieving any significant new territorial gains. They maintain that such agencies were the only alternatives to further insecurity for the United States and its allies.

In considering this argument, it is necessary to examine critically the assumption that such organizations have provided adequate substitutes for the United Nations security system. Admittedly, the United Nations has failed to develop in the way envisaged by its supporters, but is it possible to assert that the pragmatic response to this failure in the formation of regional alliances has contributed to a stabilization of international tensions? Quite the contrary. In many respects the creation of multilateral and bilateral mutual security treaties by the United States and the Soviet Union marks a return to the period before the First World War, a period of competing alliances which Woodrow Wilson believed to be the primary cause of war. Regional security systems are not only viewed by the major antagonists in the cold war as a threat to their own security, but they have also incurred the resentment and hostility of many newly independent States who see such arrangements as exacerbating rather than relieving world tensions.

With regard to NATO it is difficult to make assessments. Probably the establishment of that organization served as an important psychological warning to the Soviet that the West was prepared to resist any further encroachment in Europe. To some extent NATO has proved to be useful as a means by which the United States has shared defence burdens with her allies. But is the absence of further Soviet aggression in Western Europe and elsewhere attributable to the presence of NATO forces in numerical inferiority to Soviet troops or, more plausibly, to the delicate balance of nuclear weapons that renders any military excursion too costly? To the extent that NATO may achieve a collective nuclear capability this conclusion would have to be modified. Whether such a development would contribute to a lowering of tensions is, however, extremely doubtful.

Elsewhere the elaborate network of mutual security treaties developed by the United States contains numerous gaps. This is particularly noticeable in the Middle East where the CENTO organization is weakened by the absence of Iraq and Afghanistan. Similarly, the SEATO organization is hampered by the absence of the key States of India, Ceylon, and Burma. It has been ineffective in preventing the aggression in Laos and is militarily incapable of mobilizing sufficient forces if Communist China were to launch a full-scale attack on vulnerable Thailand or the Philippines.

The preceding discussion does not imply that the various regional alliances should be dissolved. Rather, it emphasizes some of their serious limitations as instruments of security in a world devoid of an effective universal organization to enforce the peace. Ideally, the solution to the problem of world peace requires the subordination of regional agencies to a universal agency for the maintenance of peace. Such a restatement of this maximalist approach to peace, however, only underlines the extent to which the world has strayed from the ideal of collective security suggested by Wilson—although that ideal perhaps presupposed conditions of international solidarity that are impossible to realize in a world bifurcated into conflicting political ideologies.

The restoration of a more normal equilibrium between global and regional security agencies is not in sight. The present imbalance is a symptom more than a cause of international disorder. As suggested earlier, the immediate causes of that imbalance may be traced to the change from a relatively stable to a highly unstable balance of power system, and to the appearance of divisive ideological forces. But would the normalization of relations between the Soviet Union, Communist China and the United States and the return to a complex balance of power system restore an equilibrium between universalism and regionalism? A modification of the present imbalance in world order might be realized, but the prospects of that happening appear very remote.

A more fundamental analysis by Professor Kenneth Waltz suggests that international conflict is the result of three factors that may be difficult if not impossible to modify: the nature of man; the nature of the State; and the nature of the state system.[4] Until harmony can be achieved among these three elements the possibilities for world order are not optimistic. In the meantime, it is likely that, with their success in Western Europe, non-military regional forms of international cooperation will continue to flourish, subject to appropriate internal conditions in the underdeveloped areas.

A seldom explored question is the extent to which such agencies operating in economic and social spheres oppose or complement similar activities of the United Nations and its specialized agencies. Only a tentative answer may be given in view of the absence of research on this particular issue. In theory there need be no conflict between universal and regional approaches to economic and social development.

Cooperation is often more readily forthcoming in regions where common economic and social problems present opportunities for collaboration not so easily available on a world level.

Where such regional economic integration has taken definite shape the possibility of conflict between the purposes of the regional and the universal organization is likely. Although the European Economic Community represents a substantial advance toward free trade, such an arrangement is discriminatory in States outside the Common Market area and so conflicts with the universalist ideal of expanded world trade. The creation of additional common market arrangements in Latin America, Africa, and Southeast Asia involves the threat of intesified economic protectionism unless satisfactory concessions can be worked out on an inter-regional basis. Unfortunately, the United Nations has no control over such developments and therefore cannot function as a coordinator where coordination is so vitally needed.

On the other hand, the United Nations through its technical assistance and economic development programmes has involved itself in activities embracing several distinct regions of the world. The same thing is true of the various specialized agencies operating in the fields of health, sanitation, agriculture, and education. The fact that in many of the underdeveloped areas regional cooperation has not developed to any appreciable degree has meant that States in such areas have been anxious to obtain the assistance of the United Nations and its specialized agencies.

On balance it may be said that regional economic arrangements constitute an improvement over the economic nationalism that has been a feature of international economic relations for several years, but that they represent something less than universal economic internationalism. The failure to achieve this ideal through the establishment of the International Trade Organization has in fact prompted the movement toward economic regionalism first in the prosperous and now in the underdeveloped areas. Nevertheless, the progress achieved through the International Bank and Monetary Fund, and by the GATT, in developing a multilateral framework for investments, currency stabilization and lower tariff barriers should not be underestimated.

There remains the question whether the development of regional agencies, of a military and non-military nature, marks a departure from the nation-State as the traditional unit of international relations. If so, does that development necessarily imply, as proponents of regionalism assert, that regionalism will inevitably tend toward the creation of a supra-national global order?

Although it is still too early to assess the impact of regional military and non-military agencies on the traditional system of nation-States, certain conclusions appear justifiable. Trends toward regional union cannot be arbitrarily separated into military and non-military categories. The process of integration is likely to begin with cooperation in relatively narrow spheres and, where such efforts are successful, to spill over into other areas and ultimately embrace some form of political union. Thus the experience of Western Europe since 1945 demonstrates that trans-national cooperation developed first in the military area, involving a gradual standardiza-tion of weapons systems and armed forces, without however culminating in a European Army. Then the trend toward integration spread into a relatively specialized sector of economic production with the creation of the European Coal and Steel Community. It has since spread further to include the gradual removal of all national tariff barriers and im-migration restrictions, and the development of common monetary and investment policies under the European Economic Community.

Though critics assert that the degree of trans-national cooperation so far attained in Western Europe still leaves the national sovereignty of the States pretty much intact, loyalties extending beyond the narrow confines of the member States have been slowly building up. Whether this tendency will culminate in the development of supranational legislative and executive organs, with powers binding upon the member units without their unanimous con-sent, is still uncertain. The acceleration of European unity will no doubt be affected by the intensity of Soviet hostility toward the West. As such hostility does not appear likely to abate, pressures for further unifica-tion are likely to continue. The main point is that precedents for cooperation have been established that reveal that, if the process of interdependence cannot find institutional expression on the world level in the reduction of nationalism and sovereignty, it is possible for parochial nationalism to be gradually super-seded by a regional internationalism.

The appearance of greater regional unity in the underdeveloped areas must await a greater political maturity and stability of the States located there. In many areas intra-regional rivalries act as divisive forces while nationalism also provides a deterrent to wider unity. But even in these areas regional cooperation is being advanced. The activities of the Organization of American States have been expanded into the economic field with the creation of the Inter-American Development Bank and the Free Trade Association foreseen by the Montevideo Treaty. In West Africa several States have entered into a customs union.

It is not to be expected, however, that in these areas the movement toward regional unity will proceed at the same pace as in Western Europe. Each of the underdeveloped regions is affected by political instability in vary-ing degrees—an instability resulting not only from the post-independence problem of maintaining law and order but also from the lack of adequately trained civil servants, marked gaps in standards of living between the élites and the masses, and rising populating pressures that threaten economic growth. Before regional cooperation can become effective, these pro-blems will have to be solved, or at least a start must be made toward their improvement. Finally, since regionalism presupposes a willing-ness to dilute nationalism with internationa-lism, important changes in the attitude of most of these States will be required. Many are caught up in such a wave of rising expectations for their peoples that nationalism rather than internationalism is apt to be dominant at least in the short run. All of these factors lead to the conclusion that while regional cooperation for economic and social development is under experiment in the underdeveloped areas, its rate of growth will be much slower than in Western Europe.

Altogether, then, it is doubtful whether regional entities are mainly toward the forma-tion of a supranational global order, or that the nation-State is being superseded by regional federations or confederations throughout the world. Only in Western Europe can this be said to be happening.

To the extent that regional cooperation provides for an increase in stability within regions by removing historical rivalries, settling intra-regional disputes, and promoting economic and social cooperation, it serves as a catalyst for regional peace and order. But in itself regionalism as an approach to world order is incomplete. Unless regional units are subordinated to a universal agency, regional self-sufficiency can only be damaging to inter-regional relations. It is only necessary to cite the tense inter-regional or inter-bloc conflict existing between the North Atlantic region and the Communist world of Russia, Eastern Europe, and Communist China.

In the final analysis, the world needs cooperation at both the global and regional levels. But acceptance of the need for simultaneous universal and regional cooperation, and for the existence of adequate coordinating links between the two levels, does not bring them about. A world trisected into three weakly coordinated segments, of which two are deadly hostile to each other, is not an orderly world. A revival of universalism presupposes elements of consensus and cohesion that have been notably lacking since 1945. Unless and until international politics evolves into a system in which the three great political and ideological forces of Communism, Democracy and Neutralism can function cooperatively, it is likely that the present disequilibrium between universal and regional organization will continue.

Notes

1. Lincoln P. Bloomfield, "The United States, the United Nations, and the Creation of Community," *International Organization*, Vol. XIV, No. 4, 1960, p. 511.
2. *Op. cit.*

3. *International Politics in the Atomic Age* (New York, Columbia University Press, 1959), pp. 96–108.
4. *Man, the State, and War* (New York, Columbia University Press, 1959).

Philip C. Jessup and Howard J. Taubenfeld

Functional international cooperation: patterns for the future

IN THE PRECEDING CHAPTERS we have examined some situations in which governments have acted together in groups large or small to accomplish certain ends. Why did they not act alone in these cases? Is not individual, independent, "sovereign" action generally assumed to be or to have been the dominant objective of all states strong enough to indulge in it? As suggested at the outset, the answers to such questions, even in so far as they can be hazarded, may suggest how man can most profitably explore and exploit the new frontiers of the Antarctic and of outer space. In the descriptive parts which precede, some attention

Reprinted from Philip C. Jessup and Howard J. Taubenfeld, *Controls for Outer Space*, New York, Columbia University Press, 1959, pp. 117–133.

has been paid to the occasion for each joint or multiple action and to the organizational device utilized. This summarizing chapter seeks to indicate more comprehensively those forces which have been operating in the international community during the last hundred years, the increasing momentum of which may mark the decades ahead.

The Charter of the United Nations recognizes that there is an "inherent right" of self-defense. Such an inherent right exists because of the universal instinct for self-preservation, felt not only by individuals on their own behalf but also by persons acting responsibly in governments of states. In our tendency to personify the state we are likely to attribute this feeling of government officials to the collectivity itself, to the extent that usage has made it permissible to speak in terms of the state as the actor. The response of states then to this self-protective urge has, paradoxically enough, contributed to both the solitary and the cooperative courses of action.

The contribution to the solitary course of action is so amply illustrated in day-to-day experience that it scarcely needs historical illustration. We are apt to catalogue the flow of examples under the labels "defense" and "security." Thus the Soviet refusal to subordinate its freedom of action in maintaining armaments to any system of inspection which inevitably represents a collective or cooperative approach. Thus, too, the emphasis in the United States upon the military aspects of the still uncertain uses of space and of the satellites or missiles which man may control in space. If the scholar suggests that all national claims to the moon should be foresworn in favor of the United Nations, the military strategist is bound to ask what potential military advantage he is being asked to deny himself. If one talks about an international regime in the Antarctic, one is reminded of the German naval activities in its waters during the Second World War and the strategic importance of Palmer Peninsula if the Suez and Panama Canals were blocked. In face of the impossibility, or at least difficulty, of proving in advance the specific gains to the national interest, including the guarantees of security which would flow from international cooperation, the official who believes his state possesses the means for self-defense is apt to choose the solitary in preference to the cooperative course of action.

On the other hand, it is rare indeed to find a situation in which a state is so confident of its military superiority over any possible enemy or combination of enemies that it is uninterested in the support which other states may give it. So throughout modern history the search for security has led to alliances which may be identified as cooperative courses of action to serve a protective function.* Some of the cases of cooperative action we have examined were inspired, at least in part, by defense considerations, where those interests have been served by denying a potential strategic advantage to an adversary through placing some bit of territory under an agreed international regime. The Aaland Islands, Crete, Tangier, and others are cases in which this element appears. Although an alliance in the conduct of war is recognized as a thing of necessity and not of preference, the aftermath of a war in which the great identified danger of the moment has been eliminated by joint victory may lead to temporary joint belligerent occupations and to efforts to broaden and perpetuate the alliance. Or, on the contrary, it may result in suspicion, friction, and a return to separateness. The system of collective security which the framers of the League of Nations and the United Nations sought to establish was obviously designed to substitute for unilateral defense a cooperative course of action which would in turn facilitate other measures of international cooperation. While collective security has not been secured, many of the attendant measures of cooperation have become firmly established.

These other measures of cooperation are various and much older than the two organizations established during the aftermaths of World Wars. Short of intense concern for self-defense where the strategic interest is most apparent, it has been noted that some cooperative solutions have been inspired by the need to effect a compromise between conflicting claims when the states involved felt disinclined to settle the issue by actual armed conflict. The condominiums in Samoa, Egypt, and the New Hebrides are examples, as is the proposed solution for Spitsbergen. In other instances, where the political elements are still dominant, collective decisions have been reached to prevent individual and lesser states from initiating a conflict which might spread.

---

* The story of military alliances, theories of balance of power, and the like has often been told and has not been recapitulated here, although the possibility that either space or Antarctic problems may find a solution which is neither bipolar nor universal cannot be excluded.

In this context one thinks of Memel, Leticia, and Danzig. The historical fact that from time to time throughout the modern period states have joined in some common solution of a territorial problem as an escape from conflict is quite pertinent to a consideration of Antarctica, where eight states have already, with more or less insistence, asserted claims to sovereignty. Some of those claims overlap and conflict; all of them are rejected by the two great powers, the United States and the Soviet Union. If it were not for the considerations of self-defense which have just been discussed, it would seem that every consideration of logic would impel toward an international agreement to adopt a cooperative course rather than several solitary courses of action before some new discovery suggests an immediate short-range advantage to the discoverer or to whatever state is in a position to capitalize on the discovery. Unhappily, it is the very prospect of the possibility of such a discovery which makes defense-conscious states refrain from trying their own hand, at least when the mores of their community dictate the binding force of a promise.

Although the interests of defense are primary, they are obviously not the only national interests. It will be noted later that in the Antarctic the prospect that the national economic interest may be served by territorial claims plays a significant part. In the age of discovery it was the economic motive which first led states to send explorers across the oceans. Sometimes trading stations sufficed at first to tap the economic wealth of newly discovered lands. In other circumstances, or as time passed, it seemed desirable to claim sovereignty of an area and on that base to erect the system of colonial monopoly which was characteristic of the colonial period. As it then became necessary to guard the far-flung empire and its wealth, the emphasis shifted to defense. The English interest in Egypt reflected both Lancashire's demand for cotton and the Admiralty's concern with the protection of the "lifeline" of the Empire through Suez. England for a time had to share with France control of the Suez Canal through stock ownership and the political control of Egypt through a condominium.

In spite of our ability to point to traces of a "trusteeship" concept as early as the sixteenth century, it is an inescapable fact that during long stretches of modern history (and of ancient history, for that matter) the inhabitants of a desired territory, especially if they were of a different culture or were militarily weak, were regarded merely as indigenous resources to be used (e.g., as slaves) or as natural obstacles to be overcome, as one might hack a path through a jungle or forest. Against the background of a century of development of the philosophy of the rights of man, Woodrow Wilson's conception of self-determination heralded a more effective acceptance of a political principle of responsibility for the welfare and wishes of people. As applied to the tangled ethnographic puzzles of post-war Europe this Wilsonian principle was largely inapplicable, although it found valid reflection in the protection of some minorities. In the colonial world of less-developed peoples, the resulting League of Nations mandate system did provide a precedent which, in the general stream of inclination toward the development of international organization, led to the trusteeship system of the United Nations and has now blended with a willing or reluctant yielding to the irresistible currents of contemporary nationalism. Earlier manifestations of this sensitivity to the rights of rather primitive peoples were reflected in the nineteenth-century collective approach to some of the problems of Africa, which at the same time was being carved up into colonial domains. It is these domains which are now emerging into nationhood. One can not forebear to ponder the impact on international relations of this new force, but we must note that it is not one which will in the short run influence definitively decisions about the polar and the cosmic spaces which are at present unpeopled. This is not to deny that any agreed international settlement of these two problems can be strongly influenced by the newly developed power and interests of anti-colonial voting blocs in the General Assembly of the UN. Futile to speculate at this juncture about the "inhabitants" of other planets and whether—if they exist—it is we or they who will need to be reminded of the right of self-determination.

The preceding chapters have also—without any pretense to novelty—called attention to the fact that there are many aspects of international relations which are important in themselves but which are not inextricably enmeshed in considerations of national interests, political or strategic. Even though political or other so-called vital interests are involved, they are considered separable in some manner or to some degree. They may be separable in the sense that governments are prepared to accept a temporary solution which avoids the final issue and provides a tolerable compromise for the time being. The United States proposal of May 2, 1958, for the Antarctic seems to be of this type, as will be noted later. Separability may also be found along functional lines, as where international cooperation may be accepted in the regulation and maintenance of the navigational facilities of the Danube without affecting the politics of the river basin. Communications are of vital interest to the military strategist, but various aspects of telecommunications can be entrusted to an International Telecommunications Union; one waits to see whether telecommunications with satellites are among those aspects. Although the sovereign control of a nation's superjacent airspace is jealously guarded as essential to the national safety, seventy-four states are members of ICAO, which can set certain standards in the interest of safe flight, and the Chicago Conventions contain agreements on certain reciprocal rights of overflight and landing. The economic welfare of an important segment of the population is a matter of great national interest, but it has been found possible to enter into international cooperative measures for the conservation of the resources of the sea and thus to regulate and control short-range commercial profits. Atomic energy might be selected as a prime example of a subject of the most intense importance to the national interest, but some aspects are covered by the treaties establishing the International Atomic Energy Agency, Euratom, and the European Nuclear Energy Agency. And perhaps as important as the discovery of the splitting of the atom is the political realization at which many governments have at long last arrived, that sovereignty itself can be divided, as witness the supranational institutions of the European Community and, indeed, many provisions of the Charter of the United Nations.

The institutions of the European Community have actually been given executive and judicial functions comparable to those normally possessed by national states. It is probably too soon to say whether they are successful. Judgment can be passed on some of the earlier types of dual or multipartite action, even though one cannot be dogmatic in saying that success or failure was in each case the result of the type of arrangement used. The condominium, in which two or more states by agreement divide between them the functions of government, has failed when used to govern people. A mixed administration with local participation, where background rivalries kept the powers in balance, functioned reasonably well in Tangier. In a small community like Leticia, a governing commission appointed by a world-wide international organization has succeeded, and the same may be said of the more ambitious League administration of the Saar. A similarly appointed League administrator with limited powers served a useful purpose in Danzig. In general, the case studies would seem to indicate that a crucial factor in the success of a multinational administration is the effectve internationalization of the administrative personnel.

These may appear to be cases in which states are dealing with peoples or places which, like outer space, are not already under their sovereignty and that it is different when states are asked to surrender bits of pre-existing sovereignty as, exceptionally indeed, has been done in the European community. But the amount of sovereignty restricted or surrendered may be minimal. One may look at a series of cases starting with those where the "surrender" to the international organization could scarcely frighten the most cautious guardian of the national interest.

One of the conclusions of Sayre in his early survey of functional organizations, published in 1919, in accounting for the relatively unimportant and disappointing work accomplished by such agencies was the unwillingness of states to delegate any real power to them. They were virtually impotent because of the "impossible" conditions attached to any grants of authority and the lack of real control in their administrative organs. As the preceding chapters have shown, a substantial number of these international functional organizations are limited to the collection and exchange of information. Some are charged with the effort to coordinate national activities through those means. Some, in addition, have their own research staffs or laboratories and may publish the results of their studies. Others, like FAO, may through their experts play an important advisory role in technical assistance, which is, of course, furnished only on request. A number of organizations have the power to set standards, as does ICAO. WHO's powers go somewhat further in that the Health Assembly, in addition to setting purity and related standards, may adopt regulations on sanitary and quarantine requirements, nomenclature of drugs, and on labeling of items moving in international commerce. Under the stipulations of the narcotics treaties the Drug Supervisory Body may in certain circumstances prepare estimates of national narcotic drug requirements. "This is important because the maximum of narcotics which may be imported into any country or territory is computed on the basis of these estimates and an embargo on the importation of narcotics is imposed to enforce this provision."[1] Moreover, the treaties also provide certain sanctions for the violation of some other rules of international narcotics control. The International Red Locust Control Service has men and machines at its disposal and, with local government cooperation, conducts operations to control outbreak areas in Africa and destroy the pest.

In many instances an organ which does not include all the membership, or which votes by majority, is given power to alter technical rules or standards which may for that reason be incorporated in separate annexes. The Board of Governors—or by delegation the Executive Directors—of the International Monetary Fund can prescribe a margin above and below par value for transactions in gold; members are bound by such a prescription. In the case of the International Whaling Commission, its regulations are binding on member states unless they object within ninety days.

One of the earlier examples of an agency with certain substantial independent powers and a limited right of direct "interference" in the conduct of national activities was the Permanent Sugar Commission, established in 1902. The Sugar Commission, made up of one delegate from each member, was authorized to decide whether bounties were being used in non-signatory countries and, if they were, member states were bound to apply stated countervailing duties on imports from such countries. A majority vote was sufficient to require the increased surtaxes, and there was no appeal from a second decision by the Commission. The decisions were apparently usually complied with during the decade in which the Commission flourished.[2] The existing International Sugar Council is quite different, consisting of representatives of both exporting and importing states, in which votes are weighted according to tonnage. By majority vote the Council can assign export quotas to producers, establish price limits, and assure that importers limit their intake from non-participants. Non-compliance with an established quota or failure to take agreed quantities may lead to the offender's treatment as a nonparticipant or expulsion from the organization.

Among other organizations which have had at least limited powers in the commodity field are the International Wheat Council, the International Tin Council, the Inter-American Coffee Board, and the International Tea Committee, the latter in effect a cartel arrangement of producers only.[3] The Wheat Council functions through its Executive Committee, in which exporting and importing states have weighted votes. It sets export quotas, and its decisions are binding on all members if no review is requested. A member can lose or forfeit its votes through its own actions and can be deprived of its vote, or be expelled, for breach of the Agreement.[4] The Coffee Board could, by a 95 per cent vote, in "grave" situations set quotas for the exports of coffee to the United States.[5] The sole major importer, the United States, had one-third of the votes.

Once it has been realized that the long-range national interest will be served by following a cooperative course of action, and the political decision has been made that this course can be tried without immediate prejudice to the needs of self-defense and national economic well-being, the devices which may be utilized are clearly numerous. If so-called "surrenders of sovereignty" (meaning even the slightest impairment of absolutely unfettered freedom of national action) could be measured in units, one could almost order ready-made a type of international organization to fit any number of units. Consider first the modifications in practice of what was once thought to be the sacrosanct principle of unanimity in voting in international organizations.

To a substantial degree, it can be said that existing functional organizations have replaced the rule of unanimity with that of "majoritarianism." Since a large number of these groups cannot take action which in any sense binds the members to act in particular ways, this is of course less important than its mere statement would indicate. Nevertheless, as we have seen, a number of organizations, or their organs, can make findings, rulings, or regulations, or set standards and practices, or establish quotas, which have a persuasive or even a binding effect; and it is interesting to see that the principle of unanimity has, even in these instances, generally been abandoned.

A few organizations still require unanimous agreement to effect binding changes as does, for some changes, the Postal Union. The

Inter-American Coffee Board required a 95 per cent majority to set quotas, which, in its system of weighted voting, gave the United States, the principal importer, and Brazil and Colombia, the chief exporters, a veto. In some instances a three-fourths or two-thirds vote is required,[6] but by far the most common practice today calls for a majority decision in most circumstances combined with a two-thirds requirement for certain "important" or otherwise specified questions or for decisions by certain bodies.[7]

The picture evoked by this pattern of majority decision is, of course, misleading in the sense that, with a few exceptions, the more important a state's interest the greater its reluctance to entrust decisions to international organizations operating by majority rule. Even where no outright veto exists, where an organization has in fact been given limited powers, as in the commodity arrangements, the IBRD and the IMF, and others, systems of weighted voting have been introduced which give extra votes to nations individually or as a class in accordance with their contributions, or apparent interests and roles in the fields in which decisions are made. This has been particularly true in dealing with economic matters and serves to "resolve disputes which are not too 'political' or 'important' to foreclose any method except diplomacy, but are important enough that nations prefer to avoid their decision by impartial judges or arbitrators" or by an unweighted majority of the international community.[8]

Votes have in some instances been assigned solely on the basis of the financial contribution made by a party to the organization, usually by permitting the state to choose one of a number of "classes" of membership.[9] European railroad agreements have assigned votes in proportion to length of lines, and the International Hydrographic Bureau proportions some votes to merchant tonnage. As already noted, both the IBRD and the IMF allot votes on their Boards of Governors, in part equally (250 votes per state) and in part in accordance with financial obligations undertaken, giving the United States about one-third of the total.

On both the Wheat Council and the Sugar Council, total votes assigned exporters equal the total votes assigned importers providing a veto by class if needed, but within each class votes are apportioned in accordance with a nation's guaranteed purchase or sale of wheat for a given year or average imports and exports of sugar.[10] In other instances, numbers of votes are fixed and assigned by the constitutional arrangement—the Coal and Steel Community, for example, permits Germany, France, and Italy eighteen representatives (and hence votes) each in the Assembly while giving the Netherlands and Belgium ten each and Luxembourg four. In the Council of the Economic Community, which is made up of national representatives and can make some decisions by majority vote, Germany, France, and Italy each have four votes, the Netherlands and Belgium two each, and Luxembourg one—in some cases, the majority must not only amount to twelve but it must also include the votes of any four states.

In general, to the extent that weighted votes give effect to the realities of important disparities of wealth, power, interest, and the like, and permit "necessary" states to join with some assurance of available protection, the technique will undoubtedly be used in the creation of international institutions.

Voting weighted according to financial contributions is, of course, similar to voting by shares of stock in a corporation, and governments have used the corporate device in various forms to achieve similar purposes. They could also use it for operations in space and the Antarctic. Stock has been issued in exchange for cash contributions and for noncash contributions as well. One example is the European Company for the Financing of Railway Rolling Stock (Eurofima), which came into existence as a result of the need felt to integrate the financing of railway rolling stock in Western Europe. In 1955, the railway administrations of Austria, Belgium, Denmark, France, Germany, Italy, Luxembourg, the Netherlands, Norway, Portugal, Spain, Sweden, Switzerland, and Yugoslavia signed the Basic Agreement and, on October 20, 1955, the governments of these countries signed the Convention, to which was annexed the Statute of the Company. The Company is governed primarily by both the Convention and the Statute, and secondarily by Swiss law, in so far as the Convention does not provide to the contrary. It is registered in accordance with Swiss law but, under an Additional Protocol is exempt from stated local taxes. The capital is fixed at 50 million Swiss francs and is apportioned as follows: France and Germany, 26 per cent each; Italy, 14 per cent; Belgium, 11 per cent; Switzerland, 8 per cent; Netherlands, 6 per cent; Sweden, Yugoslavia, and Luxembourg, 2 per cent each;

the remaining 3 per cent is split up among Spain, Portugal, Norway, Austria, Denmark, Greece, and Turkey. Shares are either Class A, obtained for cash and potentially subject to receipt of dividends, and Class B, for the contribution of freight cars. Class B may be converted to Class A. Each shareholder's vote is proportional to the nominal value of all shares held, and voting in the General Assembly is by majority except on certain important questions, when a seven-tenths vote of the registered capital is needed. The Administrative Council serves as the board of directors—each railway administration having at least 2 per cent of the capital is entitled to two directors who serve for three-year terms. Majority vote carries in the Council except on the question of a loan, when a three-fourths vote is needed.[11]

Like Eurofima, the International Company of the Moselle is registered under the laws of a state, in this case Germany. The Company came into existence on January 28, 1957, and is charged with the development of the Moselle River for navigation and power purposes. The Contracting Parties—France, Germany, and Luxembourg—put some DM 370 million at the Company's disposal in varying proportions. Tolls are to be collected to pay the costs of the Company and to repay loans. Actual work on the project is done by the waterway department of each territorial state on a reimbursable basis.

The Company has the status of a limited company in German law and is governed as to organization by the Convention and annexed Statute and, subsidiarily, by German law. It has special exemptions, including tax relief, under the laws of Germany and of the other participating states as well. Its General Assembly is charged with approving an annual budget, distributing profits, and amending the Charter. Decisions are taken by two-thirds majority of the registered capital except where the Convention or German law require more and except for a three-fourths majority for decisions on the auditors' report and unanimity for amendment of the Charter. There are two Managing Directors, one French and one German, who, by joint decision, direct the Company's management. If agreement is impossible, either can request a decision by the Council of Supervision, composed of fourteen members—six German, six French, and two Luxembourg—appointed by the states involved for four-year terms. Decisions are by two-thirds majority. A special protection is afforded Luxembourg in that any decision directly affecting Luxembourg's territory, taken by any organ of the Company, must be concurred in by her representatives.[12]

Eurochemic owes a good deal to the precedent of Eurofima but differs in some respects. After extensive work by committees of the OEEC, a corporate form was devised to handle the construction and operation of needed plants and facilities for processing irradiated fuels. Eurochemic, then, is an international company established by treaty and derives its legal form and status solely from the International Convention. Only where the Convention and the Statute of the Company are silent may recourse be had to the law of Belgium, the state in which the Company's plant and laboratories are located.

The Convention signed by twelve governments established the constitution of the Company while a Statute, annexed to the Convention and needing unanimous consent of the member governments for major changes, set out the allotment of the Company's capital and the Company's organization. Shares in the Company may be held by governments, public or semi-public institutions, and even private groups. The initial allotment of 400 shares, with an authorized value of a 20 million E.P.U. units of account, went to West Germany, Austria, Belgium, Denmark, France, Italy Norway, the Netherlands, Portugal, Sweden, Switzerland, and Turkey. Of this group France, Italy, Portugal, and Sweden designated agencies to act as shareholders in the Company —all are strictly government agencies except for the Swedish group, which is three-sevenths privately owned. All the shareholders constitute a General Assembly. The Assembly's approval is required for a transfer of shares except where the transfer is between persons of the same nationality and is approved by the government having jurisdiction over the persons involved. All transfers to persons of different nationality also require the approval of a Special Group of the Steering Committee of the European Nuclear Energy Agency, a body made up of government representatives. That Group may also consider and propose measures of common interest raised by the Company's operations—its decisions bind the Company. Amendments to the Statute must be approved by the Group, which also hears disputes between participating governments concerning interpretation and application of the Statute. Majorities needed on votes in the

Group vary with the matter in question. The governments thus keep a direct hand in the Company's affairs.

The Company itself is made up of a General Assembly including all shareholders plus a representative of ENEA and one of Euratom in an advisory capacity, and a Board of Directors of fifteen plus representatives from ENEA and Euratom as advisors. Each shareholder with at least 5 per cent of the shares is entitled to a seat on the Board. As usual, the Board does the actual managing of the Company.[13]

Operations by states through such corporate forms escape entirely the application of another international legal principle which used to be considered sacrosanct—the principle of equality of states. Indeed it was this principle which was invoked to justify the demand for unanimity. So firmly rooted was this principle of equality that it was necessary to include in the Charter of the United Nations a statement that the Organization is based on it. This is not the place to reopen the long argument on the definition of equality, but, at least as international practice has developed, it does not mean parity in all aspects of participation in international organization. The analysis of voting arrangements has already illustrated this. Actual provisions regulating participation in various organs are additional examples.

While many of the existing international governmental organizations are set up on the strict basis of the "sovereign equality" of the members, a significant number have recognized and given special treatment to factors which are considered especially important from the point of view of the successful (and equitable) functioning of the organization. The Security Council of the United Nations, even more emphatically than did the Council of the League, for example, gives weight to the importance of the major powers in peace preservation activities. The Trusteeship Council, too, consists of the powers administering Trust Territories plus nonadministering permanent members of the Security Council plus enough other members to balance the administrators. In the make-up of the recently convened Intergovernmental Maritime Consultative Organization (IMCO), for example, the directing Council of sixteen is to be made up of representatives of six nations "with the largest interest in providing international shipping services," six "with the largest interest in international seaborne trade," and four others elected by the

Assembly, two on the basis of interest in shipping services and two on the basis of interest in seaborne trade. The Convention establishing the IMCO did not come into effect until ratified by "21 States of which seven shall each have a total tonnage of not less than 1,000,000 gross tons of shipping...." Further, the IMCO Maritime Safety Committee of fourteen members is to include at least the eight "largest ship-owning nations."[14]

Similarly, the Assembly of the ICAO is required in electing its Council of twenty-one states to give adequate representation to states of chief importance in air transportation, to states making the largest contribution in providing facilities, and to states representing all sections of the world. The Executive and Liaison Committee of the Postal Union, too, is required to be representative of widespread geographic areas, as is the Executive Board of WHO. The International Labour Organization must include among the sixteen governmental representatives on its Governing Body eight appointed by the members "of chief industrial importance," and six of the sixteen must be from non-European states. For changes in its Constitution the ILO requires approval of two-thirds of the members, including ratification by at least five of these same important states. The Governing Board of the International Atomic Energy Agency consists of the five Agency members "most advanced in the technology of atomic energy including the production of source materials" plus five others well advanced in the art or producers of needed raw materials, with geographical distribution of importance in the selection of this group. The UN Commission on Narcotic Drugs includes fifteen members who are either important producers of raw materials, important manufacturers of narcotics, or have an important social problem in narcotics control. The IMF provides for at least twelve Executive Directors, five appointed by the five nations with the largest "quotas" and seven elected by the Governors, including two from American states and five from non-American states not otherwise included. The IBRD, similarly, gives the five members with the largest number of shares one Executive Director each but provides less specifically for the election of seven others.[15]

Thus, importance in the field to be covered, knowledge and technical ability, previously demonstrated abilities, power in general, geographic representation, and the need to include certain states to avoid important loopholes, have all been accorded weight in different ways—a challenging complex. Later chapters will suggest what special factors might appropriately be given consideration in establishing administrative arrangements in the Antarctic and outer space if new international organizations are utilized. Precedent at least does not require full equality in representation. Nor does precedent call for any particular type of organization, although many ingenious ones have been invented and tried.

If no previous type of organization is considered by governments to be helpful in meeting the problems confronted as man penetrates the frontier areas of the Antarctic and of outer space, new ones will be developed. If man's ingenuity has already met the challenge of astronautics, it may likewise grapple with the technology of international politics. But it is precisely at this point that the contrast between the exact sciences and the humanistic sciences unfortunately destroys the parallel. Even when a technically perfect solution of a problem is found, the mind and the spirit of man may conjure up reasons of pride, spite, hate, prejudice, greed, fear, or inertia which prevent common progress along an agreed road.

Notes

1. Joseph P. Chamberlain 1955, *International Organization* (Carnegie Endowment), p. 60.
2. For the 1902 Convention, see 23 Hertslet, *Treaties and Conventions between Great Britain and Foreign Powers* 579. See generally Sayre, *Experiments in International Administration* 117, 131 (1919), and Chamberlain 1955, at 130–32.
3. There are also the International Cotton Advisory Committee, the International Rice Commission, and the Rubber and Wool Study Groups, which are consultative and advisory only. The International Wine Office is also a cartel-like institution and investigates such matters as violations of price agreements, but it is essentially an information agency and probably a means for dividing the market informally.
4. The International Tin Agreement of 1953 has similar provisions in Article 17 (7).
5. See U.S.T.S. 970. Of 36 votes the United States has 12, Brazil 9, Colombia 3, and each other producing nation 1.
6. See, *e.g.*, International Whaling Commission: regulations changed by three-fourths vote, other decisions by majority vote (Art. 3(2)); WMO: generally two-thirds (Art. 10(b)).
7. For example, ILO, WHO, ICAO, IMCO, IBRD, IMF, International Sugar Council, International Wheat Council, United Nations Commission on Narcotic Drugs.
8. Metzger, *Settlement of International Disputes by Non-Judicial Methods*, 48 *Am. J. Int'l L.* 408 (1954). See generally Chamberlain 1955, at 45–52.
9. International Office of Public Health, 2 Malloy, *Treaties* 2214 (T.S. No. 511); International Institute of Refrigeration (Art. 9).
10. Under the older International Sugar Agreement of 1937, the Council was composed of all Members while the Executive Committee consisted of three representatives each of the sugar-importing, cane-sugar producing, and beet-sugar producing countries, and the United Kingdom, the United States, Cuba, and the Netherlands had to be included.

Under the Rubber Agreement of 1934, neither the Malayan rubber interests nor the Netherlands could be outvoted on any matter of importance.
11. See 75 *Rev. Gén. des Chemins de Fer* 3, 4, 6 (Jan. 1956) and see generally, *Yearbook of Int'l Org.* 1958–59 (7th ed.). See also the European Conference of Ministers of Transport, *First Report*, paras. 27, 28 (1955); *Second Report*, paras. 3, 19, 39 (1956); *Fourth Report*, paras. 54, 55, 86–94, Annex I (1958). On earlier problems of European railroads, see Masters, *International Organization of European Rail Transport*, Int'l Conciliation No. 330 (May, 1937).
12. See Ambassade de France, Note d'Information, Mar. 8, 1956; Barron's, Aug. 13, 1956, p. 9; L'Economie, Mar. 12, 1959, p. 19.
13. See ENEA and the Eurochemic Company, *First Report of the Steering Committee for Nuclear Energy to the O.E.E.C.* (1958); ENEA, *First Report to the Consultative Assembly of the Council of Europe*, (1958); British Information Service, British Record, 1959, Feb. 20, 1959, p. 2.
14. Convention, Articles 17, 18, 28, 60. On the controversy over the meaning of "shipowning nations," see Jessup, *The United Nations Conference on the Law of the Sea*, 59 *Colum. L. Rev.* 234, 255–57 (1959).
15. ICAO Convention Art. 50; UPU, Art. 15; WHO, Art. 24 and UNESCO Constitution Art. 5; ILO Constitution Art. 7 (representatives of workers and employers participate as well as those from governments); ILO, Art. 36; IAEA, Art. 6; Narcotic Drugs, ECOSOC Res. 9 (I), Feb. 16, 1946; IMF, Art. 12 (3); IBRD, Art. 5 (4).

Charles E. Osgood

The case for graduated unilateral action

IMAGINE TWO HUSKY MEN standing facing each other near the middle, but on opposite sides, of a long and rigid, neatly balanced seesaw. As either man takes a step outward, the other must compensate with a nearly equal step outward on his side or the balance will be destroyed. The farther out they move, the greater the unbalancing effect of each unilateral step and the more agile and quick to react both men must become to maintain the precarious equilibrium. To make the situation even worse, both of these husky men realize that this teetering board has some limit to its tensile strength— at some point it is certain to crack, dropping them both to destruction. So both men are frightened, but neither is willing to admit it for fear the other might take advantage of him. How are these two men to escape from this dangerous situation—a situation in which the fate of each is bound up with that of the other?

One reasonable solution immediately presents itself: let them agree to walk slowly and carefully back toward the center of the teetering board in unison. To do this they must trust each other. But these men *distrust* each other, and each supposes the other to be irrational enough to destroy them both unless he (ego) preserves the balance. But now let us suppose that, during a quiet moment in the strife, it occurs to one of these men that perhaps the other really is just as frightened as he is and would also welcome some way of escaping from this intolerable situation. So this man decides to gamble on his new insight and calls out loudly, "I am taking a small step *toward* you!" The other man, rather than have the precarious balance upset, also takes a step forward, whereupon the first takes yet another, larger step. Thus they work their ways back to safety by a series of unilateral, yet reciprocal, steps —very much as they had originally moved out against each other.

Assumptions underlying this policy. We will talk about graduated unilateral *disengagement* (rather than disarmament) to emphasize the fact that we are considering a much wider range of acts of a tension-reducing nature than the notion of disarmament includes. This policy is based on the assumption that the Russian people and leaders are sufficiently like us to accept an unambiguous opportunity to reduce the probability of mutual nuclear destruction. It also assumes that the Russian leaders are susceptible to moral pressures, both from without and from within, since such pressures are an index of the success or failure of their system. It assumes that, unlike mutual negotiations which can easily be twisted into cold-war propaganda, unilateral *acts* of a tension-reducing nature are relatively unambiguous. It assumes that each unilateral act that is reciprocated makes the next such sequence easier to accomplish. Finally, it assumes that the Communists are as convinced that their way of life will win out in non-military competition for men's minds as we are that ours will and that they would be satisfied to compete on those terms. Many statements by Communist leaders in recent years indicate that this is their view.

Nature of this policy. Although I am not competent to specify the details of a policy of graduated unilateral disengagement, I can outline its essentials and give some illustrations.

Reprinted from "Suggestions for Winning the Real War with Communism,"
The Journal of Conflict Resolution, Vol. 3, No. 4, 1959, pp. 315-324.

To be maximally effective in inducing the enemy to reciprocate, a unilateral act (1) should, in terms of *military aggression*, be clearly disadvantageous to the side making it, yet not cripplingly so; (2) should be such as to be clearly perceived by the enemy as reducing *his* external threat; (3) should not increase the enemy's threat to *our* heartland; (4) should be such that reciprocal action by the enemy is clearly available and clearly indicated; (5) should be announced in advance and widely publicized to ally, neutral, and enemy countries —as regards the nature of the act, its purpose as part of a consistent policy, and the expected reciprocation; (6) but should not demand prior commitment to reciprocation by the enemy as a condition for its commission.

In general, the initial acts of unilateral disengagement would be small in magnitude of potential risk, should they not be reciprocated, but would increase in magnitude of risk potential as reciprocations were obtained. The initial series of unilateral acts would be designed to be cumulative in their tension-reducing effect upon the enemy but non-cumulative in their effect upon our capacity to deliver massive retaliation should this policy fail—that is, the acts would not be such as to weaken us progressively in the same area or in the "survival" area at all. Progressive unilateral disengagement should be viewed as a Phase I "primer," as a means of starting a reversal in the kinds of reciprocal actions now being made (i.e., the arms race); it should not exclude other policies, such as mutual disarmament negotiations, as they become available to us. Above all, it should be a policy entered into sincerely as an attempt to probe the enemy's true intentions, not as merely another weapon in the cold war, and it should be continued consistently until it is entirely clear what the enemy's intentions actually are.

The following is intended solely *as an illustration* of what a sequence of unilateral tension-reducing acts might be like; it is *not* a proposal of what the specific acts should be. As I tried to make clear in the beginning, I do not have the necessary training or information to make concrete proposals in this area, but I am sure there are people in our government who would be fully capable of doing so.

1. The United States government announces to the world that on a date one month from that time[1] it intends to share with the Russians (and all other nations) the information it has been gathering on the conditions of outer space, on the manufacture of "clean" nuclear bombs, and on various other developments in science whose main values are peaceful and scientific in nature. We indicate that, whereas our own action is not contingent upon their prior commitment, we expect them to respond in kind by sharing information of a similar nature. We also announce that this is part of our new policy—to reduce world tensions by direct, progressive unilateral steps.

2. On the date set, this action is taken. Our next move depends upon what the Russians have done at this point. (*a*) If they have reciprocated, we take a larger step; perhaps we announce that one month from that time we intend to deactivate and withdraw from a major military base—one closest and most threatening to the Russian heartland—and we invite them to send observers to check this operation. Again, we assert our general policy and suggest appropriate reciprocation on their part.[2] (*b*) If the Russians have failed to reciprocate to our first unilateral act, we take another small step: perhaps we announce that on a date one month from this time we intend to ban for a period of one year all further tests of nuclear weapons, and again we invite their inspection. We restate our general policy and our expectation that they will reciprocate.

3. On the date set, this second unilateral action, (*a*) or (*b*), is taken. If the Russians have been reciprocating, we take still larger steps bearing on focal points of tensions. It is quite possible, of course, that by this time the Russians may be trying to outdo us in "walking inward on the seesaw"—they have already made some tentative moves in this direction (e.g., their unilateral decision to ban nuclear-bomb testing for a period). If, on the other hand, the Russians have not reciprocated, I think we should continue our series of tension-reducing but non-crippling acts until either mounting moral pressure forces them to reciprocate or their negative intention becomes completely clear.

I believe that graduated unilateral disengagement can provide the basis for a positive and consistent foreign policy, one that is appropriate to international relations in a nuclear age and one in which we can take the initiative. In recent years our foreign policy has been essentially reactive and opportunistic. This is not only ineffective but downright dangerous, because it allows others to manipulate us by simply applying the right stimuli. We could find many opportunities to apply "psycho-logic pressure" to the Russians, if we were not such blind adherents to our *own* psycho-logic—that is, always taking a posture of opposition to them, regardless of the issue. For example, we should side *with* them on issues where we can do so in good faith—which would put *their* oversimplified picture of the world under stress. Acceptance of China into the UN may be a case in point. It seems to me that we have accepted too readily the role of defending the status quo, and, in doing so, we have forgotten that our own way of life is itself a major revolution in men's minds that is just getting under way.

Consideration of some objections

THERE are many deep-seated objections to any non-aggressive policy of this sort, and it will be well to anticipate them. I have had the benefit of many critical discussions of this policy with colleagues in many fields, and they have helped shake some of the "bugs" out of the proposal. Objections tend to fall into two classes: those based on more emotional grounds and those based on more rational or practical grounds.

More emotional objections. The most deep-seated objection to the policy I have outlined goes back to what I have called the *bogy-man conception of the enemy*. Many people will argue that *any* unilateral act designed to reduce tensions would be interpreted by the Russians as a sign of weakness and, given their inherent nature, would encourage them to encroach further on the free world. I cannot deny this possibility. But, if this is their inherent nature, then we should be sure of it before the present balance of military power has shifted to any significant degree. At least, we would have made a sincere effort to test their intentions, and the increased risk should be more than offset by a gain in favorable world opinion. Surely it would be a tragedy, a cause for cosmic irony, if two of the most civilized nations on this earth were to drive each other to their mutual destruction because of their mutually threatening conceptions of each other —without ever testing the validity of these conceptions.

Some Americans would see this policy as deliberate subversion, a *Communist-inspired Trojan Horse*. They would see it as a proposal that we surrender without a fight, and anyone making such a proposal must, so psycho-logic dictates, be on the Communist side. The argument that this is a strategy designed to get us out of a dilemma and win the real war would be incomprehensible to them. The fact that this objection flows more from emotion than from reason does not minimize its effectiveness.

Many more Americans would probably see this policy as *a coward's way*, a kind of "moral disarmament," and therefore entirely distasteful. *Pacifism* has always been associated with *weakness* in the American meaning system; in times of peace it may be *good-weak* (i.e., Milquetoast), but in times of war it quickly becomes *bad-weak* (cowardly). This, too, is as illogical a criticism as it is potent. The man who throws away his gun and faces his enemy with his bare hands and his wits is certainly not a coward. Neither are the men who follow the dictates of their reason and conscience against authority or public opinion. The story of the unfaltering passive resistance of the people of Norway to the wishes of quislings and their Nazi military supporters is a heartening example of courage—courage far greater than that of the men with guns who tried to break them.

Probably many people, however, will see this policy as *an idealist's fantasy*—certainly not one that faces up to the hard realities of the world in which we live. They would say that to weaken one's own defenses in the present situation is as softheaded as it is softhearted. However, what seems realistic within one's time-bound frame of reference may seem highly unrealistic within a broader scheme of things. What we call "realistic" usually depends upon what is habitual, what we are familiar with, and immediate goals. Thus it is "realistic" to concentrate on earning a living, getting one's children through school, and getting a little fun out of life, but it is "idealistic" to concentrate on the world of the future. So, too, is it "realistic" to react to outside threat with demands for more weapons, and "idealistic" to worry about where it is all leading us. Anthropologists are familiar with cultures that, through continued blind adherence to practices that once were "realistic," are gradually committing suicide. I think we are in exactly the same spot. We are continuing to practice rites and rituals of international relations that were developed in, and appropriate to, the past—firmly believing them to be "realistic"—in a present age that renders them suicidal.

More rational objections. But there are objections to graduated unilateral disengagement that arise from considerations other than its unpopularity. Even many of those who agree with the logic of my general argument may come to the conclusion that *it is simply not feasible.* For one thing, the existing attitudes and beliefs in the public mind, coupled with my own principle of psycho-logic, make it likely that, even if such a policy were adopted and sponsored by thoughtful and courageous leaders, both it and they would be rejected by the vast majority of people in this country. And more than that—would our leaders, charged with responsibility for the security of the nation, dare to take the risks such a policy involves? My answer would be that unpopular causes have been won before. Attitudes and beliefs can be changed. During the period when Russia became our ally and bravely defended Stalingrad, some of our own research at the time [4] showed that we not only came to think of Russians as *kind, noble,* and *fair,* but even as more *Christian!* Reviewing some of the war movies of that period is quite convincing on this score. Changes in public attitudes and beliefs depend upon events—if not those that occur inadvertently in the world, then those that are produced by men whose opinions count.

But what about the objection that *graduated unilateral action involves too much risk?* Although graduated disengagement does involve progressively increasing risk—indeed, the open and explicit assumption of risk is essential for its acceptance by the enemy—I believe such risk must be taken in the interest of our long-term security. Particularly is this true because, as I have tried to show earlier, our present policies involve equal or greater risk but yet offer no long-run hope of either security or winning the real war with communism. We must simply accept it as given that *there is no policy, no alternative we can choose, that entails no risk.* The best we can do is to weigh the risks involved in different policies against the ultimate gains that might be achieved.

Another objection made on the grounds of feasibility is this: are not my conditions—(1) that acts must be disadvantageous to us in a military sense and (3) that they must not increase the threat to our heartland—incompatible? In the first place, there is no perfect correlation between the military significance of events and their psychological impact. The execution of Nagy had no military significance, but it certainly affected attitudes toward the Communists. The Russians' first Sputnik and their more recent shot to the moon did little to change the balance of military power, but they certainly had far-reaching psychological effects on people in the United States. The full implications of nuclear armaments for what does and what does not constitute military potential must be carefully considered in devising unilateral acts. Milburn [2] has argued, most wisely, I think, that there is a certain minimum capacity for retaliation that has a maximum deterrent effect on an enemy—to be able to annihilate him ten times over does not further deter him than to be able to annihilate him once! This also illuminates the essential irrationality of our arms-race mentality; just as if we were engaged in some sports event, we keep being told that we must get and then stay "ahead".

This leads to another criticism—that this policy seems to amount to *betrayal of our obligations to defend the free world.* This question needs to be studied most carefully. Although it is true that graduated unilateral disengagement would mean reducing our military support in some areas where communism is in delicate balance with more liberal political views, does this necessarily imply defeat of our way of life in these areas—particularly if we succeed in reducing tensions between East and West generally? Often what is "communist" in name is no more antagonistic to our way of life than some governments we are supporting for power reasons (e.g., Franco Spain). In the long run, the so-called "underdeveloped" countries will achieve greater security if the Russians and Americans stop using them as pawns in a global chess game. Most importantly, our own security in a nuclear age is coming to depend less and less upon allies or upon territorial control—particularly as intercontinental missiles with nuclear warheads become available. Just as we would not now risk starting a full-scale war for a remote foreign objective, so is our own liability to attack coming to be independent of geographic distance. The British are already well aware of this sobering fact. And even if we were, against our own self-interest, to engage in continuous "brush-fire wars" about the perimeter of the free world, one can reasonably ask in just what sense this "defends" other nations. In the sparring of the two giants, it is the little countries on whose soils the skirmishes take place who suffer the most severe wounds.

This is a good place to point out the essential difference between the Kissinger Plan and my own proposal. Both the limited-war strategy and that of graduated unilateral disengagement rely on our capacity for massive retaliation for ultimate security of the heartland, but also use it as the basis for other acts of foreign policy. The crucial difference is this: Where Kissinger would use nuclear deterrence as the support for further tension-*increasing* acts ("war as usual"), I would use nuclear deterrence as the support for further tension-*reducing* acts. My proposal views the United States and Russia as gradually and carefully *disengaging* themselves along the far-flung border between free and Communist worlds, rather than as gradually and dangerously engaging themselves more and more inextricably. Where my proposal seems to hold out some hope for ultimately eliminating the massive nuclear deterrents themselves (and the threat to survival they represent), the Kissinger Plan offers no such hope.

Finally, there are some questions of practicality. Even assuming we were to undertake such a policy, *would the Russians accept our unilateral acts, and we their reciprocations, as bona fide?* Applying the same arguments I brought to bear against mutual negotiations, could we not expect the Russians to perceive our acts as "cold-war" deceptions? As a matter of fact, have we not taken unilateral steps before, particularly right after World War II, and been sorry for them? I would argue, first, that there are now deep and sincere desires on both sides to escape from the present course. Many of our earlier unilateral actions were made with one hand, while the other was busily building more devastating atomic bombs— when no one else had them. Second, and most importantly, unilateral *acts*, unlike mutual discussions, have the status of *fait accompli*, just like the satellites circling our globe. It is difficult to deny the fact of their commission (particularly when they are announced in advance and publicly observed); argument over the motivation of the first act tends to be resolved by execution of the

second. As to our distrust of Russian acts of reciprocation, there is a principle of human behavior that seems very relevant here: Man A's interpretation of Man B's reaction to him depends heavily upon A's own prior behavior toward B. If American Man has made an intentional conciliatory act toward Russian Man, he is much more likely to perceive the Russian's reciprocation as bona fide than if it came unsolicited.

But what if, because of mutual distrust, *one side tried to take advantage of the other's unilateral action?* Would this not have the "boomerang effect" of even further intensifying mutual bogy-man conceptions? It would be the self-fulfilling prophecy with a vengeance. This, of course, is the risk we take, but with *graduated* unilateral acts the initial risks are small. And here again the essential difference between unilateral acts and attempts to achieve mutual agreements must be emphasized: *unilateral actions do not demand prior commitment for their execution.* Whereas mutual disarmament discussions can break down because of mutual distrust and biased perceptions of what is equable, thus fulfilling the prophecy previously made and allowing each side to blame the other for the failure, an announced unilateral action is taken regardless of prior commitment from the other side to reciprocate. Prophecies made by the other side cannot therefore be fulfilled.

Actually, I believe that the pressure of world opinion, to say nothing of the growing power of China, would soon force the Russians to at least go through the motions of reciprocating on the low-risk level at which this policy would be initiated. And here another general principle of human behavior becomes relevant: *When people are made to keep on behaving in ways that are inconsistent with their actual attitudes* (e.g., as if they really trusted each other), *their attitudes tend to shift into line with their behaviors* (cf. the "dissonance" principle of Festinger [1]). In other words, I think that, if we could initiate a series of reciprocal, tension-reducing acts and maintain them over a sufficiently long period, the basic attitudinal conditions that now prevent us from reaching significant mutual agreements would be eliminated.

Maintaining the peace

THE policy of graduated unilateral disengagement is conceived as a Phase I strategy for reversing the irrational tensions/arms-race spiral before it leads to a blowup. It is also to be viewed as a *primer*, a policy which, if successful, would gradually produce conditions where longer-term, continuing policies designed to strengthen and maintain the peace could be instituted. One of the first policies made possible in Phase II would be negotiations for mutual agreements on disarmament having greater prospects of success. Then other policies, designed to strengthen the democratic as against the totalitarian way of life, could also be developed. Since Phase II does not have the immediacy and cruciality of Phase I, I shall only briefly sketch some ideas here.

RENEWED NEGOTIATIONS FOR MUTUAL
DISARMAMENT

If my analysis of the situation has been correct, two of the major hindrances to successful negotiation—biased perceptions of what is equable and self-fulfilling prophecies—are exaggerated by the existence of high tensions between the parties (distrusts, suspicions, aggressions, anxieties). Successful execution of a series of reciprocated unilateral acts would certainly reduce these tensions, even though not eliminate them. There would still be biased perceptions of what is fair and just, but, if the parties are mutually aware of this tendency toward bias and particularly if they expect what is really equable to appear somewhat biased in favor of the other side, then successful negotiation can be conducted. It is perhaps more true of the American side than the Russian that the negotiators themselves are not sure how well they represent their own country's position, especially since that position tends to shift somewhat with national elections and the like. In any case, reduced tensions should find the press and the public more likely to make hopeful rather than dour prophecies. There would still be attempts to get the better of any bargain ("one-upsmanship"), but this is what negotiations are for.

As Singer [3] has suggested, negotiations are most likely to be successful, and should therefore begin, *on procedures for handling future issues*, rather than on present problems of conflicting interest. For example, mutual agreements on how to handle the armament of future satellite bases of Russia and the United States could probably be achieved more easily now than agreements on how to handle the Berlin situation. Similarly, negotiations might begin to nibble away successfully at testing bans and inspection systems, then proceed (as tensions reduce and confidence grows) toward cessation of stockpiling nuclear bombs, and finally turn to elimination of the capacity of both sides for massive nuclear retaliation.

At this point, however, we must stop abruptly in our analysis and look around: Can what are today the two dominant military powers eliminate their capacities for massive retaliation when tomorrow there might be a France with a nuclear arsenal, the day after tomorrow a China, and the day after that an Egypt, and so on? Obviously not. It follows, therefore, that *disarmament negotiations and agreements will of necessity become universal at some stage*. As I noted earlier, nuclear weapons will become the "great equalizer" among nations in the new age we are entering. It also follows, inevitably, that inspection and policing operations will eventually have to be world wide and therefore involve strengthening of some form of world government. Whether we like it or not, gradual reduction in national sovereignty seems to be the price we will have to pay for our continued security.

OTHER CONDITIONS THAT SUPPORT OUR WAY
OF LIFE

In the earlier analysis of the conditions that support our way of life as against totalitarian ways a number of variables were specified, even though the list was admittedly not complete. Since, as we pointed out, our way of life seems to thrive in times of peace, strengthening these conditions should also serve to maintain the peace.

Economic plenty. As our Iowan farmer and friend of Mr. Khrushchev so sagely observed, men who have good food in their bellies, good clothes on their backs, and good homes for their families are much less likely to be aggressive toward their neighbors. We who yearly have surplus crops, and factories that could easily increase their productivity, have not seen fit to use them in the cold war against communism. At a national cost much less than the armament burden, we could subsidize export trade to foreign countries where it is badly needed, at prices they could afford to bear (and thereby not harbor the "rich-uncle" resentment). The objection that this policy would enable enemy countries to further divert men and materials to weapons, it seems to me, is outweighed by the influence this would have on their way of life and their motivation toward war.

Educational opportunity. It is almost a truism (though not quite) that, the broader and more liberal a person's education, the better is he able to understand the points of view of others and even to evaluate more critically his own point of view. Although we have been expanding our programs of exchange students and scholars, the numbers have been rather closely proportional to the ease of our relationship with the countries involved. In other words, and for obvious if invalid reasons, the rate of personnel exchange has been in inverse ratio to the density of the "iron curtain." It should be just the other way around; personnel exchanges should be increased in just those places where tensions are greatest—as a way of achieving mutual understanding and thereby maintaining the peace. It has also been true that we, in our ethnocentric fashion, have been much more eager to have others learn from us than we have been eager to learn from them, and this has had unfortunate effects on our foreign relations.

Communication. The more correct information the common people in different countries get about each others' ways and views, the more likely they are to appreciate the underlying similarities and to discount the more superficial differences. Whether the mass media are controlled by the state, as in Russia, or are relatively free from government regulation, as in this country, they play the major role in disseminating cross-cultural information. And in the case of a free press, at least, playing this major role means assuming a major responsibility. In the area of international relations, this means providing a faithful picture of world events as they occur and a factual interpretive framework within which the public can make its own judgments—rather than trying to *make* the news by presetting how the public should react to present and future events, as is the way with totalitarian media. Since media people are subject to the same national pressures and "atmospheres" as the rest of us, they have a difficult job maintaining the necessary objectivity. It also behooves us to learn all we can about how people in other countries think, how they use language, and what their basic attitudes, beliefs, and values are. The more we know about these things, the better we will be able to talk to them and understand what they are trying to say to us—and the better we will be able to maintain the peace.

Summary

THE real war with communism is a pervasive conflict between two antagonistic systems of belief about the relationship between individuals and their governments. Military action is only one of the many ways this battle for men's minds can be fought. Although the increasing availability of nuclear and biological weapons has not changed the nature of the war or its goals, it has radically changed the risks involved and hence must change the weights we give to alternative strategies.

Using three main criteria—supporting our own way of life, eliminating the threat of nuclear destruction, and feasibility for our country—I have tried to make an objective evaluation of current policies. Waging preventive war, maintaining deterrence by the threat of massive retaliation, and the policy of limited war clearly do not satisfy these criteria. Negotiations for mutual disarmament fail on the ground of feasibility, as the record plainly shows—the high level of existing tensions magnifies biased perceptions of what is equable and fosters self-fulfilling prophecies about the intractability of the enemy.

Most Americans, and, I believe, most Russians as well, are fully aware of the dangers —possibly suicidal—in our present course. Yet they feel impelled toward it with a sense of inevitability. "We must learn to live with it," we are told with reference to the threat of nuclear destruction; our editorials complain about the terrible cost of military preparations but conclude that there is no alternative but to "grin and pay it." I have tried to analyze as accurately as I can the dynamic mechanisms in human thinking that seem to be forcing us along this course; they include failure to take into account the relativity of social judgments, susceptibility to the working of "psycho-logic" in producing an oversimplified picture of the world, too restricted a perspective, and distortions in the assessment of human values.

An inquiry into the requirements for policy suggests two more or less independent stages: Phase I, the most critical and delicate, requires that we reverse the tensions/arms-race spiral, both to reduce the threat to our survival and to make possible the employment of other policies. The chief tool we have available here is manipulation of the external threat perceived by the Russians. Phase II requires that we maintain the peace by instituting policies which support our way of life as against totalitarian ways on a long-term basis.

The solution of our Phase I problem is seen in terms of unilateral action. Complete unilateral disarmament is considered and rejected as infeasible; however, analysis of this possibility does reveal what is probably the deepest objection to any unilateral policy— the bogy-man conception of the enemy. I have analyzed this conception and conclude that the Russian bogy man can be cut down to more realistic size and shape. If Russian perceptions and reactions to the present situation *are* much like our own, then there is another alternative available to us—one that allows us to test the intentions of the Russians without seriously weakening ourselves in the process.

This policy is what I have called *graduated unilateral disengagement*. It sees the United States as taking increasingly significant unilateral steps designed to reduce international tensions, these steps being disadvantageous in the military sense, but not cripplingly so in a nuclear age, being publicly announced and observed, and including invitations for Russian reciprocation.

The steps taken are graduated according to the reactions of the enemy. I believe that sincere desire on the part of the Russians to avoid the eventuality of a "hot" nuclear war, coupled with their anxiety about the spread of nuclear weapons and the pressure of world opinion, would force them to reciprocate rather than take advantage of these unilateral steps. The effectiveness of the policy would depend, of course, upon the intelligence with which the steps are devised and executed.

Graduated unilateral disengagement is proposed as a *primer*, as a way of first reversing the reciprocally aggressive spiral in which we are now caught and then making more feasible disarmament negotiations and the institution of the other policies designed to support our way of life. Like the limited-war strategy proposed by Kissinger, it makes use of our ultimate capacity for massive retaliation—but as the basis for tension-reducing rather than tension-increasing acts. If under careful study by experts it can be shown to be *feasible*, then I think this policy offers definite hope for eventual elimination of massive nuclear retaliatory capacity itself and the threat to survival it represents—something which is not envisaged in the course we are currently following.

Notes

1. Time intervals between announcements of unilateral acts and their execution should be just sufficient for rational consideration by the enemy, for his preparation of reciprocating actions, and for world opinion to mobilize.
2. It probably should be pointed out that, in an age of nuclear missiles, stable military bases whose locations are well known as "sitting ducks" anyhow, since they would be the first targets in a surprise attack against us; their only value is in terms of threat or in terms of a surprise attack on our own part—which I have argued we would not launch.

References

[1]. Festinger, L. *A Theory of Cognitive Dissonance*, Evanston, Ill.; Row, Peterson & Co., 1957.

[2]. Milburn, T. W. "What Constitutes Effective Deterrence?" *Conflict Resolution*, III (1959), 138–45.

[3]. Singer, J. D. "Disarmament and National Security." Unpublished memorandum, June, 1959. (Mimeographed.)

[4]. Stagner, R., and Osgood, C. E. "Impact of War on a Nationalistic Frame of Reference. I. Changes in General Approval and Qualitative Patterning of Certain Stereotypes," *Journal of Social Psychology*, XXIV (1946), 187–215.

Gunnar Myrdal

International economic integration

International disintegration from a national point of view

IN SPITE OF WORLD WARS AND DEPRESSIONS, we have seen in each of our advanced countries a tremendous rise in productivity, security of employment, and standards of living, and also greater equality of opportunity for the individual citizens and a general equalization of incomes and wealth. In the last forty years, with all their international turmoils, these countries have witnessed a more rapid national integration than ever before in history. The ordinary citizen is apt to believe—and very largely with good reason—that the national policies by which this has been brought about are good, even if they are exactly those which are here pictured as the causes of international disintegration.

I believe we may completely misinterpret the whole problem of how the development to international disintegration may be reversed if we do not try to go deeper in our understanding of the purposes of the national policies we are bound to criticize when we apply the value premise of international integration. These policies are, indeed, mostly—by no means always—motivated by good reasons, and nationally they have on the whole been successful.

If we want to avoid their resulting in increasing international disintegration, our duty is to propose such adjustments to them as will be favorable to international integration, while at the same time taking care to protect equally well or even better the national interests that they serve. That this should theoretically be possible is implied in the faith I have expressed,

that national economic progress and integration can only reach the highest possible levels in a well-integrated world.

We might first observe that the interest in stable markets—which also implies stable employment and continuous high utilization of plant and machinery, as well as of the distribution apparatus—is naturally a very legitimate one. If we wish to prevent this interest from expressing itself in national policies implying discrimination against foreign markets, we must find the means of giving increased stability to the international economy. This special reason for a nationalistic economic policy is bound to become ever more urgent; for the importance to individual enterprises and to the national economies of stable markets—and hence the economic disadvantage of unstable markets—has been steadily increasing, and will continue to do so, as modern industry progresses toward a higher level of mechanization and capital intensity.

More particularly, full employment is a legitimate national interest, not only socially but also economically. Full employment largely explains why investment and production have been held on such very high and generally rising levels after the Second World War in most industrial countries and why productivity has been making such strides. At the high level of capital costs, typical of modern industry, enormous productivity gains follow from a high and stable level of employment. A high level of output permits higher savings, investment risks are at the same time reduced, and the more capital-intensive methods, resulting from the higher savings and investments, induce a further rise in total output.

Reprinted from Gunnar Myrdal, *An International Economy.* Copyright © 1956 by Harper & Brothers. Reprinted with permission of Harper & Row, Publishers, Incorporated, New York, pp. 44–53.

The experience of the Great Depression and the popular appeal of the type of thinking we have become accustomed to associate with the name of Keynes have been epoch-making in our countries. No well-integrated nation will now hesitate to assert its control over exports, imports, and foreign exchange, if it is a question of maintaining the level of employment. Once more, to avert national discrimination against foreign trade and restrictive controls of foreign payments, invoked to defend full employment in the individual countries, we must organize the whole world economy by concerted international action in such a way that depressing effects on national welfare from events outside a country's national boundaries are less likely to arise.

The conflict between the aims and policies of the national welfare state and the ideal of international integration becomes intense when we consider the redistributional aspects of national economic policy. All the advanced countries have embarked in recent decades upon a comprehensive complex of fiscal and social policies aimed at a fairer sharing between their citizens of the exigencies of economic fortune; but this ever more intensified solidarity stops at the national boundary.

However, the main reason why these national welfare systems tend to disintegrate the world economy is that the redistributional intentions are not limited to a direct transfer of income via the collectors of taxes and insurance contributions, but invade the whole field of national economic policy, changing the basic conditions for the operation of the price system.

Workers in the United States have a long-standing tradition of regarding protective tariffs over practically the whole industrial field as a justifiable defense of their own living standards —which they know are high—since they prevent the products of cheap foreign labor from intruding upon the American market. The fact that this argument has logical flaws, and yet, in spite of all the orthodox teachings of the theory of comparative costs by generations of professors of economics, is nevertheless so tenaciously upheld, demonstrates how solidarity is limited to the nation. Nationalism is stronger than reason.

When the redistributional policies come to be applied in the broader field of economics, this is usually, however, not the result of an intellectual mistake but, in the given setting of international relations, quite a rational

approach. In almost all the advanced countries farmers have needed state assistance to preserve their living standards on more or less the same level as other social groups and, following the principle of solidarity, the nonagricultural majority of citizens has everywhere been prepared to accept very far-reaching modifications of the price system in order to ensure some degree of "price parity" for farm production.

Such agricultural price policies have everywhere become important cornerstones in the construction of the modern welfare state, but it has never seriously occurred to any influential and politically responsible group in any country that this expression of solidarity should expand beyond the state boundary. Instead, the international market has been freely used as a dumping ground, hurting particularly those exporting countries that have narrow margins and have to count their foreign exchange carefully.

In this connection it is interesting and illustrative to compare, on the one hand, the universal acceptance by a national political majority of the obligation to support economically the farming minority at home—almost as if it were self-evident—and, on the other hand, the cold-hearted disinclination in the industrial countries to do anything at all in order to stabilize the prices of raw materials and staple agricultural commodities of the underdeveloped and very poor countries, whose whole economic and political existence is continuously in jeopardy because of their unstable export markets. We are faced here, not only with an unwillingness to accept real redistribution of incomes, like the one that has been accepted within their own countries, but also with a reluctance even to consider schemes that would merely stabilize the markets over a period of years, without any international redistribution.

Agricultural policy is only one example, but an outstanding one, because of the large number of beneficiaries and the large aggregate amount of income redistribution involved. The same principle of national solidarity and almost total disregard of the interests of the foreigner operates over the whole field of economic policy. Everywhere there is demonstrated a readiness to improve the economic basis of national production; at bottom, a social equality and welfare interest is often the driving force. This is true of the coal policy in Britain, of the regulation of the fishing industry in Norway, and of wine production in France, to mention only a few examples.

The fixing of differential tariffs by the publicly owned and publicly managed railroads offers a flexible means in most countries of reallocating the relative advantage of national industries—and of discriminating against the foreigner. The same often goes for other means of communication, like ports and airlines. The whole body of regulations in the shipping industry follows the same pattern; a Norwegian is apt to point out that the high subsidies paid to the American shipping industry and the protection given it by other means in the postwar period may have cost the Norwegian economy more than all it received in the way of Marshall aid. As the state and local authorities handle ever larger budgets and so become increasingly important as buyers in many markets, their orders for goods and services are, by law or custom, directed so as to encourage so far as possible domestic industry. In all cases the purely national interest is emphasized and the principle of national solidarity followed.

Measures against restrictive business practices are a good illustration of the nationalistic direction of economic policy. While most governments have introduced legislation against internal cartels, in order to protect the consumers from exploitation, few responsible politicians would be prepared to extend this kindly interest to the protection of the foreign buyer, and in the international markets cartels have so far been given free play. In most parliaments it would, indeed, be looked upon as a strange and almost subversive thought if somebody were to suggest that sometimes the foreigner's interests in paying less for exports from the country than he is at present obliged to might need protection. Directed toward the outside, monopolistic exploitation becomes a patriotic virtue.

To except the international cartels from control is, incidentally, often a mistake from a national point of view, In many cases the international cartels are in reality collusions of industries in different countries, agreeing to leave each other undisturbed by competition from taking what the traffic will bear in their established markets. The powerful Scandinavian pulp and paper cartel has many purposes, but one is to permit the paper industry to charge higher prices at home; for decades stationery, produced from Scandinavian raw materials and often exported in the form of paper, could be bought cheaper in London than in Stockholm.

Apart from this and other self-deceptions— and economic policy is, relatively speaking, less influenced by ignorance and emotional irrationality than foreign policy in general[1]—the nationalistic economic policies of the modern welfare state are rationally suited to their purposes: to create more stable markets and to bring about a redistribution of incomes within the nation. The greater capital intensity of modern industry tends continuously to magnify the first interest. The progressing national integration is partly a result of the pursuit of the second interest, but is at the same time continuously strengthening its driving force.

This process, by which national integration induces international disintegration, is thus cumulative. International disintegration in its turn implies that foreign markets become even more unstable, which again strengthens the rational urge to concentrate on the home market and give it better protection, for the sake of internal stability. Progressive international disintegration makes it likewise ever more difficult to visualize clearly, and to urge effectively, a policy of international, instead of national, solidarity.

The international payments problem has naturally taken its present aggravated form as a result of the international crises, with their major disturbances of the trading and payments positions. A deeper and more permanent cause, however, is the unwillingness of the national welfare states to accept the infringements on their policies of economic stability and economic equality that an automatic trade and payments system would imply if it were to bring about changes in the national economies corresponding to changes in international economic relations. The whole complex of national policies, to which I have referred above, introduces rigidities—from an international point of view—that limit the possibilities of adjustments to ensure balance of payments equilibrium without short-term controls over international trade and payments.

To restore convertibility and eliminate trade discriminations that are caused by payments difficulties and that do not, per se, represent national interests, would seem to be a first step in preventing further international disintegration. The problem is, however, whether even this very modest goal can be reached in a world where the more basic national interventions have gone so far and are backed by such strong national interests.

Internationalization of national policies

THIS general world conflict between national and international integration obviously cannot be resolved in the interest of the latter ideal simply by preaching internationalism and denouncing nationalism. No advanced country is prepared to give up, or even to risk slightly, the fruits of national integration, which remains a supreme value to its citizens. And the goal for underdeveloped countries must be to start their own processes toward national integration; their success in doing so is also a first precondition for their incorporation in a better integrated world. To deprive nations of their right to organize their own affairs and, in particular, to control and steer their internal economic development, is out of the question.

It is wrong to believe that the volume of national interventions that could be abolished in a process of simple "international economic disarmament" is large. It is true that some of them stem from misunderstandings of reality; even more of them have been instigated by special interest groups without ever having been intellectually tested by having their consequences thoroughly explained to and understood by the people. It is my view, for instance, that the strict control over international migration largely belongs to this category of measures, which it was possible to push through only because of ignorance, apathy, or nationalistic emotionalism among the general public, as does also the high protectionism of the United States, whose economy stands for various reasons in a special position.

More generally, we should note that some smaller and highly developed national welfare states, such as the Scandinavian ones, have traditionally followed a much less autarkic economic policy than the bigger ones and have nevertheless succeeded in reaching an exceptionally high level of national economic integration and in maintaining a rate of economic progress and a standard of living as high as or higher than the bigger, more autarkic countries. This should serve as an indication that there is room for reconsidering many of the present national economic policies.

We should only be deceiving ourselves, however, if we did not recognize the fact that in most cases there are valid national reasons for these policies. In many cases there exists also an interrelationship between different types of national policies which makes it difficult or impossible to abolish even those that are not strongly backed by national interests for their own sake. Most industrially advanced countries may sincerely want to abolish, if they could, those trade and payments regulations that are directly caused by payments difficulties. However, the lack of international balance revealed by the payments difficulties is itself the result not only of the changes caused by wars and the like, but also of the trend to national integration and the national policies, inherent in this trend, aimed at stability and equality. These policies the governments are not in a position to renounce. They have mostly very important national purposes, even if their total effects—direct and indirect—are disastrous for international integration.

"The fact is that we have moved far from a world in which complete international specialization of labor is possible. Some of the rigidities . . . are here to stay. . . . This means that completely free trade is not feasible." Behind this statement of a commonly accepted negative fact, which I have chosen to cite from the recent Randall Report,[2] is the more important and positive fact that national integration, though it has its essence in equalization of opportunity for people in all social groups and geographical areas, has not been achieved simply by the abolition of barriers within the country, but rather by a process of social organization.

If, therefore, we realize that it is a misdirected and, in any event, hopeless attempt to try to reach international integration unless it be as a concomitant and, indeed, as a further development of national integration, we have to draw the further conclusion that international integration in this age has similarly to imply more than a breaking down of national barriers; it has to attempt reunification and harmonization of the national policies of cooperating states.

The task for international integration becomes, then, a matter of coordination. International labor and capital movements or freer trade cannot be expected to re-emerge simply as a result of agreements to undo national policies. On both sides of every boundary practically all "markets" are now highly organized by the state and by interest groups. What is needed is *an internationalization of these national policy structures themselves, preserving the essential values they represent to the several nations.*

If governments came together intent upon

a more ambitious cooperation of this kind, some of the present policies would clearly be seen to be misdirected and irrational. In many other cases it would become apparent that national protective measures served interests which, even when not unimportant viewed unilaterally, are minor compared with the major common gains that could be realized by mutual agreement to abstain from them. This is all in the realm of what I called "international economic disarmament."

There are, though, other policies—for example, agricultural protection or other intentional support of industries as part of a national development program—that are indispensable from the national point of view. If, however, these policies were worked out on the basis of international solidarity, they could be framed so as not to lead to a competition between the countries to shift their burdens onto each other.

A primary object of cooperation would naturally be to create stable international markets and, in particular, to guarantee a stable world trend of business and production. To the extent that stability was achieved, a great number of existing national policies would prove unnecessary and, in the first instance, the quantitative trade and payments restrictions, unpopular with all governments, could be abolished.

In this new type of international relations, founded upon a widening of economic solidarity freer movement of labor and capital would play a natural role, as also would, in some measure, the sharing of burdens for common objectives, and even the giving of economic aid.

As was the case in the advanced nation-states, which offer a prototype for our model of international economic integration, this whole process would need the impetus and momentum of economic progress. Only in an expanding world economy will there exist the conditions for mutual generosity without which the integration process would not get far.

The whole movement toward international integration along these lines will have to be argued in positive terms of the wider community of interests and aspirations, not the negative ones of wanting to break up the defenses of national integration. Indeed, the stepping stone will have to be the recognition of the great accomplishment that national integration really is in a few advanced countries. The goal has to be one of transforming this national integration into a more inclusive international solidarity. It must

meet the request of actually strengthening the values of national integration—and it will have to be realized that a great hindrance to international integration is the fact that so many countries are still badly integrated nationally.

This is a technically much more difficult task than the old internationalists, who saw the problem only in terms of tearing down barriers, have ever grasped. Yet this task of coordinating national policies is the one we are actually attempting to grapple with in the international organizations when, on occasion, we succeed in proceeding one step beyond the delivery by delegates of propaganda speeches and the voting of pious resolutions. Even though our attempts so far are feeble and the results small and insecure, this is the task and there is no way around it.

The need for international solidarity

TOO often, when the internationalist denounces nationalistic economic policies, he finds himself in the company of the reactionaries, who in all our countries are waging a rearguard battle against the developing welfare state. And so he becomes allied with—and, with him, unfortunately, his ideal of international integration—historical forces which in the long run are bound to lose out.

There is to my mind no doubt that, basically, the reason why efforts toward international integration in Western Europe have achieved so little is that the deeper questions have not been faced honestly and courageously. It was assumed that international integration could be attained without the basis of solidarity that national integration required, and without accepting the consequences of such widened solidarity. Under these circumstances the common man in Europe remained cold and suspicious. He felt that this was perhaps a new way of raising obstacles to national welfare policies.

There is no retreat from the welfare state, and its further growth is intimately bound up with further progress in national integration. The events of the last two years in America under a Republican regime, where the main social advances made under the Democratic New Deal and in the entire field of economic policy have been preserved or extended, and similar features of Conservative rule in Britain, Australia, and New Zealand after an era of

Labor governments, seem amply to illustrate this point. The biggest break we can expect in the trend toward the welfare state is the flatness of an individual step in a staircase.

A social trend is never an entirely straight line but moves by fits and starts. In addition to a natural tendency for a certain slowing down after a prolonged and rapid upward movement, we have had in recent years the complicated reactions to the cold war and the heavy burden of defense expenditure. These changing historical circumstances, and the counterbalancing main trend toward the welfare state, firmly backed by the interests and valuations of a democracy, have such an overwhelming preponderance that the fluctuations of political parties and personalities in power are almost without influence, if we take the broad and long view. As a matter of fact, the break in the upward movement has not been very much larger in the United States and Britain than in those Scandinavian countries which have been continuously governed by the Labor parties, as a matter of tradition.

From an international point of view, national economic policy is not to blame for seeking stability and equalization. Its failing is that it restricts solidarity to the individual nations. We have to attempt to build a better integrated world upon states that are all, and for the most excellent reasons, continuously seeking better integration nationally. To face this issue clearly is the first requirement when attempting to tackle the problem of international integration.

I have criticized traditional internationalism —that seeks a short cut to international integration by the simple and wholesale abolition of national economic policies—as not only reactionary but also as ineffective, since it goes against an immutable historical trend, determined by people's interests and valuations in a democracy. I do not pretend that my proposed substitution—a policy of international coordination of national policies based upon a widened international solidarity—is an easy road. All the succeeding chapters demonstrate the almost insurmountable difficulties that have to be overcome; the present trend undoubtedly points in the direction of continued and increased international disintegration. I do, however, believe that while the other solution is not practical—and, in addition, would harm values that are dear to us and destroy accomplishments that are the pride of our generation—this one is, at least, a sensible goal, however difficult to reach, and one that good and well-informed people would wish to strive for.

Notes

1. Cf. my article, "Psychological Impediments to Effective International Cooperation," *Journal of Social Issues*, Supplement series, No. 6, 1952, pp. 12 ff.

2. United States Commission on Foreign Economic Policy, Report to the President and Congress, January 1954.

c. International law and organization

Inis L. Claude, Jr.

The management of power in the changing United Nations

THE CENTRAL PROBLEM OF OUR TIME is to achieve the effective management of the power relations of states. The world is constituted as a system of independent but interdependent states—independent in authority but interdependent in destiny. States are units of power. While power is a complex conception, for present purposes it may be construed in the narrow sense of force. Physical ability to kill, to damage, or to coerce, is the particular aspect of power which serves as the focus of this article. States are characterized by the possession, in varying degrees, of this capacity to damage or destroy each other. This power may be used in competitive struggle, producing destruction on a massive scale. It may be used unilaterally, producing enslavement and degradation of its victims. In short, both survival and freedom, both sheer existence and the higher values that enrich existence, are implicated in the problem of power. The national interest of every state, and the common interest of all men, in the preservation and development of civilization are threatened by the paroxysms of violence which states are capable of unleashing. Hence, the primacy of the task of controlling the use of force by states, of managing the power relations of states, cannot seriously be questioned.

I use the term, *management*, to convey the conviction that the problem of power is here to stay; it is, realistically, not a problem to be eliminated, but one to be managed. At all levels of society, human beings inherently possess and inexorably retain the capacity to do physical violence to each other. The task of socialization is not to abolish power, but to control its exercise. At the level of collectivities, I take it as a basic postulate that there will always be human groups—if no longer national states, then other social sub-divisions—which will be capable of damaging each other. They cannot ultimately be deprived of this capacity. Given brains and brawn, men can contrive instruments of lethal warfare, be they clubs or hydrogen bombs; given human social instincts and skills, men can contrive to organize their violence as the clash of collectivities. The issue will never be whether power exists; it will always be whether power is subjected to effective management.

My emphasis upon the concept of management of power carries with it the specific implication that disarmament is not the key to the problem of international violence. In the literal sense, the notion of disarmament would seem to suggest reliance upon the unattainable ideal of eliminating the potential of states for violence. Most actual disarmament efforts are, of course, more modestly conceived; they aim at checking the arms race and securing the adoption of systematic programs of arms limitation or reduction. The value of such achievements, if they should prove

Reprinted from *International Organization*, Vol. 15, Spring 1961, pp. 161–177.

possible, might be considerable. They might, by restricting the distribution of certain types of weapons and limiting the quantitative levels of power accumulation, prevent the power situation from becoming inherently unmanageable. Thus, that brand of disarmament which is more accurately characterized as arms control may be an essential prologue to, or accompaniment of, any effective scheme for the management of power in the contemporary world. Whether or not disarmament can be attained, however, the basic problem will remain that of establishing and maintaining reliable control over the exercise of power. Even if all existing weapons were destroyed and production of armaments totally suspended, the capacity to devise instruments of terrible power would remain a permanent potentiality; man cannot unlearn what he knows about the means of creating power. My basic criticism of the disarmament motif is that it tends to foster an emphasis upon abolition of power as the key to peace and security, whereas it seems to me that the problem is more realistically defined in terms of the necessity of bringing the exercise of power by states under effective and reliable control.

The theory of international relations, if one may apply that term to a literature which is more a thing of shreds and patches than a seamless garment covering our understanding of the process of international relations, contains three basic concepts which may be regarded as relevant to the problem of the management of power: balance of power, collective security, and world government. These concepts have not been defined with care, used with precision, or made to serve as bases for systematically elaborated theoretical structures; at best, they stand as rudimentary snippets of theory which have been used more for polemical than for analytical purposes. Each of them has attracted its quota of advocates and detractors, who have tended to treat the concepts competitively rather than comparatively. In short, balance of power, collective security, and world government are not terms which designate well-developed and generally understood bodies of doctrine. Nevertheless, they do represent the leading ideas regarding the problem of the management of power in international relations, and they figure as the focal points of contemporary discussion and controversy concerning this problem.

It is, of course, hazardous to try to establish definite meanings for terms which have customarily been used so loosely and inconsistently as these. Recognizing that others may exercise the right to invest them with meanings different from mine, I nevertheless venture to suggest that these three concepts can, with considerable justification derived from the literature of the international relations field, be taken as characterizing disparate systems of relationship among states—systems related to each other as successive points along a continuum and differing most fundamentally in the degree of centralization of power and authority which they imply. In this view, balance of power represents the extreme of decentralization, a kind of *laissez-faire* arrangement in the sphere of power politics. It suggests a scheme within which individual states, separate units of power and policy, operate autonomously, without subordination to a central agency for the management of power relations. Singly or in combinations reflecting the coincidence of interests, states seek to influence the pattern of power distribution and to determine their own places within that pattern. In such a balancing system, the constituent states function as coordinate managers of the power situation.

Collective security falls next in line along the scale of centralization, representing an effort to deal with the power problem by superimposing a scheme of partially centralized management upon a situation in which power remains diffused among national units. It involves a centralization of authority over the use of force, to the extent that states are deprived of the legal right to use violence at their own discretion. In its ideal form, it calls for an international organization with authority to determine when a resort to force is illegitimate and to require states to collaborate under its direction in suppressing such use of force.

Finally, world government takes its place at the opposite end of the scale from balance of power, suggesting the creation of an institutional system involving a monopoly of power, comparable to that alleged to exist in a well-ordered national state. In this scheme, both the possession of the instruments of force and the control of policy concerning their use are presumably centralized in an institution superior to the state.

Unfortunately, the differences among these concepts have more often than not been exaggerated and misstated. The case for adoption of one or another has often been argued as if a choice had to be made between totally dissimilar systems, one offering hopeful prospects for order and security, and the other leaving the world mired in hopelessness. In fact, the differences among them are far from absolute and are perhaps less interesting and significant than the similarities—to the analyst, if not to the propagandist. Having plotted them along a common scale, I would suggest that they tend to slide into each other, developing points of approximation or overlap, rather than to maintain fixed distances of separation. Both balance of power and collective security are deterrent schemes in that they rely upon countervailing power to frustrate the ambitions of powerful aggressors; moreover, the two systems are heavily dependent upon sets of prerequisite conditions which are similar in important respects. One can argue, for instance, that the balance system requires the diffusion of power among a number of major states so that no single state will control such a large fraction of the world's power resources as to make the task of counterbalancing it inordinately difficult; the same requirement can be cited for a collective security system, to avoid the possibility that any state will be invulnerable to the pressure of collective sanctions. Thus, a global power configuration marked by bipolarity is equally unfavorable to the operation of a balance system or of a collective security system. One can demonstrate that a successful balance system requires that national policies be adaptable to contingencies that may arise rather than rigidly fixed, so that old friends can be resisted when they endanger the stability of the system and former enemies can be supported when the exigencies of the power situation so require. A similar flexibility of policy, involving the capacity to switch the foci of friendship and enmity, is essential to collective security.

On the other hand, the ideal scheme of collective security is not wholly unlike that of world government. It involves a concentration of authority in a central organ giving the organ a government-like quality that can be ignored only if one dogmatically denies, as many proponents of world government do, that there are many shadings of gray between the "black" of essential anarchy and the "white" of actual government. Moreover, a scheme of world government which undertook to maintain order on a global scale by methods comparable to those used within limited boundaries by national governments would, in fact, involve reliance upon intricate and delicate processes of balancing the power of constituent units of the society. The proposition that government is a matter of exercising a literal or virtual monopoly of power over a society, rather than of presiding over a balancing process, is largely a myth, even though totalitarian dictators have sometimes gained considerable success in translating it into reality. The point is that the typical enthusiast for world government wants a system which has more in common with the balance of power system than he customarily realizes or admits.

Despite these and other points of similarity which might be cited, there are characteristic differences among the implications of the concepts of balance of power, collective security, and world government, sufficiently important to justify the proposition that they designate alternative patterns for the ordering of power relations among states. The balance of power concept allows states to maneuver freely in a competitive world. Its typical institutional expression is a set of flexible alliances within which recurrent shifts of alignment take place; its promise of order lies in the expectation that competing power urges will somehow balance and thereby cancel each other, producing deterrence through equilibration. Collective security looks to a general international organization, presiding over a collaborative, rather than a competitive, arrangement. It purports to inhibit any aggressor by making virtually all the other states the *ad hoc* allies of any state that suffers attack; thus, it promises deterrence through the mobilization of a preponderance of power against any member of the system which threatens its peace and order. World government relies upon neither the interplay of competitive states nor the collaboration of states organized to uphold the principle of order; it promises to deprive states of their standing as centers of power and policy, where issues of war and peace are concerned, and to superimpose upon them an institution possessed of the authority and capability to maintain, by unchallengeable force so far as may be necessary, the order and stability of a global community.

These are not necessarily the only conceivable patterns for the management of power in international relations. They are, however, the patterns which have become the common currency of intellectual transactions concerning world affairs in the twentieth century. Whether any of these patterns has been, or can be, or should be, fully realized in actuality is not at issue here. They constitute the standard list of theoretical alternatives; they are the intellectual pigeon-holes in constant use. . . .

The evidence leads me to the conclusion that the formulators of the United Nations Charter deliberately refrained from attempting to create an organization which would undertake to control the use of force by great powers or states supported by them, through the operation of a collective security system. They acted on the assumption that such a venture could not succeed, and ought not to be attempted. In this fundamentally important sense, the establishment of the United Nations represented the repudiation of the idea of collective security, not an unsuccessful effort to institutionalize its application.

What then was the nature of the scheme for management of power in international relations which the Charter set forth? The answer can be found only if we emancipate ourselves from the rigidity of the categories of balance of power, collective security, and world government.

The influence of the collective security orientation is evident in many of the provisions of the Charter. Aggression is prohibited, though left undefined; in principle, states are deprived of the legal right to use force against each other at their own discretion, in pursuit of their unilaterally defined interests and purposes. The legitimacy of resort to international violence is made subject to the determination of an international body; an effort is made even to hold states accountable to an international body in their invocation and exercise of the right of defensive action. Moreover, the principle is asserted that any illegitimate use of force in international relations is properly a matter of concern to all Members of the United Nations. The Security Council is expected to be equipped, through agreements to be concluded with Member States, with military forces constantly ready for action at its decision; it bears the responsibility for taking action to uphold peace and security and has a general authority to command the assistance of all member states—except that their obligation to provide military units is limited to the commitments which may be stated in their agreements with the Security Council.[1]

In its restriction of the right of states to resort to force, its espousal of the principle of collective action to repress illegal violence,

and its provision for an organ to preside over the arrangements pertaining to the use of force, the UN scheme exhibits some of the essential characteristics of a collective security system. It should be noted that it is incomplete, in that the acceptance by states of an operative obligation to put force at the disposal of the Security Council—and, consequently, the equipping of the Council to perform its enforcement role— is postponed; on this score, the Charter registers merely an agreement to agree. Nevertheless, the scheme clearly reflects the intention to create an international enforcement mechanism capable of functioning in cases which do not involve a conflict of interest and will among the great powers. It might be described as a design for a collective security system applicable only to situations of relatively minor importance as far as maintenance of the general peace is concerned. The framers of the Charter contemplated a system in which the great powers would bear the major responsibility for providing United Nations enforcement potential, with supplementary contributions by lesser states, for the purpose of dealing with aggressors acting without the support or sympathy of any of the major powers. The great powers, it should be recalled, persistently spoke at San Francisco of the "unanimity rule," not the "veto rule," thereby emphasizing the positive hope that the Security Council would be able to act decisively against aggression insofar as its permanent members could achieve unanimity in supporting such action. There was no middle ground in this arrangement. Either an act of aggression would be committed by a minor state with all the major powers ranged against it, in which case collective suppression of the misdeed would be a relatively simple matter, or it would be commited by a major power or its protégé, in which case the United Nations would be debarred from attempting collective suppression. Although the applicability of the United Nations enforcement scheme to the control of the defeated Axis powers of World War II was excluded, it was provided that this limitation might be removed at the request of the victorious allies.[2]

The key prescription of the Charter for dealing with the potential crises of greatest international importance—those involving antagonism among the great powers or aggressive action undertaken or sponsored by one or more of the great powers—is to be found in Article 51, with its recognition of "the inherent right of individual or collective self-defense" in response to armed attack. This provision may be interpreted as a declaration that it is incumbent upon states to take the necessary measures, outside the structure of the United Nations, for dealing with the most crucial threats to peace and security which might arise. The framers of the Charter were saying, in effect, that they saw no possibility of implementing collective security safely and effectively against major powers, and that some device other than collective security would have to be improvised if a major power should go on the warpath. They did not, as has often been suggested, assume that no such problem would arise; in this respect, they were hopeful but not smugly confident. Rather, they asserted the conviction that it was impossible to construct a collective security system adequate to deal with such a problem, if it should arise. The advice implicit in Article 51 is that states should establish alliances—combinations for collective self-defense—for dealing with the actuality or threat of attack by powers exempted by the veto rule from the impact of the projected United Nations enforcement mechanism.

In this vitally important respect, the Charter contemplates what is in essence a balance of power system. This was no doubt an unhappy choice for the founding fathers. Their ideological bias clearly ran not toward the balance of power but toward collective security. Their sense of realism, however, impelled them to acknowledge that they could see no way to devise a workable alternative to the balance of power system for dealing with aggressive threats posed directly or indirectly by great powers. It should be noted that the balance of power system, involving the freedom and responsibility of states to look to their own position within the international configuration of power, does not have to be adopted; it exists, until and unless an alternative arrangement for managing the power relationships of states is put into effect. Failing even to formulate—much less to put into effect—a more centralized scheme for handling conflicts in which major powers might be competitively engaged, the creators of the United Nations left states to "do what comes naturally" in such situations: that is, to develop the power and policy, individually and in alignment with others, for coping with security threats presented by dangerously powerful antagonists.

The original scheme of the United Nations for the management of power on the international scene may thus be described as one which left the balance of power system intact for cases of major importance to global peace and order, and provided for a collective security system to be applicable in cases of relatively minor significance. The Charter endorsed the *ideal* of collective security in unqualified terms, but envisaged its application in severely limited terms. It limited the legal right of states, great or small, to engage in the unfettered maneuvering which has been traditionally associated with the operation of a balance of power system, and reflected the hope that the political processes of the United Nations would inhibit the tendency of states to abuse their strength under the pretext of protecting their relative power positions. In the final analysis, however, the Charter acknowledged that the new Organization could not relieve states of the necessity of attempting on their own to match power with power, as the means of attaining security within the context of great-power rivalry. The scheme of the Charter was a curious amalgam of collective security, dominant in ideological terms, and balance of power, dominant in terms of practical application. The concept of world government, insofar as it figured at all in the consideration of the San Francisco Conference, was viewed as a distant ideal.

The history of the actual operation of the United Nations in the realm of power politics is largely a story of vacillation concerning the degree to which the implementation of collective security should be attempted, and of efforts to find other means by which international organization can be used to modify the working of a balance of power system. The reluctance with which the framers of the Charter viewed the continued dependence of the world, by default, upon the balance of power system has been shared by many of the statesmen who have shaped the subsequent development of the United Nations....

In the final analysis, then, the effort to control the use of force in international relations since World War II has been expressed in the form of a balance of power system. What has emerged is a balance system modified by a number of factors including, most significantly for purposes of this analysis, the existence of a general international organization. It would be too much to say that the United Nations "presides over" the operation of the balance of power system, but its functioning does have considerable relevance to the working of that system.

The real question for our time is not whether the United Nations is likely to develop a collective security system—or, more remotely, to institute a scheme for the management of power which would deserve the name of world government—to replace the balance of power system. The real question relates to the manner in which, and the degree to which, the United Nations can and will modify the operation of the balance system and contribute to its success as a device for preventing war. In facilitating diplomatic confrontation, fostering serious and meaningful negotiation, and providing assistance in the pacific settlement of disputes, the Organization plays a role which may be useful in mitigating the dangers of failure. In putting moral and political pressure upon states to conform to the principles of international conduct which the Charter prescribes, the United Nations may help to limit the abusive aspects of state behavior which balance of power operations may otherwise entail. In carrying out its wide-ranging activities within the economic and social sectors, the Organization may contribute to a long-term transformation of the global situation which will create new possibilities for the effective management of the power problem.

Finally, it should be noted that a role for the United Nations, more immediately and directly related to the issue of military violence, has been for some time in the process of development. In a number of instances, the Organization has secured and provided military personnel for supervising truce arrangements, patrolling armistice lines, observing developments in zones of particular instability, and otherwise contributing to the maintenance of precariously peaceful relationships. Against this background, an act of creative political ingenuity occurred in 1956, when the Organization was given the mission of mobilizing a United Nations Emergency Force, composed exclusively of military elements from states other than great powers, to function as a stabilizer of the dangerously tense situation in the Middle East. When a somewhat analogous, albeit infinitely more complex, situation arose in the Congo in 1960, the machinery of the United Nations was again used to organize and carry out a military operation. There were basic differences in the tasks required of United Nations forces in these two situations, and it may be that those differences will produce different outcomes for the two ventures; at this writing, there seems grave danger that the Congo operation will fail as clearly as the Middle East operation succeeded.

What is important for this analysis, however, is the element of similarity in the two cases. In both instances, the United Nations was used as a device for bringing into a troubled situation military contingents contributed voluntarily by smaller states and placed under the direction of the Secretary-General, for the purpose of preventing the eruption of disorders that might result in the competitive intervention of the rival great-power blocs. This is a far cry from the original notion of a United Nations enforcement system which would depend upon the unanimous participation of the great powers; it expresses the notion of a United Nations stabilization system dependent upon the unanimous abstention of the great powers.[3] Such a system cannot be forced upon unwilling great powers. It can function successfully only with their acquiescence, derived from the recognition that they have a stake in the avoidance of conflicts that might precipitate war. Intervention by the United Nations in the Middle East and in the Congo represents the experimental development of a significant role for the Organization in the balance of power system, that of assisting in its orderly operation by undertaking to insulate particular troublespots from the impact of the rivalry which dominates the relationships of the major powers. This experimentation, whatever its outcome, is a hopeful sign, for it points to the general recognition of a basic truth i.e., that the potential contribution of the United Nations in our time to the management of international power relationships lies not in implementing collective security or instituting world government, but in helping to improve and stabilize the working of the balance of power system which is, for better or for worse, the operative mechanism of contemporary international politics.

Notes

1. This summary of the scheme is based upon Articles 2, 24–25, and 39–51 of the Charter.
2. See Articles 53 and 107 of the Charter.

3. Cf. Lincoln P. Bloomfield, *The United Nations and U.S. Foreign Policy* (Boston: Little, Brown, 1960), pp. 44–45, 67.

Chadwick F. Alger

Non-resolution[1] consequences of the United Nations and their effect on international conflict[2]

Introduction

SECRETARY-GENERAL HAMMARSKJOLD has, on a number of occasions, admonished us to broaden our scope of inquiry when assessing the influence of the United Nations on international relations. For example, in the introduction to his Fourteenth Annual Report to the General Assembly in August, 1959, he declares that there is a tendency to overestimate the significance of votes on General Assembly resolutions in comparison to other consequences of Assembly meetings:

> ... whatever legal standing the Charter may provide for the results of the votes, the significance of these results requires further analysis before a political evaluation is possible. This observation applies to the composition of majorities and minorities as well as the substance of the resolutions. These resolutions often reflect only part of what has, in fact, emerged from the deliberations and what, therefore, is likely to remain as an active element in future developments ([9], p. 10.)

It is the purpose of this article to discuss some potential non-resolution consequences of the United Nations—in particular, the General Assembly. It is also a goal of this article to show how these non-resolution consequences may significantly affect international conflict.

In very general terms this discussion will assess, in an exploratory way, how the United Nations has altered patterns of communication among nations, providing new routes of contact under new conditions; how it has had an impact on national policy; and how it has altered the career patterns and possibly the future behavior of participating individuals.

The following questions reveal more specifically the areas of concern:

1. What effect does the need to defend publicly national policy in an international organization have upon the prior formulation of that policy?

2. How does experience in international organizations affect the attitudes of the participants (temporary delegates and members of permanent missions) when they move on to other national roles?

3. What is the effect of the availability of a neutral ground for inter-nation contact?

4. How do the processes of "parliamentary diplomacy" produce outcomes different from traditional diplomatic practice?

5. What effect does the automatic participation of mediators (secretariat and national delegations) have on the outcome of conflicts—in day-to-day interaction as well as on extraordinary occasions?

6. What is the consequence of increasing the number of nations actively involved in a particular problem?

7. What is the effect of creating an international center where press and other private organizations have new and different kinds of access to officials and to each other?

8. What is the significance of the new sources and kinds of information that members of international organizations obtain?

9. What is the significance of opportunities that international organizations provide for increased informal contact among diplomats?

Although this paper will not be organized in terms of these questions, all will be dealt with to some degree in the discussion that

Reprinted from *The Journal of Conflict Resolution*, Vol. 5, 1961, pp. 128–145.

follows. First, however, it might be illuminating to ask why only vague and inferential responses can be given to such important questions. A fundamental reason is the tendency to study political organizations, national as well as international, mainly in terms of their accomplishment of their explicit goals through the explicit mechanisms established for this purpose. In the case of the United Nations, this means that there is concentration on the passage or defeat of resolutions in public meetings and on extraordinary mediation attempts called for by these resolutions. However, this type of activity does not produce the only, nor necessarily the most important, impact that the organization has on relations among members. The tendency to focus upon explicit organizational goals and mechanisms for their attainment is accompanied by a tendency to attribute United Nations influence on the course of events only in cases where a problem is carried through to resolution within United Nations jurisdiction. Thereby we sometimes may miss the impact of the United Nations upon problems that at some point become the subject of United Nations concern but are not finally resolved within its jurisdiction. What, for example, was the effect of yearly United Nations debates on Cyprus on the eventual settlement elsewhere of the dispute? Would the United States–Soviet negotiations in Geneva on nuclear testing have taken place without prior debate on the question in the United Nations and without the pressure for test cessation brought by other nations on American and Soviet delegations during this debate? It is quite clear that the kind of international system in which the United Nations operates has prevented the resolution of such problems within a multilateral organization. But it is contended here that scholars have neglected the study of how multilateral organizations affect the broader international system in which they operate even when problems are not resolved within their walls.

The neglect of non-resolution consequences is, of course, not a limitation of research on international organizations alone.[3] What is known, for example, of the role of the United States Congress aside from its performance of its legislative function? How significant is the United States Congress as a nationwide communications network for local leaders? What is the effect of congressional participation upon congressmen and eventually upon local policy preferences? It may be, however, that the customary perspective in the assessment of the effects of political institutions overlooks matters of more significance in the case of organizations like the United Nations than in the case of bodies like the United States Congress. The Congress is a coercive body which, in most instances of member conflict, insures that minorities comply with the measures passed by majorities. The General Assembly of the United Nations, increasingly the most significant body in the United Nations, is not coercive. The General Assembly is a non-coercive body made up of autonomous sub-units. Its resolutions are only recommendations and cannot force minority compliance. Perhaps significant aspects of the General Assembly are being neglected by testing it against a model provided by coercive bodies. New ways may be needed for looking at this type of institution.

Lacking satisfaction with an evaluation of the impact of the General Assembly on world affairs solely on the basis of the resolutions it passes, what raw material is available for making an evaluation broader in scope? A very simple approach will be taken. What does the observer of United Nations Headquarters during a General Assembly session see? The direct observation of the behavior of persons involved in General Assembly activity may provide leads for probing the non-resolution consequences of their behavior. Some of the readily observable aspects of the General Assembly will be described very briefly and then the significance of these characteristics for international relations in general and for international conflict in particular will be examined.

Before proceeding it might be prudent to anticipate the criticism of those readers who are very familiar with the General Assembly and feel that some of what follows is a description of the mundane and obvious. In the first place, some of these things are not as well known to those who have not had the opportunity to observe the General Assembly over a period of time as more knowledgeable scholars sometimes assume. Second, the task of the scholar is not to describe and explain what is not obvious, but the significant. Particularly in the social sciences where certain fundamental aspects of human behavior are very familiar to the human participant and observer, there is a tendency to focus on the unique and dramatic instead of on patterns of behavior that are significant. The description of the "obvious" characteristics of the international community that the General Assembly brings into being may provide the raw materials for explaining significant effects of this community on international relations.

Some general characteristics of the Assembly

THE scholar who intensively observes the General Assembly for the first time is impressed by the number of participants, the intensity of their experiences, the variety of situations in which they interact, the size of the agenda debated, and the access to the delegates that is afforded external persons. The contrast between the General Assembly seen first-hand and impressions obtained from most of the literature is striking. The literature leaves an image of the General Assembly Hall with the delegations of eighty-two[4] nations, each occupying ten seats, neatly arranged in rows behind signs designating their countries. Even when committees and less public activities are mentioned, they are treated only very briefly. The Assembly of the observer, however, is a complex international community which includes approximately 1,400 national officials, portions of the some 3,000 members of the Secretariat, and hundreds of private persons: press, members of non-governmental organizations, and others interested in influencing or talking with delegates. Approximately 500 of the national officials are members of permanent missions to the United Nations, the other 900 come only for the Assembly. They come for other diplomatic posts, home government posts, and even private life. The agenda items which they consider in each session have numbered from 56 to 77 items ([16], p. 234). The items which they discuss that are not on the agenda stir the imagination and must be many times that of the formal agenda.

The complexity and variety of an Assembly session is attributable largely to the fact that it is in reality composed of the simultaneous meeting of seven "little assemblies" in which most of the work is done. These bodies are the seven committees of the General Assembly: two political committees, and one each for economic and financial, social and humanitarian trusteeship and non-self-governing territories, and legal affairs. Each member of the United Nations is represented on all of these committees, with a number of nations having two or more delegates present at meetings of some

committees. This makes it impossible for permanent missions of member states to participate in the Assembly without, on the average, almost tripling their complement.

These committees usually meet twice a day, from 10:30 A.M. to approximately 1:00 P.M. and from 3:00 P.M. to about 6:00 P.M. Occasionally there are night sessions, especially toward the end of the three months. As resolutions are passed by the committees they are brought before a plenary session of the General Assembly, a few at a time. But these plenary sessions occupy a relatively small portion of the total time spent in formal meetings. Even the plenary, when it meets to pass on committee resolutions, is often a reconstitution of the committees one at a time. For example, after the plenary deals with trusteeship items there may be a period of commotion while trusteeship committee members leave their plenary seats and return to their committee, and members from another committee take the front row seats of their delegation. In the plenary the same committee members pass again on their work, needing now a two-thirds majority to pass resolutions on important questions rather than the simple majority required in committee.

The observer of the General Assembly is immediately struck by the parliamentary atmosphere. Dean Rusk has coined the term "parliamentary diplomacy" to refer to the proceedings [18]. In this environment diplomatic rank is noticeably less a restraint on interaction than is the case in national capitals. Parliamentary roles require that diplomats who are sitting on the same committee approach each other directly even though one is an ambassador and the other is a second secretary. Contacts of Assembly members with the press, non-governmental organizations, and other outsiders are more similar to the external contacts of parliamentarians than to those of the foreign office or embassy official. Outside persons buttonhole a delegate in the corridor, page him in the Delegates' Lounge, or send a note asking for him to come out of a committee meeting, rather than seek an office appointment.

The sessions of the General Assembly are an intense and exhausting experience for the delegates. Their day begins with morning delegation meetings at the office of their country's mission to the United Nations. Then delegates go to the United Nations for morning committee sessions. Between the morning and afternoon sessions, business continues as delegates lunch together in the Delegates' Dining Room or talk in the Delegates' Lounge or at other places in United Nations Headquarters. At lunch and at other times during the day small working parties hammer out the exact wording of resolutions. Meetings of representatives of blocs are required to coordinate the positions of members of these blocs. Following the afternoon session there is usually a reception by one of the delegations, perhaps in the Delegates' Dining Room. Most likely more than one party is being held and the delegate must divide time between them. Many delegates must then return to their mission and write up the day's activities, prepare for the next day, and send cables home on important matters so that new instructions may be sent back before the delegation meeting the next morning. With what time remains, an attempt must be made to read the extensive United Nations documentation on the matters being debated. As a result, the working day for many delegates extends to nine or ten o'clock in the evening. For a large number the only respite from Assembly duties comes on the weekends.

These brief descriptive comments could, of course, be considerably extended. However, it is only intended here to describe enough to make the reader who has not observed the Assembly cognizant of the kind of evidence that stimulates an inquiry into the non-resolution consequences of this body. Does this virtually continuous interaction between representatives of most of the nations of the world for extended periods of time have significant consequences beyond the resolutions it produces? It is likely that most scholars and laymen with a reasonable amount of knowledge about the United Nations would say, "Yes." But our knowledge about these consequences does not go much beyond the assertion that "When they're debating they're not shooting," and the assumption that "it's useful to keep the communications channels open." What kind of debate or other behavior provides an alternative to violence that is considered satisfactory by conflicting parties? What particular kinds of communications channels are most useful for the kinds of ends that are pursued through the creation of international organizations? These questions lie under the clichés and we do not possess the knowledge that would enable us to answer them.

Some non-resolution consequences of the Assembly

SIX non-resolution consequences of the General Assembly have been selected for discussion here. They will be presented in the following order: (1) The impact of Assembly experience on participating national civil servants and nationals from other occupations; (2) The development of personal friendships among delegates across national lines; (3) The accentuation by the specialized committees of expert in contrast to purely political factors; (4) The formation of cooperating groups of nations that do not conform to normal political alignments; (5) The extension of the active interest of participating nations to additional geographic areas and to a broader range of international problems; (6) The new information and new sources of information that become available to participants. These factors affect the international system outside the General Assembly and also affect subsequent international relations within the General Assembly, a part of the system.

1. Impact of Assembly experience on delegates. The additional personnel that come to the United Nations for the General Assembly come from other overseas posts, foreign offices, other government departments, parliaments, and private life. For three months they are separated from their normal environment and have what is for many a quite intensive experience that places them in an extraordinarily different communications network. For some this experience is repeated for several years in succession. From posts in which most viewpoints on international relations that are encountered are from the perspective of one nation, they come to a community where they are constantly subjected to many perspectives. In addition, they are in the company of many people, members of the secretariat and others, who look at the system as a whole rather than from the perspective of one nation.

The parliamentary framework of the General Assembly provides an atmosphere that is quite different from that to which most of the delegates are accustomed, since most of them are governmental bureaucrats. For these bureaucrats to become delegates requires that they move away from a rather stationary existence behind a desk that provides, if not isolation, considerable restraints on the access to them by persons not in their own bureaucracy.

But in the Assembly, where they become mobile delegates operating most of each day away from a protective bureaucratic shell, they are directly accessible to other delegates. As has already been indicated, the lobbyist, journalist, and scholar can approach them directly as they pass from meeting hall to lounge, to dining room, and back to meeting hall in the relatively open society of the General Assembly. Although the extent of this non-delegate contact may not be great for some delegates, there is little doubt that the sources of intellectual stimulation of most delegates greatly extends that provided by the bureaucrat's incoming box and appointment calendar.

It may also be significant that delegates who participate in the General Assembly return to their normal posts with firsthand knowledge of United Nations procedures. They will be more competent to use these procedures intelligently. In the General Assembly, parliamentary diplomacy has developed into a phenomenon quite different from traditional bilateral diplomacy and is more complex than it was in the smaller League of Nations. Through participation in the General Assembly many national officials are learning parliamentary diplomacy through personal experience. This suggests the hypothesis that those who have mastered this particular kind of procedure for policy implementation are more likely to use it in the future than those who find such procedures unknown, unintelligible, and highly unpredictable.[5] This would include not only temporary delegates but permanent mission officials as well, most of whom move on to other diplomatic posts after a few years' service at the United Nations.

2. *Friendships across national boundaries.* The informality of social relations among the delegates impresses the observer who watches them in the corridors, lounges, restaurants, and meeting rooms of the United Nations. This informality may partially be attributed to the large number of persons involved. As hundreds of delegates surge into the Delegates' Lounge, the dining room, and the cafeteria following committee sessions, the social restraints associated with traditional diplomatic interchange give way to more informal patterns of behavior. Events such as the concert (followed by dancing and dinner) given by the Secretary-General and the President of the General Assembly in the 1958 session have an atmosphere of informality unexpected for such occasions. The formal attire of the perhaps two thousand persons in attendance was not matched by their informal conduct as they stood in line for Scotch and champagne, attempted to dance on the crowded dance floor, queued up for the buffet dinner, and then searched for a table at which to eat— some resigning themselves to standing up. And as the evening drew to a close there was another line to be faced as delegates obtained their coats from the check room.

In addition to the role of numbers, social interaction among delegates is encouraged by the physical environment offered by the United National Headquarters buildings. When one is enmeshed in this environment in the midst of the delegates he is tempted to rank the architect of the United Nations buildings along with the writers of the Charter in importance. The intensity of interaction of members of the General Assembly is heightened by the proximity of all of the arenas of delegate activity while they are on the United Nations premises. The General Assembly Hall, committee rooms, dining room, and lounge are all close to each other. A relatively few hallways connect the main centers of activity and delegates pass and re-pass each other frequently as they go about their tasks. One inhabitant of this system who desires to see another member on a particular day need not make a formal appointment nor look for him very energetically, for he will encounter him a number of times during the day.

Social interaction among the delegates is also encouraged by delegation receptions, with each delegation holding at least one and usually two receptions during the Assembly session. The uniformed attendant, calling out the names of the guests as they arrive, is reminiscent of the diplomatic heritage of the Assembly. Each national delegation to the Assembly must perform the representational functions of a foreign embassy as well as play parliamentary aspects of its role. It is perhaps diplomatic tradition that determines the nature of other social functions such as concerts in the General Assembly Hall, and occasional plays and other cultural events. All of these occasions add to the wide variety of situations in which members of the General Assembly encounter each other .

The sustained interaction of the delegates as well as the variety of the occasions on which they confront each other provides opportunities for the development of friendships across national boundaries that surpass those of normal diplomatic intercourse. As a result, delegates have networks of personal friends on other delegations. These networks provide opportunities for inter-nation communication that are more flexible than formal channels. The maintenance of these friendships places certain obligations on delegates, such as alerting friends to changes in policy or gradually adjusting them to change. Two United Nations delegates have themselves described the role of personal friendships:

Seldom is any vote changed by personal relations because persons, unless very senior, have little influence over national policies. It is possible however to foster a better understanding and appreciation of national positions as a result of social contacts and sometimes to affect subsequent formal exchanges and in the long run voting patterns. . . . In many eyes the personal relationships established at the United Nations have as much, if not greater, importance than the formal decisions which are reached ([8], pp. 39 and 47).

3. Participation of experts. One of the factors that contributes to the intensity of personal friendships is the camaraderie that develops among groups of delegates who are experts in the same field. Since most delegates spend their time on one committee that is handling one kind of issue, it is advantageous to nations to assign delegates to these committees who are experts in the subject matter being discussed. It is also the case that delegates assigned to these committees without previous claims of expert knowledge become experts, at least in the context of their own delegations, on the matters being considered. In addition to frequent similarities of professional training, the experts on a particular committee spend long hours together in their committee, giving them a common fund of knowledge and shared experience. For those who return to the same committee for several years common bonds are intensified. These bonds facilitate the work of the committees and at times become so pronounced as to create rivalry between committees.

Thus, it is hypothesized that the specialized committees not only create a need for experts in the conduct of assembly business but also serve as training ground for additional experts and reinforce the dedication of experts to the norms of their profession. A corollary of this hypothesis is that delegation positions in the Assembly and recommendations to home governments are affected by the professional norms of participating experts in international law, human rights, international economics, and so on.

4. Shifting majorities. One important aspect of the perspective of this analysis is that it probes below the level of national behavior in international organizations to the individual level. It has been suggested that it makes a difference who the individuals that participate are and that the effects of participation upon these individuals are important. Furthermore, it is important in the General Assembly that the simultaneous consideration of a number of issues requires nations to play a number of roles simultaneously. Coordination of the seven committee voices of a national delegation is not always easy, particularly since different issues often require cooperation with a different set of allies. It is contended that the variety of voting alignments across committees in the General Assembly introduces new elements into diplomacy within the United Nations and eventually outside as well.

In the political committees, the United States and the Soviet Union are the main protagonists, with their political allies aligning on the appropriate side and primarily some Afro-Asian nations playing a mediating role. NATO, the Warsaw Pact, SEATO, the Central Treaty Organization, OAS, and a scattering of bilateral treaties mirror basic alignments on key political questions. But in the economic committee, it is the haves against the have-nots, with the Latin Americans joining the Afro-Asians in a drive for an increase in multilateral economic programs. Often the Soviet Union votes with this group as does the Netherlands and Norway of the NATO bloc. On the social and humanitarian committee, Afro-Asian Moslems and European and Latin American Catholics cooperate on questions relating to birth control. On the trusteeship and non-self-governing territories committee the colonial nations and the newly independent countries are the main protagonists. On a matter before the legal committee related to ocean shipping, the maritime nations are lined up against non-maritime members. Finally, on the budgetary committee the lines of conflict are sometimes drawn with virtually all member nations on one side and the Secretariat on the other, as the committee assumes the typical parliamentary attitude toward the expenditures of executive officials.

Thus as one moves from committee to

committee and issue to issue, a variety of alliances is encountered. It is contended that the General Assembly, because of its varied agenda, provides opportunity for and stimulus for cooperative effort that often runs in apposition to political alignments based on organizations other than the United Nations. This cooperative effort opens up new lines of communications. It requires joint effort not only in the public sessions of committees but also in small working parties who negotiate final wordings of resolutions, and in bilateral conversations, at the United Nations and perhaps also in national capitals. These lines of communication can then be used for other purposes. These alignments and new communications routes become elements in subsequent diplomacy in the United Nations and in diplomacy conducted outside the United Nations.

5. *Expansion of nation concern.* The scope of the agenda of the General Assembly also has the effect of expanding the area of concern of participant nations. Participation in deliberations on an average of over 70 agenda items causes each nation to extend, in terms of both geography and subject matter, the range of items with which its diplomacy is directly involved. Most countries vote on almost all of these items and this requires that most of them take positions on matters that they would not have had to take stands on otherwise. It also requires public assertion of positions which might otherwise have been taken in private. Furthermore, private positions must usually be changed—if not in principle at least in emphasis and perhaps in explanation of motives—before they are made public.

It is hypothesized that this expansion of nation concern, along with the extension of the requirements for public declaration of policy, affects policy positions already held. When a nation is required to play a role in an agenda of items that covers the world, it assumes obligations that modify roles played in narrower arenas. For example, the extended participation in world affairs that the United Nations requires of the newly independent nations may be very important. After decades of foreign rule, in the first years of independence nations are inclined to be self-centered, to self-consciously assert their independence in relations with other nations and to assume little responsibility for the state of the international system as a whole. The addition of so many independent units to the interna-

tional system which is now taking place could heighten instability. The fact that United Nations participation prevents the isolation of these nations and extends their responsibilities may be diminishing the instabilities that they create in international affairs.

6. *Availability of new information.* The public debates in the General Assembly and private discussions as well provide member nations with a large volume of information on international affairs. For at least some of the smaller nations, the volume of reports sent home from their United Nations mission is greater than that from any other foreign post. Statements by participants on their nation's policy and its underlying rationale comprise a substantial portion of the voluminous documentation of the United Nations. In the "general debate" that opens the annual sessions of the General Assembly, virtually every nation of the world declares its position on what it considers to be the most important international questions. In the course of committee debate most nations participate in the "general debates" on each of the some seventy items on the agenda. Following each vote in the committees a number of nations feel the need to explain their votes. Then, when each item comes to the plenary session, nations that feel the most strongly about it may again take the opportunity to explain their positions.

In addition, there are, of course, constant explanations of positions in discussion by delegates outside the committee and plenary sessions. During the variety of occasions for delegate interaction there is considerable opportunity for detailed explanation of national positions and reasons for maintaining them. This not only includes occasions when delegates can take the initiative in making the policy of their government clear, but also occasions in which delegates can acquire information. In such cases the United Nations environment may be quite important. Much opportunity is offered for a delegate himself, or through a friendly delegate, to get information without betraying the significance of the discussion of the matter. For this reason it is hypothesized that much information is available at the United Nations with virtually no cost. Information may be obtained without revealing explicit intentions or interests to the degree that this is required to cross the more restrictive barriers of diplomacy in a national capital. A diplomat from a European country who has been at the United Nations for several years told the writer: "On the whole, this is probably the best place in the world to pick up information on other governments."

In addition, the Secretariat and special committees and visiting missions of the General Assembly collect and distribute reports on a great number of international problems. These reports, along with records of Assembly debates and other documents, provide voluminous documentation that covers virtually all international problems. To an extent never the case heretofore, a common body of documentation available to all defines the nature of major problems, supplies extensive documentation on positions of conflicting parties, and furnishes detailed background information. This documentation is, of course, more important to some nations than it is to others. For smaller nations and nations not directly involved in some issues, United Nations information sources may provide virtually all of the data on which national positions are based. This suggests the hypothesis that the growth in dependence on documentation shared by all tends to give nations a more similar view of the world.

Non-resolution consequences of the General Assembly and international conflict ·

ARE these non-resolution consequences of the General Assembly intriguing but inconsequential by-products of international relations in this community? Or do they have significance for important problems in international relations? An attempt will now be made to demonstrate that non-resolution consequences of the kind just discussed are potentially significant for what is with considerable unanimity cited as the most important problem in international relations and also as *the* problem of our age: international conflict. The primary purpose for this exploratory exposition is to show that research on non-resolution consequences is not only justified but urgently needed. In decisions so crucial as those involved in the creation of and participation in international organizations, it is not prudent for men to know only vaguely the consequences of their acts when more precise knowledge is obtainable.

To ask the relationship between the non-resolution consequences of the General Assembly and international conflict is to ask a question

that international organization scholars have not attempted to answer, except by occasional impressionistic and anecdotal accounts. This does not mean, however, that the scholar who attempts to answer this question must start from scratch. There is knowledge in the social sciences—in the literature on organizations, communications, and conflict, for example—which is useful. Possibly because the study of international organizations has become primarily the domain of political scientists, we are inclined to look at these organizations only as particular kinds of political institutions. But human behavior in international organizations is also a special case, for example, of organizational behavior, communication, and social conflict. Knowledge from these areas of social science can be usefully applied in the study of international organizations along with knowledge gained from the traditional foci of the political scientist. In the exploration of the potential relationship between the non-resolution consequences of the General Assembly and international conflict that follows, knowledge is drawn from outside the international relations area whenever possible.

The ensuing discussion indicates five kinds of ways in which the non-resolution consequences already described may have an effect on international conflict. (1) Change in the traditional patterns of inter-nation communication may affect conflict. Particularly relevant here are the changes in these patterns that personal friendships, extended national interest, and the effects of Assembly experience on delegates bring. (2) There may be a relationship between conflict and new kinds of information that the Assembly makes available. It is asserted that relationship occurs because of the greater predictability of the behavior of other nations that this information allows. (3) The third and fourth examples discuss how Assembly participation places both the nation and the individual in a more varied set of roles than before that may bind each to a larger community. In the case of the nation, the new kinds of alignments that Assembly activity brings and extended national interest are important. (4) In the case of individuals cross-pressures are encouraged by the involvement of professional norms and personal friendships. (5) Finally, the possibility is discussed that conflict in the Assembly may itself be a non-resolution consequence that substitutes for conflict elsewhere.

1. The channeling of information. When

relationships among nations are looked at as a communications system, sharp differences are discerned between the part of this system that is within an organization such as the General Assembly and that which is conducted through more traditional channels. Bilateral communications outside an international organization are conducted through the elaborate and, for the most part, extremely formal mechanisms of diplomacy. The restraints that diplomatic practices have placed on inter-nation communication have helped not only to create conditions in which there are significant areas of national ignorance about the policies and intentions of other nations, but the cost of obtaining information to eliminate ignorance has often been high. Formal requests for information may betray ignorance, reveal intentions, or expose areas of concern. These costs must be weighed against the value of the information—if it is even available. Within the General Assembly, however, a portion of the restraints on inter-nation communication are eliminated. The sustained social interaction in a variety of kinds of situations, in the context of a common institution, stimulated by such elements as personal friendships and camaraderie of experts, breaks down these restraints.

Do the new kinds of communications opportunities that the General Assembly permits have any relationship to international conflict? James March and Herbert Simon, in their recent volume summarizing the literature on organizational behavior, suggest that there is a body of knowledge that will give some insight on this question. Studies of organizations have indicated that "the greater the channelling of information-processing, the greater the differentiation of perceptions within the organization" ([15], p. 128). By channeling of information they mean limiting the number of organization members to whom any given bit of information is transmitted. Related to the proposition on the channeling of information is another which indicates its relevance to our discussion. It states that differences in the perception of reality are one of the major factors contributing to intergroup conflict ([15], p. 121).

The converse of the March and Simon propositions offer stimulating hypotheses when applied to the General Assembly. It is hypothesized that the community of diplomats in New York, largely because of their participation in the General Assembly, is an element in the international communications system where the circulation of information is more diffuse and the patterns of its distribution more complex than in the remainder of the system. Therefore it is further hypothesized that the General Assembly tends to give officials who participate in it a more similar perception of reality than they have before they participate. The information that these persons supply to the remainder of the international system when they report home and when they move on to other posts tends to give all member nations a more similar perception of reality. Thus, as a network of communications routes that supplement and sometimes by-pass traditional diplomatic patterns of communication, the General Assembly tends to lessen the intensity of conflict by causing member nations to have more similar perceptions of the world.

2. *Predictability*. As a consequence of the opportunities that the General Assembly provides for the relaxation of the communications restraints of traditional diplomacy and because of the new information available in the Assembly, it is hypothesized that participating nations know more about the capabilities and intentions of other participating nations than they would without this institution. In other words, it is contended that an organization such as the General Assembly makes the world more predictable for its members. Is there a relationship between predictability and conflict? Robin M. Williams, Jr., in a work on conflict among ethnic, religious, and racial groups in the United States, suggests that "disruption of stable expectations of interpersonal conduct tends to be productive of intergroup conflict" ([20], p. 57). Karl Deutsch has asserted the importance of predictability in the development of an international community as follows: "Insofar as members of a stable political community must be able to expect more or less dependable interlocking, interchanging, or at least compatible behavior from each other, they must be able, at least to that extent, to predict one another's actions" ([6], p. 53).

The General Assembly may not only make the world more predictable to its members as a result of opening new routes for communication and creating an environment in which nations must give extensive explanations of their policies. This extensive requirement that nations explain policies publicly may tend to make these policies more stable. Conformity with predetermined plans should be greater after these plans have been revealed publicly before most nations of the world than when dissemination has been more restricted. This would seem to be particularly true if these plans have become the basis for multilateral action within the United Nations. The reader may have noted that this is the reverse of a proposition often found in international organization literature which asserts that public debate in bodies such as the General Assembly may intensify conflict by making positions more rigid and thereby eliminating the competence of conflicting parties to compromise. But the importance of predictability to conflict suggests that public commitment may not always be a deterrent to conflict reduction. It would be valuable to know more about the conditions under which each of these seemingly contrary propositions holds true.

3. *Overlapping conflict systems.* This discussion has emphasized ways in which General Assembly processes may tend to diminish the intensity of some international conflicts. It is true, of course, that at times participation intensifies conflict between parties. In some cases, however, there may be potential beneficial effects for the stability of the system as a whole when conflict between traditional allies is intensified as a result of their being required to take a public stand on an issue on which they disagree; this may tend to relax, to some degree, tension between traditional foes who might then find themselves on the same side of an issue. For example, debate on colonial problems sometimes intensifies conflict between NATO allies when some members of NATO find themselves unable to support their allies on colonial issues. This conflict is accompanied by cooperative effort by some NATO members with nations who oppose them on other issues.

The literature on conflict often refers to the salutary effect of overlapping conflicts that in a sense tend to cancel each other out. Edward A. Ross, a sociologist writing several decades ago, described this process:

> Every species of social conflict interferes with every other species in society . . . save only when lines of cleavage coincide; in which case they reinforce one another. . . . A society, therefore, which is ridden by a dozen oppositions along lines running in every direction may actually be in less danger of being torn with violence or falling to pieces than one split just along one line. For each cleavage contributes to narrow the cross clefts, so that one might say that *society is sewn together* by its inner conflicts ([17], pp. 164–5, author's emphasis).

A mechanism whereby a "society is sewn together" by its conflicts is that of multiple group affiliations of its members which add an element of interdependence to the relations of conflicting groups. The committees of the General Assembly may be looked upon as multiple group affiliations required of the national delegations of the Assembly. Political allies find themselves at cross-purposes in economic and trusteeship committees and political enemies may at times be surprised to discover that they are allies on other issues. In the 1958 Assembly, for example, a resolution was passed urging the establishment of an international capital development fund in which the alignment was basically most NATO nations and a few more developed members of the British Commonwealth against the rest of the world. This was a significant departure from the usual alignment of the Latin American nations and others with the United States on political issues.

Multiple group affiliations bring cross-pressures that tend to restrain the pursuit of the goals of any one affiliation. It has been noted, for example, that workers in so-called "isolated" industries such as miners, sailors, fishermen, lumbermen, and sheep-tenders tend to back political extremists. This is believed to be caused by the fact that members of these groups do not have the multiple affiliations that integrate other members of society into the broader community ([12], pp. 95–6). Does the broader scope of participation that the General Assembly requires of nations serve to integrate them into a wider community and thereby modify extremist tendencies of nations formerly more isolated?

As an example we might ask whether there is any indication that the Soviet Union is to some extent integrated into the United Nations community by its multiple committee participation. Thomas Hovet, in a study of bloc voting in the General Assembly, has compiled figures that are useful. In roll call votes that Hovet classifies "collective measures, regulation of armaments, etc.," the Soviets have voted with the majority only 18.4 per cent of the time. On resolutions devoted to human rights and self-determination, however, they have voted with the majority on 50 per cent and 45 per cent of the roll call votes respectively. As a result of these percentages, and others less high, the Soviets have an over-all concurrence with majorities of 39.1 per cent ([10], pp. 68–70).

Although the Soviet Union and its allies are, to a considerable degree, isolated from the remainder of the United Nations community, we hypothesize that the overlapping system of conflicts tends to integrate them into this community. Sharing voting victories on some items makes the Assembly seem less like an institution devised solely for the frustration of Soviet ambitions and makes success in additional areas seem more feasible and worth striving for through parliamentary means. And communication is easier with delegates who, on occasion, are on your side than with delegates who constantly oppose you.

4. *Individual personalities and conflict.* As indicated earlier, study of nation participation in international organizations has rarely probed below the nation as a unit of analysis. Simultaneous with the widely held belief that individuals can change the ultimate fate of nations very little, there is the assumption that decisions of importance are made in foreign offices—delegates in international organizations being merely agents for the implementation of these decisions. United Nations delegates do, nonetheless, have a role in shaping policies that they advocate for their governments. In some cases delegates operate under general instructions with the freedom to design specific policies within this framework. However, whether the delegate's instructions be general or specific, the competence of delegates in pursuing national objectives in international bodies determines the kinds of choices that foreign office officials will have available in forming future policy. Furthermore, the delegate in an international organization selects and arranges information that is sent to the foreign office and often makes policy recommendations. The information and recommendations supplied by delegates may play a prominent role in the development of instructions that are sent back to the delegate.

Assuming that the individual delegate does have a role in the development of his nation's policies makes the effect of the General Assembly environment on delegates of some interest. Does the fact that the General Assembly to some degree consists of small international communities of experts and that personal friendships across national boundaries are encouraged have effects that are related to the role of the Assembly in international conflict? The literature on social conflict tells us that the introduction of personal factors in social rela-

tions tempers conflict. Lewis Coser, for example, suggests that the "elimination of the personal element tends to make conflict sharper, in the absence of modifying elements which personal factors would normally introduce" ([5], p. 118). This is a special case of the so-called cross-pressure hypothesis that has found its way into political studies in surveys of voting behavior ([1], p. 283; [3], p. 183). Persons who have opposing forces acting on them that engender internal conflict and indecision in voting situations have been found to be less strongly committed politically. It is not our suggestion, of course, that the cross-pressures brought to bear on General Assembly delegates will necessarily cause them to change votes or do about-faces on policy choices. The development and maintenance of personal friendships and the norms of fellow-experts may, however, alter the way in which delegates perceive situations, determine the types of contacts and sources of information available to them, and eventually affect the picture of the situation that they relay home. It is hypothesized that the development of personal friendships tends to temper the intensity of conflict which delegates feel exists between their nation and nations with whose delegates they develop friendships. Devotion by delegates to the norms of their fellow-experts on Assembly committees may produce the same effect. Those who bemoan the existence of inter-committee rivalry should not overlook the fact that it is likely caused by inter-nation cooperation!

5. *General Assembly conflict as a substitute for violence.* There is a tendency to consider all conflict as negative in its consequences. Such a perspective may prevent the perception of transformations in conflict that are taking place. It has already been indicated that conflicts among members of a subsystem may make the over-all system more stable if they tend to criss-cross a bipolar cleavage that is threatening stability. It is also possible that conflict in one form may serve as a substitute for a more violent variety.

Lewis Coser's book, *The Functions of Social Conflict,* offers a stimulating analysis of the potential positive values of conflict. In discussing the valuable information which conflict allows the antagonists to obtain about each other, Coser asserts:

> Conflict consists in a test of power between antagonistic parties. Accommodation between them is possible only if each is aware of the

relative strength of both parties. However, paradoxical as it may seem, such knowledge can most frequently be attained only through conflict, since other mechanisms for testing the respective strength of antagonists seem to be unavailable ([5], p. 137).

Earlier Coser tells us that "if alternative means are not available or are believed to be unavailable, the only way to a reappraisal of the contending parties' power is to use the 'weapon of last resort'" ([5], p. 136). Does the General Assembly at times provide a suitable alternative means for appraisal of relative strength that may make the resort to "weapons of last resort" unnecessary? It may be seen that the process here is somewhat akin to that earlier described wherein the Assembly contributes to predictability by providing more reliable information on the capabilities and intentions of opponents in conflict. But an element is added; in this instance we ask whether Assembly action might provide a substitute for other kinds of action.

Inis Claude seems to suggest that the General Assembly and the Trusteeship Council of the United Nations may be serving as arenas of final conflict over colonial questions. He reports that the most significant thing about the role of the United Nations in colonial affairs is not that it "has become the registrar of the triumphant surge of dynamic anti-colonialism, but rather that it has become the scene of conflict, the prize ring within which the battle over the future of colonialism has been fought" ([4], p. 361). In some quarters, United Nations efforts in colonial questions are judged a failure because all members are not speaking with one voice in the solution of these problems. But this conflict might be enacted in a more violent way were United Nations councils not available as a battleground. Are battles of parliamentary diplomacy substitutes for more violent battles elsewhere? It is imperative that we know much more than we do about instances in which this is the case. It is not necessarily true that an Assembly that does not reach agreements on major conflicts has been a total loss. It is crucial that we learn under what kinds of conditions conflict is amenable to transformation from violent conflict to a conflict of parliamentary diplomacy.

Conclusion

SOME non-resolution consequences of the General Assembly have been discussed with the purpose of providing direction for research that will give more complete understanding of the effect of the United Nations and other international organizations on relations among nations. It has been asserted that perceptivity to such effects may be intensified by looking at these organizations in the context of the entire international system rather than looking at them as complete systems in and of themselves. It has also been suggested that one is more perceptive to the non-resolution consequences of the General Assembly if he recognizes the fact that nations may not be the only units whose Assembly participation merits analysis. It may be significant that each nation is playing a role in seven committees simultaneously. And aspects of the behavior of individual delegates may merit consideration.

In assessing the relationship between the non-resolution consequences of the Assembly and international conflict, literature outside political science and outside international relations has been cited. This was done to show the relevance of bodies of knowledge from other areas of human behavior to the study of international organizations. The intellectual barriers that surround academic departments have cut off this study from resources outside its home base—political science. Indeed, it is only recently that the main stream of political science has begun to affect the study of international organizations. If the great gain of the past decade has been a more general recognition that there is politics in international organizations, perhaps the advance of the coming years will be the acknowledgment that people are to be found there as well.

There seem to be significant patterns of interaction in the United Nations about which we as yet know very little. These patterns were not devised by those who built the organization at San Francisco, and the writer believes that in many cases they have not been implementations of conscious planning. Often they have been the products, it would seem, of widely scattered individual decisions. They have been born out of the daily agony of individual practitioners trying to stave off cataclysm by accomplishing the seemingly impossible. Often the practitioners are so busy with their individual acts that they do not see the over-all patterns. And sometimes when they do see them they do not have time to contemplate their significance. It is up to the social scientist, building on the insights that the practitioner can give, to discern their significance in terms of their effects on international relations and the relationship of these effects to the long-range goals of international organizations.

Up to the present time, the underlying patterns have been neglected because scholars and practitioners have tended to concentrate on the explicit organizational mechanisms for conflict resolution. Changes in the basic interaction process that international organizations may effect have been overlooked. It remains to be seen whether changes have been effected that are measurable, but we may be stumbling into unplanned consequences of organizational building that equal in importance those that are planned. Ernst Haas has concluded, as a result of his study of the European Coal and Steel Community, that international "institutions are crucial causative links in the chain of integration" ([7], p. 450). They not only handle their explicitly assigned tasks but become the causes of other new factors that affect relations among their members. Haas reports that "our European lesson drives home the potential role of institutional forces in rechanneling and realigning previous group loyalties and expectations" ([7], p. 457).

Furthermore, international organizations may spur integration in a given system through making the relationships between units in the system more complicated. This may occur by the initiation of new kinds of cooperative efforts among nations that run contrary to normal political alignments, the involvement of some nations in problems that they would have ignored were they not required to act in the organization, the establishment of new channels of cooperation for governmental experts, and the establishment of new and more intense friendships among officials across national boundaries.

The creation of international organizations may thus have a two-level effect: one effect being the organization's success at attaining goals for which it is established and the other being basic changes in the international system in which it is established. A closer study of the latter may be a requisite for making international organizations more effective in the achievement of explicit goals. For example, advocates of revision of the United Nations Charter might well look at their proposals not only as revisions of Charter mechanisms but also as revisions of basic patterns of inter-nation relations. Those who voice a desire for more orderly and neatly organized General Assembly processes might also give careful consideration to the potential effects of their proposals. What would be the effects of cutting the size of the General Assembly Committees? What would be the impact of reducing the number of items on the agenda? On the other hand, more sophisticated knowledge about the non-resolution consequences of the Assembly might show opportunities for changes in procedures that could have effects as significant as Charter revision but that require neither Charter revision nor seem threatening to those sensitive to inroads on national sovereignty.

In the introduction to his Fourteenth Annual Report to the General Assembly, Secretary Hammarskjold made two recommendations for changed procedures. He asked for regular meetings of the Security Council in executive session and for the development of international economic policies in short special meetings at the ministerial level, within or under the aegis of the Economic and Social Council. How prepared are international organization scholars to predict the consequences of such innovations? Such predictions cannot be made from the data ordinarily used for international organization research: verbatim records of meetings, resolutions, handouts to the press, and journalistic accounts. These documents are only partial reflections of the consequences of the operation of political institutions. If he is to contribute anything to questions such as these beyond what the insightful practitioner and journalist can offer, the political scientist must collect other types of data and include it in his analysis. Scholars of international organizations have hardly begun the work which could enable them to provide knowledge beyond that which practitioners and journalists can supply. Under the existing documentary material above the surface lies an iceberg of unknown dimensions. Here may be unanticipated consequences of international organizational building which could make these organizations self-destructive. On the other hand, there may be elements which could be utilized to advantage.

Notes

1. Resolution here refers to resolutions passed by United Nations bodies; it is not used in the sense of conflict resolution.

2. This paper is based on field work at the United Nations in 1958 and 1959 which was supported by funds from the Carnegie Corporation in New York. Helpful criticism of an earlier draft was received from Harold Guetzkow and James A. Robinson of Northwestern University, William A. Scott of the University of Colorado, Keith S. Petersen of the University of Arkansas, and several United Nations diplomats who will remain anonymous.

3. The reader may have detected a similarity between Robert K. Merton's "latent functions" and "non-resolution consequences" ([14], pp. 19–84). Although his analysis of manifest and latent functions offered fruitful provocation, the term "non-resolution consequences" more precisely indicates the

phenomena with which this paper is concerned.

4. This paper was completed in March, 1960, before the 1960 expansion of the United Nations to ninety-nine members. [As of 1964, there are 112 members. EDS.]

5. In an attempt to assess the impact of Assembly experiences on delegates, the writer interviewed delegates to the Fourteenth General Assembly who had not served before. Delegates from thirty countries were interviewed both before and near the end of the Assembly. These data are now being analyzed. In another United Nations field study for Northwestern's International Relations Program, Gary Best studied the difference between diplomacy conducted at the site of an international organization and diplomacy in a national capital. Permanent Mission personnel from all member nations were interviewed in this study [2].

References

[1]. Berelson, Bernard R., Lazarsfeld, Paul, and McPhee, William N. *Voting.* Chicago: University of Chicago Press, 1954.

[2]. Best, Gary. "Diplomacy in the United Nations." Doctoral thesis, Northwestern University, 1960.

[3]. Campbell, Angus, Gurin, Gerald, and Miller, Warren E. *The Voter Decides.* Evanston, Ill.: Row, Peterson and Co., 1954.

[4]. Claude, Inis L., Jr. *Swords into Plowshares,* New York: Random House, 1956.

[5]. Coser, Lewis, *The Functions of Social Conflict.* Glencoe, Ill.: Free Press, 1956.

[6]. Deutsch, Karl. *Political Community at the International Level.* Doubleday Short Studies in Political Science, No. 1, Garden City, N.Y.: Doubleday, 1954.

[7]. Haas, Ernst. "The Challenge of Regionalism," *International Organization,* 12 (1958), 440–58.

[8]. Hadwen, John, and Kaufmann, Johan. *How United Nations Decisions are Made.* New York, 1958. (Mimeographed document prepared by two United Nations delegates.) Revision published, Leyden, Netherlands: A. W. Sijthoff, 1960.

[9]. Hammarskjold, Dag. "Introduction to Fourteenth Annual Report to the General Assembly on the Work of the Organization from June 16, 1958 to June 15, 1959." *United Nations Review,* 6 (1959), 8–18.

[10]. Hovet, Thomas, Jr. *Bloc Politics in the United Nations.* Cambridge, Mass.: Center for International Studies, Massachusetts Institute for Technology, 1958.

[11]. Jessup, Philip. *Parliamentary Diplomacy, An Examination of the Legal Quality of the Roles of Procedure of Organs of the United Nations,* Leyden, Netherlands: A. W. Sijthoff, 1957.

[12]. Lipset, Seymour Martin. "Some Social Requisites of Democracy: Economic Development and Political Legitimacy," *American Political Science Review,* 53 (1959), 69–105.

[13]. Mack, Raymond W., and Snyder, Richard C. "The Analysis of Social Conflict—An Overview and Synthesis," *The Journal of Conflict Resolution,* 1 (1957), 212–47.

[14]. Merton, Robert K. "Manifest and Latent Functions," *Social Theory and Social Structure.* Glencoe, Ill.: Free Press, 1957.

[15]. March, James, and Simon, Herbert, with Guetzkow, Harold. *Organizations.* New York: John Wiley and Sons, 1958.

[16]. Petersen, Keith S. "The Agendas of the United Nations General Assembly: A Content Analysis," *Southwestern Social Science Quarterly* (December, 1958), 232–41.

[17]. Ross, Edward Alsworth. *The Principles of Sociology.* New York: Century Co., 1920.

[18]. Rusk, Dean. "Parliamentary Diplomacy—Debate versus Negotiation," *World Affairs Interpreter,* 26, No. 2 (Summer, 1955).

[19]. Simmel, Georg. *Conflict and the Web of Group Affiliation.* Glencoe, Ill.: Free Press, 1955.

[20]. Williams, Robin. *The Reduction of Intergroup Tensions.* New York: Social Science Research Council, 1947.

Louis Henkin

Toward a "rule of law" community

OURS IS HARDLY A WORLD AT PEACE. If the principal "war" is a "cold war," yet there is not peace. In the tensions between East and West, aggravated by awesome destructive power on both sides, in equally sharp if less pervasive tensions among smaller nations, lie serious dangers and threats to peace. There are tensions also, and seeds of tension, in the growth of new nationalisms, in the drive of previously non-self-governing people for independence, in the demand of these peoples and other peoples for a greater share of the world's goods and a better life.

To these special sources of tension are added those ever present in a society of sovereign states with competing economic and political interests. These tensions may lead to the use or threat of force, as recently in Suez. If not force, there may be other retaliation. In any event, there is "injustice." In all events, tension results. The threat of war is pervasive. The sense of order, of justice under law, is largely lacking. There is disease among nations, which, even if it should not in fact erupt into war, poisons relations in the world family.

To cure this disease, men of good will turn to "the law," seeking in its concepts, institutions, methods and mechanics, ways to reduce the threat of war and to enhance international order. And lawyers have responded in different ways. Some have concentrated on ultimate goods, on optimum solutions and programs. They speak almost yearningly of the "rule of law." They respond to a common wish that there shall be a world community with the hallmarks and trappings of law that are known domestically in enlightened Western countries —a community observing accepted rules of conduct between nations; courts applying these rules in cases or controversies not settled amicably by the parties; police to enforce, if necessary, the law as decided by the courts. And so lawyers have formulated, and continue to refine, principles of conduct for nations in a community of nations. They have proposed and developed processes for giving effect to such principles, and programs for applying and administering these processes, and for enforcing the rules of conduct against recalcitrant nations. They concentrate on the development of new rules where none exist, or where present rules are deemed unsatisfactory. They develop and strengthen statutes for international adjudicatory tribunals. They propose new and renewed charters for international organizations and police.

Those who devote their efforts to these goals recognize that wishing for or proclaiming a rule of law does not create in fact a law of nations. They are aware that, in a society of sovereign states, an established order of laws and courts and police—which does not effectively exist even within many domestic societies —is at best a dream to be approximated, and there appears little immediate prospect that nations will agree to give up much of their present sovereignty. But those who labor in this vineyard believe that it is important to keep ultimate goals in sight; that plans and blueprints make it more likely that such a world can be achieved, at least that more progress can be made toward it; that significant educational and even political benefits may derive from reminding nations and people how the world might look.

Other lawyers, concerned for the growth and

Reprinted from Harlan Cleveland, ed., *The Promise of World Tensions*, New York, Macmillan. Copyright 1961 by Council on World Tensions, Inc., pp. 114–127.

enhancing of international order through law, begin from different positions, give different emphases. They stress that law does not create a World Community; it can only reflect such a community if it exists. In today's world, sharply polarized between East and West, there is not even the foundation for a common society to support a common law. The rule of law, in an ultimate sense, is an ideal state of health, not a prescription for achieving it. The question indeed is how, in a sorely divided world, one can achieve even a small measure of this health. If substantial order is to come without another world holocaust, it must grow from present roots. If it is to be planned, it can only be built on and projected out of the present foundations. Will East and West, with divergent and perhaps inconsistent interests, accept common standards of action, common methods and machinery for enforcing or vindicating these standards? Rules exist, but are they rules which the leading nations, and the new nations, recognize and observe? These are institutions and procedures —judicial, quasi-judicial, or political, multi-lateral or bilateral—but will nations use them and abide by their outcome?

The East and the West do not agree on many rules; they do not accept courts or other impartial forums to decide disputes; there is no power to compel either side to abide by any rules or decisions, and frequently no voluntary acceptance of them. Although the West has been far more amenable to rules, and more reluctant to incur the onus in world opinion of breaching them, it too may act in disregard of "law" where it feels important interests are at stake. Even the smaller nations find it easier to disregard law as a result of the lack of a strong fabric of a society of nations, or because of the lack of agreed force on behalf of the "law" and the world community, or because there is a big champion who might defend their violations. The nations newly come to independence may have serious question as to the meaning for them of old concepts and institutions; will they agree to accept them? Will they seek changes to which the other nations could agree?

If there is no perfect order and law in today's society of nations, some law, some standards of behavior observed, some machinery for vindicating these standards, do in fact exist. This "law" has strengths and has enjoyed successes. It has serious weaknesses and has suffered defeats. It needs strengthening. It can be strengthened in ways that reflect the world of today, that take account of power and other facts of international life, that reflect the different interests of different nations, as they see their interests.

Law can be achieved to the extent that it is in the common interest of nations, if nations can be made to recognize that it is in their common interests. In a world dominated by two powerful giants, law can be achieved if, and to the extent that, these powers believe that it is in their interests to achieve it. What is required, then, is to persuade nations, particularly the Big Powers, that order and law, at least in some areas, are in their interest. There must be an identification of areas of such coincidence of interest—common interest in having standards of conduct, explicit or tacit, upon given subjects, especially in procedures for implementing or applying these standards, as well as procedures for settling disputes in areas where there are no agreed rules.

There are in fact significant areas of coincidence of interest between East and West within which some "law" exists, and more can be developed. There are wider areas of coincidence of interest between old nations and new, and therefore hope and need for development of legal and political institutions and practices in relations between them. And, finally, there are still larger areas of even deeper coincidence of interest among the Western nations with common values and traditions where law exists and can grow importantly, which would also serve as an example and a focus for extending the rule of law to other countries, other areas and groups. The concepts, methods, and tools of law, we believe, can be invoked to increase the areas of international activity which are subject to law, and therefore contribute to the lessening or arresting of existing tensions, to the prevention of new tensions. The lawyer in close concert with economists and leaders in other disciplines concerned with the cooperation of people and communications among them, can contribute not only in his capacity as outstanding citizen and leader, but through the lawyer's skills and insights—in negotiation and adjustment, in the development and formulation of standards of conduct, in devising procedures for giving effect to such standards, in applying and administering these procedures. . . .

If there is now a clear coincidence of interest for all nations to avoid major force, it is also in their interest to make it less likely that force will be used, intentionally or accidentally.

The United States, the USSR and other leading countries must themselves refrain from initiating the use of force and exert every influence on all others also to refrain. All nations have an important interest to assure that no single nation anywhere will initiate the use of force against another.

Recognition by both sides in the global conflict that they must avoid force requires also that they recognize that any changes from the status quo must be pursuant to peaceful agreement. In some areas bristling with tension, conflicting interests may not at present permit any substantial changes by peaceful agreement. But force must be avoided, and the incitements and temptations to use force. Thus, for a current example, the Soviet Union must appreciate the circumstances which render it impossible for the West to abandon West Berlin, and which would compel the West to meet forcibly any serious jeopardy to their presence there. Subject to that limitation there may be room for some agreed peaceful change in the status of Berlin, in the presence of Western forces, in access between West Berlin and West Germany. It may be possible—again there will be call on the ingenuity of the law and of lawyers—to substitute a permanent peaceful status for the city for the present occupation status, and the likelihood of agreement may be enhanced by the symbolic, political, administrative role of the UN, or by its presence.

Despite continued failure and frustration, there is also some real coincidence of interest in efforts to control armaments, to give confidence if not assurance that nations which do not yet have them do not acquire weapons of mass destruction, and that nations which do have them will not use them. There must be intensified search, in particular, for agreement on measures to assure that there will be no surprise attack and no accidental war. There is coincidence of interest too in efforts to moderate the frantic race for new weapons of incalculable destructive power. Reliable agreements, however small and preliminary in character, can break the cycle in which tensions lead to more arms and arms increase tensions. If in a world without trust, such agreements require reliability and confidence, both sides may have to pay a price in submitting to essential verifications and inspections. Both sides must earnestly consider that there may be more security for them in known controls on armaments than in the fearful uncertainties of unbridled competition in the armaments of the future.

Areas emerging into international awareness may develop new conflicts of interest and new tensions, but nations may also be persuaded that it would be preferable for all if these areas were isolated from conflict. Agreement by the United States and the Soviet Union on the nonmilitarization of Antarctica is a small example, and an augury of hope.

The development of uses of outer space seems to offer another such opportunity. The potentialities of these uses for mutual destruction are terrifying in their uncertainty, the United States and the USSR might well consider whether it would not be preferable for both to eliminate the risks by agreement that outer space will not be used for launching weapons of destruction. The potentialities, on the other hand, of these uses of outer space for revolutionary benefits to all suggest also a coincidence of interest in cooperation for peaceful development and use. Here again, essential verifications and inspection will be necessary.

Allowing for many differences, there is reminder, if not analogy, in the early state of atomic energy, say in 1945. The tragic failure of attempts to "demilitarize" the atom and to arrange for cooperation in its peaceful exploitation must not be repeated. There is hope that the lessons of that failure, as well as the difference in the two situations, may help avoid a new failure. There is not, as there was in the case of the atom, a monopoly on one side, and a consequent fear that controls would freeze the other in a state of permanent inferiority. There has not yet been sufficient progress on either side to warrant a feeling that controls would involve a sacrifice of advantage. There can be no confidence on either side that, in the long run, a race into use of outer space for weapons would enhance its military superiority or security. It may again be difficult to persuade both sides that exchange of information, "traffic" rules and controls, and joint ventures are indeed in the interest of both nations. There can be new law here—new standards of conduct, new institutions, new procedures. And lawyers can make their contribution here as they did in the Acheson-Lilienthal Report on controlling the atom, and in subsequent, partly successful attempts to achieve cooperation on peaceful uses of atomic energy. . . .

An urgent need, even in a bipolar world, is the development of legal "substitutes for war." The United Nations Charter outlaws the use of force except in defense against armed attack.

In fact, with exceptions noted, nationals have abstained from using force in the past when force may have been justified under international law. The result has been to leave areas of international interest unprotected. There have developed no clear agreed standards of conduct, nor any clear, agreed, and effective procedure for handling those situations which in the past were dealt with by force. It is not yet clear what should happen if one nation repeatedly violates the territorial integrity of another, if nations do not meet their financial or other contractual or treaty obligations to other nations, if they mistreat the nationals of other nations, if they endanger important economic interests of other nations or of their nationals, if they defame or deceive them, if they interfere with their communications. Rights of flight over the territory of other nations at various heights are matters in dispute and sources of tension, as is the right to use international waterways which are under national control. And the national treatment of human beings and of their fundamental rights continues to evoke the concern of other nations, while the acting states continue to insist that such matters are entirely domestic and of no international concern.

If, in regard to these and other problems, force continues in fact to be avoided, tensions will remain and fester. (It would not seem desirable to bring every such instance to the General Assembly for ad hoc political consideration, especially since there are really no principles of conduct to guide the Assembly.) Ultimately, then, if the rules against self-help by force are to survive, it is important that standards of conduct and machinery for settling disputes develop quickly—particularly for areas involving important interests which nations might be tempted again to "vindicate" by force. Such developments are more difficult, but some growth appears possible, even in the shadow of the Cold War.

More work is needed to identify the areas and problems to which this concern is particularly applicable, to analyze the competing interests, to set forth or develop equitable standards of conduct, to examine existing procedures, and, if necessary, develop new ones appropriate for the settlement of disputes. It will be necessary to re-examine hitherto accepted ideas of the respective areas of domestic interest and of international concern, and relate them to a world in which many "domestic" matters arouse keen international concern.

"Domestic" transactions often have transnational character. Foreign and international acts often have profound impact on the "domestic" life of nations. It will be necessary to achieve—by agreement, or by growth of custom—rules of conduct, as well as procedures for applying them. It is hardly necessary, of course, to develop rules or even identical machinery and procedures for different problems.

In the long run, a strong deterrent to disorder in international affairs lies in the patterns and habits of peaceful intercourse which contribute to order in all nations. Among such institutions in existence are, obviously, the international postal and telecommunications systems. But the daily details of increasing transnational and international relations promise another contribution to order and an important opportunity to law and lawyers. The development, for example, of standard commercial practices, of common "forms" for contracts, bills, and notes, transcends competing ideological and political and security interests, and helps establish a common framework within which tensions recede and order grows. It is desirable to promote uniform or corresponding practices in these and related fields, in direct negotiations through private groups, and through such bodies as the Economic Commission for Europe.

Areas of a different kind also offer some possibilities for increasing order. Meeting of scientists, even in the delicate field of arms control, have proved fruitful. Scientific cooperation in other fields—the International Geophysical Year and the International Committee on Space Research—warrants encouragement for similar endeavors. The artistic and intellectual communities also have proved that they afford opportunities for building up cooperative exchange, and helping create a more open society even behind the Iron Curtain. "Opening up" of the Soviet Union could be a result of, as well as a contribution to, the strengthening of international order.

To some the goal devoutly to be wished is the submission of all disputes and differences between the United States and the Soviet Union to the International Court of Justice. It is common knowledge, however, that the Soviet Union has never used the International Court and that the United States is not over-eager to submit to its jurisdiction. Much study and effort have been devoted to developing the Court and other machinery for adjucating disputes so that they might "work" even between the United States and the Soviet Union. But the weakness is not in existing machinery for adjudication, and it cannot be cured by improving the machinery. There is no agreement between East and West on standards of conduct, and therefore no basis for decisions as to whether any given standards have been observed or violated. There is no agreement between them to submit to a process of adjudication. And the Soviet Union in particular generally rejects the notion basic to adjudication; that any court can be impartial.

It would no doubt be desirable if the United States and the Soviet Union were to submit broadly to the jurisdiction of the Court. The proposal made by a United States spokesman to add a clause to this effect to new treaties which both the United States and the Soviet Union would ratify has something to commend it, in principle; compulsory submission to the jurisdiction of the Court is in fact a common provision in recent treaties. But to be effective there must first be the substantive agreements, and these have been lacking. Indeed the addition of this clause to an agreement might even render it less likely that the Soviet Union would adhere to the agreement. United States insistence upon such a clause in any agreement might be viewed by the Russians, who do not consider the International Court of Justice "impartial," as an effort to load the scales of the agreement against the Russians.

One cannot, then, be optimistic for the future of any adjudicating process for settling disputes or relaxing tensions between East and West. But courts, we have suggested, are not the only "legal" machinery, and in international affairs today may not even be the most promising. In time of tension between big powers, representing a desire for change by at least one of them, courts tend to be an unacceptable preserver of the status quo. They are to be used for important matters; if used they are to be obeyed. If not obeyed, courts may be destroyed. Particularly in situations of tension, other forms of resolution promise better.

There are, of course, the organs of the UN, which may be used at least to confirm a resolution of a dispute if not to bring it about. There are mediatory, conciliatory, "good offices" bodies in the UN and outside it. Most important, there are the lines of direct communication, at embassies, in third countries, in the corridors of the UN—at summit level or working levels—which must be maintained as ultimately the best hope for resolving issues and relaxing tensions. For all "legal" disputes between any nations are also political disputes. Between East and West, where there exist few admitted rules of law and no agreed tribunal to apply them, all disputes are basically political to be resolved through political institutions, primarily by direct contact.

Special machinery, fundamentally political in character, may be created. Some existed and worked when both sides wished it to work, as in Germany and Austria. In Korea an armistice was ultimately negotiated. In each case it was machinery basically bilateral, a body which did not strive for impartial adjudication (which the Soviet Union, we repeat, has not been ready to accept) but a bilateral body for hard, patient negotiation. The creation of such bodies, generally of equal representation, for ad hoc negotiations or perhaps for continuing general contact and discussion, still appears to offer the best hope for relaxing tensions between East and West. This too is order, and law, and here also the lawyer needs to lend his gifts for planning, building, developing and administering institutions and procedures.

World tensions result not only from the way the big powers glare at each other, but from the quickening explosions of new nationalisms, the demand of dependent peoples for independence and a greater share of the world's wealth. The recent and contemporary history has given new vitality to the "principle of equal rights and self-determination" recognized in the United Nations Charter, although it remains for the lawyers of all nations to consider to what extent this has now become a juridical principle in the law of nations.

Basically, the new nations have set themselves three tremendous tasks: to establish a nation out of heterogeneous groups; to build this nation with meager resources, only a fraction per capita of what developing European nations (for example, Germany, Italy) had in the nineteenth century; to give their people the advantages of a welfare state. The older nations must take account of these gigantic undertakings in their relations with these nations.

The importance of the economic growth of the new nations for the reduction of tensions, and specific programs for assistance to these nations, for cooperative economic development on a bilateral basis or through the UN and other multilateral agencies, are discussed in another chapter. The machinery and procedures for economic development there suggested are, of course, political and legal institutions also. Ultimately, it is necessary for the lawyer to join the economists and others to fashion arrangements whereby the resources of the older, more developed countries are in fact made available to the newer and poorer countries. There may be need to create, or modify, or develop new international institutions and procedures. There may be need for the lawyer to help accommodate conflicting national legislation, including tax regimes and monetary regulation.

Here, we would speak also of the relation to the new nations of other aspects of "law." The new nations are, of course, members of the UN and of many specialized agencies, and are already making their voices heard there. They have entered into international relations in accordance with international practice. But there are other areas where law and legal institutions can contribute to the healthy growth of these nations and of their relations to the older nations. To suggest that there may be re-examination is not to urge rejection or to assume even that there will or ought to be important modification. Examination may well show that traditional international law was not a law for the powerful few in a private club of nations, but in fact provides basic accommodations, all generally applicable today in a society of sovereign nations.

In any event, some standard must be agreed upon and accepted. In specific areas the new nations eager for assistance from more developed nations in their struggle to preserve their independence, to develop their resources, to raise their standards of life, will have to recognize and respect the interests of those whose assistance they seek. There will have to be agreement, for example, on the rights of foreign investors, on the status of persons engaged in technical assistance to them, as well as general confidence that the new nations will abide by their agreements and by diplomatic immunities and amenities.

In their integration into an international community with even an imperfect rule of law, the new nations such as those in Africa will need sympathetic assistance. They begin "from scratch" and must come far even to begin to live by the present state of international law. There is need to assist them in their education in international matters, to help them to apply to their own situation the international law

and practice of older nations, to train their lawyers and diplomats.

The task is not made easier by the comparatively primitive state of their domestic institutions; by their poverty and large illiterate populations; by differences among the African nations themselves, including differences of language and mores which render difficult even regional grouping and federation. They will have to look to leadership within their own groups. Free nations elsewhere will have to earn leadership by exemplary behavior in accordance with law.

There is urgent need to train young leaders of these new nations in the traditions of democracy and representative government, of individual freedoms and rights under law, modified as need be to meet local needs and mores. The United States and its Western allies, in particular, should invite representatives from these nations to see and to study; they should be prepared also to welcome students to Western institutions, as well as to send teachers and other experts to advise of the establishment and growth of political institutions, the promulgation of constitutions, the training and selection of judges, the creation of a Bar of responsibility and leadership.

The nations of the West and other nations with free institutions, similar traditions, and generally common political interests undoubtedly have developed, among themselves, the most advanced legal and political institutions, and the greatest willingness to submit to the rule of law, even to the adjudicatory process. It is among these nations in particular—or among regionally associated groups of them— that we may look for new international law, new substantive agreements of a bilateral or multilateral character, greater acceptance of mediation, arbitration and adjudication, and a heartening habit of settling disputes and relaxing tensions by the process of negotiation. If where tensions exist all questions tend to become political, as tensions recede political questions can be rendered "legal," to be decided by tribunals in accordance with agreed standards. Further progress in the rule of law within this group will, of course, minimize tensions among the nations in the group—and also make it less likely that "internecine" differences will be exploited by the Soviet Union.

It will provide, also, a focus and an example for other nations to follow and to join. Immediately, even nations not as close to each other as those of the West may be prepared to accept "rule of law" for particular problems. Consequently, even nations with some hostility between them can better accept the results of an adjudication or some other form of impartial decision or recommendation rather than try to achieve the same result by compromise in negotiations. (In some areas a small group—perhaps the United States, the United Kingdom and Canada—could establish among themselves a near-"perfect" rule of law as an example to the nations. This might be achieved without incurring the dangers of "fragmentation," of new divisions within this rule-of-law bloc, which argue against some other types of regional groupings.)

There is no doubt that within this rule-of-law community there could be more use of the International Court of Justice, at least on issues not of vital moment. Among these nations it should be possible to establish that using the Court is not a hostile act. The Court would be used and its judgments respected; successful use of the Court contributing to its growth.

In this connection the United States has hardly shown a good example. Current efforts to repeal the Connally Amendment have been unsuccessful to date; this reservation has not even been abolished as between the United States and selected friendly nations.

The Connally Amendment reserves to the United States the right to determine finally that a matter is essentially within the domestic jurisdiction of the United States, and therefore not an international dispute subject to the jurisdiction of the International Court. This raises the most difficult question of all, a question that lies at the root of all efforts to develop law and order: What is essentially a domestic matter which nations are free to decide as they see the right, and what, on the other hand, is a matter of legitimate concern to other nations as to which other nations may properly make representations, seek UN consideration, or even international adjudication?

Article 2(7) of the UN Charter, which provides that the UN is not authorised to "intervene in matters which are essentially within the domestic jurisdiction of any state," has raised as many difficult political and judicial questions as any other provision in the Charter. The United States has generally taken the view that the "domestic jurisdiction" clause does not bar discussion in the General Assembly of matters which concern other nations. Surely nothing can be "essentially domestic"

and barred to the United Nations if it becomes a threat to international peace and security.

There are equally great difficulties presented by "domestic jurisdiction" as a bar to the jurisdiction of the International Court of Justice. Presumably the Court will have to take into account developments in international law in determining whether a matter is proper for international adjudication or is the private affair of the acting State. Presumably, the International Court of Justice, a conservative institution as all courts tend to be, will not be the first to see radical growth in international law. Even if there are very few questions, even "domestic" ones, that can be barred from discussion in the UN's General Assembly, it does not follow that the Court will lightly extend the jurisdiction optionally given to it by the nations to areas traditionally "domestic". Surely, the fact that there may be questions about which another nation is in controversy with the United States will not ipso facto render it "nondomestic" to the United States and therefore justiciable by the Court.

In any event, whether a matter is justiciable or not is clearly a question about the jurisdiction of the Court which should not be decided by a party to a dispute. The reservation is therefore improper in principle. Because of the applicable rule of reciprocity, it has also hurt the United States by giving the same power to deny the jurisdiction of the Court to any State whom the United States might wish to sue.

What is most unfortunate about the Connally Amendment is the appearance of isolationism, of refusal to submit to the jurisdiction of the Court even vis-à-vis its friends on a reciprocal basis. Even without this reservation there would be few cases in which the United States could be brought to the Court against its will; there are not many causes of action justiciable in the Court, and there have been few cases in which the United States has in fact been sued. Most of the few suits which might arise against the United States would probably arise out of treaties which provide for compulsory Court jurisdiction and to which the Connally Amendment would not apply. On the other hand, even with this reservation, it should be obvious that the United States, through the Executive Branch cannot properly invoke this reservation in circumstances where the matter at issue is patently not domestic but a legitimate matter of concern to another nation. The reservation then will not properly allow the United States to deny to the Court jurisdiction in the large majority of those disputes which might come to it. Even in the rare instance where invoking the reservation might be proper, the Executive Branch might well and properly decide not to invoke it because of the unfortunate consequences for the United States in world opinion. Finally, where the United States honestly believes that the matter may truly be domestic, it might be better, as has been suggested, to submit that question for a preliminary opinion by the Court.

The reservation then is not of great import to the United States. Withdrawing it would not increase substantially the extent to which the United States is subject to the Court, but would remove a continuous reminder of United States reluctance to submit to international adjudication. The reservation gives constant lie to our professions of support for the rule of law, and opens to charges of hypocrisy United States criticism of the Soviet Union for its unwillingness to submit to law. Failure to remove the reservation after the recent attempt to do so would only emphasize and aggravate the fault of the United States in the eyes of the world. We may hope that the failure is only a brief delay.

In a world of pervasive malaise and disorder the perfect "rule of law" seems remote. Treaties with ideal provisions will not be signed; courts with extensive jurisdiction over all nations and issues will not be used or obeyed, even if created. Efforts directed toward optimum solutions have their principal justification only in hope that they can be soon achieved. Fortunately for mankind, it is in the interest of all, including the Big Powers:

To avoid the use of force themselves and to exert every influence against international use of force by any nation anywhere;

To maintain the United Nations which, among other things, helps preserve the balance between East and West and serves as a bridge to the new nations.

To seek their military security through reliable, reciprocal control of armaments rather than to risk the uncertain consequences and dangers of an unbridled arms race and the ever present danger of sudden war, accidental or deliberate;

To bar the use of outer space for weapons of destruction and to cooperate in the exploration and use of outer space for beneficial peaceful purposes;

To respect and develop international law,

particularly as a common bridge to the new nations;

To develop practices and procedures as "substitutes for war" to deal with situations which in the past may have evoked the use or threat of force;

To promote cooperation and common practices and forms in the daily commerce of nations, among businessmen, scientists, artists, others; and

To keep open and to increase channels of direct communication between all nations, particularly between East and West, as the best forum for settling disputes that may arise as well as for relaxing or preventing tensions.

For the new nations the old must show sympathy and understanding, not only by assisting them in economic ways but by helping to invent useful legal and political institutions. Old and new nations must reason together about maintaining and improving the law of nations. The old must help the new to achieve at least present levels of international law and order, and to establish free institutions and freedom under law for their citizens.

The old free nations of the West with common values and traditions have even greater opportunities. Among them there can be important developments in international law, and substantial growth of international institutions, including the International Court of Justice and other adjudicatory bodies, as an example to the world. The United States must regain its leadership in this group by regaining attitudes of cooperation and submission to law at least vis-à-vis its friends; it can begin clearing its skirts by revoking the Connally Reservation.

Throughout, the responsible role for law and lawyers is clear. They can help develop the possibilities of existing institutions like the UN and help build new institutions and administer them when they are built. Individually, as citizens and leaders, and in their association, they can help meet the challenge presented by the needs of new nations, assist them in developing their domestic institutions, in moving toward regional cooperation, and toward a life under law in the community of nations. Programs for bringing students and sending teachers are an obvious need; an undertaking —say by the American Bar Association—to send books and documents of legal and political import would make an important contribution.

Lawyers have no magic formula for bringing peace and ease among nations. The specific programs suggested—development of legal

"Substitutes for force," the study of the assumptions of international law, the collection and dissemination of the facts of international practice, and new manifestations of support for the rule of law among the free nations—are indeed modest. But of such is the kingdom of law in the real world. The hope for relaxing tensions lies in the gradual recognition, especially by the Big Powers, that there are in fact substantial and important areas of common interest among them—and there is consequently a place for law as well as politics.

Grenville Clark

World order: the need for a bold new approach

IN THIS NECESSARILY BRIEF ARTICLE on a vast subject, I restrict myself, first, to a summary statement of what I take to be the essential elements of an effective plan for world order; and, second, to an appraisal of the practical prospects for the formulation and adoption of such a plan in the reasonably near future.

In my belief, the following are the fundamental requirements for genuine peace, as distinguished from the precarious armed truce which now prevails.

As a first basic condition, I place the definite acceptance by the governments and peoples of the leading powers of the concept that world order requires the same kind of legislative, executive, and judicial institutions on a world scale as the experience of centuries has shown to be necessary for the maintenance of internal order in local communities and within nations.

By all except the most ignorant, it is taken for granted that law and order in any community depend upon the existence of clearly stated laws against violence, upon reliable courts to inter- pret and apply these laws, and upon efficient police forces to deter or apprehend violators thereof. Moreover, every orderly community takes it for granted that no armed factions can be permitted. For, while the possession by individual citizens of rifles, shotguns, and pistols for purposes of sport or self-protection may be permitted, who would suppose that the existence within a community of organized and potentially hostile armed bands would be compatible with domestic peace?

In short, we have learned by long experience that the maintenance of domestic order within any organized society up to and including the nation requires not only disarmament but also legislative, executive, and judicial institutions to enact and enforce definite law against violence. And until the obvious truth is generally accepted that world order requires corresponding world institutions, there is, indeed, no chance for any reliable peace on our planet.

Assuming acceptance of the concept that enforceable world law is indispensable, what are the specific requirements to that end?

Reprinted from *The Annals of the American Academy of Political and Social Science*, Vol. 336, July 1961, pp. 154–162.

Requirements

I SUBMIT that nothing less is needed than a comprehensive plan including the following elements:

1. Universal and complete disarmament. By this is meant not only arms control or the mere limitation of armaments, but, rather, the elimination of all national armaments by every country in the world without exception, right down to the level of agreed-upon police forces for internal order only, strictly limited in number and very lightly armed, it being understood that this total disarmament must be subject at all stages to as effective an inspection system as is reasonably possible and that the accomplishment of each stage must be carefully verified before going further

2. An adequate world police force, meaning the establishment, parallel with the disarmament process, of a strong and heavily armed force of, say, 400,000 men, composed of volunteers and not of national contingents, with careful safeguards, against having any undue proportion from any nation or group of nations and in respect of command, disposition, and other factors, so as to provide every possible assurance against abuse of power by this force.

3. A world judicial, quasi-judicial, and conciliation system, under which impartial world tribunals would be constituted in order to provide fully adequate means for the peaceful settlement of all international disputes, in lieu of force or the threat of it.

4. World legislative and executive agencies, so constituted as to be fair to all nations and also workable in practice, the powers of these agencies to be carefully restricted to the end in view, namely, the prevention of war.

5. A world development authority: adequately financed and staffed, to mitigate the vast and excessive economic disparities between the "have" and the "have-not" nations.

6. An effective world revenue system to provide reliable revenues for the maintenance of the world police force and other necessary world institutions, since, without such a system, the mere establishment of those institutions would be a futility.

I cannot emphasize too strongly that every one of these elements is essential. For example, disarmament alone, no matter how complete or how efficient the inspection system, could not insure peace for the reason that many pressures for change and international disputes would still continue, with consequent rearming and fighting, unless prevented by a strong world police and trustworthy world tribunals. It is, indeed, no more sensible to expect world order without all these world institutions than it would be to expect a watch to keep time without all its essential and interrelated parts.

Practical prospects

TURNING now to the question of the practical prospects for such a program, one must recognize the formidable character of the obstacles to be surmounted.

To begin with, there is the general human tendency to resist radical change, no matter how clear the necessity; and, beyond this, there are specific and powerful adverse influences which cannot be ignored.

Probably the most important of these is the resistance of the military, not only in the United States but in many other nations.

In appraising this pervading military influence, it is necessary to recognize its good faith in most cases. The typical professional soldier does not deprecate disarmament because he is any less humane than the average civilian. He does so because his training and environment have irrevocably conditioned him to assume that his profession is indispensable. In consequence, it is simply too much to expect that the military profession as a whole will do otherwise than oppose or at least "drag their feet" in respect of all proposals for total national disarmament and all that this implies. Hence, it follows that there will be no solution for the problem of world peace until the resistance of the military profession everywhere is firmly overruled.

A less important yet significant adverse influence is that of traditional diplomacy. It must be remembered that for centuries a principal function of the professional diplomat has been to deal in power politics, that is, in such things as the making of alliances or veiled or open threats of force intended to advance the real or supposed interests of his particular country. These habits of thought are almost as difficult to shake off as those of the professional military man. Accordingly, those who seek peace through enforceable world law will do well to discount an almost certain lack of interest in many foreign offices.

In addition, there is the vested interest of the armaments industry, whose proprietors and millions of employees cannot view with complete enthusiasm the elimination of their profits and jobs, even for so great a cause as genuine peace. And, perhaps most important of all, there is the factor of mutual fears and recriminations which, as of 1961, so poison the East-West atmosphere. Unfortunately, this state of affairs is deeply rooted on both sides. It has been built up over a long period and conditions the thinking of millions of people in both East and West. There is little use in trying to assess the blame which both sides must share, and we must accept this mutually poisoned atmosphere as a fact of life which cannot be got rid of for a long time.

Taking together all these and still other adverse factors, we have a truly formidable group of obstacles. Yet they are not so formidable, I judge, as to stand against the still stronger forces making for world order.

Of these, the most powerful single force is, I suppose, the simple and natural desire of the average individual to survive. It may be arguable whether the human race is worth preserving, but the actual fact is that men and women, with few exceptions, desire to live out a normal span and even more urgently desire that their descendants shall not be prematurely cut off without a chance to experience life for good or ill.

It follows, I believe, that, as the destructive power of the new weapons increases from year to year and as, at the same time, people become more aware that the problem of removing this danger is by no means insoluble, the pressure upon those in authority to apply themselves to the formulation of an effective plan will become irresistible within a reasonably short period.

What can more definitely be said on this all-important question of timing? Are we likely to drift along with a continued arms race for a generation or so, subject to a constant risk of catastrophe? Or have we already reached the point where the danger is sufficiently great and the remedy sufficiently understood to bring about action in the immediate future?

Probabilities

I SUGGEST that the probable outcome lies between these extremes. On the one hand, the chances seem slight that the world can or will endure a continued arms race for another thirty or forty years. But, on the other hand, it is probably too much to hope that the current effort for military dominance can be brought to an end without at least five years of further strain and of education concerning the requirements for genuine peace.

Accordingly, I venture the surmise that in or about 1966–1967, following several years of intense negotiation accompanied by recurrent tensions and alarms, the time will be ripe for the agreed formulation by the leading powers of a comprehensive plan of the sort above summarized and its submission to all the other nations. And, once submitted, after the inevitably long discussions, there is good reason to suppose that the plan will have been adopted and be in operation within a few years thereafter, say, by 1971.

I venture this judgment because, by 1966–1967, the frightful consequences of all-out nuclear war should have become so apparent to all that the necessary pressures for action will probably have developed. I believe, in short, that considering the speed with which the technology of destruction is developing in 1961, five more years of progress in this field should be enough to energize the human race into effective action for its own survival, if anything can do so.

Concerning the supply of nuclear bombs and missiles, the world's stock-pile, which is fairly estimated in early 1961 as having an explosive power of 55 billion tons of TNT, will probably have increased by 1966–1967, in the absence of an arms truce, to at least 70 billion tons, or about 23,000 times the explosive power of the approximately three million tons used by all the warring powers in all theaters in World War II. This would provide over twenty-one tons for each of the estimated three and a quarter billion inhabitants of the world in 1966 and should be enough to give pause to even the most belligerent.

As to the equally important factor of accuracy, it is probable that, with five years more of practice, it will be possible consistently to land five megaton ballistic missiles within half a mile of the target point even at ranges of 7,000 miles, so that there would almost literally be no point on earth which could not be reached both from the United States and the Soviet Union.

By 1966–1967, also, both East and West should be amply supplied with nearly invulnerable means of delivery. The United States, as we are told in the *New York Times*, will then have 464 long-range nuclear missiles in a fleet of twenty-nine Polaris submarines, as well as 700 to 760 fixed-site intercontinental ballistic missiles, most of them emplaced in hardened silo or concrete underground sites. All these will be in addition to great fleets of bombers, each capable of carrying a twenty-megaton load of bombs. However, since two can play at this game, there is no reason why the Soviet Union should be behind in the race; and it is safe to assume that, while the bombing and submarine fleets of the Eastern allies may be much inferior to those of the west, this deficiency will be offset by even more land-based missile sites scattered throughout the vast land mass of those countries.

In the light of all these prospects, it is indeed hard to believe that the people will remain apathetic beyond the 1966–1967 period, if they can ever be moved at all to an adequate effort to save themselves.

This is especially so, I suggest, because the prospective increase in understanding as to the capacity of the race to destroy itself will probably be matched during the 1960's by an increasing comprehension of the world institutions necessary to prevent that destruction. The study of this subject already in progress or planned should develop in many lands a considerable number of persons equipped to formulate and administer the world security organization when the time is ripe for action. Our salvation lies, I believe, in this combination of increased concern over the danger and increased understanding of the means whereby it can be removed.

With regard to this moderately optimistic view, a skeptic might well raise the question as to where the necessary governmental leadership is to come from. He might point out that, during the whole sixteen years since World War II not a single government has taken the trouble to formulate a comprehensive and adequate plan for peace, and he might ask: Why is there are more likelihood that any government or group of governments will provide the necessary leadership during the 1960's?

My answer is that the situation has entirely changed with the advent of ballistic missiles and their constantly increasing power and accuracy and that, under the pressure of events, it is almost certain that some creative governmental leadership must soon emerge.

Leadership problems

FOR such leadership, one thinks of four possible sources: the Soviet Union, a group of neutral or uncommitted nations, the British Commonwealth, and the United States.

In the case of the Soviet Union, the difficulty will certainly not be that of insufficient zeal. For I think it clear that, because of Russia's appalling losses in war, no people or govern-

ment in the world is more anxious for disarmament and peace. In World War II alone, the Soviet Union's loss of life was not less than 15 million, or at least 8 per cent of the entire population. This loss, together with the immense losses in World War I and in the 1918–1940 period, have engendered an almost desperate desire for peace among the Russian people—to which no government, however authoritarian, can be indifferent. There is, therefore, no reason to doubt the sincerity of the Soviet proposals for general and complete disarmament; and there is every reason to suppose that the Soviet regime will continue insistently to press proposals of this sort.

Moreover, the Soviet regime has, I believe, rendered a great service in stressing the necessity for total, rather than partial, disarmament. The trouble is, however, that the Soviet government does not seem, as yet, adequately to recognize the need for a strong world police and a world judicial system as necessary conditions for the acceptance of universal and complete disarmament. Beyond this, the practical fact is that the United States and some other countries have been so conditioned to suspect and fear the Soviet regime that any proposal from that source, regardless of its merit, is under a handicap from the start. While these conditions may change, the conclusion early in 1961 must be that, however welcome any constructive Soviet proposals, there are serious doubts as to whether the Soviet Union can provide the necessary leadership during the next few years.

As to the second possibility of leadership by a group of neutral and non-aligned nations—such as Switzerland, Austria, Tunisia, India, Burma, Ceylon, and Mexico—the idea is both logical and attractive, because proposals from such a source would avoid the prejudices likely to handicap even the best plan formulated by either of the superpowers. With this in mind, a persistent effort has already been made to induce a number of eligible neutrals to consult together on a united plan for world disarmament and world development. Despite some apparent timidity and overcaution as to stepping out into the world arena on so great a subject, this possible approach is a promising one if only some powerful personality in one of these nations will summon sufficient initiative and energy.

Still more promising is possible leadership by the British Commonwealth of Nations, since, in this group of states, there are combined strong motivation, mature political capacity, and immense prestige.

Concerning motivation, the United Kingdom, by reason of extreme vulnerability in a nuclear war, must surely have the strongest possible reasons to achieve complete disarmament. With 52 million people in an area of less than one-thirtieth that of the forty-eight contiguous states of the United States, the United Kingdom has a population density of over 550 persons per square mile, while for England and Wales alone the density is no less than 790 per square mile. Remembering that, in an all-out nuclear war, Britain would certainly be a prime target and open to attack by bombing planes as well as by missiles launched from submarines and from sites inside Russia, it would seem impossible to prevent almost total destruction in Britain, no matter what was done to Russia at the same time.

In these circumstances, it seems certain that no British government can fail, under increasing popular pressure, actively to interest itself in the achievement of universal and complete disarmament. Indeed, that interest has already been shown in the striking pronouncement of the Prime Ministers of the British Commonwealth on March 17, 1961, which declared unequivocally for "total world-wide disarmament" and for the organization of a "substantial and adequately armed international military force."

Assuming the development from this foundation of a comprehensive and adequate British plan, it would doubtless command the support of all the other nations of the Commonwealth, which means a plan produced by thirteen nations on five continents with a population of about 700 million. Certainly this combination of urgent motivation with great experience and prestige makes the British Commonwealth a most promising candidate for the necessary leadership.

Concerning possible leadership by the United States, almost everything, it would seem, will turn upon the statesmanship, or lack of it, of President Kennedy. It is perfectly natural, and in no way to our discredit, that we in the United States simply cannot have the same intense aversion to modern war that we would have if we had suffered in the same way as Russia and the other nations which bore the brunt of World Wars I and II. Nevertheless, there is sufficient concern in the United States over the possible consequences of a general nuclear war to supply the President with the necessary support for a creative and comprehensive plan containing all the elements mentioned at the start of this article. Will President Kennedy, with the advice of John J. McCloy, his adviser on disarmament, decide to propose a great and really adequate plan for total disarmament and for the necessary institutions to make, interpret, and enforce world law? If so, his initiative would, I believe, be hailed throughout the world and would constitute the breakthrough whereby a system of enforceable law could and would actually be achieved. As of this writing, the omens are obscure, and we can only pray that the necessary creativity and resolve will be granted to our new President.

The approach

THE more one reflects on this whole problem of world order, the clearer it becomes that there certainly is an urgent need for a radically new approach, which will, once and for all, recognize the necessity for total, rather that merely partial, national disarmament and also for the simultaneous establishment of world institutions—legislative, executive and judicial—to fulfill the same functions in respect of world order as are fulfilled by the local legislature, local police, and local courts in any orderly community. All else depends upon the general acceptance of this basic concept.

On this basis, there will need to be established along with a stage-by-stage total disarmament plan under a careful inspection system, the other five minimum world institutions essential for the prevention of war. At the risk of repetition, I list them again as follows: A strong world police force composed of individual volunteers and carefully safeguarded against possible abuse of world power; a world judicial, quasi-judicial, and conciliation system; adequate and carefully balanced world legislative and executive agencies; a well-financed world development authority; and a world revenue system to ensure reliable financial support for the entire structure. On no lesser terms can world peace be assured, any more than domestic order can be assured without similar local and national institutions. The sooner the peoples and governments realize this simple truth, the sooner will genuine world peace be realized.

How and when

INDEED, the real question, in my view, is not as to what is needed but, rather, as to how and when the people and governments of the world can be led to formulate and put in effect the revolutionary plan which will alone suffice.

In this regard, there is a fair analogy, I believe, between the world situation in 1961 and the situation of a seriously ill but willful and obstinate man who holds back from the necessary treatment. As in the case of the world's peace problem, his trouble is entirely curable. The diagnosis is, in fact, perfectly clear. The patient needs a radical operation, together with a drastic reform in his old habits. And yet, because of inertia and willfulness, he procrastinates and withholds his consent. What, if anything, can change his mind before it is too late? Usually, so the surgeons say, only a series of physical and psychological shocks combined with some comprehension by the patient of the nature of the operation and what it can do for him will induce him to authorize it.

As I see it, very similar influences will determine the future of the world. It may well be that several more shocks will be necessary—another Congo or two, or another Cuba, or even another Korea-like war—in order further to demonstrate the risks of the arms race and the inadequacy of the United Nations. And, beyond this, there must be a much better understanding by the peoples and their governments of what is required by way of world institutions in order to effect a cure for the chronic dangers.

In summary, I suggest that what the whole question comes down to is whether the human race will show enough intelligence to make the required adjustment to the nuclear age. More specifically, the issue in 1961 is whether our human society is sufficiently resourceful to formulate and accept not only total world-wide national disarmament, but also the other necessary world institutions which must go with it in order, once and for all, to abolish war.

But this question will, in turn, depend, I believe, not so much on mankind's inherent capacity or incapacity to adjust to the new situation, but, rather, on whether a sufficient educational effort is made concerning the essentials for genuine peace. For while there is, I judge, no such inherent lack of capacity as to prevent solution of the problem, it will not be solved if the peoples are so ignorant and, consequently, so apathetic as to permit the continued domination of military and old-style diplomatic thinking.

The fact is that salvation can be found only in a truly revolutionary change in traditional thought as to the means for dealing with international disputes, a change whereby it is taken for granted that violence or the threat of it has become obsolete. And the key to such a change is, I believe, a continued and intensified process of education whereby many more people in many countries are brought to realize that only a great and comprehensive plan for enforceable world law will meet the situation.

Fortunately, this process is already well under way since, although governments have been generally neglectful, many private persons the world over have applied their minds to this problem of world peace, and there now exist carefully drafted detailed plans which can be utilized for the formulation of an adequate plan. Let this material be used by those in authority, and the task will appear less formidable to officials who often seem to approach the problem as if it were an unexplored field.

Some of this needed education will, as I have said, doubtless come from some new and disturbing experiences. And thus, through a combination of experience and mental effort, we can find the way to the formulation and adoption of the necessary plan.

Even so, the issue will be a close one, since the forces of habit and tradition are strong, and to break out of these chains will not be easy. As Arnold Toynbee has put it: "We shall have a hard struggle with ourselves to save ourselves from ourselves."

Nevertheless, when the various adverse and favorable factors are weighed against each other, my considered opinion is that the favorable factors will, subject to two conditions, outweigh the adverse. The first condition is the emergence of some creative and dynamic governmental leadership. The other is a sufficiently intelligent and persistent educational effort concerning the specific requirements for genuine world peace. With these conditions fulfilled, we can reasonably look forward to a new world order based upon universal and complete disarmament and enforceable world law within ten to fifteen years. Without them, we can expect, and perhaps deserve, nothing better than a further period of tension and frustration under a continual risk of dire catastrophe.

Part Four

National security: a field develops

Introductory note

The selections in Part I have, we hope, presented the reader with a sense of the emerging concept of national security. This Part is designed to illustrate the evolution of national security as a field of study. Some articles deal with partial and tentative attempts at theory construction; some are primarily concerned with developing and sharpening methodological tools; and others are attempts to identify and delineate broad areas for further research. Most of the theoretical approaches and methodological tools represented here are, of course, not unique to the young field of national security; rather, they are representative of recent trends in the social sciences as a whole. All in all, this picture is characteristic of the early stages in the development of any new academic discipline.

The first four articles present theoretical approaches to a limited range of phenomena in the field of national security. Boulding's first contribution applies existing organizational theory to a variety of conflictual situations. His second article draws upon economic concepts and attempts to show how a science of threat systems might be evolved by analogy with exchange systems. This would have unique applications to the problems of creating a truly stable system of deterrence. The article by North *et al.* deals with the ways in which conflict processes can serve integrative functions. Using anthropological and sociological data, the authors argue that since *intra*-group conflicts can serve to further integration, *inter*-group conflicts may also be manipulated or negotiated to integrate the hostile parties. The concept of integration is carried a step further in Deutsch's selection, which presents a theoretical scheme for the evaluation of the integration or disintegration of territorial units. Deutsch identifies the processes that create unifying habits and institutions essential to the creation of peaceful political entities (security communities).

Some possible applications of game theory to problems of national security are illustrated in the next two articles. Anatol Rapoport, using some of the methods of mathematical psychologists, creates a gaming situation to test the reaction of players to hostile and cooperative acts. The results seem to support Charles Osgood's hypothesis (pages 276–283) that chains of hostile or friendly acts may be started by small initial steps. Morton Kaplan sets up a game to demonstrate that the threat of counterattack is the best strategy against possible aggression. He tries to place the concept of nuclear deterrence on a firm theoretical ground, and urges the application of appropriate statistical and mathematical strategic models.

The article by Charlotte and George Dyer makes use of the advances in cybernetics. Since the rational formulation of policy is rendered so difficult by the extraordinary number of factors that decision-makers must consider, the authors propose the construction of an electronic "support for human thinking." This device could rationally estimate national power and intentions, they say, and test proposed policies through gaming.

The article by Leontief and Hoffenberg is another instance of the application of economic tools to national security problems. They adapt the economic method of "input-output" analysis to the problems that might be created by disarmament. This technique, they argue, could facilitate forecasting the effect on the economy of the reallocation of resources now expended for defense purposes.

The last selection opens up some new areas for research by identifying problems that might be analyzed and suggesting hypotheses that might be verified. Charles Hitch lists some of the problems created by the development of nuclear technology and suggests the economic research tools available for their solution.

Some time ago Stanley Hoffman wrote of the long and arduous road to theory in international relations. In the field of national security this road is barely a path. It is our hope that the selections in Part IV, indeed in the entire book, have illuminated the few existing milestones and have suggested some of the alternative routes.

Kenneth E. Boulding

Organization and conflict

THIS PAPER concentrates on the problem of the "parties" to conflict. Every conflict involves at least two parties or conflicting organizations. The party may be a biological individual, or it may be an aggregate or an organization of individuals. All individuals are organizations of subordinate parts: all organizations are in some sense "individuals" insofar as they have well-defined patterns of behavior and reaction. Generally, we may wish to reserve the term "competition" for the wide concept which includes interactions among unorganized aggregates (such as biological populations) and to use the word "conflict" for the narrower concept in which the conflicting parties are individuals or organizations, possessing a certain core of unity of behavior and in which each organization is in some sense "aware" of the other and makes this awareness an essential part of its behavior pattern. We think of conflict, then, as a system of interacting systems, each party to the conflict being a system in itself bound, however, to the other party by a system of communication, information, subjective knowledge, and behavior reactions. The question as to what property of such a system constitutes the "conflictual" as opposed, say, to the cooperative element is suprisingly difficult to answer and will be considered later.

A model of organization as system

LET us consider first, then, the nature of the systems which are involved in an organization. What we want here is not the organization in all its richness and completeness but rather the simple abstract model of an organization which will serve to illuminate the relationships *between* organizations. An organization, we may recall, may include things as complex as an amoeba or as simple as the General Motors Corporation! What we are looking for here is the simplest model which will enable us to study the interaction of organizations.

The first element in the description of an organization is a static structure of parts—its geography or anatomy, its organization chart or balance sheet or molecular structure. There are very interesting elements of scarcity or competition even in these static structures which may sometimes underlie conflicts—in a sense, all conflicts of interest, or "issue conflicts", arise because two things cannot be in the same place at the same time. Everything cannot be close to everything else; there is an inexorability about geography and topology which necessitates more separation in parts of large structures than in small and which imposes limits on the growth of any particular type of structure. Thus in a triangular lattice each individual part can be in direct contact with no more than six others. Fundamental also in limiting the size of organizations is the scale model, or D'Arcy Thompson principle [5], that the increase in size of a structure inevitably brings with it a change in the ratio of lengths to areas and volumes. Doubling linear dimensions of a structure quadruples its areas and octuples its volumes and hence diminishes the relative importance of those properties which depend

Reprinted from *The Journal of Conflict Resolution*, Vol. 1, No. 2, 1957, pp. 122–134.

on length (such as communications) or on area (muscular or structural strength, absorption of air or food) to those which depend on volume (weight). Hence we get the very important principle that if the relative importance of linear, areal, and volumetric properties are to be preserved, the *form* of the structure must change as it increases in size; there must be elaborations of linear networks (nerves and channels of circulation); there must be convolution of areas of surface reaction (lungs, brains, bowels), in order to increase the ratio of linear or areal dimensions to volume and weight. In social organizations (firms, states, universities), communications networks and specialized administration must increase their relative importance as the size of the organization grows.

The next step in the development of an organization model is its description as a "machine," or energy transformer. Any organization depends on some source of energy for its continued existence—food and light in the case of the biological individual, to which may be added coal, oil, and other sources in the case of manufacturing plants or armed forces. Scarcity of energy sources may be an important source of competition and issue conflict, for what is taken *by* one organization may be taken *from* another. Where the game against nature results in a "victory," and the release of another source of energy, the possibility for the expansion of all organizations together emerges, and the conflict between them is at least temporarily lessened. Surprisingly, little attention has been paid to the general description of the energy requirements of social organizations. The basic source of energy for such organizations is the same as that for the individuals of which they are composed—food. The surplus of food production over and above the consumption of the agriculturalist is perhaps the best index of the ability of a society to construct social organizations of all kinds. Savage societies cannot develop complex organizations because the food producer must spend all his time getting enough for himself and his family. In the United States today we can produce all the food we need with 10-15 per cent of the population and so release up to 90 per cent of the population for "other things."

ORGANIZATION GROWTH AND CONFLICT

The next step in the organization model is to describe it as an "open system" or, more generally, as a "growth system" or dynamic open system. A static open system is a structure which is maintained in the midst of a stream or throughput of its constituent parts. To be an open system, a structure must have the property that a "hole" in the structure produces a large attractive force or valency to pull an appropriate "occupant" from the surrounding environment into the "hole." Thus a living organism maintains its structure more or less intact in the midst of a constant throughput of atoms of matter. A social organization is a structure of "roles": any vacancy in the role structure—i.e., any role without an occupant—creates pressure to fill the vacancy with an appropriately skilled person. It is this property of being an open system which enables organizations to live longer than any of their parts—presidents, deans, and professors come and go, but the university goes on forever.

In a dynamic open system there is not merely maintenance of an existing structure but growth (or decline) in the structure itself. Not only are old jobs filled as their previous occupants pass on, but new jobs are created. The atoms in a cell, the cells of the body, can likewise be regarded as a role structure subject to a constant throughput, in which new roles are constantly added as the organism develops from the egg. The laws of development of organizations are very imperfectly understood, and this is perhaps one of the most serious gaps in our knowledge. It is clear that development never takes place haphazardly, except perhaps in pathological cases such as a cancer. Certain "organizers" of development can be identified—the gene, the chemical organizers of the embryo, the entrepreneurs, the prophets, and the heroes who are the founding fathers of social organizations. How the organization of development is actually accomplished, however, is a great mystery, and our ignorance of this machinery is evidenced by our inability to predict outcomes, except after the event. We know that an acorn grows into an oak and never into a cactus, but just what it is in the acorn which gives it this remarkable property we do not know. Similarly, we do not know what mysterious property enabled the little group of Apostles to grow into the Christian church or the little group around Hitler to grow into the Nazi state, when thousands of similar groups perish in early infancy.

Although the processes of growth remain mysterious, we do know something about the factors which limit growth, and this enables us to make some significant propositions in the theory of conflict. An important source of conflict among organizations is the attempt of two or more organizations to expand into the same field. When two firms are expanding into a limited market or two nations into the same territory or two labor unions into the same job jurisdiction, a conflict of interest is likely to arise. This "expansion conflict," to coin a term for it, has both a static and a dynamic aspect. It arises in a static sense if the number of role occupants is limited, so that, as more are drawn into one organization, fewer are available for others—the more Rotarians there are, the fewer Lions and Kiwanians; the Methodist church may grow at the expense of the Baptist; and so on. We think of the whole field of organizations as dividing among them the raw material in the shape of members, much as nations divide up the geographic area of the world, and an expansion of one inevitably means a contraction of others, unless, of course, the field itself is growing. Growth in the field itself has thus an important effect in lessening the intensity of expansion conflicts. Thus in the nineteenth century the fact that so many European countries were able to expand their power and influence in colonial Empires outside Europe may have lessened the conflict among them; the closing of the colonial field in the early twentieth century may have been one reason for the two world wars. When the labor movement is expanding and all unions are organizing the unorganized, jurisdictional disputes between them lessen in intensity; when the field is closed and one union can expand only at the expense of another, these disputes increase in intensity. An era of great missionary activity, when the churches, too, are organizing the unorganized throughout the world, also sees the decline of denominational tensions and the rise of the ecumenical movement.

We must not apply the foregoing principle too mechanically, of course, We may have a situation where something like an equilibrium or balance of power has been reached in a static situation which is completely upset by the sudden development of opportunities for expansion. Organizations which have accepted a static situation now may find themselves with opportunities for growth. The opportunity creates a habit, and the organization which has developed a habit of expansion may not be content with expanding into defenseless and unorganized regions but may turn against other organizations like itself. Thus conflict depends

on what might be called the "expansion pressure" of organizations, as well as on the nature of the opportunities which surround them. We might, therefore, identify three extreme cases. First is the situation in which the environment is static, in the sense that there is no expansion of the "raw material" of organizations, but in which there is little or no conflict because the organizations which occupy the field have no expansion pressure, are content to be stationary, and simply reproduce themselves without growth. The second case is that in which there is expansion pressure but in which there are abundant opportunities for the growth of each organization through the growth of the field itself. In this case, also, there will be little in the way of expansion conflict, as the organizations are expanding into an empty or unorganized field rather than into each other. The third case is that in which the field is static or expanding very little, but the organizations have great internal expansion pressure. Here conflict will be intense, as each organization can expand only at the expense of others of like propensities. We might perhaps distinguish a fourth case, of which the first case mentioned above is a special example, in which some organizations are expanding and some contracting in a static field but in which the contracting organizations do so willingly. In this case the expansion pressures and "contraction pressures" cancel out, and there is again little or no conflict.[1]

INFORMATION, KNOWLEDGE, AND ORGANIZATION IMAGE

Now, if we are to explore further the nature and determinants of expansion pressure, we must go to a fourth level of organization theory. This is the level of control processes involving information inputs and outputs and knowledge structures. The simplest model here is that of a cybernetic or homeostatic process, where we assume that there is a variable or, more generally, a set of variables which the organization is concerned to maintain at some equilibrium values. These variables must be in the information input of the organization, at least to the extent that the organization "knows" when there is a *divergence* of the value given by the information input from the ideal value which the organization sets out to maintain. This knowledge is reflected in behavior or action of some kind directed toward correcting the perceived divergence between the real and the ideal values of the homeostatic variables. For a system like this to operate successfully, there should also be "relational feedback"—that is, information regarding the divergence between real and ideal and especially regarding the change in this divergence, which is perceived as related to the action taken.

The theory of organizational behavior which is implied in this model might be described as the epistemic or "eiconic" theory [1]. It postulates that any organization possesses as part of its essential structure a "view of the universe" or "image" (hence the term "eiconic"). This image has many dimensions. In man, for instance, it involves a view of space and time and his position in them; it involves a relational image of cause and effect and connection: it has dimensions of reality and unreality, publicness and privateness, certainty and uncertainty, emotional effect; and over the relevant part of the field there is a value ordering according to which one part of the field can be identified as "better" or "worse" than another part. Behavior or action is then interpreted as the initiation of a cause-effect process which will move the organization toward the most highly valued part of its image of the future. Here, for instance, is a man who gets up in the morning, dresses, shaves, has breakfast, and takes a plane to New York. In explaining the behavior of this aggregation of some ten billion cells, we must postulate that he has a view of the spatial universe which includes at least his own bathroom, dining room, and the way to the airport, and in which, in spite of the agreeableness of staying in bed, moving into the bathroom and scraping his face with a razor are valued at the moment more highly than anything else which he might be doing. Similarly, he goes to New York rather than to any one of a hundred other cities because it is for him at that moment the most highly valued part of the attainable surface of the earth—for what further reason we need not inquire.

This view of behavior then raises a number of questions regarding the subordinate processes which are involved even in the simplest behavior. These concern themselves mainly with how the image, in all its complexity, is built up and especially how messages which are received by the organization result in a change in the image, for it is only through a change in the image that there can be a change in behavior. The image is not, of course, simply a pile or aggregate of messages. Most messages which are received make little or no impression on the image, or they merely serve to confirm an existing image. As I turn my head, a new message enters my eyes; it merely serves, however, to confirm the image that I am sitting in a room typing. Frequently, messages are received which merely add to the image without appreciably changing its structure; the processes of rote learning are a good illustration. Sometimes, however, a message is received which effects a revolution or reorganization of the image. A man is informed that he is promoted; this changes his image of his own role and person. A man receives overwhelming evidence that his trusted friend has deceived him; this changes his image of his friend's personality. A nation undergoes a revolution; this changes the image of the character and probable behavior of the nation, both in the minds of its own people and in the minds of others.

It is the peculiar glory, and occasionally the shame, of man that his images are built up not only by the receipt of messages from nature (signs) but also by the receipt of symbolic messages, proceeding directly from other persons in face-to-face contact or indirectly through the medium of "transcripts"—books, papers, records, movies, television, and so on. Man is the talking animal, and the complexity of his organizational world depends largely on his ability to communicate in symbols. If I hear a voice behind me, I may interpret this information as indicating the presence of a person, and the character of the voice will give me clues as to the character of the person—whether it is familiar or unfamiliar, foreign or native, male or female, etc. So far, the voice is merely a sign; it does not matter what words are spoken, and the process of building this information into an image is not essentially different from the process by which any other message from nature conveyed by any of the senses is built up into an image of the world around us—a world of rocks, trees, clouds, animals, people, buildings, and so on. The moment, however, that words are spoken which are *understood*, we pass to a "higher" and immensely complex system of symbolic communication which has the property of building up images far removed from the immediate world around us. Symbols remove the human organization from the prison of the immediate here and now, in which all lower forms of life are trapped, and the image of man therefore soars off to the galaxies, to the beginnings and the end of all things, to the realm of the impossible and almost to the inconceivable. It is because of this symbolic nature of the image of man that conflict in the human world is so much more complex than conflict in the animal kingdom, where images are built up only by signs and hence conflict is always face to face.

VALUE DIMENSIONS OF THE ORGANIZATION IMAGE

The theory of the image points to another problem underlying any theory of behavior and interaction—the problem of the determinants of the value image or, more accurately, the value dimension of the image. This is vital for a theory of behavior, for, as we have seen, behavior consists of movement into the most highly valued part of the *total* image. A shift in the value ordering, therefore, even without any change in the rest of the image, can produce profound, even revolutionary, changes in behavior. I may be all set to get on a plane for New York when I receive a telegram to say my father has died in San Francisco, the information creates a marked shift in my valuation of my image of space and time: I cancel my reservation to New York and get a plane to San Francisco immediately because this is now the most highly valued part of my image of the world of space and time. Note that the value ordering is not the same as the emotive or pleasure-pain dimension of the image; my engagement in New York may have been perceived as very pleasant, whereas my task in San Francisco may be very painful. The value ordering, however, is capable of overriding all other orderings, and it is the value ordering which dominates behavior. Notice that in this case there is no change in my general image of space and time—I still visualize New York and San Francisco as occupying the same relative positions on my inner globe. In this example we might argue that it was a change in my detailed image of space and time, especially of persons, which caused the change in the value image; thus I now visualize my father as dead, whereas previously I had visualized him as alive. We cannot always assume, however, that it is changes in some other aspect of the image which causes a change in the value image. There may be revolutions in the value image which are quite independent of any change in the rest of the image. I am asked, for instance, do I prefer tea or coffee. I say tea, and then immediately "change my mind" and say coffee. My images of tea and coffee remain the same; only my value ordering has changed.

We cannot say very much, perhaps, about so general a matter as the forces which determine the value ordering over the life of an individual. These orderings certainly originate at the biological or presymbolic level. Even though the value ordering cannot be identified with any pleasure-pain ordering, it is clear that the sheer force of natural selection produces innate value orderings which are conducive to survival and that the low positions in the value ordering which are generally given to cold, hunger, thirst, sexual abstinence, and pain are not wholly accidental. Once the symbolic image is introduced, value orderings share in the almost unlimited proliferation of the image which symbolic messages induce, and the biological origins are transcended and transformed often out of recognition. For his symbols man has been willing to endure any amount of physical discomfort and pain, even to the point of death.

In considering the value image and, indeed, the image in general, attention should be drawn to the importance of *stereotypes*, or what might be called *condensed images*. These arise mainly because the human organism, beyond a certain point, places lower and lower values on increasing complexity in the image, probably because of some limitations of capacity in the underlying biological structure. We therefore seek escape from complexity into simple, unitary condensed images. This is especially important in regard to the value image, where complexity rapidly becomes intolerable, and we constantly seek straightforward ordering. We try to divide the world into "good guys" and "bad guys" (it is unquestionably the simple value structure of the horse opera which gives it so universal an appeal). Similarly, we divide the world into "peace-loving nations" and, presumably, war-loving nations, and we divide people into simple pejorative dichotomies—Jews and gentiles, white and Negro, believers and unbelievers, the scientific and the superstitious, and so on, to the horror of the semanticist and the great confusion of man. We cannot rest content with propositions of the form "A is better than B in respect to X, but worse than B in respect to Y." We want to know where A is *altogether* better or worse than B. So we run to grade sheets; cost-of-living indexes; national, racial, and occupational stereotypes, in an attempt to escape from the intolerable multidimensionality of reality. Up to a point this simplification is a necessity—we could not act at all were we not capable of effecting these drastic condensations of the image. Condensation, however, can easily become pathological and may be an important cause of conflicts which could be resolved if the parties had a greater tolerance of complexity and ambiguity.

The danger to organizations and to the harmony and fruitfulness of their interactions, which comes from condensation of the image, arises from what might be called the principle of *linked homeostasis*. Suppose that there are two variables which must be maintained within the limits of homeostatic tolerance. If the mechanisms by which each is stabilized are too closely linked, the stabilization of one may be achieved only at the cost of the de-stabilization of the other, or they may both be stabilized only with a range outside what is regarded as desirable for both taken separately. Thus suppose we wish to stabilize both the temperature and the humidity of a building. If the apparatus for maintaining these variables is linked, we may find ourselves in the position where an attempt to raise the temperature lowers the humidity, and we find ourselves forced to choose between the warm and dry or the cold and moist, and we cannot achieve the "ideal" of warm and moist. The linkage may occur anywhere in the system, either in the information receptors, in the "image" of the control, or in the effectors (furnaces and humidifiers) by which the variables are changed. One suspects that the main source of linked homeostasis in human systems is in the condensed image. Information about two or more essential variables is condensed in the image into a single variable and can produce only a single behavior reaction in the effectors. Thus the inability to discriminate leads, paradoxically enough, to discrimination in the sociological sense. We lump together in the image things which should be separate, and, because of this, we behave toward a heterogeneous reality as if it were homogeneous and toward a homogeneous reality as if it were heterogeneous. Thus we condense the immensely complex image of personality into a few stereotypes—"Negroes," "Jews," "eggheads," "capitalists"—and classify those we meet immediately into these simple boxes and order our behavior accordingly, oblivious of the fact that our boxes are full of all kinds of different people, requiring different modes of behavior, and that a classification according to appropriate modes of behavior might be quite different.

Up to this point I have not emphasized the distinction between persons and organizations of persons, having simply a model of a "be-havior unit" without regard to its composition. There are, however, important differences between the individual person as a system and a social organization, such as a university or a corporation. It is easy to fall into a mystique of organizations and imbue them with personality, motives, and patterns of behavior in a way that is at best a metaphor and at worst a serious misconception. In a literal sense, only persons can possess images, and only persons can behave. Nevertheless, there is a sense in which an organization can be regarded, in Ralph Gerard's terminology, as an "epi-organism," possessing as a system many of the system properties of organisms. Even in the strict biological sphere, it is not always easy to tell where an organism ends and its environment begins, and for some purposes whole eco-systems can be regarded as a single organism, exhibiting division of labor, exchange, homeostasis, and so on. In the case of the social organization, what gives it "a unitary character" or "personality" is the existence of widely *shared* images, especially of the organization itself, among the participants. One should perhaps say "integrated" images rather than "shared," as the images of different persons may be very difficult and yet may fit into a unified whole. Thus the image which the president of a university has of his institution is very different from the image of the same institution in the mind of the instructor, the gardener, or the accountant. Nevertheless, all these images fit together into a role structure and a perception of appropriate behavior which makes the institution operate with a degree of unity and consistency. The instructor does not spend all his time cutting the college lawns, nor does the gardener harangue students on abstruse subjects from the college podiums. All the various images must have something in common, however vague, and an inadequate common image is a frequent source of internal disorganization. The head of a department who cannot see beyond his own department, the professor who cannot see beyond his own classroom, and any employee who has no vision whatever of the institution beyond his paycheck are all potential sources of internal strife and weakness.

ESTABLISHMENT AND DEVELOPMENT OF THE IMAGE

The question as to how common images are established is, therefore, a crucial one from the point of view of the theory of the social organization. The problem involves the dynamics of the change of the image under the stimulus of mainly symbolic messages. I am prepared to suggest as a very plausible hypothesis that common images are formed mainly through "conversation"—that is, through a dynamic process by which messages are sent back and forth among a group of people. The basic unit of conversation is the "remark." A remark always proceeds from the image of the remarker. It is heard by listeners and modifies the image of the listeners, unless there is strong resistance, in the direction of the image of the remarker. In conversation the listeners in turn became remarkers, and the images of the different individuals converge as each modifies the other in the direction of his own. For this to happen, however, I suspect that there must be a certain degree of initial similarity in the images. If the images are too divergent, a remark which is interpreted by the listener as implying a very different image from his own is regarded as a personal threat and is resisted. Under these circumstances, conversation may split up into a number of different groups, each with a convergent image, but there is no tendency for the different images of the subgroups to converge.

This theory stresses the importance of the communication network in the development of common images. The larger an organization becomes, the more difficult is the maintenance of adequate "conversation"—two-way image modifying communications among the component parts. There is a tendency, therefore, for the organization to split up into "non-conversing groups"—each group conversing within itself, but not conversing with other groups. Thus management becomes a group with much internal conversation and a converging image, and the labor force becomes another group with a different image. Much industrial conflict is a result of the differing public images of management and labor groups. It may be that one of the most important social functions of the labor movement is that it provides an intermediate group of labor leaders who participate in *both* groups and hence are able to act as intermediaries between them. The chaplain in the armed forces may perhaps have a rather similar role, participating in two potentially opposite and non-conversing groups—the armed forces and the church. The lot of the middlemen, however, is hard. Their personalities are in danger of being pulled apart by the conflict of roles in which they find themselves, or else they "sell out" to the dominant group. Thus we find labor leaders whose main function seems to be to make management decisions palatable to the rank and file and chaplains whose main concern is to whitewash the institution of war.

Implicit in the successful function of an organization is the notion of *mutual acceptance* of role images. If the participants in an organization do not accept the notion of the role *structure*, the organization is in danger of disintegrating. This does not mean that each individual must be satisfied with his own particular role. Indeed, unless there is some degree of dissatisfaction with the present role, an organization could never promote anyone, and too great satisfaction and harmony may actually lead to stagnation and decay through the failure of the "open system" aspects of organizational structure. There is a profound difference, however, between an ambition to aspire to another role and a rejection of the whole role structure as such. Thus union-management relations can be stable and harmonious only if both sides accept the role of the other. A revolutionary union, such as the old IWW, which rejects *in toto* the whole concept of a division of labor between employers and employed, cannot possibly enter into stable relations with the employer but must be in a state of constant conflict. Similarly, a revolutionary employer who is out to destroy the union and return to individual bargaining cannot establish stable relations with the union but again must be in constant warfare. Even two nations—two organizations whose main function, externally, is conflict culminating in war—can live peacefully together, like the United States and Canada, if each accepts fully the role of the other and if they share a reasonably common image of the mutual relationship.

The theory of organization and conflict

THREE CONFLICT SITUATIONS

MUCH more might be said on the subject of the theory of organization. In the interest of that conflict of space which besets every writer, however, we must now gather up the many strands of this paper to see whether the theory of organization, which we have presented here in bare outline, has fruitful applications to the theory of conflicts and their resolution. We must realize, of course, that there are many kinds of conflict situations. There is not a single concept of conflict, and therefore there cannot be a single theory of conflict. My own inquiries have led me to distinguish three different situations, each of which go by the name of conflict. We have first what Dr. Bernard calls "issue conflicts," which is what I, as an economist, might like to call "economic conflict." This is the situation in which a movement of change in a situation makes at least one party, in its own eyes, worse off and the other party better off. The theory of these situations has been elaborately developed in the theory of welfare economics, and I need not go into it here except to remark that, with two organizations, any given field can be divided into two sets, one which is called the "trading set," where movements are possible which benefit *both* parties, and the other, which is the "conflict set" (Edgeworth's "contract curve"), where a movement will benefit one party at the expense of the other.

ECONOMIC CONFLICT

An important dynamic principle emerges from this static theory, which might be called the "principle of the widening of the agenda." As long as the two parties are not in the conflict set, negotiation of a "trading" nature is possible, whereby both parties become better off. "Trading," however, inevitably moves the parties toward the conflict set and eventually lands them there. Once there, the only possibility is agreement or non-agreement; and if there is non-agreement, various rituals must be performed such as strikes, wars, etc., which will change the willingness to agree of one or both so that agreement becomes possible—assuming, that is, that the relationship cannot be avoided. Even if the parties are on the contract set in one field, however, they may get off it by widening the agenda to include variables which were not previously in discussion. Generally speaking, the wider the agenda, the greater the possibility for finding "trades," and the less chance there is of reaching an impasse on the conflict set. The principle of the widening of the agenda is exemplified in the multiplication of clauses in treaties and in union contracts. It is tempting to interpret the relative success of industrial relations as against the relative failure of international relations in terms of the greater flexibility of the agenda in union-

management negotiations as over against the hands-tied diplomat and the still more rigid soldier.

The contribution of organization theory to this part of conflict theory is to point out that it is not the "objective" situation which matters, but the subjective images of the participants, and that, therefore, the theory needs to be extended into the consideration of the dynamics of the formation and change of these images. Insofar as all issue conflicts involve utility, they are capable of resolution by changing value images as well as by a shift in the objective situation. It would be a grave error to think of issue conflicts as if they somehow involved brute facts, whereas psychological conflicts involved illusions. In the dynamics of issue conflicts especially, it is important to study the images of each party in its own mind and in the mind of the other.

INTERACTION CONFLICT

The second and third type of conflict both fall under Dr. Bernard's class of psychological conflicts, and yet they represent, to my mind, entirely different situations. The second type is what might be called "interaction conflict" as typified in the arms race, in any process of mutually heightening hostility through the reaction of each part to the behavior of the other. The pioneering analysis of these processes by Lewis F. Richardson [4] perhaps merits entitling them "Richardson processes." In the Richardson model we postulate some measure of "hostility-friendliness" (as Richardson himself points out, these models apply just as well to the process of falling in love as they do to the arms races). Then we suppose that the increase in the hostility of each party is a function, first, of some constant term which represents the underlying "grievance," and, second, of the absolute level of hostility of the other party. This gives us two simultaneous differential equations. These may have an equilibrium solution (a "balance of power"), or they may be indefinitely explosive up to some boundary at which the system breaks down in war, strike, or divorce—depending on the nature of the parameters. The less "sensitive" the parties—the less the hostility of one increases at each level of hostility of the other—the more likely is a balance-of-power solution to be found. The model can be extended easily to more complex cases involving, for instance, such variations as "submissiveness."

The Richardson process is a very general phenomenon, observable in international relations, in industrial relations, and in family relations. It may be almost unrelated to any "issue conflict," though the process takes account of this possibility through the constant term in its functions. The contribution of the theory of organization to these processes seems to be to point out the importance of the *perception* problem. It is not the "objective" hostility of the parties which is important, but the *perceived* hostility, that is, the hostility of each as perceived by the other. Consequently, again, the pattern of image formation takes a foremost place in the general theory of these processes. What are the cues, for instance, by which hostility is perceived, and how may these cues be misinterpreted? One may introduce, as an essential element in the process, the *predisposition* to perceive hostility. This is unquestionably related to internal hostility (self-hatred). The greater this predisposition, of course, the more likely are we to find unstable Richardson processes set off. The Freudian theory of displacement and aggression fits nicely into the general picture at this point. The self-hater is more likely to get into Richardson processes of mutually increasing hostility than the well-adjusted self-lover. The wisdom of the great commandment to "love our neighbor *as ourselves*" is amply justified by this impressive body of theory!

INTERNAL CONFLICT

The third type of conflict situation is that described by Kurt Lewin [2] and Neal Miller [3] and might be described as the "quandary." This is the situation in which the individual (or organization) is incapable of making a decision because it is pulled (or pushed) in two opposite directions at the same time! This is a strictly internal conflict; it does not involve two parties but the motivational forces operating on a single party. It falls into quite a different category, therefore, from either issue conflicts or Richardson processes. It is, nevertheless, relevant to the wider conflict, in that the internal conflicts may profoundly affect the conduct of external conflicts. Miller makes the extremely interesting suggestion that quandaries which result from opposing *pulls* or attractions are unstable; if the individual veers ever so slightly toward one side or the other, the side toward which he veers exerts a strong pull on him, and he soon goes over to it. Quandaries

which result from opposing pushes or repulsions are stable; as we veer to one side, the push becomes stronger and pushes us back into the quandary. Buridan's ass between two bales of hay is unstable. The slightest variation toward one bale reinforces its pull, and he goes toward it—returning then, as someone has observed, to eat the other! Buridan's ass, on the other hand, between two equally repellent skunks would be in a position of agonizing stability. As he moved toward either skunk, its repellent force would increase and would push him back towards the other.

Insofar as internal conflict of this kind produces disorganization and self-hatred, it has an important bearing on two-party conflict, as we have seen. The proposition may be ventured that those who are motivated mainly by hatred (fleeing away from what they do not like rather than toward what they like) are likely to get into quandaries and to be racked with stable internal conflicts destructive to their internal organization. Because of this, they are also likely to get involved in Richardson processes of mutually increasing hostility and are also likely to be unable to adjust their value structures (rendered rigid by their very disorganization) in the resolution of issue conflicts. Those who are motivated by "love," on the other hand, who move toward what they like rather than away from what they do not like, will be able to resolve quandaries easily, will be unlikely to get into processes of mutually increasing hostility, and can afford to have flexible value images which will help them in getting out of issue conflicts (liking what they get, instead of getting what they like).

Conflict resolution

I MAY offer one final word on conflict resolution. Perhaps the most important avenue of conflict resolution is simple *avoidance*. This is much neglected by the psychologists, though it is familiar enough to economists, and is indeed the basis for the economist's prejudice in favor of perfect competition. In a perfectly competitive market there is no conflict at all; if one arises, it is immediately avoided by switching to another buyer or another seller. It is only as markets become imperfect that conflict becomes important, as it becomes increasingly impossible to avoid particular relationships. The conflict between a professor and his dean is frequently resolved by a nice letter from another dean. In family life, divorce or separation represents conflict avoidance; here again the extreme (and inevitable) imperfection of the marriage market makes conflict in this area possibly more intense than in almost any other. In international relations, likewise, the impossibility of avoidance, especially in a world of few great powers, makes this particular solution inadmissible and forces the development of organizational solutions. Also in industrial relations, once labor is organized, avoidance becomes impossible; the individual worker can flee to another shop, but the union has to stay with the employer till death do them part.

If avoidance is impossible, the resolution of conflict depends on two factors: the reduction in the intensity of the conflict, on the one hand, and the development of overriding organizations which include both parties, on the other. The intensity of conflict can be reduced by a change in the value images of the parties toward "love" and away from "hate," by an expansion of the field into which organizations

are growing, by a diminution of their expansion pressure, and so on. Overriding organizations can develop either through sheer conquest, in which one party is eliminated (making a desert and calling it peace), or through the development of images in both parties in which there is acceptance of the role of a larger organization. Organization theory is important here in pointing out the limiting factors on the size of organization. These limiting factors may prevent the rise of uniting organizations unless the functions of these organizations are severely limited. It is clear, for instance, that world government would prevent "international" war; it is possible, however, that its very size would cause it to fall apart and render it impotent to prevent the re-formation of "non-conversing groups," with the consequent danger of civil war. It is perhaps the chief function of organization theory to warn us against simple or formal solutions and to point out the richness and complexity of conflict situations and their roots in the image-forming process.

Notes

1. These cases can be formalized into a mathematical measure of expansion conflict. Suppose we have n organizations, occupying a field of size X, apportioned among them in amounts x_1, $x_2, \ldots, x_n$. Suppose that each organization has a desired rate of growth (or decline), $r_1, r_2, \ldots, r_n$. Let R be the rate of growth of the whole field. Then expansion conflict potential may be measured by the expression $C = r_1 x_1 - RX$. If the aggregate desired rate of expansion is equal to the actual rate of growth of the whole field, expansion conflict potential will be zero.

If the aggregate desired expansion is greater than the actual growth of the field, there will be conflict: C will be positive. The greater the excess of the aggregate desired expansion over the growth of the field, the greater the potential for conflict. Negative values of C are not particularly significant and simply indicate no conflict. This is the situation where the expansion pressure of the organizations is so small that they reach their equilibrium sizes without even exhausting the available field.

References

1. Boulding, K. W. *The Image*. Ann Arbor: University of Michigan Press, 1956.

2. LEWIN, K. *Resolving Social Conflicts*. New York: Harper & Bros., 1948.

3. Miller, N. E. "Comments on Theoretical Models, Illustrated by the Development of a

Theory of Conflict Behavior," *Journal of Personality*, XXI (1956), 82–100.

4. Richardson, L. F. "Generalized Foreign Politics," *British Journal of Psychology, Monograph Supplements*, Vol. XXIII (1939).

5. Thompson, D. W. *On Growth and Form*. Cambridge: At the University Press, 1942.

Kenneth E. Boulding

Toward a pure theory of threat systems

THE WORLD OF THE ECONOMIST is organized fundamentally by exchange. This relationship, by which each of two parties gives up something to the other and receives something in return, is indeed a powerful social organizer. It is capable of organizing the division of labor and the allocation of resources, and it guides specialized production, as every elementary student of economics knows. In its general form it starts off as a conditional promise: "You do something nice to me and I will do something nice to you." If the other party to whom the communication is addressed accepts the invitation, the promises are fulfilled and the exchange is consummated. In this consummation we have a positive-sum game, provided that the exchange has been a free one in which both parties benefit, at least in their own opinion at the time. There may be later regrets which could turn the operation as it actually takes place into a negative-sum game, but the economist has generally assumed that these are small, and that such disappointments as may occur in exchange constitute a learning process by which everybody eventually learns to make wise choices among the opportunities which are open to him in the market. Exchange, furthermore, is the key relationship in what we might call unconscious or ecological economic development. It encourages the division of labor and this in turn encourages the increase in "skill and dexterity," and the growth, ultimately, of a specialized class of "philosophers," as Adam Smith called them, who practice research and development—all of which leads to increase in the "productive power of labor."

Exchange, however, is not the only system by means of which social organization is built up. Economists have always recognized that ex-change can develop a process of social organization and growth only if certain prerequisites are fulfilled in the way of institutions of property, law and order, and so on. The economist however, has tended to identify these other organizers as essentially static or given in nature and providing merely the preconditions or the framework within which exchange does the real work. Milton Friedman and the "Chicago School" (if there is one) represent the extreme of this point of view. This, however, would seem to be an unrealistic appraisal of the way in which the dynamics of most societies operate. Exchange is by no means the only human relationship which is capable of producing differentiation, division of labor, role structure, communication patterns, and all the other marks of organizational development. I distinguish at least two other types of human relationship which have the property of organizing social systems. The first of these is the threat, which is the main subject of this paper, the second may be called the integrative relationship, which involves a "meeting of minds" (that is, a convergence in the images and the utility functions of the parties toward each other). There is, of course, a negative of this relationship: the disintegrative relationship, in which the images move further apart. The integrative relationship is itself a complex of many different types of relationship, such as, for example, the teaching-learning relationship between the teacher and the student, the persuasive relationship between an orator and his audience or between an advertiser and his addressees, and a great variety of relationships, such as respect, affection, love, and so on, which lead toward similarity in value or utility functions over the domain of various states of the world in the

Reprinted from the *American Economic Review*, Vol. 53, No. 2, May 1963, pp. 424–434.

minds of the parties concerned. Economists pay very little attention to these integrative systems, and indeed have generally tended to assume, what in a dynamic sense is sheer nonsense, that utility functions are given—whereas, as Veblen pointed out, they are the product of human interaction. I would add that they are especially the product of the integrative relationships in society.

It must be emphasized that threat systems, exchange systems, and integrative systems are practically never found in a pure form. All actual social systems are likely to contain all three elements. Even under slavery, for instance, which has a high proportion of threat, there are elements of exchange and even of integration. At the other extreme, in the family, the monastery, or the utopian community, where the integrative system is dominant, there are also elements of exchange and threat. Even in the most loving family or community there is a point below which the terms of trade of an individual member cannot deteriorate without causing serious trouble, and the threat of expulsion always remains an ultimate sanction. Just as economics, however, has prospered by abstracting from the complexity of the social system as a whole a single relationship and element, that of exchange, and has built an elaborate theoretical and empirical structure on this foundation, which can then throw light on the more complex processes of the real world, so the phenomena of threat systems on the one side or integrative systems on the other can be abstracted out of the social complex and developed in a pure form. It is tempting, indeed, to try to assign the threat systems to the political scientist and integrative systems to the sociologist, as we assign exchange to the economist, though this division is too neat to correspond to the untidy facts of academic specialization.

Let us then look at the threat as an abstract human relationship, as an economist might look at exchange, and consider how this might be used as an organizer of society. Like exchange, threat in its simplest form is a relationship between two parties. Exchange, however, originates in a conditional promise to do something good if something good is done in return, whereas a threat originates in a promise to do something bad. The threat relationship begins when the threatener says to the threatened, "You do something nice to me or I will do something nasty to you." The exchange-like form of the threat can be seen in the threat of the holdup man, "Your money or your life," which looks like "Give me your money and I will give you your life." There is a real difference, however, between the commodity which is offered in exchange and the discommodity which is offered in the threat. "I will give you your life" means "I will not take away your life." In order for the threat to be perceived as a threat by the threatened, the threatener must be able to create a perception of credibility; that is of both capability and will of carrying out the threat if the threatened does not do what the threatener wants him to do. We may note that we have exactly the same problem of credibility in exchange, but it is less prominent because the information is usually more obvious. We visualize the exchanger as handing out the object which he offers to exchange. In financial exchanges, however, when what is offered is a promise to pay in the future, the problem of credibility becomes very real and takes much the same form that it does in threat systems.

The subsequent course of the system depends very much on the nature of the response to the initial threat. Four responses may be distinguished which may be labeled submission, defiance, counterthreat, and the integrative response

Submission is a not infrequent, though seldom popular, response to threat. When the holdup man threatens us we give him our wallet. When the parent says, "Don't steal the cookies or you'll be spanked," the child refrains from stealing the cookies. When the master says to the slave, "Work for me or I will kill you," the slave frequently obeys. When the state says, "Become a soldier or I will put you in prison," the young man allows himself to be conscripted. The threat-submission system is likely to be a conflict system; that is, it is likely to move the parties to a state in which the threatener is better off and the threatened is worse off than in the initial condition. The welfare situations can be illustrated in a field such as Figure 1, in which we plot A's welfare horizontally and B's welfare vertically. Suppose P_1 represents the welfare of both parties before the threat is made. The very act of making the threat is likely to change the positions of the parties in this field. They may, for instance, move to P_2, where both parties are worse off; the threat creates a state of anxiety in the minds of both parties. On the other hand it is possible that A, the threatener, may enjoy making threats, in which case the actual making of the threat might move the parties to P_2'. When submission takes place, we may move to a position like P_3, where A is better off and B is worse off. This is a typical conflict move. On the other hand, it is not impossible that B's submission to the threat may make him better off as well as A, though this is unlikely; that is, submission might move us from P_2 to a position such as P_3'. This is the situation where A is threatening to make B do something for B's own good which B would not be motivated to do in the absence of threat. The moral justification for threat frequently revolves around this hypothesis. We threaten to spank the child or to fail the student or to hang the murderer strictly for his own good, even if a little skepticism as to these protestations may not be out of order.

The threat-submission relationship has been illustrates how intertwined these two systems may be.

Threats can be perceived as legitimate only if they are also perceived as appropriate; the threatened punishment must fit the deterred crime. Even if what we are trying to accomplish is not perceived as preventing a crime by the threatened party, that is, even if the threat is not perceived as legitimate, its credibility still depends on its appropriateness. To say to a child, "If you steal the cookies I will kill you," is only credible, and only deters, if not taken literally. This is why "massive retaliation" is impotent against "salami-slicing," to slip once more into the repulsive jargon of strategic science.

The second possible response to threat is

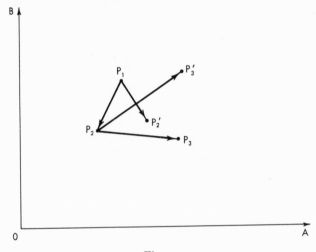

Figure 1

a powerful social organizer. It is, indeed, one of the major organizers of classical civilization insofar as this rests on slavery. It is also the foundation of a good deal of obedience to the law and of the authority of the state. As Baumol has pointed out in his *Welfare Economics and the Theory of the State*, we may quite rationally vote to threaten ourselves where there is something, like paying taxes, which everybody wants to do if everybody does it, but which nobody wants to do if other people do not. The possibility of nonconflictual threat-submission relationships, therefore, is not to be taken lightly. A key concept here is that of the legitimacy of threat. We submit to the traffic cop and the stoplight because we all recognize their legitimacy. The concept of legitimacy is perhaps more in the domain of integrative systems than of threat systems, but this only

defiance. This is somewhat analogous to the nonconsummation of exchange because of a refusal to trade. A says to B, "You give me X and I will give you Y"; B simply says, "No, it's not worth it to me," and the situation returns to the *status quo ante*. In threat systems the situation is more complicated because defiance puts a burden of response on the threatener and hence is in some sense a challenge to him. The threatener then has to decide whether or not to carry out the threat. If he does carry out the threat, this is likely to have a cost to him as well as to the threatened. We have here a very clear negative-sum game. If he does not carry out the threat his credibility is impaired; there is still a cost to him. Defiance therefore always imposes a cost on the threatener which is not found in the corresponding situation in exchange. The probability of this should presumably be taken into account by a rational threatener in deciding whether or not to make the initial threat.

The third alternative is the counterthreat; that is, "If you do something nasty to me, I will do something nasty to you." This is deterrence. This also imposes upon the original threatener a choice of whether or not to carry out the threat. If he is in fact deterred, his credibility is thereby apt to be weakened the next time he makes a threat; that is, there is a decline, as it were, in the capital value of his threat potentiality. If he carries out his original threat, there is likely to be a mutual exchange of "bads," or carried-out threats, which is very clearly a negative-sum game. This is perhaps the greatest difference between threat systems and exchange systems, for when exchange is consummated it is almost always positive-sum, whereas when threats are consummated they are usually negative-sum. This is why exchange systems have a much higher horizon of development than threat systems. This explains, I think, why in the long pull the free labor market, for instance, has always been able to outdo slavery, and why all classical civilizations have ultimately perished whereas the world of trade has grown slowly but persistently from its very origins.

Perhaps the most important single feature of systems of deterrence is their long-run instability. The whole history of threat systems is summed up succinctly in two verses from St. Luke (11:21–22): "When a strong man armed keepeth his palace, his goods are in peace; but when a stronger than he shall come upon him and overcome him, he taketh from him all his armor wherein he trusted and divideth his spoils." It is indeed a source of the basic long-run instability of all threat systems that the unilateral threat system, or the threat-submission system, which may be fairly successful for a time, almost inevitably degenerates into the bilateral threat system, or deterrence. Deterrence is successful as long as it deters, but deterrence itself seems to be unstable. The reason for this, I suspect, is that the credibility of threats depreciates with time if threats are not carried out. Hence threats occasionally need to be carried out in order to re-establish the credibility. Another reason is that threat capability declines if threats are not occasionally carried out, particularly where this capability is enshrined in complex social organizations and in apparatus such as armed forces.

For both these reasons, a state of stable deterrence is rarely stable for long. Eventually either the capability or the credibility, or both, of one of the parties will depreciate to the point where the other party will make new demands. At this point deterrence breaks down and the system slips either into submission or into defiance. Submission is particularly hard if the parties have lived under stable deterrence for a while, so the outcome of a new demand is likely to be defiance. This, then, forces on the imposer of the new demand the choice between carrying out the threat or acceptance of the defiance, which would further destroy his credibility. He is likely, therefore, to carry out the threat, which will lead to the carrying out of the counterthreat, which will result in a negative-sum game known as war. In this, it is true, one party may emerge relatively better off than the other, and indeed if the loser is very much worse off the victor may even be absolutely better off. In this case we may pass again to a unilateral threat system. This is the "successful" period of the new civilization, and this again leads to counterthreats and ultimate downfall. Thus the rise and fall of civilizations seems to be implicit in the very nature of the threat system itself—as, indeed, a pure exchange system is also likely to experience ultimate cycles of boom and collapse. It may be that, ultimately, only integrative systems can provide stability, and I am not sure even of that.

This brings us to the fourth possible response to threat, which is the integrative response. This is harder to analyze and to describe. It may take a great many different forms because of the very richness of the integrative system itself. The integrative response is that which establishes community between the threatener and the threatened and produces common values and a common interest. The integrative response may be mixed with any one of the first three responses. Submission, for instance, may be made in such a way that the threatener is eventually absorbed into a larger culture and the threat system disappears. The experience of the Negro in the United States may be such a case. By accepting and illuminating the ostensible value system of his conquerors, the Negro both made and produced an integrative response which eventually made slavery impossible. In the Gandhian experience in India we have an example of defiance mixed with an integrative response; this is the essence of nonviolent resistance. The threatened party, by defying the threatener and by accepting the consequences without bitterness or complaint, eventually undermines the morale of the threatener and the threat system disintegrates. Examples of counterthreat used as an integrative response seem to be rarer, for whereas both submission and defiance, in a sense, unite the threatener and the threatened in some sort of a social system in which integrative factors may operate, the counterthreat divides the threatener from the threatened, breaks any bond which might develop between them, and hence is apt to be disintegrative rather than integrative. This perhaps is another reason for the fundamental instability of deterrence, and its ultimate certainty of failure. It is still not inconceivable, however, that a carefully controlled counterthreat might be combined with an integrative response. We may have seen something like this happen in the industrial relationship, where the threat to fire on the part of the employer may produce either the counterthreat to quit or the more organized counterthreat of the strike. In this case, however, the very nature of the relationship and the fact that if there is to be an industrial organization at all the parties have to live together, opens up the possibility of integrative solutions to counterthreat systems. Where, for instance, the threat or even the actuality of the counterthreat is used to obtain union recognition and a contract, we see counterthreat being used as a device to establish an essentially integrative system of industrial jurisprudence. Parallel to this in international systems might be a counterthreat system used to achieve a disarmament organization of a world government.

Like exchange systems, threat systems have a geographical structure which is imposed on them by the fact that threats, like commodities, have a cost of transport. Because of this there are many striking parallels as I have pointed out in *Conflict and Defense* (Harper and Row, New York, 1962), between the competition of states by means of threats and the competition of firms by means of exchange. Thus the theory of duopoly is very much like that of a bipolar system in international relations. Each of the competing organizations has a certain "home strength" as represented by the threat capacity in the case of the nation or the cost of production at the mill in the case of the firm. As it goes away from home it has to incur a cost of transport, so that the further from home the organization operates the smaller the threat that it can bring to bear or the higher the price it must charge. In each case this represents an application of the general principle of "the further the weaker." Between two states as between two firms there is likely to be a boundary of equal strength, with each organization dominating the area between itself and the boundary. Such a situation can easily lead to an arms race or a price war, as each organization tries to push the boundary of equal strength further from its home base, either by increasing its armaments or by cutting its mill price. This is pretty clearly a negative-sum game, from which the parties can usually only be rescued by an integrative system of some kind, for instance a merger in the case of the firms, or in less extreme forms a gentlemen's agreement, and in the case of states a federation or a "security community."

These considerations lead to an interesting theory of viability which I have also expounded in some detail in *Conflict and Defense*. An organization may be said to have unconditional viability if no other organization has the capability of destroying it; that is, an organization is unconditionally viable if it is dominant over all other organizations at its home base. A system of unconditional viability is only possible if each organization is stronger than any other or any reasonable combination of others. This paradoxical result is attainable if the organizations are far enough apart and if their strength, that is, their threat capability, diminishes rapidly enough for each one as he goes away from home, that is, if there is what I call a high loss-of-strength gradient. A system of stable unconditional viability is threatened either by an increase in the number of organizations in a given field or by diminution of the loss-of-strength gradient. The less the loss-of-strength gradient, the fewer organizations can coexist in unconditional viability.

I have argued that the peculiar crisis of national defense today is a result of the loss of unconditional viability even by the largest nations in the light of nuclear threat. If we are to exist at all, it must be on conditions of conditional viability, in which each organization can destroy the other but refrains from doing so. This is not an altogether unfamiliar system—indeed, in interpersonal relations we have had to live with it. In the age of the sword, unconditional viability for the individual was at least not inconceivable, even though one had to be a pretty good swordsman to achieve it. The crossbow and, following that, firearms, ruined this system and in our personal relations we now live in a world in which we are literally all at each other's mercy. One would think that, in these circumstances, mercy would be taken seriously and studied, but this is the last thing that anyone seems to want to do. In international relations, especially, we are still living under the illusion of unconditional viability, and we may have a very rude awakening.

Concepts of liquidity and inflation which have been developed in economics have also some applicability to threat systems. The concept of generalized military capability is closely related to the economic concept of liquidity. A liquid asset is something with which anything can be bought; a military capability is something with which anything can be destroyed. It is, as it were, money for the doing of harm. Another reason for the instability of threat systems, incidentally, is that harm can be done much faster than good (I am indebted to T. C. Schelling for this observation). One might add, however, as a corollary that the ultimate victory of exchange and integrative systems over threat systems is assured by the fact that more good can be done than harm. The doing of harm has a limit of total destruction; that is, of zero good. The doing of good has no definite upper limit. The liquidity or the lack of specificity of a military capability is another factor which is likely to lead to the instability of the threat system. The military capability of A is a generalized threat directed, say, at B, C, D, and E. Each of these parties, however, perceives the threat as if it were directed wholly at him. The perception of the threat, therefore, on the part of the threatened is four times the amount of the threat on the part of the threatener at a maximum. It is not surprising that under these systems threat systems produce armament races which almost inevitably lead to the carrying out of the threat.

When threat systems become embodied in military organizations, we have problems arising which are strikingly parallel to those which develop for economics when production and exchange get to be concentrated in firms. The military organization, which I have elsewhere called the "milorg," is the equivalent in the threat system of the firm in the exchange system. It possesses many of the qualities and characteristics of the firm. It has a hierarchical organization, it is organized by a budget, it has flows of expenditures most of which are laid out in the purchase of inputs, and it has a flow of receipts. The major difference between the milorg and the firm arises from the source of the receipts: in the case of the firm, receipts are derived from the sale of a product on the market; in the case of the milorg, the receipts are derived from a government budget and ultimately from taxation or from the creation of money. The milorg, that is to say, does not produce a clearly defined product in the way that a firm does; its receipts have more the character of transfer payments than of returns from sales; that is, exchange. In this respect it is more like a philanthropy than it is like a firm. If we ask what it produces, we would have to answer in terms of a generalized threat; that is, a capability of doing harm to unspecified persons or things.

We may go further, indeed, and distinguish a number of different "commodities" which the milorg produces. One in the currently fashionable terminology is the "counterforce." This is the diminution of a potential enemy's capacity to harm the home organization. This might take the form of a defensive work such as a wall, a buffer state, a Maginot Line, or anything which would sharply increase the potential opponent's loss-of-strength gradient as he moved toward the defended center. It might also take the form of an ability to destroy the opponent's milorg or those aspects of it which have capability of destroying the home organization. Another product of the milorg might be, again in the fashionable terminology, "countervalue." This is the ability to threaten, not the threat-makers of the opponent, but the things which he values—his cities, people, social organizations, and so on. Countervalue weapons and organization are generally associated with deterrents, that is, with counter-threats, but they may also be used unilaterally to threaten the opponent into doing something which the threatener wants. The great difficulty of operating a threat system is that all these different threat-commodities are very hard to distinguish in practice, and hence an action which is intended to be one kind of threat may be interpreted at the other end as a totally different kind. Insofar as threats are used as instruments of persuasion to change people's opinions or behavior, they tend to suffer from a defect of all persuasion systems; that what is persuasive to the persuader is not always persuasive to the persuadee. The threatener or the persuader has an image of the order which is derived largely from his own experience, and hence is likely to be false in many important regards. Our threats, like our persuasions, tend to be directed at some imaginary person whom we have made in our own image, not at the real person at whom the activity is directed.

The analogue of inflation in threat systems is found in the arms race, in which both parties continually increase the amount of economic resources which they are putting into organized threats (milorgs) without changing their relative power position. Today, indeed, we may be approaching a hyperinflation of the threat system under the impact of military research and development, which effectively destroys any validity which the system once may have had. We can then look at arms control as an attempt at stabilizing the "price level" after a hyperinflation.

The subject could be pursued much further, and there seems to me to be no reason why a science of threat systems should not be developed at least as elaborately as economics builds from exchange. This science, perhaps, still has to find its Adam Smith, but one feels that so much development has gone on in it in recent years that its "Wealth of Nations" must be just around the corner. The need for this science, furthermore, is very urgent. Because of the development of the nuclear weapon and the consequent disappearance of unconditional viability, the whole threat system, that is, the system of national defense, is suffering a grave crisis—indeed, I would argue, a breakdown. The control of the threat system, therefore, is a matter of the topmost priority for the human race. Unless we do this we may not have a chance to develop any other systems. In order to control a threat system, however, we must understand it. It is one of the most astonishing features of human society that governments are willing to invest so much money in threat systems with only crude folk knowledge as to how these systems actually work, and without being at all interested, apparently, in finding out more about them. This is perhaps because the threat system is an important element in the integrative system of most societies. Nations are built on the solid foundations of violence and cruelty, threats and counterthreats Our national heroes are soldiers and our national mythology is a mythology of successful threat. A threat to the threat system, therefore, is seen as a threat to the integrity of the society itself. We love making threats and it satisfies our masculine demand for "strength" to make them, and hence a threat to the threat system is seen as a threat to that which we love. To make a science of threats, however, is to threaten the threat system itself, for a system so inefficient in producing welfare as the threat system is can only survive as long as it is supported on folk ignorance. It is little wonder, therefore, that the science of threat systems has been so slow to develop.

My thesis may perhaps be summarized in the following lines of verse:

> Four things that give mankind a shove
> Are threats, exchange, persuasion, love;
> But taken in the wrong proportions
> These give us cultural abortions.
> For threats bring manifold abuses
> In games where everybody loses;
> Exchange enriches every nation
> But leads to dangerous alienation;
> Persuaders organize their brothers
> But fool themselves as well as others;
> And love, with longer pull than hate,
> Is slow indeed to propagate.

*Robert C. North, Howard E. Koch, Jr.,
and Dina A. Zinnes*

The integrative functions of conflict[1]

HUMAN GROUPS AND ASSOCIATIONS of all
sorts—from the family, clique, clan, and
tribe to the largest religious organizations and
states—are often in conflict ([19], p. 289; 28, p.
56). The assumption is not uncommon, indeed,
that "peace within and conflict without" are
essential characteristics of group life. Closer
examination suggests, however, that conflicts
exist within the various groups themselves—
within even the most cohesive and durable—
and contribute substantially to their perpetuation ([10], pp. 123, 141; [41], p. 238; [48], pp.
1016–17; [17], p. 1).

In considering both intergroup conflict and
that occurring internally between component
parts of a single group, two kinds of effects
may be distinguished. On the one hand, conflict
may result in the destruction or disruption of
all or certain of the bonds of unity which may
previously have existed between the disputants.
On the other hand, conflict may strengthen
pre-existing ties or contribute to the establishment of unifying bonds where none before
existed. It is with the latter that we are concerned in the present paper: given the existence
of a conflict, under what conditions, if any, will
that conflict produce a stronger bond between
parties than that which existed theretofore? In
short, what are the integrative functions of
conflict?

In developing many of the ideas presented
in the following pages, it became clear to us that
scholars in a wide variety of fields at one time
or another, in one context or another, have given
thought to the possibility of the integrative
functions of conflict. To illustrate the convergence of ideas, we have added somewhat extensive
footnotes referring to sources in a wide variety
of fields.

Unit of concern

FOR the purposes of this study the unit of concern is the group. More specifically, we are
interested in the integrative function of conflicts
within and between particular groups, namely,
those which may be designated *organizations*.
Elsewhere in the paper we shall consider the
characteristics of organizations in some detail.
At this stage it will suffice simply to define an
organization, using Barnard's definition of a
formal organization, as a "system of consciously
coordinated activities or forces of two or more
persons"[2] (3, pp. 73, 78–79; 41, p. 238). In
slightly different terms, an organization consists of people who share at least one common
purpose and who are able mutually to communicate and thus to coordinate their activities.

The concept of conflict

BEFORE proceeding further, it will be necessary
to digress briefly to present several concepts
which are essential to the discussion. Because
these concepts were described in an earlier
issue of *Conflict Resolution* (23), only those
of particular relevance to an understanding of
the present paper will be summarized here.

In our terms, a *policy condition*—denoted
for convenience as c_i—is defined as an organizational purpose or goal with a time specification. In 1775, for example, the thirteen colonies
maintained the policy condition *no taxation
without representation*. The policy conditions
of an organization emerge from its decisions and
thus reflect its communication structure, that is,
its network of authority relationships or the
pattern of who communicates with whom. A
communication, in this sense, is a directive

Reprinted from *The Journal of Conflict Resolution*, Vol. 4, 1960, pp. 355–374.

which, if accepted, will influence the behavior of the recipient.

It should be noted that we further define policy conditions as being *conscious* or *unconscious*. In the latter case, according to our definition, there is no explicit declaration of the policy condition—though it can be inferred from the behavior of the organization.

Since goals (or aims) and methods (or means) are always relative to the context, it follows that any given policy condition can be either a goal or a method (or both). At any given moment an organization will entertain policy conditions with different time specifications. Such policy conditions can be classified into sets, ordered sequentially, wherein the attainment of any given policy condition in the set requires the acquisition of all those preceding it in time.

By definition, it can be said that two or more policy conditions are incompatible if they cannot obtain simultaneously. A *conflict* develops whenever policy conditions are incompatible.[3]

All policy conditions which are mutually incompatible at a given time (regardless of whether they issue from the same organization, different organizations, or a combination of both) are said to constitute a "problem" or a *conflict situation*. For convenience, a policy condition can be related to its appropriate problem area by the addition of an appropriate superscript, e.g. c_i^j. Thus, whereas the subscript serves as a label for a particular policy condition, the superscript indicates the particular dispute. In 1775, for example, the problem of taxation was a central c^j, with Great Britain holding the policy condition c_1^1—*taxation without representation*—and the colonies collaborating behind the position c_2^1—*no taxation without representation*. The quartering of troops was another problem, c_1^2, with Great Britain insisting on c_2^2 and the colonies on c_2. Hence in these terms, a conflict situation refers to all the c_i's for a particular "j".

From our definition of a conflict it follows that in any conflict situation there will be a minimum of two *parties*. In effect, a party to a conflict—that is, the participating organization or organizations upholding "one side" of a dispute—can be defined as a c_i. Clearly, then, a c_i, or party, may consist of one or more *participants*.

It is important to distinguish two types of conflict, *latent* and *overt*. In a latent conflict, no party is attempting—by any decision or overt act—to achieve its c_i. By contrast, overt conflicts are those in which one or more parties do attempt to effect some change in the situation.

A participant in any overt conflict, in our terms, can choose among four types of action: a non-violent bid, which we will designate by (m_1^j); a non-violent commission (m_2^j); a violent bid (m_3^j); or a commission of violence (m_4^j). As in the case of the c_i^j's, the "j" denotes the specific conflict in which the "m" is being used. We shall designate a general means by (m_k^j), where k goes from 1 to 4, i.e., can come from one of the four categories. This last does not represent any kind of rank order implying the more or less desirable alternative; they could be listed in any order. We differentiate, of course, between (m_k^j) and $(m_k^j)t$. An (m_k^j) simply specifies an action, while an $(m_k^j)t$ suggests that procedures from a given category of means have been designated for the resolution of issues relating to a "j" problem over time.

We define an (m_1^j) non-violent bid as an offer, proposal, or threat without implication of casualty taking. Such a bid is normally conditional in its connotation. In the sphere of international relations the means category (m_1^j) normally includes the exchange of messages and negotiations which do not imply the taking of casualties.

An (m_2^j) commission of non-violence is an act, performance, or transaction without implication or consequence of casualty-taking. Clearly, an (m_2^j) type of settlement can be used to resolve both non-violent and violent conflicts. The parties to a conflict, indeed, can decide upon (m_2^j) actions to take the place of violence; or they can establish $(m_2^j)t$ agreements to regulate and confine a violent conflict,[4] or, having fought a war, they can use an (m_2^j) settlement to formulate the new relationship. Among states the (m_2^j) category of conflict resolution includes negotiation, good offices, arbitration, conciliation, adjudication, and other recognized procedures. The addition of a time specification, $(m_2^j)t$, suggests that non-violent procedures have been agreed upon for the solution of further conflicts related to a given problem. The qualified category $(m_2^j)t$ thus embraces treaties and other international agreements and integrative instruments which depend on mutual free consent for their force.

The means category (m_3^j) bid of violence embraces all more or less conditional communications of intent—including promises and threats, whether explicit or implicit, genuine or feigned, oral, written, or symbolic—which rely upon inference of casualty-taking for their force. In this sense a sudden mobilization may be as effective a threat as a written ultimatum. An $(m_3^j)t$ relationship is again a procedure for setting issues pertaining to a given problem— but by the exercise of threats of force by one of the parties rather than by mutual voluntary agreement.

An (m_4^j) commission of violence is an act which results in one or more casualties. The qualified category $(m_4^j)t$ would emerge from a formal declaration of war, i.e., the statement by a government of its intentions to commit continuous violence in order to resolve its particular "*j*" conflict with the other party.

It should be clear that any "*m*" (means) can be viewed—in a somewhat different perspective—as a goal or policy condition. Thus a battleship is a goal for its builder and a means for its captain; the Marshall Plan, an end from one perspective and a means from another. It is always possible, then, to convert an "*m*" into a "*c*", or a "*c*" into an "*m*."

The concept of integration

THE term *integration* can be used in at least six distinctly different ways, and the concept, in consequence, tends to have remained somewhat ambiguous. Thus integration can be considered in terms of the following:

1. *Probability of violence given a conflict situation.* As used in this sense by the Deutsch study, integration can be defined as the probability that conflicts will be resolved without the use of violence. For these purposes violence is said to occur when one party produces a casualty—that is, the loss of one human being by any one of a variety of means —in another party. Thus, as the probability increases that any conflict will be resolved without the use of violence, the amount of integration between the parties increases.

2. *The frequency of conflicts between any given number of organizations.* In this definition integration is a function of the *number* of conflicts that arise between the organizations during a given span of time. Thus, as the frequency of conflicts between two organizations decreases, the extent of integration between them is said to increase. Again, integration is viewed as a continuum.

3. *Agreement on policy conditions.* Integration between *n* organizations (where $n \geqq 2$) is here a function of the number (and probably also the significance) of the compatible policy conditions. Considering two organizations, one would measure their degree of integration in terms of some average of their compatible policy conditions to their total policy conditions. Thus organization A may have a total of ten c_i's and organization B a total of fourteen, and the compatible c_i's (between A and B) may be six. To measure the integration between the two, we would take some average of $6/10$ and $6/14$. Integration, of course, is again a continuum.

4. *The degree of interdependency between n given organizations.* In this instance the integration of *n* organizations increases to the extent that their policy conditions are interrelated. Thus one organization, to achieve a particular policy condition, may depend upon the attainment by another organization of one of its policy conditions. The attainment of the United States policy condition of "containment of Russia," for example, has required a South Korean policy condition of independence from the North Korean regime.

5. *Interlocking communication systems or structure.* This definition has two implications. First, the integration between *n* organizations is a function of the number and/or significance of the communications exchanged. In the second instance, *n* organizations become more integrated as the communication structure or authority pattern tends to cross (or disregard) organization boundaries. Thus the thirteen American colonies became progressively more integrated as, first, the Articles of Confederation and, later, the Constitution established a federal authority and communication structure cutting across the old, relatively exclusive boundaries.

6. *The overlapping of membership.* Here the integration between *n* organizations increases as the overlapping of membership increases. There will be complete integration, of course, when the membership completely overlaps. This circumstance may occur in either one of two ways. In one case, an organization may contain the one beneath it. Thus the integration of the fifty states is complete within the federal structure of the United States. In the other case, all organizations may have the same membership.

Further along we shall refer to these various aspects of integration in connection with the functioning of organizations, their degrees of complexity, and their durabiliyt.

The integrative effect of conflict

THE remainder of this discussion will be concerned with three aspects of the integrative function of conflict.

In the present section we shall consider how

the bonds between two parties are affected by the conflict and its resolution—whether these bonds are strengthened or weakened, for example, and whether the duration of the relationship between the parties is likely to be relatively long or short. In the two succeeding sections we will consider, first, the circumstances under which the parties to a conflict, in the course of the resolution process, become participants in a wholly new organization—such as the public international unions—designed to regulate the problems at issue; and, second, the ways in which the resolution of a conflict can be negotiated or "engineered" to achieve what we designate as an (m_k) relationship.

A. THE INTEGRATIVE EFFECT OF CONFLICT ON TIES BETWEEN PARTIES

Some measure of integration exists in any overt conflict situation by virtue of the very fact that an overt conflict implies some contact between the parties.[5] It would be difficult, indeed, to isolate any phase of an overt conflict which does not imply interaction, communication, and, hence, the establishment and maintenance of a substantial body of ties between the conflicting parties.[6]

It should be clear from preceding pages that the resolution of a conflict between two parties may be achieved through an (m_1^j), (m_2^j), (m_3^j), or (m_4^j) procedure or through a combination thereof. The question now arises how and to what degree the extent of integration between the parties—or the durability of the relationship between them—is affected by the category of action chosen.

Our focus is upon those (m_k^j) relationships which have resulted in rules or procedures or institutions for regulating or containing or controlling conflicts in a particular issue or group of issues.[7] In these terms $(m_2^j)t$ relationships—non-violent relationships entered into by the mutual free consent of the parties—give rise to custom,[8] law,[9] and institution at every level of organization—family,[10] clan and tribe, churches, and nation-states.

It must be kept in mind, however, that throughout the course of history many organizations—and much custom and law—have had their genesis in $(m_3^j)t$ relationships which have been imposed by one party at the expense of another and which depend upon force or the threat of force for their effectiveness.

Both $(m_2^j)t$ and $(m_3^j)t$ relationships, then, may serve as mechanisms for integrating groups of a given magnitude into larger organizational units. Here, of course, we must carefully distinguish once more between (1) conflict and the resolution of conflict inside a given part to an $(m_2^j)t$ relationship; (2) conflict and the resolution of conflict between the parties to an $(m_2^j)t$ relationship; and (3) conflict and the resolution of conflict between a given $(m_2^j)t$ relationship, as an entity in itself, and other like entities. If NATO were designated as an $(m_2^j)t$ relationship, for example, we would distinguish conflicts internal to a member state, such as the United States, from conflicts among the states participating in the $(m_2^j)t$ relationship and also from conflicts between NATO and the Communist bloc.[11]

We postulate that durability of a given $(m_k^j)t$ relationship will be the function of two main variables; the relative "p" capability of each party, that is, his power or relative capacity for inflicting his will; and the amount of "d" dissatisfaction evoked by the relationship among the respective parties. For the time being, at least, we shall measure a party's dissatisfaction in terms of the "price" he is willing to pay to change his circumstances, that is, to achieve his policy conditions. When a party is faced by two more or less equally unsatisfactory—or two more or less equally satisfactory—alternatives, the relative "v" importance will also come into play as a variable.

The durability of a given $(m_k^j)t$ relationship will depend also upon the precedents, that is, upon whether or not previous agreements have worked to the satisfaction of the parties and have been generally long lasting.

It should be evident that an $(m_k^j)t$ arrangement between parties can be reached in a number of ways. The two parties may enter into an agreement of their own respective free wills; or one may dominate or conquer the other and then impose a settlement; or the parties may, through the pressure of some overriding circumstance, enter into an uneasy compromise; or one or both parties may deceptively conclude an agreement with the intent of using it for concealed ends. Against this background it is possible, by arranging the capability, importance, and dissatisfaction variables of the parties in different combinations, to suggest a number of durability and also behavior hypotheses. Illustrative of these possibilities are the following:

	A		B
p	high	p	high
v	high	v	high
d	high	d	high

Under this set of circumstances it seems probable that the durability of the agreement will tend to be long, but the effectiveness will tend to be low. Here the significant question appears to be this: at what point will the high dissatisfactions of A and B bring the $(m_k^j)t$ to an end? Will it be, perhaps, at the point where one party—correctly or incorrectly—perceives its capabilities to have risen somewhat higher than the capabilities of the other party?

A		B	
p	high	p	low
v	high	v	high
d	low	d	high

In this pattern one might anticipate high durability and—in view of B's low capability —a considerable measure of effectiveness. A, in short, will be in a position to dominate B and enforce B's adherence to the agreement. Over time, B's stored dissatisfaction may amount to a growing frustration. If, then, B's capability should begin to rise for any reason, there is a strong possibility of his striking against A even before $B_p \geqq A_p$.

If we assume, on the other hand, that B's capability will remain low and that his dissatisfaction will diminish with time, it seems reasonable to predict his gradual acceptance— as custom or law—of the once irritating settlement. This, indeed, is how time functions on the side of the invader by gradually resolving a whole range of conflicts separating him from the vanquished.

B. THE EMERGENCE OF NEW ORGANIZATIONS

At first glance it would seem that the emergence of an organization might be detected in terms of the number of j problems which the parties have resolved through $(m_2^j)t$ agreements. Under this condition the emergence of an organization beween or among parties could be specified by measuring the number of resolved j's—an organization being defined at a certain level of resolved j's, say, for example, six.

$$\left. \begin{array}{l} n \quad j\text{'s} \\ \uparrow \\ 7 \quad j\text{'s} \end{array} \right\} \text{an organization}$$

$$\begin{array}{l} 6 \quad j\text{'s} \\ 5 \quad j\text{'s} \\ 4 \quad j\text{'s} \\ 3 \quad j\text{'s} \\ 2 \quad j\text{'s} \\ 1 \quad j\text{'s} \end{array}$$

Thus it could then be concluded that parties A and B had achieved a greater degree of integration—on the basis of their $(m_2^1)t$, $(m_2^2)t$, $(m_2^3)t$, $(m_2^4)t$, $(m_2^5)t$, and $(m_2^6)t$ agreements —than parties C and D and had thereby achieved, indeed, the stature of an organization.

Further reflection suggests, however, that the number of j's is not by itself a sufficient criterion of organization. Most major powers maintain a large number of treaty relationships —even with intensely antagonistic states— without achieving any significant integration with any of them. On the other hand, highly integrated federal structures, such as the United States under the Constitution, specifically delegate the resolution of all but a relatively small number of j's to the various component parts.

It should be possible, of course, to calculate the degree of integration between or among the interacting parties in terms of the six criteria already put forward in this paper: (1) probability of violence between the parties; (2) the frequency of conflict between them; (3) agreement on policy conditions c_i; (4) the extent of interdependency of c_i's among the given organizations; (5) the extent of interlocking of communication systems or structures; and (6) the overlapping of membership. Yet measurement against these scales alone fails to provide us with a clear indication of the point where interacting parties move beyond cooperative relations as independent units and begin to merge as a single federation or other organization of a new order. Before trying to describe this point of change, we will find it helpful to consider certain definitions of organization.

According to Chester Barnard ([3], p. 83), an organization comes into being when (1) there are persons able to communicate with each other (2) who are willing to contribute action (3) to accomplish a common purpose.[12] And from a somewhat different viewpoint Kenneth Boulding ([9], p. 57) has referred to the organization as "a structure of roles tied together by lines of communication."[13]

The willingness of any participant to contribute action will depend upon the satisfaction which such participant perceives accruing from the association. According to Barnard:

If each man gets back only what he puts in, there is no incentive, that is, no net satisfaction for him in cooperation. What he gets back must give him advantage in terms of satisfaction; which almost always means return in a different form from that which he contributes. If he puts forth effort, he requires a changed condition for himself, just as he would if he put forth effort individually rather than cooperatively. Efficiency, for the individual, is satisfactory exchange ([3], p. 58.)

If incentive is insufficient to satisfy a critical number of participants, the association must find means of persuasion or perish.

Beyond this, there is also a tendency on the part of human beings to "internalize" the associations which provide them with satisfactions. At the deeper levels of such acceptance the conscience of the individual virtually speaks for the family or the church or the nation, and an attack on any of the "internalized" groups is perceived by the member as an attack upon himself.[14]

In view of these considerations, then, it seems feasible to measure any given $(m_k^j)t$ relationship along a spectrum in terms of (1) the number of roles that serve it; (2) the pattern and extent of the communications network; (3) the importance to the participants of both the relationship and the purposes; (4) the satisfactions derived from it; and (5) the degree to which the relationship, its purposes, and its other aspects have been "internalized" by the participants.

Since states, as large organizations, contain a vast variety of smaller organizations and suborganizations within their jurisdiction, a large number of conflicts in individual attachments and loyalties is inevitable—as is the appearance of incompatibilities among the various component groups. Thus, as Chester Barnard writes:

Complex organization involves competition for the contribution of individuals, and makes conflicts of loyalties unavoidable. This competition is not merely between subordinate organizations of the same rank—for example, for employees by several corporations—but also between superior and subordinate organizations. Thus the state and a subordinate corporation both compete for the support of the same individual; and similarly the corporation competes with its own department for the loyalty of the men assigned to it, of loyalties to itself directly and indirectly through its department ([3], p. 100).

As we have already suggested, an analysis of conflict and the resolution of conflict among the domestic suborganizations of a state will reveal some general propositions about conflict and the resolution of conflict between that state and other states with which it is associated. Conversely, too, we may expect a state's transactions with other states to have some effect upon its domestic subgroups—as well as upon the component groups of the other transactor states.

Pluralistic societies, for example, allow and often encourage loyalty to a large variety of institutions—the Crown or the Constitution, a church, one of two or perhaps several political parties, the family, and many other associations—and depend upon checks and balances among them for cohesion and stability. In the words of T. S. Eliot:

A people should be neither too united nor too divided, if its culture is to flourish. Excess of unity may be due to barbarism and may lead to tyranny; excess of division may be due to decadence and may also lead into tyranny: either excess will prevent further development in culture ([14], p. 50).

A country within which the divisions have cut too deep, according to Eliot, is a danger to itself, while "a country which is too well united—whether by nature or by device, by honest purpose or by fraud and oppression—is a menace to others" ([14], p. 60). On the basis of his studies among African tribes Max Gluckman has commented similarly:

The conflicts between the loyalties held by a man thus, in a wider range of relations, establish order and lead to a recognition and acceptance of obligations within law. A man's several loyalties strike at the strength of his loyalty to any one group or set of relations, which is thus divided. Hence the whole system depends for its cohesion on the existence of conflict in smaller sub-systems ([17], pp. 19–20).

One would expect that, when the various associative factors in an organization coincide, they tend to reinforce each other.[15] The use of "cross-loyalties" to weld together the parts of a confederacy is a common phenomenon. Thus:

When the exchange of goods or services, religion and nationality is coterminous, that is, is restricted to one isolated and autonomous group, the bonds within the group and the hostilities toward those outside are likely to be relatively absolute. But when positive elements overlap the boundaries of several groups, hostilities tend to be limited ([19], p. 303).

In somewhat different terms, however, multiple group affiliations within a larger body—by encouraging a proliferation of loyalties and consequent conflicts which criss-cross the society—prevent deep cleavages along a single fracture line and in this way contribute also to a general cohesion.[16] Pluralistic societies, taking advantage of this tendency, foster a multiplicity of institutions to which individual loyalties can be attached. The consequent conflicts, widely dispersed, are resolved largely by compromises, adjustments, adjudications, and accommodations among the various competing parts.

More specifically, the conflicts of a pluralistic order tend to be communicated freely and openly whenever the over-all system is unquestioned by the members—and wherever the symbol of leadership survives undamaged irrespective of the conduct of the incumbent. This, of course, is the crucial value of the Crown of Great Britain and the Constitution in the United States. "In such a system," Max Gluckman writes, "the licensed statement of conflict can bless the social order" ([17], p. 134).

Modern pluralistic states tend to divide their central authority between a part that is fixed and one that is removable. The fixed portion (throne, constitution, or other symbol) holds the loyalty, respect, and affection of the people, whereas their inevitable hostilities and discontent can be directed against the removable parts (president, prime minister, cabinet, parliament, congress, interchangeable parties, and so forth). In this way "rebellion" is licensed and waged more or less peacefully through elections, the rise and fall of cabinets, and the alternation of political parties and leaders ([40], pp. 196–97).

Monolithic societies, by contrast, find themselves unable to tolerate such free competition of loyalty and association. An attack upon the leadership in such orders is tantamount to an attack upon the whole system. In the long run, therefore, they either develop their own ways for controlling internal conflict—thus preserving the over-all $(m_k^j)t$ relationship—or they undergo revolution or disintegration. Characteristically, successful states of this sort institutionalize the "internal enemy" and the "external enemy"—usually conceived as being in close league with each other—and seek to project popular hostilities upon these scapegoats.[17]

In reality we would not expect to find any given state fitting either the pluralistic or the monolithic model.[18] Rather, we assume that states—tending toward one or the other model —move back and forth along the pluralistic-monolithic continuum depending on a variety of circumstances. Certainly in time of war we would expect a generally pluralistic state to become increasingly monolithic.

Similarly, we do not maintain at this point that a monolithic state is either more or less aggressive than a pluralistic one. Only on the basis of a careful examination of empirical evidence would such a conclusion be valid. We do postulate, however, that the institutionalizing of the outside enemy and the inside enemies[19]—whether found in a generally pluralistic or a generally monolithic state—are of great importance to both the conflict and the integrative processes.

We would expect, for example, that any conflict arising from incompatible policy conditions between states would be aggravated if either or both were traditionally inclined to identify the other as a major outside enemy. So, too, we would expect the identification of any large number of "internal enemies" to intensify aggressive external behavior of a state in time of crisis.

Conversely, the threat of an external enemy— and that of an internal enemy, too—is likely to increase the cohesion of the "in-group" organization ([10], p. 140). Thus struggle against the out-group and mutual aid within are opposite aspects of the same situation.[20] It is well known, of course, that in a monolithic state, such as Communist China, where scapegoats are institutionalized, the rank-and-file dissatisfactions—almost irrespective of their character —can be diverted by the elite against "internal enemies" and "external enemies" and thus be made to enhance cohesion.

We have postulated above that the durability of a given $(m_k^j)t$ agreement will be the function of the "p" capabilities of the parties, the "v" importance of the "j" problem to each of the parties, and the amount of "d" dissatisfaction evoked by the agreement among the various parties. The durability of a complex organization—such as a state—will be the function of similar variables, except that there may be more j's involved, and the "parties" to the relationship are likely to consist of the ruling elite, on the one hand, and an initially loose amalgamation of the "exploited masses" or other rank and file who feel that the state fails to represent their interests.

It is a common pattern for the ruling elite, being comparatively well satisfied with things as they are, to maintain policy conditions which largely embody the status quo, while the rank and file demand more and more as they begin to see possibilities for bettering their circumstances. In such circumstances the "top" and "bottom" of a state system may occupy wholly different positions on a "d" scale. Thus, if y represents the elite view of the status quo, if c_1^n stands for the combined policy conditions of the elite; if x equals the rank-and-file perception of things as they are; and if c_2^n is substituted for the combined policy conditions of the rank and file, then the system is in a potentially revolutionary situation which may be represented by Fig. 1.

On this same basis it is possible to put forward a number of propositions about the probable behavior of states and other organizations according to their internal "d" patterns and also according to the position of the state on the "d" scale. In these terms a state with a low d distributed through the system will tend to

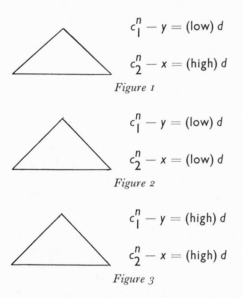

$$c_1^n - y = \text{(low) } d$$

$$c_2^n - x = \text{(high) } d$$

Figure 1

$$c_1^n - y = \text{(low) } d$$

$$c_2^n - x = \text{(low) } d$$

Figure 2

$$c_1^n - y = \text{(high) } d$$

$$c_2^n - x = \text{(high) } d$$

Figure 3

make relatively low demands upon its environment and will tend to be non-aggressive (see Fig. 2). By contrast, a state with a high d will tend to make high demands upon its environment and will tend to be aggressive—especially if its "p" capability has been low but is rising rapidly[21] (see Fig. 3). It is postulated that this tendency will obtain even though the j's at issue among the rank and file may be quite different, substantively, from those at issue among the elite.

In each case, the p (capability) of the decision-making elite to act will depend upon a certain degree of minimal support from the rank and file. When the elite loses this minimal support, the state, being unable to function, is liable to revolution or disintegration. It can be postulated, however, that a state with a relatively satisfied elite and a dissatisfied rank and file will

tend to react aggressively and even precipitously to an external challenge which the decision-makers perceive as threatening to the status quo. Both Austria-Hungary and Russia tended to fall into this category in 1914.

The negotiation of conflict

THE discussion so far has been confined to an analysis of certain processes of conflict and the way they appear to lead toward integration. At this point the question arises how and to what degree the parties to a conflict situation can be integrated by negotiation or manipulation on the part of parties to it—or by third parties acting as mediators or adjudicators.

In general, it is possible to distinguish four ways of dealing with a given conflict: (1) the parties can withdraw from contact with each other ([8], p. 133); (2) one party can dominate or even absorb or destroy the other party; (3) the parties can compromise; or (4) the parties can, to one degree or another, integrate freely on a basis of equality. In these terms it becomes evident that m_1^j, m_2^j, m_3^j, and m_4^j categories of action can all lead to domination or to compromise, whereas a true integration—integration on a free and equal basis—is achieved only through $(m_2^j)t$ relationships, that is, through voluntary consent and nonviolent means. The sole exception, noted heretofore, lies in the circumstance where an initial conquest or other act of domination becomes universally accepted by the subject people through the passage of time and through gradual "internalization."

Domination—the victory of one side over the other—is the easiest and historically, no doubt, the most prevalent way of handling conflict ([31], p. 41). Whether it is a durable way is a wholly different matter. English domination over Scotland seems to have given way to a true integration. To a large degree, on the other hand, the great conflicts of the twentieth century can be viewed as a series of struggles by subject nationalities and colonial peoples against the empires of the West.

It can be argued, indeed, that the motive power generated by domination-submission situations around the world has contributed considerably to the success of Communist expansion in many parts of the world.[22] And beyond this, communism itself can be viewed as a technique for manipulating and "engineering" such discontent for the achievement and maintenance of tightly controlled power.[23]

The resolution of conflict, other than by avoidance or conquest, depends generally on two central factors: the reduction of the intensity of the conflict and the identification or development of one (or more) overriding "c" policy conditions or—in somewhat different perspective—the achievement of a genuine $(m_2^j)t$ integration which subordinates the original incompatibility ([8], p. 133).

It is evident, on the one hand, that a conflict is always concerned with a distribution of power. Indeed, an exertion of power is prerequisite to the retention of a share in the determination of future relations—as well as for the acquiring or retaining of other benefits perceived as the "reasons" for conflict ([33], p. 400). An immediate and indispensable goal of any party to a conflict, therefore, is the achievement of victory—either complete or partial. On the other hand, it must be recognized that either or both parties can be brought to modify their original perceptions of "victory" and "defeat" ([33], p. 400). Modifications of this sort can be achieved to one degree of another, both by "compromise" and by genuine "integration."

Compromise, according to Harold Lasswell, is:

> that mode of resolving conflicts in which all parties agree to renounce or reduce some of their demand. A compromise, in contrast to a dictated solution such as involved in coercion and conformity, implies some degree of equality of bargaining power. The agreement involved in compromise is also to be distinguished from that involved in integration. In the former case each party is able to identify the precise extent of his losses and gains; in the latter, new alternatives are accepted of such a kind as to render it extremely difficult to discern the balance between concessions made and concessions received ([24], pp. 147–49).

In general, the compromise method of dealing with conflict is probably better understood than the true integration method if for no other reason than that it is the way, other than by domination, that most controversies are settled ([31], p. 31).

The first step toward compromise, as toward true integration, consists in a reduction in the intensity of the conflict. On the face of it much of this intensity derives directly from the incompatibility of the points at issue with the unsatisfied needs of each party dominating the situation ([29], p. 92). Further investigation may reveal, however, that the intensity may also be in part a function of the tension level or "social atmosphere" of the parties ([29], p. 89). Thus, as we have already had reason to imply, there is likely to be a close correlation between dissatisfactions that are inherently internal to each party and the dissatisfactions which arise from the incompatibility between them.[24] This will be particularly true of the state which customarily displaces its domestic dissatisfaction upon institutionalized "internal" and "external" enemies. Obviously, also, all these dissatisfactions with tangible inadequacies and frustrations become mixed with vague "sentiments and emotions" to endow attitudes toward the conflict at hand with an "unreasonableness" which is difficult to pin down or alleviate ([33], p. 401). It is thus common for a would-be mediator to find in each of the parties to a conflict a "fight set" which gives rise to "obscurities conscious or unconscious" ([31], p. 37). It is no accident that warlike solutions usually spring from warlike expectancies and preparation ([1], p. 63).

In a conflict situation of high intensity it can be accepted as almost axiomatic that both parties will be capable of considerable dissimulation, conscious or otherwise ([33], p. 401). It need hardly be stated, of course, that "all this applies to ourselves as well as to the other side" ([31], p. 32).

The initial step, then, is for each side to "lay its cards on the table," that is, to state its policy conditions and to enunciate clearly the nature of its own dissatisfactions. In the course of this process it will likely become evident that the parties will have some common interests, however minimal. The next step will be for each side to re-examine and perhaps re-evaluate its own desires against those of the other party and against the implication of the total situation. It may then become evident to either or to both sides that one or two formerly unperceived elements in the total situation are more important than some aspect of the proclaimed policy conditions. "Behavior," according to Kenneth Boulding, "consists of movement into the most highly valued part of the *total* image. A shift in the value ordering, therefore, even without any change in the rest of the image, can produce profound, even revolutionary, changes in behavior" ([18], p. 127).

Whereas, initially, there was a situation where

$$A \rightarrow c_1^1$$
$$B \rightarrow c_2^1,$$

it may now emerge that A will settle for $c_1^1 - x$ if B will agree to $c_2^1 - y$. This new arrangement may result from the fact that the x and y elements in the two policy conditions are perceived by the parties, on closer analysis, to be much less important to them than the aspects of the situation which they agree mutually to preserve. Or the arrangement may emerge from a new perception on the part of the two parties to the effect that the consequences of non-settlement or of violent settlement are likely to cost more than the issues are worth.

Despite the frequent use of this method for resolving conflicts, there are serious limitations inherent in it. All too frequently at least one party feels that he has been deprived of a highly important aspect of his policy condition. Dissatisfaction is likely to be stored as the deprived party awaits a favorable opportunity to redress the scale of advantages, and the new relationship may turn out to be unstable and unsatisfactory to both.[25]

The true integration of two desires—in contrast to their compromise—signifies "that a solution has been found in which both desires have found a place, that neither side has had to sacrifice anything" ([31], p. 32). This situation can be brought about either by an alteration of the desires of one or both sides or by an alteration of the problem itself—through a change of the environment or through the achievement of some other solution that transcends the original issues and provides a condition satisfactory to both parties.

With true integration, as with compromise, the first step is to uncover the conflict, face the real issues; and the next is "to take the demands of both sides and break them up into their constituent parts" ([31], p. 40).[26] The third step, again as with compromise, is for the parties to evaluate and possibly revaluate the issues. It is assumed, under such circumstances, that neither side ever "gives in" but that there often comes a moment when interests on both sides are suddenly perceived in a new perspective and "unity precipitates itself" ([31], pp. 38–39). So it frequently comes about, once an integration is effected, that the compatible, even cooperative, effort compels a change in the whole

motivation of the two parties ([3], p. 41), and a new relationship emerges.[27] In this fashion true integration becomes a kind of spontaneous "flowing together," a merging of purpose, which makes it possible for the interests of the parties to dovetail, "to fit into each other," so that all participants find some place in the final solution. Such an arrangement, over time, may lead to a mutual acceptance of role images to the point where each side knows almost precisely what to expect of the other ([8], p. 130).

In this way, once certain fundamental problems (but by no means a large proportion of the total problems outstanding) have been successfully integrated, even two nations with a history of warfare between them can perceive and tolerate each other's roles and live peacefully together as do the United States and Canada.[28]

Clearly, this kind of integration must depend upon freely conceived, freely initiated effort and not upon domination by any force whatsoever of one party over the other. Both sides must be "sincere" in regard to the particular integration, and the authority must emerge from the reciprocal, unifying process.[29] Thus legitimate authority comes to flow from coordination—not coordination from authority.[30] Under these circumstances, then, the force of the new relationship emerges from the free consent and positive cooperation of the participants and not from any outside force or from the domination of one party over the other. Each party perceives his welfare inherent in the functioning of the integrative relationship.[31] This proposition suggests that the people of the world will not be able "to make an international settlement and then erect some power to enforce it; the settlement must be such as to provide its own momentum" ([31], p. 204), its own creative coherence. To achieve true integration on a given issue, it will not be sufficient for either party merely to react to the other or merely to wait for events to take their course. The task for the statesman concerned with the resolution of conflict is not so much to predict favorable moments as it is to create favorable situations.

Notes

1. This paper has emerged from the Project on International Conflict and Integration at Stanford University.

2. "Formal organization is that kind of co-

operation among men that is conscious, deliberate, purposeful" ([3], p. 4).

3. As has been already suggested, conflicts can arise between organizations and within

organizations—both between suborganizations and between a suborganization and the organization of which it is a component.

It should also be noted that an organization can be in conflict with itself, that is, it may issue, consciously or unconsciously, c_i's which are incompatible.

4. "Sometimes each group not only centralizes itself for effectiveness, but wants its opponent centralized" ([41], p. 163); "Warfare has been the great state maker" ([41], p. 162). "The development of war is, in fact, a gradual extension of the area of peace" ([45], p. 113).

5. "The very act of entering into conflict with an antagonist establishes relations where none may have existed before. Conflict is seen as a binding element between parties that may previously have stood in no relation to each other" ([10], p. 121).

"First, quarrels arise between men because they live together in society" ([17], p. 47).

"From the elaborate regulations prescribing the way conflict shall be conducted, it appears that men who subject themselves to self-imposed rules do, to this extent at least, cooperate in carrying on conflict" ([19], p. 317).

"While the proximity of the trenches has brought intensive fighting, it has also brought its counterpart—fraternizing between the opposing sides. The men hear each other talk and sing, one side signals, the other answers, and their representatives appear and exchange tobacco, food and newspapers.

"On Christmas Day . . . the soldiers on each side agreed mutually to the cessation of hostilities . . . that until a stated hour they would shoot into the air. When that hour arrived both sides put on the mask of war, and resumed the business of killing each other" ([19], pp. 318–19).

"Trade relations, such as barter, although often leading to war because of each nation's desire to extend its markets, also tend to produce dependency between autonomous groups and thus to foster peaceful relations" ([19], p. 298).

6. "Even so optimistic a believer in the cooperative possibilities of nationality as D. G. Ritchie admitted that 'the several nations have had to become conscious of themselves by antagonism'" ([48], p. 1016).

7. "Conflict tends to give rise to regulations and norms governing its conduct and restraining the forms in which it is being fought out" ([10], p. 121).

"There was an ancient treaty between the Senecas and the Gä-quä-ga'-o-no, or Eries, who resided upon the southern shore of Lake Erie, to the effect that the Genesee River should be the boundary between them, and that when a hostile band of either nation recrossed this river into its own territories, it should be safe from further pursuit. An infraction of this treaty was one of the reasons of the long-cherished animosity of the Iroquois against them ([32], p. 328).

"A similar compact was once made with the O-ya-dä'-go-o-no, or Cherokees, by which the Tennessee River was the limit of pursuit. If a war-party of the latter had returned and recrossed the Tennessee before they were overtaken by the pursuing Iroquois, they were as safe from their attack, as if entrenched behind an impregnable rampart. The Iroquois band could still invade, if disposed, the territory of the enemy, but they passed the camp of the retreating war-party without offering the slightest molestation" ([32], p. 528).

"International law has formulated rules of belligerent procedure which define in detail the respective rights and duties of the contending parties. The state, or status, of war represents, therefore, the new legal relations arising between two or more states engaged in war" ([16], p. 443).

"In methods of warfare, as in other social situations, conduct is therefore determined by the network of relations by which the individual is surrounded and by which his behavior is affected" ([19], p. 296).

8. "Custom establishes certain conflicts between men and may thus produce quarrels among them. Custom at least controls the places where quarrels take place. But custom also brings into work mechanisms which inhibit the development of the quarrels and which exert pressure for settlement. Or the conflicts are so directed by custom that there is a change of personnel of the system, but the structure of the system persists. Finally, I examined the rituals which openly state the conflicts that exist within a social order, and yet which are believed to bless that order" ([17], p. 137).

9. "The judicial process may be considered as 'a way of inquiry set within arrangements for orderly combat'" ([18], p. 450).

"In this connection one of the characteristic institutions of common law is the method of judicial precedents which relies, for its authoritative legal material, on the judicial decisions of actual controversies" ([38], p. 54).

10. "We must remember that quarrels arise out of the very ties which link men—ties with one's wife's kin or one's own kin or one's neighbors. There is only pressure towards the establishment of peaceful relations—or, rather, the reestablishment of peaceful relations after a breach. This pressure is exerted by common interest in a mechanism of peace over a certain area, which is necessary if men are to live in any kind of security, and produce food, marry

into one another's families, or deal with one another" ([17], p. 19).

11. These various "levels" or "orders" of conflict should be distinguished also from conflicts between a given organization and the larger, perhaps somewhat looser, societal context within which it functions. Thus: "There are conflicts between the interest of different individuals within a group, and between the interests of smaller groups within a larger society. There is also conflict between society with its law and the individuals and groups which compose society" ([17], p. 37).

12. "In every event whatsoever each commune [*universitas*] promises to come to the aid of the other at its own expense as need may be with all that may be necessary for their succour to resist the attacks of their enemies and to avenge their injuries. And concerning these things they have sworn their corporal oath without guile; renewing by this oath and these presents the ancient form of confederation" (The Perpetual League between the Three Swiss Forest Communities, August 1, 1291) ([34], pp. 41–42).

"The said states hereby severally enter into a firm league of friendship with each other for their common defence, the security of their liberties, and their mutual and general welfare; binding themselves to assist each other against all force offered to, or attacks made upon them, or any of them, on account of religion, sovereignty, trade or any other pretence whatever" (Articles of Confederation of the United States of America, November 15, 1777) ([34], p. 71).

"We, the people of the United States, in order to form a more perfect Union, establish justice, insure domestic tranquility, provide for the common defence, promote the general welfare, and secure the blessings of liberty to ourselves and our posterity, do ordain and establish this Constitution for the United States of America" (The Constitution of the United States of America, September 17, 1787) ([34], pp. 80–81).

"The central government [of the Iroquoian League] was organized and administered upon the same principles which regulated that of each nation, in its separate capacity; the nations sustaining nearly the same relation to the League, that the American states bear to the Union. In the former, several oligarchies were contained within one, in the same manner as in the latter, several republics are embraced within one republic" ([32], p. 58).

"The exuberant growth of associations in African towns is a point which has often been noticed. Less attention has been given to the contribution which, in varying degrees, these associations have made to the development of national movements. First, they have made it possible for Africans to recover, within the new urban context, the sense of common purpose which in traditional African society was normally enjoyed through tribal organisations" ([20], p. 84).

13. "A social organization is a structure of "roles": any vacancy in the role structure—i.e., any role without an occupant—creates pressure to fill the vacancy with an appropriately skilled person. It is this property of being an open system which enables organizations to live longer than any of their parts—presidents, deans, and professors come and go, but the university goes on forever" ([8], p. 123).

"The first element in the description of an organization is a static structure of parts—its geography or anatomy, its organization chart or balance sheet or molecular structure" ([8], p. 122).

"The next step in the development of an organization model is its description as a 'machine', or energy transformer. Any organization depends on some source of energy for its continued existence—food and light in the case of the biological individual, to which may be added coal, oil, and other sources in the case of manufacturing plants or armed forces. Scarcity of energy sources may be an important source of competition and issue conflict, for what is taken *by* one organization may be taken *from* another" ([8], p. 123).

"The next step in the organization model is to describe it as an 'open system' or, more generally, as a 'growth system' or dynamic open system. A static open system is a structure which is maintained in the midst of a stream or throughput of its constituent parts" ([8], p. 123).

"Overlaying or embedded in the complex of informal organizations, which is the aggregate we call great national and local societies, is the network of formal organizations. If we examine this network it quickly appears that there are a few strands of formal organization that are clearly dominant and relatively comprehensive, all other formal organizations being directly or indirectly attached to and subordinate to them. They are of two types, now known as churches, that is, formally organized religions; and states, formally organized political interests" ([3], p. 96).

14. "The self typically includes more than the primary ego, which is the symbol used by a person to refer to his irreducible 'I,' 'me.' The self takes in whatever is included with the primary ego as belonging with it. The boundaries of the ego include—besides the primary ego —symbols that refer to parents, wife, children, friends, countrymen, correligionists, and other groups and individuals. These are the symbols of identification" ([25], p. 39).

"Symbols are an important factor in expectancy. Germans think of themselves as
belonging to the land of Beethoven and Goethe;
Norwegians preserve the relics of the Vikings
and in fantasy share in their fabulous exploits.
Greeks do not forget Praxiteles and Demos-
thenes. Flags, martial music, noble ruins are
profoundly significant to the citizen whose security and whose self-esteem are inseparable
from the tradition of his people.

"Now most symbols are of an exclusively
parochial order. They mark off my country
from yours. World symbols are virtually lacking: no world parks, gardens, universities, and
few symbolic world-minded documents. There
is no world currency, no genuine world capital"
([1], p. 57).

15. "In the unifications of Italy and Germany,
the division between liberals and conservatives,
or between liberals and reactionaries, cut across
state boundaries, and so in Italy did the division between pro-clericals and anti-clericals.
In Germany, moreover, the territorial changes
which had resulted from the Napoleonic Wars
had greatly increased the extent to which the
division between Protestants and Catholics
crossed the state boundaries that emerged in
1815. In Switzerland, the division between
liberals and conservatives also cut across many
cantonal boundaries in the period between
1815 and 1858, though a few predominantly
Catholic and conservative cantons took part in
the abortive attempt at secession in 1847"
([12], pp. 76–77).

"The Mohawk of the Wolf Tribe recognized
the Seneca of the Wold tribe as his brother, and
they were bound to each other by the ties of
consanguinity. In like manner the Oneida of
the Turtle or other tribe received the Cayuga
or Onondaga of the same tribe as a brother, and
with a fraternal welcome. This relationship was
not ideal, but was founded upon actual consanguinity.

"If either of the five nations had wished to
cast off the alliance, it must also have broken
this bond of brotherhood. Had the nations fall-
en into collision, it would have turned Hawk
tribe against Hawk tribe, Heron against Heron,
brother against brothers" ([32], p. 78).

[So, too, with the League of the Iroquois:]
"In the eyes of an Iroquois, every member of
his own tribe, in whatever nation, was as much
his brother or his sister as if children of the
same mother. This cross-relationship between
the tribes of the same name, and which was
stronger if possible, than the chain of brotherhood between several tribes of the same nation,
is still preserved in all its original strength. It
doubtless furnishes the chief reason of the
tenacity with which the fragments of the
League still cling together" ([32], pp. 77–78).

16. "Conflicts may be said to be 'productive'
in two related ways: (1) they lead to the
modification and the creation of law; (2) the
application of new rules leads to the growth
of new institutional structures centering on the
enforcement of these new rules and laws" ([10],
p. 126).

"A society, therefore, which is riven by a
dozen oppositions along lines running in every
direction, may actually be in less danger of
being torn with violence or falling in pieces
than one split along just one line. For each
new cleavage contributes to narrow the cross
clefts, so that one might say that society is
sewn together by its inner conflicts. It is not
such a paradox after all if one remembers that
every species of collective strife tends to knit
together with a sense of fellowship the contenders on either side" ([41], p. 165).

17. "The identification of the enemy is a condition of life in a Communist group. For the
enemy certainly exists. It remains only to be
identified and fought" ([2], p. 243).

18. The characteristics of the internal communications system may also provide useful
criteria for differentiating degrees of pluralism.
Empirical evidence suggests, for example, that
pluralistic systems tend to depend upon a maximum of "double-tracked" communications in
many directions, but especially between the
leadership and the rank and file within the
political structure. Monolithic systems, on the
other hand, tend toward "one-way" communications whereby decisions are made by the
leadership and passed "downward" as orders
or directives ([9], p. 100). The only information
moving toward the peak of the hierarchy tends
to be that which is asked for. It should be
noted, however, that states frequently transmit
"mandate" through less clearly defined channels.

"Legally [in the Chinese Empire] there was
only one track—from the top down—along
which passed imperial orders. But in actual
practice, by the use of intermediaries such as
the government servants and a locally chosen
shang-yao or functionary of the same type, unreasonable orders might be turned back. This
influence from the bottom up is not usually
recognized in discussions of the formal governmental institution of China, but it was effective
nevertheless" ([15], p. 84).

19. "The internal enemy cannot be so easily
identified as the external one, the class enemy.
That is why, in a Communist group, special
techniques have been developed for the discovery of the internal enemy. Special agents
are entrusted with the task of engaging the
Party members in discussion on various
points concerning the "line." Needless to say
these agents work on the assumption of the

necessary existence of the internal enemy. Consequently their technique is that of a 'provocateur.' The result of this is seen in the periodical 'purges' taking place in every Communist organization" ([2], p. 243).

20. "External opposition and internal uniformity have been among the most important inducements to intense political organizations" ([48], p. 1043).

"Opposition is the very breath of life to the fighting group and often it goes to pieces when it no longer has antagonists" ([41], p. 164).

21. "War between challenger and dominant nation . . . appears most likely when the challenger approaches but has not quite overtaken the dominant nation in power. In other words, an approximate balance of power increases the danger of war, while a clear preponderance of power in the hands of the satisfied nations assures world peace. However, other factors also play a role.

"War is especially likely if the challenger at its peak will roughly equal the dominant nation in power. Such a nation cannot hope to obtain a clear supremacy through internal development. Its only hope of taking the dominant nation's place is to unseat it in battle" ([36], p. 440).

22. "In Marxian doctrine, the theories of the class-struggle and of the nature of the state depend to some extent, again by implication, on the frustration-aggression principle. Surplus value, the materialistic interpretation of history, the nature of ideologies, these are subjects that can be treated adequately in a somewhat pure sociological or economic frame of reference. But when Marxists have described the dynamic human interrelationships involved in the class struggle, and in the preservation and destruction of the state, they have introduced unwittingly a psychological system involving the assumption that aggression is a response to frustration" ([13], p. 23).

23. Karl Marx perceived the central conflict between bourgeoisie and proletariat as the motivating force for revolution in capitalist countries. Extending this doctrine, V. I. Lenin concluded that in colonial and semicolonial countries the class struggle—first the proletariat and peasantry against the landowners and only later a coalition of "revolutionary classes" against the bourgeoisie—would coincide with a basic conflict between the colonial peoples, on the one hand, and their "imperialist oppressors," on the other. By developing the concept of a small, self-conscious, highly disciplined revolutionary elite, employing a body of carefully calculated strategies and tactics of operation, Lenin proposed that the international Communist "general staff"—and, indeed, all Communist leaders up and down the hierarchy

—would in every possible instance not only make use of the "ebbs and flows" of existing popular discontent but would also, in essence, create new discontents by raising "new issues," that is, new images or new policy conditions in the minds of the people.

Clearly, then, a primary function of the Communist system is conscious, organized, and purposeful conflict, and this conflict can be carried out by a variety of means ranging from the educational and psychological (so-called "brain-washing") through political subversion to economic warfare and the application of military force.

In waging its struggle along a broad front, the Communist movement depends upon its ability (a) to shape and alter non-Communist perceptions of fact; (b) to manipulate and gradually to modify or uproot and supplant non-Communist perceptions of value; and (c) to penetrate and weaken the old organizational structure from within, to attack it from without, and eventually to replace it altogether. Thus Communist tacticians seek to alter and control the behaviour of non-Communist peoples by changing both the images of fact and the images of value held by these peoples.

While seeking to change the images of people outside their own territories, Communist tacticians, once in control of an area, try to keep the images of fact and value held by subject populations under strict control and sealed off from the possibilities of alteration from influences outside.

Again, once in power, the Communist movement seeks to further, even more highly controlled, interplay of conflict and organizational processes to enhance the power of the new society and to use it as a base for the next extension of the struggle. Thus organization, quite as much as conflict, is a primary function of the Communist movement, and the way in which Communists see conflict (and destruction) carrying on its interplay with organization (and construction) is in striking respects analogous to certain biological processes.

24. "Frequently internal strife may be masked and appear as intergroup tension; this at first may contribute towards a temporary intragroup integration, but later the internal dissension begins to show, leading eventually to disorganization" ([42], p. 25).

It can be argued that something like this happened with Russia and Austria-Hungary in World War I.

25. "If we get only compromise, the conflict will come up again and again in some other form, for in compromise we give up part of our desire, and because we shall not be content to rest there, sometime we shall try to get the whole of our desire. Watch industrial

controversy, watch international controversy, and see how often this occurs. Only integration really stabilizes. But by stabilization I do not mean anything stationary. Nothing ever stays put, I mean only that particular conflict is settled and the next occurs on a higher level" ([31], p. 35).

26. "If, then, we do not think that the differing means fighting, even when two desires both claim right of way, if we think that integration is more profitable than conquering or compromising, the first step toward this consummation is *to bring the differences into the open*. We cannot hope to integrate our differences unless we know what they are" ([31,] p. 40).

27. "We progress by revolution, but usually we do not stop to examine a desire until another is disputing right of way with it" ([31], p. 38).

28. "Live peacefully together, like the United States and Canada, if each accepts fully the role of the other and if they share a reasonable common image of the mutual relationship" ([8], p. 130).

29. "Authority should arise within the unifying process. As every living process is subject to its own authority, that is, the authority evolved by or involved in the process itself, so social control is generated in the process itself. Or rather, the activity of self-creating coherence *is* the controlling activity. We see this clearly in international relations" ([31], p. 204).

30. "Authority is the character of a communication (order) in a formal organization by virtue of which it is accepted by a contributor to or a 'member' of the organization as governing or determining what he does or is not to do so far as the organization is concerned. According to this definition, authority involves two aspects: first, the subjective, the personal, the *accepting* of a communication as authoritative . . . and, second, the objective aspect—the character in the communication by which it is accepted" ([3], p. 163).

31. In this sense, legitimate authority is "the interweaving of all the experience concerned" ([31], p. 204).

References

[1]. Allport, Gordon W. "The Role of Expectancy." In Hadley Cantril (ed.), *Tensions That Cause Wars*. Urbana: University of Illinois Press, 1950.

[2]. Barbu, Zevedei. *Democracy and Dictatorship*. New York: Grove Press, 1956.

[3]. Barnard, Chester I. *Functions of the Executive*. Cambridge: Harvard University Press, 1958.

[4]. Bernard, Jessie. "The Conceptualization of Intergroup Relations with Special Reference to Conflict," *Social Forces*, XXIX (1951), 243–51.

[5]. ———. "Parties and Issues in Conflict," *Conflict Resolution*, I (1957), 111–21.

[6]. Bernard, Jessie, *et al*. The Nature of Conflict. France: UNESCO, 1957.

[7]. Bion, W. R. "Experience in Groups," *Human Relations*, I–IV (1948–51), 314–20, 487–96; 13–22, 295–303; 3–14, 395–402; 221–27.

[8]. Boulding, Kenneth E. "Organization and Conflict," *Conflict Resolution*, I (1957), 122–34.

[9]. ———. *The Image*. Ann Arbor: University of Michigan Press, 1956.

[10]. Coser, Lewis A. *The Functions of Social Conflict*. Glencoe, Ill.: Free Press, 1956.

[11]. Deutsch, Morton. "A Theory of Co-operation and Competition," *Human Relations*, II (1948), 129–52.

[12]. Deutsch, Karl W., *et al. Political Community and the North Atlantic Area*. Princeton, N.J.: Princeton University Press, 1957.

[13]. Dollard, John, *et al. Frustration and Aggression*. New Haven: Yale University Press, 1957.

[14]. Eliot, T. S. *Notes Towards the Definition of Culture*. London: Faber & Faber, 1948.

[15]. Fei, Hsiao-tung. *China's Gentry*. Chicago: University of Chicago Press, 1953.

[16]. Fenwick, Charles G. *International Law*. 2nd ed.; New York: D. Appleton-Century Co., 1934.

[17]. Gluckman, Max. *Custom and Conflict in Africa*. Oxford, Basil Blackwell, 1955.

[18]. Hamilton, Walton H. "Judicial Process," *Encyclopaedia of the Social Sciences*, VIII, 450–57.

[19]. Hiller, E. T. *Principles of Sociology*. New York: Harper & Bros., 1933.

[20]. Hodgkin, Thomas. *Nationalism in Colonial Africa*. New York: New York University Press, 1957.

[21]. Jersild, Arthur T. *Child Psychology*. New York: Prentice-Hall, Inc., 1933.

[22]. Keller, Albert Galloway. *Societal Evolution*. New York: Macmillan Co., 1915.

[23]. Koch, Howard E., Jr., North, Robert C., and Zinnes, Dina A. "Some Theoretical Notes on Geography and International Conflict," *Conflict Resolution*, IV (1960), 4–14.

[24]. Lasswell, Harold D. "Compromise," *Encyclopaedia of the Social Sciences*, IV, 147–49.

[25]. ———. *Power and Personality*. New York: W. W. Norton & Co., 1948.

[26]. Leakey, L. S. B. *Mau Mau and the Kikuyu*. London: Methuen & Co. Ltd., 1953.

[27]. Lenin, V. I. *Collected Works*. Vol. IV, Book I.

[28]. ———, *Two Tactics*, New York: International Publishers, Inc., 1935.

[29]. Lewin, Kurt. *Resolving Social Conflict.* New York: Harper & Bros., 1948.

[30]. Llewellyn, K. N., and Hoebel, A. Adamson. *The Cheyenne Way.* Norman: University of Oklahoma Press, 1941.

[31]. Metcalf, H. C. and Urwick, L. (eds.). *Dynamic Administration.* ("Mary Follett Papers.") New York: Harper & Bros., 1940.

[32]. Morgan, Lewis H. *The League of the Iroquois.* New York: Dodd, Mead & Co., 1904.

[33]. Moore, William E. *Industrial Relations and the Social Order.* New York: Macmillan Co., 1949.

[34]. Newton, Arthur Percival. *Federal and Unified Constitutions.* London: Longmans, Green & Co., 1923.

[35]. Novicow, J. *War and Its Alleged Benefits.* New York: Henry Holt & Co., 1911.

[36]. Organski, A. F. K. *World Politics.* New York: Alfred A. Knopf, 1958.

[37]. Park, Robert E. "The Social Function of War," *American Journal of Sociology,* XLVI (1941), 551–70.

[38]. Pound, Roscoe. "Common Law," *Encyclopaedia of the Social Sciences,* IV, 50–56.

[39]. Rashevsky, N. *Mathematical Theory of Human Relations,* Bloomington, Ind.: Principia Press, 1947.

[40]. Rickman, John. "Psychodynamic Notes." In Hadley Cantril (ed.), *Tensions That Cause Wars.* Urbana: University of Illinois Press, 1950, 167–208.

[41]. Ross, Edward Alsworth, *The Principles of Sociology.* New York: The Century Co., 1920.

[42]. Ruesch, Jurgen, M.D. *Disturbed Communication.* New York: W. W. Norton & Co., 1957.

[43]. Shepperson, George, and Price, Thomas. *Independent African.* Edinburgh: The University Press, 1958.

[44]. Sumner, William G., and Keller, Albert G. *The Science of Society.* New Haven: Yale University Press, 1927.

[45]. Tarde, G. *Social Laws.* New York: Macmillan Co., 1899.

[46]. Watkins, James T., IV, and Robinson, J. William. *General International Organization.* Princeton, N.J.: D. Van Nostrand Co., 1956.

[47]. Williams, Robin M., Jr. *The Reduction of Intergroup Tensions.* S.S.R.C. Bulletin No. 57. New York, 1947.

[48]. Wright, Quincy. *A Study of War,* Vols. I and II. Chicago: University of Chicago Press, 1942.

[49]. ———. "The value for Conflict Resolution of a General Discipline of International Relations," *Conflict Resolution,* I (1957), 3–8.

Karl Deutsch

Political integration and security communities

THE FUNDAMENTAL PROBLEM of international politics and organization is the creation of conditions under which stable, peaceful relations among nation states are possible and likely. Ultimately each nation's security must be assured through the existence of a community embracing all nations. Thus, as one writer has expressed it, the problem is this: "How do groups of men gain the status of security communities? ... A *security community* is considered

Reprinted from *Political Community at the International Level,* New York, Random House, 1954, pp. 33–44.

to be a group which has become integrated, where *integration* is defined as the attainment of a sense of community, accompanied by formal or informal institutions or practices, sufficiently strong and widespread to assure peaceful change among members of a group with 'reasonable' certainty over a 'long' period of time."[1]

In order to clarify this statement of the problem and to find out more about the processes leading to political integration, it is necessary to examine closely the meaning of the basic concepts which are to be employed in this study.

Concepts: integration and security community

ALL communities among people are characterized by the existence of a significant amount of transactions among them. Countries so isolated from one another as to have no significant dealings among their populations would not be members of one community at all.

Not all communities, however, are political communities, for all politics involves the possibility of enforcement of decisions. Not all political communities, again, are security communities. Within the sphere of politics, "integration" and "security community" are terms more specialized than the general terms "political unification" and "political community." The latter may include among their facilities for enforcement some organized preparations for war or large-scale violence among their participants. Integration and security community in our usage exclude such preparations, and on the contrary imply stable expectations of peace among the participating units or groups, whether or not there has been a merger of their political institutions. The processes that create such unifying habits and institutions will henceforth be called *integration*, and the territories and populations among which such integration has taken place will be called a *security community*.

The choice of a threshold in terms of the presence or absence of large-scale preparations for war is not arbitrary. It is implied in the technological character of modern warfare. Mass production of the means of violence today needs preparations on a scale as large as that required by the mass production of automobiles or airplanes. There has been no significant war or civil war in the twentieth century which did not make use of large amounts of weapons produced and assembled beforehand and of

previously trained manpower and military skills. The absence of such advance preparations for large-scale violence between any two territories or groups of people prevents any immediate outbreak of effective war between them, and it serves for this reason as the test for the existence or nonexistence of a security community among the groups concerned. The attainment of a security community thus can be tested operationally in terms of the absence or presence of significant organized preparations for war or large-scale violence among its members, and integration for us is the creation of those practices and machinery—the habits and institutions—which actually result in the establishment of a security community.

Integrative processes

SUCH security communities could be attained in a number of different ways, and have been so attained at certain times and places in the past. Each of these possible potential integrative processes, as well as their combinations, enter into the concept.

POLITICAL AMALGAMATION

The most conspicuous case is the achievement of a security community by means of *political amalgamation*, that is, the merging of several political units or enforcement agencies into one. Such amalgamation might be the result of the voluntary merging of several previously independent provinces or countries into a single unitary state. Alternatively, it might be achieved by establishing a federal union with a federal army or police force superior in power to those of its constituent units, and at the same time immune to the danger of becoming divided internally. Or it might be created by subjecting several previously sovereign states or federations to a common government having its own superior armed forces whose unity rested on their bonds of loyalty to it and to each other. In short, such amalgamation of smaller units into larger ones could be accomplished in many ways—by conquest, by explicit agreement, by gradual habituation, or by various combinations of these.[2]

Frequently, amalgamation of governments has been considered the most natural way, and sometimes the only way, of attaining integration and thus a security community. For this reason some of the inherent difficulties and limitations of political amalgamation should be kept in mind. Any amalgamation of the strongest enforcement agencies would presumably have to imply the merging of at least some of the strongest political loyalties and of some of the major symbols of political legitimacy. Beyond this, any workable political amalgamation would presumably require the merging of at least some additional political institutions and processes, such as some of those relating to legislation and taxation. It might also require a partial merging of political elites.

The extent of the range of institutions and practices that would have to be amalgamated might well be expected to expand with the steady expansion, since the last quarter of the nineteenth century, of functions and services normally performed by governments, or widely expected and demanded from them. Expansion in the depth or scope of government within a given area is quite different, of course, from the geographical expansion of a government exercising a given depth of responsibilities over additional territories or populations. The latter is sometimes implied in the concept of *expanding community* used by some students of international organization.[3] Under certain conditions, the ease of territorial expansion on the one hand, and of expansion in the scope of governmental responsibilities on the other hand, may be inversely related to each other. If so, governments sometimes may have to choose between providing many services for a smaller population or fewer services for a larger one. In any case, the main instances of voluntary amalgamation into larger political units appear to have occurred prior to the new growth in governmental regulation and services that began during the last quarter of the nineteenth century. Hence modern welfare states may perhaps need special techniques if they are to include new territories of populations without long and bitter conflict. The popular concept of a limited common government spreading over an ever-expanding territory might thus require increasingly careful qualification.[4]

Even if successful, however, political amalgamation need not lead to a security community. Subjects of a common government may feel acutely insecure and act accordingly. They may fear or expect the outbreak of large-scale violence in civil wars or wars of secession. Or, if existing institutions have become repugnant to them as an apparent threat to some of their major values or as a source of intolerable frustration to some of their desires, they may

even come to welcome such wars in preference to continued subjection to an unfriendly government or an uncongenial majority.

In this manner, the amalgamated government of the United States was faced with growing expectations of civil war during the decades after 1830, and with the reality of such a war in 1861. The amalgamated institutions of the Hapsburg Empire, after intermittent periods of relative success, failed to continue as a security community in 1848–49, and again after 1900. Again, the very limited amalgamation of Swedish and Norwegian political institutions in the Swedish-Norwegian Union was abandoned in 1905 by both countries as a hindrance rather than a help in the search for a dependable security community between them. Cases of this kind may add empirical data to the suggestion by Jacques Maritain that a common sovereign or supreme enforcement agency does not necessarily imply a political community, if by this is meant a common body politic with an effective common machinery for the creating and maintaining of consent and for the making of agreed-upon decisions.[5]

Not only may amalgamation of governments fail to last, but even while it exists it may fail to provide a security community for the peoples living under it. To account for the enduring success of amalgamation, therefore, as well as to point up alternative approaches to a security community, a number of more fundamental integrative processes must be studied.

PSYCHOLOGICAL ROLE-TAKING

First among such possible fundamental processes, a security community might be approached, in theory, by seeking to bring about an increasing acceptance and use of the same or equivalent patterns of living, thinking, and feeling among the individuals who are members of the various political units that are to make up the security community, so as to produce either a common "we-feeling" among them, or a devotion of most of them to some symbol or symbols representing this security community, or to a shared image of its population. Any of these, or a combination of them, seems implied in the notion of a sense of community mentioned in our initial definition.

Psychological acceptance of community roles, however, must arise from individual experience, and even sustained efforts at persuasion or indoctrination have only limited effects if they seem to clash with the preponderance of actual experience. Moreover, even sustained efforts at persuasion have to be organized, maintained, paid for, and protected against violent disruption.

It is not surprising, therefore, that there appears to be no case of a security community which was established solely by the appearance of a sense of community or by persuasion unaccompanied by the growth of institutions and organizations which sustained the "we-feeling" and channeled it into activities of group living; nor any security community which had only institutions and organizations but none of the psychological processes operating in and through people. In combination with the development of such institutions, on the other hand, the growth of symbols, attitudes, and expectations of community somewhat similar to what has been called "the will to form a nation"[6] has often been of great significance.

ASSIMILATION

A second approach toward a security community might be through *assimilation*, that is, a process in which participating individuals or political units become as similar as possible to one another in language, culture, political and economic habits and institutions, and, generally, the largest possible number of respects. Assimilation operates, broadly speaking, through two kinds of processes; cultural learning or diffusion which spreads common behavior patterns; and cultural unlearning, such as forgetting or repression, which eliminates patterns which make people different. Assimilation in this sense doubtless contributed to the success of political amalgamation of Italy and Germany, and to the establishment of security communities among their constituent provinces or states, as well as to the success of the American federal union between 1790 and 1830, to its triumph in the Civil War, and to its consolidation after 1865.

On the other hand, the considerable extent of linguistic, cultural, historic, and religious assimilation among the Spanish-speaking republics of Latin America has not led to any particularly successful amalgamations or security communities among them. Nor did it unite the Germans and the German-speaking Swiss, or prevent the secession of the American colonies from the British mother country.

To be sure, in all such cases assimilation was imperfect, but so it always is. Security communities have succeeded in the face of much greater linguistic or cultural diversity than

existed in the unsuccessful cases referred to above. Yet a trend toward assimilation, and particularly any political or economic pressures in this direction, may themselves provoke, or at least strengthen, reactions toward regional or national self-assertion or secession.

MUTUAL INTERDEPENDENCE

A third approach might be through the *division of labor* between unamalgamated but highly specialized or diversified political units, for instance, between a political unit specializing in paying for the protection of a military power to which they make little or no military contribution and the unit which furnishes that protection. Examples can be seen in the familiar relationships between protectorates and the protecting power in the British Empire, or in those between a highly specialized metropolitan region and its industrially undeveloped colonies or hinterlands. Interlocking relationships between protecting powers and protectorates, or between manufacturing centers and agricultural single-crop economies may lead to fuller political amalgamation, or strengthen it where it exists. They may also furnish a basis for the development of a scurity community among the regions which are critically dependent upon one another even in the absence of political amalgamation. The continuing social and economic ties between Britain and Ireland after the formal end of political amalgamation might be a case in point; and so, to a lesser extent, might be the relationship between Britain and Argentina during much of the nineteenth century when the latter was sometimes called Britain's sixth Dominion.

Arrangements of this kind imply, however, a good deal of one-sidedness and mutual dependence of the parts in the economic or political whole composed of their interlocking relationships. This one-sidedness and extreme dependence on others may of course become a major source of frustration. Demands for self-sufficiency, independence, national self-reliance, and the like may then herald developments toward the destruction of temporary security community by increasing inner conflicts and therewith the possibility of eventual secession. The secession of India and Pakistan from the *Pax Britannica* formerly imposed upon their territories, and the sessionist movements in some parts of the former French colonial empire, may serve to illustrate some aspects of this process.

MUTUAL RESPONSIVENESS

A fourth approach toward a security community might be through increasing *mutual responsiveness* among political units which need be neither amalgamated nor otherwise strongly dependent upon each other. While politic units in this category might be able to do much without each other's aid and might have no need to tremble at one another's threats, they might have acquired the political habits, practices, and institutions necessary to perceive one another's sensitive spots or "vital interests," and to make prompt and adequate responses to each other's critical needs. In a sense, interaction among different groups or peoples may be said to present an inevitable challenge to the political and social institutions and leadership of each, and their respective creativity and resourcefulness may have considerable bearing on the kind and adequacy of their response.[7] Given sufficient resources as well as resourcefulness, sovereign states with a good deal of relative economic independence, or at least immunity to each other's direct pressure, might thus succeed in developing stable security communities among themselves enduring for a century or longer. The United States and Canada since 1815 and Sweden and Norway since 1905 may illustrate this possibility. The problem of mutual responsiveness may well turn out to be crucial.

SIMPLE PACIFICATION

In theory, a fifth approach toward a security community might appear possible through *simple pacification*, that is, the voluntary or forced renunciation of war by all participating political units, accompanied or followed by disarmament and the general acceptance or imposition of some pacifist ideology, so as to make large-scale violence appear impracticable in the future. Within the community thus established, however, this approach would imply the abolition of large-scale enforcement of decisions. If it is assumed that no particular habits or machinery need have been established for the adjustment of conflicts or for the adequate perception of mutual needs and the making of appropriate responses to them, it seems to follow that simple pacification would leave many conflicts unadjusted, as well as many critical needs unanswered and often even unperceived. Thus far no record of any large-scale security community established by means of this last approach alone has been uncovered. If one should become established it could hardly be

expected to endure, not because of any conflict with some supposed "warlike instincts" in human nature, but because of its conflict with the general and basic need of human beings to have their critical needs perceived, responded to, and adjusted in some tolerable manner. No peace and no security community that failed to meet this basic need could last for long. If these needs were to be met, something more positive would be required than the mere absence of large-scale violence.

This something more would have to be present in any viable security community. For this reason the term *integration* has been chosen to highlight the positive process of growth required for its attainment through any combination of the pathways just surveyed or any others which the empirical data may disclose.

It may bear repeating at this stage that the present study is concerned with the attainment of security, in the sense of integration, among states or regions whose populations are already interdependent to some significant extent (or at least in some respects) and who show accordingly in their activities a significant extent of transaction with each other. Thus the organization of a stable peace between Thailand and Bolivia, so long as these two countries have no common borders and a minimum of mutual relations, is not of major interest. Organizations for the maintenance of peace between states that have little to quarrel about and still less opportunity to fight among each other would be trivial if not unnecessary. Rather, it is assumed that the number of opportunities for possible violent conflict will increase with the volume and range of mutual transactions.

Balance between transaction* and integration

IT is the volume of transactions, political, cultural, or economic, which throws a burden upon the institutions for peaceful adjustment or change among the participating populations. A primary focus of our study is the ways in which the institutions, processes, and habits of peaceful change and adjustment are developed in such a manner as to keep pace with the increasing volume of transaction and adjustment problems thrown upon them.

* Transaction and interaction are often used interchangeably, but some social scientists use transaction because it stresses not only interaction but also the internal changes within social groups or individual personalities which accompany the processes occurring between them.

The analogy underlying the foregoing relationship is that of the traffic load at an intersection of roads, and the burden which it throws upon the existing facilities for traffic regulations at that point or in that area. Such regulation may be carried out by a traffic policeman or by a system of traffic lights or at much higher capital cost by means of a system of overpasses such as a cloverleaf crossing. All these facilities for the movement and control of traffic—policemen, traffic lights, roads, and cloverleaf crossings, as well as the drivers controlling their individual cars—become increasingly burdened with any increase in the volume and speed of traffic. The burdens are of two kinds: some are burdens upon the physical facilities for transport, that is, for moving or transmitting traffic, such as the width of roads and so on; others are burdens upon facilities of communication, particularly upon facilities for the distribution of attention, the making of decisions, and the transmission and reception of commands. Traffic jams and eventual breakdowns at road intersections and, similarly, at telephone switchboards occur primarily through the interplay of overloads upon the physical facilities for transmitting traffic with overloads upon the facilities for controlling it, that is, the facilities of communication and decision-making. This problem of the dual overloading of the physical capabilities of a traffic system, as well as of its capabilities for attention-giving, decision-making, and responsiveness, has close analogies with certain aspects of the problem of government in general. It is these analogies—which of course should not be pushed too far—which have been utilized to some extent in the analysis offered in these pages.

What is of concern then, in the study of political amalgamation or integration, is the race between the growing rate of transaction among populations in particular areas and the growth of integrative institutions and practices among them. The concept of security community implies stability of expectations of continuing peaceful adjustment. To be stable, however, such expectation must be geared not only to the current load of mutual transaction and potential conflicts among the participants, but they must also be geared to any increase in the volume of such transactions and such possible friction among them as can be foreseen.

Although a security community implies the expectation of stability, it may not prove stable in the event. Expectations may change as conflicts grow and responses fail. Thus the security community attained by the North and South in the United States by the 1820's became jeopardized again in the decades that followed, collapsed in the War between the States, and was eventually restored during the decades that followed the Reconstruction.

As a community of political expectations, habits, and responses conducive to the flexible maintenance of peace, a security community is a particular kind of political community. The relationship between it and some other types of political community parallels to some extent that between political amalgamation and integration, discussed above. To this distinction have now been added considerations of the transaction-integration balance, and the problem of the community as a possible pathway to the attainment of a security community can now be restated in more specific terms.

Political community and integration

A *political community* may be defined as a community of social transaction supplemented by both enforcement and compliance. In this sense, it is a community of persons in which common or coordinated facilities for the making of decisions and the enforcement of commands are supplemented by habits of compliance sufficiently widespread and predictable to make successful enforcement in the remaining cases of noncompliance probable at an economically and culturally feasible cost.

The importance of compliance habits can hardly be exaggerated. They are the silent partners of every police force, and they make a good part of the difference between an accepted police force and an alien army of occupation, and between a body politic and a mere collection of groups under temporary foreign rule. The enforcement facilities may be, but need not be, amalgamated. All that matters is that they, in combination with the existing compliance habits, should be effective in maintaining expectations of continued enforcement for the future.

COMMUNITIES: POLITICAL AND SECURITY

Given sufficiently widespread compliance habits and other favorable circumstances, a political community may become effectively integrated and thus come to function as a security community, so that war among its constituent populations is neither expected nor in fact probable. Integration into a security community may be, but need not be, accompanied by a formal amalgamation or merger of political institutions. Examples of amalgamated political communities which are at the same time security communities are the United Kingdom, the United States, and many other states with stable governments.

Under less favorable conditions, however, or with less widespread habits of compliance, even a well-established political community with many amalgamated institutions may fail to function as a security community. Both its government and some of its citizens may expect the possibility of revolution or of civil war and may prepare for it on a significant scale. The actual outbreak of large-scale civil violence may be not at all improbable. Examples of political communities which are not in fact security communities are certain types of dictatorships, and countries on the eve of civil war or revolution.

TYPES OF SECURITY COMMUNITIES

A security community with few or no amalgamated institutions may be called a *pluralistic* security community. The existence of a pluralistic security community would be tested operationally by the absence of systematic advance preparations for warfare in terms of significant amounts of manpower and resources. Examples of pluralistic security communities are perhaps Sweden and Norway after 1905, and the United States and Canada after 1815.

Another international arrangement, formal or informal, might be called a *no-war* community. This is a limited political community within which, as in any security community, the only command expected and backed by relatively effective formal or informal sanctions is the command not to resort to war or large-scale violence in the settlement of disputes. In contrast to a security community, however, the possibility of war is still expected and to some extent preparations are made for it. Sanctions may include continuing defensive preparations for self-help by members, as in the no-war community of Switzerland and her neighbors, which is not a security community. A successful balance-of-power system may function temporarily as a no-war community of this type, as did the Concert of Europe between 1815 and 1853, and again between 1871 and 1914. Other examples of no-war communities might be Great Britain and

Eire after 1921, certain Italian states since between 1815 and 1858, and such a collective security arrangement among sovereign states as, with some qualifications, the League of Nations.

In the short run, a no-war community may look like a security community, but in the long run it may be disrupted by an arms race. Even without an arms race, it may be overburdened and eventually destroyed by an increase in the volume of mutual transactions among its populations, and therefore in the volume of possible disputes among them, particularly if this growing volume should come to outpace decisively the existing facilities of the community for peaceful change and adjustment. An undisrupted no-war community, on the other hand, may develop eventually into a pluralistic security community. Whether any specific security community will continue to function in the long run will depend on the ability of its facilities for peaceful adjustment to keep ahead of the strains and burdens which any growth of social transaction may throw upon them.

APPLICATION TO RESEARCH

How can these distinctions of different political arrangements be applied to research? Can they be used for more than simply the recognition of broad types of political communities? Perhaps they can, for the distinctions suggest three broad quantitative questions for every area and period which might be studied:

How much transaction?

How much integration?

How much probable security under these conditions?

The third question has been deliberately phrased to avoid the assumption of determinism. Something more human than mere reliance upon anonymous "forces of history" is involved here. Whatever such forces are believed to be, whether inflation or Islam, excessive emphasis on them tends to divert attention from the role of human decisions in the politics of history. Yet politics notoriously is both the making of decisions and the art of the possible. To judge political performance is to appraise the exercise of this art by living men and women. To do so it is necessary to assess the range of data, resources and opportunities available to those who make the crucial decision at given moments in time.

In addition to helping to assess the performance of political leaders and institutions, answers to the three basic questions would throw some light upon the stability and the capabilities of security communities and of amalgamated governments, on the one hand, and on the prospects of their breakup and the stability and the capabilities of secessionist or separatist regional governments, on the other. Judgments on the stability and capabilities of amalgamated or nonamalgamated governments in turn would reveal more about the likelihood of achieving or maintaining a security community in a given geographic area.

Conditions for a stable security community

IN all cases considered thus far it has been found that the stability of a security community depends on its continuing capabilities to produce peaceful adjustments against the growing load of social interaction and potential friction. Since every security community is inevitably a community connecting autonomous human beings and autonomous or partly autonomous social groups, regions, and populations, it appears on this view that every security community must at the same time be to some extent a *mutual-response* community. Its participants or participating groups must have continued and effective facilities for receiving signals concerning the most urgent needs of their partners, and for making responses sufficiently quick and appropriate to avoid serious conflicts or collisions. In this sense, maintaining a security community resembles driving in close convoy; both require continuous mutual attention and responsiveness. On the other hand, a mutual response community may begin to develop among regions or units which have not yet reached the status of a security community.

The development and maintenance of adequate social institutions and habits of mutual response may thus turn out to be an essential condition for any stable political integration, as well as a possible pathway toward stable integration into a security community.

Restated in these terms, the original problem now becomes: How much sense of community or how much mutual attention and responsiveness is needed to arrive at a no-war community, or at a stable security community, among a given group of territories and populations? And what is needed to make any of these communities expand in area without critical loss of its sense of community, and hence its prospects of maintaining peace? The stability of all such communities can be assessed in terms of some balance between integration loads and integration capabilities.

INTEGRATION: LOADS AND CAPABILITIES

The concept of *integration load* implies a burden both upon the capacity for attention and for decision-making on the one hand, and upon the material and human resources for implementing decisions on the other. This burden is thrown both upon the autonomous or semiautonomous groups which participate in the political community, and upon the common or central institutions which they may have developed. The extent of this burden depends at any particular time both upon the volume and range of social transaction and upon the conditions of competition, conflict, insecurity, and the like under which such transactions take place in each particular political, economic, or cultural situation.

Corresponding to this concept of integration loads is the concept of *integration capabilities*, that is, the habits, institutions, and resources by which peaceful adjustment and change can be maintained. Integration capabilities resemble in part what authors such as E. Wight Bakke have called "bonds of organization,"[8] but they represent a somewhat wider concept. They include not merely the capabilities of the central institution of the community, and the common activities or symbols shared by all or many of its members, but also the autonomous resources and capabilities of individual members or of particular groups to make the particular autonomous responses with the sensitivity, speed, and scope necessary to maintain peaceful adjustments when needed.

INDEPENDENCE: LOADS AND CAPABILITIES

Just as the probability of success in maintaining a political community can be estimated in terms of a balance between integration loads and integration capabilities, the opposite possibility of the success of the secession of some group or region from a community can be evaluated as a function, in part, of a balance between independence loads and independence capabilities.

The concept of an *independence load* also implies both the burden of attention and decision-making required to maintain independence and the burden of pressure upon manpower and resources to implement such decisions when required, accompanied by increased competition from other units and a rising level of expectations of governmental services on the part of the domestic population.

Corresponding to this concept of independence load, is naturally the concept of *independence capabilities*, that is, the material resources as well as the social institutions, facilities, and habits required to maintain independence and to accommodate the rising load of international interaction and of domestic pressures and expectations.

Since both social interaction and popular expectations have been rising sharply all over the world during the last century or more as a result of the modern growth of science and technology, it is not surprising that both the integration load and the independence load upon governments have become increasingly burdensome, and that maintaining the substance of national independence for small states has become not less desperately difficult in many cases than the maintenance of political integration in large ones.

BALANCE BETWEEN LOADS AND CAPABILITIES

The balance between independence loads and capabilities applies not only to regions or populations considering secession—or, as in the case of colonies, emancipation—but also to political units which are already independent

to meet the rising demands made upon them. Examples might be the voluntary surrender of independence by Newfoundland in 1949 in favor of joining Canada, and in the nineteenth century, the unpopularity of many of the independent German and Italian principalities prior to unification.

An example of temporary failure of integration capabilities in the face of a sharply rising integration load might perhaps be found in the case of the Civil War in the United States. A case where integration capabilities kept ahead of integration loads for more than four centuries might be that of the Austro-Hungarian monarchy; its crisis from 1900 to its final dissolution in 1918 might turn out to have been not so much a failure of integration capabilities as a fatally rapid growth of the integration loads which overwhelmed it.

Successful demonstrations of independence capabilities over a prolonged period of time can be found in both Ireland and Norway, as well as in the independence of the American colonies from Britain. Failure of independence capabilities in the face of mounting independence load, on the other hand, might be seen, as pointed out above, in the gradually declining popularity and stability of the many sovereign principalities of Germany and Italy during the nineteenth century prior to the unification of their respective countries. . . .

Notes

1. Richard W. Van Wagenen: *Research in the International Organization Field: Some Notes on a Possible Focus* (Princeton, Center for Research on World Political Institutions, 1952) pp. 10–11.
2. The dimensions of political community outlined here overlap to some extent the dimensions of world order suggested by Professor Quincy Wright for study and measurement. What has been called *amalgamation* in this study corresponds in part, though not completely, to the somewhat broader concept of *organization* used by Quincy Wright. The concept of *assimilation* similarly corresponds in part to what he calls *standardization*. Concepts of *interlocking division of labor* and of *responsiveness* together correspond perhaps in part to his term *cooperation*. The last of his four dimensions of world order, *communication*, has no counterpart among the integrative processes listed in this part of the study, since it does not seem certain that increasing communication or interaction would necessarily promote more integration or international

order rather than increasingly bitter quarrels. Accordingly communication, together with other transaction processes, is considered here as a potential load or burden on the maintenance of peaceful relations, and is discussed as a potential challenge with which the actual integrative processes must keep pace if integration is to be preserved. Apart from this qualification, agreement with Professor Wright's view that it is possible to measure some important aspects of political integration is central to the present study. Cf. Q. Wright: "Modern Technology and the World Order," in W. F. Ogburn, ed.: *Technology and International Relations* (Chicago, University of Chicago Press, 1949), pp. 174–198; and Q. Wright, ed.: *The World Community* (Chicago, University of Chicago Press, 1948), *passim*.
3. Van Wagenen: *op. cit.*, pp. 19–20. Cf. also Werner Levi: *Fundamentals of World Organization* (Minneapolis, University of Minnesota Press, 1950), pp. 15–27.
4. Cf. E. M. Carr: *Nationalism and After* (London, The Macmillan Co., 1945), pp. 1–38;

Klaus Knorr: *Union of Western Europe—A Third Center of Power* (New Haven, Yale Institute of International Studies, June 7, 1948), pp. 8–9.

5. Jacques Maritain: "The Concept of Sovereignty," *American Political Science Review*, 44: 343–357 (June 1950).

6. Hans Kohn: *The Idea of Nationalism* (New York, The Macmillan Co., 1944), pp. 15–17.

7. On broader aspects of the "challenge and response" problem in history, cf. A. J. Toyn-

bee: *A Study of History*, 2nd ed. (London, Oxford University Press, 1935–39), Vol. I, pp. 271–301; III, 368–371; IV, 5–6.

8. E. Wight Bakke: *Organization and the Individual* (New Haven, Yale University Labor and Management Center, 1952), pp. 2–5; *People and Organizations* (New Haven, Yale University Labor and Management Center, 1951), pp. 6–7; *Bonds of Organization: An Appraisal of Corporate Human Relations* (New York, Harper & Brothers, 1950, p. 8.

Anatol Rapoport

Game theory and intergroup hostility

MOTIVATION FOR THE EXPERIMENTAL PROGRAM about to be described stems from three sources. One source was ordinary curiosity. There was a seemingly simple question to be answered by a straightforward experiment, a question which seemed to us to be relevant to psychology. The answer turned out to be not simple at all, and that is why our program is now in its fourth year. The second course was a desire to test the so-called Richardson Effect. Finally, we wanted to continue the work on stochastic models of behavior, which had proved promising in learning theory and had already been extended to interaction processes by Burke, Suppes, and Atkinson, and other mathematical psychologists.

The seemingly simple question, which we thought we could answer by simple experiment, relates to what people would do if placed in a certain dilemma. In a way, the posing of a dilemma in the context of psychological theory

is an old gambit. An instance of it is found at least as early as the fourteenth century in Buridan's parable of the ass between two bundles of hay. Assuming that the behavior of the ass was governed by a simple tropism toward hay and that this tropism was related inversely to distance, Buridan argued in true scholastic fashion that the ass would starve to death, being equally attracted to either bundle. Whether Buridan was content with that conclusion or whether he designed an experiment to test it we do not know. Our interest was in another dilemma derived from the theory of games.

Our situation is known as the Prisoner's Dilemma, named after the anecdote told to illustrate it. Two prisoners, held apart incommunicado, are deliberating whether they should confess the crime with which they are charged. If both confess, both will be convicted. If neither confesses, neither can be convicted. But if one confesses, while the other holds out, then the squealer gets a reward in addition to being set free, while the prisoner who holds out gets a sentence more severe than if he had confessed. The dilemma arises from the circumstance that it is to each prisoner's advantage to confess. If the other confesses, it is better to confess in order to get the milder sentence. If the other does not confess, it is still advantageous to confess, because of the reward. Yet it is in their collective interest not to confess; for if neither confesses, neither gets convicted, while if both confess, both get convicted.

We cannot argue, as Buridan did about the ass, that in these circumstances the prisoners will "do nothing," because "doing nothing" is in fact one of the choices in the dilemma. So it seems there is no way out but to design an experiment. Logic aside, what will real people do when placed is a situation logically isomorphic with the one just described?

Our second source of motivation, I said, was the desire to test the Richardson Effect. This effect actually resolves the dilemma for Buridan's ass, even under the supposition that the ass is governed by a simple tropism. The Richardson Effect was evidently unknown to Buridan; otherwise he would have distinguished between positive and negative tropisms. If the ass were equally *repelled* by both sides, like Odyssey's crew who had to sail between Scylla and Charybdis, then he would be indeed suspended between them, for then he would be in a stable equilibrium. A slight deviation to one side would increase the repulsive force on that side and so would be corrected. This is called negative feedback. However, Buridan's ass was subjected to positive tropisms. The slightest deviation to one side would, by decreasing the distance, increase the attraction on that side and so tend to decrease the distance still further. This is positive feedback. Consequently the ass was in an unstable equilibrium: the slightest chance deviation would push him to one or the other bundle of hay.

From the point of view of the ass, this is good, since ending up at either bundle of hay suits him. However, positive feedback can operate even if one outcome is good and the other bad. Such a situation was depicted by Lewis F. Richardson, after whom the Richardson Effect is named.

Consider two countries which can assume either a friendly or a hostile attitude toward each other. Let us schematize their attitudes as a sequence of acts, positive or negative, i.e., friendly or hostile, such that the algebraic sum adds up to the current attitude, while the sign and magnitude of the next act, in turn, depends on the attitude. Starting from an attitude of neutrality, a chance deviation in one or the other direction may well be self-perpetuating. An initial hostile act is likely to evoke a hostile act in return, which makes the next act hostile and of greater magnitude. An initial friendly act, on the contrary, is likely to evoke a friendly act and so will insure the continuation of friendly acts.

Instead of magnitudes we could consider the probabilities of acts. Each hostile acts increases the probability that the next act is hostile, and vice versa. Thus whether the two countries end up as mortal enemies or as bosom friends may well depend on an initial minute chance event. Richardson interpreted increases of military budgets of blocs of allied states as hostile acts and increases of trade between the blocs as friendly acts. He showed that under certain not unreasonable assumptions the two big European blocs in the years preceding World War I were in an unstable equilibrium. According to Richardson's theory, a united Europe could have resulted if the initial impulse had been either toward greater inter-bloc trade or toward smaller military budgets. But the impulse was in the other direction, and the arms race once begun could not be stopped. World War I was the result. Richardson attributed it to the unstable nature of inter-power relations, a hypothesis contradicting the balance of power idea, which assumes a stable equilibrium.

We wanted to see whether we could reproduce the Richardson Effect on a miniature scale in a laboratory experiment. As we shall see, the Prisoner's Dilemma game does in fact seem to reproduce it.

Finally, our third source of motivation was the desire to extend the range of situations which could be treated theoretically in terms of stochastic models. As it turns out, the stochastic models which can be expected to be adequate for the interaction theory involving the Prisoner's Dilemma game are more involved than those which have been shown adequate to describe a simple learning process. By working with the more complex models, we hope to contribute to the further development of the applications of stochastic models to behavioral theory.

Our experiments all have a common feature. There are two subjects unable to communicate with one another. Each must make a choice between two acts which we shall call C (co-operative) and D (defecting). Upon making the choice, each receives a pay-off in points, to be exchanged for money. The pay-offs depend on the pair of choices as shown in Figure 1. The entries in the matrix are the respective pay-offs to the row-chooser and to the column-chooser.

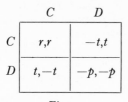

$$\begin{array}{c|c|c|}
 & C & D \\
\hline
C & r,r & -t,t \\
\hline
D & t,-t & -p,-p \\
\hline
\end{array}$$

Figure 1

Here r, t, and $p > 0$; $t > r$; $t > p$. From this we see that D dominates C for both players.

of the pressures should depend on the magnitudes of r, t, and p. Accordingly, these three parameters are the first set of independent variables. The experiments involve seven different games of this sort. These are shown in Figure 2.

Next, we might conjecture that the pressures toward the one or the other choice may depend on the experience of the players in successive choices. For example, if the same game is played many times and if the Richardson Effect operates, we might expect initial random fluctuations to drive the players toward one or the other extreme (i.e., predominantly CC or predominantly DD responses). Accordingly, in our experiments the subjects play the game several hundred times in succession. Time, as measured by the number of responses, is another independent variable. We consider each session as a sequence of 50-play blocks. In other words, we measure time in terms of successive 50-

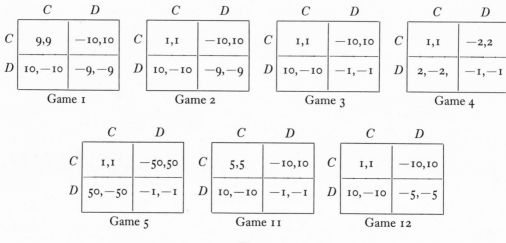

Figure 2

But if both choose D, both get $-p$ (a punishment), while if both choose D, both get r (a reward). The quantity t represents "temptation" to defect, since $t > r$. Also, since $-t > -p$, there is an inhibitory pressure on each player against trying to escape from DD. Both self-interest pressures, therefore, work in favor of D. But the collective interest pressure works in favor of C. The question is which pressure is stronger.

Independent variables

IT occurs immediately that the relative strengths

play time periods. Sessions lasted from 6 to 14 periods.

Finally, we can vary the conditions under which the games are played. In one condition, the matrix of the game being played is in front of the subjects. In another condition, it is not, although it can be inferred from the announced pay-offs. There are still other conditions, for example, one in which each subject is informed of his own pay-offs correctly but of the other's pay-offs incorrectly, attributing to the other a much larger temptation to defect (a sort of a built-in paranoia). In some conditions games are scheduled differently during the sessions.

Time will not permit the discussion of all these variations. We will, however, point out the difference between the condition in which the game matrix is displayed and the one where it is not.

To summarize, our independent variables were (1) the three pay-off parameters, (2) time, (3) the degree of knowledge, which the subjects had about the game matrix, and (4) the scheduling of the games (which will not be discussed here).

Dependent variables

THERE are, of course, a great many dependent variables to choose from. The data from each experimental session come to us in a string of successive responses of four types: CC, CD, DC, and DD. These strings can yield many statistics. The problem of relating these statistics to each other and to the dependent variables is essentially a task of data processing and no more. There are two theoretical problems. The first, a purely mathematical problem, is to construct a model (assumed to be of a stochastic type) which would hopefully involve only a few reasonable assumptions and from which as many as possible of the observed statistics could be deduced mathematically. The second is to interpret the parameters of the stochastic model in psychological terms and to relate them either to the objective experimentally controlled conditions or to the characteristics of the subjects, or to both.

Some of the statistics come immediately to mind as natural dependent variables in the context of these experiments. For instance, the frequency of the double cooperative response, CC, is an obvious index of the degree of cooperation observed in a single pair of subjects or in a population of pairs playing a particular game, or associated with a given time period or with a given condition.

We can also consider the frequency of the cooperative responses, whether bilateral or unilateral, as an index of cooperation. Obviously $CC = C + 1/2 (CD + DC)$. Thus C and CC are related. But one does not determine the other. If the responses were entirely independent we would have $CC = C^2$. But if the subjects truly interact, we cannot expect their responses to be independent. Indeed we can posit either of two interaction hypotheses: (1) that the responses of one tend to elicit *like*

responses of the other, or (2) that the responses of one tend to elicit *unlike* responses of the other. Both hypotheses seem reasonable on a priori grounds. The first one is reasonable because we expect cooperation to stimulate cooperation and vice versa; the second is also reasonable because in a Prisoner's Dilemma game we can expect cooperation to stimulate non-cooperation (it pays to be a single defector). A natural measure of either tendency is provided by the Pearson correlation coefficient

$$\rho = \sqrt{\frac{CC \cdot DD - CD \cdot DC}{(CC + CD)(CC + DC)(DD + CD)(DD + DC)}}$$

This coefficient ranges from -1 to $+1$. A positive value indicates that like responses tend to be elicited, negative values the opposite. A value of ρ near zero indicates essential independence of the responses. This correlation coefficient ρ is another of our dependent variables.

Finally we are interested in the distribution of the lengths of runs of the different responses. Consider the probability that a run of CC choices lasts at least t responses. If such runs were ended entirely by chance, like the emission of a particle from a radioactive atom, we would have for this probability

$$P_{cc}(t) = e^{-at}$$

In general we can write $P_{cc}(t) = e^{f(t)}$, where $f(t)$ is some function of time to be empirically determined. If $f(t)$ is convex downward, i.e., "stronger" than the linear function at, we could infer that the longer cooperation lasts, the more likely it is to terminate. Such processes are commonly observed. Life is one of them; the longer we live beyond a certain age, the more likely we are to die at a given moment. But it may also turn out that $f(t)$ is convex upward, i.e. "weaker" than the linear function. Of such a process we could say that the longer it lasts, the less likely it is to terminate. Such processes are also well known, for example, the length of stay in a mental hospital. Other interesting examples are found in the distributions of durations of both wars and strikes. In both of these $f(t)$ is very well approximated by $a\sqrt{t}$, which is convex upward. The character of the function $f(t)$ is still another of our dependent variables.

Several other variables could be examined, but we shall confine ourselves to those mentioned.

Results

WE would expect that if a cooperative index, say C, is compared across games, it would increase with r and with p and would decrease with t. This result is corroborated when the matrix is displayed (see Figure 3).

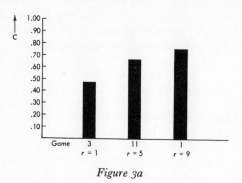

Figure 3a

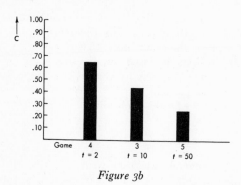

Figure 3b

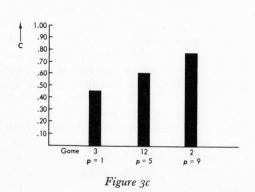

Figure 3c

Next we find that if CC or C is averaged over all games, it shows a steady increase over the time periods at least through the seventh in the same condition. On the other hand, when the matrix is not displayed, the differentiation between the games practically disappears and no "learning" is observed in the successive time periods. Also the over-all amount of cooperation is much smaller (Figure 4).

This last result surprised us. We had conjectured that the "logic" of the game, made apparent in the game matrix, would press for D. Instead we find the opposite effect. The matrix seems to indicate to the subjects (in the long run) that it pays to cooperate. We must remember that there is no way for them to reach

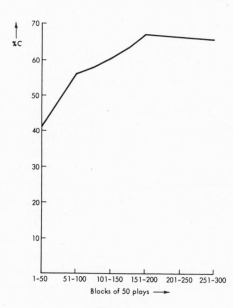

Figure 4a

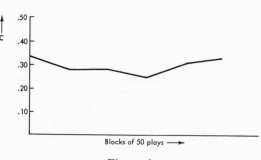

Figure 4b

an explicit agreement to cooperate. They can achieve tacit cooperation only if each trusts the other and is himself, in turn, trustworthy, i.e., resists the temptation to take advantage of the other's trust. The increasing predominance of CC responses over time indicates that they learn just that when the matrix is displayed (except for the most "severe" games, 3 and 5). They do not learn to cooperate if the matrix is not displayed, in spite of the fact that the matrix can be easily inferred from the announced pay-offs.

Examining the behavior of ρ, we find that its average also increases with time (Figure 5), indicating that the players learn to behave like each other. In other words, CD and DC responses tend to disappear.

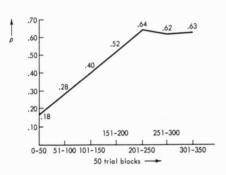

Figure 5

But all is not sweetness and light, as can be seen from the fact that the Richardson Effect operates both ways. The CC responses reinforce each other. But so do the DD responses. The more the subjects cooperate, the more they cooperate. But if they get into the DD bind, they are likely to stay in it. This can be shown as follows. We plot on the horizontal axis the number of CC or DD responses which have occurred in succession at any point in the experiment. On the vertical axis, we plot the probability that the next response will be CC (or DD) at this point. We find that both probabilities increase steadily with the number of responses of the corresponding kind that have just occurred (Figure 6).

Another way to see the Richardson Effect is in the distribution of 50-play blocks having given frequencies of CC responses. From Figure 7 we can see how strongly bimodal this distribution is. Typically a 50-trial block either has a negligible fraction of CC responses (0–10%) or a very large fraction (90–100%). Intermediate cases are comparatively rare. Thus, much evidence attests to the inherent instability of the situation, deduced by Richardson in relation to international dynamics.

Passing now to the distribution of lengths of runs, we already know what to expect; namely, that the function $f(t)$ will be convex upward, indicating a self-perpetuating tendency for these responses. This turns out to be indeed the case. The unilateral responses, on the

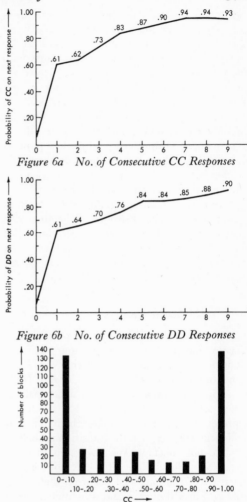

Figure 6a   No. of Consecutive CC Responses

Figure 6b   No. of Consecutive DD Responses

Figure 7

other hand, show another picture. There the function $f(t)$ is slightly sigmoid in the beginning, showing that a unilateral response is more likely to be abandoned after two such responses than after one. But if three responses have occurred, the tendency to continue again rises. However, the depletion rate is much larger in unilateral responses than in bilateral ones. Runs of unilateral responses longer than four are rare. Nevertheless, long runs do occur and are interesting in their own right. We call these long unilateral runs "martyr runs," because they result when one subject tries to induce the other to cooperate "by example," persisting in the attempt even though he takes punishment in doing so.

An interesting question relates to the end of a martyr run. We say it ends in a "conversion" if the non-cooperator begins to cooperate and is a "failure" if the martyr gives up. Also a "switch" can occur, i.e., when the defector is converted just as the martyr gives up. It turns out that failures outnumber successes about $2\frac{1}{2}$ to I, which seems like a sad commentary on the moral power of the "example." However, from another point of view, this is not so bad. When a martyr gives up, he may still be "teaching" the defector, saying to him, in effect, "If you don't cooperate, neither will I." The important thing is to combine this punishment with another chance. Our data show that it takes between two and three such unilateral attempts to induce success. On the whole, the picture is not discouraging. About 60 per cent of our pairs playing Prisoner's Dilemma with matrix displayed end up cooperating. But typically it takes a long time to achieve tacit cooperation; namely, some hundreds of repeated plays to drive the lesson home.

Stochastic models

LET us now look briefly at some possible stochastic models to represent our process. Consider the pair as a system that can be in either of four states, CC, CD, DC, or DD. If the transition probabilities between every pair of states were constant, the process would be represented by a simple Markov chain. There is evidence, however, that the transition probabilities are not constant. We have seen that the transition probability $CC \rightarrow CC$ is higher when two CC's have just occurred than when only one has occurred and still higher when three or more have just occurred. The Markov chain model could, of course, be restored by considering sequences of more than one step as the "states." The number of states would then increase exponentially with the number of steps combined into a "state." There would be 16 two-step states, 64 three-step states, etc. Then the problem of estimating transition probabilities would be made difficult by the decrease in the number of occurrences of the several states.

By way of compromise, we could assume that the probability of occurrence of the next state depends only on the previous state except when CC or DD states have been repeated, thus taking into account the Richardson Effect. Still another way would be to impose a time change in the transition probabilities of the one-step process. The latter assumption could be justified by the fact that the long unilateral runs occur more frequently toward the end of sessions. To account for this, we could simply assume that the transition probabilities $CC \rightarrow CC$ and $DD \rightarrow DD$ increase as a result not of the Richardson Effect but of the over-all experience; that is, we could assume these transition probabilities as explicit functions of time.

At any rate, several stochastic models are possible, and we can choose among them, giving preference to those which have the advantage of greater simplicity or to those which describe the observed statistics more accurately, or to some compromise between the two criteria—which are usually (but fortunately not always) inversely related.

Having chosen the "best" model by some criterion, the formal theoretical job is finished. But the heart of the theory should be content-oriented, not merely formally satisfactory. We are then faced with the task of interpreting the model.

Now a stochastic model predicts the distributions of probabilities of the states in terms of its parameters, which may be, for example, in the simplest case, the transition probabilities between single-step states. Let us suppose that this is our chosen model. How do we interpret the transition probabilities? Consider the transition $CC \rightarrow CD$. This transition occurs if one subject, having cooperated and been rewarded, continues to cooperate, while the other subject, having cooperated and been rewarded, defects. Other transitions can be similarly interpreted. This model, then, assuming the same parameters for both subjects, is built up from the following conditional probabilities, governing the behavior of the individual subjects:

$x_1 =$ probability of cooperating following rewarded cooperation;

$x_2 =$ probability of cooperating following punished cooperation;

$x_3 =$ probability of cooperating following rewarded defection;

$x_4 =$ probability of cooperating following punished defection;

as well as the complements, $1-x_1$, $1-x_2$, $1-x_3$, and $1-x_4$.

Under the assumption that the simultaneous choices of the subjects are independent of each other, we shall have the transition probability $CC \rightarrow CD$ expressed by $x_1(1-x_1)$, that of $DD \rightarrow DD$ by $(1-x_4)^2$, etc.

Introducing more general assumptions increases the number of parameters but the principle remains the same. In this way, the parameters of the model require psychological content. A behavioral theory, then, can be constructed on the basis of relating these parameters (which are really tendencies to act in certain circumstances) to either the controlled conditions of the experiments or the personalities of the subjects.

If one prefers the latter course, then the principal independent variable would become the population sample. One could compare the above-mentioned propensities in men and in women, in mental patients and in "normals," in representatives of different nationalities or cultures, in executives and in criminals, and so on. These comparisons would be of obvious interest to psychologists because the propensities mentioned, although derived as quantities on very strong scales (namely, as dimensionless numbers), are related to "deeper" psychological concepts than the hitherto quantifiable measures of behavior, such as reaction times and conditioning parameters. For, as we have seen, these propensities are related in such matters as trust and suspicion, conscientiousness and betrayal.

Our interests, however, have been so far in the other direction. We have not attempted to relate the parameters to the personalities of the players. On the contrary, in averaging over many players, we have deliberately washed out individual differences. What interests us most at present is the dynamics of the process itself. It can be shown mathematically that even in the absence of any individual differences between the players a great deal of variance among the pairs will be exhibited in the process if the Richardson Effect is truly operating. In other words, even among people of the "same kind," some can end up in tacit cooperation benefiting both, while others can end up cutting each other's throats, depending simply on how they happened to react initially, which might have been a matter of chance.

A major theoretical problem suggested by this method emerges: to disentangle these two kinds of effects; namely, the intrinsic characteristics of the participants and those determined by the dynamics of the process itself.

References

Burke, C. J.: "Two-Person Interactive Learning, a Progress Report," J. H. Criswell, H. Solomon, and P. Suppes, eds., in *Mathematical Methods in Small Group Processes*. Stanford: Stanford University Press, 1962.

Suppes, P., and R. C. Atkinson: *Markov Learning Models for Multiperson Interactions*. Stanford: Stanford University Press, 1960.

Richardson, L. F.: "Generalized Foreign Policy," *British Journal of Psychology, Monograph Supplements*, No. 23, 1939.

Morton A. Kaplan

The calculus of nuclear deterrence*

THE IMPORTANCE OF NUCLEAR DETERRENCE in the modern world does not require exposition. It became an issue of extended public discussion after the speech on massive retaliation by Secretary of State Dulles, who in the opinion of this writer came closer to an adequate theory of deterrence than most of his critics. This article will develop the view that the threat of counterattack is the best strategy against the possibility of aggression and that a nuclear counterattack is the most effective version of that strategy. The specific form this strategy ought to take will be suggested in the last portion of the article, in which a "learning" strategy will be formulated.

In the rejoinder to Dulles, the strategy of limited war (limited in objectives, area of combat, or weapons employed) was developed by various academic and military critics. It seems to me that these discussions for the most part fall into serious error because no genuine effort had been made to use the findings of any of the formal theories of strategy. This is not to assert that a correct knowledge of a formal theory of strategy is all one needs to apply to all the problems of the real world—indeed, an ultimate leap into the dark cannot be avoided—or that the statisticians and mathematicians have developed models that are completely appropriate to the subject matter of nuclear deterrence or completely unambiguous in their prescriptions. But it is not always possible to recognize the pitfalls into which one may be led to ordinary "common sense" without recourse to the strategic models which have been developed.

* I should like to thank David Wallace of the Department of Statistics and Carl Christ and T. W. Schultz of the Department of Economics at the University of Chicago for helpful suggestions in redrafting this article.

The model to be employed in this article will not be completely rigorous—indeed, I hope it will stimulate even more rigorous investigations and I invite suggestions or criticisms—but it will attempt sufficient rigor to open up the problem in a useful fashion.

The problem will be reduced to one in which two major nations or blocs are the chief contenders. It will be assumed that these nations are competitive in the sense that each desires to have at least as much control over bargains between them as the other has. In such a situation, each may reasonably ask itself under what circumstances it can deter the other side from rationally adopting a strategy which either imposes high costs on one's self or worsens one's relative bargaining position. Unless it can find such circumstances and a strategy appropriate to those circumstances, it will play a losing game.

It is obvious that any reasonably rigorous treatment of this problem must make some simplifications; otherwise, it will prove impossible to relate conclusions adequately to the premises from which they are derived. The more formally these simplifications are introduced, the easier it is to have confidence that the conclusions actually do follow from the premises. Not all simplifications are equally useful, however. Because the military problem is central to every decision in this competitive situation, the assumptions that the players have complete control over their actions and complete information concerning the consequences of any actions they take permit the most economical development of the model. These assumptions obviously do some violence to the real world, but the appropriate modifications can be introduced more easily than if other assumptions were made central to the model.

Reprinted from *World Politics*, Vol. XI, No. 1, October 1958, pp. 20–43.

To list some considerations excluded from the model will indicate the nature of the modifications which may have to be introduced when actual decisions are to be made. For instance, no consideration will be given to internal developments within nations, although it is obvious that a democratic revolution in the Soviet Union would have important consequences for United States strategy. If the United States knew that it would develop absolute offensive and defensive weapons within one year and that these weapons would not become available to the Soviet Union, it would be willing to make immediate concessions to avoid thermonuclear war that would be intolerable under other circumstances. The influences of various moves upon the network of alliances will not be taken into account. Unless otherwise stated, the difficulties of adopting given moves will not be considered.

With this preface, the game can be introduced. The conditions of the game and the rules of the game will be stated and followed by definitions, axioms, and theorems. A short informal discussion of the general conclusions of the formal exposition will then be offered, followed by an application to the kinds of warlike situations which may arise, and finally the specific "learning" strategy to be proposed will be explained.

Conditions of the game

THERE are two stocks of resources: military and non-military. Non-military resources initially are equally divided between the players. Military resources are divided into nuclear and non-nuclear stocks. At different places in the argument, the non-nuclear stocks of the players will be assumed to be either equal or unequal at the start of the game. Nuclear resources initially are in sufficient supply for each player to destroy the entire non-military stock of the other player and the entire non-nuclear military stock; but before the nuclear stock is destroyed, there will still be time for the attacked player to launch a nuclear counterattack totally destructive of human life. Nuclear weapons are in such abundance at time 1 that they may be considered costless. However, as territory and bases are lost, the probability of the totally destructive counterattack becomes progressively smaller.

Information is perfect in the sense that each player knows the outcome of each pair of moves and each player knows the resources available to the other player. However, neither player knows what the other will do, although he may acquire information which permits him to make an estimate. If this condition is changed there will be a clear statement to that effect.

Rules of the game

A MOVE consists of the use of a military resource to capture or destroy military or non-military resources of the other player or of the transformation of non-military resources into military resources.

On odd-numbered moves, players may at their own discretion attack, defend, counterattack, or do nothing with any amount or investment of their military stock. They can decrease their investment or increase it to the limit of their military stock. They may not transform non-military stock into military stock. The move comes to an end either when the players agree to a payoff and make no further investments or when their military supplies are exhausted. During even-numbered moves, non-military resources may be transformed costlessly into military resources. The players are permitted to transform only a given and equal proportion of their non-military stock. The players may make side-payments and may communicate.

Definition of total loss. Total loss = reduction to y. Total loss occurs when a given nation can no longer exist as a social entity within which minimally desirable norms of social behavior can be maintained. Thus, for the United States, total loss occurs when the fabric of democratic and liberal society is shattered and it is not possible to recreate the conditions for such a society in the foreseeable future. For the Soviet Union, total loss occurs when the Soviet system is destroyed and the possibility of re-establishing it foreclosed.

Definition of relative and absolute gains. Assume that one side has resources of $y+100$ and the other side of $y+200$. If both sides accept penalties of 10 over 10 trial periods, at the end of the 10 trials one side will have $y+100$ and the other $y+0$; that is, it will cease to exist as a player. If no considerations of domestic cost are involved and if it is assumed that the object of the game is to eliminate the other side, any loss of less than 20 for the side with 200 will represent a relative gain if the other side loses at least 10. A relative gain occurs when one side gains a greater proportion of its total holdings or loses a smaller proportion of its total holdings than the other side. Correspondingly, the actual amounts are absolute gains or losses. Thus the side with 200 that loses less than 20 when the side with 100 loses at least 10 suffers an absolute loss although it achieves a relative gain.

Axioms

Axiom 1. The value (subjective) of a move equals the values of the payoffs times their probabilities minus the values of the costs times their probabilities.

Axiom 2. Both players possess y plus the same number of units of resources They are equally strong at time 1.

Axiom 3. All units of resources of the same type are interchangeable and any unit of resources is equal in value to any other unit for both players. Thus neither player has any reason to make an equal trade or to refuse an equal trade.

Axiom 4. Players are strategically symmetrical. One man can kill one man, one tank can knock out one tank, and so forth. If forces employed in war are equal, all forces are destroyed and the unit contested can either be divided by agreement or become a no-man's-land. If forces are unequal, the larger force loses an amount equal to the destroyed smaller force.

Axiom 5. After evaluating his payoff independently of the payoff of the other player, each player introduces a discount factor for any disproportion between his payoff and that of his opponent. In other words, a payoff value is modified downward if the payoff of the opponent is greater.

Axiom 6a. Both players are symmetric in their preferences for gambles.

Axiom 6b. Both players are conservative in their preferences for gambles. Thus each player will be willing to risk the same amount for the same probability of success in gaining a unit and neither player will pay one unit to enter a lottery if he cannot do better than .5 probability of winning no units and .5 probability of winning two units.

Axiom 7. The players are symmetric in their time preferences and discount the future slightly.

Axiom 8. The total amount of resources cannot increase during the play of the game, but can decrease as a consequence of destruction.

The game is, thus, a non-zero sum stochastic game.

Theorems

THEOREM 1

EITHER defense or non-defense is a losing strategy. Assume that players have a strength of 100 each and that the military portions of the totals are equal. Assume that Player B attacks a territory of Player A which is worth 10 non-military units and that he attacks with 10 units of military resources. If Player A does not defend, the game is costless for B and B's worth becomes 110 while A's worth becomes 90. If A defends with 10 units, A and B are worth 80 and 90 respectively, assuming that the unit which was attacked becomes a no-man's-land, or 85 and 95 respectively, if it is divided. If A defends with 11 units, the values after play are 90 for A and 90 for B, which is the only good result for A so far. However, B can increase his investment. Since military resources are equal, during any move B has the option of committing as many military units as A and therefore of getting a higher payoff than A.

B can continue this process indefinitely. Since B gains' at every move, A eventually will run out of non-military stock which can be converted into military stock. A therefore has a losing game. If, however, A counterattacks a non-military resource of B, symmetry is restored. A can counterattack as long as B can attack and A can attack as many places as B, since their initial strengths are equal. However, both suffer losses of absolute strength without relative gains if this strategy is pursued. The situation may be thought of (analogically) as a Nash bargain, with this modification, that continuation of fighting on equal terms until all resources are destroyed is substituted for the Nash *status quo* point.[1] Surrender without fighting by the other player can then be viewed as the best result for each player. The Pareto optimal line would connect the two surrenders. According to the Nash criteria—invariance with respect to utility transformations, Pareto optimality, independence of irrelevant alternatives, and symmetry in the solution[2]—acceptance of the *status quo* without fighting would be the solution (see Figure 1).

The Nash function is not a prescription for rational action. However, since each player realizes that acceptance of any other solution by the other player produces a losing game for reasons already given and since fighting produces a bad result, the players have a strong incentive to coordinate on this solution.

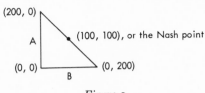

Figure 1

Schelling has discovered empirically that when two players can divide $100 if and only if they agree on the division, an offer of a $50–$50 division is usually accepted. This would appear intuitively to be more likely if several similar choices are presented over a period of time, so that a player becomes willing to believe that he cannot impose a worse solution on the other player. The stochastic aspect of this particular game greatly strengthens this conclusion.[3]

If B attacks A with 50 per cent or more of its non-nuclear forces, inaction and defense are still losing strategies. (The nuclear case does not require discussion, since the reasons given in Theorems 3 and 4 hold). But even if the defense is restricted to non-nuclear means, the argument holds. Suppose B attacks with 50 per cent of his forces. Then the case that defending with 50 per cent and counterattacking with some portion of the remainder is a losing game is clear. Suppose B attacks with 60 per cent; then unless A counterattacks with at least 60 per cent, A has a losing game for the reasons given. But, in this case, both attack and counterattack must succeed. Thus A and B exchange positions. Defense cannot do better and must do worse, since B can always neutralize a defense investment larger than 60 per cent by increasing his investment. And, in the case of the 100 per cent attack, the exchange of undamaged territory is better than the fight which leaves both sides depleted in terms of military forces and their territory ruined. If it is objected that one cannot really permit the exchange of territory in this way, since the populations would not be loyal, the obvious answer is that the counterattack would then force the withdrawal of B's military forces into defense, since he cannot afford the exchange either.

These conclusions apply particularly to two-player games. When more than two players are involved, relative losses may be accepted if there is a good chance of forming a coalition that can win at the next move. Or a winning player may not insist on his full advantage either to prevent a countercoalition or because

of fear of attack by some player who has not committed military resources in the current move. Conflicts within the coalition may also rationally prevent exhaustion of the advantages which a single player could extract from the same situation

Perhaps it appears that the advantage of the counterattack over defense follows only from the seemingly unnatural formulation of Axiom 4 to the effect that both players lose the same number of units regardless of the relative sizes of the forces committed. However, assume alternatively that the stronger player loses 2 times the ratio of the smaller player's commitment to the total forces committed multiplied by the losses of the smaller player, which are assumed to be total. Thus, if the smaller commitment is 10, for a commitment of 15, 20, and 30 respectively, the player with the largest commitment loses 8, 6 and 2/3, and 5. But this only increases the advantage of aggression and the need to equalize forces. Only by assuming that the larger force loses more than the smaller force can the conclusions above be avoided, and this assumption would certainly require justification.

It is still possible to attempt to reduce the advantage of the counterattack by assuming that the commitment of equal forces restores the *status quo ante*. This would assume that the initial aggression carries no advantages and that if all forces were destroyed, the area attacked would revert to the original holder. In addition, it would assume that the normal destruction of war would not affect the area in which the fighting occurred. The assumptions therefore are something less than natural, but, in addition, would not affect the argument to be given later where non-nuclear forces are decidedly unequal or where there are strategic asymmetries. (This argument would not hold for periods of history in which defense had strategic advantages.)

THEOREM 2

Nuclear counterattack has the same effect as non-nuclear counterattack; it produces parity. It follows from Theorem 1 that if nuclear reprisals are not employed by the weaker player where there are non-nuclear inequalities or asymmetries, the weaker player has a losing game since he has no adequate non-nuclear defense. Therefore, by the same reasoning, the weaker player in non-nuclear forces must use nuclear forces to destroy twice the value of the captured territory in order to restore parity. By the same Pareto optimal consideration as in Theorem 1, it would be optimal for the stronger player to withdraw rather than to accept this cost.

THEOREM 3

Aggression reduced the expected value of the deterrent of the aggressor. The lower the probability with which resources, such as land and the nuclear bases on the land, will be available at any move, the lower the value of the nuclear deterrent (conditions of the game) and therefore of the threat available to prevent future loss (Axiom 1). Thus, if counterattacks are not made, the aggressor can use his move 2 to transform a proportion of his resources to new nuclear weapons and bases. Since his total pool of resources is greater, it follows that the probability with which his bases can be knocked out at move 3 remains 0, while the probability that he can launch a successful surprise attack becomes greater than 0. The larger his gain, the higher the probability of successful attack. Therefore if counterattack does not occur at move 1, the deterrent value of the nuclear stock of the attacked player at move 3 is lower. The greater the loss, the lower the deterrence value. Therefore the greater the attack, the greater the probability of counterattack at move 1. And the smaller the attack, the smaller the possible gain. Since Theorems 1 and 2 have already made it unlikely that there will be no defense, there must be an absolute expected loss. But this is sufficient to reduce the expected deterrence value of the stock

of the aggressor. It creates a possibility that he may succumb to surprise attack at move 3. Moreover, he cannot have any good reason to believe that he will attack first, since the same imperatives will operate in the case of the other player. Therefore any aggression must reduce the expected deterrence value of the stock of the aggressor. This is a strong theorem, since the expected cost of an attack becomes quite high and greatly increases the danger of all-out nuclear war. Moreover, it subjects the players to the hazards of chance in a world in which all-out surprise attack is rational in order to avoid the enemy's surprise attack.

THEOREM 4

Counterattacking has the highest value of any strategy and nuclear counterattacks are more valuable than non-nuclear counterattacks. Consider a matrix giving the payoffs in resources rather than utilities for any part of a move sequence, so that if one player makes an investment, the other player attempts to estimate the payoff for any investment he makes. Let the initial stock of each player be 100; let the contested unit or units each be worth 10; let any investment by the attacked player equal the investment by the aggressor; and let the investment for aggression be 10. These assumptions are arbitrary, but it will not affect the argument if the aggressor invests more or less than the value of the unit attacked; and the aggressor has a suitable counteraction if the second player invests more (namely, to invest an amount equal to the differential). If the counterattack is nuclear, the defender must destroy twice the

PLAYER B

		Do Nothing	Attack	Defend	Non-nuclear Counterattack	Nuclear Counterattack
PLAYER A	Do Nothing	100, 100	90, 110			
	Attack	110, 90	90, 90	95, 85	80, 80	90, 90
	Defend		85, 95			
	Non-nuclear Counterattack		80, 80			
	Nuclear Counterattack		90, 90			

Figure 2

value of the relinquished units, but not more. Otherwise the aggressor will have an adequate countermove (see Figure 2).

Suppose Player B attacks. If A does nothing, he gets 90; if he defends, he gets 85; if he counterattacks he gets 80. Therefore, if Axiom 5 is disregarded and future moves ignored, A may do nothing. Suppose, however, that A asks what the consequence of this investment is for the next sequence of investments by B, who can decide to attack again, provided only that his military stock is not exhausted. Suppose A does nothing, what is B likely to do? If B regards A's failure to invest in defense as excellent evidence that he will not defend against a second attack, B must attack again. That is, B has better than an even gamble. Suppose that B estimates the probability that A will do nothing as .7, that A will defend as .2, and that A will counterattack as .1. This gives expected outcomes of .7 (110), .2 (90), and .1 (80) or an expectation of 103 (the value of relative gain is not considered).

Suppose A defends. B should hardly put the probability of future defense at less than .5. But suppose that B estimates the probabilities of defense and no defense as .5 apiece. The arithmetic expectation is 100, which, considerations of relative gain apart, is not permitted by Axiom 6. But suppose counterattack takes place. Let B estimate the expected probability of a second counterattack at the low value of .4 and the probability of defense and no defense at .4 and .2 respectively. The arithmetic sum is 90 and the probability of absolute cost without relative gain is high. There is not even a high probability of a relative gain, and the assignment of .4 probability to a future counterattack is certainly low and of .2 to no defense seems high. The power of this result is evident and does not require discussion. It would apply even if Axioms 5 and 6 did not come into consideration.

Consider the matter from the other point of view. How high must be the probability of a second attack as a consequence of non-defense in order to call forth some response other than inaction? Suppose the probability is 1. Then clearly the cost of inaction is 10, which is double the cost of defense and equal to the cost of counterattack. If the probability falls below 1, there is an immediate cost to the strategy of counterattack, if the cost of a relative decline in resources is not considered. This, however, only extends the game one move and neglects the obvious consideration that defense

lowers the probability of a second attack and that counterattack has a much stronger effect. Once this is taken into consideration, one does not need Axiom 5 to demonstrate that a counterattack would stabilize the situation very quickly and that no further attacks would be expected. Therefore the expected costs of the counterattack are lower than for any other strategy. Indeed, Axiom 5 might be derived as a theorem from this consequence. It may be noted that counterattacking produces the result so quickly that no reasonable time discount can affect it.

The fact that succeeding moves are problematical while the absolute costs of present moves are less problematical does not affect the calculus, for reasons already given, unless the players are asymmetric in their time preferences. Even asymmetry in time preferences does not change the fact that a losing strategy is the consequence of a failure to act according to the axioms. But a sufficiently high discount of the future by one player would make rational the sacrifice of the future. (It is much less likely that nations will place a high discount on the future than that individuals will.)

Note that nuclear attacks are costless, on the assumption that only nuclear resources are employed. Therefore a nuclear counterattack restores parity at no cost. Should one fear that Player B will counter-counterattack with nuclear forces, thus raising costs even higher? This assumes that the more probable higher costs become, the more willing Player B will be to risk them. It is more likely that Player A will respond again with nuclear weapons than it was that he would respond with nuclear weapons the first time. Such a sequence can gain nothing for B and can only impose absolute costs. It is true that irrational responses or responses based on mistaken information may in fact give rise to a nuclear counter-counterattack. But this requires the very same response as the initial non-nuclear attack.

Where non-nuclear strengths are not equal, the case for the immediate nuclear reprisal is even stronger. Would one engage in nuclear reprisals to prevent complete defeat? If so, the defense must be imposed in the earliest stages of the game. There is no reason to suppose that Player B will be less likely to engage in nuclear counterreprisals later in the game than earlier in the game. In such a case Player B has reason to believe that Player A is less likely to be serious, since A has accepted great losses without reprisal and since his ability to inflict punishment has declined. Therefore B is less likely to call a halt to his activities. (Incidentally, the resort to nuclear weapons is much more likely to be governed by irrational impulses in the later stages of the game, and the possibility will be reduced that the more limited demonstrations to be suggested in the last part of the paper will be successful.)

The argument is stronger still. Suppose that B does reply in kind. He has no reason to launch an unlimited nuclear attack, for then A will have no reason not to reply in kind. Thus, B would forfeit his opportunity to coordinate on a desirable outcome. This is clearly a losing move for B. Therefore he must limit his reply in kind. But A can reply in kind as long as B can. And, even if the first use of nuclear weapons did not produce that degree of belief which makes peaceful behavior rationally mandatory, the second would, as any reasonable calculation of the probabilities would establish. The willingness to engage in nuclear war to avoid a losing game is logically independent of who makes the first use of it. Therefore if A would not reply in kind when B makes a nuclear response to A's nuclear counterattack, A would have no reason to reject an initial nuclear ultimatum from B designed to change the *status quo*. It is just this difference which allows B to accept A's nuclear counterattack but which forces A to keep using this strategy as long as B attempts to maintain his aggression. If B understands the rationale of this strategy, he must accept the response, although a cheaper solution will be discussed in the last part of the paper. It is true that B may fear that his acceptance will irrationally embolden A to attempt aggression. But then he can suitably employ the same strategy employed by A. Moreover, there are other methods of communication which may permit B to solve this problem more easily.

Axiom 6 only has the function of reducing the cost before stability is reached. Actually stability is possible with asymmetry in the preferences for gambles, although extreme divergence might be unstable. The extremes necessary for instability are so unlikely that mathematical investigation is not called for. Moreover, even Axiom 5 could be eliminated if projections of possible future losses past the next move are made (in some cases, the very next move will be sufficient to make the point), unless one makes the very unlikely assumption that a pacific response will reduce the other player's estimate that the next response will also be pacific. (It is assumed that the first move

would not have been made unless the estimates made the move worthwhile.)

THEOREM 5

Where Axiom 3 does not hold, it may be difficult to use the method of Theorems 1 or 4 to produce quick stalemate (that is, inaction) and a stable solution. Assume that both players are worth 100, but that unit r, which A possesses, is worth 1 to A and 5 to B. Fighting is not optimal, for reasons already given. For any equal investment in a fight, B must gain more than A relatively and for a small equal investment—for instance, 2—B gains both absolutely and relatively, while A loses absolutely and relatively. The Nash solution is 2.5 for B and .5 for A, but the Nash criteria for bargaining situations in which the prizes are unequal are not compelling. It is true that if relative strength is disregarded, A has very little to lose and B a great deal to gain. A's best solution might seem to be to lower the value of r before relinquishing it by such means as mining r or even destroying it or furnishing the inhabitants with weapons so that Player B is forced to pay more than r is worth to Player A. It might seem that Player B has a bargaining edge because r is worth more to him and therefore that he can make a bigger investment for r. But this knife can cut the other way also. It may be possible to force B to pay more just because it is worth more to him, rather than to assume that A must give r up because it is not worth as much to him to keep it. And A can fight over r as long as B can, so that, in this sense, he has every bit as much to bargain with.

In the case given, the Nash solution is 2.5 for B and .5 for A. It is interesting to note that this totals less than the value of the prize for B and that if side-payments were permitted, a preferable solution could be found. For instance, if B were awarded the prize for a side-payment equal to the value of the Nash solution—that is, 2.5 plus .5—the net worth of both players after the bargain would be 102 and acceptance of this result may be worth more to B than the outcome of a war. This moreover would seem to represent best the players' relative bargaining strengths in terms of total military resources. In the real world, however, it may be difficult, although not impossible, to arrange side-payments. Moreover, local asymmetries in strength may be relatively great and therefore the prize may not be worth a prolonged contest if there is some natural stopping point. Taiwan, for instance, historically has been part of China, and therefore failure to prevent Chinese Communist capture of Taiwan would not necessarily convince the Communists that defenses would not be made elsewhere. In this kind of case, the calculations of Theorem 4 might not apply.

In those cases in which it costs more to hold a unit than it is worth to the other player, it may be cheapest simply to give it away. Much of the future political play may be designed to increase the costs of holding a unit. Great Communist gains in Taiwan, for instance, might create just such a situation. It is almost impossible, however, to determine what is rational in this case, and the great argument for equal division (side-payments taken into account) is the ease of coordination and the fact that both players get absolute gains without relative losses. But, since a loss here may not have future consequences, there is some ambiguity. In any case, it may be conservative to accept the solution which maintains relative parity, since this produces absolute gains for both players and relative losses for neither. The need to coordinate decisions and the costs of failure to do so may take precedence over other considerations.

THEOREM 6

The bluff is a poor weapon. If information is complete but not perfect—that is, if one knows the payoffs for different strategies but does not know how much force the other player has or whether strategic conditions are symmetric—it is less likely that coordination on the *status quo* is possible at time 1. Moreover, the less information one has to the effect that the other player will choose his best strategy, the less likely it is that coordination will occur.

Therefore the process of communication of information or even of misinformation will be important in the play of the game. The bluff is a poor device where the axioms hold, because its exposure will cause the opponent to believe that threats are not serious and therefore that the cost of aggression in absolute terms will be low or negative while the potentiality for relative gain will be high. But since this will prevent coordination on the equivalent of the Nash solution and since such coordination is better than a lack of it, the consequence will be dispreferred. However, some overstatement of one's willingness to resort to nuclear force which is sufficiently ambiguous as not to be

susceptible to exposure as a bluff may be desirable, since it will raise the probable costs of an initial action by an opponent.

It is probable that the costs of not coordinating properly may be so high that even where the applicability of the axiom set is not clear the players will find it preferable to assume, in the absence of highly probable contrary evidence, that they do apply. The *status quo ante*, moreover, as Schelling points out, may be easier to coordinate on than any other line.

THEOREM 7

If there is local strategic asymmetry, this can be compensated for by attacking where the asymmetrics are reversed or by nuclear deterrence. The reasoning is the same as for an inequality of non-nuclear forces. It is only when there is not nuclear parity and abundance that inequalities or asymmetries of strength would give rise to an unequal bargain in which the stronger side gains more. But this would also produce an eventual losing game in the two-player case.

Discussion

ONE may view the international politics of the 1930's as demonstrating the way in which action against aggression becomes more urgent while the credibility of the threatened action decreases. The equilibrium of American and Soviet strategies ultimately must rest upon the coordination of expectations and this involves a decision to employ those measures required to maintain the relative American resource position.

The problem of coordination once war has started initially on a limited basis is also important. Under the axiomatic system outlined so far, the attacked player must be willing to extend or to threaten to extend either the area of hostilities or the kinds of weapons employed to prevent defeat. Otherwise it forsakes its opportunity to regain symmetry. The thesis that both sides can coordinate on such limitations must rest upon the assumption that both sides will be willing to forego rational strategies. But this is unlikely. And if it is unlikely, there is no natural stopping point for the introduction of new weapons or new areas of conflict.

It is true that if the side accepting this limitation were the winning side, it might rest momentarily secure in this restrictive strategy—

*until the losing side decided to prevent defeat by
extension.* Thus, neither limitation to non-
nuclear weapons nor limitation to nuclear
weapons of a graduated type can rationally
serve to coordinate contending embattled nations. Moreover, if one side so restricts itself
and thus gives up its strategic advantage, the
second side, even if winning by non-nuclear
means, may still be tempted to test the will of
the first side by the introduction or the threat
of introduction of new weapons in order to
compel quick surrender. In short, restrictions
represent failures of will and evidence of such
failure reduces the probable costs to the non-
restricter of extensions of the conflict. The
attempt to restrict the bounds of conflict by
one side may itself provide a motivation to an
opponent to extend those bounds. On the
other hand, if both sides have available means
sufficient to indicate that the other cannot
achieve victory or even a relative improvement
in resource strength while, in addition, the
probability of costs becoming total is high, then
the grounds for the continuation of physical
conflict vanish and the rationale for a cessation
of hostilities becomes convincing.

In general in the more complex situations,
actual war in the nuclear age, unless it gets out
of hand for emotional reasons, may be thought
of as a testing operation in which each side
tests the seriousness of the other. Threats will
constitute probes for weakness or for lack of
concern with a particular objective. Such wars
will be complex bargaining situations. But
again the only decision upon which both sides
can easily coordinate, consonant with their
respective bargaining positions, is a *status quo*
division. In this sense, the war will not be
fought directly for gain but instead to test the
stamina and strategy of the opponent. Signs of
weakness will be exploited. Opportunities for
blackmail will be pursued. If the probes reveal
strength and determination, they will be called
off. If, on the other hand, they reveal fear of
future consequences, the temptation to extend
the area of exploit will be increased.

If one is not willing to extend the war to
prevent an enemy victory, why should one not
give up the objective if the enemy is willing to
extend it when he cannot gain victory by non-
nuclear means? Unwillingness is inherently
unstable if resources are equivalent. Thus, the
policy of limitation or restriction is inherently
different from a factual limitation or restriction
which is designed only to permit negotiation
of a settlement, with all means being held in

reserve to prevent a deterioration of the relative
resource position. The latter position is inherently stable, whereas the former rationally
impels the other side to exploit its advantage.
Thus a policy of limitation calls into question
the axiom set. It gives a strategic advantage to
an opponent and is inherently unstable.

It then follows that the object of war is not to
establish local superiority but instead to test the
resolution of the other side. Therefore the
threat to extend hostilities by communicating
firmness of will is a necessary component of a
strategy designed to reduce costs. It is doubtful
that many tests of this kind would be made in
the absence of other information which indicates a weakening of resolution. One may even
say that *any* testing of such resolution is unlikely
if a convincing determination not to limit
hostilities is demonstrated.

Strategic equilibrium, of course, is not a
necessary phenomenon. One player may have
an inherently losing game because of weakness.
An opponent may be willing to risk so much for
global conquest that he forces one to choose
between surrender and a high probability of a
war of annihilation. Provided only that a player
is willing to run a great enough risk for global
conquest, the faintest possibility that the other
side can be forced to surrender will render a
strategy of nuclear blackmail rational. It may
even turn out that surrender is the rational
response if one really prefers life as a captive
to a high risk of death. Rationality of policy
cannot be discussed apart from one's own
valuations of possible actions and those of the
opponent.

Moreover, the policy which is desirable in
the abstract may be less than desirable if in
fact that policy cannot be implemented either
because of public opinion or because of the
reactions of allies. The mere fact that such
restraints upon implementation force one into
an undesirable and even unstable strategic
situation does not change the actuality of the
restraints. If, however, the other side is not
subject to equivalent restraints, it must use the
available threats to extend its conquests. Unless
such constraints can be demonstrated as
probable, hopes for limitation of conflict
locally, to non-nuclear or even to restricted
nuclear weapons, can only be regarded as vain.
A strategy based upon such vain hopes is likely
to produce a serious underestimation of the
enemy's threats. One may entice the enemy
into an action which inflames public opinion
and leads to that all-out war which it was the

object of strategy to avoid. If one had been willing to employ nuclear weapons in an unrestricted way, the enemy could have accepted stalemate. But now he finds it advantageous to employ threats, since we rationally must surrender the position if we are so fearful of unrestricted war. Because we believe him to be subject to the same restraints as ourselves, we think the threat is a bluff and do not surrender, whereupon he uses his nuclear weapons. But now the irrational public demands conteraction and the whole war gets out of hand.

The limitation of war is possible only if the goals of war are insignificant to one or both of the parties. The general withdrawal of major problems from settlement by war stems precisely from the desirability for both parties to use reprisals to avoid the loss of relative resources. This is a quite different phenomenon from limited war. In the two world wars, the ability to inflict such costs was not clear and therefore the contending parties could bank upon chance-like elements which they might think they could estimate better than the other side to secure victory. The certainty of the destructiveness of nuclear weapons therefore immediately outlaws the attempt to accomplish major goals by military war.

If major efforts are made to change the world political structure, it will be by other means or where chance or special information may play an important role. These means will be political and economic. Military means, except where nations so lose their resolve that they become susceptible to blackmail, will not be effective for influencing this process. Thus with respect to all important areas of the world, the willingness to use nuclear weapons outlaws military warfare. In an important sense, international politics will be the continuation of war by other means. If war breaks out, the object will be not to limit it, but to call it off.

Applications

A CORRECT understanding of strategic principles —especially as they apply in the era of nuclear weapons—is an essential component of an adequate policy. The claim, however, that a strategy formulated in advance will be adequate for all situations is simply incorrect. Strategic theory is not yet completely adequate in its formal development. Even should these formal inadequacies be eliminated, problems of application will necessarily involve calculations which are specific to the individual case. Some aspects

of the matter therefore can be considered only when the case to be decided arises.

Major clash in Europe involving the Soviet Union. Unless for some reason Europe ceases to be a vital resource of the United States, the policy of limitations cannot be applied to Europe. Non-nuclear or limited nuclear weapons might be employed only to permit a period of negotiation necessarily involving the withdrawal of Soviet forces behind their original lines and partial compensation for existing damage. The Soviet Union could not be forced to concede more than this for reasons which the axioms make abundantly clear. But it must concede this much for the same reasons.

Direct attack by the Soviet Union on the peripheral zone. The response would necessarily depend upon the resource value of the zone, the applicability of Axiom 3, and the side-effects of the decision. If the value to the United States were relatively great, but the value to the Soviet Union much greater still (i.e., Axiom 3 does not apply), surrender for some side-payment might be the best strategy. If the resource value were relatively high and Axiom 3 did apply, then the threat of employment of nuclear weapons to force a *status quo* solution would be desirable. In the first case, however, if defeat or surrender so influenced allies that they defected to the Soviet Union and if this loss were vital, then nuclear deterrence might also be mandatory in this case. This would be particularly true if strategic asymmetries favored the Soviet Union.

Attack by Soviet satellites in peripheral areas. In the case of the European satellites, non-nuclear means would probably suffice to restore the *status quo ante*, although their cost might make desirable the consideration of nuclear threats. In other words, the United States might not want to employ its manpower against a second team and conceivably public opinion would not permit this—e.g., the backdown on intervention in Indochina when it became clear that manpower might be required to finish off the war. Again, however, a *status quo* solution would be mandatory, for the Soviet Union would not willingly accept the defeat of one of its satellites—first, because of the consequences flowing from the theorem set; and, second, because of the side-effects throughout its satellite and internal system.

One of the more primitive Asian satellites might not be susceptible to nuclear attack, particularly if the country the satellite attacked were occupied by it before the reprisals could be launched by the United States. Moreover, widespread attacks against civilians might cause revulsion among domestic and allied populations, leading to a deterioration of the system of alliances.

Could nuclear threats be employed against the Soviet Union in case of an attack by a satellite? Only if the Soviet Union were actively supplying arms or men or if there were an extremely high probability that such a threat would be effective in influencing the satellite. That the threat of nuclear attack against the Soviet Union would influence the satellite is not obvious and some interesting strategic problems might arise as a consequence.

Wars involving neither the Soviet Union nor its satellites. To make the problem interesting, it must follow that a victory for one of the parties would lead to a resource loss by the United States. No danger of all-out nuclear war exists unless the United States intervenes in a manner that threatens to produce a resource loss for the Soviet Union. But, in this last case, the question can be assimilated to those raised in the previous categories.

If no intervention by the Soviet Union is involved, and if public opinion is not a restraint, criteria of effectiveness alone have relevance. In all probability, the United States could easily defeat Egypt or Syria in a non-nuclear war. Whether such a victory would be worthwhile is a separate question. Colonial rule is not to be considered, for obvious reasons. But would victory have any long-term effect? What kind of governments would arise in the future and would they be any easier to deal with? What of reactions among the populace of Arab or other Oriental nations now aligned with the United States? Conceivably intervention might be necessary to forestall some overt Syrian or Egyptian military move—against Israel, for instance—but the alternatives would be nasty ones. The reasons, however, would stem from the nature of modern politics rather than from the nature of modern war. The theory of limited war has little relevance for this problem.

Suppose that the United States desired to defeat the independence movement in Algeria. It is doubtful that nuclear weapons would be useful unless the United States wished to burn out the country. Even tactical nuclear weapons would have doubtful value against that kind of guerrilla warfare. Only non-nuclear military means, supported by high firepower and great mobility, would make military sense

and even movement as long as it had the passive support of the great mass of the population.

The general question of nuclear reprisals has received only the sketchiest survey, but it seems clear that it has relevance at the present time only for wars directly involving the Soviet Union or one of the satellites or associated states of that regime or wars directly involving the resource interests of the Soviet Union. With respect to the satellites, Soviet intervention would be forced if the object were to defeat the satellite rather than to restore the prewar *status quo.* Whether the satellite could be permitted to win depends upon the applicability of Axiom 3. Whether, if it cannot be permitted to win, the threat of extension to the territory of the Soviet Union should be made depends upon the estimated degree to which decisions in the satellite are determined in the Soviet Union, or to which a threat to the Soviet Union would influence the satellite. Where the Soviet Union is directly involved and Axiom 3 holds, a policy which precludes extension both in space and in weapon types is undesirable, but a withholding of certain kinds of extensions in order to permit negotiation for a return to the *status quo* is desirable.

The reprisal strategy

AT this point interesting complications arise. The fact that bargaining demands must be made and even that they establish an equilibrium which is desirable for both sides does not prove that a pathway exists from the state of war to the state of negotiation. It has been pointed out earlier that some testing may occur if the opposing sides desire to know how serious the nuclear threats are.[5]

It is necessary that the nuclear threat be employed in such a manner that it permits the opponent to learn how to achieve an acceptable equilibrium. It is clear that a threat which upon rejection immediately led to all-out nuclear war would have a reasonable likelihood of producing total costs. No time for learning would be permitted, and if the opponent for some reason doubted the seriousness of the threat, it would not have served its primary purpose.

On the other hand, if the threat is so phrased that doubt is placed upon its seriousness, there is a high probability that it will be rejected. Thus to leave doubt about one's willingness to extend a conflict both in space and in employment of weapons is an acceptable strategy if one is not sure what one will do. This leaves open the possibility of high cost to the other side. But when one definitely intends to make the extension if the opponent does not agree to some negotiated settlement and one prefers his agreement to extension, the threat must be definite and credible in order to increase the estimate which the opponent makes of the probable costs of rejection to something approaching the real costs. To be definite, the threat need not be public—this may create other kinds of costs for the opponent that make it more difficult for him to comply with the demands that one is making—but the threat should be as definite and as credible as possible.

The question is whether some grading and timing of threats and reprisals can be achieved in order to maximize their effectiveness in those cases in which a particular line must be held, although one is in an inferior position with respect to available non-nuclear military capabilities. With respect to war in Europe, the exclusion of certain cities and zones, as proposed by Kissinger, is not acceptable as a basic premise. If one cannot afford to lose and if one cannot hold with non-nuclear military means, then some other method to force a stalemate must be found. The losing side will always be tempted to use methods that may give it some temporary advantage, but an unanticipated extension is quite likely to have uncontrolled consequences. The easiest time to halt such a war is in its earliest stages. The limitations on warfare should be designed to permit the use of types of threats that will induce the other side to agree to a stalemate. This is particularly true where the attacker chooses a local area in which he has the strategic advantage.

One alternative is a variant of a suggestion previously advocated by Szilard.[6] War cannot be confined to the battlelines or limited zones behind the lines. Nor is it desirable to attempt so to confine it. If the opponent has local superiority or even if he has only parity, but a parity that threatens to be disastrous for oneself or one's allies (for instance, consider the damage stemming from a non-nuclear war or a war with tactical limited nuclear weapons that rolled back and forth over the area of Western Europe several times running), one may rationally attempt to raise the costs of continuing the war so high that they will be prohibitive.

For reasons already clarified, nuclear war raises these costs sufficiently. However, this immediately forces an unsatisfactory solution on both players whenever an attack takes place. Instead, the threat of a series of installment reprisals that eventually progress to reprisals double the value of Europe may be employed. These should be announced in advance. For instance, the first installment may be the destruction of some central Asian city in the Soviet Union. The advance announcement may even permit the evacuation of the city to avoid widespread loss of life and the consequent inflammation of tempers that would force matters out of hand. One variation of this strategy may permit the opponent to attack one of our cities in return without additional reprisal by us. If this does not produce agreement, then the schedule becomes progressively higher. It is doubtful that an opponent would underestimate the seriousness of the threat after the first installment. It would almost certainly be the last installment.

It may be questioned whether public opinion would accept this plan despite its clear rational advantages. But one could hardly on any grounds prefer the forlorn attempt to limit a major war either as to locale or to weapons except in those cases in which both sides are in non-nuclear stalemate. This, of course, happened in Korea. But if the stalemate had not been maintained, the temptation for the losing side to extend the war would have been almost irresistible. One must remember also that it is much easier to negotiate a settlement before a war gets out of hand than afterward. One then has more time and the opposing side is less enthusiastic about potential victory than about victory within grasp. Once it has the edge, it may feel that it ought to achieve the fruits of at least partial—and perhaps complete—victory. Obviously, the strategy of reprisal is most effective if announced as general policy before war breaks out, for it may either prevent the war or increase the probability that the war can be ended by negotiations.

For areas that have less importance than Europe, the reprisals may have lower limits. The point is that the announcement of the limited series of reprisals may raise the costs so high that adventures are discouraged even if there is some prospect of ultimate successful seizure of the territory.

Where Axiom 3 does not apply, the problem is not to interdict certain areas but to establish certain costs for taking them. Even non-nuclear defense may be able to establish these costs under such circumstances. For instance, napalm bombing of Shanghai to forestall an attack on Taiwan, not as part of a defensive scheme but as part of a pre-announced program of inflicting costs, may have the military advantage that China cannot counter the move without extending both the locale of hostilities and the types of weapons employed. (Clearly China cannot retaliate against the United States mainland by non-nuclear means). But such extension may open up incalculable costs for China and may therefore be undesirable. Heavy equipping of the Nationalist air force may be even better adapted to this end. For these reasons, the means of raising the costs must be adjusted to the circumstances of particular cases.

But this also is quite different from limited war theory, for here the object is not to hold areas where Axiom 3 does not apply, but to raise the costs in such a way that military ventures will be discouraged except in those cases where national pride assumes overwhelming importance. These cases, however, are not so numerous or important to the United States that they are likely to have an unfavorable influence upon its long-term resource capabilities.

Most of these, moreover, are areas in which the Communist side has long-term political advantages—that is, these areas are likely to go by attrition. Taiwan cannot be held indefinitely, for Chiang must die, and eventually the inhabitants will choose even communism over the status of American protectorate. Therefore the raising of costs should be sufficient to discourage military ventures and to encourage dependence upon political warfare.

It seems that the areas of the world in which Axiom 3 clearly does not apply—and only in such areas does a military venture make any sense at all—are quite minor at the present time. Taiwan is one such area. It is doubtful that either Korea or Indochina comes under this rubric, at least at the present.

There may be two reasons why Axiom 3 does not apply. The first reason—the importance of the area to the attacking side—has been explored. For instance, both Chinese regimes regard Taiwan as part of China and the American "two Chinas" theory has no basis either in fact or in theory. Clearly a powerful nation will place great value on securing control over its national territory—much more so than another state can place on withholding that territory. The second reason takes effect when the territory loses value for the holding nation. If the population of some area of the world went thoroughly Communistic, a military effort to hold the area for a tottering non-Communist government would make little

sense. The costs of occupation and administration would be too high. There is no doubt that the character of Communist organizations gives the Communist nations some relative advantage in subverting an area and it may be that large and important areas of the world will go by default. But clearly the bar to unlimited war in these cases stems from the inadequacy of the remedy. If the remedy were adequate, Axiom 3 would apply and the United States could afford reprisals sufficient to deter the Communist nations.

Since this strategy of reprisal depends upon the co-ordination of decisions by the United States and the Soviet Union, it would be highly important to send a team of experts to the Soviet Union to explain the rationale of the strategy. This is a situation in which correct understanding by the Soviet Union is as advantageous to the United States as it is to the Soviet Union. But then it is no accident that this kind of game is known as a cooperative game. Indeed, it may even be that the United States should offer the secret of the "clean bomb" to the Soviet Union, since a bomb with minimal fallout enables one to play the game with greater safety and to avoid those consequences which, by virtue of certain uncontrollable factors, might lead to an extension of hostilities. Certainly it would be unwise to cease testing just at a time when we are developing those weapons which can be best used against circumscribed targets, perhaps missile bases rather than cities, with the minimal effects needed for the "learning" strategy.[7]

If, in the real world, it is not possible for political or emotional reasons to adopt the strategy indicated in this article, the calculus employed can be used to discover whether a reasonably effective alternative exists and, if so, what it is. The virtue of this kind of analysis is not that its assumptions are necessarily correct or that considerations external to the calculus will permit its employment, but rather that the assumptions are clearly stated, that they can be confirmed or disconfirmed, that the relationship between the axioms and the theorems is clear enough to be discussed rationally, and that additional factors can be considered with some assurance that any modifications indicated by them can be made in the most rational manner. When one cannot be sure what produces the result, there is little value in considering "all" factors. Although the charge that formal arguments are too restricted to deal with the problems of the real world is often correct, since mathematical reasoning is no substitute for consideration of the important and relevant factors, discursive reasoning is not an adequate substitute for accurate reasoning.

Notes

1. For a treatment of the Nash bargain, see J. F. Nash, "The Bargaining Problem," *Econometrica*, XVIII, No. 2 (April 1950), pp. 155–62. A Nash bargain represents a situation in which two players have commodities to trade. The bargaining space consists of all possible trades with "no trade"—"(0, 0)"—considered as the origin of the bargaining space. The Nash criteria given below in the text define a trade in such a way that a single point, and only a single point, of the negotiation set satisfies the criteria. The criteria seem in some sense to be the most reasonable. The situation described in this article is not quite analogous, but may be translated into the terms of a Nash bargain simply by treating complete destruction of both players as the origin of the bargaining space and any solution short of complete destruction of both as a trade.

2. Invariance with respect to utility transformations means that two versions of the same bargaining space which differ only in the point of origin and utility function can be mapped into each other by one specific utility transformation. Pareto optimality in a trade means that the payoff to one player cannot be increased without decreasing the payoff to the other player. In other words, a Pareto optimal trade must be at least as good as the *status quo*, feasible, and not bettered by any other feasible point. Independence of irrelevant alternatives means that if some feasible trades are added to a bargaining problem in such a manner that the *status quo* remains unchanged, either the arbitrated solution is unchanged or one of the new trades becomes the arbitrated solution. Symmetry in the solution means that if the players are in symmetric roles in an abstract version of the bargaining game, the arbitrated value will yield them equal utility payoffs where utility is measured in the units which made the game symmetric. See R. Duncan Luce and Howard Raiffa, *Games and Decisions*, New York, 1957, pp. 124–28.

3. Thomas C. Schelling, "Bargaining, Communication and Limited War," *Journal of Conflict Resolution*, 1, No. 1 (March 1957), pp. 19–36. Schelling also discovered that if one player offers to accept $49, the other player tries to force him even lower. This is intuitively reasonable, since it seems a confession of weakness. Such seeming weakness is even more important where non-nuclear forces are unequal and will be discussed in Theorem 2.

4. Counterattack gives (80, 80) because each player loses 15 on defense and 5 on attack. For a discussion of the stochastic game, see Morton A. Kaplan, *System and Process in International Politics*, New York, 1957, ch. 1.

5. A threat is a communication that, under stated circumstances, an action will be taken that destroys resources of the other player.

6. Leo Szilard, "Disarmament and the Problem of Peace," *Bulletin of the Atomic Scientists*, XI, No. 8 (October 1955), pp. 297–307.

7. I am indebted to Richard L. Meier of the Mental Health Institute of the University of Michigan for his exposition of the great value of continued testing of nuclear weapons.

Charlotte and George Dyer

Estimating national power and intentions

IN COMMON WITH MANY OTHER ASPECTS OF LIFE in the United States, but earlier than some, American foreign policy has reflected the chaos associated with the 180-degree change from an economy of scarcity to the "affluent society." One hundred and fifty years ago, for example, the President and the Department of State suffered from an outright lack of information upon which to base crucial decisions.[1] Now to a great extent the reverse is true, and in most areas of consideration our agencies concerned with international relations are literally flooded with an embarrassing wealth of information.[2] Why such riches should be embarrassing rather than enlightening is well described by Roger Hilsman in a recent study.[3] His "operators," though often clinging naively to the idea that their foreign policy decisions would be better if they had "all the facts," are really aware that if they did have all the facts the result would be only acute indigestion.

There are at least two underlying reasons why ulcers are the lot of decision-makers immersed in this sector of the economy of abundance. It is not just that there are too many "facts" about foreign nations available for any single human mind—or any staff collection of human minds—to assimilate. Also no over-all framework for the comparison of national "capabilities and vulnerabilities" has been established[4]—to say nothing at the moment about "intentions"—nor have there been any mechanical means devised by which the most important elements of such a comparison might be rationalized and presented in digestible form to the human mind that must, ultimately, make policy decisions. The purpose of this article is to present a proposal for such a framework and its supporting mechanization.

OBJECTIONS

Any proposal so sweeping and novel in its claims must immediately face two types of objections. The first is one advanced, notably in the Hilsman book, that "all" those facts which might conceivably have a bearing on a given foreign policy decision approach infinity as a limit. This is essentially a counsel of despair, and in justice to Hilsman it must be said that he recognizes the all-important role of selection. The present writers, while admitting that even the current price of horseshoe nails might have some bearing on the outcome of a battle or a contest for world empire, believe that a sound system of selection and emphasis can reduce the margin for error to manageable if not negligible proportions.

The second argument is the old one to the effect that "you can't add oranges and apples." This is the conceptual single track which has led previous thinkers into the intellectual cul-de-sac of trying to reduce the entire complex of national power to some over-all common denominator, such as dollars. To change the metaphor, it is on this Procrustean bed that the "facts" had to be stretched or chopped beyond any final utility. The solution offered in this article bypasses the need for a rational common denominator by providing an electronic one, and conceptualizes a model of the "perfectly" strong society against which all others may be compared in all important details; hence, in terms of relative power, each may then be compared to any other.

National power analysis

THE central ideas for this proposal are so few and so essentially uncomplicated that it might

Reprinted from *The Annals of the American Academy of Political and Social Science*, Vol. 330, July 1960, pp. 145–155.

be well to state them briefly in advance of a more elaborate exposition. One is that a system for organizing information on international relations can be devised which will comprehend data on so large a proportion of the essential elements of national strength and weakness that by means of it a trial balance between nations can be run at any time within an acceptable margin for error. Such a system is considered to be the one developed by the writers and known as *The World Analyst*.[5]

The second idea is that such a system can be expressed electronically to (1) illustrate visually the essential elements of national power so that a total relative value, in whole or for any major part, will be instantly apparent; (2) estimate with a high degree of probability the most likely of a number of possible future "courses of action," whether advantageous to us or not, by the governments or peoples of foreign nations; (3) warn in good time of other countries' dangerous hostile policies—or even "intentions"; and (4) test by means of "gaming" any new policy or plan proposed for our conduct of foreign affairs, and thus predict experimentally the efficacy of such a policy without having to risk empirical procedures.

Let us consider each of the ideas listed above. By what means would it be possible to organize this vast quantity of information in such a manner that the decision-maker could instantly strike a trial balance, and comprehend at a glance the relative strengths and weaknesses of two nations?

It must be understood initially that all events are interrelated; none stands alone. For example, the political and economic progress of any nation throughout the year might be compared to the movements of a huge ball which is slowly pushed over a flat surface, impelled by countless pressures from many directions, each exerting a different weight. These pressures may be further likened to the various elements in each of the *World Analyst* ten factors, discussed below, which are used to assess the "strengths, weaknesses, and probable course of action" of a nation. The resultant of such pressures may push the metaphorical ball to the east or west, to the north or south, toward prosperity or depression, toward alliances with other nations or war, or hold it virtually static over long periods of time.

Each time any one of these factors is changed, by increasing or decreasing its momentum and point of impact, the whole speed and direction of the movement of the "ball" may be changed.

Each factor is interrelated with every other, and may affect the others in a variety of ways. For example, if a large steel plant is built on the Delaware River, not only is steel output affected, but labor, housing, roads, water, sewage, schools, entertainment, railroads, and so forth—the list is unending—are in turn affected. Each one of these categories in turn affects others, and a chain reaction is begun.

If it were possible to show at any given moment how all other subordinate factors as well as the nation as a whole are influenced when a major change is inaugurated in one or more factors, it should help national leaders to make sounder decisions. It would be enormously helpful if such decisions could be based on an accumulation of facts, instantly recorded and visibly presented in summary, rather than on intuitive opinions derived from labored study of extensive compilations difficult to retain and balance correctly.

Also if it were possible to show the decision-maker graphically, simply, and in advance the probable results of a proposed course of action, instead of requiring him to read many "appreciations" and reports and to remember the vast number of figures and data required, he might well achieve a better understanding of the whole situation. It might even permit him to formulate policies more rapidly as well as more correctly.

Ten factors

TO accomplish the desirable results suggested above a weighted outline of the factors which affect national power in any and all nations must be established, and each nation must then be compared to this model. *The World Analyst* constitutes such a theoretical model—a simple and carefully weighted outline for the analysis of national power and intentions. The outline is divided into ten major "factors" which in turn are divided again into many subheadings of various importance.

These factors include the following fields: Geography, Sociology, Politics, Foreign Affairs, Economics, Industry, Transportation, Science, Armed Forces, History.

For the sake of clarity as well as to conserve space, the illustration of this system's application to game theory will be limited to the principal headings of one of the factors developed in, and here reproduced from, *The World Analyst*, with only one heading expanded. The letters and numbers to the left of the words

TABLE I—.D DEMOGRAPHIC (SOCIOLOGICAL) FACTOR*

.D0 Race, Ethnic Groups and Their History
.D1 Population
.D2 Language and Dialects
.D3 Temperament of People
.D4 Education
.D5 Health, Sanitation and Welfare
.D6 Recreation and Amusements
.D7 Institutions and National Culture
.D8 Religion and Philosophy
.D9 Sociological Factors Affecting Stability and Defense

Expansion of the Population (.D1) Factor Above
.D1 Population
    .D11 Census, General
    .D12 Age-Sex Distribution
        .D121 Labor Force, Statistics Only
        .D122 Armed Force, Potential, Statistics Only
    .D13 Mortality and Fertility
    .D14 Natural Increase and Projections
    .D15 Migration
        .D151 Immigration
        .D152 Refugees
        .D153 Emigration
        .D154 Internal Migration
    .D16 Spatial Distribution of Population
    .D17 Minorities
        .D171 Location, Size, Ratio to the Rest of Population
        .D172 Socio-economic Characteristics of Minorities
        .D173 Degree of Assimilation, including Ties with Mother Country by Minorities (See also .F)
        .D174 Political influence and Organization of Minorities
        D175 Aspirations of Minorities

* Charlotte L. Dyer and George B. Dyer, *The World Analyst, op. cit.*, pp. 69–70.

are simply to facilitate the filing and retrieval of material either manually[6] or by computor (see Table 1). However at this writing there are no numerical weighted values attached to the headings. Theoretical numerical values will have to be assigned to these headings and sub-headings by an operations research team of selected experts.

Assignment of values

IT is self-evident that, within the context of power politics, not all of these headings are likely to be equally important. For example, the size of the labor force (.D121) and the armed forces (.D122) is vastly more important perhaps than the refugee (.D152) problem. However, under certain circumstances—as between Israel and the United Arab Republic—the refugee problem could also have consider-able affect on the power relationships. The team of specialists, as stated above, would

have to assign a theoretical relative numerical value to each of the factors. The assigning of such numbers would be a difficult but not an impossible task and would require the services of individuals who have a wide experience in each of the disciplines most nearly represented by the factors. It is highly probable that some of the initial values assigned would be altered over a period of time, after the device had been tested with known policies for international action, the outcomes of which have been re-ported and assessed in the past. But there is no reason why a relatively workable and accurate theoretical value could not be assigned to each factor after a preliminary period of trial and error.

After these theoretical values have been assigned, their total in each component, that is, political, economic, demographic, and so on, will represent the total power possible in this field for the model nation.

When comparing the power of any two na-tions, each element within each component of each nation will be given the theoretical value assigned to that subheading, or a percent-age of it.

STEEL PRODUCTION

For example, to determine the number of points to be allocated for steel production, the theoretical number assigned for steel production in the *The World Analyst* would be considered to be equal to the greatest present production of the largest steel producing nation in the world, as well as its possible potential in one year. This number would be credited to that nation. In this case the total number of points would be assigned to the United States, the greatest steel producer at the present time. All other nations would have assigned to them a percentage of this total based on their relative position in the steel-producing scale. Thus in 1958 if the United States had 200 points representing steel, then the Soviet Union would only have 142 points, as its steel produc-tion in that year was reported at about 71 per cent of the United States total.

Conversely, with regard to the population factor, China with its probable 600 million people would have the full number of points assigned to population, while the United States, with about 175 million, would only be given 29 per cent of that number. However, in the matter of education and technological training, the tables would be reversed, and the United

States might have the optimum, and China a much lower percentage.

The factor of sea and land transportation, for example, is revealing. Where the importance of air or sea transportation looms large, those nations having highly developed systems would show an advantage, but where foot transportation was required, the nations accustomed to this mode of travel might reveal superiority on their own home territory.

It may be argued that some factors in the sociological component, such as religion, will be difficult to evaluate. Also it may be objected that some factors cannot be compared with others, such as steel with religion. With the old system of trying to reduce all values to a common denominator such as dollars, this was true. However, with this new system, the difficulty is overcome.

Sociologists are among the leaders in the quantification of elements within their areas of competence. Thus, the initial assignment of points to the various subheadings found in the sociological factor should not be too difficult for specialists in this discipline. At least it should not be any more difficult for them than for economists to assign values to the elements in the economic factor, and rather less than for political scientists, perhaps.

RELIGION EVALUATED

The method of comparing the religious element between two nations in the sociological factor will be accomplished in the same manner as steel production is compared in the economic factor. If, for example, the sociologists decided that religion is so important that it should be assigned 250 points of the total amount of points assigned for the sociological factor, then the nation whose life is most affected by religion will be given this total amount. Portugal, being a theocratic state, might very well receive this amount. It would be possible to assign the same value to one or more nations, just as in any of the elements, provided that the nation was equally affected by religion; for example, Tibet, before it was overrun by China. Other nations would be assigned a percentage of this number depending on how much their life was controlled and affected by religion. The initial assignment of these values for some ninety nations would be arduous, and would have to be done by persons who are very familiar with the nation in question. However, except in the case of a major revolution, this element would change very slowly, and would not have to be reviewed as often as, for example, some of the elements in the economic component.

The troublesome question of total number of points to be allotted to each factor will have to be decided arbitrarily for no one factor in its entirety is more important than another. In order that a country function it has to have some form of political structure, some form of economic organization, and so forth. If it lacks a whole component, such as armed forces, or scientific, it is seriously weakened, and this weakness must be reflected in the evaluation. So it is suggested that each of the 10 components be initially given the same number of points, for example, 10,000. Then each group of experts, within their discipline, will allocate these points among the elements of "their factor."

Comparative power value

IT is important to note that steel production and religion do not have to be compared. Each of the ten factors will be compared and contrasted with its opposite number in the other nation; sociology with sociology, economics with economics, and so forth. The decision-maker then has to compare and weigh only ten items against each other, instead of thousands. For example, in 1939 France's army was rated as one of the best in the world. It never occurred to anyone that it could be overrun by the Germans in six weeks. Had *The World Analyst* system been in use it would have been apparent that discontent within France was so great that the sociological factor was weakened to the point of danger as compared to the German, which was excessively strong.

Results will not be 100 per cent accurate, but the resulting estimate by the means proposed in this article will be at least much more accurate than any other method that has been devised. Previously the most varied types of information—"oranges and apples"—have not been fitted into an over-all weighted pattern which can be measured against a theoretical model. By measuring each nation against this theoretical model, they can in turn be compared to each other. Thus the economic power of one nation may be measured against the economic power of another. The morale, homogeneity, or customs, and so forth, of one nation may be seen in relation to another's and a comparative power value derived.

Electrical device

AFTER the assignment of numerical values the above system will be translated into a visual form which will indicate at a glance the following classes of information.

1. Relative over-all power of any two nations or groups of nations;
2. Potential reserve of a nation;
3. Degree of conversion of this reserve into present power;
4. Destruction by percentage of any factors in a nation and its effect on other components;
5. Acts of aggression against the United States by a nation;
6. Acts of aggression between any other two nations which might affect the United States.[7]

It is proposed that the foregoing be accomplished by substituting electric light, measured in lumens, for the numerical weights assigned to headings and subheadings of *The World Analyst* system; by using, in other words, the physical phenomena by which light intensity or electrical flow through differing resistances varies like water pressure fluctuating in a pipe; and by a combination of these types of translation from calculated numerical programs into electrical impulses, producing a device which provides a warning system, a check list for the collection of needed data, and a method for better evaluation of a given situation.

COLOR BANKS

In order to do this, it is proposed that game testing boards electrically wired be provided. Each nation under consideration should be represented by its own game board.[8] This board will consist, in a spatial-visual organization, of five vertical columns of different colors on which are arranged five banks of white lights as follows:

1. Green column lights when added together would give a number in lumens which will represent the amount of assets the nation has at the beginning of the time under consideration, as well as a number of bulbs measured in lumens equal to the probable potential which the nation could develop during a given time span. The number of lumens are derived from the addition of the theoretical values assigned to the various headings in *The World Analyst*.
2. Yellow column lights would equal the probable potential mentioned in 1 above.

National security: a field develops

3. Red column lights represent actual destruction in a nation—that is, loss from acts of God, fire, war, strike, and so forth. Here, too, the number of red column lights and their lumens exactly balance the green column lights.
4. Blue column lights represent acts of aggression between two or more nations not including the United States, but which in the long run might involve the United States. The number and intensity of the blue column lights would be representative of the power of the nations involved.
5. Purple column lights represent possible acts of aggression of any kind toward the United States, not only to include conventional war, but economic warfare, political warfare, or alliances between other nations directed against the United States, and so on. The total number and intensity of the purple column lights should balance exactly the number and intensity of the green column lights, but would not be connected with them in any way.

These five banks of lights are crossed horizontally at exactly the same place by each of the ten factor headings, as well as any subheadings which are thought to be sufficiently important to include (see Table 2).

Gaming and testing

AT the beginning of play the green "power" lights would be on. The green "potential" would be off. The yellow "potential" on. The red, blue, and purple, all off.

It would not matter whether the boards were being operated to test a proposed policy—gaming—or whether the actual power differential between nations were being measured; in either case its operations would be the same.

The green, red, and yellow boards will be connected in such a fashion that if any yellow-backed light were turned off, indicating a "potential" had been made a reality, an equal amount of light would come on in the green section. If any red lights were lit indicating some sort of destruction due, for example, to war, acts of God, major strikes, and so on, the green lights would automatically be dimmed in the various sections affected by this loss. The various sections would all be interconnected to show how a loss, for example, in rail transportation would affect the steel industry, food industry, and so forth.

The purple lights, representing acts of aggression against the United States, would not

TABLE 2—DEMOGRAPHIC

(Suggested schematic breakdown of a portion of the board*)

Green	Yellow	Red	Blue	Purple
		Race		
----- ---† ----- ---	--- ---	--------- ---------	--------- ---------	--------- ---------
		Population		
-------- --- -------- --- -------- --- -------- ---	--- --- --- ---	-------- -------- -------- --------	-------- -------- -------- --------	------- ------- ------- -------
		Language		
------ -	-	-------	-------	-------
		Temperament of People		
--------- -- --------- -- --------- --	-- -- --	---------- ---------- ----------	---------- ---------- ----------	---------- ---------- ----------
		Education		
--------- --- --------- --- --------- --- --------- ---	--- --- --- ---	----------- ----------- ----------- -----------	----------- ----------- ----------- -----------	----------- ----------- ----------- -----------
		Health, Sanitation, and Welfare		
-------- --- -------- --- -------- --- ------- ---	--- -- --- ---	---------- ---------- ---------- ----------	---------- ---------- ---------- ----------	---------- ---------- ---------- ----------
		Recreation and Amusements		
------ -- ------ --	-- --	-------- --------	-------- --------	--------
		Institutions and National Culture		
--------- -- --------- -- --------- -- --------- --	-- -- -- --	---------- ---------- ---------- ----------	---------- ---------- ---------- ----------	---------- ---------- ---------- ----------
		Religion and Philosophy		
------- -- ------- -- ------- --	-------- -- -------- -- -------- --	-------- -------- --------	-------- -------- --------	-------- -------- --------
		Total Number of Lumens for the Sociological Factor		

* The various columns would be painted the indicated color.
† The dashes represent light bulbs.

be connected with any other bank of lights, but would be turned on or off as such acts were attempted. If the acts turned out to be futile and harmless, they would only be shown on this board. But if they were actually harmful in any way, these results would show on both the red and green boards as indicated.

The blue board, representing acts of aggression between two nations other than the United States, would also show activity as it occurred. This board's activity might or might not be transferred to the red and green boards as indicated.

In gaming, a time scale will have to be applied to the operation of the boards. Thus, every minute of play might represent a certain number of days or weeks of actual time. When the boards were being operated for actual comparison, each event will be recorded as it occurs.

As the play proceeds, the beneficial as well as the harmful results of events or proposed policy will be transferred to the board, by turning on and off the various colored lights. With a photoelectric cell continually trained on the boards, it will be possible from minute to minute visually to ascertain and translate into numerical value the increase or decrease of any section of the economy, to determine the total relative strength of the nation, and also to measure its power potential.

The blue and purple lights indicate the aggressive action taken by any nation in world events and would act as a cumulative graphic warning system against this type of action. The totaling and recording of such acts, graphically shown on the entire board, would give ample warning of possible serious events.

ACCURACY OF THE RESULTS

The accuracy of the results if the game is being used to test a proposed plan will depend on the degree of accuracy of figures fed into it and the sophistication with which the initial values have been assigned. In the case of economic development, this may be forecast with a reasonable degree of precision. In the political field the forecast is much more difficult. It would have been difficult, for example, to forecast the relative displays of popularity shown to Mr. Eisenhower and Mr. Khrushchev, respectively, on their recent trips to India. It should be somewhat simpler when the happenings are recorded from day to day, as actual reporting of accomplished incidents will have the advantage of greater exactness in the allocation of values. The employment of the yellow or "power potential" bulbs should be of great utility. Had such a system been in effect before World War II the dangerous power potential and probable intentions of Germany might have been self-evident. When added to that of Italy and Japan, it should have given a warning that no one could have missed, especially since the gradual shift from potential to reality would have been striking.

Very often, small unrelated facts, which in themselves are unimportant, can, when correlated, assume great importance; for example, the development of German sailplane clubs after World War I—the future fighter pilots— the statements of Hitler's aims made in *Mein Kampf*, and hundreds of other "straws in the wind."

As soon as percentages of the red, green, blue, purple, or yellow bulbs of any nation change radically, then an immediate investigation should be made in an effort to determine the underlying causes, direction of policy, and likely outcome. The mere fact of knowing what to look for is half the battle in finding the facts, and in estimating the results from the facts found.

This type of semiautomatic assessment would prevent to some extent the errors made, as at present, by groups of people sitting around conference tables and trying—essentially through "intuition"—to estimate reality in world affairs. Very often in this situation the strongest willed, or most persuasive, speaker is able to present a relatively unimportant issue as if it were a decisive major one, and so influence the majority to his way of thinking, against the better judgment of the others.

A person able to "see the whole picture" at a glance is better able to arrive at an accurate comparison of the status of competing nations each year, is protected to some extent from special pleading, and thus may well arrive at a far more just estimate of the current world situation.

Summary

IF this device for estimating national power and intentions and testing policy through gaming were installed and kept up to date the following benefits might be expected from such a set of electronic "boards:"

1. Give a comparative measure of strengths and weaknesses between nations;
2. Provide a visual aid which not only indicates the comparative strengths between nations but graphically shows any major conversion in a nation from one type of economy to another, thus giving warning of the capability and intentions of a nation to wage war;
3. Show how an event happening in one field immediately affects related fields;
4. Show visually the cumulative increase or decrease in a nation of anti-American feeling;
5. Demonstrate graphically, and even predict, the accumulation and location of "trouble spots" in the world which might cause concern to the United States;
6. Test the efficacy of a proposed policy in order to determine whether it should be put into effect or not;
7. Analyze the effective results of any major action taken by our government in peacetime or wartime in the past.

Such an arrangement has been needed to aid our statesmen for many years, and it is believed that if the above theories were developed, a truly valuable system might be developed. Certainly some device of this sort is essential to assist in the conduct of American foreign policy and to bridge the morass of uncounted, badly organized, and unassimilable "facts."

Notes

1. S. F. Bemis, *John Quincy Adams* (New York: Knopf, 1949), Chap. XII.

2. This began early with the Department of State; see Dyer and Dyer, "The Beginnings of a United States Strategic Intelligence System in Latin America," in *Military Affairs*, Vol. 14, No. 2 (1950), pp. 65–83; amplified in "A Century of Strategic Intelligence Reporting," *Geographical Review*, Vol. 44, No. 1 (1954), pp. 49–69.

3. *Strategic Intelligence and National Decisions* Glencoe, Illinois: The Free Press, 1956), especially p. 61ff.

4. The inadequacies of previous attempts are suggested by such incomplete and unbalanced works as George B. Cressey's *The Basis of Soviet Strength* (New York: McGraw-Hill, 1945); and even in such fine efforts as Harold and Margaret Sprout's *Foundations of National Power* (2nd ed.; New York: Van Nostrand, 1951).

5. *The World Analyst: A System for Analyzing and Classifying Source Materials on International and National Affairs* (4th ed.; New Hope, Pa.; The Dyer Institute of Interdisciplinary Studies, 1958).

6. If a manual system is used, and the file folders are arranged in the suggested order, a complete report outline for a nation "in depth" is possible by simply evaluating and synthesizing the materials found in the folders. Related information will be found grouped in adjacent file sections, and the report may be written in that order.

7. A second article is in preparation which will give further details of the electrical game testing board described below, how it is wired and how it will be "played".

8. It will not be necessary to have ninety or more boards to represent the nations of the world. Being electronically controlled, a relatively few boards will suffice as they can be used first for the nations of Europe or Asia. After these results have been considered, the nations of South America or any other section of the world can be fed into them.

Wassily W. Leontief and Marvin Hoffenberg

The economic effects of disarmament

THE FEDERAL GOVERNMENT OF THE U.S. has been spending something more than $40 billion per year on the maintenance of the military establishment and the procurement of arms. These outlays have absorbed about 10 per cent of the gross national product, and they have exceeded by several billion dollars the combined net annual investment in manufacturing, service industries, transportation and agriculture. The negotiation of disarmament would eventually raise the possibility of a substantial cut in the military budget. Economists, market analysts and the makers of fiscal policy in Government and business have therefore begun to consider how the economy might otherwise employ the labor, the plant and the physical resources that now serve—directly and indirectly—the demands of the military establishment.

An increase in personal consumption, expansion of educational and medical services and facilities, acceleration of the rate of investment in domestic economic growth, enlargement of economic aid to underdeveloped countries—these are only a few of the many kinds of demand that would lay competing claims on the productive capacity made available by disarmament. There would be no problem if the goods that are listed in the typical procurement order from the U.S. Air Force missile base at Cape Canaveral also made up the shopping list of the average housewife. It would be merely a question of maintaining the total level of demand during the transition period. But swords do not serve readily as plowshares. In fact, the military shopping list is very different from the bills of goods presented by the various categories of civilian demand, and these in turn differ greatly from

one another. So even if the total level of expenditures were maintained, the shift from military to nonmilitary budgets must be expected to increase the demand for the products of some industries and reduce the demand for the products of others. Furthermore, how the sales and employment figures of various industries will respond to the shifts depends upon the proportion in which each type of civilian demand, with its characteristic bill of goods, shares in the increase in total civilian demand.

The composition of the total civilian demand could possibly inhibit the overall increase in nonmilitary expenditures and so hold the country's economic activity at a lower level following a cut in the military budget. If most of the money saved were spent on highway construction, for example, a bottleneck would quickly develop in the supply of cement; meanwhile the electronics industry, which contributes much to military output but relatively little (directly or indirectly) to road building, would remain idle. On the other hand, if funds were allocated to a more balanced pattern of demand, they would secure more nearly full employment of the available human and physical resources. In the long run, of course, any mismatch between the productive capacities of individual industries and the changed pattern of demand would be rectified by reallocation of capital and labor. But such adjustment, as is well known, is quite painful and could take many months or even several years. The loss of time would represent an irredeemable loss of real income to individual citizens and to the nation as a whole.

What is needed in order to anticipate and forestall such losses is a picture of the depen-

Reprinted from *Scientific American*, Vol. 204, No. 4, April 1961, pp. 47-55.

TABLE I—DIRECT PURCHASES BY DEMAND CATEGORY

(MILLIONS OF 1947 DOLLARS)

Production by Sector	Personal Consumption	Business Investment	Residential Construction	Public Services Construction	Maintenance Construction	Exports (except military)	Exports to India (except food)	Government (nonmilitary)	Military
1 Food and Kindred products	38,396					3,199	[5]	169	536
2 Apparel and Textile-mill products	14,532	20				1,167	[11]	109	143
3 Leather products	2,038	14				45		20	24
4 Paper and Allied products	597					184	[1]	104	
5 Chemicals and Allied products	3,879	49				1,114	[16]	412	85
6 Fuel and Power	10,943					536	[4]	556	991
7 Rubber and Rubber products	782					153	[2]	23	6
8 Lumber and Wood products	2,555	526				108	[1]	66	19
9 Nonmetallic Minerals and products	316	20				91	[2]	17	
10 Primary Metals	21					473		4	
11 Fabricated Metal products	1,109	186				330	[1]	57	106
12 Machinery (except Electrical)	968	5,957				1,651	[23]	288	166
13 Electrical Machinery	3,160	2,150				464	[6]	74	915
14 Transportation Equipment and Ordnance	5,574	2,863				962	[22]	352	9,478
15 Instruments and Allied products	389	265				122	[2]	19	22
16 Miscellaneous Manufacturing Industries	2,088	96				91		97	
17 Transportation	7,714	341				1,844	[35]	705	730
18 Trade	37,242	2,161				812	[15]	40	78
19 Service and Finance	90,025					882	[2]	11,029	705
20 Construction		16,844	12,082	5,956	10,429				967
21 Unallocated and Waste products						390	[7]		742
Expenditures (millions of 1958 dollars)	**292,956**	**46,102**	**18,893**	**7,770**	**17,713**	**22,576**	**[189]**	**37,184**	**41,585**

The figures at the bottom show the total quantities of goods and services (in 1958 dollars) delivered in 1958 to eight major categories of final demand, plus "Exports to India," a subtotal from the "Exports (except Military)" column. The demand categories approximate the breakdown of national expenditures in which the gross national product is usually stated. The figures in each column show the quantities purchased in each demand category from each production sector. Figures in each row show the deliveries made by each production sector to each demand category. The 1947-dollar figures do not yield 1958-dollar totals at bottom.

dence of various industries on military demand, plus the bill of goods of each one of the more important kinds of private and public nonmilitary demand that are likely to increase when military demand is reduced. The present study is a pilot effort to develop this information and show how it can be applied to forecasting the consequences of the transfer of expenditures from military to civilian purchases. Our research was supported in part by the Research Program on Economic Adjustments to Disarmament of the Center for Research in Conflict Resolution at the University of Michigan. The study does not attempt to predict how much the various kinds of civilian purchase might expend, any more than it tries to predict the actual magnitude of military cuts. The eight

tables of figures presented here, however, make it possible to analyze the consequences of such shifts from military to civilian expenditures as can be predicted. They should be of considerable help in spelling out the concrete quantitative implications of the alternative fiscal measures that the Government may have to take if and when disarmament becomes a fact. They should also enable business analysts to derive specific estimates of the demand for any particular goods or services or of the employment in a given industry from their own overall projections of public and private expenditure.

These tables embody insights afforded "input-output" analysis [see "Input-Output Economics," by Wassily W. Leontief: *Scientific American*, October 1951]. This technique is

TABLE 2—DIRECT AND INDIRECT DEMAND BY DEMAND CATEGORY

(MILLIONS OF 1947 DOLLARS)

Production by Sector	Personal Consumption	Business Investment	Residential Construction	Public Services Construction	Maintenance Construction	Exports (except military)	Government (nonmilitary)	Military	Total output
1 Food and Kindred products	86,166	754	462	70	351	5,766	1,362	1,513	96,444
2 Apparel and Textile-mill products	26,557	640	248	51	139	1,986	387	575	30,582
3 Leather products	3,314	117	23	8	19	113	77	116	3,786
4 Paper and Allied products	7,333	926	408	133	380	793	542	788	11,303
5 Chemicals and Allied products	10,208	1,047	380	126	853	1,960	1,183	877	16,634
6 Fuel and Power	26,530	1,969	557	553	623	1,846	1,533	2,633	36,243
7 Rubber and Rubber products	2,727	588	85	65	74	388	163	244	4,333
8 Lumber and Wood products	4,918	2,309	2,446	120	883	340	198	451	11,665
9 Nonmetallic Minerals and products	1,940	1,776	1,150	711	756	305	150	337	7,123
10 Primary Metals	8,138	7,393	1,092	651	1,434	2,445	695	3,384	25,230
11 Fabricated Metal products	5,988	4,462	1,147	428	1,438	945	382	1,281	16,071
12 Machinery (except Electrical)	3,635	7,947	205	190	204	2,237	537	823	15,780
13 Electrical Machinery	5,757	4,128	343	121	407	852	245	3,110	14,962
14 Transportation Equipment and Ordnance	10,421	4,090	145	139	131	1,443	640	10,609	27,617
15 Instruments and Allied products	786	377	23	37	22	160	61	370	1,835
16 Miscellaneous Manufacturing Industries	3,403	235	35	14	36	166	218	119	4,225
17 Transportation	15,147	2,261	951	512	675	2,658	1,418	1,486	25,108
18 Trade	44,420	4,168	1,489	254	1,334	1,350	537	735	54,287
19 Service and Finance	118,402	3,196	1,350	913	893	2,410	12,204	1,886	141,254
20 Construction		16,844	12,082	5,956	10,429			967	46,278
21 Unallocated and Waste products	9,583	2,172	490	190	433	1,270	1,143	2,144	17,426

The total—direct and indirect—dependence of the production sectors on the military and nonmilitary demand categories is shown here. The column at right shows the total outputs of the sectors. Each column to the left shows how much the outputs would be reduced if that category of demand were eliminated. The figures in each case include direct deliveries to the demand category plus deliveries to other industries needed to permit them to make their deliveries to this demand category. The figures are thus larger than those in Table 1; compare, for example, the "Rubber and Rubber products" entry in the "Military" column in these two tables.

used today in many countries by governments and private businesses to chart the state of the national economy and to appraise the implications of specific economic actions that might affect its course. It anchors forecasting in the relatively stable fine structure of the economy and develops the important indirect relationships among the interdependent elements in the system.

In the highly integrated U.S. economy, for example, many industries deliver a large part or even all of their output not to final users but to other industries; in other words, a part or all of their output serves the needs of final users indirectly rather than directly. This does not make their dependence on the level and the structure of final demand any weaker, but it does make it more difficult to measure.

In order to determine how much the demand for crude sulfur would diminish if the Army cut its purchases of trucks by $1 million, one must determine how much crude sulfur the chemical industry needs to make $1 million worth of sulfuric acid, how much sulfuric acid is used in the finishing of $1 million worth of steel sheet and how much steel sheet goes into $1 million worth of trucks. This is only one of several such linked chains connecting the output of crude sulfur to the final sales of automobiles. The input-output table of a national economy incorporates just this kind of information. The table (more properly a deck of punched cards or a magnetic tape) of interindustry relationships shows how much of the product of every other industry each industry requires to make one unit of its output. It also shows the distribution

TABLE 3—DIRECT AND INDIRECT DEMAND PER $1,000,000 DIRECT PURCHASES BY DEMAND CATEGORY

(1947 DOLLARS)

Production by sector	Personal Consumption	Business Investment	Residential Construction	Public Services Construction	Maintenance Construction	Exports (except military)	Exports to India (except food)	Government (nonmilitary)	Military
1 Food and Kindred products	294,127	16,362	24,459	9,022	19,839	255,386	[98,413]	36,623	36,374
2 Apparel and Textile-mill products	90,653	13,880	13,100	6,525	7,842	87,987	[99,471]	10,400	13,825
3 Leather products	11,312	2,534	1,196	991	1,084	5,014	[3,704]	2,063	2,777
4 Paper and Allied products	25,032	20,095	21,596	17,156	21,425	35,108	[40,741]	14,565	18,959
5 Chemicals and Allied products	34,844	22,704	20,119	16,255	48,168	86,818	[134,392]	31,823	21,087
6 Fuel and Power	90,560	42,703	29,477	71,145	35,194	81,773	[94,709]	41,219	63,309
7 Rubber and Rubber products	9,309	12,750	4,473	8,314	4,189	17,178	[25,926]	4,384	5,858
8 Lumber and Wood products	16,788	50,093	129,461	15,405	49,822	15,038	[19,577]	5,333	10,850
9 Nonmetallic Minerals and products	6,621	38,512	60,880	91,441	42,675	13,488	[23,810]	4,026	8,092
10 Primary Metals	27,778	160,366	57,794	83,745	80,929	108,279	[119,577]	18,694	81,373
11 Fabricated Metal products	20,439	96,788	60,705	55,045	81,189	41,867	[46,561]	10,284	30,812
12 Machinery (except Electrical)	12,409	172,381	10,872	24,466	11,540	99,101	[164,021]	14,439	19,788
13 Electrical Machinery	19,652	89,534	18,139	15,611	22,972	37,726	[61,905]	6,581	74,779
14 Transportation Equipment and Ordnance	35,572	88,705	7,691	17,851	7,396	63,895	[158,730]	17,206	255,126
15 Instruments and Allied products	2,680	8,184	1,228	4,736	1,225	7,074	[13,228]	1,638	8,890
16 Miscellaneous Manufacturing Industries	11,615	5,095	1,826	1,828	2,044	7,340	[4,233]	5,860	2,869
17 Transportation	51,703	49,041	50,336	65,933	38,108	117,736	[233,333]	38,129	35,729
18 Trade	151,627	90,410	78,802	32,716	75,295	59,816	[106,878]	14,439	17,667
19 Service and Finance	404,164	69,329	71,466	117,542	50,421	106,722	[91,005]	328,208	45,348
20 Construction		365,364	639,496	766,538	588,777				23,254
21 Unallocated and Waste products	32,711	47,113	25,925	24,402	24,462	56,272	[89,947]	30,739	51,567

The columns show the output required of each production sector to fulfill the direct and indirect demand (*see Table 2*) generated by $1 million of direct purchases in each demand category. One can now estimate the outputs needed to fulfill any given final demand: simply multiply each figure in a column by the total assumed demand in that category. Multiplication of the figures in the "Military" column by the 1958-dollar total military expenditure in Table 1 reproduces the "Military" column in Table 2. The figures may be regarded as ratios reflecting constant structural relations between demand categories and production sectors.

of the output of each industry to every other industry and to the various categories of final demand.

As can be imagined, the preparation of such a table represents a major fact-finding and analytical task. The last complete, detailed input-output table of the U.S. was constructed for the year 1947. A trial check shows, however, that the structural relationships shown for that year will yield a reasonably good description of inter-industry relationships in 1958. In the tables presented here the description of the interindustry relations, that is, the input-output matrix itself, has been omitted in order to bring into relief the less obvious but crucially important structural relationships between the industries

and the various kinds of demand they serve. In other words, our tables show the end product of analytical computations, not the raw statistical material that went into them.

The industries have been aggregated in 20 or 58 production "sectors." The horizontal rows in each case show the output of each sector as they are distributed to various categories of civilian and military demand. The categories of demand approximate those in which the gross national product is commonly stated and the columns under each demand heading show the input of each production sector to that category in demand.

The first seven tables constitute the set of "tools" for working out the repercussions of an assumed step in disarmament and the accompanying transfer of expenditures to other categories of demand. The eighth table shows the answers yielded by such analysis in one particular, typical case.

The basic economic data for the year 1958 are presented in the first pair of tables. The figures in Table 1 are those in which the workings of the economy are commonly stated; they show only the direct purchases from each industry by each type of demand. For technical and statistical reasons the industry-by-industry outputs are stated in 1947 dollars, the figures in the columns therefore do not add up to the totals in 1958 dollars printed in the bottom row. Conceptually it is best to regard these 1947 figures as standing for physical quantities measured not in tons, yards or bushels, but rather in units defined as "the amounts of the respective goods that could be purchased for $1 million at the prices prevailing in 1947."

Table 2 gives effect to the interindustry transactions and thus shows the true total dependence of each industry on each type of demand. At the end of each row is shown the total 1958 output of the industry in question. The entries to the left of it show by how much the total output would have been diminished if the direct purchases in that category of demand (*shown in Table 1*) had been reduced to zero. Thus the entries in the "Military" services column show that complete elimination of the military budget would have reduced the demand for "Food and Kindred products" by $1,513 million, for "Apparel" by $575 million, and so on. These figures are considerably larger than the figures in the corresponding boxes in Table 1. The reason for this is that the direct-purchase figures show only the goods delivered to the military establishment, while the figures in Table 2 show the indirect as well as direct military demand and include the goods and services that must be delivered to other industries that need these inputs in order to produce, in their turn, the goods and services demanded by the final military users. Thus, as Table 1 shows, the rubber industry delivered in 1958 only $6 million worth of its goods to the military establishment. Table 2 shows, however, that a much larger part of its total output, $244 million, depended upon military demand. All told, the $41.6 billion ($16.7 billion in 1947 dollars) of direct purchases for military purposes in 1958 generated a total of some $86 billion ($34.5 billion in 1947 dollars) of direct and indirect military demand in the economy as a whole.

In the next pair of tables the relationships developed in Table 2 are restated in a form that begins to make them useful for purposes of analysis. It now becomes possible to deal with the question of how the sales and employment of various industries would be affected by a cut in military demand and a corresponding increase in one or another category of civilian demand. Table 3 shows the quantity of goods and services each industry has to produce in order to enable the economy as a whole to satisfy $1 million worth of direct purchases in any one category of demand. With these figures it is possible to estimate the total output of each industry that would be developed under any set of assumptions about the magnitude of expenditures in the various demand categories. In other words, the figures are useful for economic forecasting in general, quite apart from the question of disarmament. All of the figures in the main body of Table 2 can be synthesized, for example, by multiplying each one of the 1958 expenditure totals in Table 1 by the entries in the corresponding columns of Table 3.

In Table 4 the output figures of Table 3 are translated into figures that show the volume of employment, industry by industry, engaged directly and indirectly in satisfying $100 million worth of direct purchases in each category of demand. This table may therefore be used along with Table 3 in estimating the detailed consequences of one or another change in the total pattern of demand. One simply multiplies the figures in each column by the assumed or given total expenditure in that demand category and thereby determines the level of employment in each industry that corresponds to that volume of expenditure. Again, as in the case of Table 3, the actual 1958 employment figures can be synthesized by performing these multiplications with the 1958 expenditure totals given in Table 1.

For the specific purpose of conjuring with the effects of a transfer of expenditures from the military to the various categories of civilian demand, Table 5 and Table 6 provide a way to short-cut the task of computation. These tables show the net effect on the sales (or employment of each industry that would result from the transfer of $1 million (or $100 million) from the "Military" column in each of the other demand columns. The order of columns and rows has been arranged in these tables so as to segregate the bold figures—the negative changes in output and demand—above the diagonal falling from left to right. (The regular figures

TABLE 4—TOTAL EMPLOYMENT PER $100 MILLION DIRECT PURCHASES BY DEMAND CATEGORY

(1958 MAN-YEARS)

Employment by sector	Personal Consumption	Business Investment	Residential Construction	Public Services Construction	Maintenance Construction	Exports (except military)	Exports to India (except food)	Government (nonmilitary)	Military
1 Food and Kindred products	498	21	28		20	374	[128]	56	53
2 Apparel and Textile-mill products	658	80	72	35	41	502	[560]	66	86
3 Leather products	107	24	11	9	10	47	[34]	19	27
4 Paper and Allied products	121	97	104	85	105	170	[197]	71	91
5 Chemicals and Allied products	180	128	94	85	211	481	[660]	168	128
6 Fuel and Power	359	163	114	236	127	283	[318]	172	220
7 Rubber and Rubber products	54	74	27	49	24	100	[151]	26	34
8 Lumber and Wood products	141	421	1,084	126	420	126	[164]	45	92
9 Nonmetallic Minerals and products	60	348	548	828	385	123	[217]	36	73
10 Primary Metals	133	782	262	435	380	496	[599]	88	364
11 Fabricated Metal products	160	695	387	386	500	333	[392]	90	258
12 Machinery (except Electrical)	97	1,379	85	175	88	755	[1,301]	108	169
13 Electrical Machinery	145	781	110	91	153	313	[513]	51	662
14 Transportation Equipment and Ordnance	156	466	38	73	36	370	[991]	78	2,467
15 Instruments and Allied products	36	110	17	63	16	94	[177]	22	119
16 Miscellaneous Manufacturing Industries	103	45	16	14	17	65	[37]	52	25
17 Transportation	518	488	506	669	380	764	[1,523]	383	322
18 Trade	2,674	1,600	1,369	616	1,297	1,060	[1,900]	258	322
19 Service and Finance	3,715	705	665	856	391	937	[883]	9,296	584
20 Construction		2,091	3,658	4,396	3,364				134
Employees in Business Establishments	9,915	10,499	9,193	9,228	7,965	7,394	[10,746]	11,086	6,230
Households	870								
Government: Civilian								9,649	1,977
Armed Forces									6,329
Total Employees	10,785	10,499	9,193	9,228	7,965	7,394	[10,746]	20,734	14,536

The columns show the total employment (in 1958 man-years) required in each production sector to satisfy the direct and indirect demand generated by $100 million of direct purchases in each demand category. With these figures one may estimate the employment required in each production sector to fulfill any given final demand: multiply each figure in a column by the assumed demand in that category. Multiplication of figures in the "Military" column by the 1958-dollar total military expenditure in Table 1 shows this expenditure sustained 1,026,300 jobs in "Transportation Equipment and Ordnance" and 2,591,700 total "Business" jobs.

—the positive changes in output and demand— fall correspondingly below the diagonal.) The tables bring out clearly the pronounced differences in the responses of the various industries and the equally pronounced differences in the capacity of the various types of civilian demand to absorb the goods and services now serving final military demand.

The "Transportation Equipment and Ordnance" industry emerges in the **bold face** figures at the top of these tables as the one that depends most heavily upon military demand. This group of industries includes the aircraft, motor vehicle, shipbuilding and railway-equipment industries along with ordnance proper. It

is followed in the hierarchy of dependence upon military demand by "Instruments and Related Products" and "Electrical Machinery." On the other hand, in the lower rows of the table, the regular figures opposite the "Transportation," "Trade" and "Service and Finance" industries show that their outputs are bound to increase whichever type of civilian demand lays claim to the resources that are released from military needs.

The reader will note that the industries appear in a slightly different order in the two tables, suggesting that an increase in output could be accompanied in some cases by a decrease in employment. This apparent in-

TABLE 5—PRODUCTION BY SECTOR AFTER REALLOCATION OF $1,000,000 DIRECT MILITARY PURCHASES (THOUSANDS OF 1947 DOLLARS)

Production by sector	Exports to India (except food)	Exports (except military)	Business Investment	Personal Consumption	Public Services Construction	Residential Construction	Maintenance Construction	Government (nonmilitary)	Military
14 Transportation Equipment and Ordnance	96	191	166	220	237	247	248	238	255
15 Instruments and Allied products	4	2	1	6	4	8	8	7	9
13 Electrical Machinery	13	37	15	55	59	57	52	68	75
1 Food and Kindred products	62	219	20	258	27	12	17		36
3 Leather products	1	2		9	2	2	2	1	3
2 Apparel and Textile-mill products	85	74		77	7	1	6	3	14
12 Machinery (except Electrical)	144	79	153	7	5	9	8	5	20
6 Fuel and Power	31	18	21	27	8	34	28	22	63
10 Primary Metals	38	27	79	54	2	24		63	81
16 Miscellaneous Manufacturing Industries	1	4	2	9	1	1	1	3	3
7 Rubber and Rubber products	20	11	7	3	2	1	2	1	6
9 Nonmetallic Minerals and products	16	5	30	1	83	53	35	4	8
11 Fabricated Metal products	16	11	66	10	24	30	50	21	31
5 Chemicals and Allied products	113	66	2	14	5	1	27	11	21
4 Paper and Allied products	22	16	1	6	2	3	3	4	19
8 Lumber and Wood products	9	4	39	6	5	119	39	6	11
17 Transportation	198	82	13	16	30	15	2	2	36
18 Trade	89	42	73	134	15	61	58	3	18
19 Service and Finance	46	61	24	359	72	26	5	283	45
20 Construction	23	23	342	23	743	616	566	23	23

This table, Table 6 and Table 7 are designed to short-cut the computations involved in analysis of the consequences of disarmament. The columns here show the net increase or decrease (*bold figures*) in the output of each production sector resulting from the transfer of $1 million of demand from the military to each of the eight nonmilitary categories of demand. The figures were obtained by subtracting from the entries in each of the first eight columns in Table 3 the corresponding entries in the "Military" column shown at far right. In this table the columns and rows have been rearranged to segregate bold and regular figures.

consistency is a consequence of the necessarily gross "product mix" involved in summarizing the industrial economy in only 20 sectors; it reflects the fact that the principal increases in output are coming in these cases from industries having a lower ratio of labor to output. Since employment is necessarily foremost among the concerns in any economic forecast, the industry-by-industry employment figures are shown in the fine detail of a 58-industry breakdown in Table 7.

What would be the effect on employment of a 20 per cent, or $8 billion, cut in a $40 billion military budget if this cut were accompanied by an equal increase in nonmilitary expenditures? Taking the simple case of the transfer of the entire expenditure to one or another category of civilian demand, one need

only multiply the figures in the chosen category in Table 7 by 80. Thus on the unlikely assumption that the entire expenditure is moved into the "Government" column (which comprises all governmental demand except for military and construction activities of the Government), as many as 329,000 jobs held in private business establishments would be eliminated, and this would be offset by the creation of 717,000 new jobs in other private industries. The equally unlikely shift of demand to "Exports" to foreign countries would cause far less strain as measured in turnover of the labor force (only 249,000 jobs would be lost and 342,000 new jobs created). As this result suggests, exports draw upon much the same industries as the military, though for different products. The column "Exports to India," which appears in all the tables except 2 and 8, makes it possible to perform similar

TABLE 6—EMPLOYMENT BY SECTOR AFTER REALLOCATION OF $100 MILLION DIRECT MILITARY PURCHASES

(1958 MAN-YEARS)

Employment by sector	Exports to India (except food)	Exports (except military)	Business Investment	Personal Consumption	Public Services Construction	Residential Construction	Maintenance Construction	Government (nonmilitary)
14 Transportation Equipment and Ordnance	1,476	2,097	2,001	2,311	2,394	2,429	2,431	2,389
15 Instruments and Applied products	57	25	9	83	56	102	103	97
13 Electrical Machinery	149	349	119	517	571	552	509	611
2 Apparel and Textile-mill products	473	416	6	572	51	14	45	20
3 Leather products	8	20	3	80	18	16	17	8
6 Fuel and Power	98	63	57	139	16	106	93	48
12 Machinery (except Electrical)	1,132	586	1,210	72	6	84	81	61
1 Food and Kindred products	75	321	32	445	53	25	33	3
16 Miscellaneous Manufacturing Industries	12	40	20	78	11	9	8	27
7 Rubber and Rubber products	117	66	40	20	15	7	10	8
10 Primary Metals	235	132	418	231	71	102	16	276
5 Chemicals and Applied products	532	353	0	52	43	34	83	40
9 Nonmetallic Minerals and products	144	50	275	13	755	475	312	37
11 Fabricated Metal products	143	75	437	98	128	129	242	168
4 Paper and Allied products	106	79	6	30	6	13	14	20
8 Lumber and Wood products	72	34	329	49	34	992	328	47
18 Trade	1,578	738	1,278	2,352	294	1,047	975	64
19 Service and Finance	247	353	121	3,131	272	81	193	8,712
17 Transportation	1,147	442	166	196	347	184	58	61
20 Construction	134	134	1,957	134	4,262	3,524	3,230	134
Net Increase in Business Employment	4,516	1,163	4,268	3,685	2,997	2,963	1,735	4,855
Total Negative Change	1,625	2,471	2,108	3,325	3,203	3,480	3,523	3,854
Total Negative Change (from Table 7)	2,897	3,117	2,768	3,610	3,724	3,746	3,911	4,114

The columns in this table show the net increase or decrease (*bold figures*) in employment (in 1958 man-years) in each production sector resulting from the transfer of $100 million of demand from the military to each of the seven nonmilitary categories of demand. The "Net Increase in Business Employment" figures are net after subtracting the negative changes shown in this table and totaled in the "Total Negative Change" row below. The "Total Negative Change (from Table 7)' row shows that a larger number of job holders would have to seek re-employment than is indicated by the coarser industrial breakdown in this table.

computations with the quite different bill of goods that would be involved in a substantial increase in economic aid to underdeveloped countries.

Table 8 shows the effects upon employment in the 58 industries that follow from a more reasonable assumption: the projected $8 billion cut in the military budget is here transferred pro rata to the various categories of civilian demand, leaving their relative magnitudes unchanged. As can be seen, a total of 253,815 jobs would be eliminated in 19 industries and a total of 541,855 new jobs would be created in the other 38 industries—a net gain of 288,040 jobs. For purposes of comparison, it may be observed that during the recession of 1957 and 1958, employment fell in 54 and expanded in only four of the 58 industries; the combined loss of jobs amounted at that time to 1,411,000 man-years and the gain to only 7,000.

The net increases in "Business Employment" indicated in the transfer of expenditures from military to civilian demand are important, for it is likely that disarmament would be accompanied by the release of large numbers of civilian and uniformed personnel of the Department of Defense. If the cuts in personnel were directly proportional to the cut in the budget, then each $100 million cut would be accompanied by the release of 1,977 civilian workers and 6,329 uniformed men. Not one of the net increases in total business employment computed in Tables 7 and 8 would be adequate to absorb entirely this addition to rolls of job seekers. The tables provide the means, however, for trying out sets of assumptions different from the simple one demonstrated here.

The analytical methods employed in this

(1958 MAN-YEARS)

		Exports (except military)	Exports to India (except food)	Business Investment	Personal Consumption	Public Services Construction	Maintenance Construction	Residential Construction	Government (nonmilitary)
14	Aircraft and Parts	1,653.5	1,554.7	1,652.9	1,703.8	1,707.1	1,707.1	1,707.1	1,705.0
14	Ordnance	341.7	341.7	341.7	341.7	341.7	341.7	341.7	341.7
14	Ships and Boats	275.1	267.6	271.0	338.5	349.1	343.6	343.0	343.9
13	Radio	408.3	352.6	238.9	433.3	497.3	466.8	497.3	482.8
10	Aluminium	7.6	9.9	4.0	25.1	21.7	12.2	20.4	26.4
15	Instruments	24.3	58.3	9.1	82.7	55.5	102.2	101.7	96.8
2	Apparel	5.0	23.1	24.3	390.6	27.1	27.1	27.1	.2
10	Copper	8.0	7.9	12.0	30.8	19.2	12.0	12.0	32.9
5	Plastics	51.8	14.4	4.7	27.1	27.7	19.3	26.4	34.6
17	Overseas Transportation (Water)	103.3	228.0	9.7	6.6	9.7	10.0	10.2	7.5
17	Other Transportation	33.8	9.7	64.3	73.7	44.0	66.9	64.4	50.5
6	Electric Light and Power	14.8	2.1	11.2	72.2	21.8	29.9	23.9	23.1
19	Professional and Services	219.6	189.9	10.3	1,011.0	185.1	246.5	26.1	8,555.7
13	Motors, Generators	.6	60.2	61.0	67.2	62.3	66.5	68.9	76.2
10	Other Nonferrous Metals	4.4	18.8	16.9	31.6	25.3	13.3	22.7	38.0
11	Metal Stamping	1.9	55.4	18.9	51.2	66.8	64.1	68.5	67.9
12	Machine Tools	66.3	337.3	150.0	37.3	37.6	43.0	42.9	39.6
6	Petroleum	1.4	63.2	75.9	4.5	3.7	74.2	91.5	86.8
12	Power Transmission Equipment	24.5	77.5	31.3	8.3	3.6	13.7	14.2	12.5
12	Engines and Turbines	83.5	108.3	50.4	10.8	9.8	13.7	14.0	6.7
11	Metal Containers	16.3	11.0	2.0	7.2	5.6	3.0	6.2	7.2
13	Electrical Equipment (N.E.C.)	50.2	94.6	222.3	9.1	14.0	8.3	6.3	17.5
12	Industrial Machinery	116.6	162.6	531.9	29.9	33.2	26.5	25.3	29.5
3	Leather and Leather Products	20.7	6.9	2.6	80.0	17.7	16.5	15.6	7.6
1	Livestock, Poultry	42.1	27.6	14.1	113.8	19.5	12.1	15.3	1.2
14	Railway Equipment	47.7	440.2	33.1	5.8	3.0	6.0	5.7	3.2
10	Iron and Steel Forging	12.2	82.0	63.8	56.8	36.7	38.4	38.5	63.6
11	Cutlery, Tools	25.9	28.8	56.5	41.0	7.8	5.8	17.2	54.1
5	Medical Supplies	62.6	142.0	9.0	23.5	10.1	8.8	9.5	22.0
1	Food Products	218.7	5.5	21.8	271.0	30.2	24.6	24.9	3.7
13	Insulated Wire and Cable	1.8	45.6	71.1	29.0	9.5	28.7	13.5	33.7
10	Iron and Steel	115.3	152.2	329.7	86.3	100.7	92.1	8.7	114.7
5	Organic Chemicals	90.2	117.2		9.3	8.7	3.8	8.2	4.4
7	Rubber and Rubber products	66.0	116.6	40.4	20.4	14.8	9.8	7.1	8.3
11	Plumbing Fixtures	5.8	4.1	28.2	1.6	3.8	149.4	95.4	9.6
16	Miscellaneous Manufacturing Industries	39.5	11.9	20.1	77.8	11.0	8.3	9.3	27.2
2	Textile Mill	421.0	497.1	17.8	181.1	24.5	18.0	13.3	19.9
1	Grain and Feed Crops	9.6	1.7	.3	5.0	1.0	.1	.1	.2
4	Paper and Allied Products	79.0	106.0	6.8	30.6	5.7	14.4	13.7	19.9
5	Inorganic Chemicals	63.8	60.2	.3	7.1	4.4	2.5	3.5	62.8
11	Fabricated Metals	25.4	43.6	335.6	14.6	212.5	165.3	91.2	29.5
9	Nonmetallic Minerals	49.8	144.0	274.8	12.9	754.6	312.1	475.5	36.6
19	Business Services	200.0	389.7	50.0	465.2	197.4	18.0	3.7	14.1
14	Motor Vehicles	125.9	247.5	231.6	78.8	7.3	33.0	31.4	5.3
12	Farm, Building, Mining Machinery	198.6	242.0	347.0	.8	76.2	5.6	2.8	27.7
5	Miscellaneous Chemicals	84.0	198.5	13.0	28.9	7.6	104.2	13.6	5.9
8	Lumber, Wood products	33.9	71.9	328.9	49.2	34.2	328.1	991.6	47.0
12	Pumps, Compressors	96.6	204.5	99.6	15.2	13.9	10.3	15.3	.7
13	Electrical Appliances	5.9	3.2	3.1	20.8	12.0	3.4	6.1	1.5
18	Trade	737.9	1,577.5	1,277.0	2,351.6	294.0	974.9	1,046.2	64.9
1	Tobacco, Alcoholic Beverages	50.3	40.4	3.9	55.4	2.4	3.8	14.5	.3
17	Railroads, Trucking	373.5	983.4	240.8	129.0	401.4	135.4	258.6	18.7
6	Coal and Coke	73.0	30.4	25.5	28.2	27.5	9.3	6.2	14.5
6	Gas Utilities	2.9	6.0	4.2	42.4	5.6	1.3	2.5	1.3
19	Auto and other repairs	15.0	19.7	39.0	83.4	177.2	44.4	37.2	14.1
19	Banking, Finance	138.9	79.7	42.4	714.6	82.3	27.2	73.3	30.2
19	Restaurants, Hotels, Amusements	218.4			856.3				97.6
20	Construction	133.7	133.7	1,957.1	133.7	4,262.7	3,229.9	3,524.2	133.7
	Business Employment: Increase	4,280.7	7,413.1	7,036.0	7,294.9	6,722.1	5,646.2	6,709.2	8,968.8
	Decrease	3,117.4	2,897.0	2,767.8	3,610.4	3,724.5	3,910.9	3,746.0	4,113.9
	Net Change	1,163.3	4,516.1	4,268.2	3,684.5	2,997.6	1,735.3	2,963.2	4,854.9
	Total Employment: Increase	4,280.7	7,413.1	7,036.0	8,165.3	6,722.1	5,646.2	6,709.2	16,641.0
	Decrease	11,423.2	11,202.8	11,073.6	11,916.2	12,030.3	12,216.7	12,051.8	10,443.0
	Net Change	7,142.5	3,789.7	4,037.6	3,750.9	5,308.8	6,570.5	5,342.6	6,198.0

The columns in this table provide the same information as Table 6; that is, they show the net change in employment resulting from the transfer of £100 million of demand from the military to each of the non-military demand categories. But they relate this information to a finer breakdown of 58 production sectors. The key numbers at left show to which of the 20 larger sectors in the other tables each of these production sectors belongs. The figures at bottom show that the net increase in business employment would be offset in all but one demand category by release of uniformed and civilian personnel directly employed by Department of Defense.

TABLE 8—EMPLOYMENT AFTER REALLOCATION OF $8 BILLION MILITARY
PURCHASES TO OTHER DEMAND CATEGORIES

(THOUSANDS OF 1958 MAN-YEARS)

		Change in employment	Per cent change in employment
14	Ordnance	27,336.0	19.24
14	Aircraft and Parts	135,600.0	17.90
14	Ships and Boats	26,320.8	10.99
13	Radio	33,036.8	6.07
10	Aluminium	1,707.2	2.82
15	Instruments	5,944.0	2.42
10	Copper	2,022.4	2.36
13	Motors, Generators	4,086.4	2.04
10	Iron and Steel Forging	3,050.4	1.31
10	Other Nonferrous Metals	1,920.0	1.31
11	Metal Stamping	3,526.4	1.06
5	Plastics	1,152.8	.70
11	Cutlery, Tools	1,924.0	.70
13	Insulated Wire and Cable	1,035.2	.61
12	Machine Tools	1,055.2	.47
6	Petroleum	1,988.8	.38
12	Power Transmission Equipment	258.4	.29
17	Overseas Transportation (Water)	139.2	.27
10	Iron and Steel	1,711.2	.26
12	Engine and Turbines	38.4	.04
4	Paper and Allied products	1,945.6	.36
11	Metal Containers	344.0	.44
5	Organic Chemicals	800.8	.46
17	Other Transportation	3,064.8	.60
7	Rubber and Rubber products	1,592.0	.63
17	Railroads, Trucking	12,338.4	.67
13	Electrical Equipment (N.E.C.)	1,388.0	.67
6	Electric Light and Power	3,609.6	.73
5	Inorganic Chemicals	1,048.0	.74
12	Industrial Machinery	2,915.2	.74
11	Fabricated Metals	3,062.4	.78
9	Nonmetallic Minerals	5,231.2	.81
6	Coal and Coke	2,186.4	.92
11	Plumbing Fixtures	1,073.6	.93
5	Miscellaneous Chemicals	2,328.0	.94
8	Lumber, Wood products	9,634.4	.98
19	Business Services	26,111.2	1.00
14	Motor Vehicles	6,437.6	1.01
3	Leather and Leather products	4,108.0	1.15
5	Medical Supplies	1,694.4	1.17
16	Miscellaneous Manufacturing Industries	4,548.0	1.21
2	Textile Mill	11,252.0	1.24
12	Pumps, Compressors	2,124.8	1.26
20	Construction	36,086.4	1.36
1	Livestock, Poultry	5,940.8	1.40
1	Grain and Feed Crops	297.6	1.40
13	Electrical Appliances	1,187.2	1.44
12	Farm, Building, Mining Machinery	3,953.6	1.44
19	Professional and Services	108,730.4	1.46
6	Gas Utilities	2,317.6	1.47
18	Trade	144,533.6	1.51
19	Auto and Other Repairs	5,402.4	1.51
1	Food products	14,848.0	1.53
2	Apparel	20,199.2	1.61
19	Banking, Finance	39,332.0	1.66
1	Tobacco, Alcoholic Beverages	3,225.6	1.69
19	Restaurants, Hotels, Amusements	46,824.8	1.81
14	Railway Equipment	99.2	1.95
	Business Employment: Increase	541,855.2	1.42
	Decrease	253,815.2	6.85
	Net Change	288,040.0	.69
	Total Employment: Increase	639,376.5	1.41
	Decrease	760,135.2	11.99
	Net Change	120,758.7	.22

The figures here reflect the changes in employment by the 58 production sectors that would follow from a 20 per cent, or $8 billion, cut in
military expenditure and reallocation of this demand proportionally to
other demand categories. The totals show a net increase of 288,040 job
openings under "Business Employment" but a net deficit of 120,759 job
openings under "Total Employment," resulting from release of personnel by the military.

study can obviously be used to answer many further questions. How would the industrial impact of disarmament be felt in various parts of the country? What would be the magnitude—and the effect on other industries—of the short-run production bottlenecks that could prevent some industries from supplying the additional output called for by changes in the composition of demand? How would the creation of the additional productive capacities required to meet such increased demand affect the level of output in industries supplying the requisite capital goods?

In making use of the material presented here, and in formulating additional questions, it is most important to keep in mind the fact that military expenditures constitute only one factor affecting the state of the U.S. economy. Since a substantial portion of the economic resources now serving military needs could be used to increase private or public investment, the question of the economic implications of the disarmament necessarily leads to the more general problem of economic development and growth. In so far as foreign trade, and in particular foreign aid, enter into the picture, the effects of reduced military expenditures would have to be traced beyond the borders of our own national economy. This means that the present study does not pretend to answer all the questions, and suggests the nature of the fact-finding labor that is required if major economic changes are to be subjected to concrete, quantitative analysis.

Charles J. Hitch

National security policy as a field for economics research[*]

I

PROBLEMS OF NATIONAL SECURITY are in no sense novel for the application of economic analysis. Adam Smith, in a well-known passage in *The Wealth of Nations*, was concerned with the allocation of resources between "defense" and "opulence"—what we would call the prob-

lem of the size of the national security budget. There has been great interest among economists, especially during and following the First and Second World Wars, in problems of industrial mobilization during war, including the associated problems of economic stabilization. In fact, to many economists during the past generation this set of mobilization problems

[*] This article was written at the request of the Committee on National Security Policy Research of the Social Science Research Council. It is not an attempt to provide a comprehensive or definitive outline of a program of research, but a highly personal essay which I hope will stimulate interest and have some influence on the direction of national security policy research among economists. It does, however,

reflect the suggestions made at a conference on Economic Research on National Security convened by Klaus Knorr for the Social Science Research Council in New York, January 31 and February 1, 1958. I have developed some of my views at greater length in a book, *The Economics of Defense in the Nuclear Age*, by C. J. Hitch and R. N. McKean, Harvard University Press.

Reprinted from *World Politics*, Vol. XII, No. 3, April 1960, pp. 434–448.

constituted *the* economics of defense. Books were published with titles like *Economics of Defense* that dealt with little else.

My principal theme in this research note is that changes in the technology of war have so degraded the significance of wartime mobilization problems that these are no longer very interesting or important for economic policy research; but that these same changes in technology have brought to the fore a new set of problems that constitute an opportunity for and a challenge to economists.

I am referring, of course, to the development of nuclear weapons and advanced systems for delivering them at great distances—long-range bombers, nuclear-powered submarines, and intercontinental missiles. I will here simply state, without attempting to marshal the evidence,[1] that either the United States or the USSR has the power to destroy the industrial mobilization potential of the other in a matter of hours, and within a few years will be able to do so in a few minutes. So may other powers.

In consequence, what matters most in all-out war is the *forces-in-being* at the outset. The initial exchange of thermonuclear blows is likely to be decisive. Even if it is not, nothing remotely like the industrial mobilization of World War I or World War II will follow.

I am by no means implying that future wars will necessarily be all-out (or "general" or "thermonuclear") wars.[2] If deterrent forces are made invulnerable, other kinds of war are certainly more likely to occur. Since the end of World War II there have been many "limited" wars of various sorts—wars in which the major nuclear powers had limited (even if important) interests and objectives, and so were willing to fight by proxy, or, if as principals, with self-imposed constraints on weapons and/or the geographic area of combat. There is every reason to expect that similar wars, like the Korean, the Indo-Chinese, and the Greek civil war, will threaten our security in the future. It is even possible that the loss of the U.S. nuclear monopoly makes serious but less than all-out military challenges more likely in the future than they have been in the past. In addition, we are currently engaged in a contest with the Soviet bloc which is appropriately known as "cold war," using diplomatic and economic weapons, with military moves restricted to threats, feints, displays, and deployments. This kind of contest also seems likely to persist for an indefinite period.

Both limited wars and cold war present important and interesting problems for economics research. These problems tend to be very different from those associated with all-out nuclear war, but are like them in not being problems of industrial mobilization.

What then are the economic problems of national security in the nuclear era? Or, more precisely, what are the economic aspects of national security problems?

One complication in answering this question is that no one has ever defined the content of economics to the general satisfaction of economists, and there exists in consequence some disagreement about what is and what is not an "economic" problem or aspect of a problem. There have been two general classes of definitions: (1) The first relates economics to the *economy*—to a complex of producing, marketing, distributing, and consuming institutions and activities. (2) The second relates economics to *economizing*—to a certain kind of rational choosing and behaving, to making the most of one's resources in achieving one's objectives, in whatever kind of institutional framework.

Of course, there is a large area of overlap between these two classes of definitions. We assume, almost certainly correctly, that men in their wealth producing and acquiring activities are especially inclined to *economize*, i.e. to minimize costs, or to maximize the achievement of objectives with given resources, in a careful and explicit way. But people in other activities, outside the institutions of the economy as these are usually understood in the first class of definitions, also economize in this manner, or want to, or in some important sense ought to. These include people concerned with national security, and in consequence a lot of economic theory—of the analysis of economizing—can be applied, if appropriately adapted, to the solution of their problems. The design of a system for ordering and stocking spare parts for aircraft is an economic problem, whether the aircraft are owned by a commercial airline or by the U.S. Air Force, although there are important differences stemming from the fact that the services of the former are sold on a market while the services of the latter are not. So is the choice between Bomarc and Nike-Hercules: which missile (or combination of the two) will provide the most economical (i.e., efficient) air defense of the United States? So, too, is the choice between military aid, on the one hand, and a larger budget for our own military forces, on the other.

II

I WILL now review the major national security areas where I think economic research— research concerned with the economy or with economizing—has something substantial to contribute to the understanding or solution of national security problems.

THE ANALYSIS AND MEASUREMENT OF ECONOMIC STRENGTH FOR WAR

In the period between the two world wars we grew accustomed to talking of "economic war potential," meaning the fully mobilized war-production capacity of a nation. The concept of maximum wartime output is no longer very important, but economic strength is still vital for national security. It is the source of the forces-in-being needed to deter or fight a general nuclear war. It makes it possible to meet less than all-out challenges and it deters limited aggression that may stimulate translation of potential into military strength. Economic capacity also provides the sinews of many of our cold war moves—including the aid program and measures to reduce the West's vulnerability to economic pressure by the Soviet bloc.

But the economic strength that is important in all-out nuclear war is not potential, but translated strength.[3] And there is no reason to presume that the relation between the two will be the same in different countries. A sizable national product is necessary, but not sufficient. The proportion of national product that a country allocates to national security will depend upon its surplus over demanded living standards, upon its comprehension of the challenge confronting it, and upon its resolution. The USSR, with a national product perhaps a third that of the United States, has been allocating a similar quantity of resources to its military forces.[4] Western Europe, with an aggregate product substantially in excess of that of the USSR, has been allocating much less.

We need a new analysis of the likely (and dangerous) kinds of wars, of the factors that are important in determining their outcomes, and of the way in which economic strength is related to these factors. We need new methods of measuring and comparing the economic strengths for war of different powers. How can the USSR maintain such formidable military power? Why cannot Western Europe? How important will it be a generation hence that

Russia's rate of industrial growth today appears to be substantially greater than ours?

These questions are not purely economic; they involve considerations of science and technology, of politics and psychology. But their economic aspects are substantial, and economists are probably in the best position to design the analysis and define and assemble inputs from other disciplines. On some of the technical problems of measuring and comparing national products and the military sectors of national products, economists have recently done some pioneering research.[5] But this is just a beginning.

IMPLICATIONS OF LARGE DEFENSE BUDGETS IN TIME OF PEACE

Until World War II the United States had characteristically devoted 1 or 2 per cent or even less of its national product to military purposes in time of peace. After World War II we demobilized rapidly. But the Korean War, beginning in 1950, and the accumulating evidence of the Russian military threat led to national security budgets in the United States ranging from 10 to 15 per cent of national product. Now, nine years later, they are still around 10 per cent. A new international crisis could send them higher, and there is little prospect of substantial reductions.

Military budgets of this magnitude have serious economic consequences that demand analysis if we are to understand them and mitigate those that are unfavorable. Some of the consequences are simply the result of high total government expenditure—e.g., the implications of the necessary high tax rates on incentives. Others (e.g., implications for stabilization) stem jointly from the high level and the fluctuating character of expenditures. Still others are more intimately related to the fact that the expenditures are military and are made within a specific institutional framework.

Economists have, of course, done a great deal of work on the incidence and effects of different kinds of taxes. Much of this work, however, has been a relatively barren effort to deduce effects from simple general psychological assumptions. It has long been known, for example, that even the sign of the effect of a progressive income tax on the supply of effort could not be determined by such methods; yet little empirical work has been undertaken to supply the needed answers.[7] Moreover, most economic research on taxation has been undertaken in an environment in which tax rates were lower than now, and the assumption of low average rates, made consciously or unconsciously, reduces the relevance of the conclusions in a situation in which 25 per cent, 30 per cent, or more of national income must be collected. In particular, distortions of incentives that are tolerable with low rates or temporarily high rates (as during short wars), may seriously disrupt the efficiency of the economy when rates are permanently high. An entirely new sort of compromise between the claims of equity and those of efficiency may be indicated.

Most economists believe that a very high level of government expenditure has an inflationary impact on the economy even if the budget is balanced by taxation. The same high level makes it easier to counter any deflationary movement by adjusting tax rates, although defense expenditures themselves, with their characteristically long lead-times, are no more promising than many civilian public works as a counter-cyclical device. Perhaps the more interesting and less well-understood problems involving stabilization are those resulting from large-scale and sudden changes in defense spending in either direction.

Associated with the stabilization problems are the problems of controls—direct vs. indirect. Are there any circumstances in which direct controls (of what type?) should be utilized during lengthy periods of preparedness or during periods of transition to higher or lower levels of expenditure?[8]

Finally, there are the special implications of high defense expenditures for the functioning of a free enterprise economy. One peculiarity of defense procurement, at least in this era of rapid technological advance, is the extremely limited scope for competitive bidding. There appears to be none whatever in the vast domain of research and development, and very little in the purchase of production quantities of weapons. Negotiated contracts of a "cost plus" character are the rule rather than the exception. In consequence a large sector of the American economy, including some of the most rapidly growing and technologically oriented industries, are largely removed from the guidance and incentive provided by the price system. The military departments attempt to prevent pocket lining and profiteering, in the absence of competitive bidding, by contract renegotiation, and by techniques of what are elsewhere regarded as management prerogatives. What long-run effects will negotiation, cost-plus, renegotiation, and control have on the efficiency

of the American economy, and what, if anything, can be done to find more suitable substitutes for the market mechanism?

Of course, not all effects of military expenditure are deleterious. The technological spillover into the civilian economy of military expenditures on research and development has been substantial, as has been the training by the military services of technicians, many of whom retire to civilian employment after their training has been completed. It would be interesting to try to compute some "net" cost of the peacetime defense budget.

HOW LARGE "SHOULD" THE DEFENSE BUDGET BE?

Public and Congressional debates on this question tend to center on two relatively sterile questions: How large a defense budget do we require? How much can the economy stand? Economists could perform a considerable service here (as elsewhere on this list) by simply illuminating the nature of the problem in publications and in terminology that will have some impact on officials. Allocation problems cannot be solved, except in rare special cases, by looking at the demand side alone or the supply side alone.

What do we require for national security? To be secure again, as we were in the nineteenth century, requires more than all the income and wealth in the United States. Absolute security has become unattainable. No practicable level of defense expenditure can insure against grievous damage from thermonuclear warheads. It may be that no practicable level of expenditure can insure "winning" in a meaningful sense.

And how large a budget can the economy stand? During World War II the military budget took 40 per cent of GNP. There is no economic reason why we cannot spend much more than 10 per cent (the current level) if we want to and are willing to make the sacrifices, and are clever enough to mitigate the worst effects by appropriate tax and fiscal measures. There have been various efforts to demonstrate this thesis, and to find possible limits beyond which different types of controls would be desirable.[9]

There is no escape from the necessity of comparing *at the margin* net costs to the economy (in other goods sacrificed, in inflationary pressures, in deleterious effects on efficiency) with net gains in security. That imponderables, incommensurables, and uncertainties make it impossible to perform this comparison as an explicit economic calculus does not mean that nothing interesting and useful can be said about it.[10]

Another promising line of attack for economists to pursue is to devise techniques for presenting costs and gains in more meaningful fashion to facilitate the exercise of judgment by officials, Congress, and the public. Traditional federal budget categories, which classify appropriations by such objects of expenditure as "personnel," "major equipment," "construction," etc., instead of by end-use functions, make it difficult or impossible to trace the effects on security of either cutting or increasing appropriations.[11]

EFFICIENCY IN USING AND MANAGING DEFENSE RESOURCES

The Department of Defense is, in effect, an enormous firm which buys factors of production and intermediate products, subject to budgetary constraints, and produces national security or "military worth." How can we help it accomplish this task efficiently—maximizing military worth for given resources, or minimizing resources for given military worth?

This is an economic problem (of the economizing sort) that requires attack at several different levels, and with different techniques. With very large defense budgets and the steadily increasing danger and destructiveness of war, it has become a tremendously important problem. At one extreme there is need for imaginative conceptual and theoretical work on the general problem of promoting efficient use of resources in an environment in which the market pattern is incomplete. While the defense departments usually purchase factors and products in markets (sometimes highly imperfect cost-plus markets), there are no markets for valuing the outputs (military capabilities or worths) they produce, and very few for valuing intermediate products within the government structure. There is a lot of ready-made economic theory that is applicable to this problem, but it requires development and adaptation. At the other extreme there is need for a great deal of applied economic research to contribute to the solution of specific national security problems like the design of efficient (i.e., economical) systems for deterrence.[12]

The incompleteness of the market structure means that prices cannot perform their function of facilitating commensurability: the gains and costs of military expenditures are seldom commensurable in any generally acceptable way; in addition there are often diverse incommensurable (if not imponderable) gains. This makes the selection of criteria and the design of economizing analyses more difficult than within a market economy.

There are other complications in finding efficient solutions to national security problems. There are formidable technological and strategic uncertainties in comparing, for example, alternative weapon systems. There is always an enemy to complicate our analyses as well as our lives. National security problems are not unique in any of these respects, but they provide a challenge for the development and application of decision theory, organization theory, probability theory, game theory, and operational gaming, and the relating of these to the efficient use of economic resources.[13] Economists have been slow in learning how to incorporate uncertainties in economic analysis. In defense economics, as elsewhere, dodges like "certainty equivalents" do not help.

Economists will be successful in tackling defense problems only if they accept modest objectives. Optima are unattainable in a world of incommensurables and uncertainties. But economizing does not necessarily require optimizing, in the military or in the economy. It simply requires finding *better* solutions than those that would otherwise be adopted. And this, in very many cases, is both a feasible and a practically important objective.

INSTITUTIONAL ARRANGEMENTS TO PROMOTE EFFICIENCY

In general, economists attempt to promote efficiency in that part of the economy subject to the price mechanism by suggesting improvements in the institutional environment rather than by the calculation of optimal allocations. There are somewhat similar possibilities within the military (and civil) bureaucracy that merit our attention. How can markets be simulated to advantage (as with stock and industrial funds)? Should there be more or less contracting with private industry (as opposed to "in-house" capability)? How can contracting with private industry be made more conducive to efficiency (incentive contracts, etc.)? How can budgeting and accounting techniques be improved to facilitate economic calculus? What is the appropriate role of specialized operations-research groups and of economists within them? How can perverse incentives in a bureaucracy (e.g., to spend effort in maximizing a budget instead of economizing within a budget) be reduced? What is the optimal compromise between centralization and decentralization of decision-making? How can bureaucratic bargaining be made to serve an economic function?[14]

MILITARY RESEARCH AND DEVELOPMENT

Research and development are a vitally important part of investment in which economists are beginning to take a serious interest.[15] How much should be spent on research and development? Is there a tendency for a competitive economy to underallocate for certain kinds of research and development? How should one choose among alternative development projects? How much duplication is desirable and in what circumstances? Military-sponsored R and D is a large proportion of total R and D and poses some special management problems.[16]

MILITARY LOGISTICS

Logistics is the business side of military preparedness and operations. It is concerned with procurement, spare parts supply, inventory policy, maintenance, transportation, and other aspects of business (or businesslike) management. It provides an opportunity for the fairly direct application of many facets of business economics.

But there is the usual difference—the principal objective of logistics is combat capability, present or future; and since combat capability is not sold on the market, it is impossible to apply a simple profit-maximizing criterion in designing, say, an optimal inventory policy. Within limits this difficulty can be overcome, or sidestepped, by designing an inventory policy that minimizes the cost of a given combat capability; and by examining the trade-offs between the cost of such an inventory and that of other elements affecting the same combat capability, like increased maintenance or the procurement of additional operational aircraft. But we are likely to be left with subtle problems like: Is a central reserve inventory of $1\frac{1}{2}$ X for two geographically separated units equal in contingency value to an inventory of X held by each unit? Even problems of this kind frequently yield to economic analysis if the analyst is content with simply doing better rather than finding an *optimum optimorum*.[17]

THE ECONOMICS OF MILITARY ALLIANCE

The problems of military alliance are closely analogous to the problems of international trade. What are the potential gains from taking advantage of comparative cost differentials and division of labor within an alliance, and to what extent can or should these gains be forsaken in view of the lack of perfect correspondence among the national objectives of the members of the alliance? It is important here to draw a distinction between specialization in military *function* (e.g., long-range missile force vs. infantry) and specialization in the *production* of weapons and equipment. In general, nations will be much more willing to rely on allies for supplies, even essential ones, than for essential forces, and this willingness should increase as forces in being gain in importance. It is less essential than it used to be that the "arsenal of democracy" be concentrated in an industrial nation far removed geographically from potential aggressors, since no nation is now far enough removed. But this same fact should provide increased opportunity for specialization in military production that is desirable on strictly economic grounds.

Other important politico-economic problems of military alliance relate to the sharing of the burden of defense. There have been attempts to apply tax theory to those problems.[18]

ECONOMIC WARFARE AND ECONOMIC FOREIGN POLICY[19]

Economic warfare, old style, was tied intimately to the notion of mobilization base. Its weapons were trade denial, preclusive buying, blacklisting, etc. The United States (and the whole West to a lesser extent) is still using trade denial and boycott against the Soviet bloc, particularly China, but the significance of such measures has declined and is declining. They damage the economic strength of both sides to a limited extent, and their net effect on relative strength is problematic and certainly small. They can exert powerful leverage only on countries highly dependent on external trade, not on large, nearly self-sufficient blocs.[20]

On the other hand, the competition for the support (or at least neutrality) of the uncommitted areas, and for the continued support of allies, has become of tremendous importance for the cold war and has obvious economic aspects. The principal "weapons" are aid in its manifold forms (including public and semi-public loans) and trade and investment policies.

There has been a tendency, both in the administration of aid programs and in their analysis, to distinguish military, economic, and political aspects. In fact almost all aid programs have mixed objectives, and all have mixed effects. Regardless of how the aid is parceled and what each parcel is called, we should design and judge the aid program in the light of all effects. When we give military or "defense support" aid to a country, we are likely to release indigenous resources for other purposes. When we give economic aid, we (hopefully) contribute to political stability and sometimes to military strength as well as to economic growth. Have we been overemphasizing *aid* as compared with *trade* policy? What is the relation between economic growth, political stability, and Western orientation?[21] How can we help to reduce the vulnerability of our less self-sufficient allies to economic pressure by the Soviet bloc (e.g. the threat of deprivation of Middle East oil)? Will some increase in Soviet (or bloc) trading with uncommitted areas increase or diminish their relative influence in such areas?[22] What kinds of accretion of military strength in recipient countries will contribute most to the national security of the United States? It is apparent that a worth-while analysis of our aid and trade policies requires knowledge and judgment of a wide range of national security questions.

MOBILIZATION

I have not meant to imply that the concept of mobilization is completely outmoded. It is even conceivable that we will have a long, large-scale war, without effective strategic bombing by either side, in which mobilization potential will weigh heavily in the scales of victory, although I would argue that this contingency should be ignored in allocating the defense budget, on the ground that it is both unlikely and lacking in danger to the United States. Even this proposition, however, is important to ponder and investigate, for we are still spending hundreds of millions annually on military reserves and mobilization potential that would be useful mainly in such a contingency.

The kind of mobilization potential that would permit a very rapid build-up of forces and production for limited wars (of the Korean type) would appear to me to make much more sense. So would preparatory steps to permit rapid mobilization in crises. What kind of reserves and what kind of industrial mobilization measures would these capabilities require? What should be the composition of the stockpile? What kinds of excess productive capacity would be optimal, and how should it be provided and financed?

CIVIL (OR NON-MILITARY) DEFENSE AND RECUPERATION

To date the United States has spent virtually nothing on civil defense and acquired virtually no worth-while capability. At the same time we have spent billions on active air defences (interceptors and missiles). Since the two forms of defense are to some extent substitutes and to some extent complements, is this a sensible (economic) allocation of the defense budget?[23]

Civil defense has been justified on two grounds: that it contributes to deterrence by demonstrating our seriousness of purpose, and that it lessens the destruction of population and industry if deterrence fails and war comes. The first is a dubious argument and should be questioned and studied: deterrence may well be at a maximum when the cities on both sides are exposed and vulnerable, while the striking forces are hidden, buried, or otherwise rendered invulnerable. The second argument is sound enough in principle; the relevant question is how much destruction can be reduced by what kinds of amounts of expenditure.

The gains and costs of various possible civil defense measures (fallout shelters, blast shelters, evacuation, stockpiling, dispersal of industry and population, etc.) must be assessed and compared in various combinations against a range of enemy threats. This involves a sophisticated economic analysis of alternative ways of using resources to which very few persons appear to be devoting their efforts.

Economic analysis is also required to estimate the ability of the economy to recuperate following various patterns and magnitudes of attack, and ways in which its recuperability can be enhanced by pre-attack planning, stockpiling, etc.

"DISARMAMENT" AND ARMS CONTROL

"Disarmament" is the term now commonly used to include all kinds of mutual arrangements with potential enemies to reduce the risk or violence of war—whether or not they involve disarming. Despite the frustrations of years of unsuccessful negotiating with the Soviet bloc, the possible payoff from success is so great, and the possible disaster from misconceived arrangements so monstrous, that the subject and its problems deserve far more intense, unemotional, and rigorous study than they have yet received.

While economic motives (budget savings) have provided a good deal of the steam behind disarmament negotiations, it is far from clear that an effective plan, e.g., to prevent surprise nuclear attack, would reduce national security expenditures and it might well increase them.

The formulation of effective "disarmament" plans is incredibly difficult because they must be *mutually* advantageous to be acceptable. While the core problem is not an economic one, it is possible that economists can make an important contribution from their studies of what causes equilibria to be stable or unstable, and of analogous bargaining and "game" situations.

III

THERE are difficult problems of access to data in conducting some kinds of national security research. One of the barriers is security classification. Another is privileged information—restricted to the originating firm or agency for competitive reasons. Still another is the inaccessibility of the kind of information that can only be gained from experience in or close association with a functioning organization. There is no doubt that these are formidable barriers to attacking some national security problems, and that their existence has discouraged many scholars with keen interest in the subject.

Without in any way belittling these barriers,

there are two points I should like to make about them. The first is that they are much more formidable in some problem areas than in others. They are relatively unimportant in studying the implications of large defense budgets, perhaps most important in studying efficiency in using and managing defense resources. But even in this latter area there are relatively unrestricted subareas; for example, useful theoretical analyses of optimizing with incomplete markets may be possible with only a general acquaintance with governmental and military institutions. Information of logistics is relatively open, as is information on trade, aid, mobilization, and civil defense.

My seond point on access is that the difference between national security and a good many other important areas for economics research is, if anything, a matter of degree. Once we leave the most abstract levels of general theory, research in economics is likely to require specialized factual and institutional knowledge that is difficult to acquire. There are few security classifications in the private economy or the civilian side of the government, but rules governing the use of privileged information are frequently just as restrictive. We have tried to go too far in economics on too few data and too little experience. The economist who is serious about applied research in national security or almost any other field should expect to devote much time and effort to acquiring specialized information, and preferably, if he does not already have it, some specialized relevant experience. In the case of national security, there are now several ways in which he can do this.

Notes

1. This has been done by many writers in open sources. See, for example, Henry A. Kissinger, *Nuclear Weapons and Foreign Policy*, New York, Harper and Brothers, 1957; and The RAND Corporation, *Report on a Study of Non-Military Defense*, Report R-322-RC, July 1, 1958.

2. Neither, on the other hand, do I believe in what Walter Millis calls the "hypertrophy of general war." There has been an alarming amount of wishful thinking that all-out wars won't happen because they constitute "mutual suicide." The best demonstration of the fallacy of the mutual-suicide theory is an article by Albert Wohlstetter, "The Delicate Balance of Terror," *Foreign Affairs*, XXXVII, No. 2 (January 1959), pp. 211–234.

3. To the extent that we may be confronted with *faits accomplis*, forces in being may be more important than potential in limited wars.

4. Although apparently not a much higher proportion of its national product measured in rubles. The USSR has a comparative advantage in the production of military goods and services.

5. See especially Milton Gilbert and Irving B. Kravis, *An International Comparison of National Products and the Purchasing Power of Currencies*, Paris, Organization for European Economic Co-operation, n.d.

6. On this and several other topics mentioned here, see Committee for Economic Development, *The Problem of National Security*, A Statement on National Policy by the Research

and Policy Committee, New York, July 1958.

7. For discussions and references, see *Federal Tax policy for Economic Growth and Stability*, Subcommittee on Tax Policy, Joint Committee on the Economic Report, 84th Congress, 1st Session, Washington, D.C., U.S. Government Printing Office, 1956; and Gershon Cooper, "Taxation and Incentive in Mobilization," *Quarterly Journal of Economics*, LXVI, No. 1 (February 1952), pp. 43–66.

8. See Tibor Scitovsky, Edward S. Shaw, and Lorie Tarshis, *Mobilizing Resources for War*, New York, McGraw-Hill Book Co., 1951; Gerhard Colm and Manuel Helzner, "General Economic Feasibility of National Security Programs," National Planning Association, March 20, 1957, published in *Federal Expenditure Policy for Economic Growth and Stability*, Hearings before the Subcommittee on Fiscal Policy of the Joint Economic Committee, 85th Congress, 1st Session, Washington, D.C., U.S. Government Printing Office, 1958; Aaron Director, ed.; *Defense, Controls, and Inflation*, Chicago, University of Chicago Press, 1952.

9. See especially Colm and Helzner, *op. cit.*

10. For a responsible and useful attempt to assess net gains in security from larger expenditures, see Rockefeller Brothers Fund, Inc., *International Security—The Military Aspect* (Special Studies Report II), New York, Doubleday Headline Publications, 1958.

11. See Arthur Smithies, *The Budgetary Process in the United States*, New York, McGraw-Hill Book Co., 1955, ch. 11.

12. For a general discussion, see Roland N. McKean, *Efficiency in Government Through Systems Analysis*, New York, John Wiley and Sons, 1958. For more on the role of economists and economics, see my article, "Economics and Military Operations Research." *Review of Economics and Statistics*, XL, No. 3 (August 1958), pp. 199–209.

13. See, for example, Thomas C. Schelling, "The Strategy of Conflict: Prospectus for a Reorientation of Game Theory," *Journal of Conflict Resolution*, II, No. 3 (September 1958) pp. 203–264.

14. On the last point, see Charles E. Lindblom, *Bargaining: The Hidden Hand in Government*, The RAND Corporation, Research Memorandum RM-1434-RC, 1955; and Alain Enthoven and Henry Rowen, "Defense Planning and Organization," a paper presented at the Universities/National Bureau Conference on Public Finance, April 1959, published in the *Proceedings* of that conference in 1960.

15. A number of papers on economic aspects of research and development will be presented at the conference on inventive activity to be held at the University of Minnesota in May 1960 under the joint sponsorship of the Universities/National Bureau Committee and the Committee on Economic Growth of the Social Science Research Council.

16. See Burton H. Klein and William H. Meckling, "Application of Operations Research to Development Decisions," *Operations Research*, VI, No. 3 (May-June 1958), pp. 352–363; and Burton H. Klein, "A Radical Proposal for R. and D.," *Fortune*, May 1958, pp. 112–113, 218, 222, 224, 226.

17. See Stephen Enke, "An Economist Looks at Air Force Logistics," *Review of Economics and Statistics*, XL, No. 3 (August 1958), pp. 230–239; and Horst Mendershausen, "Economic Problems in Air Force Logistics," *American Economic Review*, XLVIII, No. 4 (September 1958), pp. 632–648. A great many books and articles have been written on specific logistics problems like transportation, procurement, inventory policy, etc. See, for example, Thomson M. Whitin, *The Theory of Inventory Management*, Princeton, N.J., Princeton University Press, 1953.

18. As a general reference, see Malcolm W. Hoag, "Economic Problems of Alliance," *Journal of Political Economy*, LXV, No. 6 (December 1957), pp. 522–534.

19. For research suggestions on economic foreign policy, many of which have national security implications, see Charles P. Kindleberger, "United States Economic Foreign Policy: Research Requirements for 1965," *World Politics*, XI, No. 4 (July 1959), pp. 588–613.

20. I am not denying that they have adversely affected the industrialization of China. The Chinese economy is not yet large, and in its industrializing stage is far from self-sufficient.

21. The relation is by no means a simple one, as some economists have been prone to assume. For one attempt at a partial answer, see Charles Wolf, Jr., *Foreign Aid: Theory and Practice in Southern Asia*, Princeton, N.J., Princeton University Press, 1960.

22. See Albert O. Hirschman, *National Power and the Structure of Foreign Trade*, Berkeley, Calif., University of California Press, 1945.

23. For a general discussion, see *Report on a Study of Non-Military Defense, op. cit.*

Selected bibliography

THIS BIBLIOGRAPHY is more than a list of suggested readings for the interested student. It is designed, first of all, to give some sense of the variety and scope of the developing literature in the field. We hope that it will shed further light on the topography of the discipline of national security and on the lines of inquiry pursued in it. We have also used the bibliography to fill some of the unavoidable gaps in our selections. There are, for instance, sections on diplomacy and intelligence, neither of which is directly covered in this book although they are, of course, highly relevant to national security. Our attempt to present all relevant topics has forced us to sacrifice some selectivity to increased comprehensiveness. Many of the entries may seem marginal to the concept and field of national security as defined by us. But since our definition is not the only one, we have found important materials in a large number of sources, classified under a variety of titles. We have tried to bring the best of these together and to place them in our organizational scheme. This should enable the researcher to sidestep much of the painful, time-consuming routine that was previously needed to locate materials relevant to national security. Finally, since the bibliography does follow the conceptual scheme of the book, it can and should serve as a guide to further student reading, assigned by each instructor according to his special needs.

General references

Bibliographies

Bemis, S. F., and C. G. Griffin. *Guide to the Diplomatic History of the United States, 1775–1921*. Washington, D.C.: Government Printing Office, 1935.

Collart, Yves. *Disarmament: A Study Guide and Bibliography on the Efforts of the United Nations*. The Hague: Nijhoff, 1958.

Foreign Affairs Bibliography 1919–1952. Three volumes. The Council on Foreign Relations, New York.

Hald, Marjorie. *A Selected Bibliography on Economic Development and Foreign Aid*. Santa Monica, Calif.: The RAND Corporation, 1957.

Hazlewood, Arthur. *The Economics of "Under-Developed" Areas: An Annotated Reading List of Books, Articles, and Official Publications*, 2nd ed. London: Oxford Univ. Press, 1959.

Huntington, Samuel P. "Recent Writing in Military Politics—Foci and Corpora," in *Changing Patterns of Military Politics*, Huntington, S. P. (ed.), New York: The Free Press, 1962.

Journal of Conflict Resolution, Ann Arbor, Mich.: Periodic Bibliographies Reviewing Current Literature in the National Security Field.

Moskowitz, Harry, and Jack Roberts. *Disarmament: A Bibliographic Record, 1916–1960*. Washington, D.C.: Government Printing Office, 1960.

Plischke, Elmer. *American Diplomacy: A Bibliography of Biographies, Autobiographies, and Commentaries*. College Park, Maryland: Bureau of Governmental Research, College of Business and Public Administration, University of Maryland, 1957.

———. *American Foreign Relations*. College Park, Maryland: Bureau of Governmental Research, College of Business and Public Administration, University of Maryland, 1955.

Rips, Rae E., ed. *United States Government Publications*, 3rd ed. rev. New York: H. W. Wilson Company, 1949.

Shubik, M. "Bibliography on Simulation, Gaming, Artificial Intelligence and Allied Topics." *American Statistical Association Journal*, LV (1960), 736–751.

United States Government. *U.S. Government Publications — Monthly Catalogue*. Washington, D.C.: Government Printing Office.

United States Department of the Army. *Military and Strategic Implications of Technological Progress*. (Special Bibliography No. 17.) August 1, 1958.

United States Senate. Subcommittee on Government Operations. *Organizing for National Security: Bibliography of National Security Materials*. Washington, D.C.: Government Printing Office, 1960.

United States Senate. Subcommittee on National Security Staffing and Operations of the Committee on Government Operations. "Administration of National Security: A Bibliography." Washington, D.C.: Government Printing Office, 1963.

United Nations. Headquarters Library. *United Nations Documents Index*.

United Nations. *Ten Years of United Nations Publications, 1945–1955*.

Documentary collections

A Decade of American Foreign Policy: Basic Documents, 1941–1949. Senate Document No. 123. Washington, D.C.: Government Printing Office.

Department of State. *Documents and State Papers* (Monthly). Washington, D.C.: United States Department of State.

Department of State Bulletin (Weekly).

Documents on American Foreign Relations. New York: Harper & Row, Publishers, Annual Volumes (1933–1963). Washington, D.C.: Government Printing Office.

United States Department of State. *American Foreign Policy 1950–1955*: Basic Documents (2 Vols.). Department of State Publication No. 6446, Washington, D.C.: Government Printing Office.

United States Department of State. *Foreign Relations of the United States* (Annual Series). Washington, D.C.: Government Printing Office.

United States Senate. Subcommittee on Government Operations. *Organizing for National Security: Selected Materials and Documents*. Washington, D.C.: Government Printing Office, 1960.

United States Senate, Subcommittee on National Security Staffing and Operations of the Committee on Government Operations, "Administration of National Security: Selected Materials and Documents." Washington, D.C.: Government Printing Office, 1963.

Periodicals devoted to national security and related fields

Air Force
American Political Science Review
Annals of the American Academy of Political and
    Social Science
Armed Forces Management
Army
Bulletin of Atomic Scientists
Current History
Foreign Affairs
Foreign Service Journal

International Affairs, London
International Conciliation
International Journal, Toronto
International Organization
Journal of Arms Control
Journal of Conflict Resolution
Journal of International Affairs
Journal of Politics
Military Review
Orbis
Political Science Quarterly
Survival, London
United Nations Review
World Affairs
World Politics
Scientific American

National security: a concept emerges

Beard, Charles A. *An Economic Interpretation of the Constitution of the United States.* New York: The Macmillan Company, 1941.

———. *The Idea of National Interest.* New York: The Macmillan Company, 1934.

———. *The Open Door at Home: A Trial Philosophy of the National Interest.* New York: The Macmillan Company, 1934.

———, and Mary R. Beard. *The Rise of American Civilization.* New York: The Macmillan Company, 1934.

Bentley, Arthur F. *The Process of Government,* 1949 ed. Bloomington, Ind.: Principia Press, 1908.

Carr, E. H. *The Twenty Years Crisis, 1919–1939.* New York: St Martin's Press, Inc., 1949.

Downs, Anthony. *An Economic Theory of Democracy.* New York: Harper & Row, Publishers, 1957.

Easton, David. *The Political System.* New York: Alfred A. Knopf, Inc., 1953.

Friedrich, Carl J. (ed.). *The Public Interest.* New York: Atherton Press, 1962.

Grassmuck, George L. *Sectional Biases in Congress on Foreign Policy.* Baltimore: Johns Hopkins University Press, 1951.

Kaplan, Morton. *System and Process in International Politics.* New York: John Wiley & Sons, Inc., 1957.

Latham, Earl. *The Group Basis of Politics.* Ithaca: Cornell University Press, 1952.

Lippmann, Walter. *The Phantom Public.* New York: Harcourt, Brace & World, Inc., 1930.

———. *The Public Philosophy.* Boston: Little, Brown and Company, 1955.

Mackinder, H. J. *Democratic Ideals and Reality.* New York: Holt, Rinehart & Winston, Inc., 1942.

Mahan, A. T. *The Influence of Sea Power Upon History, 1660–1783.* Boston: Little, Brown and Company, 1928.

Meyerson, Martin, and Edward C. Banfield. *Politics, Planning and the Public Interest.* New York: The Free Press, 1955.

Morgenthau, Hans J. *In Defense of the National Interest.* New York: Alfred A. Knopf, Inc., 1951.

Niebuhr, Reinhold. *Moral Man and Immoral Society: A Study in Ethics and Politics.* New York: Charles Scribner's Sons, 1932.

———. *The Structure of Nations and Empires.* New York: Charles Scribner's Sons, 1959.

Osgood, Robert E. *Ideals and Self-Interest in American Foreign Relations.* Chicago: Univ. of Chicago Press—Phoenix Books, 1964.

Schubert, Glendon. *The Public Interest: A Critique of the Theory of a Political Concept.* New York: The Free Press, 1960.

Simon, Herbert A. *Administrative Behavior: A Study of Decision-Making Processes in Administrative Organization,* Rev. ed. New York: The Macmillan Company, 1957.

Snyder, Richard C., H. W. Bruck, and Burton Sapin. *Decision-Making as an Approach to the Study of International Politics.* (Organizational Behavior Section, "Foreign Policy Analysis Series," No. 3.) Princeton: Princeton University Press, 1954.

Spykman, Nicholas. *America's Strategy in World Politics.* New York: Harcourt, Brace & World, Inc., 1942.

———. *The Geography of the Peace.* New York: Harcourt, Brace & World, Inc., 1944.

Truman, David B. *The Governmental Process.* New York: Alfred A. Knopf, Inc., 1951.

Waldo, Dwight. *The Administrative State.* New York: The Ronald Press Company, 1948.

ARTICLES

Bailey, Stephen K. "Public Interest: Some Operational Dilemmas," in Friedrich (ed.) *The Public Interest,* New York: Atherton Press, 1962.

Cassinelli, C. W. "Comments on Frank J. Sorauf's 'The Public Interest Reconsidered,'" *Journal of Politics,* XX (1958), 553–556.

———. "The Public Interest in Political Ethics," in Friedrich (ed.) *The Public Interest,* New York: Atherton Press, 1962.

———. "Some Reflections on the Concept of the Public Interest," *Ethics,* LXIX (1958), 48–61.

Cleveland, Harlan. "The Executive and the Public Interest," *Annals of the American Academy of Political and Social Science*, CCCVII (1956), 37–54.

Colm, Gerhard. "The Public Interest: Essential Key to Public Policy," in Friedrich (ed.), *The Public Interest*, New York: Atherton Press, 1962.

Cook, Thomas I., and Malcolm Moos. "The American Idea of International Interest," *American Political Science Review*, XLVII (1953), 28–44.

Dahl, Robert A. "The Concept of Power," *Behavioral Science*, II (1957), 201–215.

Dickinson, John. "Democratic Realities and Democratic Dogma," *American Political Science Review*, XXIV (1930), 283–309.

Friedmann, W. "The Changing Content of Public Interest: Some Comments on Harold D. Lasswell," in Friedrich (ed.), *The Public Interest*, New York: Atherton Press, 1962.

Helms, E. Allen. "The President and Party Politics," *Journal of Politics*, XI (1949), 42–64.

Lasswell, Harold D. "Current Studies of the Decision Process: Automation versus Creativity," *Western Political Quarterly*, VIII (1955), 381–399.

———. "The Public Interest: Proposing Principles of Content and Procedure," in Friedrich (ed.), *The Public Interest*, New York: Atherton Press, 1962.

Latham, Earl. "The Group Basis of Politics: Notes for a Theory," *American Political Science Review*, XLVI (1952), 376–397.

Leys, Wayne A. R. "Philosophy and the Public Interest," *PROD*, II, September, 1958: 12–13.

Mackinder, H. J. "The Geographical Pivot of History," *Geographic Journal*, XXIII (1904), 421–444.

Montgomery, John D. "Public Interest in the Ideologies of National Development," in Friedrich (ed.), *The Public Interest*, New York: Atherton Press, 1962.

Morgenthau, Hans J. "Another 'Great Debate': The National Interest of the United States," *American Political Science Review*, XLVI (1952), 961–988.

Niemeyer, Gerhard. "Public Interest and Private Utility," in Friedrich (ed.), *The Public Interest*, New York: Atherton Press, 1962.

Pennock, J. Roland. "The One and the Many: A Note on the Concept," in Friedrich (ed.), *The Public Interest*, New York: Atherton Press, 1962.

Schattschneider, Elmer E. "Political Parties and the Public Interest," *Annals of the American Academy of Political and Social Science*, CCLXXX (1952), 18–26.

Schubert, Glendon. "Is There a Public Interest Theory?" in Friedrich (ed.), *The Public Interest*, New York: Atherton Press, 1962.

———. "'The Public Interest' in Administrative Decision-Making: Theorem, Theosophy, or Theory?" *American Political Science Review*, LI (1957), 346–368.

———. "The Theory of the Public Interest," *PROD*, I, May, 1958: 34–36.

Sorauf, Frank J. "The Public Interest Reconsidered," *Journal of Politics*, XIX (1957), 616–639.

Sprout, Harold, and Margaret Sprout. "Environmental Factors in the Study of International Politics," *Journal of Conflict Resolution*, Vol. I, No. 4, 1957: 309–328.

National security and international conflict

a. The military problem

1. GENERAL STRATEGY AND GENERAL WAR

Blackett, P. M. S. *Atomic Weapons and East-West Relations*. New York: Cambridge University Press, 1956.

Brodie, Bernard. *Strategy in the Missile Age*. Princeton: Princeton University Press, 1959.

———. (ed.). *The Absolute Weapon*. New York: Harcourt, Brace and World, Inc., 1946.

Dinerstein, Herbert S. *War and the Soviet Union*. New York: Frederick A. Praeger, Inc., 1959.

Furniss, Edgar S. (ed.) *American Military Policy: Strategic Aspects of World Political Geography*. New York: Holt, Rinehart & Winston, Inc., 1957.

Gallois, Pierre. *The Balance of Terror: Strategy for the Nuclear Age*. Translated by Richard Howard. Boston: Houghton Mifflin Co., 1961.

Garthoff, Raymond L. *The Soviet Image of Future War*. Washington, D.C.: Public Affairs Press, 1959.

———. *Soviet Military Doctrine*. New York: The Free Press, 1953.

———. *Soviet Strategy in the Nuclear Age*. New York: Frederick A. Praeger, Inc., 1958.

Gavin, James M. *War and Peace in the Space Age*. New York: Harper & Row, Publishers, 1958.

Gouré, Leon. *Civil Defense in the Soviet Union*. Berkeley: University of California Press, 1962.

Kahn, Herman. *On Thermonuclear War*. Princeton: Princeton University Press, 1960.

———. *Thinking About the Unthinkable*. New York: Horizon Press, Inc., 1962.

Kaufmann, William W. (ed.). *Military Policy and National Security*. Princeton: Princeton University Press, 1956.

Kaufmann, William W. *The McNamara Strategy*. New York: Harper & Row, Publishers, 1964.

King-Hall, Stephen. *Defense in the Nuclear Age*. London: Victor Gollancz, 1958.

Kingston-McCloughry, E. J. *The Direction of War*. New York: Frederick A. Praeger, Inc., 1958.

Kissinger, Henry A. *The Necessity for Choice*. New York: Harper & Row, Publishers, 1961.

———. *Nuclear Weapons and Foreign Policy*. New York: Harper & Row, Publishers, 1957.

Liddell-Hart, B. H. *Deterrent or Defense.* New York: Frederick A. Praeger, Inc., 1960.

———. *Strategy.* London: Faber & Faber, 1954.

Medaris, John B. *Countdown for Decision.* New York: G. P. Putnam's Sons, 1960.

Miksche, F. O. *Atomic Weapons and Armies.* New York: Frederick A. Praeger, Inc., 1955.

Morgenstern, Oskar. *The Question of National Defense.* New York: Random House, Inc., 1959.

Pokrovsky, G. I. *Science and Technology in Contemporary War.* Translated by Raymond L. Garthoff. New York: Frederick A. Praeger, Inc., 1959.

Rostow, W. W. *The United States in the World Arena.* New York: Harper & Row, Publishers, 1960.

Singer, J. David. *Deterrence, Arms Control and Disarmament: Toward a Synthesis in National Security Policy.* Columbus: Ohio State University Press, 1962.

Slessor, Sir John. *The Great Deterrent.* New York: Frederick A. Praeger, Inc., 1958.

———. *Strategy for the West.* New York: William Morrow & Co., Inc., 1954.

Snyder, Glenn H. *Deterrence and Defense.* Princeton: Princeton University Press, 1961.

Sokolovskii, V. D. *Soviet Military Strategy.* Englewood Cliffs, N.J.: Prentice-Hall, Inc., 1963.

Taylor, Maxwell. *The Uncertain Trumpet.* New York: Harper & Row, Publishers, 1959.

Waskow, Arthur I. *The Limits of Defense.* Garden City, N.Y.: Doubleday & Company, Inc., 1962.

ARTICLES

Amster, Warren. "Design for Deterrence," *Bulletin of the Atomic Scientists,* XII, May 1956: 164–165.

Brodie, Bernard. "Nuclear Weapons and Changing Strategic Outlooks," *Bulletin of the Atomic Scientists,* XIII, February, 1957: 56–61.

———. "Nuclear Weapons: Strategic or Tactical," *Foreign Affairs,* Vol. 32, January 1954: 217–229.

Burns, Arthur Lee. "From Balance to Deterrence: A Theoretical Analysis," *World Politics,* Vol. 9, July 1957: 494–529.

———. "The International Consequences of Expecting Surprise," *World Politics,* Vol. 10, July 1958: 512–536.

———. "The New Weapons and International Relations," *Australian Outlook,* XII, June 1958: 32–42.

Deutsch, Karl W. "The Impact of Science and Technology on International Politics," *Daedalus,* LXXXVIII, Fall 1959: 669–685.

Dinerstein, Herbert S. "The Revolution in Soviet Strategic Thinking," *Foreign Affairs,* XXXVI (January 1958) 241–252.

Gallois, General Pierre M. "A French General Analyzes Nuclear-Age Strategy," *Realités,* No. 96, November 1958: 19–22, 70–72.

Gilpatric, Roswell L. "Our Defense Needs: The Long View," *Foreign Affairs,* Vol. 42, No. 3, April 1964: 366–378.

Kahn, Herman. "Strategy, Foreign Policy and Thermonuclear War," in *America Armed,* Robert Goldwin (ed.), Chicago: Rand McNally & Co., 1963: 43–70.

King, James E. "Airpower in the Missile Gap," *World Politics,* XII (July 1960), 628–639.

Milburn, Thomas W. "What Constitutes Effective Deterrence?" *Journal of Conflict Resolution,* III, June 1959: 138–145.

Schelling, Thomas C. "Dispersal, Deterrence, and Damage," *Operations Research,* IX, May–June, 1961: 363–370.

Singer, J. David. "From Deterrence to Disarmament," *International Journal,* XVI, Autumn 1961: 307–326.

———. "The Strategic Dilemma: Probabilities versus Disutilities," *Journal of Conflict Resolution,* Vol. V, June 1961: 197–205.

———. "Stable Deterrence and Its Limits," *Western Political Quarterly,* XI, September 1962: 449–464.

Weisner, Jerome B., and York, Herbert F. "The Test Ban," *Scientific American,* Vol. 211 (October 1964), 27–35.

Wohlstetter, Albert. "The Delicate Balance of Terror," *Foreign Affairs,* Vol. 37, January 1959: 211–234.

Wolfe, Thomas W. "Shifts in Soviet Strategic Thought," *Foreign Affairs,* Vol. 42, No. 3, April 1964: 475–486.

2. LIMITED WARFARE

Halperin, Michael. *Limited Warfare in the Nuclear Age.* New York: John Wiley & Sons, Inc., 1963.

Kissinger, Henry A. *The Necessity for Choice.* New York: Harper & Row, Publishers, 1961.

———. *Nuclear Weapons and Foreign Policies.* New York: Harper & Row, Publishers, 1957.

Knorr, Klaus. *Limited Strategic War.* New York: Frederick A. Praeger, Inc., 1963.

Osgood, Robert E. *Limited War.* Chicago: University of Chicago Press, 1957.

ARTICLES AND PAMPHLETS

Brodie, Bernard. "Unlimited Weapons and Limited War," *The Reporter,* v. 11 (Nov. 18, 1954), 16–21.

Burns, Arthur Lee. "The Rationale of Catalytic War," Center of International Studies, Princeton University Press, 1959. (Research Monograph No. 3.)

Kissinger, Henry A. "Limited War: Nuclear or Conventional? A Reappraisal," *Daedalus,* v. 89 (Fall 1960), 800–817.

Royal Institute on International Affairs. *On Limiting Atomic War.* 1956.

Schelling, Thomas C. "Bargaining, Communication, and Limited War," *Journal of Conflict Resolution,* v. 1 (March 1957), 19–36.

———. *Nuclear Weapons and Limited War.* (Pamphlet 1620) Santa Monica, Calif.: The RAND Corporation, February 20, 1959.

3. UNCONVENTIONAL WARFARE

Atkinson, James D. *The Edge of War.* Chicago: Henry Regnery Co., 1960.

Crozier, Brian. *The Rebels*. Boston: Beacon Press, 1960.

Dixon, C. Aubrey and Otto Heilbrunn. *Communist Guerrilla Warfare*. New York: Frederick A. Praeger, Inc., 1954.

Eckstein, Harry. *Internal War*. New York: The Free Press, 1964.

Guevara, Ernesto. *On Guerrilla Warfare*. New York: Frederick A. Praeger, Inc., 1962.

Miksche, F. O. *Secret Forces: The Technique of Underground Movements*. London: Faber & Faber, 1950.

Modelski, George. *The International Relations of Internal War*. Center of International Studies, Princeton Univ., May 24, 1961. (Research Monograph No. 11).

Osanka, F. M. (ed.). *Modern Guerrilla Warfare: Fighting Communist Guerrilla Movements, 1941–1961*. New York: The Free Press, 1962.

Paret, Peter, and John W. Shy. *Guerrillas in the 1960's*. New York: Frederick A. Praeger, Inc., 1962.

Pye, Lucian. *Guerrilla Communism in Malaya*. Princeton: Princeton University Press, 1956.

Strausz-Hupé, Robert, William R. Kintner, *et al.* *Protracted Conflict*. New York: Harper & Row, Publishers, 1959.

ARTICLES AND PAMPHLETS

Bjelajac, Slavko N. "Unconventional Warfare in the Nuclear Era," *Orbis*, v. 4, Fall 1960: 323–337.

Girardet, Raoul. "Civil and Military Power in the Fourth Republic," in Huntington, S. P., *Changing Patterns of Military Politics*. New York: The Free Press, 1962.

Huntington, Samuel P. "Patterns of Violence in World Politics," in Huntington, *Changing Patterns of Military Politics*. New York: The Free Press, 1962.

Kelly, George A. "Revolutionary War and Psychological Action," *Military Review*, v. 11 (October 1960), 4–13.

Ney, Virgil. "Guerrilla War and Modern Strategy," *Orbis*, v. 2, Spring 1958: 66–82.

Papagos, Alexander. "Guerrilla Warfare," *Foreign Affairs*, v. 30, January 1952: 215–230.

Paret, Peter. "The French Army and La Guerre Revolutionnaire," *Journal of the Royal United Service Institution*, v. 104, February 1959: 59–69.

4. HISTORY AND ANALYSIS OF WAR

Aron, Raymond. *The Century of Total War*. New York: Doubleday & Company, Inc., 1954.

Clark, Sir George. *War and Society in the Seventeenth Century*. New York: Cambridge University Press, 1958.

Earle, Edward Mead. *Makers of Modern Strategy: Military Thought from Machiavelli to Hitler*. Princeton: Princeton University Press, 1943.

Falls, Cyril. *A Hundred Years of War*. New York: The Macmillan Company, 1954.

Fuller, J. F. C. *A Military History of the Western World*. New York: Funk & Wagnalls Co., Inc., 3 vols., 1954–1956.

Huntington, Samuel P. (ed.). *Changing Patterns of Military Politics*. New York: The Free Press, 1961.

Nef, John U. *War and Human Progress*. Cambridge: Harvard University Press, 1950.

Preston, Richard A., Sydney F. Wise, and Herman O. Warner. *Men in Arms: A History of Warfare and its Interrelationships with Western Society*. New York: Frederick A. Praeger, Inc., 1956.

Richardson, Lewis F. *Statistics of Deadly Quarrels* (Quincy Wright and Carl C. Lienau, eds.). Chicago: University of Chicago Press—Quadrangle, 1960.

Ropp, Theodore. *War in the Modern World*. Durham: Duke University Press, 1959.

Tucker, Robert. *The Just War*. Baltimore: Johns Hopkins Press, 1961.

Waltz, Kenneth. *Man, the State, and War: A Theoretical Analysis*. New York: Columbia University Press, 1959.

Wright, Quincy. *A Study of War* (2 vols.). Chicago: University of Chicago Press, 1942.

b. The economic problem

1. THE ALLOCATION AND MOBILIZATION OF RESOURCES

Blackman, J., A. Basch, S. Fabricant, M. Gainsbrugh, and E. Stein. *War and Defense Economics*. New York: Holt, Rinehart & Winston, Inc., 1952.

Burkhead, Jesse. *Government Budgeting*. New York: John Wiley & Sons, Inc., 1956.

Colm, Gerhard. *Can We Afford Additional Programs for National Security?* National Planning Association (Planning Pamphlet No. 84), October 1953.

Committee for Economic Development. *The Problem of National Security*. (Statement by Research and Policy Committee) July 1958.

Eckstein, Otto. *Trends in Public Expenditures in the Next Decade*. A Supplementary Paper of the Committee for Economic Development. New York: Committee for Economic Development, April 1959.

Federal Expenditure Policy for Economic Growth and Stability, Hearings before the Subcommittee on Fiscal Policy of the Joint Economic Committee, 85th Congress, 1st Session, 1958.

Galbraith, J. K. *The Affluent Society*. Boston: Houghton Mifflin Company, 1958 (especially Ch. XII).

Harris, Seymour E. *The Economics of Mobilization and Inflation*. New York: W. W. Norton & Company, Inc., 1951.

Hitch, Charles J. and Roland N. McKean. *The Economics of Defense in the Nuclear Age*. Cambridge: Harvard University Press, 1960.

Huzar, Elias. *The Purse and the Sword: Control of the Army by Congress Through Military Appropriations, 1933–1950*. Ithaca: Cornell University Press, 1950.

International Stability and Progress: United States Interests and Instruments. New York: The

American Assembly, Columbia University, June 1957.

Knorr, Klaus. *The War Potential of Nations.* Princeton: Princeton University Press, 1956.

Lincoln, George A. *et al. Economics of National Security,* 2nd ed. Englewood Cliffs, N.J.: Prentice-Hall, Inc., 1954.

Millikan, Max F., and W. W. Rostow. *A Proposal: Key to an Effective Foreign Policy.* New York: Harper & Row, Publishers, 1957.

A Modern Concept of Manpower Management and Compensation for Personnel of the Uniformed Services (The Cordiner Report), Defense Advisory Committee on Professional and Technical Compensation, 1957. Washington, D.C.: Government Printing Office.

Rowen, Henry. *National Security and the American Economy in the 1960s.* Study Paper No. 18, Study of Employment and Price Levels. U.S. Congress Joint Economic Committee, 86th Cong., 2nd Sess., January 30, 1960.

Schelling, Thomas C. *International Economics.* Boston: Allyn and Bacon, Inc., 1958.

Schlesinger, James. *The Political Economy of National Security.* New York: Frederick A. Praeger, Inc., 1960.

Smithies, Arthur. *The Budgetary Process in the U.S.* New York: McGraw-Hill Book Company, 1955.

Soviet Economic Growth: A Comparison with the United States. Prepared for the Subcommittee on Foreign Economic Policy of the Joint Economic Committee by the Legislative Reference Service of the Library of Congress, 1957.

Smith, Ralph E. *The Army and Economic Mobilization.* Washington, D.C.: Office of the Chief of Military History, Department of the Army, 1959.

Post-Attack Resource Management, by Marshall K. Wood and John D. Norton, a report to the OCDM by the National Planning Association, August, 1959.

ARTICLES

Breckner, Norman. "Government Efficiency and the Military 'Buyer-Seller' Device," *The RAND Corporation,* Paper P-1744, July 8, 1959.

Davenport, John. "Arms and the Welfare State," *Yale Review,* LXVII, No. 3, Spring 1958: 335–346.

Durham, J. A. and B. Caplan. "Stabilization Planning Under the National Security Act," *Law and Contemporary Problems,* v. 19, No. 4, 1954: 477–485.

Fisher, Gene H. "Weapon-System Cost Analysis," *Operations Research,* IV, No. 5, September–October 1956: 558–571.

Gumz, Donald G. "The Bureau of the Budget and Defense Fiscal Policy," *U.S. Naval Institute Proceedings,* 85, April 1959: 80–89.

Hitch, Charles. "An Appreciation of Systems Analysis," *Operations Research,* III, No. 6, November–December 1955: 466–481.

Hoag, Malcolm W. "Some Complexities in Military Planning," *World Politics,* XI, No. 4, July 1959: 553–576.

Foldes, Lucien. "Military Budgeting and Financial Control," *Public Administration Review,* v. 17, Winter 1957: 36–43.

Katzenback, Edward L., Jr. "Bubud's Defense Policy," *The Reporter,* 22, June 23, 1960: 25–30.

Krout, John A. (ed.). "Mobilizing American Power for Defense," *Academy of Political Science Proceedings,* v. 24 (May 1951), 287–439.

Lipsey, R. G., and K. Lancaster. "The General Theory of Second Best," *Review of Economic Studies,* XXIV, No. I, 1956–1957: 11–32.

Livingston, J. Sterling. "Decision Making in Weapons Development," *Harvard Business Review,* XXXVI, No. I, January–February 1958: 127–136.

Silberman, Charles E., and Sanford S. Parker. "The Economic Impact of Defense," *Fortune,* June 1958: 102–105, 215–216, 218.

Tobin, James. "Defense, Dollars, and Doctrines," *Yale Review,* LXVII, No. 3, Spring 1958: 321–334.

2. FOREIGN AID AND TRADE

Allen, Robert. *Soviet Economic Warfare.* Washington, D.C.: Public Affairs Press, 1960.

Anderson, C. Arnold *et al. Research Needs for Development Assistance Programs.* Washington, D.C.: Foreign Policy Studies Program, Brookings Institution, 1961. 1 v.

Baran, Paul. *The Political Economy of Growth.* New York: Monthly Review Press, 1957.

Bauer, P. T. and Basil S. Yamey. *The Economics of Under-Developed Countries.* Chicago: University of Chicago Press, 1957.

Berliner, Joseph. *Soviet Economic Aid.* Frederick A. Praeger, Inc., 1958.

Brown, William Adams, Jr. and Redvers Opie. *American Foreign Assistance.* Washington, D.C.: Brookings Institution, 1953.

Furniss, Edgar S., Jr. *Some Perspectives on American Military Assistance.* Center of International Studies, Princeton University, June 18, 1957. (Memorandum No. 13.)

Heilbroner, R. *The Great Ascent: The Struggle for Economic Development in Our Time.* New York: Harper & Row, Publishers, 1963.

Jordan, Amos A. *Foreign Aid and the Defense of Southeast Asia.* New York: Frederick A. Praeger, Inc., 1962, p. 272.

Liska, George. *The New Statecraft: Foreign Aid in American Foreign Policy.* Chicago: University of Chicago Press, 1960.

The Military Assistance Program of the United States. Prepared at the request of the Special Committee to Study the Foreign Aid Program, U.S. Senate. Washington, D.C.: Government Printing Office, 1957.

Montgomery, John Dickey. *The Politics of Foreign Aid: American Experience in Southeast Asia.* Published for the Council on Foreign Relations. New York: Frederick A. Praeger, Inc., 1962. p. 336.

Myrdal, Gunnar. *An International Economy: Problems and Prospects.* New York: Harper & Row, Publishers, 1956.

———. *Rich Lands and Poor: The Road to World Prosperity.* New York: Harper & Row, Publishers, 1957.

Pentony, De Vere (ed.). *The Underdeveloped Lands: A Dilemma of the International Economy.* San Francisco: Chandler Publishing Co., 1960.

———. *United States Foreign Aid: Readings in the Problem Area of Wealth.* San Francisco: Chandler Publishing Co., 1960.

Political Development. The Brookings Institution, Reprint No. 65, Washington, D.C., 1962. p. 23.

Price, Harry B. *The Marshall Plan and Its Meaning.* Ithaca: Cornell University Press, 1955.

Ransom, Harry H. (ed.). *Foreign Military Assistance and National Policy: Some Background Materials.* Harvard Defense Policy Serial No. 114, April 1957.

Rockefeller Brothers Fund, Inc. Special Studies Project. *Foreign Economic Policy for the Twentieth Century,* 1958.

Rostow, W. W. *The Stages of Economic Growth: A Non-Communist Manifesto.* New York: Cambridge University Press, 1960.

Staley, Eugene. *The Future of Underdeveloped Countries: Political Implications of Economic Development.* (2nd ed.). New York: Frederick A. Praeger, Inc., 1961.

U.S. Senate Special Committee to Study the Foreign Aid Program. *The Military Assistance Program of the United States: Two Studies and a Report.* Committee Print., 85th Cong., 1st Sess., 1957.

Wiggins, J. W. and Helmut Schoeck (eds.). *Foreign Aid Reexamined—A Critical Appraisal.* Washington, D.C.: Public Affairs Press, 1958.

Wolf, Charles, Jr. *Foreign Aid: Theory and Practice in Southern Asia.* Princeton: Princeton University Press, 1960.

ARTICLES

Balogh, T. "The Strategy and Tactics of Technical Assistance," *Public Administration,* v. 37, Winter 1959: 327–342.

Bowles, Chester. "Basic Principles of Foreign Aid," *Department of State Bulletin,* v. 47, August 6, 1962: 207–213.

Connery, Robert H. and Paul T. David. "The Mutual Defense Assistance Program," *American Political Science Review,* v. 45, June 1951: 321–347.

"Foreign Aid and Foreign Policy: A Symposium," *Current History,* v. 33, Sept. 1957: 129–192.

Galbraith, John Kenneth. "A Positive Approach to Economic Aid," *Foreign Affairs,* v. 39, April 1961: 444–457.

Haviland, H. Field, Jr. "Foreign Aid and the Policy Process: 1957," *American Political Science Review,* v. 52, September 1958: 689–724.

Heilbroner, Robert L. "Dynamics of Foreign Aid: Problems of Underdeveloped Nations Plague Assistance Program," *New Leader,* v. 44 (September 18, 1961), 18–21.

Johnston, Bruce F. "Farm Surpluses and Foreign Policy," *World Politics,* v. 10, October 1957: 1–24.

Jordan, Amos A., Jr. "Military Assistance and National Policy," *Orbis,* Summer 1958: 241–244.

Lincoln, George A. "Factors Determining Arms Aid," *Academy of Political Science Proceedings,* v. 25, May 1953: 263–272.

Montgomery, John D. "Gilded Missiles: Reflections on the Politics of Foreign Aid," *Far Eastern Survey,* v. 28, June 1959: 81–89.

Morgenthau, Hans J. "A Political Theory of Foreign Aid," *American Political Science Review,* June 1962: 301–309.

Phillips, William T. "New Frontiers in Foreign Aid," *SAIS Review,* v. 5, Spring 1961: 37–43.

Pickell, Clyde V., and Thomas C. Musgrave. "Investment in Security," *Military Review,* v. 40, December 1960: 50–59.

Pye, Lucien W. "Soviet and American Styles in Foreign Aid," *Orbis,* v. 4, July 1960: 159–173.

Reuss, Henry S. "The United States Foreign Aid Program," *The Annals,* v. 336, July 1961: 23–29.

Rippy, J. Fred, "Foreign Aid and the Problem of Non-Intervention," *Inter-American Economic Affairs,* v. 11, Winter 1957: 23–47.

Rostow, Walt W. "The Future of Foreign Aid," *Foreign Service Journal,* v. 38, June 1961: 30–35.

Schatz, Sayre P. "The American Approach to Foreign Aid and the Thesis of Low Absorbtive Capacity," *Quarterly Review of Economics and Business,* v. 1, November 1961: 55–62.

Shaffer, Helen B. "Peace Corps Expansion," *Editorial Research Reports,* v. 2, No. 20, November 28, 1962: 855–872.

Symposium. "The Underdeveloped Areas," *Current History,* v. 33, August 1957.

Thorp, Willard L. "Trade, Aid, or What?" Baltimore: Johns Hopkins Press, 1954.

Viner, Jacob. "Economic Foreign Policy on the New Frontier," *Foreign Affairs,* v. 39, July 1961: 560–577.

Windle, Charles, and T. R. Vallance. "Optimizing Military Assistance Training," *World Politics,* v. 15, October 1962: 91–107.

Wolf, Charles, Jr. "Economic Aid Reconsidered," *Yale Review,* v. 50, June 1961: 518–540.

Wurfel, David. "Foreign Aid and Social Reform in Political Development: A Philippine Case Study," *American Political Science Review,* v. 53, June 1959: 456–482.

c. The political problem

I. THE GENERAL POLICY PROCESS

Bell, Wendell, Richard J. Hill, and Charles R. Wright. *Public Leadership.* San Francisco: Chandler Publishing Co., 1961. p. 242.

Brookings Institution, International Studies Group. *The Administration of Foreign Affairs and Overseas Operation; A Report Prepared for the Bureau of the Budget, Executive Office of the President.* Washington, D.C., 1951.

Buck, Philip W. (ed.). *Control of Foreign Relations in Modern Nations.* Philip W. Buck and

Martin Travis, Jr. (eds.) (1st ed.) New York: W. W. Norton & Company, Inc., 1957.

Frankel, Joseph. *The Making of Foreign Policy: An Analysis of Decision Making.* New York: Oxford University Press, 1963.

Goss, H. P. *The Administration and Execution of United States Foreign Policy, 1960–1975.* Santa Barbara: General Electric Company, Technical Military Planning Operation, 1959.

Haviland, H. Field, Jr. *The Formulation and Administration of United States Foreign Policy.* Washington, D.C.: Brookings Institution, 1960.

Huntington, Samuel P. *The Common Defense: Strategic Programs in National Politics.* New York: Columbia University Press, 1961.

Katzenbach, Edward L., Jr. *The Separation of Powers and National Security.* New York: 1960. p. 29.

Kissinger, Henry A. *The Necessity for Choice.* New York: Harper & Row, Publishers, 1961. p. 370.

Mailick, Sidney, and Edward H. Van Ness (eds.) *Concepts and Issues in Administrative Behavior.* Englewood Cliffs, N.J.: Prentice-Hall, Inc., 1962. p. 201.

McCamy, James L. *The Administration of American Foreign Affairs* (1st ed.) New York: Alfred A. Knopf, Inc., 1950.

Macmahon, Arthur W. *Administration and Foreign Policy.* Urbana, Ill.: Institute of Government and Public Affairs, 1957.

Marx, Herbert L. (ed.) *Defense and National Security.* New York: H. W. Wilson Co., 1955.

Millett, John D. *Government and Public Administration: The Quest for Responsible Performance.* New York: McGraw-Hill Book Company, 1959. p. 484.

Price, Don K. *The New Dimension of Diplomacy: The Organization of the U.S. Government for Its New Role in World Affairs.* New York: Woodrow Wilson Foundation, 1951.

Schilling, Warner R., Paul Y. Hammond, and Glenn H. Snyder. *Strategy, Politics, and Defense Budgets.* New York: Columbia University Press, 1962.

Seabury, Paul. *Power, Freedom and Diplomacy: The Foreign Policy of the United States of America.* New York: Random House, Inc., 1963.

Selznick, Philip. *Leadership in Administration: A Sociological Interpretation.* New York: Harper & Row, Publishers, 1957.

Simon, Herbert A. *Administrative Behavior; A Study of Decision-Making in Administrative Organization.* New York: The Macmillan Company, 1947. p. 259.

Snyder, Richard C., H. W. Bruck, and Burton Sapin. *Decision-Making as an Approach to the Study of International Politics.* Princeton: Princeton University Press, Organizational Behavior Section, 1954.

United States Foreign Policy: Compilation of Studies. Prepared under the direction of the U.S. Senate Committee on Foreign Relations. Washington, D.C.: Government Printing Office, 1961.

Westerfield, Bradford. *The Instruments of America's Foreign Policy.* New York: Thomas Y. Crowell Company, 1963. p. 538.

ARTICLES

Acheson, Dean. "The Responsibility for Decision in Foreign Policy," *Yale Review*, v. 44, September 1954: 1–12.

Bourbon-Busset, Jacques de. "How Decisions are Made in Foreign Politics: Psychology in International Relations," *Review of Politics*, v. 20, October, 1958: 591–614.

Bowie, Robert R. "Formulation of American Foreign Policy," *The Annals*, v. 330, July 1960: 1–10.

Cohen, B. C. "Foreign Policy Making: Modern Design," *World Politics*, v. 5, April, 1953: 377–392.

Elliott, William Y. "Governmental Organizations for Foreign Policy Decisions," *Social Science*, v. 30, October, 1955: 209–216.

Frankel, Joseph. "Towards a Decision-Making Model in Foreign Policy," *Political Studies*, v. 7, February, 1959: 1–11.

Fulbright, J. William. "American Foreign Policy in the 20th Century Under an 18th Century Constitution," *Cornell Law Quarterly*, v. 47, Fall 1961: 1–13.

Halperin, Morton H. "The Gaither Committee and the Policy Process," *World Politics*, v. 13, April 1961: 360–384.

Hamilton, William C. "Some Problems of Decision-Making in Foreign Affairs," *Dept. of State Bulletin*, v. 37, September 9, 1957: 432–436.

Hilsman, Roger. "Planning for National Security: A Proposal," *Bulletin of the Atomic Scientists*, v. 16, March 1960: 93–96.

———. "The Foreign Policy Consensus: An Interim Research Report," *Conflict Resolution*, v. 3, December 1959: 361–382.

Hoffman, Stanley. "Restraints and Choices in American Foreign Policy," *Daedalus*, v. 91, Fall 1962: 668–704.

Huntington, Samuel P. "Strategic Planning and the Political Process," *Foreign Affairs*, v. 38, January 1960: 285–299.

Jackson, Henry M. "Organizing for Survival," *Foreign Affairs*, v. 38, April 1960: 446–456.

Kennan, George F. "America's Administrative Response to its World Problems," *Daedalus*, v. 87, Spring 1958: 5–24.

Larrabee, Eric. "The Politics of Strategy," *Bulletin of the Atomic Scientists*, v. 17, March 1962: 16–21.

Lindsay, F. A. "Planning in Foreign Affairs: The Missing Element," *Foreign Affairs*, v. 39, January 1959: 279–290.

McCamy, James L. "The Administration of Foreign Affairs in The United States," *World Politics*, v. 7, January, 1958: 315–325.

Marshall, Charles Burton. "Organizing our Foreign Policy," *New Republic*, v. 145, December 25, 1961: 13–16.

Morgenthau, Hans J. "Decision-making in the Nuclear Age," *Bulletin of the Atomic Scientists*, v. 18, December 1962: 7–8.

Nitze, Paul. "Political Aspects of a National Strategy," *Survival,* v. 2, November–December 1960: 219–226.

———. "National Policy-Making Techniques," *SAIS Review,* v. 3, Spring 1959: 3–8.

Perkins, James A. "Administration of the National Security Program," *Public Administration Review,* v. 13, Spring 1953: 80–86.

Rogers, Lindsay. "The Political Setting of American Policy," *Journal of International Affairs,* v. 6, Spring 1952: 135–144.

Rostow, Walt W. "Ideas and Action," *Department of State Bulletin,* v. 47, July 9, 1962: 59–63.

Souers, Sidney W. "Policy Formulation for National Security," *American Political Science Review,* v. 43, June 1949: 534–543.

Strang, Lord. "The Formation and Control of Foreign Policy," *Durham University Journal,* v. 49, June 1957: 98–108.

Taylor, Maxwell D. "Security Will Not Wait," *Foreign Affairs,* v. 39, January 1961: 174–194.

Thompson, C. L. "Formulating Foreign Policy," *Current History,* v. 30, March 1956: 166–171.

Wood, M. K. "The National Security Dilemma: Challenge to Management Scientists," *Management Science,* v. 7, April 1961: 195.

2. THE ROLE OF THE PRESIDENT AND THE EXECUTIVE OFFICE

Binkley, Wilfred E. *The Man in the White House: His Powers and Duties.* Baltimore: Johns Hopkins Press, 1959.

Coffey, Joseph I., and Vincent P. Rock. *The Presidential Staff.* Washington, D.C.: National Planning Association, April 1961. p. 102.

Egger, Rowland. *The Unsettled Limits of the American Presidency.* New York: 1960. p. 49.

Fenno, Richard F., Jr. *The President's Cabinet.* Cambridge: Harvard University Press, 1959. p. 327.

Finer, Herman. *The Presidency: Crisis and Regeneration.* Chicago: University of Chicago Press, 1960. p. 374.

Henry, Laurin L. *Presidential Transitions.* Washington, D.C.: The Brookings Institution, 1960. p. 755.

Koenig, Louis W. *The Invisible Presidency.* New York: Holt, Rinehart & Winston, Inc., 1960. p. 438.

May, Ernest R. *The Ultimate Decision: The President as Commander in Chief.* New York: George Braziller, Inc., 1960.

Millis, Walter. *The Constitution and the Common Defense.* New York: Fund for the Republic, 1959. (Free Society, series)

Nash, Bradley De Lamater. *Staffing the Presidency.* Washington, D.C.: prepared for the National Planning Association, 1952. (Planning pamphlets, No. 80).

Neustadt, Richard E. *Presidential Power, the Politics of Leadership.* New York: John Wiley & Sons, Inc., 1960. p. 224.

———. *Reorganizing the Presidency in 1961.* A preview of the issues, prepared for the 1960

Annual Meeting of the American Political Science Association, New York: 1960.

Rossiter, Clinton. *The American Presidency.* New York: Harcourt, Brace & World, Inc., 1960. p. 281.

Stanley, Timothy W., with H. H. Ransom. *The National Security Council.* Harvard Defense Policy Seminar Serial No. 104, Jan. 12, 1957.

Tugwell, Rexford G. *The Enlargement of the Presidency.* New York: Doubleday & Company, Inc., 1960. p. 508.

ARTICLES

Alsop, Stewart, and Charles Bartlett. "In Time of Crisis," *Saturday Evening Post,* v. 235, December 8, 1962: 15–20.

"The American Presidency in the Last Half Century: A Symposium," *Current History,* v. 39, October 1960: 193–236.

Anderson, Dillon. "The President and National Security," *Atlantic Monthly,* v. 197, January 1956: 42–46.

Bailey, Stephen K. "The President and His Political Executives," *Annals of the American Academy of Political and Social Science,* v. 307, September 1956: 24–36.

Bresica, Peter F. "The National Security Council: Integration of American Foreign Policy," *Columbia Journal of International Affairs,* v. 4, Spring 1950: 74–77.

Clark, G. Edward. "Executive Branch of the Government: Dynamics in a Cloister," *Foreign Service Journal,* v. 34, February 1957: 22–23, 48.

Cutler, Robert. "The Development of the National Security Council," *Foreign Affairs,* v. 34, April 1956: 441–458.

Driggs, Don. W. "The President as Chief Educator on Foreign Affairs," *Western Political Quarterly,* v. 11, December 1958: 813–819.

Fairman, Charles. "The President as Commander-in-Chief," *Journal of Politics,* v. 11, February 1949: 145–170.

Fenno, Richard F., Jr. "Now is the Time for Cabinet Makers," *New York Times Magazine,* November 20, 1960: 12, 88, 91–94.

Frankel, Joseph. "Rational Decision-Making in Foreign Policy," *Year Book of World Affairs,* 1960: 40–66.

Gordon, Bernard K. "The Top of Policy Hill," *Bulletin of the Atomic Scientists,* v. 16, September 1960: 289–291.

Gray, Gordon. "Organizing for Total Defense," *General Electric Quarterly,* v. 3, July–September 1960: 4–10.

Halle, Louis J. "Lessons of the Cuban Blunder," *New Republic,* v. 144, June 5, 1961: 13–17.

Hammond, Paul Y. "The National Security Council as a Device for Interdepartmental Coordination: An Interpretation and Appraisal," *American Political Science Review,* v. 54, December 1960: 899–910.

Henry, Laurin L. "Transferring the Presidency: Variations, Trends, and Patterns," *Public Administration Review,* v. 20, Autumn 1960: 187–195.

Hirschfield, Robert S. "The Power of the Contemporary Presidency," *Parliamentary Affairs,* v. 14, Summer 1961, 353–377.

Hobbs, Edward H. "The President and Administration — Eisenhower," *Public Administration Review,* v. 18, Autumn 1958: 306–313.

Irish, Marian D. "The Organization Man in the Presidency," *Journal of Politics,* v. 20, May 1958: 27, 96–98.

Kesselman, Mark. "Presidential Leadership in Congress on Foreign Policy," *Midwest Journal of Political Science,* v. 5, August 1961: 284–289.

Kintner, William R. "Organizing for Conflict: A Proposal," *Orbis,* v. 2, Summer 1958: 155–174.

Kirkpatrick, H. P. "Advisers or Policymakers: The National Security Council," *American Perspective,* v. 2, February 1949: 443–450.

Kuic, Vukan. "Theory and Practice of the American Presidency," *Review of Politics,* v. 23, July 1961: 307–322.

Lay, James S., Jr. "The National Security Council," *American Foreign Service Journal,* March 1948: 7–8.

———. "National Security Council's Role in the U.S. Security and Peace Program," *World Affairs,* v. 115, Summer 1952: 37–39.

Legere, Lawrence J., Jr. "Military Advice for a Strong President," *Army,* v. 11, June 1961: 22–28.

Longaker, R. P. "President as International Leader," *Law and Contemporary Problems,* v. 21, Fall 1956: 735–752.

McClure, W. "Presidency and World Affairs: Mobilization of Assistance," *Journal of Politics,* v. 11, February 1949: 206–217.

Morgenthau, Hans J., "Can We Entrust Defense to a Committee?" *New York Times Magazine,* June 7, 1959: 9, 62–66.

Neustadt, Richard E. "Presidency and Legislation: The Growth of Central Clearance," *American Political Science Review,* v. 48, September 1954: 641–671.

———. "Presidency and Legislation: Planning the President's Program," *American Political Science Review,* v. 49, December 1955: 989–1021.

———. "Staffing the Presidency: the Role of White House Agencies," *Indian Journal of Public Administration,* v. 8, no. 3: 270–281. Reprinted in U.S. Congress. Senate. Committee on Government Operations. Administration of National Security. Selected papers. Subcommittee on National Security Staffing and Operations, 87th Cong., 2nd Sess. Washington, D.C.: U.S. Government Printing Office, 1962: 127–136.

Nitze, Paul H. "The Modern President as a World Figure," *Annals of the American Academy of Political and Social Science,* v. 307, September 1956: 114–123.

Norman, Lloyd. "The Commander in Chief and National Security Policy," *Army,* v. 12, February 1962: 46–49.

Reston, James. "The Security Council at Work: The Commander-in-Chief's Group of Policy Coordinators," *Reporter,* v. 1, May 10, 1949: 8–10.

Rosenau, James S. "Consensus, Leadership and Foreign Policy," *SAIS Review,* v. 6, Winter 1962: 3–10.

Smith, Roger. "Restraints on American Foreign Policy," *Daedalus,* v. 91, Fall 1962: 705–716.

Stuart, G. H. "Presidential Control of Foreign Policy," *Current History,* v. 22, April 1952: 207–210.

Truman, Harry S. "My View of the Presidency," *Look,* v. 22, Nov. 11, 1958: 25–31.

———. "The President's Responsibility," *Military Review,* v. 42, September 1962: 2–4.

Vile, M. J. C. "The Formation and Execution of Policy in the United States," *Political Science Quarterly,* v. 33, April–June 1962: 162–171.

Wyeth, George A., Jr. "The National Security Council: Concept of Operations; Organization; Actual Operations," *Journal of International Affairs,* v. 8, No. 2, 1954: 185–195.

3. THE DEPARTMENT OF DEFENSE

Biadasz, Francis E. *Proposals for Defense Reorganization: Analysis and Evaluation.* Washington, D.C.: Naval War College, 1958.

Enthoven, A. C., and H. S. Rowen. *An Analysis of Defense Organization.* Santa Monica, Calif.: The RAND Corporation Research Paper P-1640, 1959. p. 55.

Hammond, Paul Y. *Organizing for Defense: The American Military Establishment in the Twentieth Century.* Princeton: Princeton University Press, 1961.

Hittle, James D. *The Military Staff, Its History and Development* (rev. ed.) Harrisburg, Pa.: Military Service Publishing Co., 1949.

Job-Concept of the Civilian Secretary. Harvard Defense Policy Seminar Serial No. 93, November 8, 1956.

Kast, Fremont Ellsworth, and James E. Rosenzweig. *Management in the Space Age; An Analysis of the Concept of Weapon System Management and Its Non-Military Applications.* New York: Exposition Press, 1962. p. 183.

Kintner, William R. *Forging a New Sword.* New York: Harper & Row, Publishers, 1958.

Leach, W. Barton. *The Job of a Service Secretary.* Harvard Defense Policy Seminar Serial No. 103, December 1956.

——— and H. H. Ransom. *Department of Defense Reorganization—1958.* Harvard Defense Policy Seminar Serial No. 131, October 6, 1958.

McClendon, Robert Earl. *Changes in Organization for National Defense, 1949–1953.* Maxwell Air Force Base, Ala.; Documentary Research Division Research Studies Institute, Air University, 1956. (U.S. Air University, Documentary Research Study, AU-256-54-RSI.)

Millis, Walter. *Arms and Men: A Study of American Military History.* New York: G. P. Putnam's Sons, 1956.

Mosher, Frederick C. *Program Budgeting: Theory and Practice, With Particular Reference to the*

U.S. Department of the Army. Chicago: Public Administration Service, 1954.

Ransom, Harry Howe. *Government Secrecy and National Security: An Analysis.* Harvard Defense Policy Seminar Serial No. 123, January 1958.

Rockefeller Brothers Fund. *International Security, the Military Aspect: Report of Panel II of the Special Studies Project.* New York: Doubleday & Company, Inc., 1958.

Stanley, Timothy W. *American Defense and National Security.* Foreword by Robert Cutler. Washington, D.C.: Public Affairs Press, 1956.

Taylor, Maxwell D. *The Uncertain Trumpet.* New York: Harper & Row, Publishers, 1959. p. 203.

ARTICLES

Baldwin, Hanson W. "Changes in Joint Chiefs," *New York Times,* June 1, 1955: 16.

———. "Joint Chiefs—Fulcrum of the 'Islands' Debate," *New York Times,* April 10, 1955: 3E.

———. "Scope of Command: Joint Chiefs' Definition of the Authority of Unified Operation Heads Called Vital," *New York Times,* February 5, 1959: 12.

Bolles, Blair. "Joint Chiefs of Staff and U.S. Policy," *Foreign Policy Bulletin,* v. 31, March 15, 1952: 3.

Borklund, C. W.. "The Case for Reorganization," *Armed Forces Management,* v. 7, March 1961: 18–21.

Brodie, Bernard. "The Scientific Strategists," *Monograph No. 7 of the Council for Atomic Age Studies, 1962.* Reprinted in U.S. Congress. Senate. Committee on Government Operations. Administration of National Security. Selected papers. Subcommittee on National Security Staffing and Operations, 87th Congress, 2nd Sess. Washington, D.C.: Government Printing Office, 1962: 190–201.

Connery, Robert H. "Financial Management in the United States Army," *American Political Science Review,* v. 43, February 1949: 38–52.

Church, Albert T., Jr., and Lloyd R. Vasey. "Defense Organization Issues," United States Naval Institute Proceedings, v. 87, February 1961: 23–31.

Collins, J. Lawton. "Our Modern Military Establishment," *Military Review,* v. 42, September 1962: 17–30.

Cutler, Robert. "Defense Organization at the Policy Level," *General Electric Defense Quarterly,* v. 1, January–March 1959: 8–15.

Davis, Kyle. "Command and Command Relationships," *Military Review,* v. 34, February 1955: 24–33.

"Department of Defense: Annual Report," *Armed Forces Management,* v. 8, November 1961: 7–120.

"Department of Defense: Annual Report," *Armed Forces Management,* v. 9, November 1962: 1–114.

Drucker, Peter F. "Defense Organization: New Realities and Old Concepts," *General Electric Defense Quarterly,* v. 2, January–March 1959: 4–7.

Duffield, E. S. "Organizing for Defense: To Give Proper Scope to Businessmen as Well as to Handle the Vast Complexity of its Operations, the Department of Defense Will Have to Decentralize," *Harvard Business Review,* v. 31, September 1953: 29–42.

Dupré, J. Stefan, and W. Eric Gustafson. "Contracting for Defense: Private Firms and the Public Interest," *Political Science Quarterly,* v. 77, June 1962: 161–177.

Eliot, George Fielding. "Interservice Competition," *Ordnance,* v. 44, January–February 1960: 558–561.

Enthoven, Alain C. "Systems Analysis and Decision Making," *Military Review,* v. 43, January 1963: 7–17.

Foldes, Lucien. "Military Budgeting and Financial Control," *Public Administration Review,* v. 17, Winter 1957: 36–43.

Frye, W. "National Military Establishment," *American Political Science Review,* v. 43, June 1949: 543–555.

Hammond, Paul Y. "Effects of Structure on Policy," *Public Administration Review,* v. 18, Summer 1958: 175–179.

Henry, A. F. and others. "Armed Forces Unification and the Pentagon Officer," *Public Administration Review,* v. 15, Summer 1955: 173–180.

Hensel, H. Struve. "Changes Inside the Pentagon," *Harvard Business Review,* v. 32, January–February 1954: 98–108.

Hitch, Charles J. "Programmer to Bridge Defense Plans Gap," *Armed Forces Management,* v. 7, April 1961: 46, 50.

Huntington, Samuel P. "Interservice Competition and the Political Roles of the Armed Services," *American Political Science Review,* v. 55, March 1961: 40–52.

Huzar, Elias. "Reorganization for National Security," *Journal of Politics,* v. 12, February 1950: 128–152.

Janowitz, Morris. "Military Mission: Key to Military Organization," *Air Force,* v. 43, March 1960: 54–58.

Kintner, William R. "Progress in Defense Organization," *Journal of Public Law,* v. 9, Spring 1960: 73–95.

Kissinger, Henry A. "Strategy and Organization," *Foreign Affairs,* v. 35, April 1957: 379, 394.

McCullough, Hugh. "New Concepts in Defense Planning, Programming and Budgeting," *Federal Accountant,* v. 12, September 1962: 70–84.

McDonald, William G. "The Changing Management Role of the Military Departments," *Air University Quarterly Review,* v. 13, Summer 1962: 45–55.

Millett, John D. "The War Department in World War II," *American Political Science Review,* v. 40, October 1946: 863–897.

Mosher, Frederick C. "Old Concepts and New Problems," *Public Administration Review,* v. 18, Summer 1958: 169–175.

——— and others. "Decision-Making in Defense:

The Role of Organization," *Public Administration Review*, v. 18, Summer 1958: 169–188.

"The Question of National Defense Organization; A Quarterly Review Study," *Air University Quarterly Review*, v. 12, Summer 1960: 52–134.

Rosen, Harris N. "Control of the Army Budgetary Process," *Military Review*, v. 34, February 1955: 14–23.

Waters, Ace L., Jr., and Jack L. Rogers. "The Reorganization of the Department of Defense," *Armor*, v. 48, January–February 1959: 17–21.

Yost, Carl R. "Management Control," *Armed Forces Management*, v. 8, December 1961: 40–42.

4. DIPLOMACY AND THE DEPARTMENT OF STATE

Barnes, William, and John Heath Morgan. *The Foreign Service of the United States*. Washington, D.C.: Government Printing Office, 1961, p. 430.

Barron, Bryton. *Inside the State Department: A Candid Appraisal of the Bureaucracy*. New York: Comet Press Books, 1956.

Beal, John Robinson. *John Foster Dulles: A Biography*. New York: Harper & Row, Publishers, 1957.

DeConde, Alexander. *The American Secretary of State: An Interpretation*. New York: Frederick A. Praeger, Inc., 1962.

Elder, Robert E. *The Policy Machine: State Department and United States Foreign Policy*. Syracuse, N.Y.: Syracuse University Press, 1961.

———. *The Foreign Leader Program: Operations in the United States*. Washington, D.C.: The Brookings Institution, 1961.

Fleming, D. F. *The Cold War and Its Origins, 1917–1960* (2 Vols.). New York: Doubleday & Company, Inc., 1961.

Graham, Stuart H. *The Department of State*. New York: The Macmillan Company, 1949.

Haviland, H. Field, Jr. *The Formulation and Administration of United States Foreign Policy*. Washington, D.C.: The Brookings Institution, 1960.

Kennan, George F. *American Diplomacy 1900–1950*. Chicago: University of Chicago Press, 1951.

———. *Realities of American Foreign Policy*. Princeton: Princeton University Press 1954.

Kertesz, Stephen D. *American Diplomacy in a New Era*. Notre Dame, Ind.: University of Notre Dame Press, 1961.

———, and M. A. Fitzsimons. *Diplomacy in a Changing World*. South Bend: University of Notre Dame Press, 1959.

Mid-America Assembly. *The Secretary of State*. The Mid-America Assembly, November 16–19, 1961. A Conference jointly sponsored by The University of Missouri and The American Assembly of Columbia University. New York: Columbia University Press 1961.

Plischke, Elmer. *Conduct of American Diplomacy*. Princeton: D. Van Nostrand Co., Inc., 1962.

Price, Don K. (ed.) *The Secretary of State*. Englewood Cliffs, N.J., Prentice-Hall, Inc., 1961.

Steiner, Zara S. *Present Problems of the Foreign Service*. Princeton: Princeton University, Center of International Studies, March 1961.

———. *The State Department and the Foreign Service: The Wriston Report—Four Years Later*. Princeton: Princeton University, Center of International Studies, 1958. (Memorandum No. 16.)

Williams, William Appleman. *The Tragedy of American Diplomacy*. Cleveland: The World Publishing Company, 1959.

ARTICLES

Bowles, Chester. "Toward a New Diplomacy," *Foreign Affairs*, v. 40, January 1962: 244–251.

"The Department of State, 1930–1955: Expanding Functions and Responsibilities," *Department of State Bulletin*, v. 21, March 21, 1955: 470–486.

Elder, Robert E. "Country Desk Officer Low Man on the Totem Pole," *Foreign Service Journal*, v. 35, May 1958: 38–46; June, 1958: 18–21.

Gerber, William. "Organizational Reform Since World War II," *Foreign Service Journal*, v. 36, November 1959: 25–27.

Hannah, Norman B. "Craftsmanship and Responsibility: A Restatement of the Generalist-Specialist Problem," *Foreign Service Journal*, v. 39, April 1962: 21–24.

Kennan, George F. "Diplomacy as a Profession," *Foreign Service Journal*, v. 38, May 1961: 23–26.

———and others. "Planning in the Department of State," *Foreign Service Journal*, v. 38, March 1961: 20–24.

Laves, Walter H. C., and Francis O. Wilcox. "The Reorganization of the Department of State," *American Political Science Review*, v. 38, April 1944: 289–301.

Marshall, Charles Burton. "Making Foreign Policy on the New Frontier," *The Annals*, v. 342, July 1962: 138–146.

McCamy, J. L. "People of the State Department and Foreign Service," *American Political Science Review*, v. 38, December 1954: 1067–1082.

McGhee, George C. "The Changing Role of the American Ambassadors," *Department of State Bulletin*, v. 46, June 25, 1962: 1007–1011.

Montgomery, John D. "Crossing the Culture Bars: An Approach to the Training of American Technicians for Overseas Assignments," *World Politics*, v. 13, July 1961: 544–560.

Morgan, George A. "Planning in Foreign Affairs: The State of the Art," *Foreign Affairs*, v. 39, January 1961: 271–278.

Morgenstern, Oskar. "Decision Theory and The State Department," *Foreign Service Journal*, v. 37, December 1960: 19–22.

Osborne, John. "Is the State Department Manageable?" *Fortune*, v. 55, March 1957: 110–113, 267–276.

"The Policy Planning Staff—What It Is—What It

Does," *Foreign Service Newsletter,* v. 123, May 1957: 4–6.

Rossow, Robert. "The Professionalization of the New Diplomacy," *World Politics,* v. 14, July 1962: 561–575.

Saltzman, Charles E. "The Reorganization of the American Foreign Service," *Department of State Bulletin,* September 27, 1954: 436–446.

Stuart, G. H. "A Streamlined State Department: The Effects of Reorganization," *Current History,* v. 18, February 1950: 71–75.

Scigliano, R. "They Work for Americans: A Study of the National Staff of an American Overseas Agency," *American Sociological Review,* v. 25, October 1960: 695–703.

Thayer, Charles W. "Our Ambassadors: An Intimate Appraisal of the Men and the System," *Harper's Magazine,* v. 219, September 1959: 29–35.

Waters, Maurice. "The Ad Hoc Diplomat: A Legal and Historical Analysis," *Wayne Law Review,* v. 6, Summer 1960: 380–392.

Wriston, Henry M. "The Special Envoy," *Foreign Affairs,* v. 38, January 1960: 219–237.

5. THE ROLE OF CONGRESS

Acheson, Dean G. *A Citizen Looks at Congress* (1st ed.). New York: Harper & Row, Publishers, 1957.

American Academy of Political and Social Science. *Congress and Foreign Relations.* Edited by Thorsten V. Kalijarvi and Chester E. Marrow. Philadelphia, 1953. (Its Annals, v. 289).

Bailey, Stephen K., and Howard D. Samuel. *Congress At Work.* New York: Holt, Rinehart & Winston, Inc., 1952.

Carroll, Holbert N. *The House of Representatives and Foreign Affairs.* Pittsburgh: University of Pittsburgh Press, 1958.

Cheever, Daniel S., and H. Field Haviland, Jr. *American Foreign Policy and the Separation of Powers.* Cambridge: Harvard University Press, 1952.

Dahl, Robert A. *Congress and Foreign Policy* (1st ed.). New York: Harcourt, Brace & World, Inc., 1950.

Dennison, Eleanor E. *The Senate Foreign Relations Committee.* California: Stanford University Press; London: Oxford University Press, 1942.

Farnsworth, David N. *The Senate Committee on Foreign Relations.* Urbana: University of Illinois Press, 1961.

Galloway, George B. *The Legislative Process in Congress.* New York: Thomas Y. Crowell Company, 1953.

Green, Harold P., and Alan Rosenthal. *The Joint Committee on Atomic Energy: A Study in Fusion of Governmental Power.* Report by the JCAE Study Project. Washington, D.C.: George Washington University, 1961.

Griffith, Ernest S. *Congress, Its Contemporary Role.* (3rd ed.). New York: New York University Press, 1961.

Huzar, Elias. *The Purse and the Sword: Control of the Army by Congress Through Military Appropriations, 1933–1950.* Ithaca, N.Y.: Cornell University Press, 1950.

Kofmehl, Kenneth Theodore. *Professional Staffs of Congress.* Purdue University Studies: Humanities Series. West Lafayette, Ind.: Purdue University, 1962.

Matthews, Donald R. *U.S. Senators and Their World.* Chapel Hill: University of North Carolina Press, 1960.

Robinson, James A. *Congress and Foreign Policy-Making: A Study in Legislative Influence and Initiative.* Homewood, Ill.: Dorsey Press, 1962.

———. *The Monroney Resolution: Congressional Initiative in Foreign Policy Making.* Eagleton Institute, Cases in Practical Politics. Case 8. New York: McGraw-Hill Book Company, 1960.

Wallace, Robert Ash. *Congressional Control of Federal Spending.* Detroit: Wayne State University Press, 1960.

Westphal, Albert C. F. *The House Committee on Foreign Affairs.* New York: Columbia University Press, 1942; London: P. S. King and Staples, 1942.

Young, Roland A. *The American Congress.* New York: Harper & Row, Publishers, 1958.

———. *Congressional Politics in the Second World War.* New York: Columbia University Press, 1956.

ARTICLES

Bradshaw, Mary E. "Congress and Foreign Policy Since 1900," *Annals of the American Academy of Political and Social Science,* v. 289, September 1953: 40–48.

Brown, Ben H., Jr. "Congress and the Department of State," *Annals of the American Academy of Political and Social Science,* v. 289, September 1953: 73–83.

Brown, McAlister. "The Demise of State Department Public Opinion Polls: A Study in Legislative Oversight," *Midwest Journal of Political Science,* v. 5, February 1961: 1–17.

Clark, Joseph S. "The Influence of Congress in the Formulation of Disarmament Policy," *The Annals,* v. 342, July 1962: 147–153.

Cohen, Benjamin V. "The Evolving Role of Congress in Foreign Affairs," *Proceedings of the American Philosophical Society,* v. 92, October 25, 1948: 211–216.

Colegrove, Kenneth. "The Role of Congress and Public Opinion in Formulating Foreign Policy," *American Political Science Review,* v. 38, October 1944: 956–969.

"Congress and U.S. Foreign Relations," *Congressional Digest,* v. 30, February, 1951: 35–64.

"Congressional Influence in Foreign Policy," *Congressional Quarterly Weekly Report,* v. 17, October 30, 1959: 1442–1445.

Dawson, Raymond H. "Congressional Innovation and Intervention in Defense Policy: Legislative Authorization of Weapons Systems," *American Political Science Review,* v. 56, March 1962: 42–57.

Farnsworth, David N. "A Comparison of the Senate and Its Foreign Relations Committee on Selected Roll-Call Votes," *Western Political Quarterly,* v. 14, March 1961: 168–175.

Gillette, Guy M. "The Senate in Foreign Relations," *Annals,* v. 289, September 1953: 49–57.

Goodwin, George, Jr. "Subcommittees: The Miniature Legislatures of Congress," *American Political Science Review,* v. 56, September 1962: 596–604.

Gordon, Bernard K. "The Military Budget: Congressional Phase," *Journal of Politics,* v. 23, November 1961: 689–710.

Gould, James W. "The Origins of the Senate Committee on Foreign Relations," *Western Political Quarterly,* v. 12, September 1959: 670–682.

Graebner, Norman. "Politics in Foreign Policy," *Current History,* v. 28, January 1955: 7–14.

Green, Harold P., and Alan Rosenthal. "Fusion of Governmental Power," *Bulletin of the Atomic Scientists,* v. 18, June 1962: 12–16.

Griffith, Ernest S. "The Place of Congress in Foreign Relations," *Annals,* v. 289, September 1953: 11–21.

Halperin, Morton. "Is the Senate's Foreign Relations Research Worthwhile?" *American Behavioral Scientist,* v. 4, September 1960: 21–24.

Henkin, Louis. "The Treaty Makers and the Law Makers: The Law of the Land and Foreign Relations," *University of Pennsylvania Law Review,* v. 107, May 1959: 903–936.

Hickey, John. "The Role of the Congress in Foreign Policy," *Inter-American Economic Affairs,* v. 14, Spring 1961: 67–89.

Hilsman, Roger. "Congressional-Executive Relations and the Foreign Policy Consensus," *American Political Science Review,* v. 52, September 1958: 725–744.

Humphrey, Hubert H. "The Senate in Foreign Policy," *Foreign Affairs,* v. 37, July 1959: 525–536.

Jewell, Malcolm E. "The Senate Republican Policy Committee and Foreign Policy," *Western Political Quarterly,* v. 12, December 1959: 966–980.

Kalijarvi, Thorsten V. "The Future of Congress in Foreign Relations," *Annals,* v. 289, September 1953: 172–177.

Kampelman, Max M. "Congressional Control vs. Executive Flexibility," *Public Administration Review,* v. 18, Summer 1958: 185–188.

Kennedy, John F. "Congress: How it Works Toward a More Organized Defense Effort," *General Electric Defense Quarterly,* v. 2, January–March 1959: 19–21.

Kesselman, Mark. "Presidential Leadership in Congress on Foreign Policy," *Midwest Journal of Political Science,* v. 5, August 1961: 284–289.

Kilday, Paul J. "The Office of the Legislative Branch in the Formulation of National Security Policy," extension of remarks, *Congressional Record,* v. 101, Feb. 24, 1955: A1195–A1199.

"The 'Military Lobby': Its Impact on Congress, Nation," *Congressional Quarterly Weekly Report,* v. 14, March 24, 1961: 463–478.

Morton, Thurston B. "Congress and Foreign Affairs," *Social Science,* v. 30, October 1955: 236–238.

Moss, John E. "The Crisis of Secrecy," *Bulletin of the Atomic Scientists,* v. 17, January 1961: 8–11.

Nelson, Randall H. "Legislative Participation in the Treaty and Agreement Making Process," *Western Political Quarterly,* v. 13, March 1960: 154–71.

Perkins, James A. "Congressional Investigations of Matters of International Import," *American Political Science Review,* v. 34, April 1940: 284–294.

Ramey, James T. "The Joint Congressional Committee on Atomic Energy and the Civilian Control of Atomic Energy," Paper delivered before the American Political Science Association Annual Conference, New York, 1960, 22L.

Richards, James P. "The House of Representatives in Foreign Affairs," *Annals,* v. 289, September 1953: 66–72.

Robinson, James A. "Another Look at Senate Research on Foreign Policy," *American Behavioral Scientist,* v. 4, November 1960: 12–16.

Rourke, Francis E. "Administrative Secrecy: A Congressional Dilemma," *American Political Science Review,* v. 54, September 1960: 691–693.

Wiley, Alexander. "The Committee on Foreign Relations," *Annals,* v. 289, September 1953: 58–65.

Wright, Q. "Congress and the Treaty-Making Power," *American Society of International Law Proceedings,* 1952: 43–58.

Younger, Irving. "Congressional Investigations and Executive Secrecy: A Study in the Separation of Powers," *University of Pittsburgh Law Review,* v. 20, June 1959: 755–784.

6. THE ROLE OF PARTIES, PUBLIC OPINION, AND NONGOVERNMENTAL GROUPS

Almond, Gabriel A. *The American People and Foreign Policy* (1st ed.). New York: Harcourt, Brace & World, Inc., 1950; New York: Frederick A. Praeger, Inc., 1961.

Baker, Roscoe. *The American Legion and American Foreign Policy.* New York: Bookman Associates, 1954.

Bailey, Thomas A. *The Man in the Street: The Impact of American Public Opinion on Foreign Policy.* New York: The Macmillan Company, 1948.

Bauer, Raymond A., and Ithiel de Sola Pool. *American Businessmen and International Trade: Code Book and Data from A Study on Attitudes and Communications.* New York: The Free Press, 1960.

Beloff, Max. *Foreign Policy and the Democratic Process.* Baltimore: Johns Hopkins Press, 1955.

Cater, Douglass. *The Fourth Branch of Government.* Boston: Houghton Mifflin Company, 1959.

Cohen, Bernard C. *Citizen Education in World Affairs.* Princeton: Princeton University, Center of International Studies, 1953.

————. *The Influence of Nongovernmental Groups on Foreign Policy-Making*. Studies in citizen participation in international relations, v. II. Boston: World Peace Foundation, 1959.

————. *The Political Process and Foreign Policy: The Making of the Japanese Peace Settlement*. Princeton: Princeton University Press, 1957.

Dawson, Raymond H. *The Decision to Aid Russia, 1941: Foreign Policy and Domestic Politics*. Chapel Hill: University of North Carolina Press, 1957.

Elliott, Osborne. *Men at the Top*. New York: Harper & Row, Publishers, 1959.

Gaither, Rowan H., Jr. *The Ford Foundation and Foreign Affairs*. New York: Harper & Row, Publishers, 1956.

Graebner, Norman A. *The New Isolationism: A Study in Politics and Foreign Policy Since 1950*. New York: The Ronald Press Company, 1956.

Hero, Alfred. *Americans in World Affairs*. Studies in citizen participation in international relations, vol. 6. Boston: World Peace Foundation, 1959.

————. *Mass Media and World Affairs*. Boston: World Peace Foundation, 1959.

Hunter, Floyd. *Top Leadership U.S.A.* Chapel Hill: University of North Carolina Press, 1959.

Isaacs, Harold R. *Scratches on our Minds: American Images of China and India*. New York: The John Day Company, Inc., 1958.

Key, Valdimer O. *Politics, Parties, and Pressure Groups* (5th ed.). New York: Thomas Y. Crowell Company, 1963.

————. *Public Opinion and American Democracy*. New York: Alfred A. Knopf, Inc., 1961.

Lasswell, Harold D., Daniel Lerner, and C. Easton Rothwell. *The Comparative Study of Elites*. Stanford: Stanford University Press, 1952.

Lippmann, Walter. *Public Opinion*. New York: The Macmillan Company, 1922.

————. *The Public Philosophy*. Boston: Little, Brown and Company, 1955.

Matthews, Donald R. *The Social Background of Political Decision-Makers*. New York: Doubleday & Company, Inc., 1954.

Mills, Charles Wright. *The Power Elite*. New York: Oxford University Press, 1956.

Perkins, Dexter. *The Perkins Lectures*. (Popular Government and Foreign Policy). Pasadena, Calif.: Fund for Adult Education, 1956.

Rosenau, James N. *Public Opinion and Foreign Policy*. New York: Random House, Inc., 1961.

Savord, Ruth, and Donald Wasson. *American Agencies Interested in International Affairs*. New York: Council on Foreign Relations, 1955.

Scott, William A., and Stephen B. Withey. *The United States and the United Nations: The Public View, 1945–1955*. New York: Manhattan Publishing Co., 1958.

Seldes, George. *The People Don't Know: The American Press and the Cold War*. New York: Gaer Associates, 1949.

Westerfeld, Bradford. *Foreign Policy and Party Politics: Pearl Harbor to Korea*. New Haven: Yale University Press, 1955.

Williams, William A. *The Tragedy of American Diplomacy*. New York: Harcourt, Brace & World, Inc., 1958.

Windmuller, John P. *Foreign Affairs and the AFL-CIO*. Ithaca, N.Y.: State School of Industrial and Labor Relations, 1956. (Reprint Series, No. 44).

ARTICLES

Acheson, Dean G. "Parties and Foreign Policy," *Harper's*, v. 211, November 1955: 29–34.

Adler, Kenneth P., and Davis Bobrow. "Interest and Influence in Foreign Affairs," *Public Opinion Quarterly*, v. XX, Spring 1956, pp. 89–102.

Almond, Gabriel A. "Public Opinion and Space Technology," *Public Opinion Quarterly*, v. XXIV, Winter 1960: 553–572.

Bauer, Raymond A. "The Communicator and the Audience," *Journal of Conflict Resolution*, v. II, March 1958: 78–89.

Blaisdell, Donald A. "Pressure Groups, Foreign Policies, and International Politics," *Annals*, v. 319, September 1958: 149–157.

Brogan, D. W. "Politics and United States Foreign Policy," *International Affairs*, v. 33, April 1957: 165–175.

Dexter, Lewis A. "What do Congressmen Hear: The Mail," *Public Opinion Quarterly*, v. XX, Spring 1956: 16–27.

Donovan, John C. "The Political Party and Foreign Policy-Making: A Note of Speculation," *World Affairs Quarterly*, v. 28, April 1957: 62–75.

Emeny, Brooks. "Nongovernmental Organizations in International Affairs," *Social Science*, v. 30, October 1955: 239–243.

Feld, M. D. "Political Policy and Persuasion: The Role of Communications from Political Leaders," *Journal of Conflict Resolution*, v. II, March 1958: 78–89.

Gable, Richard W. "Political Interest Groups as Policy Shapers," *Annals*, v. 319, September 1958: 84–93.

Hilsman, Roger. "The Foreign Policy Consensus: An Interim Research Report," *Journal of Conflict Resolution*, v. III, December 1959: 361–383.

Kissinger, Henry. "The Policymaker and the Intellectual," *The Reporter*, v. 20, March 5, 1959: 30–35.

Klingberg, Frank L. "The Historical Alternation of Moods in American Foreign Policy," *World Politics*, v. 4, January 1952: 239–273.

MacClellan, David S., and Charles E. Woodhouse. "Businessmen in Foreign Policy," *Southwestern Social Science Quarterly*, v. 39, March 1959: 283–290.

Murphy, Robert D. "Labor's Concern with Foreign Affairs," *Department of State Bulletin*, v. 32, January 17, 1955: 84–86.

Pye, Lucian W. "Effects of Legislative and Administrative Accessibility on Interest Group Politics," *Prod*, v. 1, January 1958: 11–13.

Riesman, David. "Private People and Public Policy," *Bulletin of the Atomic Scientists*, v. 15, May 1959: 203–208.

Sussmann, Leila. "Mass Political Letterwriting in America," *Public Opinion Quarterly*, v. 23, Summer 1959: 203–212.

Welles, Sumner. "Pressure Groups and Foreign Policy," *Atlantic*, v. 180, November 1947: 63–67.

Wilson, Howard E. "The Role of the University in International Relations," *Annals*, v. 301, September 1955: 86–92.

Windmuller, J. P. "Foreign Affairs and the AFL-CIO," *Industrial and Labor Relations Review*, v. 9, April 1956: 419–432.

7. STRATEGIC INTELLIGENCE, PROPAGANDA, AND PSYCHOLOGICAL WARFARE

Carroll, Wallace. *Persuade or Perish*. Boston: Houghton Mifflin Company, 1948.

Daugherty, William E. *A Psychological Warfare Casebook*. In collaboration with Morris Janowitz. Baltimore: published for Operations Research Office, Johns Hopkins University. Baltimore: Johns Hopkins Press, 1958.

Dulles, Allen W. *The Craft of Intelligence*. New York: Doubleday & Company, Inc., 1963.

Hilsman, Roger. *Strategic Intelligence and National Decisions*. New York: The Free Press, 1956.

Holt, Robert T., and Robert W. van de Velde. *Strategic Psychological Operations and American Foreign Policy*. Chicago: University of Chicago Press, 1960.

Johnson, Haynes. *The Bay of Pigs*. New York: W. W. Norton & Company, Inc., 1964.

Katz, Daniel, Dorwin Cartwright, Samuel Eldersveld, and Alfred McClung Lee (eds.). *Public Opinion and Propaganda*. New York: Dryden Press, 1954.

Kent, Sherman. *Strategic Intelligence for American World Policy*. Princeton: Princeton University Press, 1949.

Linebarger, Paul M. A. *Psychological Warfare* (1st ed.). Washington, D.C.: Infantry Journal Press, 1948.

MacMahon, Arthur W. *Memorandum on the Postwar International Information Program of the United States*. Prepared in cooperation with the Office of Public Affairs. Washington, D.C.: The Department of State, 1945. U.S. Department of State, Publication 2438.

McGovern, William M. *Strategic Intelligence and the Shape of Tomorrow*. Published in cooperation with Foundation for Foreign Affairs, Inc. Chicago: Henry Regnery Co., 1961. (Foundation for Foreign Affairs Series, No. 5).

Platt, Washington. *Strategic Intelligence Production; Basic Principles*. New York: Frederick A. Praeger, Inc., 1957.

Qualter, Terence H. *Propaganda and Psychological Warfare*. New York: Random House, Inc., 1962.

Ransom, Harry H. *Central Intelligence and National Security*. Cambridge: Harvard University Press, 1958.

Scott, John. *Political Warfare*. New York: Harper & Row, Publishers, 1957.

Thomson, Charles A. H. *Overseas Information Service of the United States Government*. Washington, D.C.: Brookings Institution, 1948.

Tully, Andrew. *The CIA*. New York: William Morrow & Co., Inc., 1962.

Wise, David, and Tom Ross. *The Invisible Government*. New York: Random House, Inc., 1964.

ARTICLES

"Automation Aids Intelligence Flow," *Armed Forces Management*, v. 8, July 1962: 64–69.

Blumenfeld, F. Yorick. "Intelligence for Security," Washington, D.C.: *Editorial Research Reports*, v. 2, No. 24, 1961: 937–954.

Bruce, D. K. E. "National Intelligence Authority," *Virginia Quarterly Review*, v. 22, July 1946: 355–369.

Cook, Fred J. "The CIA," *Nation*, v. 192, June 24, 1961: 529–572.

DeWeerd, H. A. "Strategic Surprise in the Korean War," *Orbis*, v. 6, Fall 1962: 435–452.

Dulles, Allen W. "Dulles Outlines C.I.A.'s Intelligence Role," *Aviation Week*, v. 74, February 17, 1960: 87–97.

Evans, Allan. "Intelligence and Policy Formation," *World Politics*, v. 12, October 1959: 84–91.

———, and R. D. Gatewood. "Intelligence and Research: Sentinel and Scholar in Foreign Relations," *Department of State Bulletin*, v. 42, June 27, 1960: 1023–1027.

Evans, John W. "Research and Intelligence: The Part They Play in Foreign Policy," *Foreign Service Journal*, v. 34, March 1957: 24–25, 34, 40.

Fitch, Alva R. "Intelligence and Security—the Army's Newest Basic Branch," *Army Information Digest*, v. 17, August 1962: 2–8.

Hilsman, Roger. "Intelligence and Policy-Making in Foreign Affairs," *World Politics*, v. 5, October 1952: 1–45.

Oliver, Revilo P. "Intelligence in Intelligence," *American Opinion*, v. 9, November 1961: 37–46.

Ransom, Harry H. "How Intelligent is Intelligence?" *New York Times Magazine*, May 22, 1960: 26.

Stanford, N. "The Role of the CIA," *Foreign Policy Bulletin*, June 15, 1960: 148.

Stewart, Charles T., Jr. "Who is Mine Enemy?" *Military Review*, v. 41, October 1961: 14–20.

Taylor, Rufus L. "Command and the Intelligence Process," *U.S. Naval Institute Proceedings*, v. 86, August 1960: 27–39.

Wasserman, Benno. "The Failure of Intelligence Prediction," *Political Studies*, v. 8, June 1960: 156–169.

8. SCIENCE, SCIENTISTS, AND TECHNOLOGY

American Academy of Political and Social Science, Philadelphia. *Perspectives on Government and*

Science. Special Editor Norman Wengert. Philadelphia, 1960. (Its Annals, v. 327).

Amrine, Michael. *The Great Decision: The Secret History of the Atomic Bomb.* New York: G. P. Putnam's Sons, 1959.

Baxter, James Phinney. *Scientists Against Time.* Boston: Little, Brown and Company, 1946.

Blair, Clay, Jr. *The Atomic Submarine and Admiral Rickover.* New York: Holt, Rinehart & Winston, Inc., 1954.

Brewer, M. Carey. *Science and Defense: Military Research and Development in the United States.* Ph.D. Thesis, Harvard University, 1956.

Brodie, Bernard. *The Absolute Weapon.* New York: Harcourt, Brace & World, Inc., 1946.

———. *Sea Power in the Machine Age.* Princeton: Princeton University Press, 1941.

Bush, Vannevar. *Modern Arms and Free Men.* New York: Simon and Schuster, Inc., 1949.

Dahl, Robert A., and Ralph S. Brown, Jr. *Domestic Control of Atomic Energy.* New York: Social Science Research Council, 1951. Pamphlet 8.

Dupré, J. Stefan, and Sanford A. Lakoff. *Science and the Nation: Policy and Politics.* Englewood Cliffs, N.J.: Prentice-Hall, Inc., 1962.

Emme, Eugene M. *Hitler's Blitzbomber.* Research Studies Institute, Air University, December 1951.

Gilpin, Robert. *American Scientists and Nuclear Weapons Policy.* Princeton: Princeton University Press, 1962.

———, and Christopher Wright (eds.). *Scientists and National Policy-Making.* New York: Columbia University Press, 1964.

Higham, Robin. *The British Rigid Warship, 1908–1931: A Study in Weapons Policy.* London: Foulis, 1961.

Holley, Irving B. *Ideas and Weapons: Exploitation of the Aerial Weapon by the United States During World War I.* New Haven: Yale University Press, 1953.

Jungk, Robert. *Brighter Than a Thousand Suns: A Personal History of the Atomic Scientists.* New York: Harcourt, Brace & World, Inc., 1958.

Lindveit, Earl W. *Scientists in Government.* Washington, D.C.: Public Affairs Press, 1960.

McCamy, James L. *Science and Public Administration.* Tuscaloosa: University of Alabama Press, 1960.

Ogburn, William F. (ed.). *Technology and International Relations.* Chicago: University of Chicago Press, 1949.

Peck, Merton J., and Frederic M. Scherer. *The Weapons Acquisition Process: An Economic Analysis.* Cambridge: Harvard Business School, 1962.

Price, Don K. *Government and Science: Their Dynamic Relation in American Democracy.* New York: New York University, 1954.

Research for Public Policy. Brookings Dedication Lectures. Washington, D.C.: The Brookings Institution, 1961.

"Science and World Politics" (A Symposium), *Journal of International Affairs,* v. 13, 1959.

Snow, C. P. *Science and Government.* Cambridge: Harvard University Press, 1960.

Stewart, Irvin. *Organizing Scientific Research for War: The Administrative History of the Office of Scientific Research and Development* (1st ed.). Boston: Little, Brown and Company, 1948.

Stover, Carl F. *The Government of Science.* Santa Barbara, Calif.: Center for the Study of Democratic Institutions, 1962.

U.S. House of Representatives Subcommittee on Military Operations. *Organization and Administration of the Military Research and Development Programs.* House Report No. 2618, 83rd Cong., 2nd Sess. August 4, 1954.

———. *Organization and Administration of the Military and Development Programs.* Hearings, 83rd Cong., 2nd Sess., 1954.

U.S. Senate, Committee on Foreign Relations. *Developments in Military Technology and Their Impact on U.S. Strategy and Foreign Policy.* (Study No. 8). A study prepared by the Washington Center of Foreign Policy Research, December 6, 1959.

Waldo, Dwight. *The Research Function of University Bureaus and Institutes for Government-Related Research.* Berkeley: University of California, Bureau of Public Administration, 1960.

ARTICLES

Blumenfeld, F. Yorick. "National Science Policy," Washington, *Editorial Research Reports,* v. 1, No. 19, May 18, 1960: 361–378.

Brode, Wallace R. "Development of a Science Policy," *Science,* v. 131, January 1, 1960: 9–15.

———. "National and International Science," *Department of State Bulletin,* v. 42, May 9, 1960: 735–739.

Brooks, Harvey. "Long Range Planning for Science in the Federal Government," *Nuclear News,* v. 5, August 1962: 3–5.

Denny, Brewster C., and Emmanuel G. Mesthene. "Science and Statecraft," Santa Monica, *The RAND Corporation Research Paper,* P-2462-1, January 1962.

Dickinson, William B., Jr. "Government Research and Development," Washington, D.C.: *Editorial Research Reports,* v. 1, No. 3, January 24, 1962: 43–60.

"Evolution of the Organization of the Federal Government for Scientific Activities: 1947 to the Present," *Science,* v. 128, Nov. 28, 1958: 1329–1331.

Fozzy, Paula. "Research Coordination," *Bulletin of the Atomic Scientists,* v. 17, March 1961: 29–31.

Gilpin, Robert G., Jr. "The Politics of American Scientists, 1945–1960," Ph.D. Thesis, University of California (Berkeley), 1960.

Glass, H. Bentley. "The Scientist as Politician," *Johns Hopkins Magazine,* v. 13, May–June 1962: 24, 26–29.

Greenberg, D. S. "Science and Foreign Affairs: New Effort Under Way to Enlarge Role of Scientists in Policy Planning," *Science,* v. 136, May 25, 1962: 698–700.

Haller, George L. "Industry's Role in Defense Planning," *General Electric Defense Quarterly*, v. 2, October–December 1959: 13–17.

Halmos, E. E., Jr. "IDA's 'Brain Factory' Guides Weapons Choices," *Missiles and Rockets*, v. 5, January 5, 1959: 20–21.

Hanks, L. M., Jr. and others. "The Scientist and U.S. Foreign Policy," *Saturday Review*, v. 39, June 2, 1956: 41–47.

Holzman, Benjamin G. "Basic Research for National Survival," *Air University Quarterly Review*, v. 12, Spring 1960: 28–52.

Hutchinson, Charles E. "An Institute for National Security Affairs," *American Behavioral Scientist*, v. 4, September 1960: 31–35.

Kaplan, Norman. "The Role of the Research Administrator," *Administrative Science Quarterly*, v. 4, June 1959: 20–42.

Katzenbach, Edward L. "Ideas: A New Defense Industry," *Reporter*, v. 24, March 2, 1961: 17–21.

Killian, James R., Jr. "Science and Public Policy," *Bulletin of the Atomic Scientists*, v. 15, April 1959: 168–172.

Kistiakowsky, George B. "Science and Foreign Affairs," *Bulletin of the Atomic Scientists*, v. 16, April 1960: 114–116.

Klein, Burton. "A Radical Proposal for R. and D.," *Fortune*, v. 57, May 1958.

Livingston, J. Sterling. "Decision Making in Weapons Development," *Harvard Business Review*, v. 36, January–February 1958: 127–136.

Mainzer, Lewis C. "A Public Place for American Science," *Virginia Quarterly Review*, v. 37, Summer 1961: 398–413.

———. "Science Democratized: Advisory Committees on Research," *Public Administration Review*, v. 18, Autumn 1958: 314–323.

———. "Scientific Freedom in Government-Sponsored Research," *Journal of Politics*, v. 23, May 1961: 212–230.

Price, Don K. "The Scientific Establishment," *Science*, v. 136, June 29, 1962: 1099–1106.

———, J. S. Dupré, and W. E. Gustafson. "Current Trends in Science Policy in the United States," *Impact of Science on Society*, v. 10, 1960: 187–213.

Schilling, Warner R. "The H-Bomb Decision: How to Decide Without Actually Choosing," *Political Science Quarterly*, v. 76, March 1961: 24–46.

———. "Scientists, Foreign Policy, and Politics," *American Political Science Review*, v. 56, June 1962: 287–300.

"Science, Scientists and Society," *American Behavioral Scientist*, v. 6, December 1962: 2–28.

"Scientific Progress and the Federal Government," *Science*, v. 132, December 1960: 1802–1815.

Seaborg, Glenn T. "Higher Education and the Atomic Energy Commission," *Higher Education*, v. 18, December 1961: 3–6, 19–23.

Shannon, James A., and Charles V. Kidd. "Federal Support of Research Careers," *Science*, v. 134, November 3, 1961: 1399–1402.

Solow, Robert A. "Gearing Military R&D to Economic Growth," *Harvard Business Review*, v. 40, November–December 1962: 49–60.

Speyer, Edward. "The Brave New World of the Scientists," *Dissent*, v. 8, Spring 1961: 126–136.

Sponsler, George C. "Needed: Scientists on Top," *Bulletin of the Atomic Scientists*, v. 18, June 1962: 17–20.

Steinbach, H. Burr. "Scientists and Public Policy," *Bulletin of the Atomic Scientists*, v. 17, March 1962: 10–14.

Stewart, Bruce. "Science and Social Change," *Bulletin of the Atomic Scientists*, v. 17, September 1961: 267–270.

Trudeau, Arthur G. "R&D—Key to National Security," *Army Information Digest*, v. 15, May 1960: 38–49.

Wolfle, Dael. "Government Organization of Science," *Science*, v. 131, May 13, 1960: 1407–1417.

Wolk, Herman S. "Scientists, Politics, and the Bomb," *Air Force*, v. 45, October 1962: 44–46, 48.

9. THE PROBLEM OF CIVIL–MILITARY RELATIONS

Amrine, Michael. *The Great Decision: The Secret History of the Atomic Bomb*. New York: G. P. Putnam's Sons, 1959.

Andrzejewski, Stanislaw. *Military Organization and Society*. London: Routledge & Kegan Paul, 1954.

Cohen, Bernard C. *The Political Process and Foreign Policy: The Making of the Japanese Peace Settlement*. Princeton: Princeton University Press, 1957.

Coles, Harry L. (ed.). *Total War and Cold War: Problems in Civilian Control of the Military*. Columbus: Ohio State University Press, 1962.

Cook, Fred J. *The Warfare State*. New York: The Macmillan Company, 1962.

Ekirch, Arthur A. *The Civilian and the Military*. New York: Oxford University Press, 1956.

Feis, Arthur A. *The Road to Pearl Harbor: The Coming of the War Between the United States and Japan*. Princeton: Princeton University Press, 1950.

Finer, Samuel Edward. *The Man on Horseback: The Role of the Military in Politics*. New York: Frederick A. Praeger, Inc., 1962.

Fox, William T. R. *The Struggle for Atomic Control*. New York: Public Affairs Committee, Inc., 1947. (Public Affairs Pamphlet, No. 129).

Friedrich, Carl J. (ed.). *American Experiences in Military Government in World War II*. New York: Holt, Rinehart & Winston, Inc., 1948.

Goodrich, Leland M. *Korea: A Study of U.S. Policy in the United Nations* (1st ed.). New York: Council on Foreign Relations, 1956.

Herring, Edward P. *The Impact of War: Our American Democracy Under Arms*. New York: Holt, Rinehart & Winston, Inc., 1941.

Holborn, Hajo. *American Military Government: Its Organization and Policies*. Washington, D.C.: Infantry Journal Press, 1947.

Huntington, Samuel P. *The Soldier and the State: The Theory and Politics of Civil-Military Rela-*

tions. Cambridge: Belknap Press of Harvard University Press, 1957.

Janowitz, Morris. *The Professional Soldier and Political Power: A Theoretical Orientation and Selected Hypotheses.* Bureau of Government, Institute of Public Administration, Ann Arbor: University of Michigan, 1953.

————. *The Professional Soldier: A Social and Political Portrait.* New York: The Free Press, 1960.

Kerwin, Jerome G. (ed.). *Civil-Military Relationships in American Life.* Chicago: University of Chicago Press, 1948.

Langer, William L. *Our Vichy Gamble.* New York: Alfred A. Knopf, Inc., 1947.

Lasswell, Harold D. *National Security and Individual Freedom.* New York: McGraw-Hill Book Company, 1950.

Masland, John W., and Laurence I. Radway. *Soldiers and Scholars: Military Education and National Policy.* Princeton: Princeton University Press, 1956.

May, Ernest R. (ed.). *The Ultimate Decision: The President as Commander-in-Chief.* New York: George Braziller, Inc., 1960.

Millis, Walter. *Arms and the State.* New York: Twentieth Century Fund, 1959.

————. *Arms and Men: A Study in American Military History.* New York: G. P. Putnam's Sons, 1956.

Mills, C. Wright. *The Power Elite.* New York: Oxford University Press, 1956.

Minnesota World Affairs Center. Institute on Military Factors in Foreign Policy, Sept. 29, 30, and Oct. 1, 1952. *Proceedings.* Edited by William C. Rogers, Director. Minneapolis: University of Minnesota, Center for Continuation Study, 1953.

Rapoport, David C. *Praetorianism: Government Without Consensus.* Ph.D. Thesis, Berkeley: University of California, 1960.

Read, Thornton. *Command and Control.* Princeton: Princeton University Center of International Studies, June, 1961.

Sapin, Burton M., and Richard C. Snyder. *The Role of the Military in American Foreign Policy.* New York: Doubleday & Company, Inc., 1954. (Doubleday Short Studies in Political Science, 7.)

————, and H. W. Bruck. *An Appropriate Role for the Military in American Foreign Policymaking: A Research Note.* Princeton: Princeton University, Organizational Behavior Section, 1954 (Foreign Policy and Analysis Series, No. 4).

Shepley, James R., and Clay Blair, Jr. *The Hydrogen Bomb: The Men, the Menace, the Mechanism.* London: Jarrolds, 1955, 1954.

Smith, Louis. *American Democracy and Military Power: A Study of Civil Control of the Military Power in the United States.* Chicago: University of Chicago Press, 1951.

Stein, Harold J. *American Civil-Military Relations: A Casebook.* University, Ala.: University of Alabama Press, 1964.

Tarr, David W. *National Strategy and Military Technology: Towards the Reformulation of the Problems of Civil-Military Relations.* New York, 1960. 17 L. Paper delivered at the Annual Conference of the American Political Science Association, 1960.

Toulmin, Harry A. *Diary of Democracy: The Senate War Investigating Committee.* Introduction by Harley M. Kilgore. New York: R. R. Smith, 1947.

Wood, Marshall, W. B. Leach, and H. H. Ransom. *The Budgetary Process and Defense Policy.* Harvard Defense Policy Seminar Serial No. 122, Nov. 18, 1957.

Zink, Harold. *The United States in Germany.* Princeton: D. Van Nostrand Co., Inc., 1957.

ARTICLES

Fox, William T. R. "Civilians, Soldiers, and American Military Policy," *World Politics,* v. 7, April 1955: 402–418.

————. "Representativeness and Efficiency: Dual Problem of Civil-Military Relations," *Political Science Quarterly,* v. 76, September 1961: 354–366.

George, Alexander L. "American Policy-Making and the North Korean Aggression," *World Politics,* v. 7, January 1955: 209–232.

Halle, Louis J. "The Role of Force in Foreign Policy," *Social Science,* v. 30, October 1955: 203–208.

Harsch, Joseph C. "The Place of the Armed Forces in the Making of National Strategy," *Information Service for Officers,* v. 4, June 1952: 25–45.

Hittle, J. D. "Military Planning at the Seat of Government," *U.S. Naval Institute Proceedings,* v. 83, July 1957: 713–721.

Hoag, Malcolm W. "Some Complexities in Military Planning," *World Politics,* v. 11, July 1959: 553–576.

Hoopes, Townsend. "Civilian-Military Balance," *Yale Review,* v. 43, December 1963: 218–234.

Huntington, Samuel P. "Civilian Control of the Military: A Theoretical Statement," in Eulau, Heinz, Samuel J. Eldersweld and Morris Janowitz (eds.). *Political Behavior: A Reader in Theory and Research.* New York: The Free Press, 1956, pp. 380–385.

————. "Civilian Control and the Constitution," *American Political Science Review,* v. 50; September 1956: 676–699.

"The Impact of the Military on American Life," *Social Action,* v. 28, February 1962: 3–30.

Katzenbach, Edward L., Jr. "Military Policy as a National Issue," *Current History,* v. 31, October 1956: 193–198.

————. "Should Our Military Leaders Speak Up?," *New York Times Magazine,* April 15, 1956: 17, 36–39.

Kintner, William R. "War, Politics, and the Military," *U.S. Naval Institute Proceedings,* v. 77, February 1951: 129–133.

Lasswell, Harold D. "The Garrison-State Hypothesis Today," in *Changing Patterns of Military*

Politics, Samuel P. Huntington (ed.). New York: The Free Press, 1962, pp. 51–70.

Lincoln, George A. "Planning Military Requirements," *American Economic Review,* v. 42, May 1952: 438–452.

Lyons, Gene M. "The New Civil-Military Relations," *American Political Science Review,* v. 55, March 1961: 53–63.

Mallalieu, William G. "The Origin of the Marshall Plan," *Political Science Quarterly,* v. 73, December 1958: 481–504.

Mansfield, Harvey C. "Civil-Military Relations in the United States," *Current History,* v. 38, April 1960: 228–233.

Marshall, George B. "Present-Day Relationship Between Military Power and Civilian Authority," *Department of State Bulletin,* v. 27, September 1952: 348–352.

Marshall, S. L. A. "Politicians and the Military," *New Leader,* v. 45, February 5, 1962: 3–5.

Masland, J. W. "National War College and the Administration of Foreign Affairs," *Public Administration Review,* v. 12, no. 4, 1952: 267–275.

May, Ernest R. "The Development of Political-Military Consultation in the United States," *Political Science Quarterly,* v. 70, June 1955: 161–180.

"The Military and U.S. Foreign Policy Planning," *Journal of International Affairs,* v. 7, no. 2, 1954: 139–222.

Morris-Jones, W. H. "Military Power in Politics," *Durham University Journal,* v. 53, June 1961: 107–116.

Morton, Louis. "The Decision to Use the Atomic Bomb," *Foreign Affairs,* v. 35, January 1957: 334–352.

———. "National Policy and Military Strategy," *Virginia Quarterly Review,* v. 36, Winter 1960: 1–17.

Murphy, Robert. "Interlocking Elements in our National Security," *Department of State Bulletin,* v. 36, March 25, 1957: 475–479.

———. "The Interrelationship of Military Power and Foreign Policy," *Department of State Bulletin,* v. 31, August 1954: 291–294.

———. "The Soldier and the Diplomat," *Foreign Service Journal,* v. 29, May 1952: 17–19, 49–50.

Radway, Laurence I. "Uniforms and Mufti: What Place in Policy?," *Public Administration Review,* v. 18, Summer 1958: 180–185.

Rapoport, David C. "A Comparative Theory of Military and Political Types," in *Changing Patterns of Military Politics,* Samuel P. Huntington (ed.). New York: The Free Press, 1962, 71–101.

Reinhardt, George C. and William R. Kintner. "Policy: Matrix of Strategy," *U.S. Naval Institute Proceedings,* v. 80, February 1954: 144–155.

Schilling, Warner R. "Civil-Naval Politics in World War I," *World Politics,* v. 7, July 1955: 572–591.

Schratz, Paul R. "A Look at Civilian Control," *United States Naval Institute Proceedings,* v. 88, June 1962: 34–43.

Snyder, Richard C., and Glenn D. Paige. "The United States Decision to Resist Aggression in Korea: The Application of an Analytical Scheme," Evanston, Ill.: Graduate School, Department of Political Science, Northwestern Univ., 1959: 341–378. (Mimeographed.)

Stimson, Henry L. "The Decision to Use the Atomic Bomb," *Harper's,* v. 194, February 1947: 97–107.

Sunderland, R. "The Soldier's Relation to Foreign Policy," *U.S. Naval Institute Proceedings,* v. 69, September 1943: 1170–1175.

Zuckerman, Sir Solly. "Judgment and Control in Modern Warfare," *Foreign Affairs,* v. 40, January 1962: 192–212.

National security and international order

a. Disarmament and arms control

Abt, Clark C. *Disarmament Appraised as a Strategy.* Paper. Ann Arbor: International Arms Control Symposium, University of Michigan, December 1962.

———, Thomas O'Sullivan, Melvin M. Kessler and Vahakn Dadrian. *Theoretical Aspects of Unilateral Arms Control.* Report, Raytheon Company, January 1963.

Barnet, Richard J. *Who Wants Disarmament?* Boston: Beacon Press, 1960.

Batten, James K. *Arms Control and the Problem of Evasion.* Monograph. Princeton: Center of International Studies, Princeton University, 1962.

Beaton, Leonard, and John Maddox. *The Spread of Nuclear Weapons.* New York: Frederick A. Praeger, Inc., 1963.

Bechhoefer, Bernhard G. *Postwar Negotiations for Arms Control.* Washington, D.C.: The Brookings Institution, 1961.

Benoit, Emile, and Kenneth E. Bouldings. *Disarmament and The Economy.* New York: Harper & Row, Publishers, 1963.

Bethe, Hans A., Douglas F. Dowd, Walter F. Lafeber, Mario Einaudi, Philip Morrison, and Jay Orear. *Problems of Disarmament.* New York: Monthly Review Press, 1962.

Bloomfield, L. P. *The Politics of Arms Control: Troika, Veto and International Institutions.* (Special Studies Group, SM-3). Washington, D.C.: Institute for Defense Analyses, October 6, 1961.

Brennan, Donald G. (ed.) *Arms Control, Disarmament, and National Security.* New York: George Braziller, Inc., 1961.

Bull, Hedley. *The Control of the Arms Race.* New York: Frederick A. Praeger, Inc., 1961.

Etzioni, Amitai. *The Hard Way to Peace: A New Strategy.* New York: Collier Books, 1962.

Feld, Bernard T. *et al. The Technical Problems of Arms Control.* (Program of Research No. 1). New York: Institute of International Order, 1960.

Forbes, Henry W. *The Strategy of Disarmament.* Washington, D.C.: Public Affairs Press, 1962.

Frisch, David H. (ed.) *Arms Reduction Program and Issues.* New York: The Twentieth Century Fund, 1961.

Hadley, Arthur T. *The Nation's Safety and Arms Control.* New York: The Viking Press, 1961.

Halperin, M. H. *A Proposal for a Bank on the Use of Nuclear Weapons.* (Special Studies Group, SM-4.) Washington, D.C.: Institute for Defense Analyses, October 6, 1961.

Henkin, Louis (ed.). *Arms Control: Issues for the Public.* Englewood Cliffs, N.J.: Prentice-Hall, Inc., 1961.

———. *Arms Control and Inspection in American Law.* New York: Columbia University Press, 1958.

Jesup, Philip, and Howard Taubenfeld. *Controls for Outer Space and the Antarctic Analogy.* New York: Columbia University Press, 1959.

Lefever, Ernest W. (ed.) *Arms and Arms Control: A Symposium.* New York: Frederick A. Praeger, Inc., 1962.

Melman, Seymour. *Inspection for Disarmament.* New York: Columbia University Press, 1958.

———. *The Peace Race.* New York: George Braziller, Inc., 1961.

Millis, Walter. *The Abolition of War.* New York: The Macmillan Company, 1963.

National Planning Association. *1970 Without Arms Control.* (Planning Pamphlet No. 194.) Washington, D.C. 1958.

———. *Strengthening the Government for Arms Control.* Washington, D.C.: National Planning Association, July, 1960.

———. *The Nth-Country Problem and Arms Control.* Washington, D.C.: National Planning Association, 1960.

Noel-Baker, Philip. *The Arms Race: A Programme for Disarmament.* New York: Oceana Publications, 1960.

Nogee, Joseph. *The Diplomacy of Disarmament.* New York: Carnegie Endowment for International Peace, January 1960. (Pamphlet No. 526 in the series "International Conciliation.")

Osgood, Charles E. *An Alternative to War or Surrender.* Urbana: University of Illinois Press, 1962.

Schelling, Thomas C., and Morton H. Halperin. *Strategy and Arms Control.* New York: The Twentieth Century Fund, 1961.

Singer, J. David. *Deterrence, Arms Control, and Disarmament: Toward a Synthesis in National Security Policy.* Columbus: Ohio State University Press, 1962.

Spanier, John W., and Joseph L. Nogee. *The Politics of Disarmament: A Study in Soviet-American Gamesmanship.* New York: Frederick A. Praeger, Inc., 1962.

Spingarn, Jerome H. *New Approaches to Disarmament.* Pamphlet. Foreign Policy Association, 1962.

Strachey, John. *On the Prevention of War.* New York: St Martin's Press, Inc., 1962.

United National Economic and Social Council. *The Economic and Social Consequences of Disarmament: Report of the Secretary-General Transmitting the Study of his Consultative Group.* E/3593, February 28, 1962.

U.S. Congress, Joint Committee on Atomic Energy. *Technical Aspects of Detection and Inspection Controls of a Nuclear Weapons Test Ban.* May 1960.

U.S. Department of State. *A Chronology of the Development of United States Disarmament Policy: 1953–1960.* (Historical Office Research Project, No. 502.) March 1961.

———. *Freedom from War: The United States Program for General and Complete Disarmament in a Peaceful World.* September 1961.

———. *Disarmament: The Intensified Effort: 1955–1958.* (Publications of the United States Department of State, No. 7070). October, 1960.

———. *Documents on Disarmament, 1945–1959.* 2 vols. 1960.

U.S. Arms Control and Disarmament Agency. *The Economic and Social Consequences of Disarmament.* Washington, D.C., 1962. EC 121(13).

Wadsworth, James J. *The Price of Peace.* New York: Frederick A. Praeger, Inc., 1962.

Warburg, James P. *Disarmament: The Challenge of the Sixties.* New York: Doubleday & Company, Inc., 1961.

ARTICLES

Abt, Clark C. "The Problems and Possibilities of Space Arms Control," *Journal of Arms Control, v.* I, no. 1, January 1963.

Barnet, Richard J. "The Soviet Attitude on Disarmament," *Problems of Communism,* May–June, 1961: 32–37.

Bethe, Hans A. "Disarmament and Strategy," *Bulletin of the Atomic Scientists,* September 1962.

Dougherty, James E. "The Disarmament Debate: A Review of Current Literature," *Orbis,* Part II, Winter 1962.

Feld, Bernard T. "Amospheric Testing," *Bulletin of the Atomic Scientists,* January 1962.

Finklestein, Lawrence S. "Arms Inspection," *International Conciliation,* no. 540, November 1962: 5–89.

———. "The United Nations and Organization for the Control of Armaments," *International Organization,* Winter 1962.

Foster, Richard B. "Unilateral Arms Control Measures and Disarmament Negotiations," *Orbis,* Summer 1962.

Gardner, Trevor. "Organizing for Peace," *Bulletin of the Atomic Scientists, v.* 16, September 1960: 297–300.

Humphrey, Hubert H. "Government Organization for Arms Control," *Daedalus, v.* 89, Fall 1960: 967–983.

Inglis, David R. "Evolving Patterns of Nuclear Disarmament Proposals," *Centennial Review, v.* 6, 1962.

———— *et al.* "A Specific Proposal for Balanced Disarmament and Atomic Control," *Centennial Review*, v. 6, 1962.

Jacob, Philip E. "The Disarmament Consensus," *International Organization*, Spring 1960: 233–260.

Kalkstein, Marvin. "Proliferation of Nuclear Weapons," *Bulletin of Atomic Scientists*, 1963.

Katz, Amron H. "Good Disarmament—and Bad," *Air Force and Space Digest*, May 1961.

Kelly, George A. "Arms Control and the Military Establishment," *Military Review*, v. 41, January 1961: 62–72.

Kissinger, Henry A. "Arms Control, Inspection and Surprise Attack," *Foreign Affairs*, July 1960: 557–575.

Levine, Robert A. "Breaking the Arms Stalemate," *Bulletin of the Atomic Scientists*, June 1962.

————. "Arms Agreements, A Model of Stalemate." *Journal of Conflict Resolution*, December 1962.

Morgenstern, Oskar. "Goal: An Armed, Inspected, Open World," *Fortune*, July 1960: 93–95, 219–227.

————. "The Nth-Country Problem," *Fortune*, March 1961: 136, 137, 205–208.

Nanes, Allan S. "Disarmament: The Last Seven Years," *Current History*, May 1962.

Orear, Jay. "Safeguarded Zonal Disarmament," *Bulletin of the Atomic Scientists*, February 1963.

Phelps, John B. "Information and Arms Control," *Journal of Arms Control*, January 1963.

Schelling, Thomas C. "Arms Control: Proposal for a Special Surveillance Force," *World Politics*, October, 1960.

————. "Surprise Attack and Disarmament," *Bulletin of the Atomic Scientists*, December 1959.

Singer, Eugene. "A Bargaining Model for Disarmament Negotiations," *Journal of Conflict Resolution*, v. 7, 1963.

Sohn, Louis B. "A Way to Disarmament," *New Republic*, February 23, 1963.

————. "Zonal Disarmament and Inspection: Variations on a Theme," *Bulletin of the Atomic Scientists*, September 1962.

U.S. Senate, Committee on Foreign Relations. "Attitudes of Soviet Leaders Toward Disarmament," Washington, D.C.: Government Printing Office, 1957. (Staff Study #8)

Van Atta, Lester C. "Arms Control: Human Control," *American Psychology*, January 1963.

Wildavsky, Aaron B. "Nuclear Clubs or Nuclear Wars," *Yale Review*, March 1962.

Wolfe, Thomas W. "Soviet Strategy of Disarmament," in Hahn, Walter F., and John C. Neff (eds.). *American Strategy for the Nuclear Age.* New York: Doubleday & Company, Inc., 1960: 135–151.

b. *International organization, law, and regionalism*

Asher, Robert E. and others. *The United Nations and Promotion of the General Welfare.* Washington, D.C.: Brookings Institution, 1957.

Bailey, Norman A. *The Inter-American Peace and Security System for Dealing with Threats to the Peace and Breaches of the Peace, 1948–1959.* Ph.D. Thesis, Columbia University, 1962.

Bailey, Sydney B. *The General Assembly of The United Nations.* New York: Frederick A. Praeger, Inc., 1960.

Benoit, Emile. *Europe at Sixes and Sevens.* New York: Frederick A. Praeger, Inc., 1961.

Bloomfield, Lincoln P. *International Military Forces.* Boston: Little, Brown and Company, 1964.

————. *The United Nations and U.S. Foreign Policy: A New Look at the National Interest.* Boston: Little, Brown and Company, 1960.

————. *Evolution or Revolution? The United Nations and the Problem of Peaceful Territorial Change.* Cambridge: Harvard University Press, 1957.

Corbett, Percy E. *Law and Society in the Relation of States.* New York: Harcourt, Brace & World, Inc., 1951.

Claude, Inis L. *Swords Into Plowshares: Problems and Progress of International Organization.* New York: Random House, Inc., 1963.

Dallin, Alexander. *The Soviet Union at The United Nations.* New York: Frederick A. Praeger, Inc., 1964.

Deutsch, Karl W. *Political Community and the North Atlantic Area.* Princeton: Princeton University Press, 1957.

————. *Political Community at the International Level.* New York: Doubleday & Company, Inc., 1952.

De Visscher, C. *Theory and Reality in Public International Law.* Princeton: Princeton University Press, 1957.

Eagleton, Clyde. *International Government.* New York: The Ronald Press Company, 1957.

————. *The United Nations and The United States.* Dallas: Southern Methodist Univ. Press, 1958.

Falk, Richard A. *Law, Morality and War in the Contemporary World.* New York: Frederick A. Praeger, Inc., 1963.

Goodman, E. R. *The Soviet Design for a World State.* New York: Columbia University Press, 1960.

Goodrich, Leland M. *The United Nations.* New York: Thomas Y. Crowell Company, 1959.

————, and Anne P. Simons. *The United Nations and the Maintenance of International Peace and Security.* Washington, D.C.: Brookings Institution, 1955.

Green, James F. *The United Nations and Human Rights.* Washington, D.C.: Brookings Institution, 1956.

Haas, Ernst B. *The Uniting of Europe.* Stanford: Stanford Univ. Press, 1958.

Holcombe, Arthur N. *The United Nations and American Foreign Policy.* Univ. of Illinois Bulletin, v. 55, no. 16, October, 1957, issued by Institute of Government and Public Affairs. Urbana, Ill.: Univ. of Illinois.

Hovet, Thomas, Jr. *Bloc Politics in the United*

Nations. Cambridge: Harvard University Press, 1960.

Jessup, Philip. *A Modern Law of Nations.* New York: The Macmillan Company, 1948.

Kaplan, Morton, and Nicholas deB. Katzenbach. *The Political Foundations of International Law.* New York: John Wiley & Sons, Inc., 1961.

Kraft, Joseph. *The Grand Design: From Common Market to Atlantic Partnership.* New York: Frederick A. Praeger, Inc., 1962.

Lawson, Ruth. *International Regional Organizations; Constitutional Foundations.* New York: Frederick A. Praeger, Inc., 1963.

MacIver, Robert M. *The Nations and The United Nations.* New York: Manhattan Publishing Co., 1959.

MacLaurin, John. *The United Nations and Power Politics.* New York: Harper & Row, Publishers, 1951.

Mayne, Richard. *The Community of Europe; Past, Present and Future.* New York: W. W. Norton & Company, Inc., 1962.

McDougal, Myres S., and Florentino F. Feliciano. *Law and Minimum World Public Order: The Legal Regulation of International Coercion.* New Haven: Yale University Press, 1961.

Miller, Richard I. *Dag Hammarskjold and Crisis Diplomacy.* New York: Oceana Publications, Inc., 1961.

Millis, Walter, Reinhold Niebuhr, and others. *A World Without War.* New York: Washington Square Press, 1961.

Moore, Ben T. *NATO and the Future of Europe.* New York: Harper & Row, Publishers, 1958.

Murray, James N. *The United Nations Trusteeship System.* Urbana, Ill.: Univ. of Illinois Press, 1957.

Myrdal, Gunnar. *An International Economy.* New York: Harper & Row, Publishers, 1956.

The National Studies on International Organization, Carnegie Endowment for International Peace:
The U.S. and The United Nations: The Public View, 1945–1955.
The U.S. and The United Nations: Promoting the Public Welfare, 1945–1955, 1960.

Nicholas, H. G. *The United Nations as a Political Institution.* New York: Oxford University Press, 1959.

Nogee, Joseph L. *Soviet Policy Toward International Control of Atomic Energy.* Notre Dame, Ind.: University of Notre Dame Press, 1961.

Northrop, F. S. C. *European Union and United States Foreign Policy.* New York: The Macmillan Company, 1954.

———. *The Taming of the Nations: A Study of the Cultural Bases of International Policy.* New York: The Macmillan Company, 1954.

Perkins, Dexter. *America's Quest for Peace.* Bloomington: Indiana Univ. Press, 1962.

Riggs, Robert E. *Politics in the United Nations: A Study of United States Influence in the General Assembly.* Urbana, Ill.: Univ. of Illinois Press, 1958.

Schiffer, Walter. *The Legal Community of Mankind: A Critical Analysis of the Modern Concept of World Organization.* New York: Columbia University Press, 1954.

Sharp, Walter R. *Field Administration in the United Nations System.* New York. Frederick A. Praeger, Inc., 1961.

Slick, Tom. *Permanent Peace: A Check and Balance Plan.* Englewood Cliffs, N.J.: Prentice-Hall, Inc., 1958.

Stone, Julius. *Aggression and World Order: A Critique of United Nations Theories of Aggression.* Berkeley: Univ. of California Press, 1958.

———. *Quest for Survival: The Role of Law and Foreign Policy.* Cambridge: Harvard University Press, 1961.

Wilcox, F. O., and H. F. Haviland (eds.). *The United States and The United Nations.* Baltimore: Johns Hopkins Press, 1961.

ARTICLES

Asher, Robert E., and others. "Economic Cooperation Under United Nations Auspices," *International Organization,* Summer, 1958.

Beloff, Max. "National Government and International Government," *International Organization,* v. 13: 538–549, Autumn 1960.

———. "Federalism as a Model for International Integration," *Yearbook of World Affairs,* v. 13, 1959: 188–204.

Bloomfield, Lincoln P. "Arms Control and World Government," *World Politics,* July 1962.

———. "The United Nations and National Security," *Foreign Affairs,* v. 36, July 1958: 597–610.

———. "Law, Politics and International Disputes," *International Conciliation,* no. 516, Jan. 1958: 257–316.

Burton, J. W. "Regionalism, Functionalism and the United Nations," *Australian Outlook,* v. 15, Autumn 1960: 538–49.

Claude, Inis L., Jr. "United Nations Use of Military Force," *Journal of Conflict Resolution,* v. 7, 1963.

———. "The United Nations and the Use of Force," *International Conciliation,* no. 632, March 1961: 325–384.

Crane, Robert D. "Law and Strategy in Space," *Orbis,* v. 6, no. 2, Summer 1962.

———. "Soviet Attitudes Toward International Space Law," *American Journal of International Law,* v. 56, no. 3, July 1962.

Diebold, William, Jr. "Theory and Practice of European Integration," *World Politics,* v. 11, no. 4, July 1959: 621–628.

Finkelstein, Lawrence. "The United Nations and Organization for the Control of Armaments," *International Organization,* Winter, 1962.

Fisher, Roger. "Responding to Disarmament Violations," *Bulletin of the Atomic Scientists,* September 1962.

Freeman, Alwyn V. "The Development of International Cooperation in the Peaceful Use of Atomic Energy," *American Journal of International Law,* v. 54, no. 2, April 1960: 383–392.

Fulbright, J. W. "For a Concert of Free Nations," *Foreign Affairs,* v. 40, October 1961: 1–18.

Goldstein, Walter. "The Peaceful Limitation of Disputes: Police Powers and Problems," Paper.

International Arms Control Symposium, Ann Arbor: University of Michigan, December 1962.

Haas, Ernst B. "Regionalism, Functionalism and Universal Organization," *World Politics,* v. 8, Jan. 1956: 238–263.

———. "Regional Integration and National Policy," *International Conciliation,* no. 513, May 1957: 381–442.

———. "The Challenge of Regionalism," *International Organization,* v. 12, Autumn 1958: 440–458.

———. "International Integration: The European and the Universal Process," *International Organization,* v. 15, Summer 1961: 336–393.

Halderman, John W. "Legal Basis for International Armed Forces," *American Journal of International Law,* October 1962.

Hoffmann, Stanley. "International Systems and International Law," *World Politics,* v. 14, October 1961: 205–237.

———. "The Role of International Organization: Limits and Possibilities," *International Organization,* v. 10, August 1956: 357–372.

Ikle, Fred C. "Alternative Approaches to the International Organization of Disarmament," Report. The RAND Corporation, February 1962.

Jackson, Elmore. "The Future Development of the United Nations: Some Suggestions for Research," *Journal of Conflict Resolution,* v. 5, no. 2, June 1961.

Jenks, C. Wilfred. "World Organization and European Integration," *European Year Book,* v. 1, 1955: 173–186.

Jordan, William M. "Concepts and Realities in International Political Organization," *International Organization,* v. 11, Autumn 1957: 587–596.

McClelland, Charles, and Quincy Wright. "Prospects for Novel Control Systems in International Politics," Paper. *International Arms Control Symposium,* Ann Arbor: Univ. of Michigan, December 1962.

Padelford, Norman J. "Political Cooperation in the North Atlantic Community," *International Organization,* August 1955.

———. "Regional Organization and The United Nations," *International Organization,* May 1954.

Schacter, Oscar. "The Use of Law in Conflict Resolution," Fortieth Annual Meeting, *American Orthopsychiatric Association,* Washington, D.C., March, 1963.

Sohn, Louis B. "The Role of International Institutions as Conflict-Adjusting Agencies," *Univ. of Chicago Law Review,* v. 28, Winter 1961: 205–257.

Wright, Quincy. "Power Politics or a Rule of Law?," *New Republic,* December 29, 1962.

Theories and methodologies

NOTE: Probably the most important single source for material on theoretical approaches and methodological innovations is the *Journal of Conflict Resolution: A Quarterly for Research Related to War and Peace,* published since 1957 by The Center for Research on Conflict Resolution, The University of Michigan, Ann Arbor, Michigan. In addition to significant individual contributions, it also publishes, from time to time, comprehensive surveys of existing literature. An individual listing of relevant contributions appearing in this *Journal* would be so voluminous that we have, for the most part, omitted them from our bibliography. The interested researcher should examine the Index to the *Journal* for easy access to these articles.

Boulding, Kenneth. *Conflict and Defense: A General Theory.* New York: Harper & Row, Publishers, 1962.

Deutsch, Karl W. *The Nerves of Government.* New York: The Free Press, 1963.

———. *Nationalism and Social Communication.* New York: John Wiley & Sons, Inc., 1953.

Fox, William T. R. *Theoretical Aspects of International Relations.* Notre Dame, Ind.: University of Notre Dame Press, 1960.

Guetzkow, Harold. *Simulation in International Relations: Developments for Research and Teaching.* Englewood Cliffs, N.J.: Prentice-Hall, Inc., 1963.

Hoffman, Stanley. *Theory and International Relations.* Englewood Cliffs, N.J.: Prentice-Hall, Inc., 1960.

Kaplan, Morton. *System and Process in International Politics.* New York: John Wiley & Sons, Inc., 1957.

Knorr, Klaus, and Sydney Verba. *The International System: Theoretical Essays.* Princeton: Princeton University Press, 1961.

Lasswell, Harold, and Abraham Kaplan. *Power and Society: A Framework for Political Inquiry.* New Haven: Yale University Press, 1950.

Liska, George. *International Equilibrium: A Theoretical Essay on the Politics and Organization of Security.* Cambridge: Harvard University Press, 1957.

———. *The New Statecraft: Toward a General Theory of Foreign Aid.* Chicago: University of Chicago Press, 1960.

McDonald, John. *Strategy in Poker, Business & War.* New York: W. W. Norton & Company, Inc., 1950.

Modelski, George A. *A Theory of Foreign Policy.* New York: Frederick A. Praeger, Inc., 1962.

Morgenstern, Oskar. *The Question of National Defense.* New York: Random House, Inc., 1959.

——, and John Von Neumann. *Theory of Games and Economic Behavior.* Princeton: Princeton University Press, 1944.

Myrdal, Gunnar. *Value in Social Theory: A Selection of Essays on Methodology.* New York: Harper & Row, Publishers, 1958.

Orcutt, G. H., M. Greenberger, J. Korbel, and A. Rivkin. *Microanalysis of Socioeconomic Systems: A Simulation Study.* New York: Harper & Row, Publishers, 1961.

Rapoport, Anatol. *Fights, Games and Debates.* Ann Arbor: University of Michigan Press, 1960.

——. *Strategy and Conscience.* New York: Harper & Row, Publishers, 1964.

Richardson, Lewis F. *Arms and Insecurity.* Chicago: Quadrangle Books, 1960.

——. *Statistics of Deadly Quarrels.* Chicago: Quadrangle Books, 1960.

Riker, W. *The Theory of Political Coalitions.* New Haven: Yale University Press, 1962.

Schelling, Thomas C. *The Strategy of Conflict.* Cambridge: Harvard University Press, 1960.

Shubik, Martin (ed.). *Game Theory and Related Approaches to Social Behavior.* New York: John Wiley & Sons, Inc., 1964.

Siegel, S., and L. E. Fouraker. *Bargaining and Group Decision-Making.* New York: McGraw-Hill Book Company, 1960.

Simon, Herbert A. *Models of Man: Social and Rational.* New York: John Wiley & Sons, Inc., 1957.

Snyder, Richard C., and James A. Robinson. *National and International Decision-Making.* New York: The Institute for International Order, 1962.

Van Wagenen, Richard W. *Research in the International Organization Field: Some Notes on a Possible Focus.* Princeton: Princeton University Press, 1952.

ARTICLES

Benson, O. "Simulation of International Relations and Dipomacy," in H. Borko (ed.). *Computer Applications in the Behavioral Sciences.* Englewood Cliffs, N.J.: Prentice-Hall, Inc., 1962.

Bloomfield, L. P. "Political Gaming," *United States Naval Proceedings,* v. 86, 1960: 57–64.

Boguslaw, R. "Situation Analysis and the Problem of Action," *Social Problems,* v. 8, 1961: 212–219.

Brody, R. A. "Some Systemic Effects of the Spread of Nuclear Weapons Technology: A Study Through Simulation of a Multi-Nuclear Future," Doctoral dissertation, Northwestern University, 1963.

Coleman, J. "The Simulation of Processes in Social Controversy," in H. Guetzkow (ed.). *Simulation in Social Science.* Englewood Cliffs, N.J.: Prentice-Hall, Inc., 1962, pp. 61–69.

Dawson, R. E. "Simulation in the Social Sciences," in H. Guetzkow (ed.). *Simulation in Social Science.* Englewood Cliffs, N.J.: Prentice-Hall, Inc., 1962, pp. 1–15.

Deutsch, Karl W. "Toward an Inventory of Basic Trends and Patterns in Comparative and International Politics," *American Political Science Review,* v. 55, 1960: 34–57.

——. "Game Theory and International Politics," *The Canadian Journal of Economics and Political Science,* v. 20, 1954: 76–83.

Ellis, J., and T. Greene. "Contextural Study: A Structural Approach to the Study of Political and Military Aspects of Limited War," Santa Monica, Calif.: The RAND Corporation, P-1840, 1959.

Grace, H. "A Quantitative Case Study in Policy Science," *Journal of Social Psychology,* v. 41, 1955: 197–219.

Haywood, O. G., Jr. "Military Decision and Game Theory," *Journal of the Operations Research Society of America,* v. 2, 1954: 365–385.

Jones, Stephen. "A Unified Field Theory of Political Geography," *Annals of the Association of American Geographers,* v. 44, no. 2, 1954: 111–123.

Kindleberger, C. "Scientific International Politics," *World Politics,* v. 11, 1958: 83–88.

Lasswell, H. "Technique of Decision Seminars," *Midwest Journal of Political Science,* v. 4, 1960: 213–236.

Maccoby, M. "Social Psychology of Deterrence," *Bulletin of the Atomic Scientists,* v. 17, 1961: 278–281.

McClelland, Charles. "Systems and History in International Relations: Some Perspectives for Empirical Research and Theory," *General Systems Yearbook,* v. 3, 1958.

Morgenstern, Oskar. "Effective and Secure Deterrence: The Oceanic System," *Royal Canadian Air Force Staff College Journal,* 1960.

Osgood, C. E. "Graduated Reciprocation in Tension-Reduction: A Key to Initiative in Foreign Policy," *The University of Illinois, Institute of Communications Research,* Urbana, December 1960.

Pool, I., and R. Abelson. "The Simulmatics Project," *Public Opinion Quarterly,* v. 25, 1961: 167–183.

Snyder, R. C. "Experimental Techniques and Political Analysis: Some Reflections in the Context of Concern Over Behavioral Approaches," in J. C. Charlesworth (ed.), *The Limits of Behavioralism in Political Science,* a symposium sponsored by The American Academy of Political and Social Science, October 1962, pp. 94–123.

——. "Some Recent Trends in International Relations Theory and Research," in A. Ranney (ed.), *Essays on the Behavioral Study of Politics.* Urbana, Ill.: University of Illinois Press, 1962, pp. 103–171.

Sutton, O. Review of Lewis F. Richardson's "Arms and Insecurity and Statistics of Deadly Quarrels," in *Scientific American,* v. 204, 1961: 193–200.

Index

Index